Desert Landscape Architecture

John C. Krieg

Edited by

Nancy R.H. Sappington

Photographs by

Charles Sappington

CRC Press
Boca Raton London New York Washington, D.C.

Library of Congress Cataloging-in-Publication Data

Krieg, John C., 1951-
Desert landscape architecture/by John C. Krieg; Nancy R. H. Sappington, editor; photographs by Charles Sappington.
p. cm.
Includes bibliographical references and index.
ISBN 1-57444-225-2 (alk. paper)
1. Desert landscape architecture I. Sappington, Nancy R. H. II. Title.
SB475.9.D47K75 1998
712'.0915'4--dc21
98-40872
CIP

St. Lucie Press is an imprint of CRC Press

International Standard Book Number 1-57444-225-2
Library of Congress Card Number 98-40872
Printed in the United States of America 1 2 3 4 5 6 7 8 9 0
Printed on acid-free paper

Contents

Foreword

The unique environment of the Southwest desert is so different that it requires one to seek guidance to help meet the requirements of appropriate landscape design and horticultural reality. John Krieg, through considerable research, sensitivity, and practical experience, has developed an appropriate vehicle that provides a tremendous source of detailed information that can be used as a guide for landscape architects, students, contractors, developers, and home gardeners in pursuit of desert excellence. It is a well known fact that Westerners do things differently and *Desert Landscape Architecture* is definitely in that category. The author has gathered a deep well of information from his own landscape design and on site experience on many types of landscape projects and from his astute awareness of important details that help projects come to successful conclusions.

There was a time when the "green stuff" (coastal-oriented plants) was the norm. Now the use of native and introduced dry-climate plants has made valued additions to the new philosophy of natural and water conserving landscaping which had its roots in Arizona where the author gained valued experience.

The organization of this book provides detailed information on every facet of landscape design, environmental concerns, water issues, cultural issues, and plant material use. Line drawings add to the great scope of details. This dedicated book provides the reader and user with answers to many questions.

Eric A. Johnson

Biographies

Author/Illustrator

John C. Krieg is a registered landscape architect in Arizona, California, and Nevada. Mr. Krieg is also a licensed landscape contractor and swimming pool contractor in California. He has 18 years of experience as a desert landscape architect, having opened his office as a private practitioner in Phoenix, Arizona, in early 1979. He remained in professional practice in Phoenix for over 10 years before relocating to the Palm Springs area in late 1989. In the early part of his career, Mr. Krieg concentrated primarily on commercial and multifamily housing projects. Today, he is involved with country club and resort type development owner of Natural Effects, a full-service design/build company. In addition, he is Southern California's representative for Native Resources International. Native is an indigenous plant material devegetation/revegetation and native seed gathering company. His office is in Palm Desert, California.

Editor

Nancy R. H. Sappington has been a desert horticultural consultant for over 10 years. She is past editor of *Landscape Design* magazine, produced by Adams Publishing Company in Cathedral City, California. She is currently a staff editor for *Pool and Spa News*, based in Los Angeles.

Photographer

Charles Sappington has been a professional nature photographer for 20 years. His work has appeared in several periodicals including *Palm Springs Life.* His office is in Bermuda Dunes, California.

Foreword

Eric A. Johnson has over 58 years of experience in landscape architecture, horticulture, and landscape contracting. He is recognized as an authority on landscape architectural practices in the desert southwest, the Coachella Valley in particular, and has authored or coauthored eight books on the subject. He was Southwest Garden Editor for "Sunset Magazine" from 1955 until 1968, and is a contributing author to *Sunset's Western Garden Book.* His most current literary contributions are *Beautiful Gardens* (1991) and The Low Water Flower Gardener (1992). Mr. Johnson's guide to gardening plants for the arid west — *Pruning, Planting & Care* — was published by the Ironwood Press in Tucson, Arizona. Mr. Johnson has served as a former member of the Design Review Board — City of Palm Desert, and as a consultant to Coachella Valley Water District, Desert Water Agency, and the City of Indian Wells. He currently holds a position as Landscape Design Consultant to the City of Palm Desert Public Works Department.

Acknowledgments

I would like to thank the following individuals for their assistance in developing this book. For review and comment on the entire manuscript: John Steigerwaldt, Landscape Architect, Palm Desert: Mr. Jack E. Ingels, Professor of Landscape Architecture, S.U.N.Y., Cobleskill, New York: Mr. Kenneth Struckmeyer, Professor of Landscape Architecture, W.S.U., Pullman, Washington: Mr. Dennis Scholtz, Landscape Architect for the City of Phoenix, Department of Engineering, Phoenix, Arizona: Mr. Bill Rowe, Landscape Architect for the City of Henderson, Parks Department, Henderson, Nevada: Mr. and Mrs. Gary Alexander of Imperial Tree Service, Palm Springs, California: Mr. David Eppele, President, Arizona Cactus and Succulent Research, Inc., Bisbee, Arizona: John Patten Guthrie, A.I.A., author of *The Architect's Portable Handbook*, Phoenix, Arizona.

Mr. Ron Gass of Mountain States Nursery, Phoenix, Arizona, and Mr. Phil Furnari of California Desert Nursery, Bermuda Dunes, California, for review of the Planting chapter and horticulture terminology.

Mr. Ruben Villegas of Santa Rosa Irrigation Designs, La Quinta, California; Mr. Jack R. Donis, Irrigation Consultant, Tucson, Arizona, Mr. Scott Powell of United Green Mark, Inc., Palm Desert, California; and Mr. Sam Toby of Salco Drip Irrigation Products, Inc., Hawthorne, California, for their invaluable input on the Irrigation Design chapter.

Mr. Michael Divel, Electrician, Palm Desert, California, for review of the Lighting Design Chapter; Mr. Mark Rosbottom, Landscape Contractor, Rancho Mirage, California, for suggestions on improving the Lighting chapter.

Mr. Alan Renwick of Del Webb's Sun City Palm Springs Maintenance Division, for review of the Installation and Maintenance chapter.

Mrs. Karen C. Jones of KCJ Editorial and Graphic Services, Palm Desert, California, for typing, computer graphics, and formatting.

May God bless you all and hold you in the palm of his hand.

Introduction

The target audience for this book is:

- Planning personnel, design and engineering professionals, especially other landscape architects.
- Landscape contractors, nurserymen, suppliers, and any other members of the landscape industry.
- Developers, builders, and anyone else considering commissioning the services of a landscape architect.
- People entering the field, especially students.
- Homeowners with a thirst for more knowledge than that generally available in most do-it-yourself books.

It is assumed that the intended readership has at least a rudimentary knowledge of what a landscape architect is and what his/her role is in the design field. Note that the text occasionally addresses other landscape architects in the first person. This is not to exclude the other readers, but should only serve as a reminder that the book is, after all, about landscape architecture.

The book is written from the perspective of a private practitioner. There are several areas of landscape architecture that may not be touched upon here. Regional and large-scale site planning, for example, are not frequently discussed. What this book does attempt to do is to give the reader an understanding of desert environments, their climatic conditions, and unique physical beauty. It also attempts to provide insight into how the built environment is designed and installed in order to cope with such a harsh and unforgiving physiographic area. Every attempt has been made to provide useful day-to-day information.

The format of the book is much like the development of any given project. First, a desert landscape architect should know something about deserts. Second, when one sets up in business, he should endeavor to learn as much as he can about the geographical, cultural, social, and political climate of the area where he works. In order to provide a clientele with a good design product, a proven process that has a reasonable chance of assuring positive results should be undertaken.

The Design chapters (Chapters 3, 4, 5, 6, and 7) follow in much the manner that a complete and functional set of working drawings would in order to install a finished project. The final chapter on "Installation and Maintenance" gives the reader some guidelines as to how a project should go into the ground and how to keep the site functional, the plants healthy, and the project upkeep cost efficient.

To facilitate reading, the chapters are set up to present text, drawings, and then illustrations. The glossaries have been placed at the ends of the chapters so they can be studied while the subject is still fresh in mind. Hopefully, this format will help provide for easy future reference.

The design chapters are structured to:

1. Define that area of design.

2. Tell why that area is important.

3. Describe techniques and methodologies.

4. Explain how this information is depicted in a set of landscape architectural working drawings.

The Appendix contains useful tables, charts, and graphs that bridge areas of information found in or missing from the separate chapters.

Chapter 1

North American Deserts

Teddybear Cholla forest

Introduction

There are 23 major deserts in the world, 5 of which are in North America. Worldwide, deserts occupy 12% of the Earth's land area and 3% of the North American continent. Deserts occur on a consistent basis north and south of the equator loosely aligning themselves with the Tropic of Cancer and the 30°N parallel and the Tropic of Capricorn and the 30°S parallel. This is not a coincidental phenomenon. We know (since the days of Columbus) that the earth is round and rotates around the sun on an oval track. A complete rotation takes one year and the distance closer to or farther away from the sun on the oval track is what causes seasons. In addition, the earth spins on its axis as it revolves around the sun. One complete spin takes 24 hours and is evidenced by night and day. Imagine that this axis is a north/south stake driven directly through the center of the earth. If you are having a hard time visualizing the earth's axis, look at a globe mounted on a metal stand. The stand grips the globe (Earth) at the North and South Poles which are the exit points of the imaginary axis.

Generally, it is warmest at the equator because this represents the widest part of the earth as it faces, and is therefore closest to, the sun. The Arctic and Antarctic are so cold because they are the farthest away from the sun. The earth rotates in an easterly direction and this spinning causes turbulence which gives rise to intercontinental winds (the tradewinds) and cold ocean currents. These two physiological events, in conjunction with mountain ranges, account for the majority of deserts on earth.

First, the tradewinds or, more specifically, the clouds they carry: clouds are most intense at the equator. Because the equatorial band is the widest latitudinal point on earth, it must spin the fastest in order to keep up. This is why footballs spiral. These wind-driven clouds rise, and as they do, they drop their moisture in prodigious amounts. This accounts for the tropical rainforests. Now lighter and higher in the atmosphere, the clouds fan out and literally float towards the tropics of Cancer and Capricorn. Gravity, being what it is, eventually pulls these clouds down. This creates high atmospheric pressure which, in and of itself, creates dryness.

The cold oceanic currents, for whatever reasons, travel along the western continental shelves of the continents. This, for geological reasons, is where the majority of the Earth's great mountain ranges also occur. When the clouds pass over those parts of the oceans carrying the cold currents, they drop their moisture in response to cooler air temperatures. Continuing east along their way, they now abut the coastal mountain ranges and once again have to drop most of their remaining moisture in order to lighten themselves and rise up over the peaks. The wet westerly side of these ranges is called the "windward side" while the dry easterly slopes are referred to as the "leeward side." In any event, the lands which lie immediately to the east at the base of these ranges is unlikely to receive any significant amount of moisture and are said to exist in a rain shadow. This gives rise to the deserts of the world.

All or parts of the five main North American deserts occur within the territorial boundaries of the U.S. The five American deserts are located predominately between two major mountain ranges. Furthest west representing barrier ranges, are the Sierra Nevadas of California and the Cascades of Oregon and Washington. To the east lie the Great Rocky Mountains. The northernmost of the deserts is the Great Basin Desert. Immediately below the Great Basin is the Mohave Desert. East of the Mohave lies the Painted Desert. Directly south of the Mohave and southwest of the Painted Desert is the Sonoran Desert so named after the Mexican state of Sonora. Situated east of the Sonoran Desert, is the Chihuahuan Desert, again named after the Mexican state of Chihuahua. Diagrams of geographic locations are provided at the end of this chapter.

Within any major desert can be found subdeserts which may sometimes differ greatly from their parent environment. Take, for example, the Coachella Valley where I currently live and work. This area occurs in the extreme western end of the Sonoran Desert. This portion of the Sonoran is referred to locally as the Colorado Desert. The Colorado Desert was so named by early Spanish explorers, because the Colorado River serves as its eastern boundary. The Sonoran is the most variable of North American deserts, being either extremely lush, as deserts go, or extremely hot and dry.

In terms of mean annual rainfall and temperatures, the Colorado Desert compares favorably with the Great Sahara Desert of North Africa and the Western and Arabian Deserts of the Middle East. What causes the Colorado Desert to be so hot is its low elevation. Several areas within the Coachella Valley itself are below sea level. The town of Thermal, in fact, is more than 100 feet below sea level. Two main factors cause the Colorado Desert to be so dry. First, winter rains approaching from the west are blocked by extremely high mountain ranges. Second, the summer monsoon rains originating in the Gulf of Mexico and blowing inland usually only travel as far west as Central Arizona. Thus, while the Northern Mexican and Arizonan parts of the Sonoran Desert rate among the lushest desert environments on earth, the Colorado section is truly desolate.

Any number of physical or environmental factors can cause any given area of any given desert region to differ from what is considered the norm. Research of local conditions is critical as is an appreciation for any subtle natural nuance that may impact the native or built landscape.

Climate

The desert environment is marked by extremes: hot and cold; day and night; summer and winter; wet and dry. As harsh as conditions may seem, the desert is a very sensitive environment. It takes a long time for perennial plants to become established and animal populations to become stable. The life spans of all desert organisms are determined by one major limiting factor — *water.*

The availability of water, as it pertains to desert environments, is not always just a measurement of mean annual precipitation, but also is a function of the rate of evaporation. If water brought into an ecosystem evaporates before it can be utilized, the ecosystem exhibits aridity and can thus be classified as a desert. Factors contributing to evaporation are heat, wind, and solar radiation. Deserts occur where the rate of evaporation meets or exceeds the rate of precipitation. The rate of evaporation is measured from exposed surfaces. Life can exist in this type of environment because the ground plane is not always completely exposed. Also, on brief occasions, rainfall is intense enough to percolate below the ground surface to be stored within the soil for longer periods of time.

Even in deserts there is a noticeable difference in the availability of water. Parts of the Sonoran Desert, for example, receive 8 to 10 inches of rain annually. The Mohave receives only 4 to 6 in. of annual rain, while the Chihuahuan is considered the wettest North American desert.

In all instances, no North American desert receives more than an average of 10 in. of annual precipitation.

Rain clouds travelling from the equator or originating over the Pacific Ocean and moving eastward do reach desert environments, either with less moisture or through mountain passes. The trade winds which carry these rain clouds travel in currents or tracts. Due to the spinning of the earth on its slightly tilting axis, these winds, known as the "westerlies" exhibit a seasonal shift. They travel over Mexico and the southwestern U.S. in the winter months and shift northward into Canada during the summer. As the westerlies shift to the north in July, storm cells oftentimes occur in the Gulf of Mexico and are drawn northwestward into desert regions. The northern and western deserts receive winter rain, while southeastern deserts receive summer rain, and some intermediate deserts, most notably parts of the central Sonoran, receive bi-seasonal rain.

In terms of annual mean temperature, North American deserts can be classified as being either cold or hot. These classifications are primarily related to latitude. The Great Basin, Painted, and northern parts of the Mohave deserts are frequently categorized as cold deserts. The southern Mohave, Sonoran, and Chihuahuan are categorized as hot deserts. This cold or hot classification pertains to how a desert environment receives precipitation. Most of the moisture available to cold desert organisms comes in the form of snow melt. Hot deserts receive their moisture predominantly in the form of rainfall.

Daily temperatures in any given desert environment can vary widely, sometimes by as much as 50 degrees. Because deserts infrequently have cloud cover, thermal energy from the sun is shallowly absorbed by the desert surfaces and rapidly re-radiates back into the atmosphere at night. That is, there is no cloud cover to hold heat closer to the ground surface at night.

A desert environment's mean annual temperature is also affected by altitude. Temperature rises or falls by 3 degrees for every 1000 feet of elevational change. Thus, record high temperatures have been recorded at Bad Water Basin in the Death Valley portion of the Mohave Desert, which lies at 232 feet below sea level. This is quite atypical of the rest of the Mohave which lies predominately at 4500 feet above sea level. The Mohave, in general, is considered quite temperate as deserts go. Another interesting fact to note is that freezing temperatures are often a more major limiting factor to desert adapted organisms than is extreme heat. During winter freezes, warm air which always rises, will travel up the side slope of hills at the same time cold air is conversely falling to the desert floor. Proof that this temperature inversion does indeed occur can be evidenced by plant materials of the same size and species freezing on the desert floor and surviving unharmed just 500 feet upslope. Temperature, especially nighttime temperature, is influenced by sun orientation. A north- or east-facing slope that lies in afternoon shade is cooler considerably earlier in the evening than a south- or west-facing slope. If you have ever camped in the desert or ever intend to, this is a fact well worth remembering.

Physiography

The physical geography of North American deserts falls into the area that is known as the Basin and Range Province. In terms of land area, the basins usually exceed the ranges, sometimes by as much as 70%. Visually, the mountain ranges dominate the landscape. Elevational changes can be dramatic. Mountain ranges in this provence often exceed 13,000 feet above sea level. With the highest basins occurring at 5,000, feet there can be over 8,000-foot high mountains in any given desert environment, and elevational differences of over 10,000 feet are not uncommon.

Mountain ranges consist of several individual mountains, and between these mountains are voids or canyons. Over centuries of time and occurring into the present, water running down these canyons carries soil and debris. Canyon walls generally become less steep as the elevation drops towards the canyon's mouth. When water, soil, and debris reaches the canyon's mouth it spreads out in an inverted "V" or fan-like pattern. This area at a canyon's mouth is referred to as an "alluvial fan."

Where several mouths of several canyons merge, a gently sloping land mass known as a bajada occurs. The gradient of bajadas is generally very consistent, as this land mass descends to the lowest available elevation known as the desert floor. The importance of bajadas will become evident when indigenous desert plant material is discussed. In terms of deposited soil mass, bajadas resemble the delta areas of rivers. Bajadas differ from river deltas in that surface-borne water in the desert evaporates so fast that it usually cannot accumulate at the bottom reaches of the bajada. In fact, the further up the slope of the bajada one travels, the wetter the surface environment gets. These wetter surface areas, coupled with cooler air due to the elevation rise, contribute to a greater diversity of plant material and accompanying animal life on the upper bajada.

"Desert floor" is the term usually given to what is actually the bottom of the basin areas. At the lowest depressions within these basins, lakes often occur. A few lakes are water-filled year round, as is evidenced by Great Salt Lake, Utah in the Great Basin desert. The great majority of desert lakes are water filled only during times of brief intense rainfall and then dry out. Often when these lakes dry, their bottoms become cracked and fissured. The areas between these cracks and fissures are often quite geometric. These geometric ground surface areas are called "playas."

Soils

Most desert areas were once ancient oceans, and the lowest portions of today's deserts contain extremely saline soils. When water is introduced into these areas and then evaporates, the process literally sucks salts to the ground surface, thus forming a phenomenon know as a salt flat. Desert soils are varied and unpredictable. Soils are formed from eroded rocks and other inert matter. Many desert soils are relatively new to the evolutionary process and thus not as fertile as more aged soils. In addition, owing to the sparseness of vegetation, there is relatively little leaf litter falling on the ground plane and contributing to organic matter. Several desert soils have been carried by wind or water from other areas and deposited over older soil and rock areas. At any given desert location, a sample of soil strata or layers can show quite a variety of soil types and degrees of permeability. A problem soil known as "caliche" occurs as clay soils bake and dry. Caliche can often be found several feet below the present soil surface. It formed and then was covered by deposited soil. Other desert soils are very sandy and quite fine. The finest is known as blowsand and does not contain enough organic matter to support most life forms.

Life forms that blowsand can support are algae and fungi which are found even in deserts. They are quite prevalent in sand dunes because sand holds water more loosely than other soil types, making the moisture available to whatever the sand can support. Because of their shifting and loose nature, sand dunes usually do not allow larger and more biologically sophisticated plants to gain a foothold. Algae and fungi, however, can grow and reproduce quickly and need only the soil surface for support. In fact, these organisms, wet and dried, combine with other natural processes to form a crust. This crust actually holds the soil surface in place and stabilizes the upper soil layer so that other plant seeds can germinate and higher plants can become established. This crust is quite sensitive to foot traffic and, once broken, it becomes an area susceptible to wind and water erosion.

Soil type, air temperature, and most important, the quantity and quality of available water, affect all living organisms. Given these elements, even in limited or extreme degrees, organisms will find a way to evolve and adapt within and to their environment. Desert flora and fauna have developed a myriad of adaptations to survive within their harsh surroundings.

Animal Life

By far, the most prevalent desert animals are insects and reptiles. Both groups are dependent on air temperature to control their own body temperature. They are incapable of regulating their body temperatures but, rather, possess internal mechanisms that allow them to function at optimum temperatures and shut down when temperatures are either too hot or too cold. Desert reptiles have a slow heart rate, which in turn slows their entire metabolic rate. While the ground surface may seem the hottest place for snakes and lizards, these creatures have adapted marvelously, either with methods by which they do not actually come into contact with the ground or by physical adaptations that allow them to break through the hot soil surface to cooler subsurface areas.

There are relatively few desert amphibians, although a small number of frog and toad species do exist. Frog species are found in association with riparian environments. Toads, especially the spade-foot toad, flourish in the desert, living a life of fleeting activity followed by long periods of dormancy. Immediately following a cloudburst, adult toads emerge from their burrows and quickly enter into a croaking chorus followed by a mating frenzy. Eggs hatch rapidly, tadpoles are born within two days, and mature to adults within a month in temporary, fast-drying pools. As the immediate environment becomes more arid and pools eventually disappear, these desert newcomers emulate their parents and burrow beneath the soil following the last of the moisture. When the soil's suspended moisture becomes inadequate to maintain these amphibians' lives, they are capable of secreting a gelatinous substance which hardens and encases their body and so prevents further moisture loss. This substance softens and breaks when the next rain comes with enough moisture to start this cycle over again.

There are also fish species that exist in the desert — not only freshwater fish that live in association with freshwater riparian environments, but also fish adapted to the saline desert pools and lakes. The tiny pupfish, for example, can exist in water several times saltier than the Pacific Ocean and up to a temperature of 115°F. These curious little fish can be found at the bottom of Death Valley in marsh areas of standing water surrounded by salt flats.

Bird species are not as numerous as in other ecosystems, but birds are found quite frequently in the desert. The body temperature of birds is quite warm, sometimes as high as 110°F. Thus desert air temperatures must exceed this reading before birds begin to exhibit heat stress. Birds, being mobile, simply fly to shaded areas or rise to a higher and cooler altitude.

Of all the desert animals, mammals are the least internally adapted for coping with life in arid regions. A great many mammals do make their homes in the desert, however. The simplest survival strategies include exhibiting nocturnal habits and the utilization of burrowing to escape the hottest part of the day. Other adaptations include specialized coats, sweat glands, and kidney structures. The kidneys of several desert animals have an increased renal capacity. That is, the processing tubes coiled within the kidney are longer in length and are more efficient than those of nondesert species. So efficient are these kidneys, in fact, that several desert mammals pass urea in a dry form. This means that all the moisture available to the animal is utilized before the animal needs to drink again. Several desert animals, rodents in particular, can go an entire lifetime without an actual drink of water. Water is extracted from that contained in the plant food they eat. Larger mammals like the kit fox can derive a large amount of their moisture-content requirements from the rodents they eat.

Positioned at the bottom of any food chain is plant material. This is particularly true in the desert food chain. The amount and type of vegetation will form the basis for the hierarchy of animal life within the desert ecosystem.

Plant Life

Desert plants have adapted predominantly by the way they manufacture and store carbohydrates as food. This food is produced as a result of the photosynthetic process. Put simply, photosynthesis is the basis for all life on earth. The technical definition of photosynthesis is the process by which plants manufacture carbohydrates (food) from light, air, and water. The photosynthetic process usually takes place in the leaves, which are exposed to air and light. Water is transported to the leaves through roots and conductive stem tissue. In the desert, the main limiting factor to this process is the quantity of available water.

Root systems are distinguished by long, deep taproots and/or very shallow and wide-spreading surface roots. The surface roots capture shallow soil moisture before it evaporates. Deep taproots draw water as it slows and settles while leaching through progressively thicker and usually more absorbent layers of soil.

Trees, shrubs, cacti, and other plant types (most notably the Ocotillo) will produce leaves rapidly in wet periods and drop these leaves just as quickly in dry spells. These plants are referred to as being "drought deciduous." A plant's leaves are the fastest and best producers of carbohydrates. They also expend the bulk of a plant's energy in the respiration and transpiration processes. When water is plentiful even for short periods, it benefits a plant to produce carbohydrates with leaves. Conversely, when water becomes scarce, the plant needs to stop expending excessive amounts of energy by slowing its rate of respiration and transpiration. The Ocotillo is a perfect example of this phenomenon. Travellers in the desert have come to call the Ocotillo the "desert barometer" because the plant will produce leaves after a minimal amount of rain and drop its leaves when the moisture leaches below the root zone.

Trees such as the Palo Verde store carbohydrates in their green trunks, which are shaded and cooled by the tree's canopy. The tree's trunk also presents less surface area to the sun than do leaves, which limits evaporation.

Cacti such as the Prickly Pear and Saguaro have developed a method of shrinking and swelling their stems in response to water loss or intake. These cacti develop very shallow but wide spreading root systems. When it rains in the desert it frequently occurs as an intense downpour of short duration. The roots of these cacti absorb as much water as possible as quickly as possible. Since a large amount of water is being piped into the body of the cactus at a rapid rate, the body must swell to accommodate it. The center of these cacti, known as the pith, has a cellular structure that simply stretches and gradually compresses back to normal form. The outer perimeter, called the cortex, expands or contracts to accept the swelling and shrinking of the underlying pith. Saguaro and Barrel Cacti have also developed hairy heads which rapidly absorb rainwater directly into the pith. Knowledgeable plantsmen actually irrigate transplanted Saguaros through their heads until such time as they can develop new root systems capable of sustaining life in the more conventional fashion.

At the outer surface of the cortex, all cacti will produce a waxy surface substance or cuticle. The amount of cuticular wax is greater in the taller cacti such as Saguaros or the cacti less protected by a profusion of shade giving thorns, such as the Prickly Pear. The purpose of the cuticle is to retain water. Thus when the cactus closes its stomata, the surface cells which allow the exchange of water and gases through the cactus wall, the cuticle protects against water loss through transpiration and simple evaporation. The side of the cactus exposed to the hottest sun orientation will be more apt to succumb to thermal pressures and respond by emitting cooling moisture. Cacti have adapted to this by producing a thicker cuticular layer on their more vulnerable sides. This is important to remember when transplanting cacti. Always orient the cactus as it was positioned prior to transplanting. If the thin side of the cuticle receives intense sun exposure it could greatly damage or even kill the plant.

Cacti, Yuccas, and Agaves all utilize the same tactics to survive in the desert. They quickly take up moisture through shallow root systems. Then they will swell their stems and leaves to store water. Finally and most importantly, they will prevent the loss of water by sealing-off their outer skins. Since their skins or cuticles are sealed during a great portion of the day, air cannot pass through the walls of these cacti. As defined earlier, air (most notably carbon dioxide) is required in the process of photosynthesis. With a sealed cuticle, a cactus still can utilize sunlight and internal water, but must draw its carbon dioxide from other sources. The cacti have evolved a chemical process called crassulacean acid metabolism (CAM), which allows them to take in carbon dioxide during the cooler evening hours and convert it to a chemical that can be applied to the photosynthetic process during daylight hours.

Desert trees and shrubs not capable of CAM must perform the photosynthetic process during the day. Since this process will occur during periods of extreme heat and intense solar radiation, the plants have developed mechanisms to cope with these elements. Acacias and Mesquites develop extremely tiny, pinnate leaves in great profusion. Because the leaves are small, they present less surface area to the sun and so transpiration loss is minimal. The thorns of many cacti were once leaves that became rolled, smaller, and harder as the cacti developed other means of carrying on photosynthesis. The fact that these cacti possess stored water is not lost on many desert animals, and the thorns are needed in modern times for protection.

Creosote Bush, the most common and widespread desert shrub, utilizes not only tiny leaves, but also manufactures an oily substance within these leaves that tastes quite bad to animals thereby discouraging grazing. Creosote has a wide-spreading root system which prevents other plants, even other Creosotes, from invading its perimeter. It is believed this occurs because the roots of one plant emit a toxin that repels the roots of other plants, even Creosotes. This accounts for the often geometric pattern of this plant's distribution on desert floor areas referred to as Creosote flats.

The most common method of survival that plants have developed, not only in deserts but in other ecosystems, is the phenomenon of annualism.

Annuals are plants which complete their entire life cycle within one growing season. Any given annual's growing season is determined by conditions conducive to its growth. In deserts there are winter annuals and summer annuals depending upon the time of the rainy season. The annuals are capable of germination, growth, flowering, fruiting, and producing seeds all within a 6-week to 3-month period, depending upon the species. Thus, through a process called avoidance annuals live out their lives and set seed for the next generation during a favorable weather period and simply wait out unfavorable weather. It is the seeds that are truly remarkable. The seeds of desert annuals are programmed to germinate at the right time when conditions for the plant's survival are optimum. In addition, seeds of the same species are programmed not to all germinate at the same time. This allows for ecological misjudgment and helps to assure the survival of the species.

The color of desert plant materials is another adaptation designed to repel solar radiation. Many plants take on a bluish tone and exhibit a glaucous or waxy buildup on their exterior surfaces. It is believed this glaucous buildup functions to a lesser degree than does the cuticle on cacti.

Riparian Environments

A riparian environment refers to any grouping of plants and animals that exist along a permanent body of water. A desert riparian environment occurs most commonly along rivers and streams but can occur at springs. There are specialized riparian environments that support unique species. Take, for example, the exotic California Fan Palm, the palm in Palm Springs which grows at the base of many canyons throughout the San Jacinto wilderness and also takes advantage of groundwater fissures along parts of the San Andreas fault. This stout palm, often 3 feet wide at the base and rising over 30 feet in height, can be found throughout the western portion of the Colorado Desert. A grove at Fishtail Canyon in the secluded Kofa Mountains in northwestern Arizona is believed to have descended from parent trees dating back to a prehistoric era. Groves at the Death Valley Monument in the Mohave desert are not given much botanic consideration as they are believed to have been planted by the hands of man as recently as the 1900s. The groves that can be found in the isolated side canyons of the Coachella Valley are, however, considered quite botanically significant. The palm played an important part in Cahuilla Indian culture, providing not only a food source, but also a reliable roofing material, made from its fronds. In one of the earliest forms of North American agriculture, the Indians understood the role of fire (natural and purposely set by Cahuillas) in the regeneration and survival of the groves.

Water, a scarse commodity in the desert, is also the terrain's most erosive element. The erosion process is what forms the water body's main channel and embankments. The banks of desert rivers and streams and the populations of organisms they support are usually comprised of two distinct elevational levels. The first level accepts occasional flooding up to 10-year storms. The second and higher level is usually defined by 50- and 100-year storms. Plants called water spenders are technically *phreatophytes* which take in and transpire water at rapid rates. As odd as this may seem in the desert, plants such as Cottonwoods, Sycamores, and Desert Willows send roots into a permanent water source and literally suck water constantly through their structures. Mesquites exist on the upper bench in much the same way but, due to other adaptations, can venture further away from a permanent water source. Mesquite bosques are prevalent along desert rivers. Desert riparian environments, while few and far between, support diverse populations. The Desert Bighorn Sheep, for example, must drink from a permanent water source at least every three days during the hottest summer months. Fish, most amphibians, muskrats, beavers, and waterfowl are exclusively dependent upon and confined to riparian environments. Because of their importance to the survival of a myriad of desert organisms, riparian environments need to be zealously protected and those that have been altered need to be restored.

Conclusion

Deserts are environments undergoing constant change. In the process of evolution the cactus has reduced its leaves to mere appendages or thorns. The thorns serve a useful purpose — discouraging animals from eating the stems which shrink and swell with stored water. The Saguaro has elevated this process of survival to become a dominant species. Young Saguaros live underneath the shading canopies of Palo Verdes. As their cuticles thicken and their root systems spread, the Saguaros crowd out the Palo Verdes by stealing surface rainwater before it can reach the deeper Palo Verde root systems. The Palo Verdes die out and the Saguaros reign supreme. The desert woodpecker has a beak long and thin enough to avoid the thorns and penetrate the cortex of the Saguaro. It hollows a cavity into the wall of the cactus. The woodpecker rears its young and abandons its nest. The cavity then becomes the home of an owl. The owl feeds on the kangaroo rat which keeps its population in check. With the rodent population regulated, desert grasses and annuals grow at a moderate rate sufficient to hold and retain surface moisture to be used by other desert inhabitants. Into this moist and stabilized soil falls the seed of a Palo Verde soon to be followed by the seed of a Saguaro. Life goes on in the desert, studied and measured; and it endures.

World Deserts and Geography

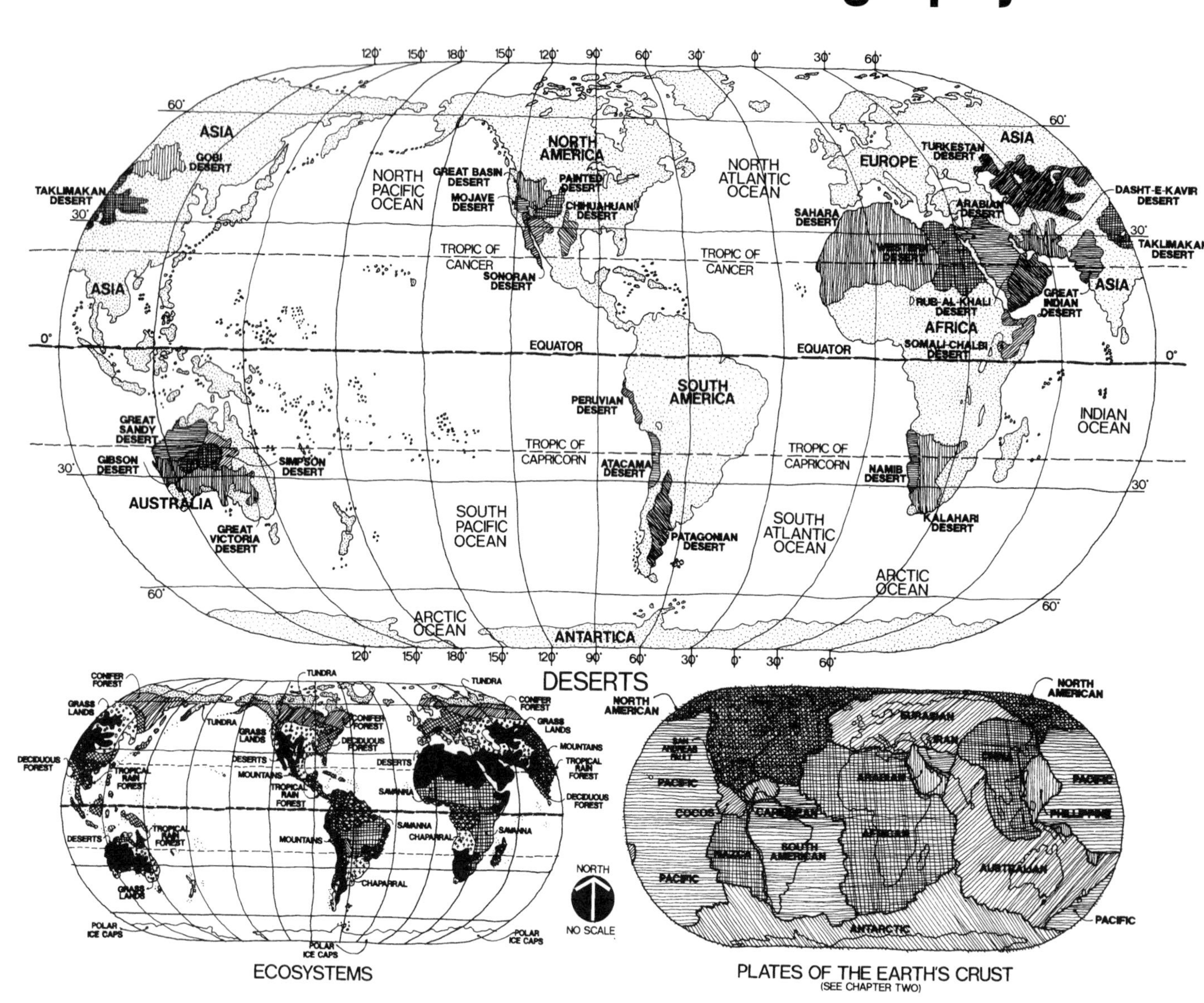

North American Deserts

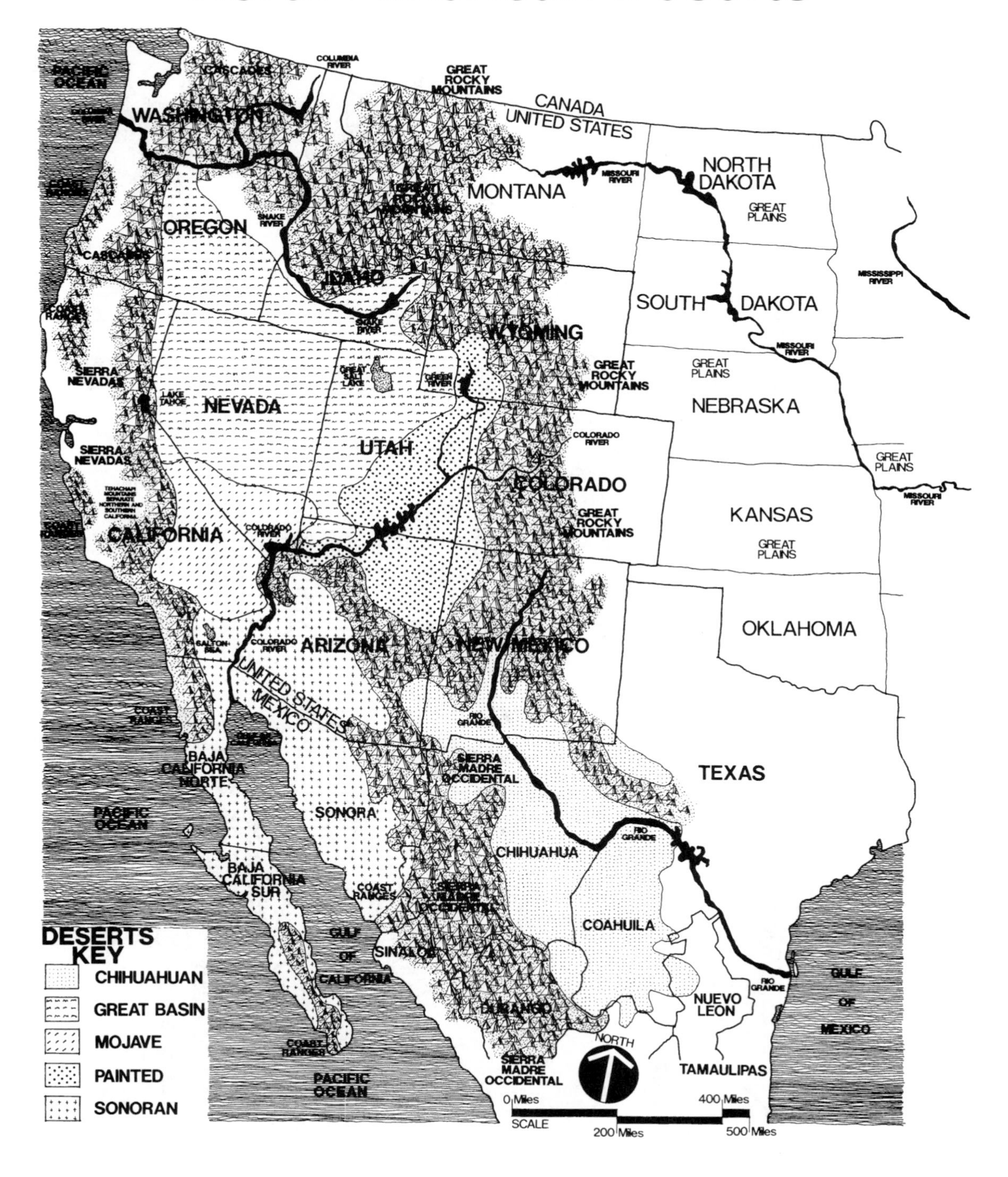

Southwest U.S. Deserts

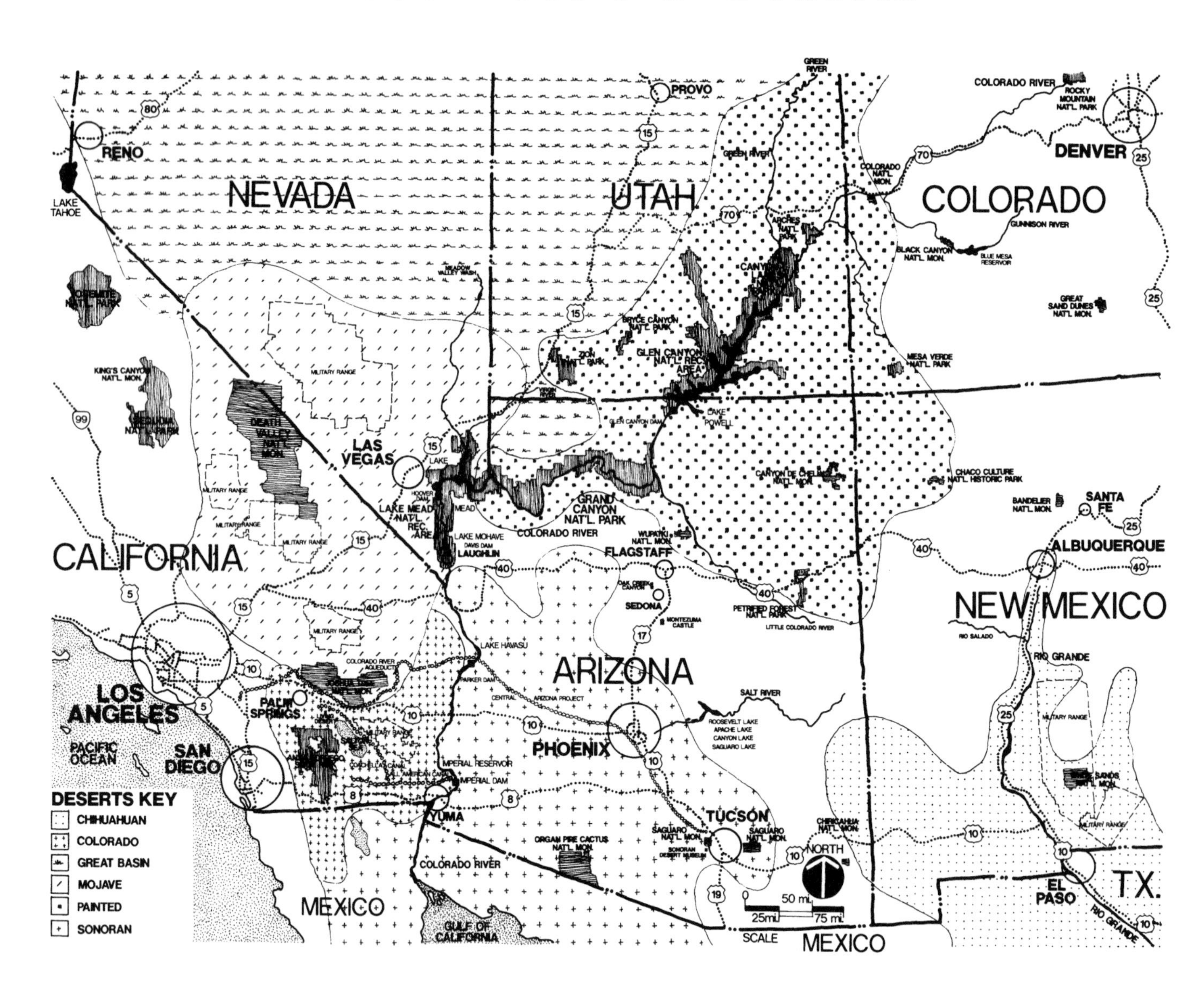

Indian Petroglyphs

Desert Landforms

Gradual slope alluvial fan

Bajada

Desert floor

Creosote flat

Desert Vegetation

Ocotillo (Sonoran Desert)

Joshua Tree (Mohave Desert)

Beavertail Cactus (Colorado Desert)

Agave (Palm Desert, CA)

Desert Riparian Area

Desert Succession

Glossary

Alluvial fan: Sediments deposited at the mouth of canyons due to the effects of water erosion. These deposits spread out in a fan-like or an upside down "V" pattern upon exiting the canyon.

Altitude: Vertical elevation above sea level.

Amphibians: Animals that are capable of living on land or in water and whose development includes an external egg, larval (tadpoles), and adult stage. Body temperature is regulated by surroundings.

Annualism: A desert survival strategy whereby many plant materials will complete their entire life cycle in one growing season. The growing season occurs during optimum periods of temperature and moisture. The plant sets seeds which are dispersed and then dies, thereby avoiding less optimum growing conditions (heat and drought). This is a strategy often referred to as avoidance.

Arid: An exceptionally dry place.

Axis: North/south line through the center of the earth around which the planet revolves.

Bajada: A slope occurring at a generally consistent gradient that is formed as the result of deposits from two or more merging alluvial fans. A bajada can also be formed from debris and/or eroding material. The one factor constant in bajadas is that they are noticeable slopes.

Basin and Range Province: Geographic term used to describe an area of approximately 300,000 square miles contained between the east slopes of the Sierra Nevadas and Cascades and the west slope of the Rocky Mountains. Land surface is characterized by large, flat or depressed areas (basins) penetrated by some 200 mountain ranges. Basins predominate, which make the mountain ranges even more visually dominant. All five north American deserts fall within the confines of the Basin and Range Province.

Birds: Animals characterized by feathers and wings which are used for flying. Their growth cycle includes an external egg (embryonic), juvenile, and adult stage. Very high body temperature is regulated by a rapid heart rate.

Caliche: Soil with large amounts of calcium carbonate that form hard, virtually impenetrable strata. This strata of caliche must be cut or bored through to guarantee adequate surface drainage.

CAM (crassulacean acid metabolism): An adaptation evolved by cacti and succulents which enables them to convert carbon dioxide to a chemical that can be used in the process of photosynthesis during daylight hours. This enables these plants to manufacture food with their stomata closed and thus not lose moisture due to the process of transpiration. (Note: See Chapter 5 glossary for related definitions.)

Chihuahuan Desert: Named after the Mexican state of Chihuahua. Occupies southern New Mexico and the panhandle of Texas, extending far into Mexico. Characterized as a hot desert.

Cloud: Atmospheric vapor in visible forms. Their shapes indicate weather patterns. When enough accumulated vapor becomes heavy enough to turn to water, it rains.

Cold desert: A desert which receives the predominance of its moisture in the form of snow melt.

Colorado Desert: A subdesert. Name given to the westernmost portion of the Sonoran Desert that is bordered on the east by the Colorado River and predominately bordered on the west by the Santa Rosa Mountain range.

Colorado River: Third largest river in the U.S. Named because its headwaters originate in the state of Colorado. Numerous dams supply water to the states of Colorado, New Mexico, Utah, Nevada, Arizona, and California. The river has been aptly called "the West's last watering hole."

Cortex: The outer perimeter of a cactus that encloses the inner pith. Often the cortex has accordion-like folds that can accommodate the shrinking and swelling of the pith as a response to the absence or presence of water.

Creosote flats: Desert floor areas where Creosote Bush is the most prevalent and therefore the dominant species. Often very geometric in pattern, owing to the plant's rooting strategy.

Cuticle: Outermost noncellular layer of a cortex or leaf of waxy composition. Seals off and protects inner fleshy tissue.

Desert floor: Term given to lowest and most level parts of the desert.

Diurnal: Active during daylight hours.

Dormancy: Plant or animal life in a state of inactivity. In the dormant state, far less energy is used by the organism.

Drought deciduous: Survival strategy employed by desert and chaparral-type plant materials. Leaf drop occurs as a response to drought conditions, which greatly reduces the process of transpiration.

Ecology: Ecology is a study of how organisms fit into and function within their environment.

Ecosystem: The ecological relationship between air, water, soil, and plant and animal communities within a given geographic area.

Environment: Similar to the term ecosystem, but differs in that the term is usually used in a broader sense. Also, a term applied to describe all the external forces that influence the life of any given organism.

Equator: Exact horizontal center of the earth occuring at right angles to its north/south axis.

Evaporation: In the drying of a liquid, the process of turning into a vapor in the air.

Evolution: The process by which organisms adapt to their changing environment over broad periods of time.

Fauna: All animal life on earth.

Fish: Animals that exist in water, obtaining oxygen through organs known as gills. Growth includes an external egg stage, juvenile, and adult. Body temperature is regulated by surrounding water.

Flora: All plant life on earth.

Glaucous buildup: Waxy, often white, substance that covers the cuticles of many desert plants, especially cacti and succulents. Aids in repelling solar radiation and in sealing of stomata.

Great Basin Desert: Northernmost of the North American Deserts. Occurs entirely within the U.S. Occupies southwestern Oregon with extensions into Washington state. Also occurs in southern Idaho, eastern Utah, and all but the southern tip of Nevada. A cold desert.

Gravity: Tendency of any body to be pulled toward the center of the earth.

Hot desert: A desert that receives its moisture from rainfall. This includes winter rains originating over the Pacific Ocean or summer monsoons from the Gulf of Mexico.

Latitude: Horizontal line of reference north or south of the equator.

Leeward: Direction away from that in which the wind blows. Opposed to *windward.*

Mammal: Highest group of animals on earth. Man is a mammal. Growth includes an internal embryonic stage, juvenile, and adult. Warm blooded. Body temperature is regulated by heart rate and increased or decreased energy usage. Cooling is by some manner of sweat glands.

Mohave Desert: Desert occurring entirely within the U.S. Occupies southern Nevada and most of southern California. Generally a high desert with average elevations of 4500 feet. Primarily considered a cold desert.

Niche: In ecological terms, the area within an ecosystem that a specific organism occupies, feeds within, and completes most of its growth and life functions in. Many organisms can live within an ecosystem because they occupy different niches. Niche selection lessens competition among species.

Nocturnal: Active during nighttime hours.

Painted Desert: Cold desert occurring entirely within the U.S. Occupies western Utah, extreme eastern Colorado, northwestern New Mexico, and northeastern Arizona. Known for its unique rock formations in a wide array of shapes and colors.

Phreatophytes: Plants that occur primarily in association with riparian environments. Their rooting strategy is to send deep tap roots into a permanent water source and transpire (drink) continually during daylight hours.

Pith: Central stem tissue used for water storage. In desert plant material (including cacti) it is capable of shrinking and swelling rapidly in response to the presence of water.

Playas: Low points and depressions on the desert floor. Either ancient lakes that have gone dry or shallow temporary lakes that occur during brief rainfalls. When these lakes dry out they leave a characteristic fissured geometric pattern.

Precipitation: Rainfall.

Radiation (Solar): Intense direct rays from the sun.

Rain: Atmospheric vapor (clouds) that condenses into water and then falls to earth by the forces of gravity.

Rain shadow: Deserts that exist on the leeward side of mountain ranges are said to be in a rain shadow because clouds drop their rain on the windward side of the mountains to become light enough to pass over them. Thus, rain shadow deserts receive little moisture.

Renal capacity: Degree to which processing tubes are coiled within the kidneys of animals.

Riparian: Adjacent to a river or lake.

Salt flat: Depressions on the desert floor where prehistoric oceans once occurred. Occasionally evaporating rain water draws the soil salts to the soil surface where it becomes encrusted, sometimes in jagged patterns.

Sonoran Desert: So named after the Mexican state of Sonora. Occupies much of southwestern Arizona and the tip of southern California before extending well into Mexico. A hot desert that is the most tropical desert on earth.

Temperature inversion: Cold air flowing under warm air and down a slope to a low-lying area. Although the slope is higher and typically colder, in the event of an inversion, it will be warmer.

Tropic of Cancer: Northern latitude to which the sun comes closest once a year.

Tropic of Capricorn: Southern latitude to which the sun comes closest once a year.

Water: H_2O. A colorless, odorless, tasteless liquid responsible for all life on earth.

Westerlies: Name given to North American continental winds which always flow from west to east across the surface of the Earth as it spins on its axis.

Wind: Any movement of air.

Windward: In the direction from which wind blows. Opposite of *leeward.*

Chapter 2

Landscape Architectural Design

Big Horn Country Club residence

Introduction

More than anything else, design is a process. It is a study in logic before being an exercise in taste. It involves assembling information and elements to create an order and flow. It is chaos and turmoil refined to a simple end product. It involves art, but must be tied to reason. It provokes the emotional but must remain calm. It starts out as a great challenge and ends up a mere undertaking.

In attempting to explain design, we will start with the process, recognize human use areas, define known components, and then apply techniques. Landscape architectural design, or any design field for that matter, is an evolution through these steps to a final solution. The beginning of the process is more logical, while the end is more creative. Points along the way and the role they play will determine the quality of the design. It should always be remembered that landscape architecture is a living art form. Buildings, cars, and clothes are what they are immediately after they are assembled. In many ways a landscape design is what it will become. Plants grow, flower, die, and recycle. Water is a fluid medium affected by any form of motion. Sunlight, much like the wind, is in a state of constant play and restlessness as it enters and dances through a garden. We are guiding and being guided by nature — and nature is never static.

The Design Process

The design process, while not as rigid as that of other disciplines, can be defined. The following outline is very closely aligned with what any landscape architect would incorporate (in abbreviated form) as the scope of services in a contract proposal.

Client Interview (Programming)

Whether the project is a shopping center or a private courtyard, there is always one common thread: the design should be developed to accommodate the needs of the eventual enduser(s). This involves interviews, research, trial and error, and, most important, open and constant communication. This dialogue is necessary to determine everything from facility production methods to residential lifestyles.

At the end of this process, a program should present itself. This program will act as a point of departure in establishing a design direction. This is the most important step. Without a thoughtful effort made at this juncture, all work to follow will run the risk of criticism, misunderstanding, and continual change.

Site Inventory

The landscape architect should always visit the site to get a feel for the lay of the land. Environmental concerns, gradient, drainage patterns, and existing vegetation should be noted. Site features such as rock outcroppings, individual boulders, existing structures, or equipment from previous users should be recorded. Any running water or even obvious washes should receive special consideration in a desert area. Roadways and other circulation systems to and on the site are important. Study areas adjacent to the site as well as significant views. What is the design character of neighboring properties? Can the plant materials and design elements on adjacent properties be incorporated into the upcoming design to create neighborhood continuity? Visit the site at night to gain a perspective on evening usage. Above all, whenever on site, be observant. When you live in the desert, observation involves getting up early. The sunrises can be just as spectacular as the sunsets. Plant life glistens and bustles in the cool morning air, while the last of the nocturnal animal life retreat to their hiding places and burrows. Birds echo a chorus of joy that will let you know whether this site has any potential at all. Now is the time you will realize it.

Site inventories can be done on scratch paper or on actual plans provided by owners, architects, or civil engineers. Tract and tax maps can be put into service. Aerial photos or U.S. Geological Survey maps are a big help, especially on larger sites.

Review Agency Analysis

The Southwest, especially Southern California, is probably the most environmentally and aesthetically conscious area of the nation. In order to maintain this commendable stature, various levels of governmental restrictions and review processes have been implemented. Many designers, myself included, have seen these turn into a gut-wrenching nightmare. However, we must ask ourselves, where would the region, the states, and their respective municipalities be without some system of review and design control? State and county agencies and even cities have the right to request an Environmental Impact Report on any site they deem necessary. Such reports are usually required on larger, more complicated projects or on especially sensitive sites.

Most of the cities in the Southwest issue design standards including some or all of the following:

Landscape Standards

- Number of trees per lineal foot of street frontage.
- Number of shrubs per project square footage.
- Parking lot tree standards, with emphasis on providing shade.
- Incentives for less use of turf and for using water-efficient plant material.
- Vision triangles or sight distance lines at street intersections.
- Screening of street frontage parking from public view.
- Site signage standards.
- Site lighting standards.
- Incentive for artwork in conjunction with an outdoor art program.
- Minimum acceptable planting details, hardscape details, and grading and drainage details.
- Sample of acceptable landscape, hardscape, and grading and drainage specifications.
- Request for a sign-off on plant materials list from various county agricultural commissioners.
- Request for sign-off of landscape and irrigation plans from appropriate governing water agencies.
- Request for sign-off of plans from any number of adjacent municipal and county jurisdictions.

Irrigation Standards

- All plant material in public right-of-way required to be irrigated with an automatic irrigation system.
- No overthrow of water onto public property or pedestrian walkways.
- Moisture sensing devices (tensiometers) encouraged.

- Emitter/drip systems encouraged; no polytubing mainlines or spaghetti tubing is usually allowed.
- Brass valves preferred over plastic.
- Multiple program controllers preferred.
- Minimum acceptable irrigation details.
- Sample of acceptable irrigation specification.
- Approval from governing water districts required on all projects.

Maintenance Standards

- Landscaping, irrigation system, outdoor lighting, related hardscape, sculpture, and water features to be maintained in healthy condition or in full working order.
- City to impose penalties for noncompliance to this section; refer to city codes.

Any given state's Department of Transportation has very specific criteria for work within its right-of-way areas. Fees for installation permits are assessed and performance bonds need to be posted — sometimes for as long as 20 years. When working on public streets, the governing municipality often handles the agreement with the state agency, but not always. Frequently the project developer (owner) must coordinate directly with the Department of Transportation. It is wise to know how this issue is to be addressed going into the project.

In addition to the above, work frequently occurs within the physical and legal confines of private country clubs. These clubs usually have design standards and a private review staff, both of which must be satisfied.

Several cities and other design review bodies often restrict plan sheet sizes for ease in storage and retrieval. The graphic scale(s) that will be allowed is often limited to ease in plan readibility. Although these may seem like minor issues, they are good to verify before embarking on a set of drawings.

As if trying to wade through all these standards and review agencies is not enough, the *procedure* for doing so with plan submittals and personal interviews is not always clear. It is easy to see and cannot be emphasized enough that analyzing the review agencies and the myriad of governmental criteria has now become a major step in the design process.

Coordination with Other Design Disciplines

Landscape architecture does not exist in a void. It is interrelated with and often dependent upon information, physical design, and input provided by other professionals.

A landscape architectural firm may be commissioned to design a segment of a site that has an existing master plan developed by a multidisciplinary firm that specializes in regional, city, or large-scale site planning. It will be the responsibility of the landscape architectural firm to coordinate with the planning firm through meetings, review, and adherence to their established guidelines, and subjugation of its own design style in an attempt to mesh with the original design intent.

Eighty percent of the projects acquired by a landscape architectural firm will have already had an architectural and civil engineering firm selected. These firms frequently have sited buildings, located site infrastructure and circulation systems, and essentially been given or taken the design lead. Even when there is disagreement with the direction of the existing work, certain things will have to be accepted in a spirit of cooperation. The landscape architect should try to fit in and do the best he can with what he has to work with.

Architects provide building floor plans which, with their room arrangements and window and door locations, quickly define obvious use areas and site circulation. Sometimes the layout of exterior spaces is performed by the architect and sometimes it is performed by the landscape architect. This is a matter of owner or designer preference and the contractual scope of services.

Civil engineers provide site surveys, grading and drainage plans, and street and subdivision layouts. They also establish the pad elevation for structures based upon criteria from governmental review agencies and/ or 100-year storm information. Their imput is extremely important to the shaping of the site. They also assume the lion's share of the liability concerned with the actual physical layout of the site as contractors build and locate curbs and gutters, streets, drainage structures, and a wide variety of other site features in accordance with information provided on the civil plans.

Interior designers are occasionally the project lead. This is especially true in high end residential work, where the bulk of the design budget will be directed towards interior elements, finishes, and furnishings. In this event, the theory of transition is important for both the landscape architect and interior designer to grasp. Transition, or flow, allows a person to pass from interior to exterior space and vice versa with little noticeable disruption to the senses. That is, the transition should not be abrupt. Transition is created by allowing materials and finishes to continue across the doorway penetrating into and being repeated throughout both interior and exterior spaces. The landscape architect's careful coordination with a project interior designer will benefit the project immensely by providing a measure of elegance and taste.

The landscape architect often needs to consult with other disciplines to a lesser degree and should try to identify who they are and what they are needed for early in the design process. Walls and trellises should be reviewed by a structural engineer. Soil samples are often sent to testing laboratories for stability and fertility analysis. A water feature designer is frequently brought into the design process to review hydraulics and design efficiency. Irrigation designers are gaining a respected position and are becoming more frequently commissioned as water conservation becomes a more pressing issue.

The presence of and need to work with other disciplines should not be viewed as a deterrent to creativity or become a clash of egos. Each discipline is necessary to bring the project to fruition and, it is hoped, some measure of excellence.

Conceptual Design

This involves very loose, broad-stroke, freehand graphics and a brainstorming thinking approach. Using balloon or bubble diagrams, the most desirable relationships of use areas to one another, circulation systems, and site linking to adjacent sites are graphically depicted. Once this is accomplished, this ultimate site usage diagram, is looked at in terms of how it fits within the realities of the actual site. Using a base sheet, which is a scaled drawing of the site from any given source, the designer overlays flimsy transparent paper and superimposes use area bubbles where the site seems to accept them. This may differ from the predetermined ultimate diagram but is necessary to determine if the design program is feasible.

When working with conceptual design, remember to think big, then little. The idea is to take a candy store approach — what would you want if you could have it all? With a solid concept, the ensuing details often fall into place.

Often landscape architects are brought into the design process or onto the design team after the building has been laid out and the architect has sited the structure. In this case, certain elements are locked in. It is up to the landscape architect to still take a conceptual approach to the areas that he has left to work with and to be free thinking before narrowing his ideas to a structured layout. It's in the conceptual stage that great ideas, later to be distilled to no more than a mere detail, are born.

Schematic Design

With seasoned landscape architects this is frequently when drawings start to be generated. Use areas have been identified, elements of the client's program addressed, and site limitations noted. On flimsy or tracing paper, alternatives and evolving ideas about more detailed areas and elements are explored and explained at client presentations. Too often, in the haste necessitated by a tight schedule, this phase is glossed over and, as a result, the project suffers or the client ends up unhappy. It is in the schematic stage where the client's input should be sought. These drawings are easy to back away from and any new and different directions which need to be taken will be the most painless. The main purpose of doing schematics is to make sure the client understands what is proposed and is in agreement before drawings take on a more hardlined nature and changes start to create unnecessary conflicts.

Preliminary Design

It is at this stage that the plan starts to become hardlined and accurate. Preliminary designs are often requested by the various plan review agencies elaborated upon above. For this reason, they are often graphically pleasing with nice line work, shadow effects, varying tones, etc. Preliminary work is frequently colored for presentation purposes. Many cities, in fact, require color-rendered preliminaries as a part of their initial design review process. Because the working drawings to follow are usually refinements and more explanatory extensions of the preliminary, the preliminary design is done to scale. This scale is usually larger (more feet to the inch) than that of the ensuing working drawings. Note that "large-scale" means that the boundaries of the actual drawing become smaller with each increase in scale. Larger scales are used because detailed areas are not as important at this stage as the overall picture is, and it is easier to show the overall site on one sheet or as few sheets as possible. This benefits the reviewer who can view the site at a glance.

The information provided on the preliminary plan(s) should be sufficient to clearly define design intent, use areas, location of trees, and placement of major site elements. This being the case, cost estimates generally start to be generated at this point in the process. To the more graphically oriented designer, preliminary design is probably the most fun part of the process.

Working Drawings

This is the culmination of all the previous steps. Hopefully, the client knows the design direction and understands all the facets of the preliminary design. If the client does not (and they frequently do not) it is risky to proceed into this step without further explanation of all the steps that have come before.

Working drawings can include any or all of the following:

- Grading and Drainage Plans
- Hardscape (Staking) Plans
- Planting Plans
- Irrigation Plans
- Lighting Plans

These will all be explained at length in other chapters. Occasionally, a specialty type of plan, such as an Existing Tree Preservation, Site Demolition, or Boulder Placement Plan will also be required, but the plans noted above apply 90% of the time.

In conjunction with the plans, appropriate details which show materials and methods of installation are provided. These details are usually arranged to follow the path of construction. That is, they are sequenced in a manner consistent with the time when they will be utilized by the various construction trades. Inseparable from details are the specifications.

Specifications are written descriptions of how a project is to be built. By and large most of today's specifications are Performance Specifications. This type of spec outlines the results to be achieved in the installed design and does not attempt to tell the installer how to go about his work. Performance Specifications are written in three sections:

1. **General Information** — Describes the work, calls for any licenses, bonds, or insurances that the contractor must carry. Lists submittals to be made by the contractor to the landscape architect. Stipulates any guarantees or warranties to be provided by the contractor.
2. **Materials and Products** — Describes items to be used, sometimes by brand name. Outlines quantities and quality of some furnished items.
3. **Workmanship or Implementation** — Sets minimum acceptable standards for the outcome of the finished installation.

I believe that the specifications are the quality assurance part of the job. It is a fact of life, however, that they are frequently not read! For this reason I highlight what is said in the specs on my plan notes. This is contrary to most conventional schools of thought that say, "Keep the drawings generic and the specs descriptive." The theory is to keep information in one area only in case there are (and there often are) changes. If information is in two areas, the chance exists that the change will only be picked up in one spot, giving rise to conflicting information. I recognize this school of thought, but believe that the many good contractors who do not read specs do read plan notes. My rule is: if a specification changes, check your plan notes, and if you change or delete a plan note check your specs. I don't really worry about duplication or, for that matter, providing too much information. If something is described two, three, or even five times, that's fine with me if the message is consistent. The more times the message occurs, the more likely it is to be absorbed. My goal is to always make it easier for plan reviewers and contractors to understand the project — not to make their lives more difficult.

Field Observation

Until about 12 years ago, this part of the process was referred to as field inspection. A succession of lawsuits caused this verbiage to change when courts started finding designers guilty of negligence on the basis that if they were in fact inspecting a job then they were in fact responsible when something went wrong. Observation implies that you are merely observing and off to the side of the on-site decision-making process. Landscape architects — make no mistake about it — a good attorney will tear this little protective wall of words apart. It doesn't matter if you are inspecting, administering, or merely observing; if you issue a field report, then you are in it up to your eyeballs as far as most attorneys, arbitrators, judges, and juries are concerned.

Let's examine the purpose of field observation. The landscape architect is to review the work to see if it complies with the plans and specifications. He issues field reports to that end — as a function necessary to get the job constructed properly. This should ease the mind of the owner and provide clarity and direction to the contractor. If at the time of writing the contract a landscape architect is unsure of who these owners are or who the contractors are going to be, he should give himself an out. This can be done by qualifying in the scope of services under which conditions he will or will not perform field services.

Sometimes economics forces a landscape architect to perform field work he would rather forget, but in most instances field observation represents only 5% of the typical contract amount. If an owner is not willing to select from, say five qualified contractors on a bid list provided, should the landscape architect be required to play policeman for him while at the same time putting his financial future on the line?

A final message to designers concerning all disciplines: Louis L'Amour once said in a television interview that "There were good cowboys and bad cowboys and there were good Indians and bad Indians." The same could be said for contractors and designers. Try not to look upon contractors as bumbling, beer-guzzling buffoons, but rather as people with a job to do. With this being the case, work with contractors who have the same goals as you hopefully do — to do the job right.

Project Closeout

At the completion of the construction process, the end user (the owner) or the end user's maintenance staff will inherit the project. The landscape architect should try to leave them with the proper information and resources to perpetuate the design. If in the ensuing months and years an owner or a member of his maintenance staff calls for some advice or direction, don't be stingy. After all, completed projects that catch the public's eye and the referrals of satisfied owners are the best sources of new work.

Human Use Areas

Entries: Whether its a formal tree-lined boulevard leading to a large corporate headquarters or a simple entry walk to a middle-class residence, this is where the owner's statement is going to be made. This is the area where all visitors will come onto and leave the site. First impressions are lasting, and last impressions are memorable. For this reason, it is important to establish a sense of entry that will evoke the owner's pride and visitor's praise. A formal, even symmetrical entry heralds guests, while an informal "S" curved, or free-form entry invites surprise. You can learn a lot about the people on the other side of an entry door by observing the sequence of elements that lead to that door. Often, in this case, you can judge a book by its cover.

Living Spaces: This area of design invariably receives the most attention, if only because it is where users spend the majority of their time. In the desert, this area will demand the most climate control. Probably the highest concentration of hardscape elements will be located in this area. Swimming pools, spas, outdoor barbecues, and firepits will require careful planning. In commercial design, provisions will need to be made for gathering places, and site furniture will need to be situated. In no other use area will the outdoor room concept, to be explained later, need to be more skillfully applied. This area will probably chew up the largest amount of site area and, accordingly, the installation budget; so painstaking thought is needed.

Service Areas: These are the areas of the site where items necessary for maintenance, storage, and waste disposal are given design consideration. In addition, these areas frequently house the mechanical, air-conditioning, heating, and pool/spa equipment systems. Storage sheds for lawn mowers and garden equipment are often located here. Gardens themselves, especially when utilitarian in nature, are frequently located in the service area. In commercial settings, large trash dumpsters, grease pits, and maintenance equipment are found in the service area. In fact, these areas often are called maintenance yards. Think of this use area as being the heart of the design — something that is not outwardly seen but upon which all functions depend.

Play Areas: These areas include either active or passive recreation and, frequently, both. In park and school design they can take the form of recreational ballfields or court games. In the residential setting, the play area could be a simple panel of turf for frisbee tossing, golf putting, or casual relaxation. Families with small children will want play areas within full view from the kitchen, family, and living rooms while definitely being separated or fenced from pools and spas. Other site areas can be used for play - a basketball court in the entry drive or a volley ball net across the pool, for example. One thing is certain, play is an important part of our lives and accomodations for it should be incorporated into the initial design stages and not left to afterthought.

Privacy Areas: These areas are for individual or limited use. Contemplation and theme gardens are often located in privacy areas. In the residential setting, they can be off the master bedroom or study. In the workplace, a privacy garden can serve as an outdoor conference room or dining area for small groups. One thing is common to all privacy gardens, because they are passive they should be intimate in scale. This is a place for fine sculpture, exotic plant material, or an intricate fountain to be studied, touched, and fully appreciated. Privacy areas should possess the innate ability to take users far from the madding world and return them refreshed.

Viewing Areas: These include enclosed atriums around which a building centers, a garden outside a bathroom, or even a staging area from which distant views are seen. In the design of viewing gardens, the angle of perspective becomes extremely important. If the viewer is looking down from above, a Mimosa tree which flowers very profusely across the top of its canopy may be a good subject. This same tree could be a poor choice if viewed from below. In this case, a tumbling vine or cascading water feature that falls to meet the viewer's eye level would probably be a better choice. Distant or borrowed views should be given special consideration as they expand the limits of the garden in the viewer's perception.

Public Areas: These are often the areas at the front of buildings that are left over in terms of human usefulness. Commercial owners, however, consider these areas great image makers, and the better part of an installation budget can be used up here. There is nothing wrong with embellishing architecture per se. The streetscape is important. It would be just be nice to see as much importance attached to the places where people gather as to the places that people see. In the residential setting, the public areas (front yards) of houses do much to establish the neighborhood character. The money spent here is typically in more realistic proportion to other home use areas, as the residential user is usually more concerned with how he lives than how he looks.

Design Components

It is very difficult to arrange the following design components in any given order. They certainly are not listed in order of importance. If anything, they are listed according to the physical mass they occupy in space, and move in descending order to that which has no mass but high visual impact, such as color.

Form: Form, or the shape of an element, relates to its physical and perceived qualities. "Round," "square," "angular," etc., are words used to describe forms. Shape represents the outer edge of solid or displaced forms. Designers use the terms form and shape interchangeably although, technically, they are different. Whether an object is described as having a form or shape, this relates to its physical appearance in space. The various forms of trees can have several different design applications. Rounded, wide-spreading canopies block wind, provide privacy, and draw the eye closer to the ground plane. Vertical (conical) conifer trees lead the eye upward and their upright character makes them good choices for view enframement and entry definition. The ground-plane form of planting beds, swimming pools, and the like is very important, as it is the basis or template around which all the other aspects of the design will revolve.

Scale: Scale, as it applies to the built environment, refers to the relative size of an object. For our purposes, this size is measured or comprehended in proportion to the human body. Mountain ranges have extreme scale, tall buildings have large scale, most trees have perceivable scale, and 6-inch river rocks have ground-plane scale. Humans and objects, of the same or nearly the same size, have human scale. Objects that are used in everyday functions and are designed to fit human dimensions — tables, chairs, televisions, and cooking utensils — are also often said to have human scale. For comfort, the closer an object is to a person, the better it is to be of human or below human scale. The further away larger objects are, the less intimidating their scale becomes.

Space: Space, as it relates to the design professions, is either a physical (as with a room) or a perceivable enclosure (looking down into a valley). Even the wide-open spaces are enclosed, as far as the human eye is concerned, because we see the ground plane and horizon merge. Human-scale spaces create comfort. Medium perceivable scale spaces such as an auditorium cause awareness in that one is more cognizant of his immediate surroundings and focuses on elements within those surroundings for visual balance and stability. Large-scale spaces such as the manmade canyons of buildings in Manhattan inspire awe. Extreme-scale spaces such as the Grand Canyon elicit not only awe, but wonder and reverence. Man seems to be the most impressed by elements and spaces outside the realm of his physical control. Creating the appropriate space by arranging items in the right proportions to one another is perhaps the designer's greatest task. The visual or physical merging of objects (such as two walls) creates space. The voided area between these items creates volume, while the items themselves are defined as mass. The positioning of masses that create voids defines space.

Rhythm, Line, and Harmony: Rhythm is the movement of the eye across a space marked by the regular recurrence of elements within that space. Rhythm may be achieved in several ways. Repetition of a shape or element moves the eye in a line of sight from one thing to the next. Although an effective means of achieving rhythm, repetition may become monotonous, in which case alternation of line and shape can liven up a design. The principles of unity and variety are important to rhythm. Unity aids the visual flow, and variety adds interest to a design. Continuity induces movement in a slow manner while holding the interest of the observer. A break in the continuity may occur, creating a point of interest. Progression is a third way of achieving rhythm. Changes in shape, size, direction, or color create flow throughout the design. This type of rhythm is usually more dynamic than the others, but can also be misused more easily.

Lines provide direction, movement, and speed to any design. Horizontal lines lying at rest with the ground and offering little opposition to gravity produce a peaceful calm environment. Vertical lines are more dominant, moving the eye upward. The more domineering the vertical line, the more forceful the movement, and hence, the greater the sensation. Diagonal and zigzagging lines are less static and due to their multidirectional qualities, offer liveliness and activity to a design. Curvilinear lines, often smooth and meandering, produce a slow and gentle atmosphere. Vertical lines narrow and horizontal lines widen — a fact frequently exploited in women's fashions.

Viewers need to perceive objects or spaces with logic and understanding. This may stem from man's basic need to find reason with and relate to that which he experiences from day to day. Order in his surroundings is beneficial for peace of mind and tranquility. Where unity is essential to a space, monotony must be avoided. Variety must exist to interrupt the boredom created by too much order. A touch of variety or disorder is sometimes necessary for man to exercise his senses. It must be remembered, however, that an overabundance of variety could create chaos and confusion in a design. Unity and variety must exist in a fragile equilibrium, and when they do, harmony exists.

Balance: Balance is the relation of objects within a space that create a sense of completeness. Three main types of balance exist with relation to exterior spaces: symmetry, asymmetry, and radial balance. Balance is said to be symmetrical when objects of the same kind are placed equidistant from a center line, or axis point, and align with one another. Symmetry is formal in nature and usually results in precise order. Asymmetry is much less formal, and is often referred to as occult or active balance. There is no obvious center line which divides the space into two parts. Due to its informal nature, asymmetry offers the designer much more freedom in regards to imagination and creativity. With radial balance, the objects of a space revolve around a central point. Balance of this kind often serves the purpose of accentuating objects, either along the perimeter or in the center of the space.

Emphasis: Emphasis, or focalization of interest, is an important factor in any exterior space. Emphasis involves assigning varying degrees of dominance and subordination to objects within a space. There should be no more than one major point of interest, often called the focal point, with all other objects becoming subordinate or exhibiting minor degrees of dominance to it. Contrast between different colors, textures, shapes, sizes, and details determine the level of emphasis among elements. Caution must be taken to avoid conflict among objects by allowing each to exhibit equal or near-equal emphasis. The major point of interest should be chosen before the completion of the design. Varying degrees of dominance and subordination may occur within the design, while not competing visually with this focal point.

Texture: Texture can be tactile (touch), visual, or dimensional. In all three cases, texture is most clearly defined as the surface characteristic of an object. Varying degrees of texture exist, ranging from smooth to rough. Smooth surfaces reflect light, while rough surfaces absorb it. Rough textures, when working with exterior spaces, tend to be domineering and, in turn, a bit crude. Smoother textures are more subtle and produce a casual effect. When trying to comprehend visual and tactile texture, think of varying grades of sand paper.

Light: This is an extremely difficult element to define. To say that light is the medium which allows us to see may seem like an understatement but it does exactly that. Outdoor natural light is approximately 1000 times brighter than indoor artificial light. Outside, in the open desert, the light is extremely clear, bordering on brilliant. Desert light can provide crisp highlights and deep, well defined shadows. The eye always is drawn to and focuses upon the most intensely lit object. Owing to the difference in sun angle, the appearance of an object will change markedly through the course of the day. As various design features are subjected to the play of sun and shadow, their colors will change in intensity through the passing of the daylight hours. A carefully conceived outdoor space can exploit this phenomenon and display a kinetic quality, to the delight of the users. Night lighting provides safety, channels visual interest, and creates a sense of drama. As such, it is a powerful design tool.

Color: Color is perceived and defined in terms of hue, value, and intensity. Hue is the actual name of a color. There are primary, secondary, and tertiary colors. These are what are shown on a color wheel. The primary colors are red, yellow, and blue. These primary colors are mixed with one another to create the secondary colors of green, orange, and purple. Varying amounts of primary and secondary colors are mixed together to form the tertiary colors that are mostly pastels and earth tones. Value describes the amount of light within the hue and can run from white to black. Intensity or chroma of a color describes its strength or weakness as it absorbs or repels light. Think of water colors when trying to visualize intensity. The more water (light) the less actual color (intensity). Color is a very potent design tool because it is capable of manipulating or altering the psychological mood of the people experiencing the space. Warm colors (red, yellow, and orange) advance, while cool colors (blue and white) recede. White expands volume and black reduces volume. Green is considered a neutral color because it does very little of either, evoking calm emotions. Good design can be negated with poor color selection and bad design can be salvaged, to some degree, with good color selection. No other design tool will have a more immediate impact upon viewers or create immediate emotions of like or dislike. Any quality art store or paint supplier can supply color charts to aid a designer in choosing the appropriate hue.

Desert Design Techniques

The desert environment affords unique opportunities for outdoor living. Seasoned desert dwellers can live comfortably outdoors 8 to 9 months out the year. The intensely hot summer months of June, July, and August can be made tolerable, even enjoyable, with some design forethought and degree of climate control.

The landscape architect should be aware of the varying daily sun exposures, the difference between summer and winter sun angles, and how this creates microclimates. Microclimates can refer to the thermal difference between valley and hillside, position on a hillside, or nearness to an insulating or cooling body of water. Most frequently, however, the term is used to describe the difference between the north, east, south, and west exposures of a building. This temperature difference at any given point in time can be surprisingly significant. Sometimes 10- to 15° F variations can be recorded, especially if the north exposure is shaded and the west exposure is exposed. The need to address microclimatic areas will affect the location of shade structures and hardscape, plant material selection, and hydrozone application — all to be discussed in detail in other chapters.

Wind control is another environmental factor that will influence design. The strongest desert winds usually flow from late winter through early spring, February to late May. This does not preclude summer wind storms caused by air movement due to low pressure areas on the desert floor or from occasional tropical storms originating in the Pacific Ocean or Gulf of Mexico. Plant materials, walls, fences, and upwind buildings all play a part in blocking or reducing the flow of wind onto any given site.

Assuming that the landscape architect knows how to assign the various use areas to the site, is well versed in the usefulness of design components, and has considered known environmental factors, it is then time to apply them on paper, graphically utilizing design techniques to arrive at a workable design solution.

Speak the local vernacular: "Vernacular" means being of a native or common place or group. In design, it means applying indigenous plant and building materials. The Santa Fe style evolved in New Mexico because clay soils made adobe readily available and large poles from Sycamores and Cottonwoods were supplied by nearby riparian areas. The Mission style of Southern California came about because the coastal trails and the Pacific Ocean afforded dependable supply routes for roof tile from Mexico and frame lumber from the Pacific Northwest. Desert architecture in territorial Arizona and California borrowed from these two emerging styles, but incorporated more of the readily available rock, tin, and copper from early mining operations. Desert architecture and early gardens quickly transformed into a style that reflected what the average Apache and Cahuilla Indian had known for centuries — provide shade in summer and fire in winter, stay out of the wind, and conserve water.

Enlist the outdoor room concept: The rooms denoted on a building's floor plan all contain a specific function for living, sleeping, bathing, etc. Likewise, knowing that the site a building sits on has functions (use areas), it is not unreasonable to contain these functions within rooms. Outdoor rooms are not as hard or enclosed as interior rooms. In fact, many outdoor rooms are simply implied. The elements on the ground plane, either natural or manmade, act as the room's floor. Property line fences, hedges of plant materials, or earth berming can be employed to serve as walls. An overhead trellis, canvas screening, tree canopy, or beautiful desert sky can become the ceiling. The strength of the outdoor room concept is that once the designer has use areas identified as rooms it becomes easier to place or organize elements within these rooms.

Let the circulation system dominate: Site circulation, or flow, links outdoor rooms and defines important transition areas. By allowing a free and open circulation pattern starting with vehicular access to the entry, entry to the interior, interior to the exterior and then back again, a person feels unrestricted and space appears larger. Site furnishings fall to the sides and end of this dominant swath, thus providing order. Design components, especially lines, can add to the sensation of movement within the circulation system. Elements that impose on the circulation system are more noticeable and thus gain importance. The decreasing width and also the decreasing hardness of the circulation system indicate less use, lower importance, or privacy. Good site circulation is more important on larger or commercial sites as they must transport greater numbers of users, but also plays a part in smaller scale design in organizing and identifying spaces.

Consider the value of the oasis, transition, "feather-to-desert" theory: This theory originates by just studying the pattern of human habitation in any desert region. Humans settle in an area with a dependable supply of water and plant gardens for enjoyment — *the oasis*. They simultaneously plant agricultural fields and groves of trees for survival purposes. Indigenous vegetation invades at the periphery of the agricultural zone utilizing the more abundant soil moisture — *the transition*. In varying degrees, the density of the native vegetation decreases as the terrain moves away from the human development until conditions are the same as they always were — *feather to desert*.

Applying this theory to landscape architectural design is easy and beneficial. Planting around the building is relatively thick. Plant material selection, while responding to microclimate, is greener and its moisture content cools the ground plane and/or provides shade to the structure — *the oasis*. Planting that extends out into other use areas thins while plant species selection is towards less water demanding to near drought tolerant — *the transition*. Hydroseed mixes for seasonal color, thicker than normal native cactus plantings, and eventually raw desert occurs as you fade further away from the building — *feather to desert*.

Another application of this process can be used when building upwards on a bajada from a developed desert floor area. Development at the toe of the slope can be the greenest, blending with previous development. Middle slope planting can be transitional in nature. The top of the bajada should be preserved or re-established in a native condition.

Theme Garders Evoke Emotions. Among other things, theme gardens are areas that deal with a subject, promote an idea, or pay tribute to something. Theme gardens can be nothing more than a celebration of color. If a client's favorite color is red, white, yellow, pink, or violet it is an easy thing to assemble plant material that flowers in that color and group them together for viewing pleasure. A patriotic theme garden may emphasize red, white, and blue colors and an American flag. A cactus garden with one species in various stages of growth and decline, even to a few standing skeletons, could revolve around the theme of life and death.

A Christian religious theme garden could center around the common names of plants or the stories that can be related to them. Jerusalem Thorn, Our Lord's Candle, Joshua Tree, Crown of Thorns, and Passion Vine are all somewhat self explanatory. Olives are a sign of peace and were frequently planted around missions. Date palms, grapes, figs and pomegranates were all agricultural staples in the early formation of the Holy Land as they are today.

Theme gardens can be miniature ecosystems, mathematical patterns, or a small-scale memorial to a variety of people or things. Although they can easily be turned into something cute or trite, they can also be gardens that bring out the best in people.

Apply the Unusual. Try to develop an eye for those things that are not common to most ordinary forms of development. Certainly sculpture is not found in the everyday garden. The same can be said for sundials, mounted telescopes, and weathervanes. Large boulders are hard for everyone to obtain. Colorful windsocks and banners not only lend visual impact, but are also relatively inexpensive. Wind chimes of all shapes and sizes are not only visual but auditory. One of the most underused landscape elements in the desert is fire for viewing. Fire adds a primitive feeling to any environment, and when applied with sculpture, can create a kinetic vertical movement unlike wind or water.

Establish a hierarchy of importance: With all the processes and elements that go into a design, it is easy to get confused or produce a product that is confusing to others. This can be avoided by prioritizing in two areas. The first is to determine the relative value of each use area in the design. The second is to determine what is the most important part or element within each use area. When the comparative importance of the outdoor rooms is determined and the value of all the items in each room is decided upon, then the designer is in the position to select items to fill the rooms. Another technique is to create a focal point. The focal point, due to its importance, draws first attention and, likely, the most attention. All other items around the focal point are subordinate to it. When there are no competing focal points, the viewer can comprehend the design in an orderly and relaxed fashion.

Employ mimicking and repetition of form: To mimic means to imitate. By mimicking the style, material, or detail of an architectural element within the landscape design, a landscape architect can establish a design continuity which ties the site to the architecture. A three-tiered wall system that repeats the feel of three distant mountain ranges is a good example of mimicking. Using the stone found around the inside fireplace as a coping material for the outside firepit is mimicking. Repetition of form differs from mimicking in technique, yet is similar in results. Patterns found in the architecture — triangular, rectangular, or circular — that are repeated in the hardscape, on wall surfaces, or to define a planting bed would be repetition of form. Repetition of form, like mimicking, adds continuity to the design. Unlike mimicking, repetition of form is not as apt to be misused or used in a cute or silly manner. Both can be powerful design tools if applied with a measure of restraint and taste.

Consider the power of the axis: An axis is a straight line that connects two points. An axis is a line created by man, usually to establish order, but sometimes to create awe. It has been applied to some of the most monumental designs in history, especially by the Renaissance French and Italians. The axis has a beginning and usually a terminus. A strong terminus such as sculpture, a vertical tree, or a magnificent fountain increases the power of the axis. Often a terminus is implied, such as the peak of a mountain range or the steeple of a church in the distance. What makes a terminus a terminus is that it terminates one's view. The eye stops looking and fixes on the terminus. They are most always centered on the center line of the axis. The axis and the terminus are usually bilaterally symmetrical and elements at the sides of the axis are frequently, but not always, symmetrical. Axes are powerful and quite formal. Consider their application carefully. An axis can be valuable in creating the formal entry or leading the eye or the viewer to a dramatic view or element. Axes also can be used to define governmental plazas and other larger than life spaces.

Maximize views: Views can be created on site or borrowed from elements occurring off-site. The most important thing to remember about a view is how it is set up and presented. To set up a view, consider the optimum position of the viewer. If the view is the most important element of the design it should be seen from a staging area located within the most important site use area. In addition, the viewer should be brought to or placed in the staging area in a sensitive manner so that the view opens up before him. Views at a distance are more likely to hold an onlooker's gaze. Distant views need only be interesting, while foreground views have to be attention grabbers.

View presentation is an art in itself. Most views, especially distant and panoramic ones, have more impact when they are framed like a picture. The human mind finds it difficult to comprehend something that the eye cannot immediately focus on. View enframement allows the eye to focus and the mind to grasp and appreciate quickly. Views can also be presented in segments or a series of sequential vistas as one winds up a road or staircase. When designing such a view progression, the time and the place should come when the onlooker can stop and take it all in.

Introduce water: Water is a precious commodity in the desert. With increasingly stricter conservation standards, the use of water for purely aesthetic purposes needs to be justifiable and efficient. Because it is so precious, water literally commands people to be drawn to it. In the desert, especially in enclosed spaces, it does not take a lot of water to make an impact. The sound of water can be just as compelling as the sight of it. The fluidity and reflective qualities of water can be manipulated in thousands of ways. Water adapts to any design style from postmodern to completely natural. Sometimes it is the display of water in an unnatural application, such as with upward spurting jets that has special appeal. Sometimes attention to natural principles connects us to a garden in a subconscious way. Water in the natural state seeks its own level. Left unrestricted, water flows to the lowest point in any given terrain. By lowering a fountain or basin or stepping down to a spa or swimming pool, we can stir memories of visits to other natural places. In the desert, nine times out of ten, one steps down to find water.

As a means of climate control, micromist systems have come to the fore. They introduce atomized water particles to the overhead plane. This can cool the area under that plane by as much as 20°F. Employment of vertical canvasses or fiberglass screens in the path of natural or fan-blown wind with water dripping over them is another environmental cooling device. The utilization of these two climate modification systems in more creative ways will add liveability to future outdoor rooms.

Perception equals rate of movement and distance: The level of detail of an object or within a setting changes or blurs as the speed of the perceiver increases. This is why highway signs have big letters and graphics and very short messages. Conversely, a quiet meditation garden off a residential study can contain a great many objects for the observer to experience. This is not only because he can walk slowly, but also because of his physical proximity to the objects. Taking into account where a site or subject is and how it will be seen will often dictate the design approach.

Invite wildlife: These are nature's freebies. Animals can be encouraged to enter into the outdoor room from the wild, or they can be brought in and enclosed. Hummingbirds, doves, quail, lizards, and even the desert tortoise can be encouraged by emulating their natural habitats or providing food or both. Koi, goldfish, birds in a large aviary, and even cats and dogs are examples of animals that are introduced. Also, truly wild animals found off-site can become part of the design scheme through view channelization into areas where they normally congregate or feed. Agricultural animals on a large rural site can be viewed in a setting without fences by use of an unseen drop in grade called a haha.

Gardens that attract hummingbirds are enjoyed by everyone. Introduce hummingbird feeders — glass containers filled with colored dyes. Use a variety of colors in addition to the commonly used red. Hang these containers at varying lengths using clear, monofilament fishing line so they appear to float in space. Into this poor man's "stained-glass" forest will fly winged jewels that dazzle and delight.

Remember: Rules were made to be broken! Designers through years of professional training and, too often, nonprofessional chastisement, arrive at a design style. They come to a thinking process and drawing methodology that works for them, the overriding critical factor being commissions or gainful employment. It is unfortunate that what creates success frequently promotes stagnation. Designers get idea-lock or style lock and their projects start to look and function the same. This happens because rules of thumb and personal design standards become a habit which, in the face of schedule and financial constraints, assures survival.

When and if given the luxury to break out of this mold, there are ways to get back on the creative track. The easiest way is to develop a system of checks and balances much as a detective would. For every theory, position, or idea generated, look at the exact opposite. For example, if you want to emphasize the foreground ask yourself, "what would happen if I emphasized the background instead?" If you feel an area should receive cool colors — why not warm colors? Consider smooth texture, rough, and so forth. The point is — challenge yourself. If you cannot find an acceptable reason to discount the converse, perhaps the first proposition is a weak one. Just because something has always been done a certain way, it does not mean that it has to continue that way. Reserve, above all else, the right to change your mind.

All of this challenging and mind-changing, however, can create enough turmoil and indecision to immobilize a designer. If an honest effort has been made early on in the inventory and analysis part of the design process, then the concepts generated are probably solid and strong; good concepts usually take care of the majority of the details. No two designers look at things or approach problems the same way. For this reason no two design solutions will ever be the same. Who is to say that one design or designer exceeds another? If the program has been met and the clientele satisfied, then the designer has done his duty. Design, like art, as it is perceived by the individual, is a matter of personal preference and taste.

Design Process

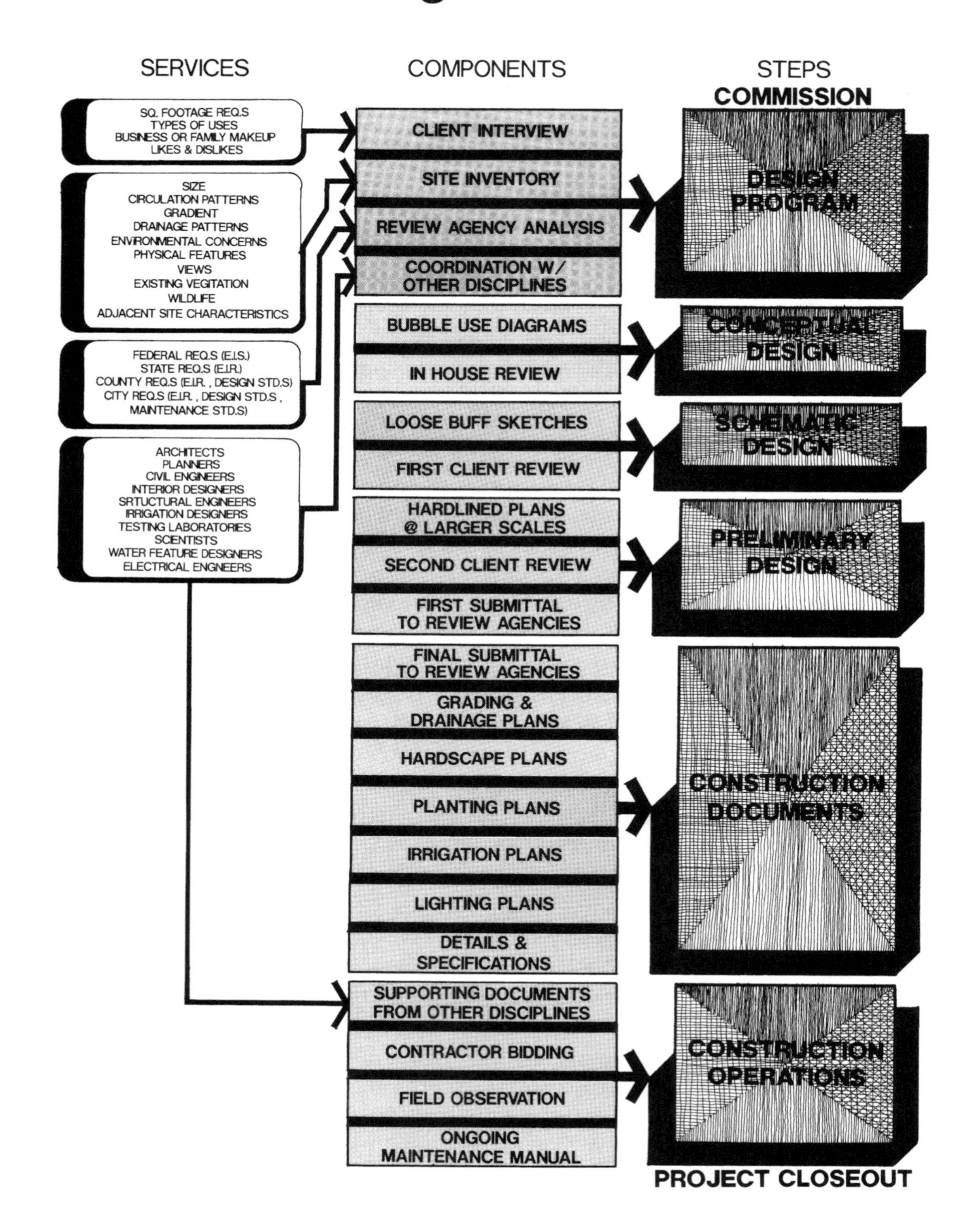

Design Elements

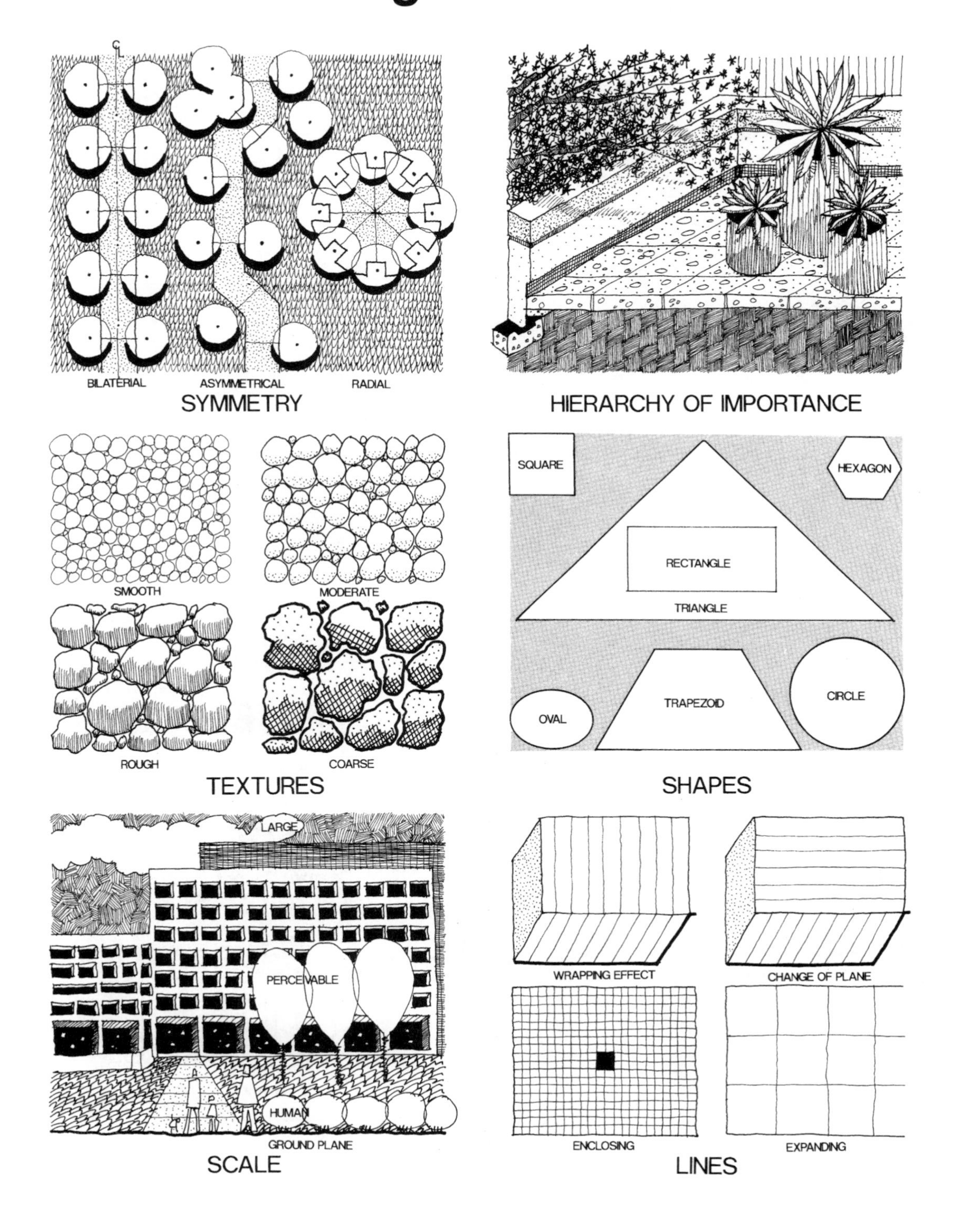

Solar Orientation

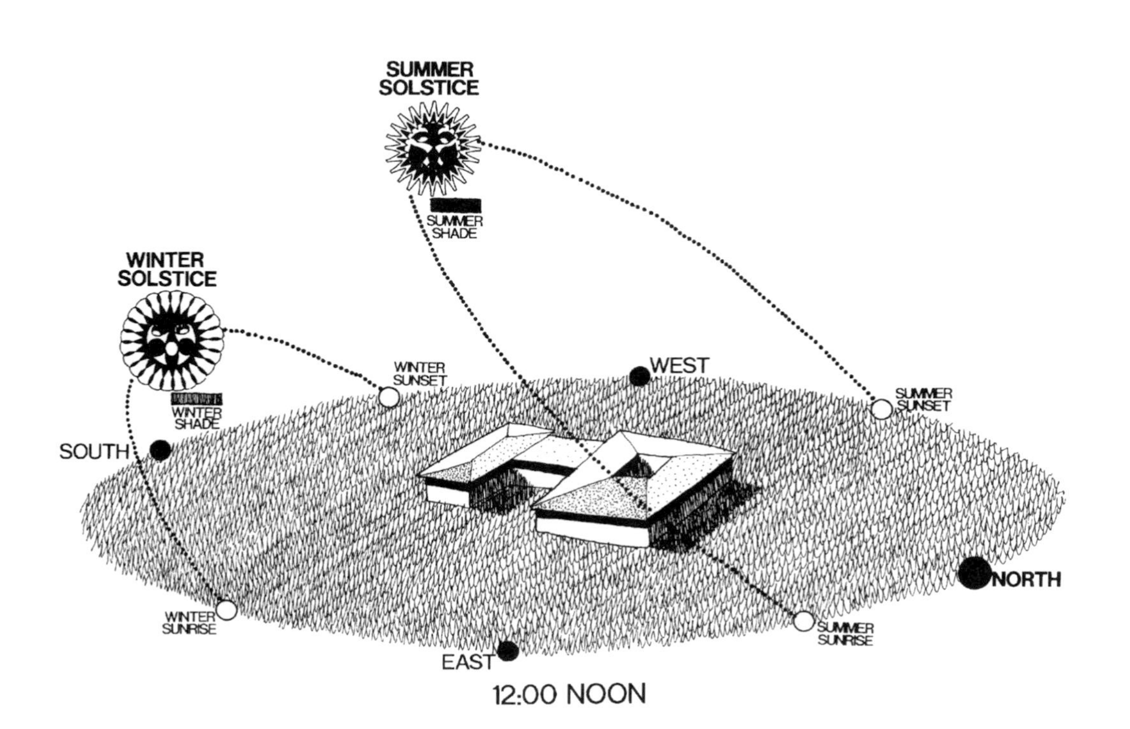

12:00 NOON

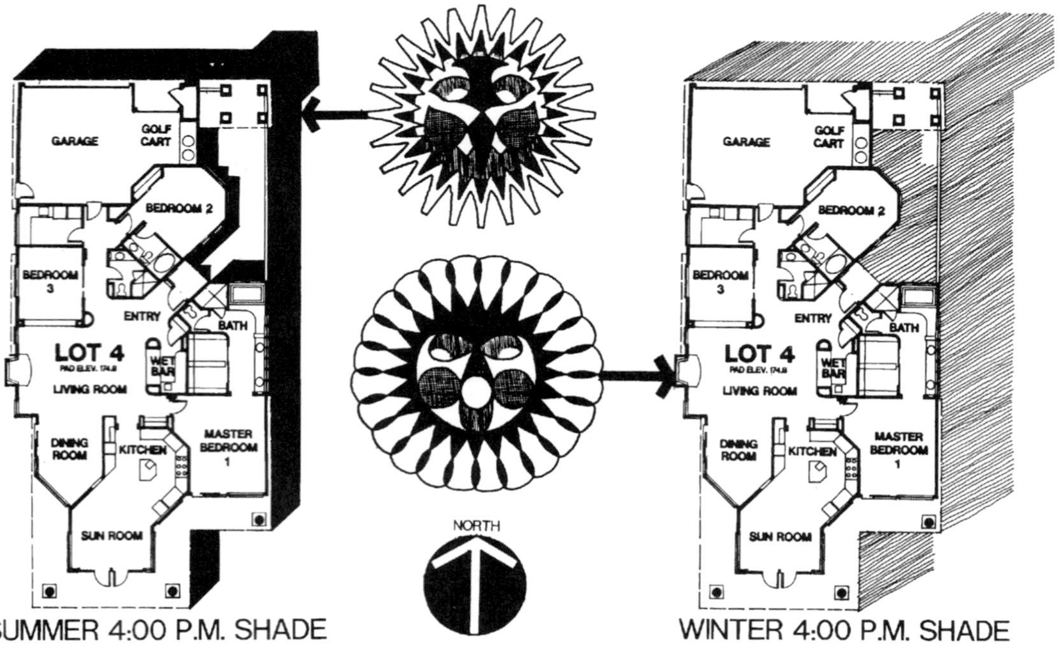

GARAGE
GOLF CART
BEDROOM 2
BEDROOM 3
ENTRY
BATH
LOT 4
PAD ELEV. 174.8
WET BAR
LIVING ROOM
DINING ROOM
KITCHEN
MASTER BEDROOM 1
SUN ROOM

SUMMER 4:00 P.M. SHADE

NORTH

GARAGE
GOLF CART
BEDROOM 2
BEDROOM 3
ENTRY
BATH
LOT 4
PAD ELEV. 174.8
WET BAR
LIVING ROOM
DINING ROOM
KITCHEN
MASTER BEDROOM 1
SUN ROOM

WINTER 4:00 P.M. SHADE

Schematic Design

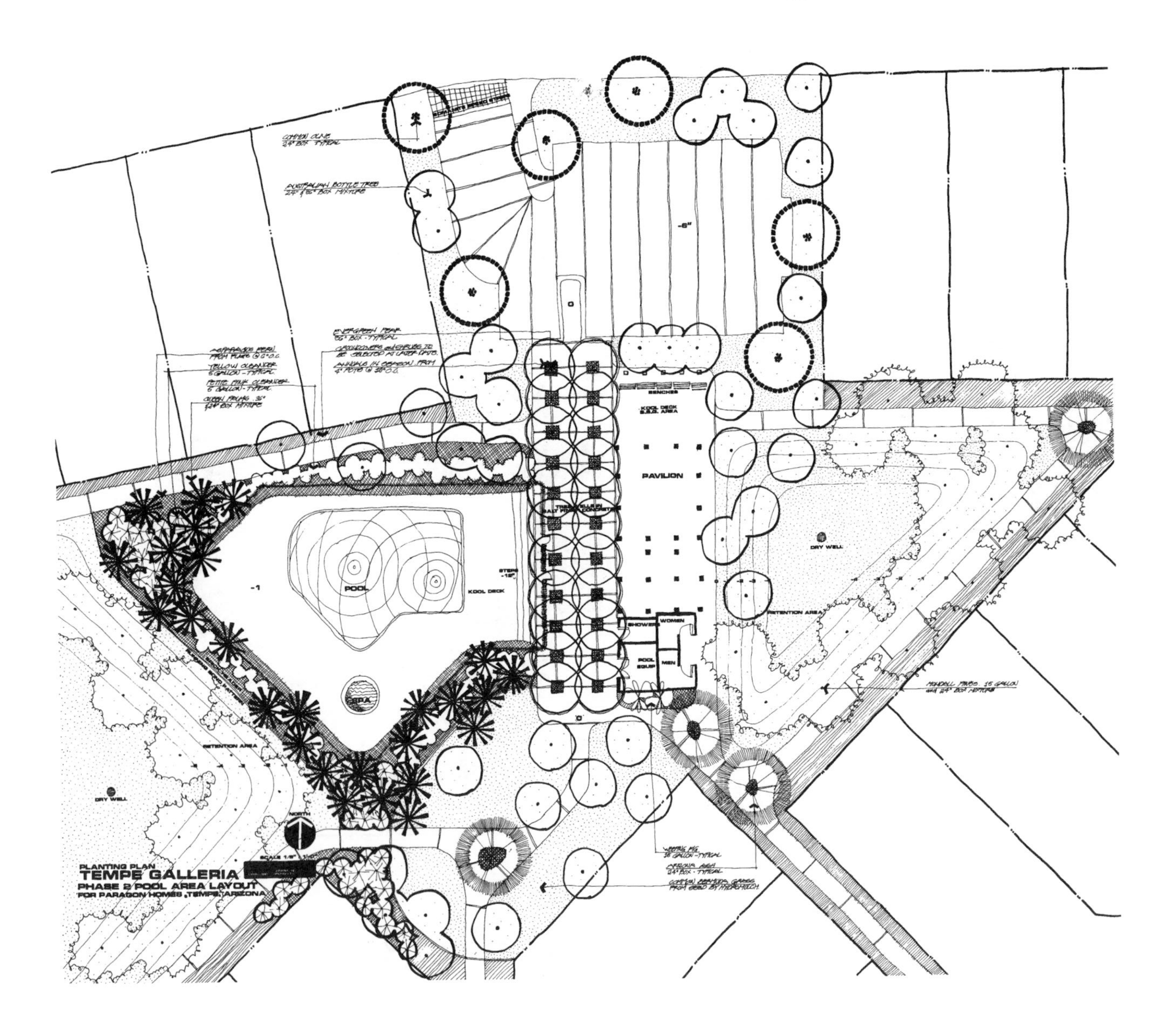

Preliminary Design

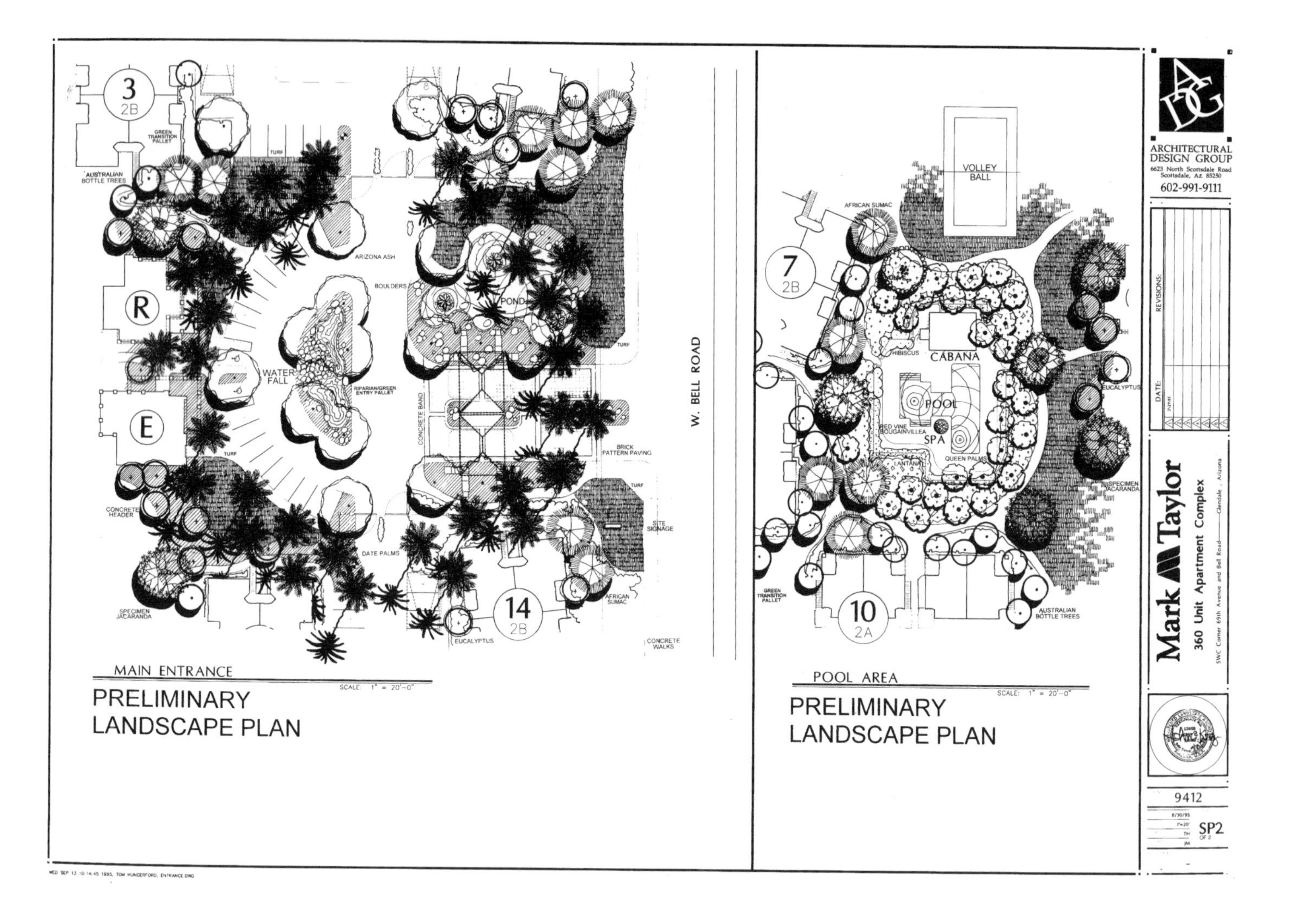

Preliminary Design

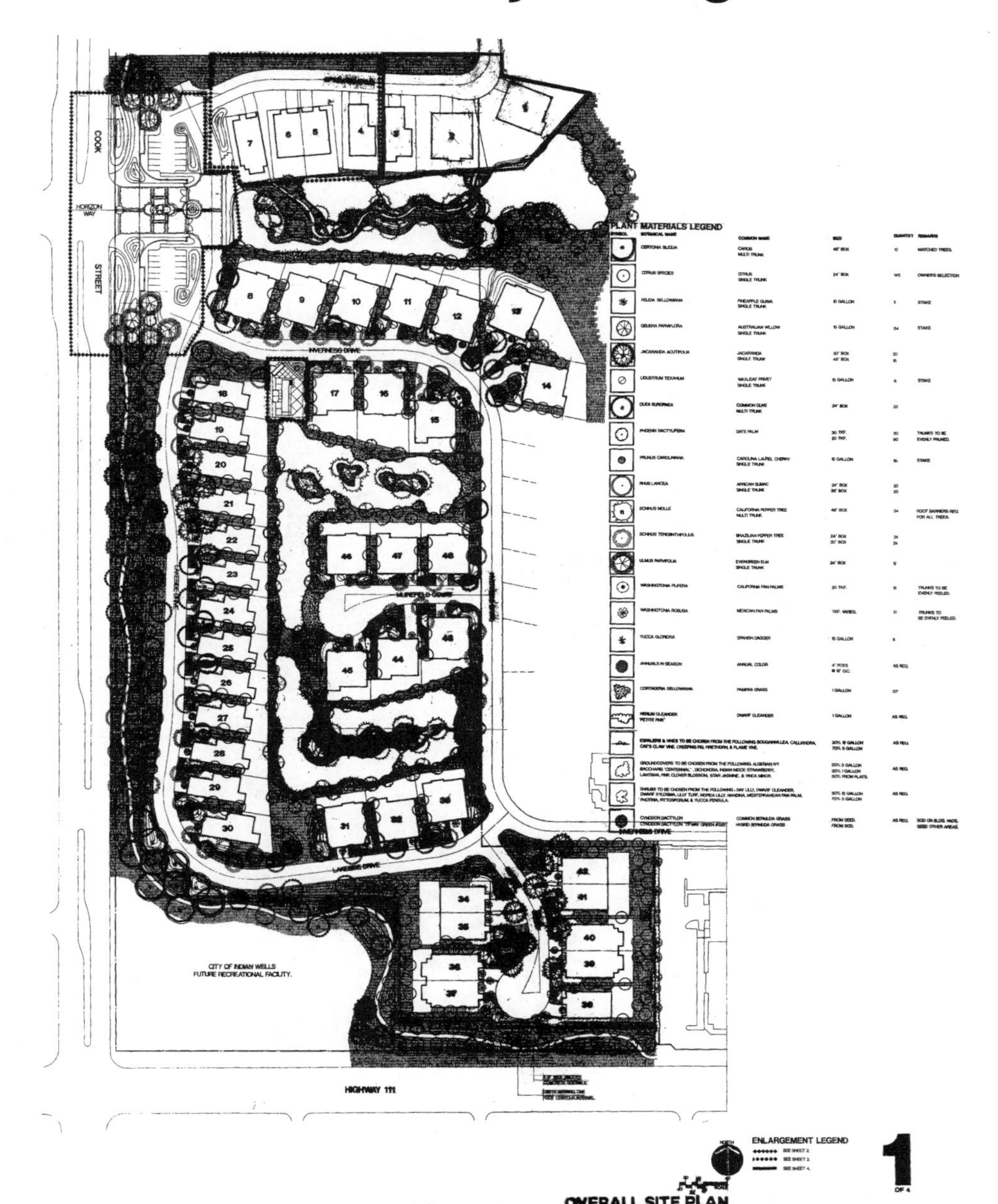

Landscape Master Plan

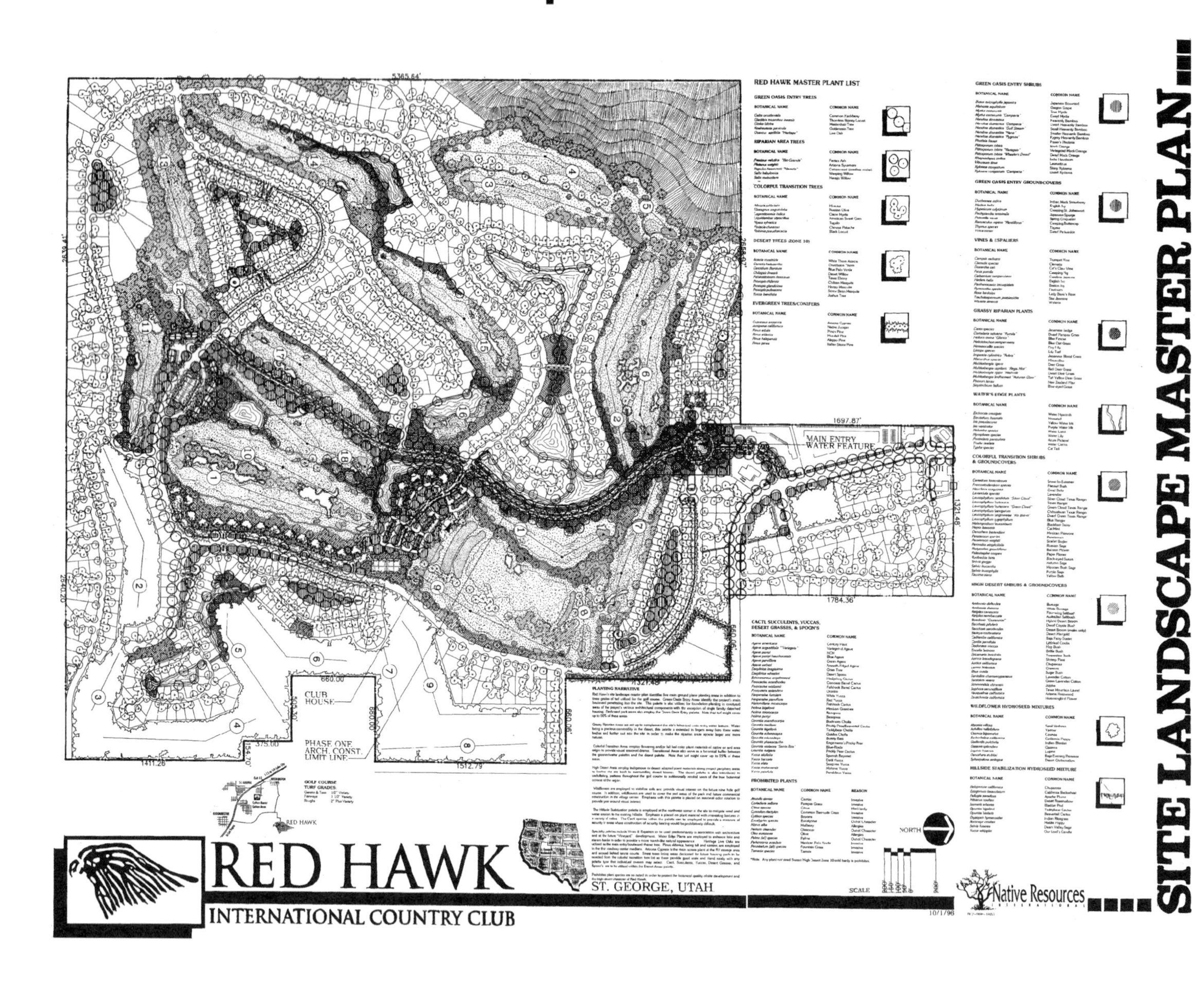

Preliminary Design

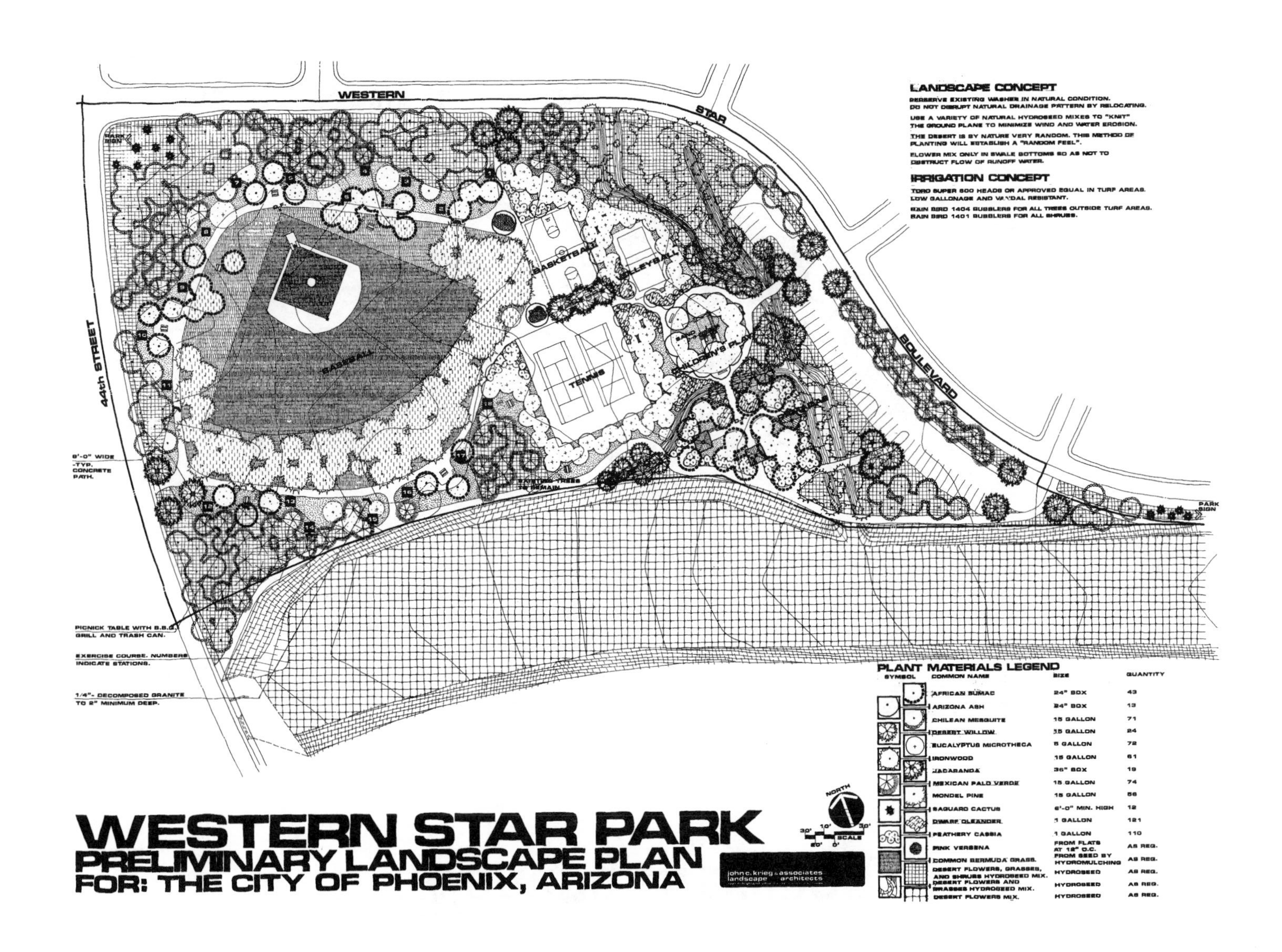

Working Drawings

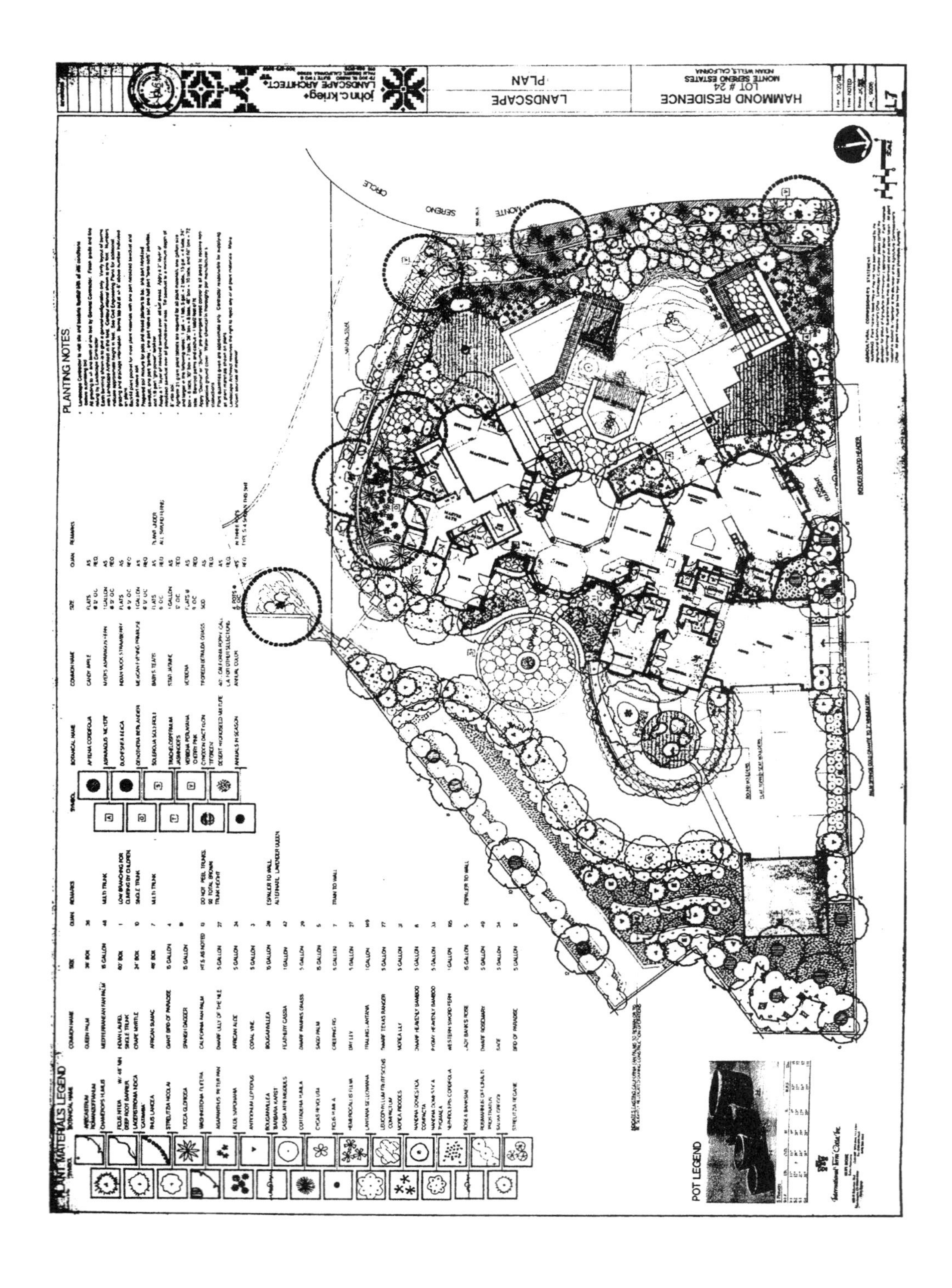

Working Drawings

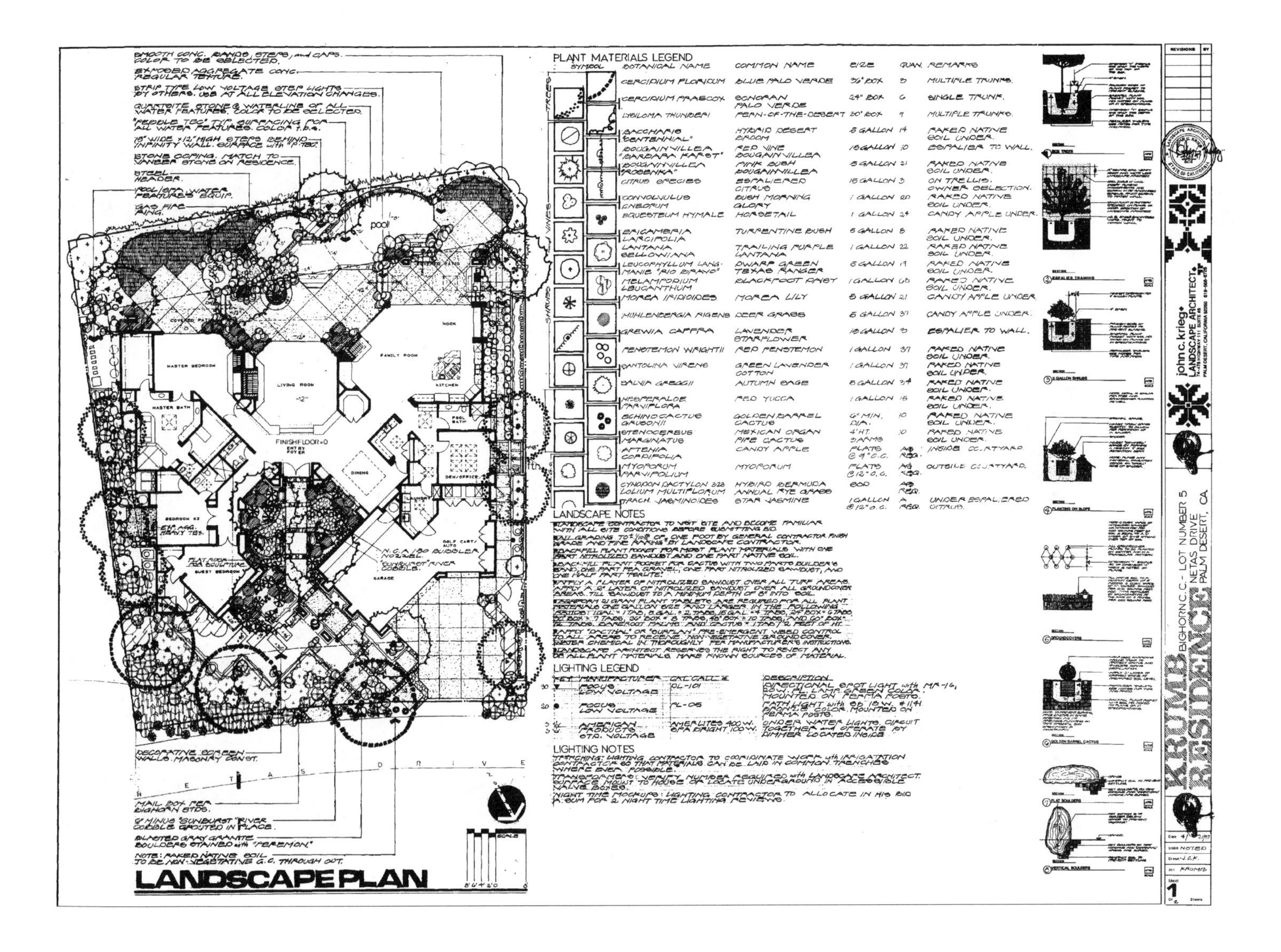

Design Components

Typical entry statement

Common area pool

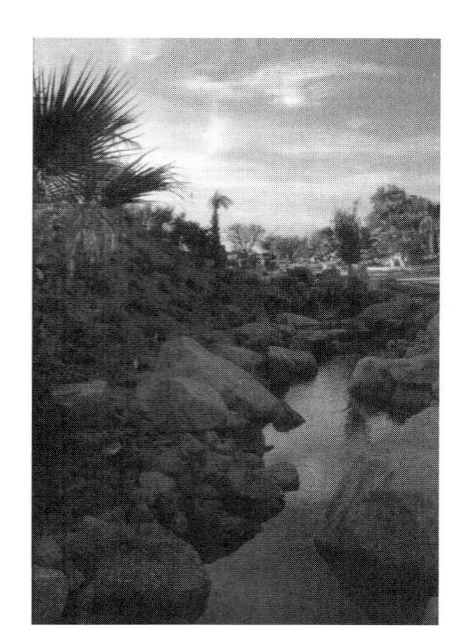

Stream head

Low water use planting

Glossary

Aerial photo: A photograph taken from above the earth's surface. Professional aerial photography services can provide photos at a defined scale, usually 1" = 100' or 1" = 200'. Very useful for broad overview information.

Architect: An individual licensed by law to design buildings and related structures.

Axis: A straight, unbroken line. Usually an axis has a beginning and an end (terminus).

Balance: Harmonious distribution of objects or forms. Items complement one another and appear appropriate in size, texture, etc.

Balloon diagram: Fast, sketchy drawings showing the relationship of defined-site uses to one another.

Base sheet: A drawing that can be done on any number of mediums (vellum, mylar, etc.) that reflects site elements that are common to different drawings. For example, property lines, building locations, walks, and drives are all base sheet items. It would be inefficient to draw the same thing over as they never change. Therefore, reproducibles are run for a variety of plan types (grading and drainage, hardscape, landscape, irrigation, lighting, etc.). Sometimes referred to as a footprint.

Circulation: Refers to vehicular or pedestrian movement. A good circulation design aids efficient traffic flow. A circulation pattern can also dictate placement of other design elements.

Civil engineer: An individual licensed by law to design site structures and systems (bridges, roads, parking lots) and to lay out grading and drainage systems.

Client interview: Initial step in the design process and one of the most important. Information garnered from this interview aids in formulating a program that is based on the client's needs.

Color: The surface appearance of an object as it appears to the retina of the human eye. This is not shape or form, but wave lengths of radiant energy capable of stimulating neural responses. Also referred to as hue.

Design process: Logical series of steps taken to arrive at a design solution that is responsive to defined program elements.

Details: Scaled drawings of specific elements or structures which show how they are constructed and what materials, textures, and colors comprise their physical makeup.

Drafting: The mechanical drawing process by which design solutions are graphically expressed on paper.

Drafting scale: An instrument in which smaller increments represent much larger increments (1/8" = 1' 0" or 1" = 20' 0"). An architect's scale utilizes feet and inches, while an engineer's scale is calibrated in tenths of a foot.

Emotions: Human feelings often expressed by bodily and/or facial expressions. Design elements can evoke emotions.

Emphasis: Drawing attention to specific design elements

Enframement: Arranging foreground design elements so that they frame background elements and views.

Entry: As it applies to design, this is the point where one comes onto a site or into a building.

Field observation: That point in the design process where the landscape architect observes events during the construction sequence and isues objective reports to the client as to the quality of the installation and the degree of adherence to construction documents.

Flimsy paper: Also called buff, or tissue paper. Very thin paper that accepts a variety of drafting mediums (ink, pencil, markers, etc.). Sketches, ideas, diagrams, and rudimentary designs are most frequently expressed on this inexpensive and expendable paper.

Focal point: The object of primary visual interest in a design sequence or outdoor room. Can be natural or manmade.

Form: The physical size and makeup of an object that determines its outer shape. (See Shape.)

Haha: An unseen drop in grade from a viewing area or platform. Developed during the period of Romantic English design when pastoral settings were often artificially used. The haha separated man from animals. The same concept is frequently used today in zoos and wild animal parks to create a more natural setting.

Harmony: An equilibrium that is reached by arranging objects and design elements in such a manner that they are noticeable and pleasing to the senses.

Hierarchy: Arranging design objects so that they are assembled in order of importance within the overall composition.

Indigenous: Of or specific to a place or region.

Infrastructure: Elements basic and essential to a site. Underground utilities and roadways are considered infrastructure. In most types of development, this term embodies all those elements necessary to access the site and begin building construction.

Interior designer: An individual who by training and/or experience is knowledgeable and adept in designing the interior surfaces and spaces of buildings.

Irrigation designer: An individual who by training and/or experience is knowledgeable and adept in the design of irrigation systems capable of maintaining plant material in a healthy condition.

Landscape architect: An individual who by training, experience, and licensing is capable of designing outdoor spaces, doing environmental studies, and selecting plant materials suitable for a specific region. A landscape architect is primarily concerned with resource conservation and stewardship of the land so that it serves its highest and best purpose.

Light: A source of illumination which is either natural (sunlight) or manmade (lamps). Light is necessary in order for objects to be seen.

Living spaces: The area within the exterior environment where site users will spend the majority of their time.

Macroclimate: Climatic conditions specific to an area or region. Temperature variables and other conditions usually change slowly and are expressed as an average (mean) set of conditions.

Microclimate: Climatic conditions specific to a site. Microclimates most frequently are created by building orientation to sun exposure.

Mylar: Drafting medium that is of a plastic type origin. Very tough and durable and, accordingly, the most expensive medium on which to draw. Accepts ink very well.

Oasis: A green area in a desert. Plant life is supported by ground water or artificial irrigation.

Perception: How individuals view their surroundings and anything that effects their senses or intellect.

Plan notes: Notes of key importance or the highlights of a more lengthy specification that are shown directly on the plan to which they pertain.

Play areas: Areas that are purposefully dedicated to either active or passive recreation.

Preliminary design: Intermediate step in the design process. Most typically a refinement of a schematic, but a level of detail below a working drawing.

Prints: Medium on which plans are reproduced. Colors of most commonly used prints in ascending order of expense are bluelines, blacklines, and brownlines.

Privacy areas: Areas to be used individually or by small groups. Quite, secluded, and intimate in scale.

Project closeout: The end of the design process when the landscape architect is no longer involved with the design, installation, or upkeep of the project.

Public areas: Areas of a site within public view.

Radial axis: A straight line originating at a central point and moving away from that point.

Rhythm: Repetition of elements, forms, colors, or lines which create a noticeable sensation of movement to the eye.

Scale: The size of an object in proportion to other objects.

Service area: A site area that serves the more utilitarian functions, such as trash or tool storage or vegetable gardening.

Shape: The outer periphery or profile of a form.

Site analysis: Compiling site inventory information in conjunction with researching of legal and jurisdictional constraints. This information is important in defining the initial design program.

Site inventory: An on site review of physical site conditions. A comprehensive site inventory is essential in developing a congruent design program.

Soil testing laboratory: A facility that runs tests for either the structural stability or overall fertility of site soil samples.

Space: An area or volume created by two or more enclosing elements.

Specifications: Written documents that complement working drawings. Specifications provide general information, call for specific materials and products, and prescribe acceptable standards for workmanship.

Structural engineer: An individual licensed by law to design physical support systems for buildings and structural elements such as bridges and retaining walls.

Symmetry: A type of balance. Perfect proportion. All sides divided by a center line are mirror images of each other.

Tax map: Simple maps usually showing property line locations only. Used by the County Recorder for the purpose of assessing property taxes.

Texture: The tactile, visual, and dimensional surface characteristics of an object.

Tract map: Legally recorded document, usually prepared by a civil engineer, showing exact property line coordinates accompanied by precise legal descriptions. Tract maps must be approved by the respective governing agencies before other plans can be submitted.

U.S.G.S. map: Maps complied and drawn by the U.S. Geological Survey. Among the most accurate and well-done large-scale maps available.

Vellum: Frosty clear paper drafting medium which is particularly good for pencil and produces good prints.

Vernacular: Specific to a particular locality or region.

View: Something that is seen from a particular vantage point. As it applies to this chapter, a view seen from a specific site is something that should be inventoried and preserved.

Viewing area: That location or vantage point from which a view is best seen.

Vista: Views of a smaller scale that are displayed by enframement and/or sequencing.

Working drawings: The final stage in document preparation and interlinked with written specifications. The drawings from which the project is physically constructed.

Chapter 3

Grading Design

Atrium grate

Introduction

For the purpose of this chapter, "grade" means the surface of the ground and "grading design" refers to the interpretation and manipulation of this surface. Grading design is the canvas or mold upon which the rest of the seen landscape architectural design is painted or formed. Consider the painter — he arrives at an idea or subject for his painting, but must determine the actual physical dimensions of the canvas before he can start his picture. The landscape architect must know the actual size of his canvas (site) before he can begin his work, but must also know the nature of the gallery (adjacent sites) where his work is to be displayed. The potter at his wheel must throw the clay at just the right thickness to maintain structural strength and in a form that will assure the stability of the piece: too thin and clay will buckle, too wide and the clay will wobble off the wheel. By achieving the right proportion, his piece is well formed and pleasing to the eye, and so it is with grading design.

No other area of landscape architecture requires as much of a sense of feel as does grading design. If you do enough of it, you can sweep your hand, palm down, above and across a plan rising, falling, stopping and stepping in air where the ground will do these same things on the site. This simple procedure will enable a designer to ascertain the flow of the ground plane and whether it meets the desired effect. Seasoned grading designers have the experience and graphic ability to place themselves visually on the surface of this plan and envision the site in three dimensions. In a drafting room, if you have ever seen a designer bend or squat until his eye level was the same as that of the plan, this is exactly what he was doing — sighting along the sheet to feel the lay of the land.

Site Drainage

Surface drainage is the term applied to the method or methods by which runoff water is handled or disposed of as it flows over the ground plane. The land area within a site's property lines is referred to by civil and hydraulic engineers as being that particular site's watershed. Whenever rain or irrigation water falls onto a watershed, a certain amount of runoff will occur. Runoff is defined as the water falling on a site that does not naturally pond, is not absorbed by soil or plants, and does not immediately evaporate. The amount of runoff on concrete can be 95%, on asphalt 80%, on rocky desert terrain 75%, and in a typical desert urban environment as high as 60%.

The runoff rate is expressed as a percentage called a coefficient and is used as such in the formula Q = CIA. This formula is applied to determine the amount of runoff water that falls on an individual site over a specific period of time, and that will need to be disposed of.

Q = Volume of water expressed in cubic feet per second.
C = Percent of rain that runs off (coefficient).
I = Rainfall intensity in inches per hour.
A = Site area expressed in acres.

A non-mathematician might express the formula as:

$$C \times I = \_\_ \times A = Q$$

It is very important to know what the volume of runoff water is, as it will affect all surface aspects of the site design.

Most desert cities have no, or only a limited, stormwater sewer system. Most state laws and municipal codes do not allow drainage from one site directly onto an adjacent site. It therefore becomes the individual's responsibility to handle stormwater and irrigation water runoff on his own site. In limited cases, usually in country club developments, the water from the front yards can be run to the streets which act as a sheet flow (wide, thin layer of water) drainage system. In most cases, however, complete on site retention or partial retention must be accomodated before the drainage water will be allowed to flow to off site watersheds or into subsurface public or private drainage systems. The easiest and sometimes the only way to accomplish retaining this predetermined volume of water is to depress grades into hollowed-out retention basins.

Often owners and/or architects employ civil engineers to perform the site grading layout necessary to locate the building pad and retention basins. The landscape architect is brought into the process later and inherits the civil engineer's basins, and this is where a lot of conflict can sometimes arise. Many times these basins are square or rectangular in configuration and sections through them look very rigid. Soil, especially sand, does not stay at right angles on the horizontal plane. While these square basins make it easier for the civil engineer to calculate volume which determines the size, depth, and/or number of retention basins needed on site, it is obvious they won't work from a practical standpoint and redesigns by either the landscape architect or the civil engineer become necessary. A square basin, even with rounded corners, is not particularly natural looking on the ground plane.

Most municipalities set the volume of runoff water to be retained at that which would be present if the site were subject to a 100-year storm. A 100-year storm is defined as the rainfall of the greatest volume in a 100-year period. The grading and drainage designer is required to hold the entire volume that falls on the site within the confines of that site in order to meet retention calculations that must be approved by the governing agency. In an effort to reduce the area required for retention basins and sometimes just to handle the 100-year storm design volume, a drainage structure known as a drywell has come to the fore. Drywells are simply drainage culverts standing on end, with their sidewalls cored on specific centers to allow for the passage of water into soil strata. Drywells consist of concrete pipe 4 to 6 feet in diameter that penetrate 10, 20, and even 30 feet into the soil. Most municipalities will not allow the area inside the drywell to be used as part of the retention volume calculation. What drywells usually do is increase the rate at which runoff water is able to percolate into the site soil. Recall $Q = CIA$. By increasing the rate of soil saturation, drywells reduce C (percentage of runoff), which in turn will reduce Q (volume of water to be retained on site), which, in the final outcome, will reduce the size of retention basins. It is a sad fact that many lower budget type developments have a site so maxed out (buildings and parking occupy the maximum allowable square footage of the site) that every available planting area becomes a retention basin with a drywell.

Drainage Structures and Equipment

On sites that are fortunate enough to connect to some form of storm sewer system, there is a variety of equiupment that catches and carries water to these systems. In addition, there are structures that must be installed to channel or block the flow of overland and roof drainage. These include:

Area drains: Wrought iron, steel, or plastic grates with a threaded pipe collar that screws into an underground pipe that leads to the underground drainage system. Use bronze or like-colored (match to adjacent material) grates in hardscape. Black looks best underneath shrubbery, as does green in turf and low ground cover areas. Also, for grates located in paving, consider the type of paving. Use square grates within square grids and round grates in natural stone. Round grates are used because the installer does not know how an irregular edge is going to abutt the grate, and abutting to a rounded edge will look the least awkward.

Catch basins: Underground concrete or plastic structures, whose depth depends upon anticipated water volume, with a steel or plastic grate at grade that lifts for cleaning purposes. Sometimes direct entry of surface water is allowed and, by design, it simply flows through the grate. Usually, this is not the case. Catch basins have an inlet pipe that brings water from a curb cut or area drain to the catch basin. Catch basins have an outlet pipe that carries water from the catch basin to other points in the underground drainage system. The outlet is always slightly higher than the bottom of the inlet inside the catch basin itself. This is done to maximize the volume of the catch basin. The rate of fall of the outlet pipe out of the catch basin is greater than that of the inlet pipe until the elevation of the downstream pipe is lower than the inlet pipe. Then the downstream pipe continues at a more normal gradient. Catch basins are used as temporary water-storage structures and to break the rate of water velocity that builds in the upstream pipe. Acceptable velocity in drainage pipes is 2 1/2 feet per second (fps). Pipes are usually sloped at 1%, but design limitations and site conditions sometimes infringe upon this gradient standard. Under no circumstances should velocity exceed 5 fps. If there were not catch basins along the course of the drainage system to break velocity and allow air to enter the line, a back pressure would build up and water would back up at the point of entry (the area to be drained in the first place). Catch basins are located as far from structures and critical site areas as possible — the reason being that the stormwater volume is occasionally greater than the design volume, and the water could back up through the catch basin grate and flood the surrounding area.

Bubble boxes: Similar to catch basins, but they have no outlet pipe. They are utilized to break water velocity and allow the water to bubble or seep through the grate or through an opening to its discharge point — usually a curb opening or lake. Bubble boxes are used extensively in country club design.

Dry wells: As explained earlier, these can also function in the same manner as catch basins or bubble boxes, the difference being that they store a far greater volume of water before discharging or sending it through an outlet to points downstream.

Head wall and end walls: Walls, usually of concrete or masonry construction. They hold large concrete or metal pipe (culverts) in place at the start (head) and end of a drainage system.

Roof gutters and scuppers: These elements are frequently forgotten about during the project design stage and become issues of much lament the first time it rains. Gutters catch rainwater that falls on roofs and vent it at grade or, optimally, in a below-grade drainage system. Scuppers are openings in roof parapets that simply allow rainwater to exit and fall to the ground. In the case of gutters that vent at grade or roof-mounted scuppers, it behooves the landscape architect to verify whether the architect or civil engineer has made adequate provisions for splash blocks or other elements to break the fall of water, as this can be a very erosive element. If such provisions have not been made or are inadequate, the landscape architect will need to generate a workable design solution.

In designing underground drainage systems, always be judicious in equipment selection and determining actual need. Costs always increase as equipment is added to a system.

Subsurface Drainage

To illustrate the subject of subsurface drainage, there is a reverse analogy between drainage pipe and the pipe in an irrigation system. This analogy is used because desert landscape architects should be well versed in irrigation principles. In an irrigation system, the highest volume of water is at the valve where the water first enters the system. This volume lessens the farther the line travels from the valve and as water is dispersed through the irrigation heads. Downstream pipe size, therefore, also decreases because the pipe is required to hold less water. In a subsurface drainage system, the situation is exactly opposite. The area drains (heads) flow towards their point of destination (valve). The volume of water increases as each drain adds more water into the system. Pipe size must, therefore, increase to hold the higher volume of water.

It's a lot easier for beginners to grasp the theory of pipe sizing in a drainage system than in an irrigation system because of the next comparison. Think of a river system. The river starts out small and as it travels towards its destination it widens as water from tributaries (area drains) converge with the main river. The river has to get deeper and wider to accomodate the increasing volume of water. As the river flows through a granite canyon it picks up speed (velocity) because the size of the river's trough (pipe) is narrower and the water volume must pass quickly or the river backs up.

Drainage design is especially important in high-end jobs. On a project with a generous construction budget, higher grade surface materials are often used because their inherent aesthetic qualities lend class and elegance to the design. This often means expensive limestone, granite, slate, or textured concrete for the floors of the outdoor rooms. These floors, costing what they do, are to be treated with the same level of concern as an interior floor. The exterior floor, being exposed to the elements, or frequently being cleaned by means of hose and water, has to drain. But also being costly, the floor has to appear to be level or nearly level. This dictates very slight gradients (slopes) to a water discharge point or an area drain. Oftentimes, sheet flow over the floor's surface is out of the question. This occurs when to sheet in one direction would make the gradient noticeable over the length of the drop in grade or when there is nowhere to sheet to. The patio is locked in by walls, the pool coping, higher adjacent slopes, etc. Then patio surfaces have to be tipped or tilted towards centrally located area drains. The larger the patio (deck) is, the more area drains will be required. This is not because one area drain could not handle all the volume but (because of a series of very slight gradients) all the volume is not directed toward any one drain.

Many individuals, in an honest effort to control construction costs, have challenged the use of area drains, arguing that it does not rain very often in the desert. True, but desert rainstorms, when they do occur, are frequently very intense. Studies of the dynamics of these rainstorms bear out that the maximum intensity and thus highest volume of water occurs at the beginning of the storm and decreases as the storm abates. Even a brief desert cloudburst can drop a huge volume of water, if only onto a limited area. If the subject site is within this area, then fast and efficient drainage is going to be a big issue.

Another drainage consideration is the difficulty encountered in the actual routing of the drainage line (pipe). This is particularly true in high-end residential design. Great attention is given to front yard and streetside image and backyard livability. Drainage pipe, pool equipment areas, air conditioning equipment, and many other service type features are crammed into the narrow side yards. For aesthetic (viewing), climatic (shading and wind protection), and privacy (screening) purposes the landscape architect is frequently faced with trying to fit trees into the side yards also. It is important for the landscape architect to note or coordinate with the drainage designer (often civil engineers) the routing of drainage lines away from or around tree rootballs. This is not rocket science. The size of the rootball and the location and depth of the drain line are both known factors. Either they interfere with each other or they don't. The tree size will have to be reduced or the drain line moved or the tree eliminated altogether. For this reason, it behooves the landscape architect to draw the dimensions of rootballs on his or over the civil's grading and drainage plan and try to develop a realistic solution by routing drain lines around or under rootballs.

Desert Soils

Before delving into a more in-depth discussion of grading terminology and grading design, let's examine the types of desert soil to be built on, moved around, and planted in. In the Southwest, there are two broad categories of soil: sand and clay. Varying degrees of gravel are found in both soils, but, except in terms of permeability and compaction, gravel content is not a major concern. Sandy soils are frequently found on bajadas and desert floor areas. Clay soils are usually found at the mouth of some canyons, owing to centuries of alluvial deposits originating in the mountain ranges. Maximizing and managing soil fertility will be addressed in the planting chapter.

Clay soils require more elaborate grading and drainage and are more difficult to calculate for cut and fill purposes because of an increased shrink/swell factor. Also, any type of import soil set over a clay base soil stands a good chance of sliding. Obtaining a conclusive soils report from a soils engineer and enlisting the aid of a qualified civil engineer would be wise when working with clay soils.

Geologically speaking, sandy soils are relatively new soils. Soil is really broken and weathered rock (parent material) that has mixed with weathering and decomposed organic matter (humus). Sandy soils have often been transported by the forces of wind and water erosion. The finer the sand particle, the more weathered and less likely it is to have humus and nutrient matter affixed to its surface. Sand gets blown about continually in windy desert areas. Depressions and landlocked canyons that become filled with fine-particled blowsand are unstable and unfertile environments. They require quite a bit of stabilization and/or environmental control to become useful for construction purposes. Most of the Southwest desert cities have enacted laws and codes which require and regulate dust control on new construction sites. Dust control is accomplished chiefly by the use of water trucks or temporary above ground irrigation systems. On large construction sites or sites that are cleared and then take years to complete on a phased building program it would aid the cause of water conservation to seed the area with native wildflowers and grasses. While this plant material does require some method of temporary watering, the volume of water required is much less over the buildout life of the project. These natives would help knit the soil, re-stabilize the ground plane, add seasonal color to an otherwise drab area, and most important, require less precious water to be used. It's an idea that is worth considering. The reason it's so often forgotten is that everyone assumes a short term construction period. Sometimes short terms lengthen with delays and, even if on schedule, the normal buildout time frame is months, even years. Native desert plant materials, because they exhibit annualism, can germinate in a 2-week period. Even when they die out, their root systems hold soil in place. As one drives around the various desert developments watching massive quantities of valuable water being pumped out over dry construction sites one has to wonder if a $0.05 to $0.07 per square foot native seed mix doesn't make sense.

Sandy soils are very good soils for building upon as, once compacted, they exhibit little settling. These soils are also very predictable when calculating cut and fill if wind erosion can be controlled. There is virtually no shrink/swell factor with properly compacted displaced sandy soils.

Landscape architects and contractors should know the source of all import soil brought to their job sites. All too often it's the kind of soil the other guy was more than happy to get rid of. Even on a site that has inherent good soil, the placing of clay soils and blowsand over the surface will adversely affect plant growth — particularly turf and groundcover establishment due to their shallow root systems. What is often saved up front on these poorer soils is later lost in maintenance costs as expensive fertilizers are added in an attempt to improve soil quality.

Grading Design

Let us now return to the subject of above-ground grading design. Go outside and stand on open ground. Look down at your feet. The point where the surface of the ground meets the soles of your shoes is your personal benchmark and your feet are at grade. Everything that you survey is above, below, or even with your benchmark. This is exactly what happens when a civil engineer or surveyor does a site survey. They work from a known benchmark and everything they shoot (survey) is assigned an elevation either above or below that benchmark. The benchmark the surveyor uses has been previously located by the U.S. Geological Survey. The U.S.G.S. personnel assigned the level of the benchmark as being either above or below sea level. Water, when contained, seeks its own level. The sea is assigned 0'-0". This is datum. Technically, a datum is defined as a reference plane used in surveying for the purpose of establishing a starting elevation. For our purposes, datum is the Pacific Ocean.

Now abandon your personal benchmark and go back inside. Go to the kitchen and fill a clear glass half full of water. Hold the glass up and look at the water line. Imagine that you are now looking at a contour line. Contours are the basis for developing any real understanding of grading design. Contours, as they exist on earth, are imaginary and always level. Tip the glass — the contour stays level. Think of the sides of the glass as mountain ranges and valleys. Although they slope, the contour always stays level. Now, still holding the first glass (half full), fill a second glass three quarters full with water. Set the two glasses side by side on the counter. The difference between their water levels (contours) is the contour interval. In grading design, contours are drawn on paper and the contour intervals are shown in 1- foot, 2-foot, 5-foot, 10-foot, or additional units of 5-foot increments. The contour interval on any given plan is always consistent, and every fifth contour is a heavier line for graphic clarity.

On plans drawn for grading design, existing contours representing the surface of the site before construction are shown as dashed lines. Proposed contours depicting grade changes to the site, to accommodate new construction, are shown as solid lines. Where the two differ and separate is indicated by a tick mark. On plans drawn to record topographic information for general reference, the contours are frequently shown as solid lines as it is not anticipated that they will be altered without some form of professionally prepared grading and drainage plan to be submitted to the appropriate governmental and/or legal jurisdictions. The U.S. Geologic Survey produces excellent quality maps called quadrangles that show contours at large scales. You can get U.S.G.S. maps at map and hiking stores. Purchase a map of the town where you live, as this should be the area you are most familiar with. At a very large scale, the map will show cities, mountains, valleys, rivers, and roads. Study the U.S.G.S. map carefully, because it was prepared and drawn by professionals who rank among the best in the world.

Notice on the U.S.G.S. map that the contours stop or end at the edge of the sheet. In reality, contours always close. Go back to the glass. In this next analogy imagine that the glass itself is the Earth's atmosphere and where the water line (contour) touches the atmosphere is the surface of the Earth. The contour does close upon itself and it is always level. As you learn to read contour lines on a map, you will begin to develop a few graphic rules of thumb such as: they do not merge or cross except at vertical or overhanging surfaces. The closer together they are, the steeper the ground. The more closely parallel they are, the smoother and more regular the ground surface. In rolling land, they take on flowing curves; in broken land they wiggle; over plane surfaces they run in straight lines. Contours form a "V" shape at valleys and ridges. A tight "V" always indicates a stream valley (desert wash) or a pronounced ridge. The bottoms of these "V's" point up stream valleys and down ridges. Water always flows perpendicular (at a right angles) away from contours, towards the next lowest contour and will continue to flow until contained, at which point it will seek its own level.

Put the glass away, grab a shoebox, and go back outside to your personal benchmark. Bend over and set the box down on the ground. Imagine that the box is an important architectural structure. On a grading and drainage plan you would have to locate the building or it could not be built. You locate the building (shoebox) by noting the elevation (above or below the benchmark) of each of its four corners. These are called spot elevations. Spot elevations are used to clarify the exact location of building floors, tops and bottoms of walls, sidewalks, the water line of pools, etc. Spot elevations will determine the height of all the elements on the site and also show the difference in elevation between elements. For example, the top and bottom of a string of steps would be called out by spot elevations and the difference in height could be easily determined by subtracting the lower spot from the higher spot.

While discussing steps, this is a good place to introduce how they are incorporated into the design. That portion of a step that goes up vertically is called a riser (R). The portion of a step that runs horizontally (where you put your foot) is called a tread (T). Outdoors, the formula for designing steps is 2R + 1T = 27 inches. This is called the riser/tread ratio. Verbally expressed, a riser, a tread, and the next riser, when measured, should come out to 27 inches. Ignore texts that say "the riser tread ratio should not exceed 27 inches". This statement implies that it would be okay for the total dimension be less than 27 inches but such is not the case. The reason for this is usually that the tread would not be long enough to step on comfortably. In designing steps, do not allow the riser to go below 4 inches or above 6 inches in height. Less than 4 inches is a toe tripper, and above 6 inches means the tread will again be too short.

The reason for steps, in the first place, is to accommodate a grade change that was too steep to ramp or traverse by means of gently sloping the terrain. The degree or rate of a slope can be expressed as a percentage or a ratio.

Slope Standards

Material	Slope Percentage Min.	Max.	Opt.	Ratio	Horiz. Dist.	Vert. Dist.
Smooth concrete	.05	3.0	1.0	.05	1 ft	1/16 in.
Loose granite	2.0	5.0	3.5	3.5	1 ft	7/16 in.
Stone paving	1.0	3.0	2.0	1.0	1 ft	1/8 in.
Asphalt	2.0	5.0	3.5	2.0	1 ft	1/4 in.
Roads	1.5	5.0	3.0	6.0	1 ft	3/4 in.
Parking	5.0	2.5	1.0	2.5	1 ft	5/16 in.
Main entry walk	.05	4.0	1.0	—	—	—
Collector walk	1.0	8.0	4.0	4.0	1 ft	1/2 in.
Sloped turf	5.0	33.0	2.0	5.0	1 ft	5/8 in.
Hand-mown turf	—	33.0	—	33.0	3 ft	1 ft
Tractor-mown turf	—	20.0	—	20.0	5 ft	1 ft
Swales	2.0	10.0	5.0	10.0	10 ft	1 ft
Groundcover w/ stabilization	—	50.0	—	10.0	1 ft	1 ft

Slope Formulas

All information needed to determine a slope gradient, vertical height, or ground plane distance can be found by applying one of these three formulas: $G = D/L$ or $L = D/G$ or $D = G \times L$. Non-mathematicians note:

G = D (this top number is divided by
L this bottom number)

G = gradient in degree of slope
D = vertical distance between two points
L = the horizontal length between two points

Slope Ratios and Percentages

In referring to slopes by ratio, the horizontal distance is always written or spoken before the vertical dimension. The percentage of slope is graphically shown as the resulting angle when the furthest horizontal point is connected to the highest vertical point. Thus:

1:1 = 100%	4:1 = 25%	7:1 = 14.31%
2:1 = 50%	5:1 = 20%	8:1 = 12.50%
3:1 = 33.33%	6:1 = 16.67%	9:1 = 11.11%
10:1 = 10%	30:1 = 4%	50:1 = 2%
20:1 = 5%	40:1 = 3%	100:1 = 1%

12:1 = 8.33% is the maximum allowed by law for handicapped ramps. Ramps as well as other handicapped site features and considerations are required on all new public works and projects deemed to be frequently used by the public. This issue will be discussed further in Chapter 4.

Following are conversion tables that will prove quite useful when performing any grading exercise:

Conversion of inches in a foot to tenths of a foot:

1/8" = .01'	1" = .08'	5" = .41'	9" = .75'
1/4" = .02'	2" = .16'	6" = .50'	10" = .83'
1/2" = .04'	3" = .25'	7" = .58'	11" = .91'
3/4" = .06'	4" = .33'	8" = .66'	12" = 1.00'

Conversion of tenths of a foot to percentage of inches in a foot (for ease of graphic scale conversion):

1 tenth of a foot = 1.2 inches	6 tenths of a foot = 7.2 inches
2 tenths of a foot = 2.4 inches	7 tenths of a foot = 8.4 inches
3 tenths of a foot = 3.6 inches	8 tenths of a foot = 9.6 inches
4 tenths of a foot = 4.8 inches	9 tenths of a foot = 10.8 inches
5 tenths of a foot = 6.0 inches	10 tenths of a foot = 12.0 inches

The graphic aspects of the grading design process are most often schematic, preliminary, and final (working) drawings.

Schematic Design

Observe the site to see if it has any aspects that fit with the program. Centrally located high spots are obvious areas for structures and other critical elements. Low spots could lend themselves to retention basins or aid in reducing swimming pool excavation. Can existing vegetation be preserved from or relocated prior to grading operations? Can the existing drainage pattern (often in conjunction with existing vegetation) be utilized or will it have to be reworked? Above all, try to take what the site gives. Decisions at the schematic level can be made on a U.S.G.S. topographic survey map, on a civil engineer's site survey, on a base sheet, aerial photograph, or by freehand sketch.

Preliminary Design

Working on a scaled base sheet of the site, the next step is to draw in existing contours and assign spot elevations to the corners of the property, while noting any natural features to be preserved, and any high or low spots. If the design includes structures, determine the best location and assign a pad elevation. Pad elevation is always 6 inches below the building's finish floor and is followed by earthwork contractors so that they leave the site ready for the builder to start immediately on formwork. Assign a finish floor elevation. Finish floor elevation is always 6 in. higher than the pad elevation and is usually the most important elevation in the design. Positive drainage must be provided away from finish floor to protect the building from flooding. Next, assign top of curb, top of bench, top of wall, top of drainage structure rim, and pool coping elevations. Determine and assign waterline elevations of pools, spas, and water features. This is normally 6 in. below the top of coping. Six inches is used because most tile adhering to the edge of the pool is 6 in. square and butts to the bottom of the coping. The waterline is encouraged to cover one half of the tile (3 in.), which leaves 3 in. of tile exposed that when added to a normal coping thickness of 3 in. makes the waterline 6 in. below the top of coping. This is important to note and make adjustments for when using a thicker coping material or a larger tile.

Dimensions to consider when assigning spot elevations (discussed in depth in other chapters)

Measurement	Description/Function
1"	Usual minimum difference (drop in grade) between finish floor elevation and top of adjacent outdoor pavement. This elevation will be the starting point at which to show positive drainage away from a structure.
1 1/2"	Minimum grade drop between top of headers, curbs or pavement, and finish grade in turf and planting areas.
3" to 3 1/2"	Normal pool coping thickness at exposed edge.
4"	Difference between top and bottom of a roll curb. Minimum riser height of a step.
6"	Difference between pad and finish floor of a structure. Difference between top and bottom of a conventional curb. Maximum height of step riser. Normal difference between top of pool, spa and fountain copings, and waterline.
9"	Comfortable difference between top of coping and tread of first pool or spa step.
10" to 12"	Maximum comfortable riser height in pool and spa steps. Riser tread ratio underwater is not to exceed 2R + 1T = 36". Note that underwater movements are much different than on dry land.
14" to 18"	Comfortable pool or spa seat depth below waterline.
16"	Optimum outdoor seating (bench) height.
24" (2')	Minimum depth for fountains that receive lighting.
28" to 30"	Optimum outdoor counter (desk) height.
32"	Optimum outdoor leaning (butt) height.
32" to 34"	Outdoor rail height.
36" (3')	Handicap rail height. BBQ counter height.
42"	Minimum water depth for raising koi fish. Usual depth of spas.
48" (4')	Optimum rail height for resting of elbows when standing or leaning. Minimum safety rail height from dangerous heights.
60" (5')	Good screen wall height for equipment yards.
72" (6')	Minimum privacy wall height. Usually maximum wall height allowed by most Southwest municipalities. Code allowance is usually based upon height as measured from subject property.

Taking into account the physical size of the client's or the project's end users and their personal preferences for noncode dimensions would be wise. A child's playground would require different design standards than a retirement center's recreation area. Spa jet locations for a tall person will be different than those for a short person. It's a matter of fusing research with common sense.

Once spot elevations are assigned, it is time to route new contours where the existing contours will not work with the design. Remember that all new contours of the same elevation must tie back to or meet with existing contours on site within the property lines. Also note that how contours are routed affects cut and fill, and it is more cost-effective to balance cut and fill so no import or export of soil will be needed. Graphically, a cut is depicted when a lower numbered contour crosses (cuts) a higher numbered contour. Conversely, when higher numbered contours cross (pile over) lower numbered contours a fill situation occurs. In plan, the amount of cut and fill can be graphically ball parked by using different line hatchings, shades, or colors in the areas where cut contours and fill contours cross existing contours. Try to visually balance the two opposite symbols. There are other and much more accurate methods of calculating the amount of cut and fill. Three such methods are: (1) planimeter; (2) grid (or borrow-pit); and (3) average end area (site sections). These methods are explained in depth in several of the books cited in the bibliography. It is rare that a landscape architect is given the responsibility (or accepts the liability) of calculating cut and fill. It is done preliminarily so that coordination can begin with the civil engineer and/or grading contractor, who will eventually estimate the quantities of earth needed to be brought to or taken away from the site.

Also, it is usually not within the landscape architect's scope of work to perform roadway and parking lot design. Sometimes the plan layout of these features is done by the landscape architect on a preliminary (study) basis to maintain the same aesthetic quality and sensitivity that is expressed in the rest of the site design. The final design work and exact calculations are usually done by the project civil engineer. There are a few aspects of road and parking lot design that it would be helpful to know in order for landscape architects to communicate and coordinate ideas more effectively with the client and the civil engineer.

Roadway Design Considerations

- Most urban roads are raised in the centerline (middle). This is called a crown and storm water flows in two directions to the curbs. Roadways with a center median (many freeways) are often depressed to the centerline and water is directed to the median. Country and rural roads frequently are raised at one side and water flows across the road to a collection curb or open roadside ditch at the lower side. This is called a cross- or transverse-sloped road.
- In roadway design, where two roads meet or cross, it is always better to have the intersection align at right angles and any curve should not be located within 300 feet of the intersection. Offset "T"-type intersections should be a minimum of 150 feet apart at their centerlines. Provide clear viewing at any intersection by not allowing any vertical obstruction above 3 feet high within the confines of a 33-foot by 33-foot "vision triangle" as measured from the face of curbs at both sides of the subject street.
- Do not change the radius of a curve within itself. The entire curve should be consistent. Avoid continuous and sharp "S" curves. On curves in opposite directions, separate the curves by at least 100 feet of straight-of-way. When "S" curves must be used, both halves of the "S" should be equal.
- Maximum depth for a cul-de-sac should be 700 feet. Cul-de-sacs should have a 40-foot minimum clear turning radius for fire engines and garbage trucks.
- Roadway elevations are shown at stations. The first station is usually the center of the intersection, called 0+ elevation, and then stations occur every 100 feet (1+ elevation, 2+ elevation, etc.).
- At guard gates, drive-throughs, and banking facilities allow a 60-foot minimum of protected roadway (out of the flow of any other traffic) for stacking of three cars.
- A typical parking space is 10 feet wide by 20 feet deep. Handicapped spaces are 12 feet by 20 feet minimum and are always clearly marked by some form of the international handicapped symbol. Compact parking spaces are frequently 8 1/2 feet by 17 or 18 feet. A backout space or drive width of 24 feet is considered comfortable in all cases.

- The closer the parking angle is to perpendicular (90°) the more difficult the actual parking manuver. 45° parking is the easiest; 90° is the most efficient in terms of the number of spaces that can be obtained.
- Always check local codes for ratio of handicap spaces to conventional spaces.
- Many municipalities require 50% shade on parking lot surfaces. This necessitates cut outs and islands for trees. Most cities prefer at least one planter per every run of 10 spaces. It is advisable to use root barriers for all trees in parking lots.
- Any shrub or groundcover in a parking lot planter higher than 3 feet becomes a visibility hazard.

The preliminary grading design also will determine whether there is a need to terrace grades or whether some retaining walls will be required to accommodate abrupt grade changes. Grades that require steps will also frequently require retaining walls. Walls and steps of any height over 24 feet should cheek (turn) back to accept the soil which is rising vertically at the end points and needs to back slope or be contained against something solid. More about retaining walls and steps will be forthcoming in Chapter 4 on Hardscape Design.

Working Drawings

By the time the grading and drainage design reaches to the working drawing stage, it should only require some minor massaging to arrive at and depict a workable solution that fits budgetary and physical constraints, while also maintaining the thrust of the original concepts and some semblance of design sensitivity.

Only elements and information that is not shown on the other discipline's plans (civil, structural, architectural, etc.) or is essential to the viewer's interpretation of the landscape architect's grading and drainage plan should be addressed. Contours are never shown through buildings and not usually shown through paving areas, as these areas are controlled by spot elevations. Arrows should show the direction of water flow for aboveground swales and underground drainage lines.

Graphics should be clear, easy to read, and accompanied by a legend which may include some or all of the following:

Legend:

FFE	Finish floor elevation
172.00	Finish elevation
TC	Top of curb elevation
BC	Bottom of curb elevation
TW	Top of wall elevation
BW	Bottom of wall elevation
WL	Water line elevation
T	Top of drain elevation
2%	Direction of slope and percent
	Bubble box or drain line daylight: indicate rim elevation
	Catch basin: indicate rim elevation
	Drywell: Indicate rim elevation
	Area drains: indicate rim elevation
	Lawn areas: AP 961 8" dia. green
	Grate with corresponding catch basin. See Specs.
	Planting areas: AP 954 4" Dia.
	Black atrium grate with corresponding catch basin. See Specs.
	Floor drain in irregular stone or concrete paving: JOSAM 5A-2, 5" dia. round satin bronze grate. See Specs.
	Floor drain in cut stone and paver areas. JOSAM 5S-2, 5" square satin bronze grate. See Specs.
	Strip drain. Deck-o-drain mark 2 with stainless steel cap. See Specs.
	Drain line direction of flow
	Existing contour
	Proposed contour

Check the civil site survey for existing gas, sewer, electric, cable TV, and water lines. If the grading and drainage design affects them, show and label them on the plan. As a courtesy to other trades and as a measure of liability protection to the landscape architect, all grading and drainage plans should include a note referring to a "blue stake" service that is frequently provided by local utility companies. This service is usually free. Many companies provide preprinted warning labels that can be affixed directly to plans. Upon a customary 24-hour notice, workers from the local utility(ies) come out to the site and stake the locations of underground lines and other important objects.

Before closing, I would like to point out something that happens in the field 75% of the time. The general contractor and landscape contractor cannot come to a meeting of the minds as to who is responsible for and what the extent of the final grading is. This occurrence plagued me for the first 10 years of my career. It's something that just won't go away. Usually a landscape architect's Grading Plan will note: "All grading to ± one tenth of one foot (rough grade) by general contractor. All finish grades and fine raking by landscape contractor." This seems simple enough, but unless the civil engineer's grading plan states the same thing or somehow refers to the landscape grading plan, a conflict can arise. What happens is that the landscape architect is often brought in later than the civil engineer. The civil firm has already completed their plan and the landscape architect adds berming (mounds) for design aesthetics over the grades already established by the civil firm. The civil engineer is unaware of this, and the landscape architect thinks everyone will pick up on his grading note. This is not the case. First of all, the mass grading contractor is often long gone by the time the landscape contractor sets foot on the site. Second, both civil engineer and landscape architect have forgotten to note who is responsible for import of planting soil, parking lot islands, raised planters, etc. It seems that this should be interpreted as rough grading — but by whom? Once again, the mass grading contractor is out of the picture by the time the question comes up.

Landscape architects, do yourselves a favor! Unless you can coordinate with the civil engineer early and have a clear meeting of the minds, and can see the necessary notes on the civil engineer's plan before bidding begins, forget that there is such a thing as finish grade. Call for all import of planting soil and soil for earth berming by the landscape contractor. It may put some costs back into the landscape construction budget but, by and large, it will save you some massive headaches.

Contour Interpretation

Gradients

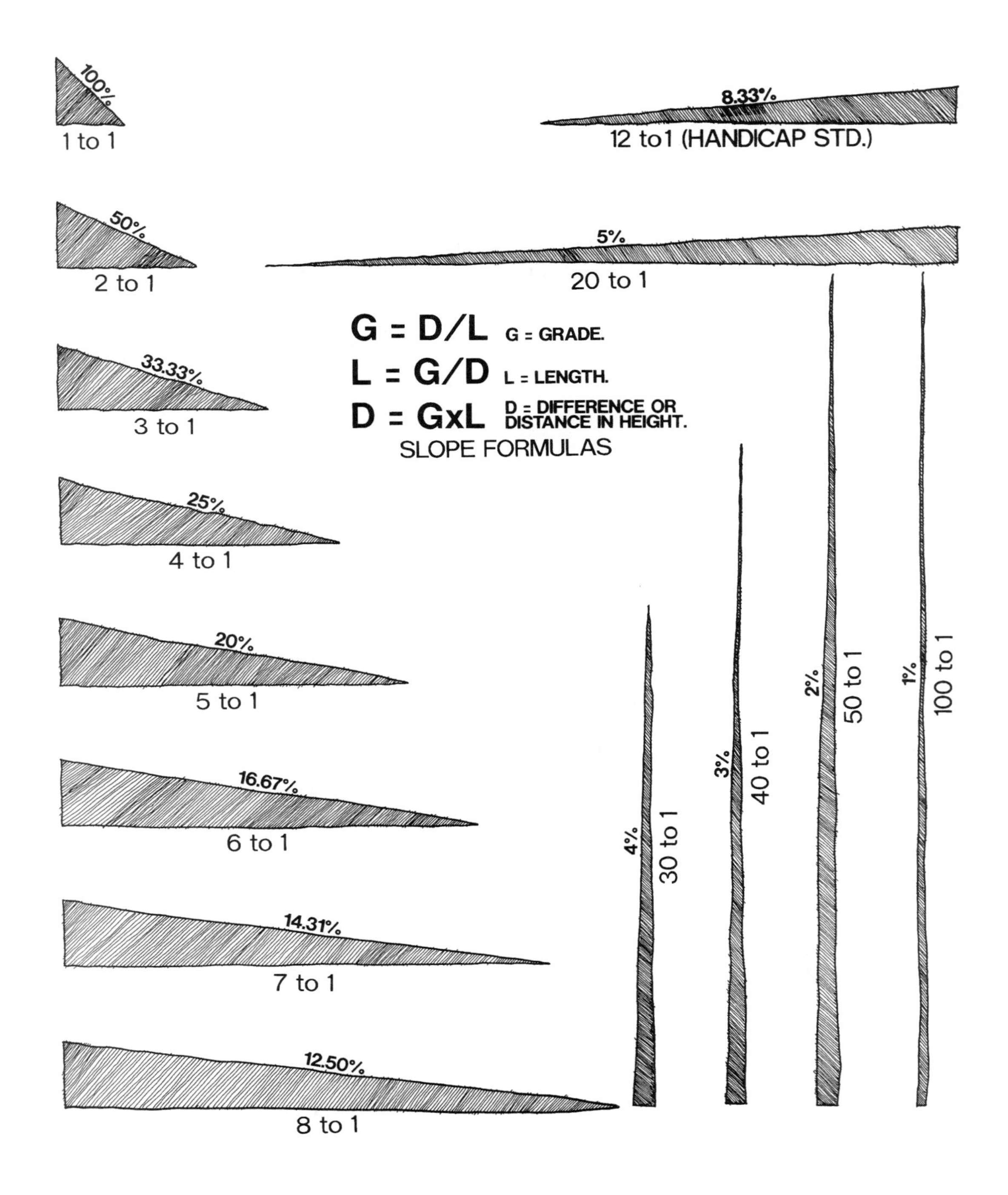

100%
1 to 1
50%
2 to 1
33.33%
3 to 1
25%
4 to 1
20%
5 to 1
16.67%
6 to 1
14.31%
7 to 1
12.50%
8 to 1
8.33%
12 to1 (HANDICAP STD.)
5%
20 to 1
G = D/L G = GRADE.
L = G/D L = LENGTH.
D = GxL D = DIFFERENCE OR DISTANCE IN HEIGHT.
SLOPE FORMULAS
4%
30 to 1
3%
40 to 1
2%
50 to 1
1%
100 to 1

Drainage Structures

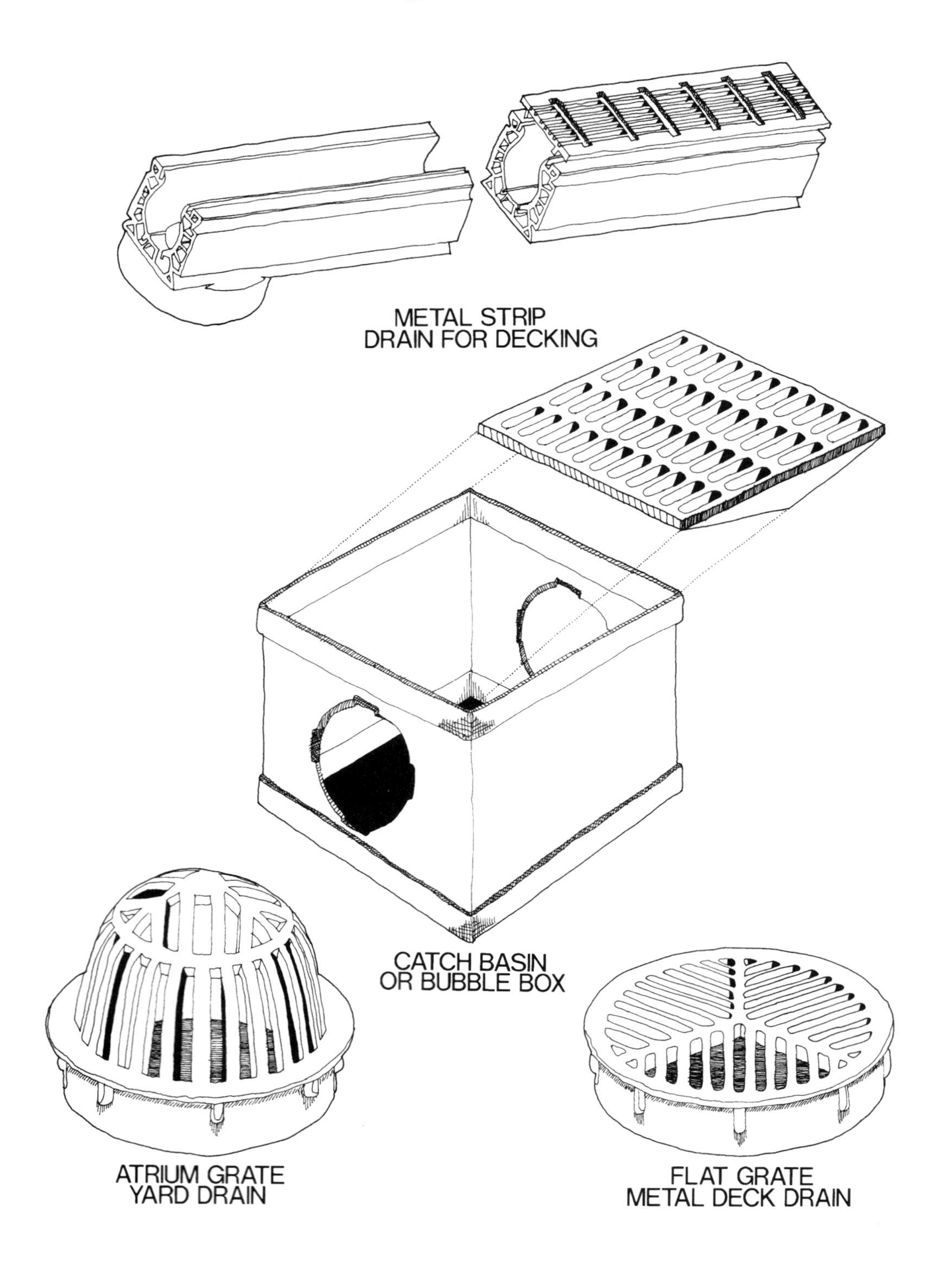

Roadway Design

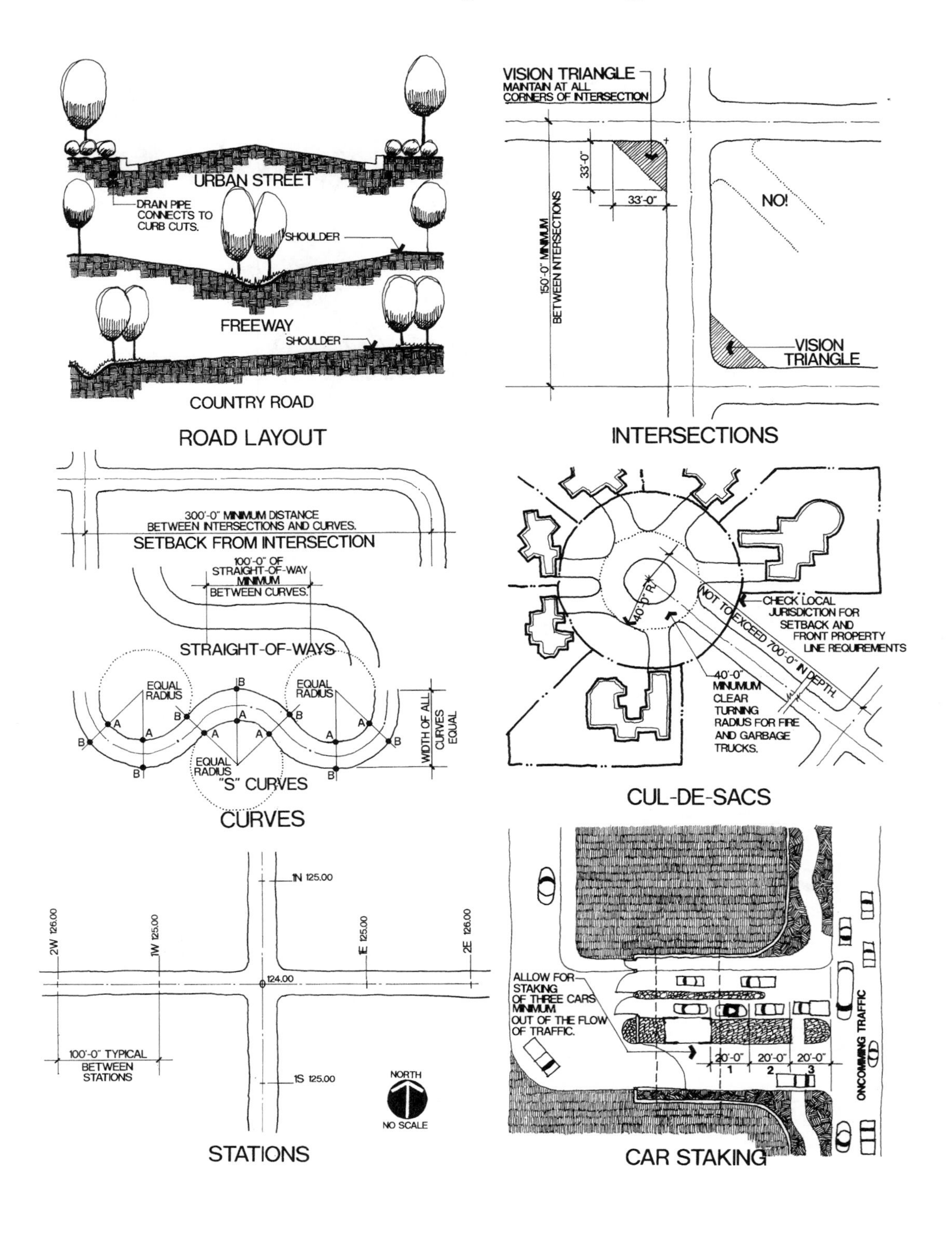
URBAN STREET
DRAIN PIPE CONNECTS TO CURB CUTS.
SHOULDER
FREEWAY
SHOULDER
COUNTRY ROAD
ROAD LAYOUT
VISION TRIANGLE
MAINTAIN AT ALL CORNERS OF INTERSECTION
33'-0"
33'-0"
150'-0" MINIMUM BETWEEN INTERSECTIONS
NO!
VISION TRIANGLE
INTERSECTIONS
300'-0" MINIMUM DISTANCE BETWEEN INTERSECTIONS AND CURVES.
SETBACK FROM INTERSECTION
100'-0" OF STRAIGHT-OF-WAY MINIMUM BETWEEN CURVES.
STRAIGHT-OF-WAYS
EQUAL RADIUS
EQUAL RADIUS
EQUAL RADIUS
WIDTH OF ALL CURVES EQUAL
"S" CURVES
CURVES
40'-0" R.
NOT TO EXCEED 700'-0" IN DEPTH.
CHECK LOCAL JURISDICTION FOR SETBACK AND FRONT PROPERTY LINE REQUIREMENTS
40'-0" MINUMUM CLEAR TURNING RADIUS FOR FIRE AND GARBAGE TRUCKS.
CUL-DE-SACS
1N 125.00
2W 126.00
1W 125.00
1E 125.00
2E 126.00
124.00
100'-0" TYPICAL BETWEEN STATIONS
1S 125.00
NORTH
NO SCALE
STATIONS
ALLOW FOR STAKING OF THREE CARS MINIMUM OUT OF THE FLOW OF TRAFFIC.
20'-0"
20'-0"
20'-0"
1
2
3
ONCOMMING TRAFFIC
CAR STAKING

Grading and Drainage Plan

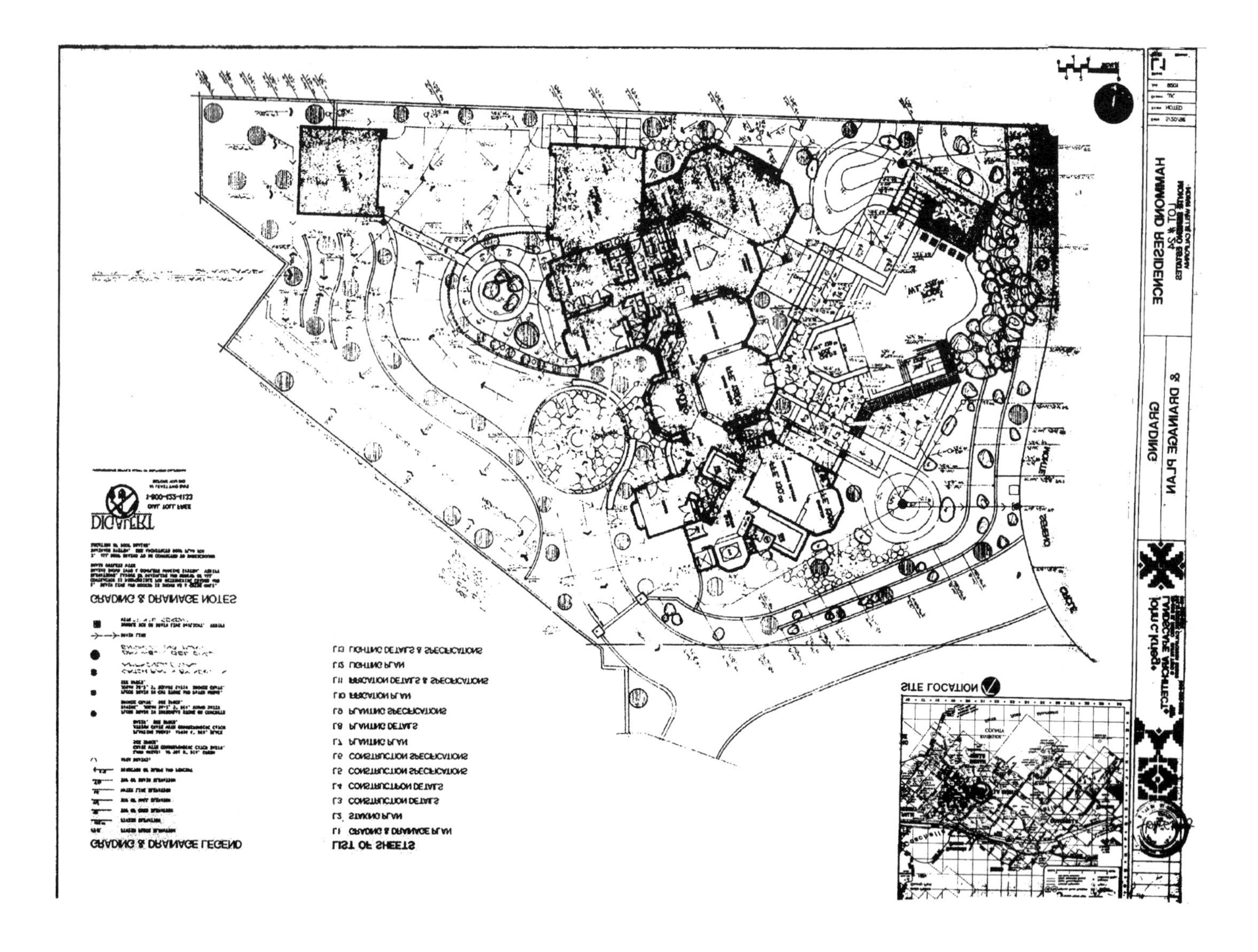

Flood Plain

Drainage Structures

Steep alluvial plain

Armored White Water River channel

Overflow drain

Floor drain

Drainage Equipment

Drainage parts

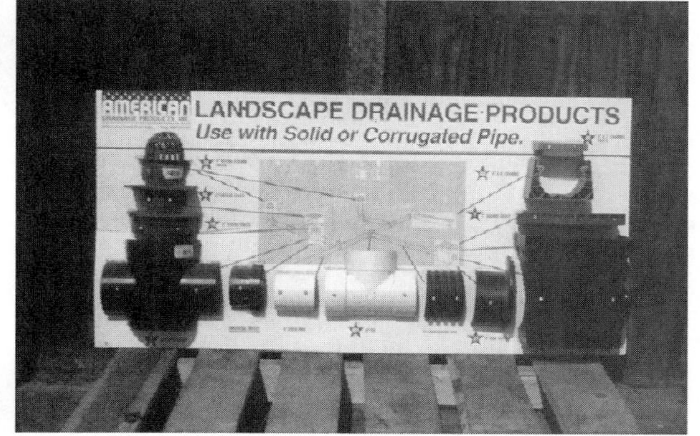

Drainage equipment

Deck grates

Planting grates

U.S.G.S. Map

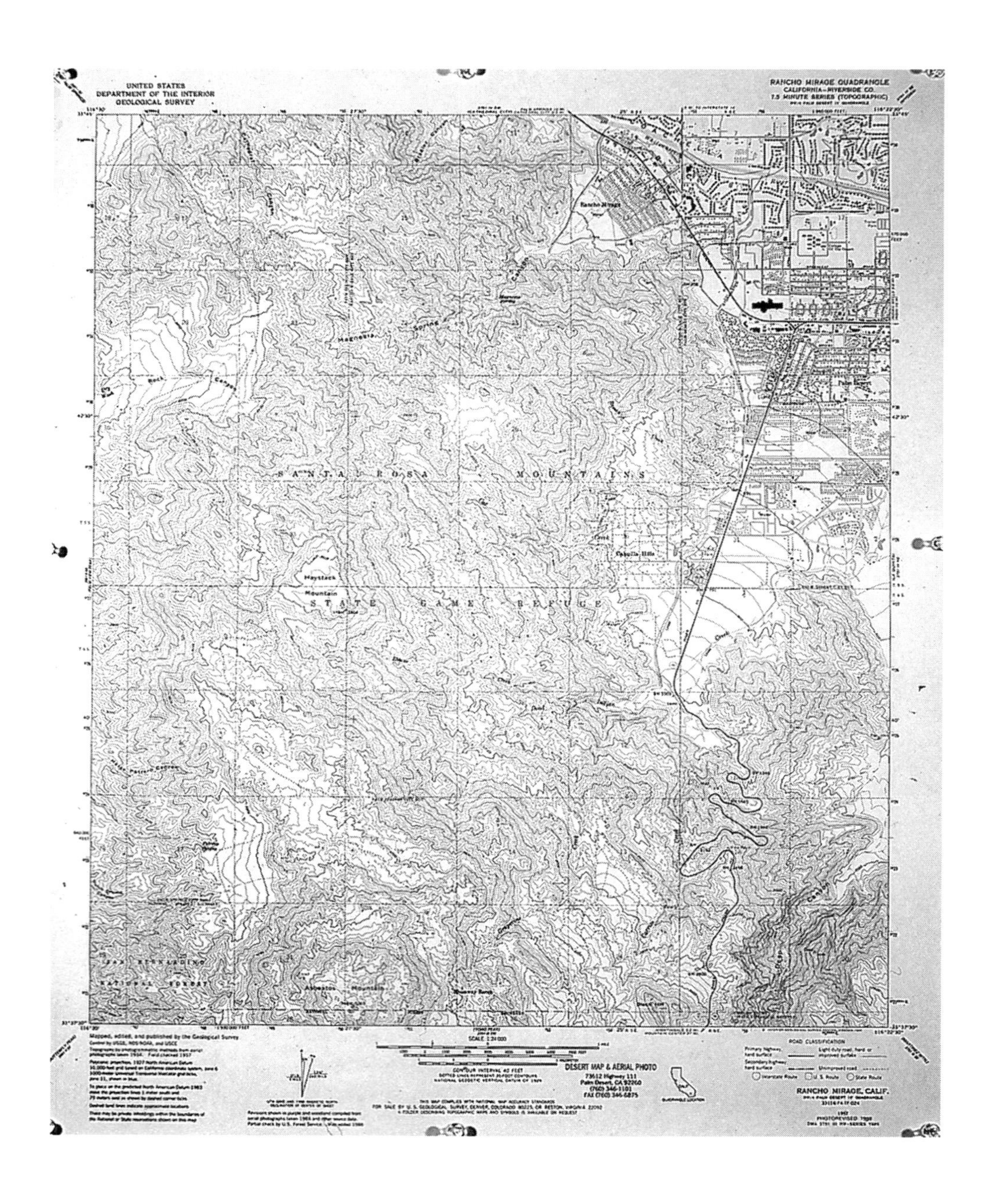
UNITED STATES
DEPARTMENT OF THE INTERIOR
GEOLOGICAL SURVEY
RANCHO MIRAGE QUADRANGLE
CALIFORNIA—RIVERSIDE CO.
7.5 MINUTE SERIES (TOPOGRAPHIC)
S A N T A   R O S A   M O U N T A I N S
S T A T E   G A M E   R E F U G E
Haystack
Mountain
DESERT MAP & AERIAL PHOTO
RANCHO MIRAGE, CALIF.

Glossary

Area drain: A smaller-size drain which provides for drainage of a smaller area. Usually connects to a larger drainage system before a downstream discharge point is reached.

Benchmark: A permanent marker of known elevation above or below sea level (datum). A benchmark for a specific site acts as a reference point or point of beginning for site surveys.

Bubble box: A drainage structure, usually occurring at the end of a system, which allows water within the system to discharge (bubble) out of the structure.

Catch basin: A drainage structure of medium size into which runoff from a moderate size area is collected. Catch basins are also used as clean out points along a drainage line.

Civil engineer: An individual licensed by law to design site structures and systems (bridges, roads, parking lots) and to lay out grading and drainage systems.

Clay soil: Any soil that is 50% to predominantly clay particles in content; a soil that will drain slowly and retain an excessive amount of moisture.

Coefficient: A number used in mathematical equations that is usually multiplied by other numbers.

Contour: Imaginary line through space that is always level unto itself above or below an assigned datum or sea level.

Culvert: A manmade drainage structure which occurs under roadways or through embankments.

Cut: Slicing through soil. Most frequently applies to removing soil from an existing slope.

Datum: Point above or below which other points can be assigned an elevation. The most commonly referenced datum is sea level at 0'-0".

Drainage: The removal of water from the area where it first occurs.

Dry well: Extremely large underground drain water collection device. Dry wells are often the point of termination in a manmade drainage system.

Elevation: A measurable point above or below a datum (usually sea level).

End wall: A structure (usually concrete) which supports the opening at the low end of a culvert.

Fill: Soil added to or placed over existing soil.

Fine raking: Removing debris and stone up to 1/2 inch in diameter from raked soil.

Finish grade: Final grade called for on the grading and drainage plans. The soil is fine raked, leveled, and consistently smooth.

Finish floor: The final elevation of any given point on a building's floor.

Formula: An exact assemblage of numbers or events to arrive at a predictable and consistent result. If always applied in the correct sequence, the elements which make up the formula will always produce the same outcome.

Gradient: Degree of slope expressed as a percentage.

Grading: The physical moving of site soil to accommodate the placement of new elements on the ground plane.

Gutter: A channel run along and set immediately below a roof's eave to catch rain water to be discharged at or below grade.

Head wall: A structure (usually concrete) which supports the opening at the high end of a culvert.

Humus: Decomposed organic matter (leaves, manure, etc.) found in soil. Humus improves the fertility and workability of a soil.

Inlet: A point where water enters a drainage structure, system, or pipe.

Loam: A soil that contains equal or near equal amounts of clay, silt, and sand in conjunction with a measurable amount of organic matter. Loam soils are usually quite fertile and an ideal planting medium for most types of plants.

Mass grading: The term given to initial and, frequently, the most intensive site grading operations.

One hundred year storm: The largest rainstorm that can be expected to fall within an area in a 100-year period. This is based upon recorded historical weather data.

Outlet: A point where water exits a drainage structure, system, or pipe.

Pad elevation: The elevation assigned to the area where a building's floor will eventually be constructed. Pads are typically 6 inches below finish floor elevation.

Planimeter: A mechanical calibrated device used to measure areas on flat surfaced drawings. Frequently used to calculate cut and fill.

Ramp: A consistent gradient between two points. Handicap ramps in most states cannot exceed a slope ratio of 12 to 1 or 8.33%.

Ratio: The relationship between two or more known quantities or numbers. Ratios are used to express portions of a mix or amount of one element as opposed to another.

Retention basin: A basin created in the ground for the express purpose of catching and holding runoff water.

Retaining wall: A wall designed and engineered to accommodate fill or a slope against one side while also being capable of resisting lateral sheer forces.

Riser: The vertical face which accommodates the elevational rise in a step.

Rough grade: The grade (soil surface) that exists prior to the addition of soil preparation materials and subsequent fine raking. Usually considered to be 1/10 foot below finish grade.

Runoff: Rain or irrigation water falling on a site and which does not naturally pond, is not asorbed by soil or plants, and does not immediately evaporate.

Saline soil: Soil containing a sufficient level of concentrated or soluble salt as to be detrimental to plant growth.

Sandy soil: Any soil that is 50% to predominately sand particles in content. A soil that drains rapidly and requires frequent irrigation to support most types of plant life.

Scupper: An opening in a roof parapet which allows rain water to flow from the roof. Splash blocks are placed below scupper openings to break the fall of this roof drainage.

Shrink/swell factor: Displaced soils will shrink when drying and swell when wet. A factor must be applied to compensate for this, depending on whether more or less soil is critical to the grading design intent. Fill soils tend to shrink while cut soils tend to swell.

Slope: Any inclination. Any grade that is not level.

Soils engineer: An individual licensed by law to study soils for suitability for building or other forms of construction.

Soils report: The findings of a soils engineer are usually compiled in this written document.

Spot elevation: The elevation of an exact point (spot) in space.

Steps: Composed of vertical risers and flat treads. Steps traverse gradients.

Survey: As it applies to this chapter, the property line location and topographic notations needed to define a specific site. Done by a licensed surveyor or civil engineer. A survey serves to provide the basic information from which tract maps and other plans are generated.

Surveyor: An individual licensed by law to perform land surveys and issue drafted information of such on paper.

Topsoil: Technically, the top layer of soil resting at grade. Commonly thought to be the most fertile soil, due to its having the highest humus content. The term topsoil as it is most often used, refers to fertile, workable soil adequate to support plant life.

Tread: The horizontal surface which accommodates the lateral distance in a step.

Watershed: The entire land area within the boundaries of a specific site that will receive rain or irrigation water.

Chapter 4

Hardscape Design

Seat wall design

Introduction

Hardscape, as it pertains to landscape architecture, embodies those design elements and features which are hard. These elements are ground plane surfacing, site walls, overhead elements, site furniture, and water features. Water features are classified as hardscape because, although the water is soft, the shell that contains the water is a hard material.

Hardscape elements are usually fixed. Owing to their size, weight, and physical structure they are considered permanent once installed or located in a setting. Because something like concrete, for example, cannot easily be reworked or rearranged after it has been installed, great care and forethought must be given to its initial use and placement.

A diligent landscape architect will make every effort to communicate his design thoughts concerning the hardscape as early as possible in the design process. The ground plane layout of entry walks, patios, etc., and the location of walls, steps, and ramps will affect the way the site circulates, functions, and feels. Once satisfied that the client knows and understands the purpose and the extent of all hardscape areas and features, the landscape architect must determine exactly how this information is to be presented to contractors, manufacturers, and suppliers.

In no other area of landscape architectural design and construction is accuracy, clarity, and meticulous attention to detail more important than they are here. Hardscape working drawings or staking plans require accurate dimensions, angle, and curvature information, finish schedules for material descriptions, and comprehendible details. Hardscape and water features can easily comprise over 50% of the exterior construction budget. They are installed immediately after the site grading is completed and set the tone for the quality of, or lack thereof, for the rest of the project. How the design intent affects the choice and application of materials or how the material selection impacts design decisions is so interrelated that the normal design axiom of "develop concepts then details" is hard to adhere to with hardscape.

This chapter will first describe materials, how they are used, and factors to consider in their selection and installation. Once a good grasp on what materials are available is obtained, we will then embark on tying all the different elements together within the confines of the outdoor room to arrive at a workable (and liveable) hardscape design solution. Then site furnishings and features will be discussed. Finally, how all this information is depicted in a set of working drawings that contractors can read and comprehend will be examined.

Hardscape Materials

- **Adobe:** Adobe, in historic terms, is an indigenous clay that was molded into blocks and used extensively in New Mexican and Arizonan territorial style architecture. It is not a building material used in areas where soils are predominately sandy. Today, the adobe clay is stabilized with asphalt emulsions to improve strength and moisture resistance. Adobe is primarily used in block form with available sizes comparable to that of masonry block. Texture of adobe can be very irregular and earthen, owing to its clay content. Even with water-proofing, it is probably better used for walls than for patios where it can be subject to standing (and erosive) water.
- **Aluminum:** This metal is nonmagnetic and very lightweight in comparison to other metals. Used extensively as a corrugated roofing material and in window and door frame manufacturing. Also used quite frequently in the manufacture of outdoor lighting fixtures. Do not use aluminum below grade in some types of sandy soils, as they are capable of decomposing the metal. While not as frequently employed for ornamentation as other metals, aluminum can be easily shaped and formed. Being the most abundant metal within the earth's crust, it is highly likely that even more creative uses for this material will continue to be developed.
- **Asphalt**: This ground plane surfacing material is comprised of bitumens that are left as an afterproduct of petroleum distillation. Inherent moisture content directly affects the level of softness or hardness of the material. Heated asphalt

is quite malleable and easily spread and formed. Dried and coated with a sealer, the material is attractive in a utilitarian way. Used primarily in roadway and parking lot construction, it could be employed more creatively in recreational and urban plaza design. Asphalt will accept admixtures for coloration and a limited amount of texturing. Asphalt must be laid on a well-compacted subbase to be effective. Positive drainage off of asphalt will prolong its life. The material will decay when subjected for prolonged periods in standing water.

- **Bomanite:** Bomanite® is a concrete coloring and texturing process patented by the Bomanite Corp. (Modesa, CA). Bomanite is so frequently specified and used that it has taken on an identity of its own. The Bomanite process is franchised to a number of contractors worldwide. Refer to the "Concrete" listing for further information about concrete and concrete processes.
- **Boulders:** Boulders, especially as they are used in high end residential and resort hotel work, should be considered a part of the hardscape design. When specifying boulders, it is important to know the source and the quantity that is available from that source. Some boulders are rough and angular while others are smooth and rounded. Colors range quite a bit from one type to another. With the advent of desert varnishes, which stains the boulder to a natural color by replicating the chemical process that happens in nature at a greatly accelerated pace, boulders can be matched to one another on site or matched to adjacent rock formations. Boulders are extremely heavy and very expensive. The expense is not so much associated with the material itself but with the equipment required to handle it. Special equipment, including cranes, is needed to move the larger specimens. For this reason, care and judgment should be exercised in their design application. When specifying boulders be consistent in dimensional call-outs. Angular boulders can be specified by height, width, and length, while rounded boulders are usually called out by diameter. To appear natural, boulders often have to be buried up to one third their height. Do not let concave areas show. Try to make the boulder appear as if it has always been a part of the site and not just set there recently. Because of the difficulty and expense

encountered in acquiring and working with natural boulders, processes for making artificial boulders have been developed and continue to improve. The level of quality in artificial boulders can vary greatly and a company's track record should be carefully studied when contemplating the use of their product. It is extremely difficult to tell some artificial boulders from the real thing, while others can look ridiculously fake.

- **Brick:** Classic building material. Usual size is 2 inches thick by 4 inches wide by 8 inches long, although several other sizes are available. Brick set on a concrete subslab and tacked and grouted with cement mortar can be as thin as 3/4 inch. Brick is made of clay or shale and has wide variety of colors. Colors range from yellowish beige, to tan, to brown, to terracotta, to deep red. Clay is molded and wire-cut for precise edges and then fired until burnt in a kiln. Shale is pulverized to powder and then treated the same as clay. The relatively small dimensions of brick guarantee firing through the entire clay body of the brick. Hollowed-out or cored brick is lighter to use and provides ground-plane drainage if set on sand. Two exterior grades are SX and SW. SX is stronger and more water resistant. Both grades are fine for desert applications. Common brick is the most frequently used red brick in the Southwest. New interlocking shapes are being offered for exterior use on the ground plane. The interlocking feature is especially useful for installation on sand-setting beds.
- **Cast Iron:** This material is used extensively for garden ornamentation. Tables, benches, and all manner of other outdoor furniture are all made from cast iron. In addition, functional and ornamental tree grates are almost exclusively formed from this product. Lamp posts, building columns, ready-for-assembly fountains, and gates stretch the limits of this material's tensile strength. The beauty of the material is the intricacy of detail that can be achieved with it. In its molten form, cast iron is as flexible as wet plaster and can flow easily into the smallest molds. It should be remembered that cast iron is extremely heavy and will rust if not maintained properly, which often means yearly paintings.
- **Ceramic Tile:** Ceramic tile is made from high-quality clay that is often dried, fired, pulverized, and refired to give it the

finest and smoothest consistency. Ceramic tile is fired at extremely high kiln temperatures. This yields a very hard tile of high compressive strength with fairly exact edges. Ceramic tile is very water and abrasion resistant, which makes it especially valuable in swimming pool and spa construction. With the artistic use of colorful and patterned glazes (to be discussed later) these tiles can add beauty and elegance to the hardscape.

- **Clay:** Clay, in and of itself, is not a building material. However, once it is shaped and dried it is useful in a variety of building materials and site elements. Adobe and brick discussed earlier are composed primarily of clay. Clay, as discussed here, applies to pottery. Pots, while they seem rather common, can enhance any design with their size, shape, and placement. Pots in desert design are the logical place to introduce bright but limited annual color. Soil mixtures and water conservation are easily controlled with pots. The reason pots seem so common is that they are so readily available and shapes are somewhat standard among the various manufacturers. Landscape architects can design their own shapes or coordinate work with private potters to arrive at new, unusual, limited edition, and one-of-a-kind pots. It is one of the most cost-effective ways to infuse practical art into the hardscape.
- **Concrete:** Concrete is the term applied to a mixture of cement, sand or aggregate, small amounts of lime, and water. In its liquid or plastic state it is quite flexible and will mold to the shape of the form containing it, much as a cake in a decorative tin takes on the shape of the pan. Concrete is often the best selection for a flowing or free-form design. Where a curvilinear edge would require special cutting and odd angles in brick or wood, concrete accepts this configuration naturally.

Two properties of concrete are important to consider when contemplating its use. First is its strength. Concrete is known to be very high in compressive strength and very weak in tensile strength. That is, it can accept heavy loads, but must not be put in a situation where it will have to bend or stretch. The extremely high temperatures encountered on the desert floor during the summer months cause concrete to expand (stretch) which, unless designed to accommodate this action, will cause the concrete to crack. In desert landscape architecture, heat expansion is the critical factor in concrete installation. Expansion joints are very important and no slab or field of concrete should exceed 400 square feet without receiving some form of expansion joint. Steel reinforcing bar and wire can be placed within concrete to improve its tensile strength, which they do, but these elements will not counteract the forces of heat expansion, as they will expand themselves when exposed to heat. The second significant factor of concrete usage is how the material forms. As previously stated, concrete is a mixture of ingredients. These ingredients are mixed with and suspended in water. The wet concrete mixture hardens as water evaporates from the mix during a process known as *hydration*. Proper hydration in concrete causes the cement inherent in the mixture to adhere to sand and aggregate. If hydration happens too fast, water-suspended particles in the mix will rise to the surface of the slab leaving a chalky film which discolors, cracks, and fissures. If hydration occurs too slowly, the bonding process of cement to sand and aggregates is retarded and the concrete weakens. In the desert, rarely does concrete cure too slowly. To retard the rapid evaporation of water during the hydration process, the surface of the concrete is kept wet or covered with plastic sheeting. When using plastic sheeting, it is important to allow no air bubbles between the surface of the concrete and the bottom of the plastic as this will cause discoloration. Concrete strength is usually tested at 7 and 28 days. Normal acceptable compressive strength at the end of 28 days is 3,000 $lb./in.^2$ In water features, the strength is often increased to 6,000 $lb./in.^2$ The stronger the concrete is, the less porous it is. That is, the surface of the stronger concrete will be more waterproof, which discourages leaking. Concrete strength is greatly increased by using lesser amounts of water in the mix. A very dry concrete known as gunite is used extensively in water-feature designs throughout the Southwest and will be discussed in greater depth under its own heading.

Because of its original liquid nature and degree of workability as it hardens, concrete lends itself to a myriad of design uses. Concrete can be colored in a wide array of hues. Color additives are simply incorporated into the mix. Concrete can have stone aggregates exposed on its surface. The stone is either added to the mix and washed clean as the concrete hydrates or is seeded and tamped into a semi-stiff pour. Last, concrete can accept innumerable textures and patterns during its curing process. Trowel-finish, broom-finish, salt-finish, and all manner of cutting, stamping, and scoring add infinite variety and interest to concrete surfaces.

- **Copper:** This metal is extremely popular in the Southwest. Copper is used as a plate material for roofing and formed into all sorts of garden elements. Copper can maintain its distinctive color through chemical treating or frequent wire brushing or it can be allowed to develop a chalky, green patina. Sheet copper is also used to form a natural weir in water features. Do not use copper or any other metal in water features that contain fish, as these metals are toxic to the animals. Copper was mined extensively in Arizona at the turn of the century and less productive mines exist there to this day. This is a material that speaks quite easily to the local vernacular.
- **Decomposed Granite:** Decomposed or crushed granite is mostly used as a topping in planting beds. In some cases it is used as a paving material for lightly traveled walks and in equipment yards. Decomposed granite is becoming increasingly more available from sources throughout the Southwest in quite a few colors from tan, to brown, to mauve, to deep red, and black. Normal sizes are 1/4 in. minus, 1/2 in. minus, and 3/4 in. minus. Three-quarter inch minus and the less available larger sizes are more suitable for high-wind areas where the 1/4 inch minus has so many fines that the majority of the granite would be literally blown away. The 1/4-in. granite is useful in equestrian facilities and trails as it is small enough not to catch in horses' hooves, while 3/4-in. granite will. On steep slope areas, where grades approach or exceed two to one it is advisable to employ a chemical stabilizer to bind granite together. Stabilizer works much better on 1/4-in. minus granite. The smaller the size of the granite, the easier it is to roll into a tightly compacted surface. Normal depth of granite is two inches. It is costly to place visqueen plastic sheets under large areas for weed control. In areas over 1,000 $ft.^2$ it is more efficient to apply a chemical such as Dacthal or Surflan and water it in thoroughly through the granite to the soil surface. For larger orders, suppliers will incorporate and mix the chemical into the granite before bringing it to the job site.
- **Expansion Joints:** Material for expansion joints varies from felt, to foam, to plastic with stainless steel caps, to sand. They are all grouped under one heading here because expansion of concrete and masonry elements is extremely impor-

tant in the desert. For Californians, earthquakes, although customarily mild in intensity, occur on a regular basis. In all desert areas, heat expansion of concrete slabs is the number one reason for cracking. While there are some excellent products to accommodate the need for expansion, two design axioms will help more than the expansion materials themselves. First, minimize large expanses of unbroken decking and, second, do not butt decking to vertical elements such as walls and columns. The more gap or float areas around a slab the less likely it is to experience stress from any given direction. More expansion will always be better than too little, as even an expansion joint is more pleasing to look at than a crack.

- **Fiberglass Screening:** Environmental control is of primary concern during a desert summer day where temperatures on the exposed ground plane can exceed 130°F. Complete shade can cool temperatures by 15 to 20 degrees, depending on the sun exposure, while filtered shade can make a difference of 10 degrees. Fiberglass screens hung over or lashed to an overhead trellis of wood, pipe, or tautly drawn cable can provide 30 to 95% shade, depending on the density of the screen's mesh. These screens are lightweight so the trellis structure need not be as structurally elaborate as that required to support other materials. Fiberglass screens are also colorful, available in a wide range of hues. These colors can be coordinated to the color scheme of adjacent architecture quite nicely. In high-wind areas, these screens should be demountable or be 50% mesh or less to allow the wind to pass through them.
- **Flagstone:** Flagstone derives from the same metamorphic rock and sedimentary clays as slate, but is softer in composition due to a higher sand content. For this reason, flagstones are usually cut thicker than slates. Flagstone colors are usually more uniform and paler than slate colors, making it a good choice in the subtle garden. It is a fine stone for stepping pads or decking. Flagstone can be cut into 12-in. by 12-in. squares or can come in random sizes up to 3 ft by 3 ft and beyond. In addition, extremely thick (10 in. and larger) flagstone in lengths up to 6 ft are used for freestanding bridges with dramatic natural effects.

- **Glass Block:** This modular material is seeing increased use in exterior design. Their compressive strength is an issue because they are not as strong as standard masonry block. This material is used by landscape architects in walls for aesthetic purposes and to diffuse bright light and glare. It is also used in water features to create translucent effects and as a water weir material, an is probably one of the most high tech elements in the desert designer's arsenal of construction materials. Glass blocks are either hollow- or solid-formed. Hollow block has more selections in colors and surface textures. Consider backlighting glass block for dramatic night-time silhouetting of design features.
- **Glazes:** As addressed here, glazes are the finishes that ceramic tiles and pottery receive. Glazes are comprised of fine sand particles with powdered pigments added which are suspended in liquid. This liquid dries over and is slightly absorbed by the clay body it is applied to. Once fired in a kiln, the glaze becomes hard and waterproof like glass, because it is, in fact, nothing more than colored freeform glass. Glazes are either gloss or matte finish. Their importance here is in color and texture coordination with other design elements. If one accepts the premise that pottery is underrated and often unimaginative in outdoor applications, then one must also accept the same premise for the glazes that cover the pottery. As with pottery, new creative approaches to glazes can approach the realm of fine art.
- **Granite:** This igneous rock is of volcanic origin and extremely hard. Due to the expense encountered in quarrying the material, it is not usually used in slab form in landscape applications. Granite is one of the finest most durable materials to sheath a building with. Outdoors, on the ground plane, granite is usually comprised of square sets or irregular rectangular Belgian blocks. These granite modules are either set on compacted sand or on a concrete subbase and grouted in place with mortar. Granite is not frequently used in desert design, and when it is, the amount is usually limited to bands and borders. It is, however, a material with a rich history and a rugged natural quality that is rarely out of place.
- **Gunite:** Gunite is an extremely dry and stiff form of concrete used in swimming pool, spa, and water feature construction.

Having a lower water to cement ratio causes gunite to be up to three times stronger than conventional concrete. On the vertical plane, gunite is usually set thinner (6 in. vs. 8 in. minimum) than conventional concrete and, because of its thinness, receives more steel reinforcement. This added steel reinforcement increases the tensile strength of gunite to the point where entire swimming pool shells can be formed without the need for any expansion joints. Gunite is applied as a spray. Dry cement and tiny aggregates are pumped through a hose and water is added just before the mix exits the nozzle. An experienced applicator can literally spray the shell in a matter of hours. Because of its dryness, gunite is very rough textured. This is a benefit in water feature construction where plaster is applied over the gunite to waterproof the shell. The gunite's rough texture provides a receptive surface for the plaster to adhere to. Because of its expense and its rough surface texture, gunite is not really practical for ground plane applications. However, for special features, such as freestanding sculpture, it has unlimited possibilities.

- **Lake Linings:** Contrary to what one would expect for the desert, there is a large amount of lake construction in the Southwest. High-dollar country club and residential construction demands this amenity. While the landscape architect must satisfy his clientele, he should also do his part in taking a leadership role in the area of water conservation. In the area of lake construction, the best thing anyone can do is to try to minimize leaking. Most lake construction consists of a concrete freeboard (coping) around the lake's edge that penetrates below the lake surface from 2 to 3 feet and then continues at a maximum 5:1 slope for an additional 4 or 5 feet. It is necessary to make a lake a minimum of 7 feet deep to significantly discourage algae growth. Before the concrete edge is poured, a 20-mil minimum and up to 40-mil thick polyvinyl chloride (PVC) liner is set in place and turned down just under the surface of the soil at the top of the freeboard. This liner continues on into the hollowed out lake shell. Where the liner cannot be run continuously to the other side of the lake, a joint becomes necessary. Sheets of polyvinyl chloride are overlapped 2 feet minimum and solvent welded to prevent leaking. Gunite and concrete are not cost effective for large lakes and liners are the only practical solution. On firmly compacted soil they work fine. Care must be taken during installation to prevent slits and holes from being formed in the liner. To protect the liner, 6 inches to a foot of sand is placed over it. In cases where humans or higher quality species of fish will be swimming in the lake, layers of silica sand and diatomaceous earth are used over the liner to increase water filtration and clarity.

- **Limestone:** Limestone is composed primarily of sedimentary rock. Not as many colors are available as with other stone. Colors are predominately creams, buffs, and tans with some grays to bluish grays. Limestone has a rich earthy feel. It is a very expensive material. Due to the relative softness of the stone, it is easily cut into dimensioned pieces, and it is also easy to finish its surface, bevel, and even radius its edges. Be careful when using limestone adjacent to water features. The stone can be quite absorbent and can be very slick to walk on. Due to its expense, limestone is often used in limited areas for banding, fountain copings, or as insets within larger fields of stone.
- **Marble:** Marble is, or more appropriately was, limestone that has metamorphosed. "Metamorphic" is the term used to describe rock that has been exposed to extremely high temperatures. This exposure changed the rock's density and crystalline structure. Therefore marble is harder and shinier than limestone. Marble is also more colorful. Colors range through a broad spectrum and veins of darker colors add beauty and character to the stone. Marble is the classic building material of ancient Greece and Rome. It is used primarily as a cut stone and in sculpture. It is extremely expensive, even more so than limestone. Except for pedestals and accent features it is not frequently used outside, and is rarely used on the ground plane. When it is used, it is usually in the unpolished state. As much care should be taken with marble as with limestone around water features, as it becomes very slippery when wet.
- **Masonry:** In historic terms, masonry is described as the art of joining together of building modules (brick, stone, block, etc.). For the purposes of this definition within this chapter, masonry is discussed as concrete block. Concrete block is usually classified as heavy or light owing to the weight of the inert material used in conjunction with cement to make the

block. Standard practice in detailing or specifying block is to call out dimensions by width, height, and length. This is what the contractors and suppliers are familiar with so it is wise to stick with tradition. Block used for structural purposes is usually in lengths or units of four (4 in., 8 in., 12 in., 16 in.). Block for walls is frequently elongated to 18 in. which results in fewer blocks and less hand labor needed to construct the wall. Do not use 18-in.-long block for structural items. Masonry block also comes in a variety of surface textures and sometimes the block itself is formed in an ornamental pattern. Caps for walls are normally half the height of the blocks in the wall runs and often wider so that the overhang will cause a shadow line which adds the effect of depth to the wall design. Colors and textures vary due to inconsistencies in material from one gathering site to the next. When depending on a special look from a special block, order all block made at one site and in one run so that they will be consistent. Concrete blocks are hollow. These hollow areas are called cells. Steel reinforcing bar is run from solid concrete footings or foundations vertically through these cells and frequently connect to steel rebar running horizontally through special notched courses in the top row of the blocks. These horizontal bars are called *bond beams* as they bond the grid of reinforcing bar together. The cells of the wall where the vertical rebar occurs are grouted solid. In walls requiring more strength, especially retaining walls, which are load bearing walls, all the cells are grouted. Expansion in a masonry wall is as important as in a concrete slab. Walls receive vertical expansion joints or a simple gap is left to accommodate movement. Masonry block can be stuccoed or painted. When applying paint, especially in hot weather, it is a good idea to wet the surface of the wall first. This enables the paint to dry over the surface consistently rather than being literally sucked in by the porous block.

- **Paints:** Paints for exterior use are classified in two main groups: Latex and oil based. Oil-based paints are receiving less and less use due to the difficulty encountered in cleaning brushes and spraying apparatus. Latex-based paints can be cleaned with water and are much easier to use. In some cases, oils are more suitable, as in finishing some woods. When specifying any paint, consider the characteristics of the surface to be painted and the desired final result. Certain finishes and colors reflect light and create glare while others will absorb light and make an object appear dull. Painting for environmental protection is not necessarily the same thing as painting to create a nice color scheme. For quality results, outdoor painting on bare surfaces almost always requires three coats. The first, or prime coat, seals the surface of the element for the second, or intermediate coat; and the third, or finish coat provides a consistent color and surface texture. Paint, especially oils, are toxic to plant materials when introduced wet into the soil. This is an item to be closely monitored during field observation.

- **Pebble Tec:** Pebble Tec® is a patented water-feature sealing process that had its origins in Australia, but now has several franchises in the U.S. (Pebble Technology, Inc.). Small pebbles are worn smooth in a mechanical tumbler and then introduced to a plaster/epoxy mix. Applied like plaster, it is hand troweled in place and the surface of the exposed pebbles is washed smooth. It has a very natural effect that looks especially good with boulders. The material can be applied right up to the base of pool/spa and water featuring copings, thus eliminating the need for tile. Pebble Tec is especially useful in stream design, as the material can come up out of the water, turn down, and meet grade. It simply follows and coats the gunite, in what is called a "rolled-bond beam." A wide array of color choices are available. This is a material whose popularity will skyrocket in the next 10 years.
- **Plaster:** Plaster is comprised of high-grade Portland cement, fine sand, and lime or gypsum mixed with water to a paste-like consistency. Plastering, as we will address it here, applies to the surfacing of gunite pool, spa, and water-feature shells for waterproofing and aesthetic purposes. In its normal state, plaster is off-white in color. It is the addition of water, which in turn reflects the sky above, that turns a swimming pool its characteristic shade of blue. For the more natural and infinity edge-type pools, or when a more reflective surface is desired, colors are mixed integrally with the plaster to provide darker hues. Quality pool contractors feel that plaster is the only sure way to seal gunite shells. The very best way to place boulders into a pool is to set them on a gunite shelf that has been pre-plastered. To set a boulder onto a bare gunite shelf and then try to plaster up to the surface of the boulder will guarantee a leak every time, due to the surface texture

and porousness of the boulder itself. Proper plastering assures water conservation — apply it generously.

- **Quartzite:** Quartzite is a very high-density sandstone. That is, during eons of time it has been compressed to a greater degree than conventional sandstone. In the process of this compression silica sand cemented with quartz crystals. It is these crystals that give quartzite its reflective, glinty quality. Massive quantities of quartzite flat stone is being mined in Idaho, making the material increasingly more affordable and available. It is primarily cream, tan, gray, and rust to golden in color, and makes a fine cut stone. Because of its density, it is a good choice for driveways and other heavy use areas.
- **Reinforcing Bar:** Steel reinforcing bar is a critical element for adding tensile strength to concrete slabs and masonry walls. The bar is sized or graded by a numbering system. Each higher number represents a 1/8 inch increase in diameter. Thus a No. 4 rebar is 1/2 in. in diameter. No. 4 rebar is quite common in desert wall design. Welded wire mesh is used for concrete slabs. Eight by eight by ten welded wire mesh means 8-in. squares with No. 10 steel. When designing retaining or load-bearing walls it is always wise to employ the services of a structural engineer who will specify the size and location of reinforcing bar and provide details on how to utilize the material for maximum strength and efficiency. Any liability concerning wall failure will then rest with the structural engineer.
- **Riverstone:** This is a favorite material of landscape architects in a desert setting. Grading plans frequently employ directional swales and retention basins to accommodate surface drainage. Riverstone makes a natural and somewhat cost-effective surface liner in these areas. A lot of simulated desert washes are used for aesthetic effects. Done properly, the design can be stunning. Done improperly, the results can be quite tacky. One of the cardinal rules in creating a dry riverbed is to arrange the stones as they would appear in nature if the river were actually flowing. In Arizona and California, riverstone comes from four main sources and in four main colors. Sunburst riverstone is rust to golden orange and comes from the Colorado River (Big Red). It is somewhat flattened and very smooth. La Paz stone is jet black, comes from the La Paz River in Mexico, and is very flat and

smooth. La Paz stone can be striking due to its rare color. Salt River stone comes from the Salt River in Arizona. Colors range from light gray to mauve and, at a distance, it takes on a pinkish tint. It is rounded and angular in shape. Whitewater riverstone comes from the Whitewater River outside Palm Springs and its white color gives the river its name. It is a rounded and rough textured granite stone. All these stones come in a variety of sizes so it is important to call out diameter when specifying. Common sizes are 3 in. minus, 6 in. minus, 12 in. minus, and oversized.

- **Saltillo Tile:** This is the common Mexican tile used so frequently as a paver throughout the Southwest. The name comes from their place of origin, Saltillo, Sonora, Mexico. Other tiles come from other Mexican cities, but Saltillo tile is by far the most abundantly available. Saltillo tile is a sun-baked clay either formed in rough molds or laid directly on the ground and cut like cake. The latter can be quite irregular with 1/2-in. warps not uncommon. For this reason it is not recommended that Saltillos be set on sand. Their best application is when set on a concrete subslab and placed on a minimum 3/4-in. mortar setting bed. This allows the installer some leveling area. The tile is porous and needs to be water sealed frequently, especially outdoors. The relatively inexpensive unit cost of the tile is often adversely offset by the high installation costs due to increased labor. The Saltillo cannot be surpassed for earthiness and warmth and its popularity iscertain to continue.
- **Sandstone:** Our discussion concerns two sandstones. Both are readily available from sources in Mexico. Sandstone, as its name implies, is primarily compressed sand with surrounding clays acting as a bonding agent. Adoquin and cantera are the two sandstones commonly used. Adoquin is a harder, denser stone and better surface material. Cantera stone is softer, lending itself to the hand carving of a multitude of architectural caps, moldings, balustrades, and columns. Both stones are cut extensively for use in fountains and all manner of garden ornaments. Colors range from tan, to coffee, to black. There is also a light orange and a magnificent pink available. For gardens that emphasize the local vernacular, either of these two stones would be an excellent selection.

- **Slate:** This metamorphic rock offers the largest variety of colors and surface textures among paving stones. This sedimentary clay with suspended sand and minerals is harder than flagstone, its close relative, because it was exposed to higher temperatures and heavier compressive loads. Like flagstone, it built up over centuries in flat layers that are easily split into pavers and veneers. Some blackboards in schools come from slate. Unlike flagstone, slates possess varied colors which run in veins and swirls throughout their structure. Slate can be obtained in just about any thickness and color. Grays, greens, and browns are the most common slates. When using large random sized slabs with varying edge thicknesses always get full sized samples or hand pick the pieces. Larger pieces of slate can contain a lot more black than one would expect. Slate used for pool and spa copings should be ground smooth to the touch on the edges as it can often be very sharp in its natural state. While quite strong in compression, slate is brittle and will break easily if not properly supported. Slate is one of the most earthy and colorful materials available and, although not cheap, its price is not so high as to preclude its wide and abundant use. On an existing installation where the decking goes nowhere and seems to do nothing, slate can liven up the job and salvage the most mundane of layouts.
- **Steel:** This is a material that most landscape architects will not be involved with on a regular basis. The three steel products that are most commonly used are plate steel for wood fasteners and connections, rolled steel for somewhat flexible landscape headers, and stainless steel for pool and spa handrails. Stainless steel is the only steel product that (like its name) will not rust. Even plate steel that has been galvanized (zinc or iron coated) will rust over time when exposed to outdoor elements. For this reason, plate steel should be painted and maintained unless the rust is a desired feature (as in sculpture). Steel wire is used for tying and bundling, and like reinforcing bar, always increases in size with each increase in numerical designation.
- **Stucco:** Stucco is nothing more than plaster with a texture added. Frequently a tackifier or epoxy is incorporated in the mixture to provide adhesive quality and enhanced waterproofing characteristics. Stucco is used extensively in the

Southwest. Mixed with colors and sprayed or trowelled onto buildings and walls, it will create, in two or three steps, a beautiful and watertight skin. Because stucco contains paint, it is toxic to plant materials, so care should be taken during its application to landscape features. Stucco's primary benefit, besides ease of application, is the wide variety of surface textures that can be achieved with the medium. It also lends itself well to covering curvilinear walls.

- **Tin:** This is a metal that dates back to ancient Babylon. Today Bolivia and Central America along with Southeastern Asia are the largest tin producers. It was used extensively in historical Mexican architecture. This metal can be rolled very thin, which allows it to be bent, pressed, pounded, and drilled into a variety of shapes and patterns. Tin is most frequently used as a rough roofing material and as a decorative cover for exterior lighting. Being a material that fits well into the local vernacular, tin could receive more creative uses in all types of garden ornamentation.
- **Water Sealers:** For the purposes of this discussion, water sealers are defined as liquid chemical compounds that are sprayed or brushed over concrete, masonry, or wood surfaces. "Thompson's Water Seal™" is well known, but several similar products from other manufacturers are on the market. What must be understood is the importance of water sealers and waterproofing in general. Wood, in a desert environment, experiences extreme heat stress. Under normal conditions, dried wood contains 10 to 15% of its mass in the form of water volume. This water volume rises or shrinks slightly, adjusting to the surrounding atmosphere. In effect, wood, although the tree is dead, continues to breathe moisture. With extreme desert heat, so much moisture evaporates from the wood so quickly that the wood will twist and crack (split). If the wood's moisture content drops below a critical limit (± 7%) the wood will dry rot and exhibit a loss of structural strength as it starts to literally disintegrate. Water sealers applied to wood in the desert are to keep moisture in rather than out. Concrete, brick, and stone contain inherent salts and minerals which can evaporate towards their surfaces. This process is called efflorescence, which is technically defined as encrusted salts deposited upon a surface. Efflorescence can be caused by water that is drawn through

a material or by the evaporation of water that has been resting on a surface. Concrete subslabs can contain quite a bit of salts so when putting expensive stone over the subslab it is wise to treat the entire stone with water sealer. With this process (usually dipping) water cannot be drawn up from below (wicking) or penetrate from above. Efflorescence is hard to treat and eliminate once it gets started so it is always better to take preventive measures from the outset of construction.

- **Wood:** Wood for construction comes from two orders in the plant kingdom. Hardwoods come from the angiosperms which are the broadleaf and predominately deciduous trees. Softwoods come from the gymnosperms and are represented by conifers (pines), cedar, and redwood. The reason softwoods are called "soft" is that they contain more resinous growth (sap) which allows wider annual rings. Hardwoods are usually slower growing and their annual rings are closer together. There is less suspended moisture in the trunk; thus the wood is harder. There will be a more lengthy explanation of plant growth, in general, in the planting chapter. What is important to note here is that the annual rings are important in construction. Wood will bow up or cup down in the circular direction of its annual rings. When building a deck, point the rings up so that water cannot stand in the cup. This is true for trellises and building fascias. Point (face) the convex rings towards the predominant viewers. Slight bowing is much less noticeable than slight cupping. Most wood used for landscape purposes is redwood or cedar. Redwood is the more prominent of the two. Wood is classified by manufacturers and suppliers to fit within various grades. Information readily available from the California Redwood Association or the Western Wood Products Association will tell you all you need to know about lumber classifications. Hardwoods, owing to their tight grains, are extremely valuable and are usually not considered for exterior use. The two most common woods for landscape purposes are clear heart redwood for decking and exposed lattice work and construction grade redwood for headers. All wood, with the exception of headers, should be thoroughly treated with a wood sealer. When detailing or specifying lumber, remember that finished dimensions are different from the dimensions commonly used to describe the piece:

Common Call Out (inches)	Finished Dimensions (inches)
2 × 4	1-1/2 × 3-1/2
2 × 6	1-1/2 × 5-1/4
2 × 8	1-1/2 × 7-1/4
2 × 12	1-1/2 × 11-1/4
4 × 4	3-1/2 × 3-1/2
6 × 6	5-1/2 × 5-1/2
8 × 8	7-1/4 × 7-1/4

(Always verify lumber dimensions with the supplier to assure accuracy.)

- **Wrought Iron:** Wrought iron is a purer form of iron than cast iron. The two start out the same but when the molten iron (pig iron) is mixed with a glass-like slag material, it becomes more malleable, especially for extruding. Although wrought iron can be formed into sheets for plating elements, its primary usage in landscape architecture comes as an ornamental fencing and gate material which is relatively inexpensive. Because it can be poured thin and joined by welding, wrought iron is much lighter than cast iron and almost as capable of achieving the same level of intricate detail. When using wrought iron fencing, make sure to specify that the pickets be no more than 4 inches apart. If ithe space is any wider, a child's head can get caught between the pickets and create a dangerous situation.

Now, let us see how these materials are applied to the hardscape design by utilizing the outdoor room concept.

The Outdoor Room

The Floor Plan

This includes walks, patios, steps, stairs, ramps, bands, curbs, headers, driveways, and parking lots. Most elements on the ground plane are a function of design program, shape of property, interaction with the penetration points of architecture, and physical constraints of the site grading plan. Most ground plane surfacing for parking areas and drives is asphalt or concrete. Drives of more expensive structures may be of brick or stone. Walks and living areas (patios) are usually concrete or masonry laid over a concrete subbase or compacted sand. The magic number to remember in concrete and masonry floor layouts is 4. Brick and most precast masonry units are manufactured in units of 4 inches. Lumber used for formwork of concrete is dimensioned in units of 4. Irrigation heads interior to the spaces created are mostly designed to radii set in units of 4. In fact, 4 feet is the cutoff point between using spray heads and having to go to bubblers to water narrower areas in irrigation design. Four feet is a good minimum walk width and 4 inches is the minimum riser height in a set of steps. By using the rule of 4 a designer can make the installer's job a lot easier and material usage much more efficient.

In their quest to create just the right amount of space, many designers make outdoor floor areas too small. When in doubt about decking, too much will always be better than too little. The great outdoors will shrink perceptible scale and what seems right indoors will often seem tiny outdoors. Think of the times you or a friend have bought a little Christmas tree only to find out it was not so small indoors. Conversely, what seems like a big indoor room may not have as much impact outside.

Another common mistake is the use of too many surface materials on the ground plane. Three materials within the same viewing space is usually considered appropriate. Rules are made to be broken and this one often is. Remember that it is easier to create elegance with simplicity, and complexity often creates chaos. It is also important to integrate materials tastefully. Exposed aggregate concrete abutting salt finish can create an annoying edge. Separating these two finishes with a smooth concrete or brick band makes a more pleasing transition. Two different colored concretes are better separated by a neutral colored band than being allowed to abut. A change of grade is always a good place to change materials, as is a change in use area. Remember, in decking design, a logical transition between different materials always creates smooth visual transition.

Steps and ramps are considered part of the outdoor floor. Except at entry stoops, one step is uncomfortable and can create accidents. This is particularly true if the step is placed indiscriminately within a large expanse of decking. In this case, there is not enough visual warning to let the user know there is a grade change. Three steps is a good grade change and there should always be a landing after five steps. Never vary the height of risers or width of treads within a given run of steps. A band element at least the width of the step treads is a good idea at the top of the run to provide visual warning that the steps are forthcoming. On approaching steps, a recess or reveal in the risers creates a shadow line that lets the user know the steps are coming and how many there are.

Ramps are required throughout the Southwest for all new public construction to provide for handicap access. Maximum gradient for ramps is 8.33% (1:12). On gradients above 6% (1:15), slip-resistant surfaces are required as are 30- to 34-inch high handrails. Six feet of level approach area is required, and a minimum 5-foot-long landing is mandatory at the end of any run that exceeds 30 feet in length. Five feet of landing is also needed at the top of any ramp before accessing a building or adjacent space. Ramps are to be a minimum of 4 feet wide (rule of four). If a landing area is also used to accommodate a change in direction it must be 6 feet long.

In the design of floor areas, the concept of "linking" can either visually or physically add harmony and logic to the design. Walk and patio edges should line up with building edges. Bands should maintain the same width as building columns and mow strips the same width as bands. If the bands are wide enough (18 inches minimum) they can determine the width of pool or spa copings. Grout lines of tiles or pavers which align with score lines or expansion joints of adjacent concrete are visually pleasing. Score lines of walks should run at right angles to the walk edge. Avoid odd angles whenever possible. Remember that lines themselves create motion and can shorten or lengthen a space. Consider how the shadow lines from an overhead trellis will orient to the lines on the ground plane. Rectangular proportion will create movement to or away from the viewer. Square proportion will create static space with a sense of repose. A large grid expands from a central point, while a small grid encloses to the central point. If repeating material from the ground plane onto an adjacent vertical (wall) plane, consider alignment of score or grout lines and whether they are to run with or against the prevailing ground plane pattern. "With" creates a wrapping effect while "against" creates a defined edge. Above all else, when desiring to create a smooth transitional flow from interior to exterior, coordinate ground plane surfaces with the interior designer. The simplest and easiest thing to do is to use the same material across the door threshold. This creates strong linkage, widens space, and inspires a compelling emotional pull to circulate from one space to the other. Unfortunately, nine times out of ten, this is ignored and not done. In design there are precious few givens that will assure aesthetic success, and this is a sure waste of a given.

The Wall Plane

This is the vertical plane, the wall of the outdoor room. Walls are the great definers of space. Inappropriately placed, they are the great eliminators of space. Walls create privacy and security. Walls define property lines, which emotionally reinforces the feeling of pride of ownership. Walls screen us from unwanted views, noise, wind, and intruders. Robert Frost wrote, "Fences make good neighbors," and he was certainly right about that.

Walls, on the exterior, extend architectural mass and can add a sense of proportion (or destroy it). This often happens by enforcement in many desert cities as most building codes specify allowable wall height and that the color and material is to match the adjacent architecture. The great majority of walls in the desert are block and stucco and rather ordinary in appearance.

The Spanish hacienda emphasized the entry court, defined by low walls and an intricate gate. This occurs often enough in high-end resort homes, but is a rarity in typical tract development. Entry courts help to establish the sense of entry and support a sense of well-being by physically separating man from the automobile.

Like classic architecture, good wall design is composed of three elements; base, middle (wall), and cap. A base, when desired, establishes a noticeable line where the horizontal and vertical planes meet. It can also be the logical place to incorporate a neutral material before changing to a vertical facade material that differs from the ground plane. In this way a wall's base can greatly aid in design transition.

Many of the design axioms that were applied to ground plane materials apply to the surface area of a wall. Most important are that three materials are usually enough and special attention should be given to the directional impact of score and mortar lines. Also, be practical about the construction budget. If the wall is for privacy, and not for viewing, it may be better to build it inexpensively and visually buffer it with plant material.

Wall caps and their impact are often overlooked. A cap that protrudes beyond the face of a wall will always leave a shadow line. This will impart a strong horizontal line which can lead or stop the eye. It will also reveal the wall's relative height in proportion to all the elements in front of and beyond it.

Retaining walls, in comparison to conventional block walls, require more reinforcing bar, wider and/or deeper footings, and provisions for drainage on the retaining side of the wall. When designing a retaining wall, there are three basic approaches. First is to simply beef up the conventional inverted T-shaped footing. Second is to have an L-shaped footing with the bottom of the footing opposite the direction of the load (earth retained). Third is a gravity wall. Here, the sheer weight and mass of the wall itself resists the load behind it. Gravity or buttress walls have a large butt and batter (taper) to a cap or top that is usually a minimum width equal to one half the width of the butt. These are the stone-faced walls that comprised hahas in romantic English design.

Walls that work with the prevailing wind patterns are also often overlooked in desert design. Panels of wood, plexiglass, or metal can be incorporated in sections of the wall. These elements, if designed to pivot like doors, can let wanted cooling winds in and lock hostile dust storms out. The concept also works for providing wanted viewing or desired privacy at appropriate times. Whenever use flexibility can be incorporated into design function, the outdoor room becomes that much more liveable.

The Ceiling Plane

This is what lies overhead, and consists of trellises, overheads, lattices, or canopies. Although dictionaries provide no differentiation, in standard industry jargon, a "trellis" is thought of as a vertical element, while a "lattice" typically represents an overhead horizontal element. The deeply recessed building overhangs prevalent in desert architecture are designed to provide shade. Open air porches are common, as are completely covered patios. The landscape architect often has a solid overhead plane provided by the architecture to work with and play off of. This is especially true in residential design. Roofs of structures often cantilever over open areas to rest on columns that are matched with the details inherent in the architecture. If more overhang area is needed, the column design can be mimicked and a lattice supported by beams may be run from the building facia board out to or beyond the new columns.

Sometimes it is more desirable to have a freestanding overhead in another area of the garden. This free-standing lattice can be of completely different material than the architecture or mimic a few of its details. Free-standing gazebos and pavilions of remarkable quality are available in kits from several manufacturers. These gazebos are usually of redwood construction and emphasize intricate trellis work.

Often, overheads are post-and-beam construction with lath or smaller frame lumber suspended across the beams. It is important to design the wood members so that the dimensioned lumber is neither too thick nor too thin in comparison to related details in the architecture. For larger post-and-beam connections, steel plates of various shapes and sizes provide structural stability. Steel stirrups that support the posts above the ground are a good idea in termite-laden areas. Assuming that the post-and beam-detailing is well done, the lath or lumber that rests on top should be run in a direction that will allow the shadow lines to complement ground-plane elements.

Galvanized pipe frames with lashed fiberglass screening are increasing in popularity. The screening is extremely lightweight in comparison to other overhead systems. It is also flexible, which can accommodate arched, circular, and free-flowing shapes. This flexibility also allows the material to be retracted and slid about to provide alternative shade patterns.

All overhead structures can do double duty by providing support for hanging plants, lights, fans, and mist systems. What the designer must determine in the design of overhead canopies is how much is for shade, how much is for spatial definition, and how much is for show. Remember that the shadow pattern of the overhead element is not only important to the ground plane, but the play of shadow and light on an adjacent wall surface should also be taken into account. Furthermore, the pattern of the element itself and the amount of positive and negative light that is seen as the canopy is looked through from below has an effect on the perceptions and emotions of the ground plane viewer.

Not every outdoor room needs a defined ceiling. The understory of canopy trees can provide shade or dancing filtered light. The clear blue desert sky itself is probably the ultimate outdoor ceiling.

Site Furnishings

Site furnishings include those elements that occupy the outdoor rooms. They provide an aesthetic quality and/or functional liveability. There are so many elements that could be categorized as site furnishings that any list could be arguably incomplete. Here is a brief list of favorites.

- **Banners:** Colorful cloth or canvas windsocks or seasonal announcements. Attached to buildings, poles, or suspended by ropes or cables over streets or pedestrian malls. Not employed enough as a design element outdoors.
- **Barbeques:** Outdoor cooking units. Can be portable or fixed in place. Charcoal units are the least expensive initially but the most maintenance intensive. Gas and electric units are expensive but are more practical for frequent use. Gas is considered a better source of heat. See Outdoor Kitchen heading.
- **Benches:** For rest and relaxation. Can be used to define space and direct pedestrian circulation. Should be an integral part of the early design process. Too often they are an add on and they look like it. Optimum outdoor seat height is 16 inches. Benches with backs are more comfortable. Radius all exposed edges for comfort. Exposed aggregate is not a good bench material as it is uncomfortable to sit on. A wide variety of quality prefabricated benches are on the market.
- **Bike racks:** Prevalent in school and campus design. Several prefabricated types are manufactured. Be careful when locating, since bike racks can be terrible ankle breakers for unsuspecting pedestrians.
- **Bird feeders and houses:** Range from simple, as is the case of liquid-filled hummingbird feeders, to intricately detailed

birdhouses. Several pre-manufactured and aesthetically pleasing units are commercially available. These represent one of the easiest ways to invite wildlife into the garden.

- **Bollards:** Short concrete, metal, or wood pillars. Used to prevent vehicular or direct pedestrian circulation. The lighted bollard enjoys widespread popularity.
- **Clocks:** Not frequently used in everyday design as most people that are concerned about time wear a watch. More an aesthetic item. Some ornate cast-iron clocks are made commercially.
- **Drinking fountains:** In the desert, drinking fountains are not used nearly enough. Countless manufactured units are available. Handicapped drinking fountains are a good idea. These units are set away from the pedestrian circulation system and the bowl cantilevers out for use. Nice effect that could be expanded on with other design elements.
- **Flags and flag poles:** Very similar to banners. Adds sense of national or regional pride to a space. Aesthetic flagpole design is severely lacking and could use lots of improvement.
- **Gazebos:** Outdoor structures that were alluded to earlier in this chapter in the discussion on the ceiling plane of the outdoor room. Several fabricators make gazebos of outstanding quality. In fact, it is a very competitive part of the industry. As an element intended primarily to enhance rest and relaxation, gazebos have a place in residential design.
- **Hardware:** An all encompassing term for metal or wood fasteners and all manner of door handles and gate latches. Mentioned here as several companies offer very ornate pieces that are worthy of closer scrutiny.
- **Kiosks:** Round, hexagonal, or square — human-scaled (6 to 8 feet high) structures that are often roofed. Like bike racks, usually an element used in institutional design. Used to display posters and personal messages. Some good prefabricated units are available but this is an element that can easily be designed to mimic the surrounding architecture.
- **Light poles:** Several pedestrian-scale poles available. Most are Tudor style. Some of the more generic cast-iron poles could be incorporated into Southwest and desert design themes, with a little more creativity directed at the globe.

- **Mailboxes:** The forgotten element. Too often the last thing designed or completely ignored. Not a nice way to treat the first thing that sets the tone for most residential drives and entries. Few pre-manufactured mailboxes are acceptable, so they usually will have to be designed. Check postal standards when designing. Most are mounted flush with the back of walk or curb and set 40 inches from grade to the bottom of the box. When trying to uplight mailbox numbers, remember that shadows are cast upward. Any surface projections located below the numbers will cast a shadow which covers them.
- **Micro-mist systems:** While more a building system than a furnishing, these environmental systems are beginning to receive widespread use and need to be discussed. Primarily an adaptation of drip-irrigation systems as micro-misters and emitters operate on the same principle. Small amounts of water forced through tiny openings place water in a smaller area where it can be used more efficiently. With emitters, water is directed to the root zone of plant materials. With misters, the water is in the atmosphere immediately adjacent to human-use areas. In mist systems, water forced through pipes or tubes at relatively high pressures atomizes in the air. This cooling effect reduces temperatures by as much as 20°F, even in areas of intense sunlight. While water conservation is a primary concern in the desert, one has to take a serious look at what a mist system could mean to the year-round liveability of an outdoor room. The atomized water dries so quickly that people sitting directly underneath are not wet. This has proven to be a boon for outdoor cafe and restaurant owners and for outdoor pedestrian malls. With thermostats set to regulate the operation of the system only during the hottest parts of the day, the causes of water conservation and climate control can be jointly served. The areas where these systems are to be installed should be closely examined. Water constantly applied to the wood fascias of buildings or to wood lattices will cause paint to peel and wood to twist and eventually rot. The pipes and misters should be suspended or attached away from wood and masonry products which are known to efflorescence. These systems also receive use in water-feature and tropical garden design as they are an effective alternative to actual fog. Micro-misters are also utilized in greenhouses

for humidity and for outdoor dust and odor control. Micro-mist systems are here to stay and should receive more creative thought as to their design use and application.

- **Outdoor kitchens:** This could be anything from a simple barbecue unit to a full-blown food service station, including sinks, wet bars, ovens, refrigerators, etc. All of these elements are usually set in an outdoor counter and are regularly requested in high-end residential design. Gas barbecues are better outdoors than are electric. Check the site survey or with local utility companies for availability of natural gas. Outdoor kitchens are a very specialized area of design and equipment suppliers should be consulted often, even to the point of being asked to provide shop drawings for clarification. Well done, outdoor kitchens can add additional enjoyment to the outdoor room. Done poorly, the cost of the equipment alone, coupled with a client's dissatisfaction can cost a landscape architect his commission.
- **Pots and planters:** These items can make or break a design, especially on the small property where space is limited. By planting with pots, the varying soil and moisture requirements of dissimilar plant materials can be accommodated, thus allowing groupings and arrangements not usually possible in the open ground. Pots add a lot of flexibility as they can be changed and moved. They are also the best places to rotate annual color. Pots placed in unusual places, such as at the top of walls or climbing a staircase add drama to otherwise ordinary places. Pots can lift or suspend tiny blossoms and intricate foliage to eye level. Larger-size pots are often referred to as planters. Due to their weight and importance to the overall design scheme, planters are considered permanent. As such, accommodations for irrigation and drainage should be made. This includes leaving cutouts or sleeves in decking and through walls. A little forethought in this area, will reduce a lot of maintenance time and headaches later.
- **Recreation equipment:** There are too many items to go into detailed descriptions here. In terms of function, wood is not a good selection. Wood dries and splinters in the desert and requires constant treatment. Synthetic rubber coated galvanized steel pipe is the best selection for high use playgrounds. A second choice would be similarly coated wood. The coating lessens heat buildup to a tolerable level and,

with integral color, lessens painting maintenance requirements. Several soft synthetic surfaces for playground use are now coming to the fore. When designing playgrounds utilize the concept of "linked play." Here, elements connect to or flow from one to the other, creating a play circuit which allows a child little time for boredom or confusion. A great many companies supply recreational equipment. As always, selection should be a function of budget, needs, and taste.

- **Sculpture:** Could be anything and often is. "Beauty is in the eye of the beholder," frequently applies to sculpture and artwork in general. The subject matter, the way the sculpture works in context to its setting, and the way the piece relates to surrounding architecture and the region are all somewhat vague, but useful, criteria for evaluating the appropriateness of a piece. Scale is important with sculpture. A large piece in a small space will dominate and a small piece in a large space will be lost. Design is a study in logic and for that reason I believe that design can be, and often needs to be, explained by the designer. Sculpture, as a design area, can be explained. I don't really buy it when a sculptor says his work is over our collective heads. Again, personally, if I know what the underlying concept of a sculptural piece (or any design) is and I can buy into it, then I can feel comfortable with the work. Those who commission sculpture are going to have to decide for themselves where they stand on this issue of accountability and live with the beauty or the consequences.
- **Signage:** The provision of basic information should be the primary criterion of sign design. The fewest words possible that deliver the intended message make the best signs. Most municipalities restrict sign design in the two main areas of overall square footage and maximum letter height. Also, limitations are usually placed on setback from street, maximum height above grade, mounting to architecture, and method of lighting. Sign designers should take into account the speed at which the viewer is traveling and the maximum distance he will be away from the sign. This will determine size, letter height, colors, and verbiage. Consider, also, the neighborhood character and prevailing style of architecture. Signage, and its overwhelming importance to some commercial users (auto lots, strip centers), can severely hamper the

landscape architect, especially in the area of planting design. Most desert cities have mandated 50% tree shading for parking lots. This is a commendable aesthetic and environmental stance. It creates a virtual uproar, however, among some commercial business owners whose fear of trees blocking signage can verge on phobia. There are two methods of appeasement. The first would be to use low-lying monument type signage at the street. Second, and worthy of more consideration, is the use of deciduous trees. Trees that drop their leaves during the winter leave facia and wall-mounted signs exposed to view. This happens during the Southwest's tourist season when a much higher volume of shopping is done. In a case of reverse paranoia among landscape architects and the tourism industry, in general, it is believed that all trees should be green and beautiful during this season. While true in a resort-type residential area, it is not true in a shopping district. The branch structure of trees is beautiful. Deciduous trees are much less susceptible to the freezing that causes the dreaded winter brownouts and some trees provide a fall (leaves) and spring (flowers) color show. Shade is provided during the hot summer months which is the primary intent of the municipalities. Welcomed, warming sunlight is allowed to penetrate to the ground plane in winter. Even in more middle class areas with a more established population, being visually exposed to signage four months out of the year enables people to learn where stores are in their neighborhood. Using deciduous trees can save a designer from the severe verbal beratements of shop and store owners who feel their livelihood depends on their sign.

- **Sundials:** Usually constructed of high quality brass or bronze. Good feature for use in the theme or contemplation garden. The function of this element connects the viewer with other earth forces in a psychological way. Several attractive pre-manufactured units are available.
- **Tables:** Primarily used in recreational and gathering areas. Card tables for vest-pocket parks and small cafe tables are available premanufactured and coordinated with other site furniture. In very tight urban spaces, rounded corners are more comfortable as they can be slid around rather than banged into. Picnic tables for recreational use run the gamut from aluminum to fine redwood. Study the project budget,

local history of vandalism, and user characteristics when selecting a picnic table.

- **Trash containers:** Used primarily in recreational and public places. Several good prefab units are available, mostly coordinated with other site furniture. Use tough units, preferably with weighted bases and locking tops in high wind areas. Open topped containers, if they don't catch all the trash thrown towards them, at least serve to concentrate trash in one area for easier pick up by maintenance personnel.
- **Tree grates:** Many times these represent site function and site ornamentation combined into one. Tree grates are made of cast iron or concrete, with cast iron being more popular by a ratio of three to one. Some cast iron manufacturers supply grates with intricate patterns. The grates do protect tree roots but primarily protect users from tripping over and into hardscape cut outs. A 2- inch to 4-inch high curb will twist and break a lot of ankles in a high pedestrian use area. Grates also protect irrigation heads from being broken and accommodate the rims of uplighting fixtures. Several quality companies supply round, square, hexagonal, and customized grates.
- **Umbrellas:** Available in canvas, nylon, and limited molded plastic construction. Plastic is destroyed by ultraviolet light in the desert. Umbrellas provide shade, style, color, and some movement to the landscape. Some units like the Newport umbrella border on fine art. In high wind areas, use a heavily weighted base and an umbrella that collapses when not is use. Consider using umbrellas in combination with lighting and small-scale (individualized) micro-mist systems.
- **Water features, swimming pools, spas:** These water elements have two main things in common — a mechanical system which handles water and an electrical system to operate the mechanical system and provide underwater lighting.

The mechanical system of a pool will usually have a filtration system, drainage system, and water-level control device. Spas and fountains not only have all of the above, but also have a water-effects system. In fountains, this water-effects system pumps water for jets, weirs, or sprays. In spas, the water-effects system pumps water for jacuzzi jets. The only real difference between a spa and a fountain is that a spa's jets are emitting water that is heated and that has had air injected into it and the water effect is underwater rather than coming out from or flowing into the main pool of water.

Pools, spas, and water features appear to be very complicated, but actually, they are quite simple. All that equipment sitting in an equipment yard or room looks very involved — something to be comprehended only by engineers, technicians, and the analytical mind. All that equipment is really two or three sets of equipment designed to perform separate functions.

Think of any water feature as water sitting in a shell. All the mechanical equipment does is move water into, out of, and around the shell. Each function is different, and the equipment for each operates independently of the other.

A filtration system consists of a filter, usually composed of sand or diatomaceous earth. In residential swimming pools, easy cleaning cartridge filters are most frequently employed. In order for the filter to clean water, the water must pass through it. A recirculating pump sucks water from the pool through a skimmer and main drain and then through pipe to the filter and then pushes the water from the filter back to the pool through return pipes to inlets in the side of the pool. That's all the system does — move water. In heated pools, the water in the return pipe passes through heated coils. The same is true for spas, except that the heater may have more thermal capacity or the ability to heat water more quickly. Skimmers for these water features usually have a surface mounted lid about 8 to 12 inches in diameter. Care should be taken in locating the skimmer lid. If the lid cannot be centered on score lines or set aesthetically in decking, consider the less popular side inlet skimmers which mount below the coping. In all cases, paint exposed surface lids the same color as the adjacent decking. This seems like a minor point until you see a white plastic lid set off-center in a field of slate or limestone. When the decking can accommodate it, place skimmers at the most downwind point of the pool. The wind helps circulate water and debris to the skimmer location, thus saving unnecessary wear and tear on the recirculating pump. Inlets carrying water from the filter back into the pool or spa shell should be placed at the point farthest from the skimmer. This allows cleaned water to pass the longest distance through the pool before being recirculated again. It's a matter of efficiency. Why reclean cleaned water when there is dirty water downstream waiting to be cleaned? The main drain serves two purposes. First, it acts as the pool's bottom skimmer, and second, it does as its name implies — drains the pool. Main drains are covered with a plate called an antivortex plate. A vortex is defined as a downward suction which, in the case of water, means a whirlpool. A large volume of water travels through the main drain and conceivably people (especially children) could drown if the antivortex plate did not break this downward pull. One final note about filtration: after a period of continual use the filter itself gets dirty and needs to be cleaned. Through a system of valves and redirecting of pipe, water driven by the recirculating pump and under high velocity is reversed through the filter, thus backwashing it. The backwashed water exits the filter through a screened hole and is directed by pipe or hoses to the underground drainage system. Residential home owners, as well as project maintenance personnel, can utilize backwash water for irrigation of some plant materials. Citrus, for example, does not seem to mind chlorinated water, nor does Bermuda Grass.

The drainage system in water features consists of the main drain and an overflow drain. Most pool main drains are used via the recirculating pump's backwash feature. Most main drains for pools are lower than the pipe in the underground drainage system and are definitely lower than the surrounding grade, so the only way to get the water out of the pool is to pump it up and out. On projects with higher construction budgets, underground equipment vaults are used to save space, deaden equipment noise, and hide equipment from view. Often vaults must be connected directly to a drywell. Occasionally, in a system like this, water can gravity flow from the main drain to the drywell. Overflow devices in pools usually drain by gravity flow. It would be a patent waste of water to simply allow water to enter the pool and simply overflow. In addition, if a pool were filled and the water shut off, evaporation would soon cause the water level to sink below the skimmer and return lines and cause the filtration pump to work so hard it would be damaged or burn out. A level control device (autofill) assures that neither condition can exist. Level controls operate on the same principle as a toilet bowl float does. In a pool, level controls are usually side mounted just below the coping. In lower budget residential pools, level controls are often not included, as the on site user can monitor and control the water level.

With water-effects systems, fountain and spa design starts to become a little more complex. Two basic things happen with a water effect. First, the water must have velocity to have motion. This velocity is generated by a dry or submersed water effect pump. Second, this water under velocity must have someplace to go. Spas have an air blower which forces air into the waterline just before it enters the spa shell. This creates the bubbling jets. Fountains have bubblers, sprays, and weirs. This is where the water from the water-effects pump goes — out to the various nozzles or over various edges to create the desired effect. Hydraulics play a big role in designing fountains, especially volume calculations and relationships between static water level in a basin and the impact of displaced water on the actual volume of water in the water effect when it is operating. Most electronic water-level devices can be set to maintain the water level in a pool lower than the normal static setting when the water effect is operating. When the water effect is shut down, the water from the effect rests in the pool at normal level. Water is saved because it is not allowed to overflow.

Surge or wave-like motions of water occur as water in the air falls into water in the basin below. Surge is greatest in small and/or round fountain basins. A wave reaches the side of the pool before it can dissipate at or near water level and splashes against the side. This may be undesirable, especially if water splashes out of the basin or into the overflow drain and is wasted. Surge is not a problem with spritzer- or fan-jet fountains because the volume of displaced water is actually very small. Surge is, however, often a concern in bubbler-type fountains since a high volume of water is being displaced and reenters the basin at one time. Surge can be controlled by using baffles or wire mesh to break the waves. Appropriate basin sizing, however, is the best way to prevent or minimize surge. With bubbler-type fountains, wind is also a design consideration. Winds in the desert are often strong enough to blow a bubbler's stream of water completely away from the basin below. When designing fountains with bubblers, be sure to include a wind speed sensor which will automatically lower the height of the bubbler as the wind speed increases to a point were it will completely shut the bubbler down. A good rule of thumb is that the width of the basin should be four times the height of the bubbler jet for efficient operation.

Weirs are controlled waterfalls or, simply put, an even flow of water over a level edge. In order to have a weir there must be an upper and a lower basin. The volume of water that flows over the weir is called the nappe and the surface of water is called the weir's crest. The weir itself must be very thin or somehow notched on its underside to make the water fall free and evenly off its outer edge. A 1/2 inch depth of water (nappe) flowing over a 1 foot width of weir will require about 20 gallons of water per minute. Figure 30 gallons per minute for 1 inch of water over a 1 foot width. Once you start getting over one inch of nappe, you are getting into the realm of waterfalls and it's time to consult with a water feature specialist. To keep the weir nappe from splashing out of the lower basin, the size of the basin should be at least as wide as the weir is high. In weir and waterfall design, consider where the water in the upper basin will go when pumps are shut down. The entire surface area of the upper basin to a volume equal to the depth of the weir will now fall to the lower basin. Because of this phenomenon, the lower basin must be larger than the upper basin to accommodate this occasional additional water volume.

The infinity edge pool is beginning to gain popularity. Here water flows over a weir that is not cantilevered but is in actuality the top of a wall. The water flows quietly over the weir, down the wall, and into a collection trough. The water is then pumped out of the trough and recirculated through the pool to start the process all over again. The concept is that the water appears to flow on to infinity or connects to another water feature further away. This works well, for example, in residential country club design where lake features are often a part of the site amenity package. For flood control purposes, housing pads are already elevated above the lake. By extending an infinity edge pool towards the lake with the edge away from the viewer, the illusion can be created that the pool is flowing into the lake beyond. This illusion only works if the line of sight between the two elements is unbroken and plant materials are not planted behind the trough. Anything that projects above the infinity edge, breaking the line of sight, will negate its purpose. Infinity-edge pools can be a powerful design tool when employed correctly.

There are several good references to consult on water feature design, but hydraulics is another matter. Water feature contractors and designers can provide shop drawings and equipment lists to aid in making a design a reality. The landscape architect must, however, have a rudimentary knowledge of the concepts behind water features to evaluate the merit of these submittals.

Water feature designers should concern themselves with two aspects of water feature electrical design. First, coordinate with the electrician to provide enough power and outlets at the equipment room to operate the equipment. Second, underwater lighting is expensive, and due to the cost of electrical runs, junction boxes should be located as close to the light fixture as possible. Code restrictions limit all aboveground electrical service connections (and lights) to a 5 foot minimum from edge of pool. The landscape architect should locate the junction boxes for pool, spa, and water feature lights on his hardscape (staking) plan or they will be located for him, often to the dismay of all.

The design of water elements should reflect the proportion and style of the surrounding hardscape. They should look as if they fit into, rather than have been dropped onto a site. Copings for pools should cantilever 2 inches minimum over the edge so swimmers can get a hand hold. Copings for spas should not exceed a 1/2 inch overhang or the edge of the spa will be uncomfortable to lean against. Plastered steps should receive a row of 2-inch tile on the treads just in front of the adjacent riser for safety purposes. Lights should always be oriented in such a manner so as not to shine directly into the eyes of viewers and be pointed away from residences. Benches, swimouts, and other human use gimmicks should be scaled to the bodily dimensions of the users whenever possible.

Water-feature design is a big business in the Southwest. There are more swimming pools in the desert than anywhere else in the country. There are likewise more unused and poorly maintained pools than anywhere else. On small lots, for homes with small children, or for limited landscape budgets, a swimming pool may not always be practical. Users should examine how they really use a pool. If all a person does is plunge into the pool to cool off and then get out, then a well-placed outdoor shower may be more appropriate. An outdoor shower costs much less, uses less water, takes up much less space, prevents drownings, and offers cooler water. Be careful to set up the outdoor shower so that hot water that has been standing in the pipes is allowed to pass before the user gets under the shower. The money saved by choosing an outdoor shower can be put toward purchasing a spa. A spa, in comparison to a pool, has an entirely different physical purpose, takes up less space, uses less water, and can be more easily covered for safety and energy (thermal) conservation. Spas also require half the maintenance of a pool. If someone wants a pool, fine. All I'm trying to point out is that there are other options which offer some nice bonuses. If a residential homeowner opts to do without a pool, and resale value is an issue, be sure to design the outdoor room in such a manner to allow a swimming pool to be incorporated at a later date.

- **Weather vanes:** These are definitely a specialty item. Most are made from some type of metal and are usually quite ornate. Used to monitor wind direction and to provide architectural adornment.
- **Wind chimes:** Used primarily in residential applications, these can range from simple to elaborate. The demeanor of other site users and adjacent site users should be taken into account when considering the use of wind chimes as some people find the noise(s) created by them to be annoying. Wind chimes can add the element of movement and surprise into a garden.

Working Drawings

Once the hardscape elements have been selected and their placement in the landscape has been decided, the landscape architect must now convey his design ideas into working drawings so that the design can be constructed and become a reality.

The plan layout of hardscape elements is shown on what is called the “hardscape" or "staking plan(s).” On these plans, critical dimensions are given, while items to be shown in sections or in details are called out with graphic symbols. A finish schedule is often provided, which describes items, materials, colors, etc., and may refer to details of elements where the finish is found. The finish schedule may also list telephone numbers and addresses of manufacturers and suppliers of some items to assist contractors in obtaining hard-to-find items or to acquire information considered to be outside the realm of common knowledge. On projects where pots are integral to the hardscape design, a “pot legend” may also be provided. The pot legend describes the size, color, finish, texture, quantity, and manufacturer of all significant pots used in the project. This legend is a good reference for contractors, who will often need to order the pots months in advance to give the manufacturer enough lead time to make and ship them.

Staking plans are usually dimensioned in one of three ways:

1. Dimensioning of critical elements from known reference points (building corners, property lines, etc.).
2. Establishing a grid of equal sized squares (4 feet, 8 feet, 10 feet, 16 feet, 20 feet, etc.) that extends from a known reference point (a monument from the site survey) across the plan. The grid system is very useful for curvilinear and freeform designs. Golf course architects frequently employ this method. The contractor simply measures over so many grids and then constructs what he sees within the grid on paper on his expanded grid on site.
3. Running dimensions from a baseline or baselines. Baselines are straight lines that run between two known points. Once the baseline is located, measurements can be taken along it from its point of beginning to where it ends. Upon finding the desired point along the baseline, straight or angled dimension lines are run to locate critical elements. The baseline system works well, for example, where a curvilinear walk runs alongside a straight roadway curb. At equal or dimensioned increments along the curb, dimension lines can be perpendicularly run over to the walk, thus locating it in relation to the curb.

In all types of dimensioning, one thing is key. A known reference point or point of beginning must be established and located. If this point cannot be fixed, then the information that flows in all directions from this point cannot be fixed.

In landscape architecture, dimensional call-outs are from outside face of one element to the outside face of another element. This is important in establishing a consistent format. Dimension lines should not cross and if they sometimes must, one should be broken where it crosses the other to show that it is passing over or underneath the other line.

When running a string of dimensions across two previously located elements, say a building and a property line wall, let one side float. That is, do not assign the last dimension on the string, as this space is existing and it will be whatever existing conditions and the total of the other dimensions allow and may not be the dimension you want to assign it. Sometimes a dimension floats in the middle of the string, especially if the element is not critical to construction or is hard to determine.

Dimension only what is needed to construct the design. Do not provide information that is provided elsewhere, as the information may conflict. If a dimension is given from the wall of a house to a face of a bench it will not be necessary to dimension the width of the bench if the bench is picked up in a detail and the dimension is on the detail. If both items (plan and detail) were to receive dimensions and the detail were to change and the change was not reflected on the plan, a conflict would arise and the bench could conceivably be built incorrectly.

There are two ways to address dimensions that are not fully known at the time the drawing is prepared or cannot be completely controlled because of unknown conditions in the field. The great catchall word "verify" instructs the contractor to tell the landscape architect what the field condition is when construction is to the point where that condition starts to become apparent. The other dimensional convention is the word "equal". If there is a patio with three squares of concrete across its width and its ending point could not be determined due to, say, the location of a wall beyond to be built by others, the landscape architect would run a dimension line through the squares and call out "equal, equal, equal" at each square. This would tell the contractor that no matter what the final width of the patio turned out to be, the three squares would be of equal width. If the patio were 9 feet wide, each square would be 3 feet wide. If the patio were 9 feet 9 inches wide, the squares would each be 3 feet 3 inches wide.

Last, dimensions and strings of dimensions can conflict if the landscape architect double dimensions. This occurs when the same item receives a dimension on the same surface but the dimension lines originate from different reference points. Remember when we discussed letting the last dimension on a string of dimensions float. When two strings of dimensions approaching from opposite directions connect at an item, sometimes an impropriety that would have been accommodated in the float is now reflected at the double-dimensioned item. Careful plan checking and a policy of only showing critical dimensions can wipe out the dreaded double dimension.

Details accompany the hardscape or staking plan. Details show the size of materials used and placement of an object. Details are usually sections through an object or a profile of its outside edge. For clarity, the details of smaller projects are usually shown on one sheet or on sheets grouped together at one location in the working drawing set of sheets. On larger projects with a lot of details, the details are often put in a separate "construction manual." Try to choose the method that is easiest for the contractor/installer. If this individual can easily find a detail, he will be more apt to refer to it. The numbering of details usually follows the anticipated path of construction. That is, details should occur in the same sequence as construction events will occur. Detailing an item involves three main processes:

1. Show the detail at a defined scale
2. Dimension the physical proportions of the item and any important connections it has to adjacent items
3. Describe the item by material, texture, color, and finish callouts (notes)

When detailing an item, try to mentally picture how it will actually be built. Visualize form work, site access to the object, conflicts with other trades, sequence in the construction schedule, and availability of materials. Also consider the capabilities of the contractors who will do the job. It is asking for trouble from the outset if contractors are asked to come out of their comfort zone and do something they have not done before or have done before but would prefer not to do again. Try to be practical, simple, and guiding when detailing.

Finally, the working drawing specifications should follow the Construction Specifications Institute's (C.S.I.) format, since most catalogues and suppliers' information are based on it and most contractors are familiar with it. Also, every section of every specification should have a provision for cleanup. This is very important, as it lets every contractor know, in writing, that he is responsible for removing his own mess and excess materials from the job site. A cleanup provision in every section of every specification will endear the landscape architect to owners, general contractors, and the municipality where the job is located.

The Outdoor Room

Human Dimensions

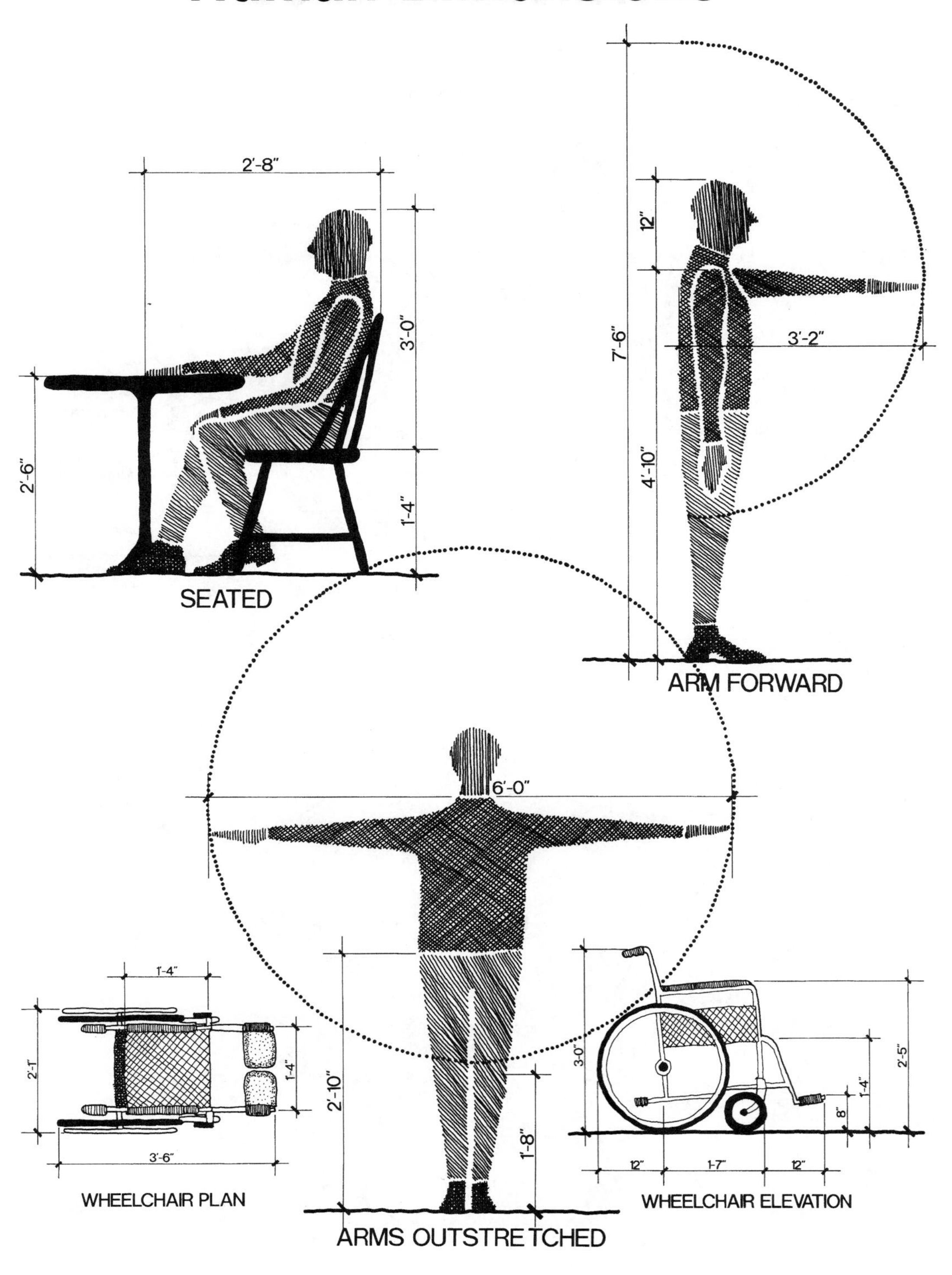

Water Features

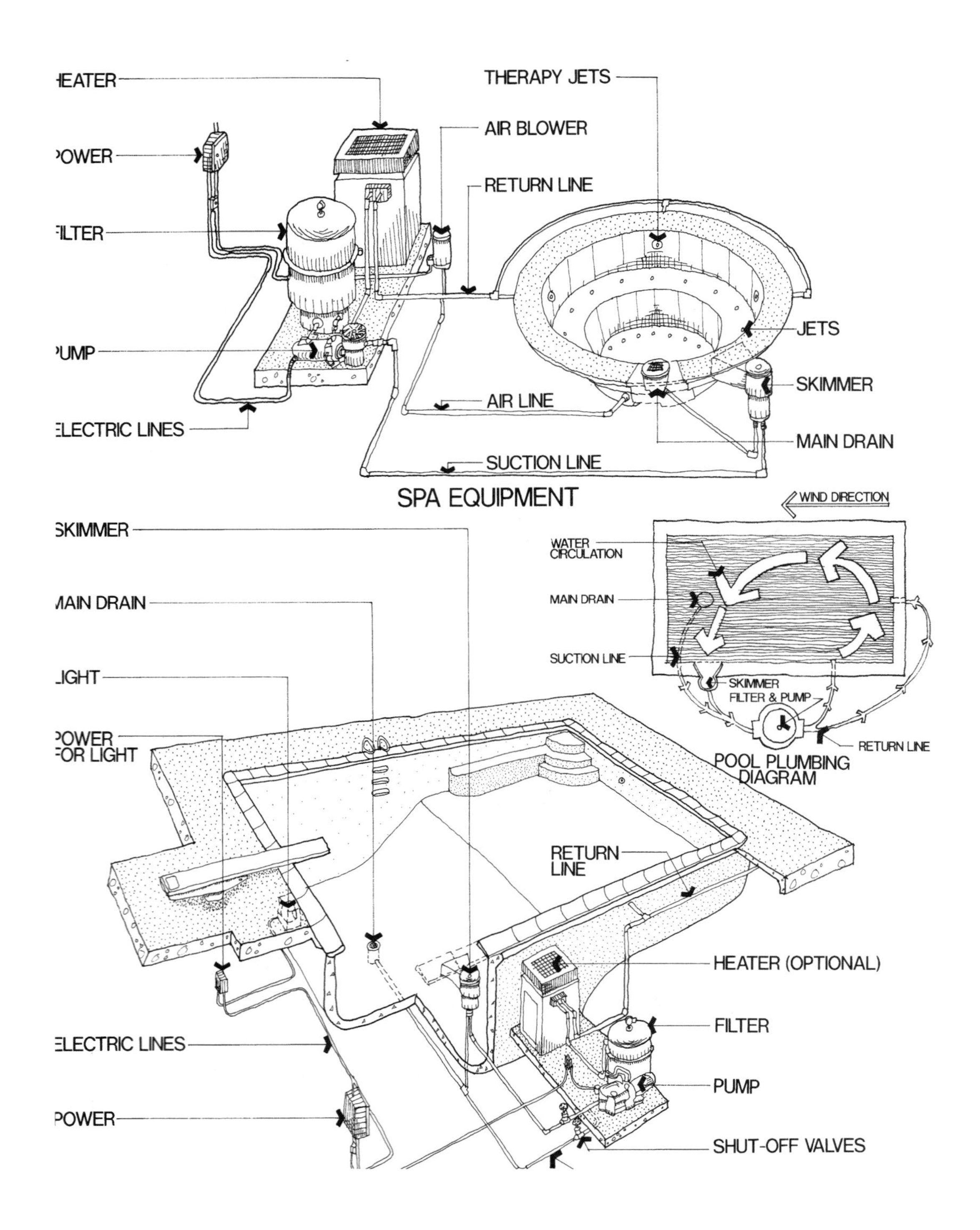
THERAPY JETS
AIR BLOWER
RETURN LINE
JETS
SKIMMER
AIR LINE
MAIN DRAIN
SUCTION LINE
SPA EQUIPMENT
WIND DIRECTION
WATER CIRCULATION
MAIN DRAIN
SUCTION LINE
SKIMMER
FILTER & PUMP
RETURN LINE
POOL PLUMBING DIAGRAM
RETURN LINE
HEATER (OPTIONAL)
FILTER
PUMP
SHUT-OFF VALVES

Staking Plan With Dimensions

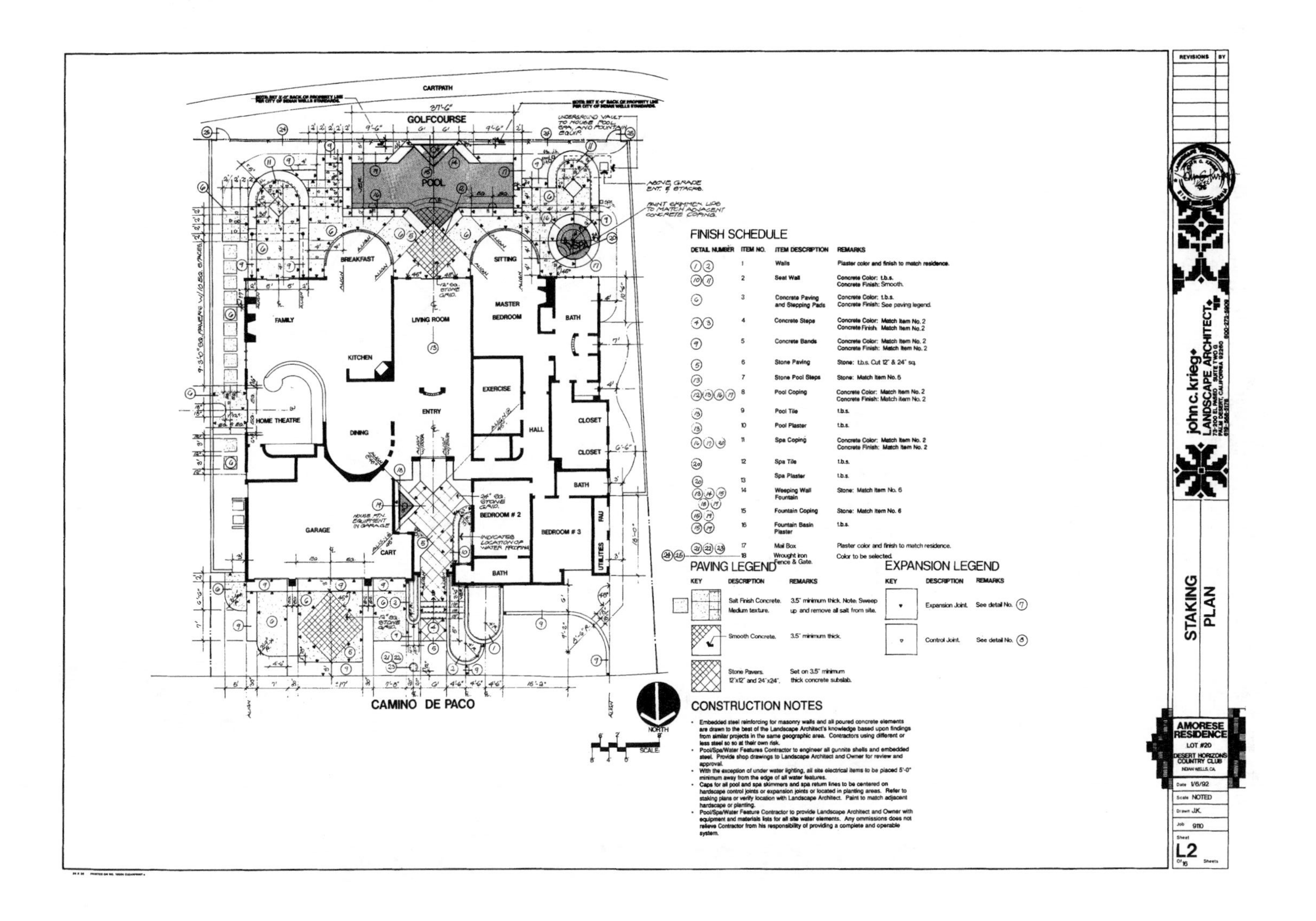

FINISH SCHEDULE

DETAIL NUMBER	ITEM NO.	ITEM DESCRIPTION	REMARKS
1, 2	1	Walls	Plaster color and finish to match residence.
10, 11	2	Seat Wall	Concrete Color: t.b.s. Concrete Finish: Smooth.
6	3	Concrete Paving and Stepping Pads	Concrete Color: t.b.s. Concrete Finish: See paving legend.
4, 3	4	Concrete Steps	Concrete Color: Match Item No. 2 Concrete Finish: Match Item No. 2
9	5	Concrete Bands	Concrete Color: Match Item No. 2 Concrete Finish: Match Item No. 2
5	6	Stone Paving	Stone: t.b.s. Cut 12" & 24" sq.
13	7	Stone Pool Steps	Stone: Match Item No. 6
12, 13, 16, 17	8	Pool Coping	Concrete Color: Match Item No. 2 Concrete Finish: Match item No. 2
13	9	Pool Tile	t.b.s.
13	10	Pool Plaster	t.b.s.
16, 17, 20	11	Spa Coping	Concrete Color: Match Item No. 2 Concrete Finish: Match Item No. 2
20	12	Spa Tile	t.b.s.
20	13	Spa Plaster	t.b.s.
13, 14, 15, 18, 19	14	Weeping Wall Fountain	Stone: Match Item No. 6
15, 19	15	Fountain Coping	Stone: Match Item No. 6
15, 19	16	Fountain Basin Plaster	t.b.s.
21, 22, 23	17	Mail Box	Plaster color and finish to match residence.
24, 25	18	Wrought Iron Fence & Gate.	Color to be selected.

PAVING LEGEND

KEY	DESCRIPTION	REMARKS
	Salt Finish Concrete. Medium texture.	3.5" minimum thick. Note: Sweep up and remove all salt from site.
	Smooth Concrete.	3.5" minimum thick.
	Stone Pavers. 12"x12" and 24"x24".	Set on 3.5" minimum thick concrete subslab.

EXPANSION LEGEND

KEY	DESCRIPTION	REMARKS
	Expansion Joint.	See detail No. 7
	Control Joint.	See detail No. 8

CONSTRUCTION NOTES

- Embedded steel reinforcing for masonry walls and all poured concrete elements are drawn to the best of the Landscape Architect's knowledge based upon findings from similar projects in the same geographic area. Contractors using different or less steel so so at their own risk.
- Pool/Spa/Water Features Contractor to engineer all gunnite shells and embedded steel. Provide shop drawings to Landscape Architect and Owner for review and approval.
- With the exception of under water lighting, all site electrical items to be placed 5'-0" minimum away from the edge of all water features.
- Caps for all pool and spa skimmers and spa return lines to be centered on hardscape control joints or expansion joints or located in planting areas. Refer to staking plans or verify location with Landscape Architect. Paint to match adjacent hardscape or planting.
- Pool/Spa/Water Feature Contractor to provide Landscape Architect and Owner with equipment and materials lists for all site water elements. Any ommissions does not relieve Contractor from his responsibility of providing a complete and operable system.

Staking Plan "Builder' Set"

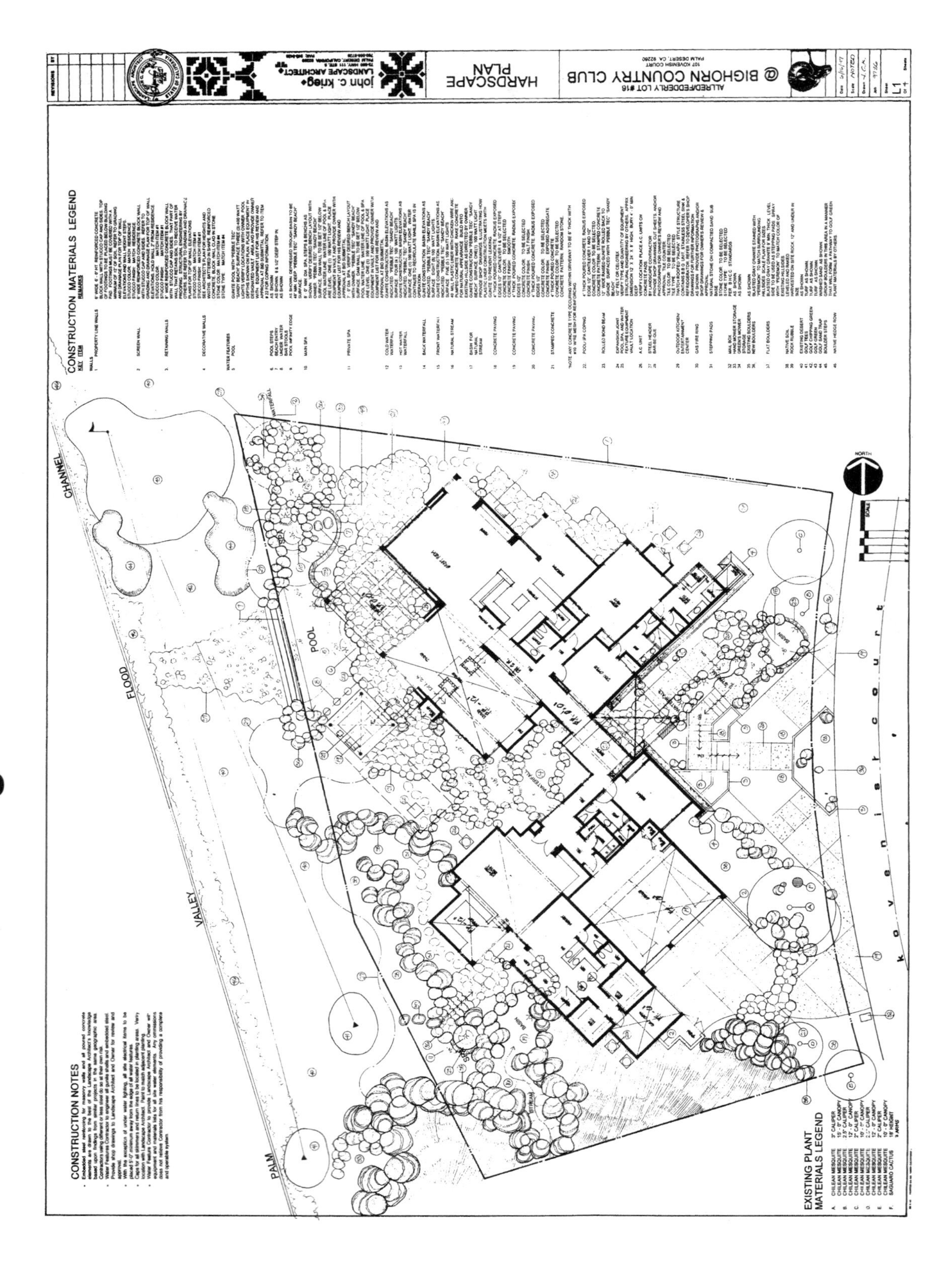

Construction Details

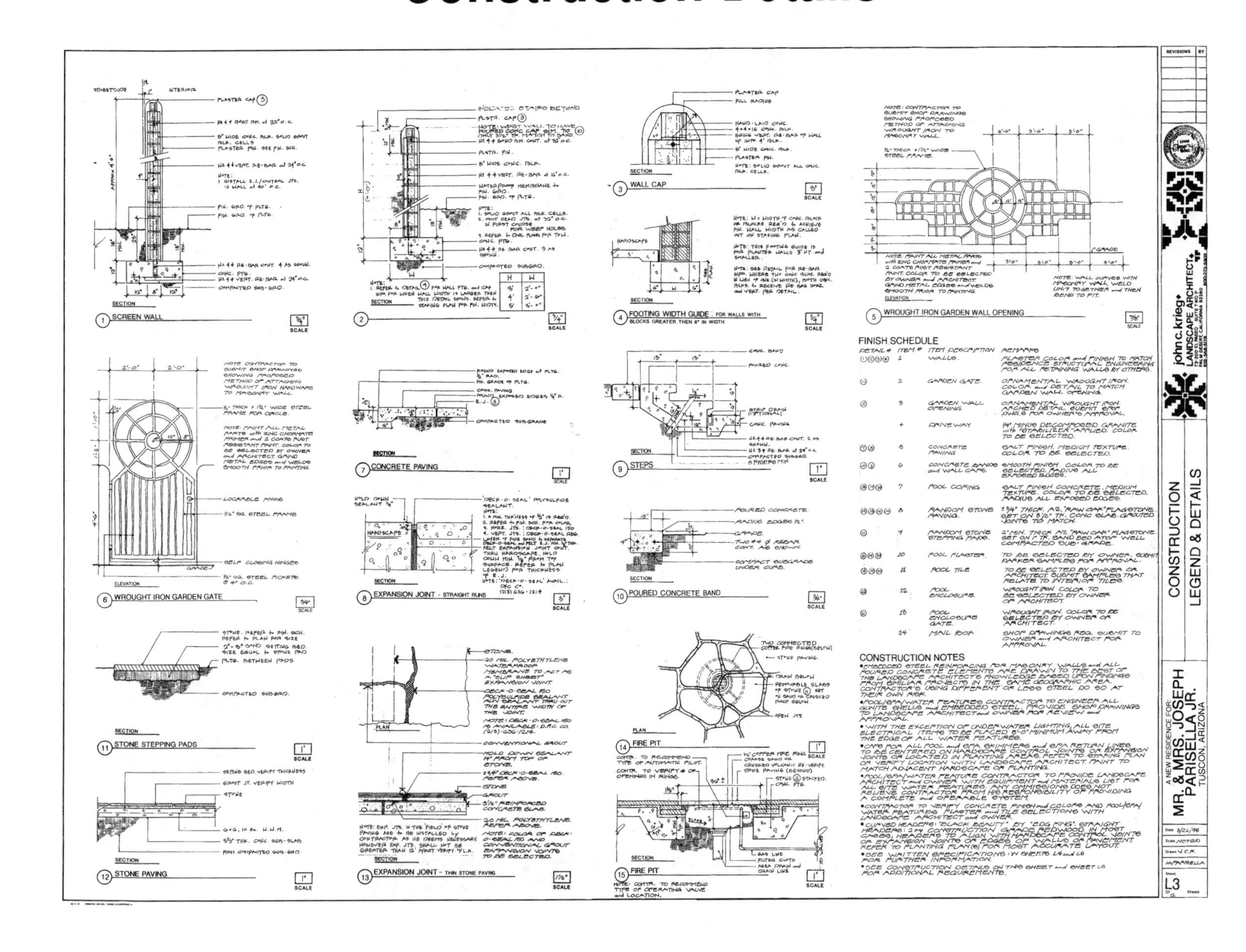

Water Feature Sections

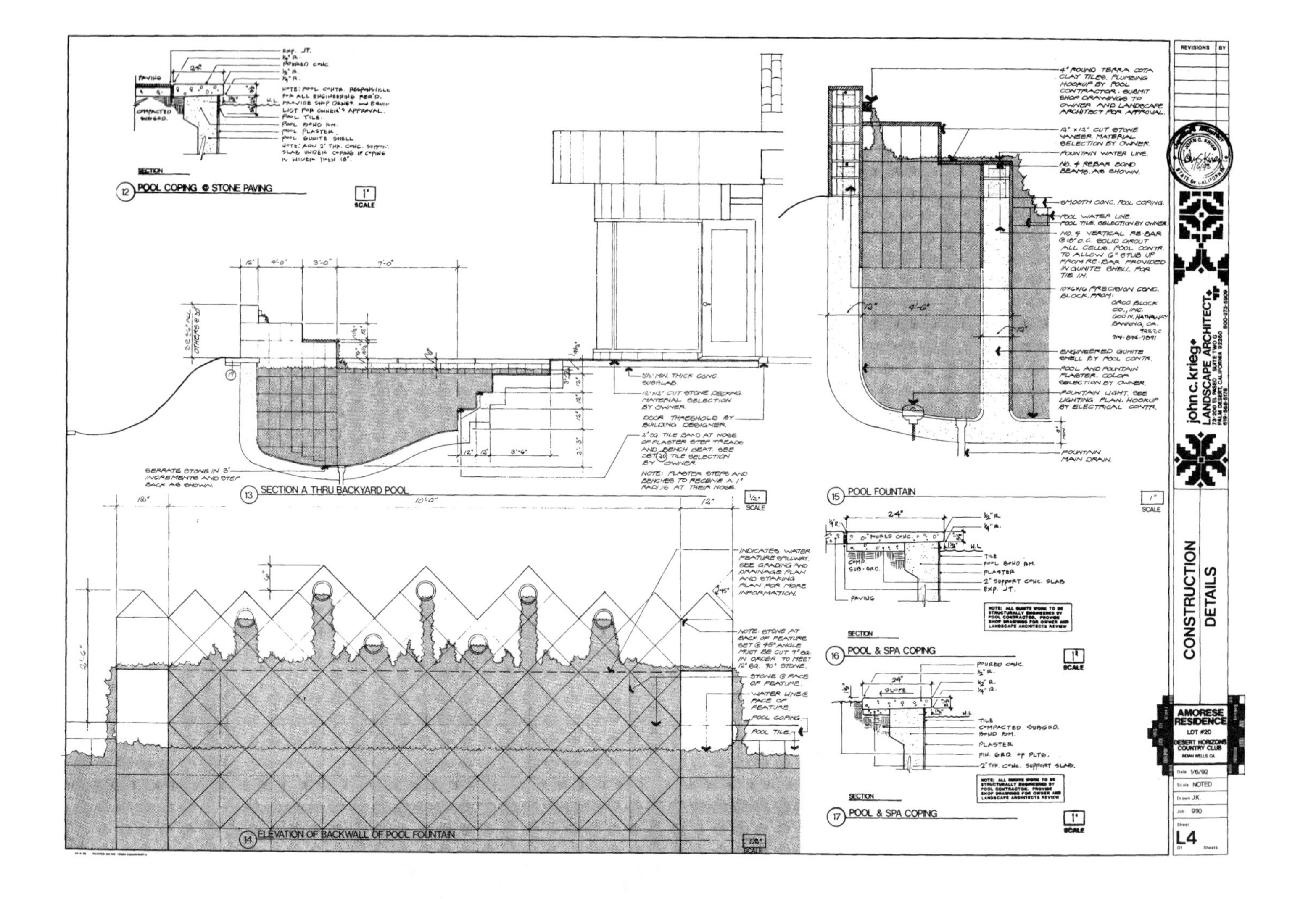

Free-Form Design with Grid

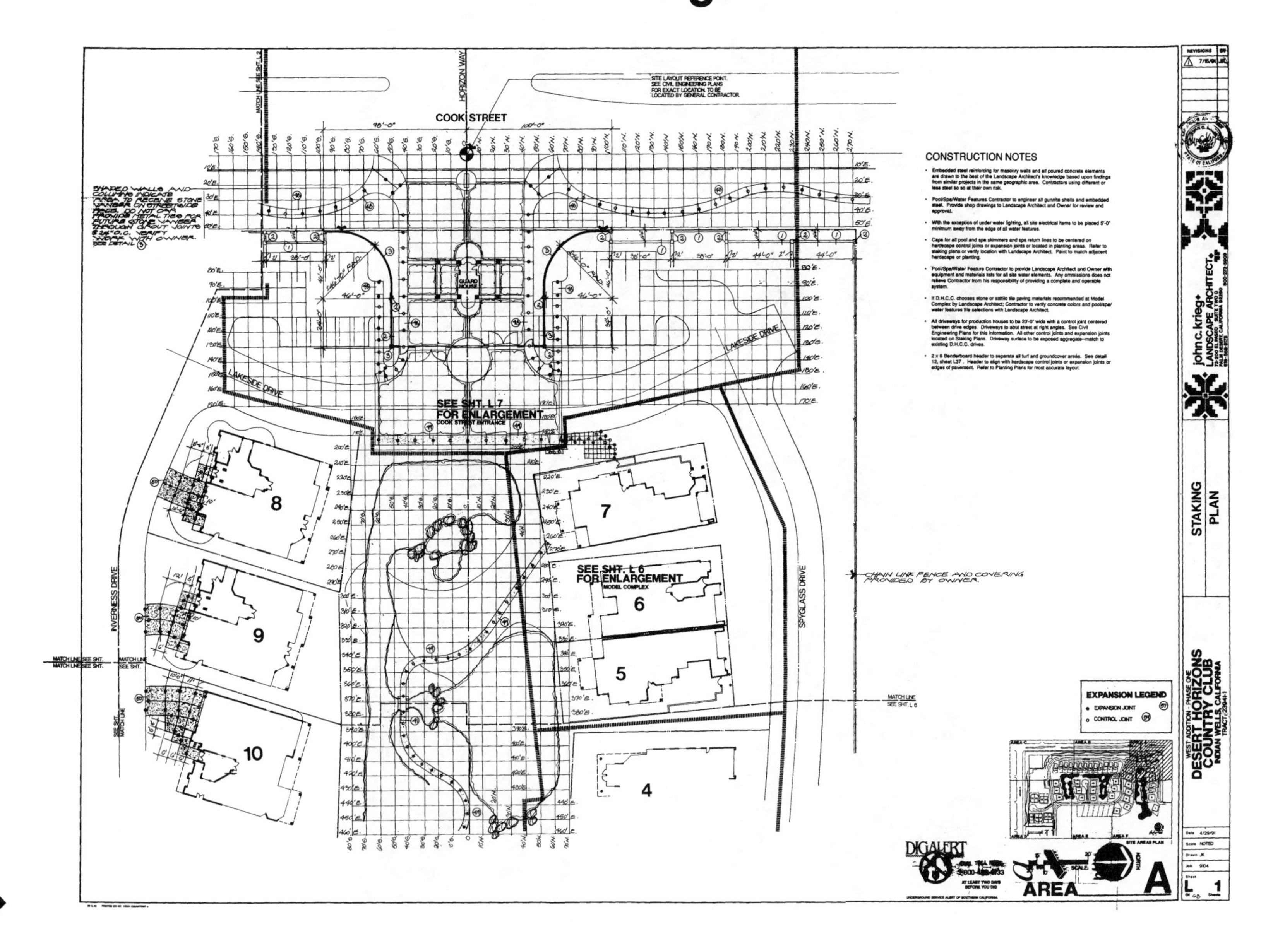

Concrete Form Work

Construction Materials

Granite samples

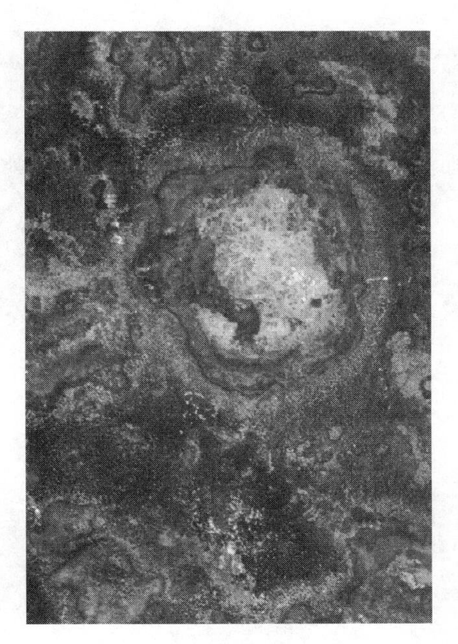

Slate sample

Boulders

Custom ceramic pot

Construction Installations

Concrete finishing

Stamped concrete

Salt finish concrete

Exposed aggregate

Water Accents

Wall fountain

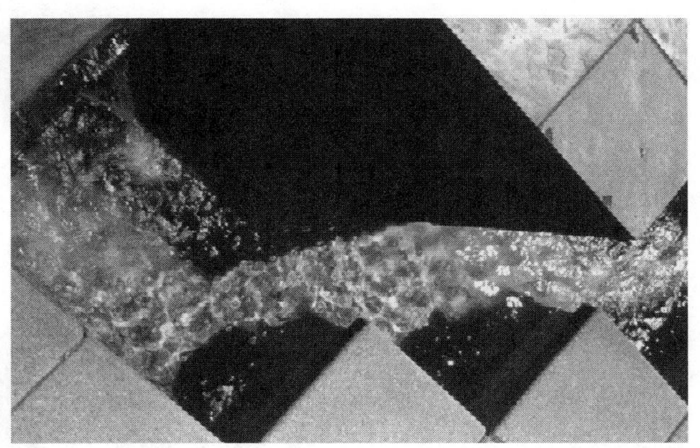

Courtyard fountain

Raised spa and stream

Stream and pool

Pool and Spa Details

Gunite pool steps

Gunite spa shell

Skimmer construction

Spa construction

Infinity Edge Pool

Glossary

Adhesive: A substance that causes the surface of one element to stick or bond to the surface of another element.

Admixture: Elements added to concrete with the exception of water. Aggregates, curing accelerators or retarders, and color pigments are all admixtures.

Aggregate: Any type of stone added to a mix of concrete.

Arch: Curved construction over an opening that closes and structurally completes the opening allowing for lateral construction above the arch.

Beam: Horizontal support member designed to handle traverse loads.

Column: Vertical support member similar to a post but usually more ornate. Columns frequently support arches. Columns played a key role in classical architecture.

Contraction: To become smaller (shrink) in area or thickness.

Curing: The process by which concrete hardens. Curing concrete is usually tested for strength at 7 and 21 days.

Cutout: Term used to describe void areas in concrete or decking. Cut outs are most frequently employed to insert planting and/or accept area drains and outdoor lighting fixtures.

Decking: Term used to described any expanse of hardscape on the ground plane.

Diatomaceous earth: Earth containing the remains of prehistoric one-celled plants and animals. Used in water feature filtration systems. Also frequently used as a bottom to artificial lakes that will be used for swimming.

Dimension: A measurable unit such as length, width, or thickness.

Efflorescence: Deposits of encrusted salts on the surface of masonry, concrete, or stone work. Caused by soluble salts within these elements rising to the surface due to the forces of evaporation or capillary action (wicking).

Expansion: To become larger (swell) in area or thickness.

Filter (water): A device assembled to remove solid soil, plant, and animal particles that are suspended in water from the water. As such, a filter is a device used to clean water.

Finish schedule: A listing shown on the plans which describes all hardscape elements, particularly colors and textures.

Footing: Usually the concrete base of a wall. A footing is a widened area used to distribute a vertical load.

Foundation: Concrete, soil, or rock upon which a building rests. Like a footing, foundations distribute vertical loads.

Hydration: Chemical reaction that occurs between water and cement as water evaporates and concrete is formed.

Lattice: Diagonally crossed strips of thin metal or wood. Usually implies an intricate overhead element.

Legend: A chart or accounting of items shown on a plan with descriptions.

Key: Discloses information. Similar to a legend but usually briefer in format and content. For example, a key plan is typically an overall site reduction used to provide broad information such as to what part of the site the plan sheet pertains.

Nappe: The volume of water that flows over a weir.

Plinth: A noticeable, low lying, square or round base to support a column or wall, or in the case of landscape architecture, pots or sculpture.

Post: Vertical steel, masonry, stone, or wood member which usually supports a horizontal beam, but can support any manner of lateral construction.

Pump: Mechanical device that pushes or draws (sucks) water or other fluids. Note that a pump cannot draw water higher than 33.94 feet because this is the limit of atmospheric pressure.

Skimmer: In pool and spa design, a device that receives surface water before it is sucked through the filtration system. Skimmers catch larger insects, leaves, etc. before they reach the filter and impair its effectiveness. Skimmers must be accessible because they require frequent cleaning.

Sleeve: As it applies to this chapter, a pipe or conduit under decking or through walls. Wire, gas, and irrigation lines, etc., are routed through the sleeves and can be pulled out of them to make repairs.

Tackifier: Sticky material that enhances the bonding capacity of one element to another.

Trellis: Similar to a lattice. Diagonally crossed thin wood or metal members that are used for vertical support and ornamentaton on the wall plane.

Vortex: Downward sucking motion. In water, a whirlpool.

Waterproofing: General term used to imply that an element should be made impervious to water.

Wier: An even sheet of water flowing over a defined edge.

Chapter 5

Plant Materials and Planting Design

California Desert Nursery

Introduction

Plant materials and planting design are the essence of landscape architecture. It is what separates the profession from the architectural and engineering disciplines and more closely aligns it with the natural sciences. To truly know and understand plant materials, one must have working knowledge of botany, soils, and chemistry. In addition, a comprehension of ecology will enable a landscape architect to see how the cellular structure and morphology of plants fit into a far greater picture and, indeed, form the basis of all life on earth.

Cultural Factors

Plant growth depends on air, soil, water, temperature, and light. While some plants are grown hydroponically (exclusively in water), this is primarily an agricultural application which we will not concern ourselves with here. Photosynthesis, simply explained, is the process by which plants manufacture food/energy for internal growth.

Air provides carbon dioxide needed in the process of photosynthesis. Oxygen, which plants give off as a waste product of photosynthesis, diffuses into the air. Oxygen is essential to the survival of all animal life and also combines with hydrogen to make water.

Soil holds nutrients and water in suspension for plants to utilize. On a more practical note, soil provides the medium that plants anchor themselves into before beginning vertical growth.

Water is fundamental to all plant and animal life on earth. Most living organisms, including man, are made up of from 60 to 20% water. Water is one of the main ingredients in photosynthesis. It is the medium that holds soil nutrients and manufactured enzymes in suspension as they are transported throughout the plant.

Temperature is a major limiting factor in plant growth. It determines plant zones and regions. A plant's hardiness is determined by its response to cold temperatures; more specifically, the temperature at which it freezes. Changes in temperature determine the rate of growth, indeed the method of growth, within a specific hardiness zone.

Light is essential in the process of photosynthesis. Light is the energy source that allows the plant to produce sugar from carbon dioxide and water, acting in the presence of chlorophyll, while releasing oxygen. Varying durations and intensities of light sources determine plant growth rate, density, and species variation.

Plant Categories

In the practice of landscape architecture, plant materials are usually grouped into five main categories: (1) trees; (2) shrubs; (3) vines and espaliers; (4) ground covers; and (5) turf grasses. There are specialty plants such as palms, cacti, and succulents, but they are usually grouped under the heading of either trees or shrubs. Likewise, water plants (cattails, water lilies, and lotuses) are usually referred to as shrubs.

Trees are the dominant visual and physical elements in the landscape. They play a major role in defining and enclosing outdoor space. Trees are most notably defined by their size, shape, and number of trunks. Any vertical plant material over 15 feet high could be considered a tree. With a single trunk and some form of crown (head) it would almost certainly be classified as a tree.

Shrubs are smaller than trees and typically have many stems. Shrubs are the most human-scale plants in the landscape, being at or near eye level. Shrubs usually define the walls of the outdoor room and often act as individual accents.

Vines and espaliers are frequently classified as shrubs but many landscape architects like to break out these unique plants into a separate category. Vines are plants that climb by twining stems, utilizing tendrils, or employing suckers. They lie flat against a wall or will spread horizontally across a trellis. The majority of desert vines are fast growers. Vines serve a very useful purpose in that they provide foliage in tight spaces and grow in limited soil areas where it would be virtually impossible to locate other types of plant material.

Espaliers are plants that would normally be shrubs or small trees, but are pruned and trained to lie flat against a wall. They serve a similar purpose as vines, but usually offer thicker growth, an occasional flower show, edible fruit, or a pleasing aroma. In most cases, the growth of espaliers can be controlled, often in geometric or architectural forms.

Just as it is difficult to discern the difference between a small tree and a large shrub; it is oftentimes hard to establish a cutoff point between what is a low shrub or a high ground cover. Ground covers, as the name implies, cover the ground — usually with a profusion of stems that are covered with foliage or flowers. I consider any spreading plant material under 18 inches high as a ground cover. This is more for the sake of simplicity than for any scientific reason.

Turf grasses are, in reality, the lowest lying of ground covers. Because of the maintenance they receive and their high water requirement, they become a separate category.

Some other categories will be addressed in the Plant Compendium. They are described in greater detail in the explanation of how the compendium is organized.

Plant Life Spans

In terms of life span, plants are classified as: (1) annual; (2) biennial; and (3) perennial. Annuals are plants whose entire life cycle is expended in 1 growing season. Biennials are plants that require 2 growing seasons to complete their life cycle. With biennials, seeds or seedlings are planted in spring or fall, the plant grows through the first season, flowers and sets seed the next season, and then dies. A perennial is any plant that lives for over 2 years. Technically, trees and shrubs are perennials, but the term is used to describe an entirely different group of plants within the industry. In the landscape trades, "perennials" refers to plants that usually lose their top growth or go dormant in winter and revegetate the following spring and summer. For this reason the term perennial, as it is commonly applied, usually encompasses clumping and grassy types of plant material.

Plant Origins

Plants, as they occur within any given ecosystem, are described as belonging to one of the following three groups: (1) native, (2) naturalized, or (3) exotic. Native or indigenous plant material are plants that have originated and evolved within the confines of a particular region. They are ideally suited to the environmental factors inherent to that area and are arguably the best selection, at least in terms of survival, for any site within the same region that closely emulates all the conditions where it is found in the wild.

Naturalized plants are plants that have been introduced into an area by outside forces, most frequently man. Similar or parallel environments or ecosystems occur throughout the world. Because of the oceanic separation of continents, plants that have evolved in one continent were isolated to that continent. Though quite capable of living on another continent, plants had no viable way of physically reaching a parallel environment. With the coming of man and his transportation systems this all changed. Plants from Australia and South Africa are ideally suited to the Southern California climatic and soil conditions and vice versa. While the interchange and naturalizing of foreign plants adds a greater selection to the landscape palette, it can also present some severe environmental problems. The diversity of life within an environment is determined by a system of checks and balances with each life form occupying a certain environmental niche. A plant's natural enemies in its native environment, which keeps its population in check, may not be present in its new environment and it can become a rampantly spreading nuisance. In addition, plants from one region may be capable of surviving indigenous pests and diseases which they carry into their new region. Plants existing in the new region have not been exposed to these pests and diseases and have not developed the adaptations necessary to combat them and thus fall prey to them. Horticultural and economic catastrophes have occurred throughout agricultural areas because of this phenomenon. For this reason, among others, many states have set up county agricultural commissioners' offices in several intensively farmed areas. Such a body governs all plant material brought into or taken from an area. These offices usually have a list of all plant materials banned within a region and should be consulted before any new or unknown plants are contemplated for design use within that region.

Exotic plant material refers to plants that are not native to a region and, if left to their own devices, would not be capable of naturalizing in that region. These are plants that, because of their unique beauty or agricultural importance, are brought to an area and aided by man in their survival. This may include providing supplementary water and environmental protection and oftentimes both. The harshness of the desert environment makes 80% of the plant material grown technically exotics. When landscape industry people refer to plants as exotics they are usually talking about a much narrower range of material. In Southwest nursery jargon, the term exotic most often refers to plants that could be more technically classified as tropical or specialty plant material.

Plant Growth

Botany is the science of plant life and, as such, is the most important science related to the profession of landscape architecture. In a brief overview of botany, as it is needed to serve this chapter, the following will be examined: (1) seeds, (2) root systems, (3) stems, (4) leaves, and (5) flowers and fruits.

Seeds

With the possible exception of ferns (grown from spores) the majority of ornamental plant material applied in landscape architecture can be started from seeds. Faster and more reliable methods of plant propagation are often employed in the nursery industry, but the fact remains that plants used for commercial landscape purposes can be grown from seed. This is true even of plants that you would normally consider grown from easily recognized vegetative processes. Consider Orchids grown from rhizomes or Tulips grown from bulbs. When growers want to create new or better varieties of these plants they will cross-pollinate flowers by hand and raise the ensuing hybrids from seed. These hybrids must often be vegetatively propagated since their seeds are frequently sterile, or fertile seeds often contain traits that revert to the parent plants.

Seeds vary greatly in size, but all are encased in some form of hard capsule (seed coat). Inside this capsule an embryonic root (radicle) and modified leaves (cotyledons) are separated by an embryonic stem (hypocotyl). When the right frequency or sequence of environmental factors occurs the miracle of germination takes place. Germination, simply defined, is the process whereby a seed develops into a seedling. Germination is predominantly triggered by temperature and the availability of moisture. When these conditions are right, the radicle breaks through the seed coat and progresses downward in a response to gravity (geotropism) and water (hydrotropism).

In their initial stages of development, seedlings draw their energy from a store of food (endosperm) housed in the seed capsule. Growth of seedlings is quite rapid as the size of endosperms and the amount of energy they contain is usually limited. The radicle develops quickly and is considered a true root by the time it starts to put out secondary root hairs.

About the time these secondary root hairs start to develop, the hypocotyl has broken through the seed coat and begins to push in an arching fashion through the soil surface. Attached to the hypocotyl and soon to follow it out of the seed coat and into the air above the soil surface are the cotyledon(s). Seedlings with one cotyledon are known as *monocots* while seedlings with two cotyledons are known as *dicots*. This is extremely important later on in the growth process in the way stems and trunks are formed in the order of flowering plants known as the angiosperms. Angiosperms are plants that develop seeds within some form of fruit which is, in reality, a mature ovary structure. The other group of plants used extensively in landscape architecture is the gymnosperms, represented primarily by pines and other conifers. There are many differences between angiosperms and gymnosperms, starting at the seedling stage (gymnosperms have many cotyledons) and expanding into differences in trunk structure, leaf structure, flowers, and subsequent fruit production. Gymnosperms have no enclosed ovary (fruit) and seeds are usually encased in cones.

By the time the seedling has depleted its store of food housed in the endosperm, it has formed true leaves capable of independent food production. Given the presence of continued water and soil nutrition, the newly formed plant is well on its way to survival.

Root Systems

In a rough comparison, the root system does for a plant what the intestinal system does for an animal. Assuming that soil is the food source for plant growth, roots penetrate and draw nutrients and moisture from this source just as the villi within the intestine draw nutrients from food. These nutrients, in both cases, act as the fuel that keeps the organisms running.

There are two general types of root systems — fibrous roots and taproots. A fibrous root system has a profusion of roots, all about the same length and they are wide spreading. As a matter of practicality, fibrous root systems are usually (but not always) typical of lower growing and monocotylenous plants. Taproot systems, found more frequently in dicotylenous woody plants, have a deep main root and several secondary roots. The main taproot not only draws moisture from deeper underground water tables but also helps to anchor the plant, which is especially helpful in the case of tall trees.

Root structure, in cross section, is quite similar to stem structure, which will be discussed next. Longitudinally, a root consists of a hard root cap at its very end. The cells that comprise the root cap are constantly being worn away as the root moves through the soil. New cells growing behind the root cap replace the cells that have worn away. These cells are known as the root's meristematic tip, and just behind this tip are elongated cells. These elongated cells act as conductors that allow the aboveground stems and leaves to literally pull water and nutrients through them to other areas within the plant.

The extent of a plant's root system is often massive with the tiny root hairs making up a surprising amount of the overall root system surface area and performing a good deal of the work. These single cell thick, tiny root hairs are the actual points of absorption. These root hairs often exist in a symbiotic relationship with soil borne fungus. The structure of root hairs in association with fungus is called a mycorrhiza. The fungus helps the root hairs take in water and phosphorus and apparently use something in the chemical conversion process to enhance their own growth. Mycorrhiza associations exist in a wide variety of desert plant materials, and research is ongoing to see how they can be used to benefit plant establishment and water conservation.

Debate has been going on for years as to whether roots search for water or simply grow when water is present. (Personally, I believe that most perennial desert species have developed some mechanism to seek water or they would not have survived in the open desert.) Whatever the case, one fact is clear. Roots will be most abundant in areas where water is most abundant. This is an important fact to remember when designing an area for trees or when contemplating the moving of existing trees. The greatest profusion of roots, especially root hairs, will lie directly at the edge of a tree's canopy. This area is commonly referred to as the tree's "dripline." Even though desert rains are infrequent, they are often intense. Tree canopies have a tendency to divert large volumes of falling rainwater over their leaves and towards the outer edge of their canopy. Think of the tree's canopy as an umbrella and the rainwater running to the edges of the umbrella and then falling to the ground.

When placing trees in cutouts in pavement or in narrow parking lot islands, it is necessary to provide supplemental and deep watering to encourage roots to go down and not out. It is also advisable to enlist the aid of a root barrier to obtain this objective. If the root system is allowed to follow its natural tendency and grow towards the edge of the tree's canopy, the tree's growth could become stunted due to the lack of water under the pavement. The roots could also crack or heave the pavement in search of water. When moving existing trees, it is helpful to try to get the width of the top of the rootball as close to the width of the tree's canopy as possible. The less damage to these surface feeder roots, the better the plant's chances of surviving the move. The same rule applies to lowering or raising the existing grade around a tree. Disturb as little of the area under the tree's canopy as possible.

Stems

Stems are the support and duct system for the plant's leaves or leaf canopy. The cross section of stems or trunks is similar to the cross section of roots. All stems have a hardened outer coating that ranges in toughness from outer cells hardened with fibrous lignin to woody bark. The outermost cellular layer of any stem, leaf, or root is technically called the epidermis. Layers of cells just inside the epidermis are known as the cortex. Inside the cortex in various arrangements, depending on plant type, lie the three primary stem tissues — the phloem, cambium, and xylem. In some monocots and nonwoody dicots these conductive tissues are found in bundles, but in woody dicots and larger monocots, they are located in layers. Most trees that develop leaves and the conifers are termed "woody" and a cross section of their stems from interior to exterior consists of xylem, cambium, phloem, cortex, and epidermis.

The cambium, which lies between the xylem and phloem, is the most important tissue in this group of woody plants. The cambium is one cell thick and is composed of meristematic cells, which initiate growth. All xylem and phloem cells originate at and then separate from the cambium. Xylem primarily stores water and conducts it upwards to the leaves. Phloem tissue conducts manufactured carbohydrates, sugars, and starches throughout the plant, thus stimulating root and leaf growth. The xylem layers are much thicker than the phloem layers owing to the vast quantities of water needed to produce a relatively small amount of food. When you count a tree's rings to determine its age you are actually counting xylem layers. The ring is the difference between summer (active) and winter (dormant) growth. In large trees, the innermost and very dark rings of xylem represent tissue that has outlived its conductive purposes and, after being fortified with fibrous cellulose, is used solely for support. This tissue is called the "heartwood" (e.g., clear heart redwood) and is highly prized in the production of quality lumber.

All stems have a terminal bud at their outermost point. All buds inward of or below the terminal bud are called "lateral buds." Lateral buds initiate leaf and flower growth and often twig and branch growth. In cacti, these lateral buds are modified and called aereoles, which, in turn, produce thorns. The terminal trunk of a tree always strives to be the highest point in response to a genetic trait called apical dominance. This trait is what makes a tree grow upward defying the forces of gravity. If the branch or trunk (leader) that holds the apically dominant bud is damaged, other branches will vie to take its place until one eventually wins out. The buds on a stem, branch, or twig that have not developed or are latent are separated by sections of stem. The buds are called nodes and the distance between nodes is called an internode. This is important to know when pruning. Cuts should always be made just above a node and not within the internode. The internode is living tissue and will expend the plant's energy as it dies back to the nearest available bud (node). This will always occur since the internode has no meristemic cells to initiate new growth and once cut off from serving any useful purpose, will die back to the next growth point.

As stated above, the cambium layer of cells is ultimately important. Remember that the cambium initiates the growth of xylem and phloem as well as other tissue. When plants are propagated from cuttings, the stem is cut at a 45-degree angle to allow more cambium cells to be exposed to new life-giving sources of soil and water. If the cambium layer of trees is completely severed in a process called girdling, the tree will die. This, unfortunately, happens all too frequently when maintenance personnel use string trimmers to remove turf and weeds at the base of trunks. It also occurs when wire ties are not removed from the trunks of smaller trees that were staked for support at the time of installation. Landscape architects and maintenance contractors, do yourselves a favor and try to avoid these needless hazards.

Leaves

The leaves serve as a plant's food-processing facility. With the exception of some unique stem adaptations (e.g., Palo Verde Trees and Saguaro Cactus), the process of photosynthesis takes place in the leaves. Leaves are usually broad thin structures, with the notable exception of conifer needles which are modified leaves.

Plants that hold their leaves year-round are called evergreens. Pines and conifers are well represented here, although it should be noted that not all conifers are evergreen. Plants which hold their leaves year-round in all but the coldest winters or hottest summers are said to be semievergreen. Plants that predictably drop their leaves every year on a seasonal basis and have a defined dormant period are deciduous.

Conventional leaves are comprised of three main physical parts which aid greatly in plant identification: (1) blade or lamella, (2) petiole or leaf stalk, and (3) stipules (paired blade-like appendages at the base of the petiole.)

The leaf blade is usually very thin and has distinct differences between its upper and underside. Both top and bottom of the blade are surfaced with a thick, waxlike substance called a cuticle. Lying inside the cuticles are the upper and lower epidermis. Inside the upper epidermis are vertically arranged cells, collectively called palisade tissue, where carbohydrates are most frequently manufactured. Interior to the palisade tissue is a spongy tissue which is used primarily for storage of water and nutrients. Routed through this spongy tissue and lying just underneath the palisade layer are leaf veins, which are actually specialized xylem and phloem cells. These veins are housed in a sheath, which could be compared to the plant's outer stem or bark. As with conductive stem tissue, the xylem transports water while the phloem brings nutrients into the leaf and transports manufactured sugars (food) out to other areas of the plant. The spongy tissue is backed by the lower epidermis and then the underside of the leaf blade. Amazing openings called stomata (singular, stoma) penetrate through the lower cuticle and lower epidermis. Air containing carbon dioxide passes into the leaf structure through these stomata, while oxygen is dispelled from the leaf by way of the stomata as a by-product of the photosynthetic process. Surrounding each stoma are guard cells which, by either shrinking or swelling, can close or open the stoma. This opening and closing is in response to guard cell moisture content, which creates what is known as turgor pressure. The guard cells are aptly named as they are essential to individual leaf survival and, ultimately, the life of the plant. The primary function for the stoma is to allow for the passage of gases (carbon dioxide, oxygen) to and from the leaves as the plant utilizes energy through a process termed respiration. Water vapor also passes through the stoma in a process called transpiration. In some species, up to 95% of all water taken into the plant is lost to the atmosphere through the transpiration process.

During the day, especially in the desert, as air warms it becomes drier and progressively more receptive to absorbing moisture. Dry air literally sucks water vapor from leaves. As guard cells lose moisture they lose their turgor pressure, which causes them to collapse and the stoma to close. Unfortunately, in some cases, the stomata do not close fast enough and transpiration continues at such a rapid rate that the plant reaches a permanent wilting point and dies. Transpiration is greatly accelerated in the presence of progressively drier air and/or wind. Trees and shrubs being transported should be laid flat and covered to prevent wind transpiration. It is not a bad idea to spray the cover (tarp) with water as an added transpiration prevention measure. As discussed in the chapter on deserts, cacti have developed a physiological process of storing a special acid (malic acid) that allows them to carry on the process of photosynthesis with their stomata closed during the daylight hours and then open at night to exchange essential gases. This process is called crassulacean acid metabolism (CAM) and is critical to the survival of several species. The importance of transpiration to the more conventional plant species is a subject of much debate among botanists. It is a scientific fact that transpiration is a cooling mechanism and does help to speed the drawing of water and nutrients up through the root and stem tissue and into leaves. The ultimate survival of most plants, however, does not depend on either of these two factors and transpiration is viewed more as a hinderance than a help to survival. When planting new materials, oil sprays called antidesiccants or antitranspirants are sometimes sprayed on leaves to reduce the effect of moisture loss through transpiration.

On deciduous trees many latent leaf buds occur as an adaptation to frequent (annual) leaf drop. When planting these trees during the hottest summer months I recommend stripping all the leaves from the branches by hand. The reason for this is two-fold. First it eliminates immediate transpiration loss. Second, energy wasted on what would soon become dying leaves can now be utilized for new root and bud growth.

The leaf petiole is the stalk like structure which holds the leaf blade to a branch or stem. Leaves that have no petiole and attach directly to stem surfaces are said to be sessile. In some plant species there are one or two small blade like (modified) leaf parts called stipules that are found at the base of the petiole where it attaches to the stem. The importance of these appendages is not completely known. The size, shape, and position of stipules do aid in plant identification.

The biggest aid in keying (identifying) plant material is to note how the petiole relates to the leaf blade or blades. A single leaf on a petiole with no indentations is called entire or simple. A single leaf that is indented is said to be lobed. A petiole that contains more than one leaf (leaflets) belongs to a compound leaf. The stalk-like (petiole-like) extension between the first leaflet and succeeding leaflets is called a rachis. Leaflets that are opposite one another and separated by one or more rachises in a bilateral pattern until terminating at a single leaf tip are defined as being part of a pinnately compound leaf. A palmately compound leaf has leaflets that meet at a common point just above the petiole. A myriad of descriptions are applied to the differences in leaf tips, edges, bases, and overall shapes. A working knowledge of these descriptions aids greatly in plant identification and often in recognizing related or unrelated cultural requirements among various species. Note that the leaf structures of many desert plant species are very small and are often pinnately compound. This reduces the amount of surface area exposed to solar radiation, heat, and wind, all in an attempt to minimize transpiration. In addition, many desert species have evolved the adaptation of being drought deciduous. That is, they drop their leaves during the hottest and driest summer months and utilize the phenomenon of dormancy to survive the harshest time of year.

Flowers and Fruits

Flowers, in their truest sense, are the reproductive organs of the angiosperms. Fruit mainly relates to the mature ovary of angiosperms in which seeds are housed, but in a larger, if unscientific, sense can also be used to describe pine cones and their place in the life cycle of conifers. Of the six main groups of vascular plants that have evolved over millions of years and are still on earth to this day, the angiosperms and gymnosperms are, by far, the most advanced and most commonly used for landscape architectural purposes. These are the two groups addressed here.

Angiosperm reproductive (sex) organs are borne on flowers. An individual flower that bears both male and female parts is called a perfect flower (a complete flower, by contrast, must also include both petals and sepals) and the parent plant is technically classified as a hermaphrodite. There are several kinds of plants that have unisexual flowers. That is to say that male and female sex organs are on different flowers. When a plant is a hermaphrodite or has unisexual flowers on the same specimen, it is said to be monoecious (all parts on one plant). Dioecious (separate parts on two plants) plant material defines species that support male and female flowers on separate plants. Dioecious plants are either definitely male or female. While the vast majority of angiosperms are monoecious, it is an odd quirk of nature that several of the plants of agricultural importance are dioecious. Since the male dioecious plant does not bear fruit it is of little use to the farmer except to be kept around in such numbers as necessary to guarantee the pollination (fertilization) of the female flowers. Occasionally this works to the landscape architect's advantage, as the messy fruits and objectionable sex of some dioecious plants (e.g., the carob and ginkgo trees) can be avoided altogether by specifying that only male or female plants be used. Dioecious plants offer a little flexibility; with monoecious plants you take what you get.

For ease of explanation, a complete flower of a monoecious plant in the angiosperms will be described. Flowers are borne on specialized stems. At the end of this stem is an enlarged fleshy organ which fuses stem to floral parts. This is the receptacle. Appendages that grow from the receptacle that appear to be either leaves or petals are in fact neither. These are sepals, and in some species, colored sepals actually outstage and outgrow the petals (e.g., the Bougainvillea vine). Upstream of the sepals are the petals which are usually the pretty and colorful part of most flowers. Sepals joined collectively together are called the calyx. Petals joined together are referred to as the corolla. That portion of the flower that includes the calyx and the corolla is called the perianth. These are important terms to remember when reading texts on plant identification. Arrayed inside the petals are long string-like upright organs with tiny heads. These are the male sex organs, called stamens. The string is called the filament and the head at the end of the filament is called the anther. Pollen, the botanic equivalent to the animal kingdom's sperm cells, is borne on the anther and is frequently yellow to gold in color.

While the flower may have several stamens, it usually has only one pistil. The pistil is the female reproductive organ and is frequently somewhat vase shaped. The pistil is in the center of the flower and its biggest, roundest, part, the ovary, nests on top of the receptacle. Extending upwards out of the ovary is the style, which is similar to the throat of a vase. Terminating the style is a rounded, thicker, and somewhat wider tissue called the stigma.

When the ovaries are ripe and the pollen has matured, the stigma often becomes sticky. This occurs for the purpose of catching pollen, which is transported to the stigma by wind, bees, other insects, flies, and/or hummingbirds. The process by which pollen is transported to stigmas is called pollination and is truly an everyday miracle of nature. Flowers have adapted numerous forms which cause insects and other animals to simultaneously brush against pollen laden anthers and sticky stigmas to achieve pollination. Many insects actually eat pollen but, in the process, distribute it to stigmas. Nature, in her infinite wisdom, always seems to provide more pollen than the insects can eat. To attract bees and hummingbirds, many flowers secrete a sweet liquid nectar from glands called nectaries, usually located at the base of the ovary. The pollinators literally have to brush against and disturb the anthers to get to the nectaries. The most recognizable product manufactured in the animal kingdom from flower nectar is honey, produced by bees. As ovaries mature, and the seeds within develop, the members of the angiosperm class set fruit. Fruit can be elaborate, with pronounced seeds such as with watermelon or squash or elaborate with nearly unnoticeable seeds as with banana or strawberry. Both fruit and seed can be inconspicuous, as is the case with many eucalyptus. There is no apparent correlation between flower size and fruit size or fruit size and seed size. A knowledge of fruit types often aids a landscape architect in plant identification and can provide some basic insights into soil type and soil moisture levels.

Fruits can range from vegetables and citrus to items one would not ordinarily associate with being a fruit. Nuts are actually fruits, as are dates and grain crops (e.g., Wheat). The dried winged samaras of Maples are fruits, as are the spiked buttonballs of Sycamores. The angiosperms did not necessarily evolve fruit as a food substance to assure the survival of the animal kingdom, but rather to assure their own. Edible fruits encourage animals to ingest and later disperse seeds. Barbed fruits are carried on the coats of mammals. Lighter winged fruits are dispersed by the wind. A myriad of adaptations have evolved to assure the thing that is always foremost in the plant kingdom — survival of the species.

The gymnosperms are second only to the angiosperms in being the most recent plant class to appear on the evolutionary calendar. Even at that, the gymnosperms are considered prehistoric relics. Conifers, the ancient Ginkgo, and the exotic Sago Palm are representative gymnosperms. For the purposes of this chapter, the pines and their method of reproduction will be examined.

Pines do not flower or fruit, per se, but they do develope pine cones which at their inception can be compared to flowers and at their maturity can be likened to fruit. Pines produce staminate (male) and carpellate (female) cones. The staminate cones are generally smaller and sometimes significantly smaller than the carpellate cone. They are nonwoody and short-lived. Carpellate cones are woody, house the female sexual components and eventually seeds. In the earlier stages of their development, the male and female cones can be roughly compared to the separate male and female flowers on a monoecious plant of the angiosperm order. It is how these elements mature, fertilize, and eventually form seeds that make gymnosperms radically different and quite unique.

The staminate cone produces two microsporangiam (sporangia producing tiny spores) on the under side of each of its scales. The microsporangium is basically a pollen sac with the spores within going through numerous divisions which eventually generate winged pollen that develops the micro-gametophytes. This pollen is manufactured in massive profusion and is wind distributed and can be easily seen blowing about by the naked eye.

The carpellate cone produces scales which are technically called megasporophylls. Each megasporophyll houses two ovary-like megasporangia on their undersides. Through a series of cellular divisions these two megasporangia each eventually form a single megaspore which developes into a female gametophyte containing a functional egg. The male pollen (sperm) is wind blown into an opening on the female gametophyte called the microphyle, where it produces a pollen tube which grows to the internal structure of the female gametophyte, where fertilization takes place. The resulting seeds mature on the scales of the carpellate cone, which themselves open further and become continuously more woody. The seeds develop wings and are eventually blown from the cone scales and dispersed to the surrounding soil. Their function completed, the carpellate cones eventually fall to the ground.

With their natural ability to form seeds, the angiosperms and gymnosperms have become the dominant dry land plants. Both groups and every species within them vie to occupy their own ecological niche and, with an eternal slowness, evolve the mechanisms and processes necessary to insure their continued survival.

Ecology

As stated at the beginning of the chapter, an understanding of the principles of ecology would serve a landscape architect well. Ecology is the study of the relationship of living things (plants and animals) to their environment (physical surroundings). The environment and all the living things within it comprise an ecosystem.

A diagrammatic breakdown of all the components adding to the concept of an ecosystem would look something like this:

CELL → TISSUE → ORGAN → SYSTEM → ORGANISM →

POPULATION → COMMUNITY → ECOSYSTEM

A short definition of each of these components before an attempt at an explanation of the broad concept of ecosystem would be in order:

Cell: The basic subunit or building block of any living organism, the simplest unit that can exist as an independent living organism.

Tissue: An aggregation of similar cells having the same physiological function.

Organ: A discreet structure composed of tissues which have one or more specific functions; morphologically distinct from adjacent or adjoining organs.

System: A specialized organ or group of organs in conjunction with specialized tissues which perform a specific function within an organism.

Organism: Any living individual.

Population: A grouping of individuals of the same organism type within a given area.

Community: A grouping of different populations within an area.

Ecosystem: A grouping of communities plus abiotic factors (e.g., wind, light, water, oxygen, carbon dioxide, etc.) within an area.

The major component of an ecosystem is energy. All organisms compete for and utilize some form of energy. Ecosystems can be looked at as closed systems with energy generated from the sun being the only energy form that passes through. Biological and chemical properties are rotated or recycled within this closed system. There are definite chemical cycles which exist within any given ecosystem type. Nitrogen, phosphorus, sulfur, potassium, etc. are reused over and over again by organisms in these ecosystems. Carbon dioxide, hydrogen, and water are constantly recycled within the earth's biosphere.

The only organisms capable of making their own food are the green plants, and even they compete for the greatest amount of the sun's energy, for soil nutrients, and for available water. The energy entering our atmosphere (all energy on the earth is originally derived from the sun) is transferred through a series of steps: sun to plant (through the process of photosynthesis), to herbivore (plant eater), to carnivore (meat eater). Each advancing step in this process is called a trophic level. At each trophic level, the remaining amount of original energy is decreased. Of a hundred units of sun energy, only one unit of that energy may actually become plant tissue. (The unit value used here is arbitrary.) The other 99 units are lost in the form of heat, reflected light, and energy demands of the plants. When a plant is eaten, only a fraction (0.1) of the one unit retained by the plant may actually be used to make the herbivore's body tissue. The other 0.9 units are converted to body heat and other forms of lost energy.

Because of the dramatic decrease in available energy at each higher trophic level, there will always be fewer living things at each step. This is one explanation for the fact that there are more carnivores that eat herbivores than carnivores that eat other carnivores. If an organism can omit intermediate steps and go directly to the plants, it will have more usable energy available to it. A diagrammatic food chain is often used to illustrate the fact that a carnivore eats a herbivore or a smaller carnivore in order to obtain energy or simply to survive, when in actuality, a diagrammatic food web is a much better explanation of what really goes on.

The amount of energy available in an ecosystem at any one time is limited; thus the number of organisms that can utilize this energy is limited. This limited energy is called an ecosystem's carrying capacity. If the carrying capacity is exceeded by too many energy seekers (overpopulation), mass starvation ensues with populations responding by migrating to different areas if possible, or simply dying if not, until a workable carrying capacity is once again reached. When an ecosystem is able to stay within its carrying capacity over an extended period of time, it is said to have reached a steady state.

Ecosystems which display a great amount of diversity are believed to be healthy ecosystems in that they support more life forms. Diverse ecosystems are hard to knock out with disease and pestilence because not all the organisms will be affected and they will aid in the regeneration of the ecosystem. Because energy or food/nutrients is limited in an ecosystem, the organisms within it have devised specialized habitats and niches to reduce competition. The term "habitat" refers to where a population lives, while "niche selection" refers to what a plant or animal within a habitat does to obtain food/nutrients. Diurnal and nocturnal feeding habits of different animals can be viewed as a niche preference. Also, the food/nutrient preferences of organisms are in direct relationship to niche (e.g., seed eating finches as opposed to fish-eating ospreys or shallow rooted desert grasses vs. deep rooted Mesquite trees.)

All ecosystems undergo a process known as entropy which simply means they age. Entropy in a climax desert ecosystem may not be noticeable, but the process does occur. Over very long periods of time, mature trees and cacti age, weaken, and die. They are succeeded by younger plants which are most likely to be of the same species, but the dead plant material is succeeded just the same.

The process of succession is also characteristic of ecosystems. In the formation of any given ecosystem, there is a definite series of steps undertaken to reach the climax or steady state stage. In forest ecosystems the steps are represented by the decline and fall of various types of seral vegetation until the climax plant association is reached. Remember in the opening desert chapter, the Palo Verde to Saguaro cactus cycle was noted. This is a prime example of recurring succession.

In a small forest meadow, trees on the outer edge will usually infiltrate the meadow with seeds and reestablish the forest proper. In large forest meadows, which may have come into being due to clear cutting practices or forest fires, the succession to the climax vegetation community will require many more steps. First, grasses will appear. These will prevent splash erosion of soils to a great extent and form an organic layer which will encourage shrub species to germinate and grow. These, in turn, will contribute organic matter to the soil in the form of leaf litter. As the soil fertility increases, the lower deciduous trees will come into the area and likewise (through leaf litter) contribute organic matter to the soil. Eventually the climax trees will infiltrate and, later, the area will become a climax forest area. In order to speed the process of succession in a desert ecosystem it is always advisable to restore the ground plane through hydroseeding of native annuals and grasses.

Disclimax occurs when, for some reason, an ecosystem is prevented from reaching the expected climax community type. The reasons are usually microclimatic, such as temperature and moisture variations as well as soil types. Disclimax can be man induced. An example of this is the massive coniferous forest regions found in the southeastern U.S., most notably the Carolinas and Georgia. Man, through the use of fire, prevents the invasion of hardwoods as they are burned in the understory fires. The conifers of this region do not crown out until they are about 15 to 20 feet above ground. Consequently, the fires cannot reach the crowns. Also, the trunks of these trees are very fire resistant. Thus, man keeps the conifers in and the hardwoods out due to the fact that the conifers are much more economically valuable to him in this particular region. Cahuilla Indians employed fire to manage *Washingtonia filifera* groves in an effort to reduce competition for water from other species which increased fruit production and removed annoying ground plane litter. In all cases, as ecosystems undergo change, the number and types of plant and animal species found within will fluctuate and change. There is reason for this: as the ecosystem changes, so do the niche types and their availability. Living organisms are specific to their environments.

It should be remembered that everything that applies to organisms will usually apply to populations, but populations have characteristics that do not apply to organisms. Every organism lives within a range of preferences for certain conditions. These ranges of preferences are called limits of tolerance and the conditions are known as limiting factors. Limiting factors would include all the things that an organism requires to live. A partial listing of limiting factors for plants and animals would include the following:

LIMITING FACTORS

Plants

1. Light
2. Temperature
3. Amount of water and its quality
4. Amount of air and its quality
5. Nutritional requirement in form of solid nutrients primarily available from soil
6. Wind velocity
7. Soil types

Animals

1. Light
2. Temperature
3. Amount of water and its quality
4. Nutritional requirement in form of vitamins primarily available from plant life
5. Wind velocity

It should be noted that different environments have limiting factors which are much more specific to their functions than to other environments (e.g., salinity in the oceans and tidal estuaries). Organisms or populations with a narrow range of tolerance to some or all the limiting factors previously listed are said to be "steno", while those with a broad range of tolerance to these same factors are said to be "eury." Thus, a brook trout would be said to be stenothermal if its acceptable temperature range was compared to that of the carp. Eurythermal, or having a broad temperature range, would describe the carp's limits of tolerance to temperature. In desert environments Saguaro is "steno" and Creosote is "eury." Organisms also display optimum preference ranges for each limiting factor listed in which they function at their best. The law of the minimum likewise applies to organisms. This simply means that if all the factors an organism requires to grow and function are at an optimum level, except for one, then that one factor will retard the organism's growth. An example is a tree that has its optimum water, sunlight, temperature, and air requirements filled, but is planted in poor soil. Despite the optimum factors present, the soil will retard the plant's growth. Thus, the organism's growth will be no better than that allowed by its minimum limiting factor. Frequently organisms will compensate for limiting factors or, in plain language, do the best with what's available. Take, for example, an orchid that prefers full sun when in cooler temperature regions, but grows under trees in the tropics. It sacrifices the optimum sun, but stays alive due to the cooling shade provided by the trees. As stated previously, populations have characteristics that apply to them and not to specific organisms. A listing of these characteristics would look like this:

Density — Number of same organism species in a given area.

Mortality — Death rate.

Natality — Birth rate.

Age distribution — The important aspect of this category is the percentage of individuals that are at optimum breeding age as they will most likely determine the near future of the population.

Distribution — Habitats and ranges.

Growth form (rate) (Do not confuse with birth rate.) — The rate at which the overall population is growing (or declining).

To see how populations of specific organisms evolved and survived in a process called natural selection, a simplified breakdown of Charles Darwin's *Origin of Species* would be in order:

1. All average organism populations tend to overproduce.
2. Yet, population sizes stay more or less constant.
3. Therefore, some of the over-produced numbers die.
4. Not all individuals within a certain population are alike. Some are superiorly adapted.
5. The superiorly adapted ones tend to survive in greater numbers.
6. These will tend to find similar superiorly adapted mates and pass the better traits on to the offspring. (Today we know that genetics is the reason for this.)
7. In time, a superiorly adapted or even a new species arises from the accumulation of different superior traits.

Plant Communities

A look at plant communities is important at this juncture. Plants with similar environmental preferences and with characteristics which mutually benefit the survival of one another will group together in an association which botanists call a community. Formation and types of plant communities are easier to notice and describe in a mountainous northeastern hardwood forest than they are in deserts, but be assured, although less noticeable than other regions, desert plant communities do exist. In the hardwood forest, vegetation groupings are decidedly different on north- or south-facing mountain slopes. This is due to differences in sun exposure, rainfall, temperature, and evolved soil type. In addition, there are different levels (layers) of plant materials with a clearly defined upper story (trees), understory (smaller trees and bushes), and occasionally groundcover (ferns, mosses, vines). Leveling of desert species also occurs, but instead of being a response to light, as in the hardwood forest, it is a response to soil moisture. Different plant species in a desert plant community develop varying root depths in order to create their own niche. By utilizing different rooting strategies desert plant communities slow the progress of gravitational water, usually but not always to the mutual benefit of all. Once established, desert plant communities exhibit some of the associations that occur in other plant communities. Upper story plants provide leaf and flower litter to lower story plants as a source of nutrients, while lower story plants knit the ground plane, preventing wind and splash erosion. Midsize plants provide ground plane shadowing over wide spreading root systems. As with all plant communities, note that desert plant communities exist in a delicate balance. This balancing of one organism to another, so that life can coexist, is really the essence of ecology.

Desert Survival Strategies

Desert plants have developed marvelous adaptations to allow them to cope with their environment. Broadly defined, the three main types of desert plant material are: avoiders, tolerators, and water spenders.

The avoider group includes annuals and drought deciduous plants, which simply do not live through or go dormant during the hottest, driest summer months. They kick in their more important life processes during the cooler, wetter winter months.

The tolerators are simply plants that survive year-round. These plants include trees and shrubs (e.g., Ironwood and Creosote) which have deep and wide spreading root systems to find what little water that is available. Also included are the cacti, which have adapted their entire growth process and physical form to more efficiently utilize and store water during the long periods between rains. The cacti utilize leaflessness, crassulacean acid metabolism (CAM), sponge like stems, and either shallow and/or deep root systems which absorb rain rapidly as survival mechanisms.

The water spenders are those plants that grow in association with riparian environments and simply employ the process of unimpeded transpiration. Examples are Cottonwood and Ash and, to a lesser degree, Mesquite. Plants that use water at very high rates are called phreatophytes. Some debate has occurred as to whether the removal of phreatophytes would make more water available for man, livestock, and agricultural plants. Most objections to phreatophytes have been quelled for three reasons. First, these plants aid in soil stabilization and, more important, flood control. Second, they cool their immediate understory environment, providing habitat for numerous plant and animal species, in particular, larger desert mammals. Third, the leaf litter from larger-scale riparian trees restores soil nutrients to the surrounding environments. Most environmentalists believe that the phreatophytes in direct association with ground surface water are more a help to the desert ecosystem than a hinderance.

Soils

No study of plant material and plant communities would be complete without a discussion of soil types and soil nutrition as it relates to plant growth.

Three aspects of soil, for the purposes of planting, that concern the landscape architect are soil texture, soil reaction, and soil fertility. The texture of soil is rated by particle size, with clay being the smallest and sand being the largest. Due to their proximity to alluvial fans, many desert soils often contain varying sizes and percentages of gravel. Soil scientists classify soil in twelve textural classes which are depicted on a triangle. For our purposes, we shall identify five soil ranges: clay, silt, fine sand, medium sand, and coarse sand. The determination of various percentages of each type of particle in a given soil area is called a mechanical analysis. When the two soil types of clay and sand are in equal or near equal percentages, then a third soil classification called "loam" is created. Loam soils are considered ideal for most planting situations.

Soil reaction is the term given to a particular soil's degree of acidity or alkalinity and is expressed on a scale of 1 to 14 called "pH value." The pH value is really a measurement of the hydrogen ion concentration within the soil solution. A pH value of 7 is termed neutral, while 0 to 6.9 is referred to as an acidic soil, and 7.1 to 14 is alkaline. Most desert soils are moderately to highly alkaline. Most plant material, especially introduced plants, in new desert landscapes prefers a slightly acid soil (6.0 to 6.5 is considered ideal). The addition of acidic products or gypsum reduces alkalinity while the addition of lime will raise alkalinity.

While not normally considered a component of soil reaction, a soil_s salinity is closely related to pH. Many desert soils are quite saline. Deep watering or leaching of salt laden soils is the best way to literally flush salt out of surface soils and away from root zones.

Soil fertility, as it applies to planting, is a measurement of organic matter and nutrient levels. There are three main macronutrients in soil: nitrogen, phosphorus, and potassium. Nutrients of secondary importance are calcium, magnesium, and sulfur. Iron, manganese, and zinc are considered micronutrients. Organic matter includes leaf mold, manures, bone meal, cottonseed hulls, and the various remains of once living organisms. While many of the nutrients listed above can be obtained from organic matter as it decomposes, these materials are more important for what they lend to a soil's structure. Organic matter and often inorganic matter (perlite, vermiculite, and pumice) as well, will increase air space in soil which, in turn, increases a soil's ability to absorb and hold water. Both air spaces and the availability of water allow the root systems of plants to spread freely, adding to their overall growth rate and health.

Of the three macronutrients, nitrogen is the most heavily used by plant materials. Nitrogen promotes growth in all parts of the plant, but has the most effect upon leaf growth. Since the leaves usually represent the largest growing surface area of the plant, a lot of nitrogen is required. Phosphorus primarily aids conductive tissue, root, and stem growth. Potassium promotes top growth, especially leaf and flower bud formation.

Micronutrients often act as catalysts in a number of growth processes and interact with secondary nutrients to form chemicals that allow macronutrients to function more efficiently. Of the micronutrients, iron is sometimes hard for desert plants to obtain. This is not usually because iron is not present in the soil, but rather it is in a form that the plants cannot access. Iron becomes tied up when lime is either present or added to soil. A condition known as *chlorosis* occurs when an iron deficiency is present. Chlorosis is recognized by yellow leaves with green margins. Chlorosis can be combated with iron sulfate or iron chelate. Chelated fertilizers are chemical fertilizers that are soluble in water. These fertilizers make iron readily available to root systems or can be applied to leaves as a foliar spray.

To supplement inherent soil fertility, commercial fertilizers have been developed to be incorporated into tilled soil. Commercial fertilizers can be either organic or chemical but are always specified the same way. The basis of commercial fertilizers is the macronutrients which are always listed as N (nitrogen), P (phosphorus), and K (potassium). A typical fertilizer label lists these nutrients as a percentage of overall weight. This listing is called the fertilizer's guaranteed analysis. Thus a 20% nitrogen fertilizer in a 10 pound bag contains 2 pounds of actual nitrogen (10 lb. × .20 = 2 lb.). Fertilizer with only one or two macronutrients is called a simple fertilizer. Fertilizer that contains all three macronutrients is called a complete fertilizer. The higher the percentage of macronutrients in any given fertilizer, the greater the concentration of that element within the mixture. Fertilizers of higher concentrations frequently are applied in lighter (by weight) applications, reducing maintenance time and storage space requirements.

Fertilizers are available bagged, granular, powdered, and water-soluble. Natural fertilizers are frequently used by home gardeners following aging by composting. It is always difficult to determine the guaranteed analysis of natural fertilizers and, for that reason, they are infrequently used on large-scale projects or for initial installations. Slow-release and controlled-release fertilizers are gaining in popularity as they are useful for containerized and newly transplanted plant materials.

Before applying or depending heavily on fertilizers for plant growth, the landscape architect should employ the service of a soil-testing laboratory, consult with local horticulturists, and confer with the local county agricultural extension agency to learn all he can about the site's existing soil capabilities and obvious deficiencies. If you are new to an area, it is advisable to observe plant materials in the ground and to talk with local nurserymen and installers about growth rates. The same species can sometimes exhibit dramatic differences in its overall physical proportions from one soil type to another.

Some desert localities have soils of high clay content that are occasionally stratified with compressed hardpan layers called caliche. Caliche is found in all desert areas, but is most often associated with clay soils. Caliche is formed when calcium carbonate hardens to an almost impervious layer that prohibits drainage. When a layer of caliche is found during planting operations, it must be broken through to more permeable underlying layers of soil so that planting basins will drain and root systems can spread downward.

Another phenomenon which frequently occurs in foothill desert areas, especially in box canyons and cove areas, is blowsand. These fine wind blown sand particles are deposited in enclosed canyons and can build up layers several feet thick. Blowsand is very low in nutrient value and quite unstable in structure. Wherever blowsand is encountered it will have to either be removed or heavily amended.

Before closing the subject of soil, let us examine the capability of soils to retain water for plants to utilize. Every soil particle has the ability to make water adhere to its surface. A given volume of clay is wetter than an equal volume of sand, due to the fact that it has twice as many particles and thus twice the actual surface area for water to adhere to. The adherence of water to soil particles is called cohesion. As a result of cohesion, soil particles will actually fight root systems for water at a given point. When rapidly transpiring plant materials try to draw up water faster than the soil is willing to release it, the plant starts to wilt and the soil has reached a permanent wilting point. Without cooling to slow plant transpiration or addition of soil moisture to combat soil cohesion, the plant will also shortly reach its permanent wilting point and die. A tensiometer is a device used to measure relative soil moisture and its use will aid in recognizing when a soil is approaching its permanent wilting point.

Water introduced to soil is either lost to drainage (gravitational water) or held by the soil. The volume of water held by the soil is called its field capacity. It is my belief that by increasing a desert soil's field capacity, water can be conserved and plant growth somewhat enhanced. Manufacturers are beginning to introduce sponge-like particles called polymers into the marketplace. In their dry state the particles are small, but when they are wet they can expand to ten times their original size. The incorporation of these particles into planting backfill mixes and raised planters will prolong field capacity. Research is ongoing as to the life span of these soil polymers. More discussion on soil moisture retention and related issues will take place in the irrigation chapter.

The installation and maintenance of plant material will be discussed in succeeding chapters also. A solid understanding of plants, how they grow, and the environment that they will be placed into is indispensable to the landscape architect.

Plant Classification

Of utmost importance to the landscape architect is a working knowledge of plant taxonomy and nomenclature. Taxonomy is the science of plant and animal classification. Latin is the universally accepted language of science. All plants have a botanical or Latin name and, usually, a common name. Because common names can vary from region to region, the Latin name is always used in the preparation of professional planting plans.

A Lady Bank's Rose is used to study the taxonomic breakdown of a plant for the purpose of scientific classification. The breakdown below includes the categories most important to the landscape architect. Two categories that occur between kingdom and class, division and phylum, are not examined, as they are so broad in definition that they are of little use to practical design applications.

Lady Bank's Rose	*Rosa banksiae "Lutea"*
Kingdom:	Plant
Class:	Angiosperm
Family:	Rosaceae
Genus:	*Rosa*
Species:	*banksiae*
Cultivar:	"Lutea"

Among living organisms there are six recognized kingdoms. The two most important kingdoms, and the ones we will concern ourselves with here, are plants and animals. The primary difference between these two kingdoms is in cellular function. Plant cells are capable of internal food production while animal are not.

Classes are differentiated by methods of reproduction, as we examined earlier when discussing angiosperms vs. gymnosperms.

Families are made up of genera, all of which are related by a set of similar characteristics. It should be remembered, however, that these similarities are very wide in nature and that plants within the same family may not lead one to generally think of them as relatives. For example, Roses are in the family Rosaceae, and so are Apples.

A genus is a division of plants of the same family but refined to a narrower set of similar features. In practical applications, the genus is the point of beginning for the everyday classification and description of plants within the profession of landscape architecture. In most texts that describe plant materials (this one included) the first point of reference is the genus. Species within a genus share at least one noticeably common characteristic and are also noticeably different in one or more respects.

The species name is the second word in the typical botanical name. Species define unique individuals which have at least one characteristic that is theirs and theirs alone. A species is totally separate from any other species and, for this reason, plant classification by genus and then species is the most exact way of obtaining the correct individual plant. Cultivars, for the purposes of this chapter, encompass subspecies and varieties that are either natural or man-induced hybrids of the species. Most cultivars came into being after the advent of hybridizing by hand pollination. Frequently the cultivar is named by or after the breeder. Whatever the case, cultivars are specialized plants within a species. The specialization is usually in size, color, texture, fruit production, or disease resistance. Frequently they are distinguished by two or more of these features.

A Swedish botanist Carolus Linnaeus (1707–1773) developed the most frequently used system of plant classification, even to this day. Linnaeus's system, in part, is the one described above, and botanists the world over have added over 350,000 species of plants to the recognized list. There are still thousands of plants unclassified, with many yet to be found. Many future plants are also yet to be created, and no doubt will be as hybridization methods and genetic engineering continue to advance. We owe a lot to this great early day botanist for bringing order to a science that could easily wallow in chaos. It's exciting to work with a design medium more diverse than the painter could ever imagine and to realize that the plant material at our disposal is constantly expanding and improving.

Arboretums are living museums of plants and plant culture. They serve as records of a species' characteristics and range. Arboretums should be frequently visited, supported, and, above all, enjoyed.

Planting Design

Planting design should be a response to both the aesthetic and the functional. As a design medium, plant materials are never static but, rather, constantly changing. This adds a kinetic quality to designing that is not possible with many other mediums. Although dramatic results can be achieved by adhering to hard and fast design rules, it is hard to incorrectly design with plants. Most plants are inherently beautiful. A fine line often exists between what is good or bad design. If healthy and well maintained, plants will often hide the planting person's inadequacies. The more appropriate planting design is to the specific requirements of a site, the higher the level of emotional response to that design. Most viewers react, if only on a subliminal level, to good planting composition.

All design principles that apply to architectonic elements apply to the utilization of plant materials. Mass, scale, proportion, juxtapositioning, and above all, composition allow plants to delineate space. Foliage and floral color infuse life into and evoke attention towards the design. Visual and tactile textures of leaves and stems can be employed as design tools.

The shape of trees and shrubs is called a plant's habit or form. Some commonly used tree habit descriptions are columnar, oval, round, vase, weeping, and pyramidal. Shrubs are often said to be vertical and upright or horizontal and spreading. Ground covers are uniform, irregular, low spreading, or billowy.

Trees, especially multiple trunk specimens, can act as living sculpture. Orientals believed that the bottom one third of a tree was the most beautiful part. Trees also provide scale and emphasis for a space. Trees are used to add beauty and visual continuity to the streetscape. Trees and shrubs can act as windbreaks, stabilize soils, provide visual screening, delineate space, link spaces, accent spaces, frame views, herald entries, and define property ownership.

In areas large enough to employ groups of trees, consider the desired effect. For natural and freeform applications, scrutinize how trees occur in nature. In forests, they compete for light, grow taller than usual, and are somewhat consistent in their spatial relationship to one another. In meadows, they usually infiltrate at the fringes in informal drifts and stands with one or two stragglers from one species randomly overlapping into a grouping of another. Nowhere in rolling or hill country will you see a tree growing at the very apex of a land farm. They ride the side slopes and congregate on the flatter bench areas. In trying to emulate the natural in the manmade, stagger groups of trees in irregular triangles and let a few risk-takers venture a little further away from the safety of the main group. If employing more than one species, let a few overlap one another. Vary box sizes of the same species when you can, because rarely do all trees in a natural setting start their life spans simultaneously.

Trees in the urban environment can be utilized in entirely different manners. In plaza design, in particular those within intense pedestrian circulation, it is little use trying to pretend that one is shoreside at Walden Pond. Here, formal grids of trees called bosques take on a collective life of their own. As in the forest, they will compete for light and exhibit vertical growth if not topped. If topped, they will spread until their canopies and feeder roots touch and then they will maintain that size. This can provide startling beautiful and architectural effects.

Leveling is a strategy frequently employed in planting design. Taller plants are used as a backdrop for medium height plants which, in turn, form a backdrop for even lower plants. The theory is to either cause the eye to uplift or sweep downward. The uplifting process calls attention to even taller elements beyond the plant groupings. Sweeping downward brings far away spaces and elements closer to the viewer and, if appropriately employed, can help create human scale from the viewer's point of reference. Massing of similar plant materials provides flow and continuity which adds to rhythm, line, and harmony.

The arrangement of dissimilar plant materials, deciduous with evergreen for example, can provide variety, accent, and drama.

When massing shrubs in linear areas, such as along street frontages, one technique to consider is to create throw away areas. These are voids in front of or behind the main mass where an accent shrub, usually something colorful like a Mexican Bird-of-Paradise can be introduced. If the shrub freezes (and many flowering shrubs do), it can be cut to the ground (thrown away) and will not be too badly missed as it was an accent but not essential to the main composition. When the shrub grows back it adds life and variety to the design as well as the element of surprise. This technique can be used with cactus species such as Ocotillo which look good for brief period, but cannot carry a design by themselves. While massing creates unity and order it can also create a lack of ecological diversity. When using just a few species in any given design, you run the risk of entire stands of trees or groupings of shrubs being wiped out by a single infestation of insects or disease.

One rule of thumb frequently applied, with respect to the diversity of the plant palette, is that the number of species and level of detail increase as the project's size and ultimate number of users decrease. The plant palette for a shopping center will be significantly less numerous than that of a high-end residential project. This is due to the viewer's time of perception and is also a reflection on maintenance budgets.

Employing an environmental and climatic approach to planting design can greatly aid in assuring the overall success of the project. Plants with similar climatic and soil requirements should be grouped together. This is not only logical in terms of watering but also in terms of maintenance requirements, especially scheduling. Consider the use of winter deciduous trees in combination with a dormant winter lawn; or summer drought deciduous plants in association with cacti to minimize summer watering requirements.

Plants with different rooting strategies and rotating growth periods should be used for erosion control on steep slopes. Shallow-rooted, fast-growing plants (usually annuals) will initially knit the soil and restore the ground plane. As more permanent plants grow and take over, their varying root depths will assure stabilization of successive underground soil layers.

When conducting a site analysis, it is important to take note of any existing plant materials, especially natives. These plants serve as indicators of environmental and cultural conditions. A landscape architect can make some broad-scale determinations as to soil type, sun exposure, and moisture availability based on what the indicator plants reveal.

Plant material employed to provide screening should be suited to the task. Plants chosen for visual screening are not necessarily the same plants one would choose for wind screening. Visual screening requires plants with a tight branch structure and dense foliage. Space allowing, it is better to try to diffuse the wind rather than to stop it abruptly. In the open desert where 40-mph winds are commonplace and 60-mph winds are not uncommon, a single dense planting will often receive heavy damage trying to break the wind. It is better to use separate rows of progressively higher and tighter material starting with short and filtered plants at the head of the windbreak and progressing to tall and dense plants as the final row of defense. The shorter plants encourage the wind to rise under its own momentum and the progressively higher plants further reinforce the uplifting process. Trees with multiple trunks, are better suited to high wind areas than single-trunk trees, because they are generally stouter at the base.

While plant materials are very useful for environmental protection it should be noted that little to no evidence has been presented to support the commonly held notion that they will block or absorb sound. The best material for absorbing sound is earth — the more the better. Trees in association with earth berming may psychologically separate people from sound, but it should be remembered that the berming is what is really absorbing the noise.

Desert Planting Techniques

The nursery industry in the Southwest has evolved to the point where most plant material offered is containerized stock. Some bare-root material still exists, being provided mostly from Eastern and Midwestern mail-order houses catering predominantly to a residential clientele. It is seldom encountered in large-scale, production-type landscaping and, when it is, its planting technique is much the same as that for container plants except to say that proper timing is of critical importance. In the low desert, if you can not plant bare root stock in January or February — forget about it, as the chances of survival during hotter periods is minimal. You may have more time in the high desert, say to the end of March, but that's the extent of it.

The very best time of year for planting trees and shrubs in the desert is in the early fall, specifically late September and early October. Second choice would be the spring months of March and April. At these times, soil temperatures are warm enough to be most receptive to new root growth. The fall, in particular, usually avoids the occasional late season

100°F day and allows two months of relatively mild air temperatures before an early winter frost may occur. With any luck at all, the initial growth spurt can continue into January before the near certainty of cold weather will impede it.

As a rule of thumb, assume that any time that more than 1 solid month of good air temperatures can be counted on, is prime planting time. In the commercial arena, however, where the need to acquire an occupancy permit overrules the desire to plant at the optimum time, it is a fact of landscape life that planting can occur during any season — even the height of summer or the dead of winter. Under these circumstances, the landscape architect must be diligent in specifying that plant material that stands the best chance of surviving the season in which it is put into the ground.

Three things are of key importance. The first is to provide healthy plant material. The second is to properly prepare the soil into which the plant is to be placed. Third, and ultimate to desert survival, is adequate irrigation. All these issues are covered at length in other chapters and sections, except a little should be said about plant material selection and the preparation of the actual planting hole or plant pocket as it is referred to on details and by professionals.

Minimum size of any given plant pocket for any given size of containerized plant is double the dimension of the top of the container for its width and 1 1/2 times the height of the container for its depth. Note that this is a minimum standard and should be looked upon as simply a point of beginning. An axiom well worth remembering is that in arid land soils, the bigger the hole the better. When backfilled with viable and well-draining soil, this allows fast growing feeder roots to get a foothold and the taproot to get a quick head start.

A word about the selection of plant material, in particular trees, shrubs, and ground covers. *Do not be swayed by size alone.* Look for vigor and form. Taller trees and shrubs may have been set too close together in tight nursery rows and grown vertically in competition for light. Or perhaps they bolted when induced by far too generous applications of fertilizers. In general, the thicker the leaf canopy the thicker the root mass. Have growers set material out in the open so you can view it from all angles to be sure its head is well formed. I will always opt for smaller plants with better character, especially if they have been grown in quality soil.

Check to be sure that material is not root bound. If roots are coming out of the holes in containers or the cracks in boxes, it is a good indication that the plants weren't moved up to a larger container size when they should have been. If there is an air gap between the root ball and the sides of the container, it is a sure sign that the plant is root bound. Roots, when contained, will start to circle and, if given time, will literally choke themselves. This is a point to remember, not only at the nursery but also when planting in hard clay soils where the plant pocket, especially if pre-dug and allowed to bake in the hot summer sun, is little different than a large clay pot — it will restrict root growth. With shrubs, choose plants that stay in the container when tipped upside down and that will slide when you deliver a firm hand slap to the bottom. With trees it is a little harder. Note the general condition of the nursery itself. If what you can see is sloppily maintained, just think about what you can't see. The larger a plant material is when you buy it, the less you can do to improve its growth subsequent to its purchase. Great soil preparation and superb irrigation will be of little consequence if you start with poor stock. To have award-winning landscapes, one must begin with quality plant material.

In actual planting operations, second only in importance to the size of the hole is adequate preparation of the backfill mix. Remember that desert soils contain relatively little organic matter, owing to the fact that sparse natural vegetation contributes small quantities of leaf litter to the ground plane. Soil preparation is an issue that I'm an absolute fanatic about. While not as important with transplanted native trees and cacti, it is critical to the survival of plants from domesticated nursery conditions that are being introduced into what equates to the wild.

Most specifications call for a plant pocket backfill mixture of one part native soil (what was dug out) and one part soil amendment, which is usually nitrolized sawdust. It is vital that these two ingredients be thoroughly blended together into a new improved soil. Again, this is just a minimum requirement and should be viewed as just a point of departure. I like to use potting soil with the standard mix for annual color, peat moss for acid loving plants, granular fertilizers (especially slow release) with ground covers, and gravel and perlite with cacti. The point to remember is that this is the opportunity to give the plant a fighting chance in life. Don't skimp on soil amendments.

Wet the bottom of the plant pocket prior to adding backfill mix. Take the bottoms off of box trees prior to placing them in the holes. Always place the top of the root ball as it occurred in the container. Adjust the level of the container with shovels or steel pry bars and make sure it won't settle prior to filling up the sides of the hole. Remove the rest of the box and check for circling roots. Cut away any that you find.

Have a hose running at the same time you backfill and push the shovel handles or pry bars about in the new soil to break up lumps and eliminate air pockets. Forget about a surface level water well unless you're a homeowner. In commercial applications, it just doesn't happen. For trees, drop the grade 4 inches below the adjacent grade at the point where it aligns with canopy line in planting beds and shave the grade out from this area in turf until the ground level continues on as intended. This adjusted grade must correspond to the top of the rootball. This depression will hold more than enough irrigation water. Insert shovel handles about 12 inches into the new soil and push fertilizer tablets, again with the shovel handle, into the holes. Be sure to space tablets evenly around the circumference of the rootball to assure even application.

In projects where the plant is to be viewed from predominantly one location, choose the best side and face it toward the eventual viewers prior to placing it in the hole.

With plant materials on sloping land, adjust the downhill grade into a slight berm so that water will pond around the uphill plant.

Thin out the canopy if it doesn't hurt the overall appearance of the plant. No matter how clean the planting operation, transplanting is a lot of stress for the plant and it will need to adjust to its new home. The task will be easier if the roots have less leaf mass to support.

Double-stake 15 gallon trees as a matter of course, and stake box trees on an as-needed basis. Always coat wire with rubber hose at the point where it rubs against trunks. Remember to remove the wire as the tree matures, for failure to do so will girdle the cambium and kill the tree.

One situation that frequently occurs with vines and espaliers is that the space for an ideal planting hole is restricted by a wall foundation. This also occurs where a planting strip squeezes between a wall and adjacent hardscape. In this case, the root ball, as is, is just too large. If you can, try to downsize to a smaller container, as this is always the best course of action. When you must, the only other option is to reduce the size of the root mass by cutting it with a sharp knife or, if loose enough, by knocking soil away from roots with your fingers. In either case, work evenly around the circumference of the ball. Do not take soil and roots from just one side. Get a plant, so treated, into the ground immediately. Water it in heavily, remove as much leaf mass as you can stand, and hope for the best.

Sometimes, despite our best efforts and intentions, plants don't survive. A postmortem should reveal whether there was an error in the planting technique or if the species was inadequate for the space. In the case of the latter, bite the bullet and make another selection. Any serious individual in this field does not like to witness or contribute to the death of plants.

Micro-Planting Zones

Eric A. Johnson and David Harbison suggest, in their Coachella Valley manual *Lush and Efficient,* three main planting zones around a structure. In addition to these three zones, I would like to define two more that are commonly created to cope with arid region living.

These zones are defined by solar orientation and their somewhat arbitrary boundaries move subtly with the constantly changing azimuth of the sun. Generally, west and south exposures are grouped together as **Zone A**. This is the hottest area and usually receives some form of architectural treatment such as overhangs and enclosed porches to create shade. When shade is not available, it is important to note proximity to the building when selecting and placing plant material. Certain plants which encounter no difficulty 10 feet away from a building wall will literally cook when placed immediately adjacent to the same wall due to radiated heat.

Zone B addresses the building's east exposure. While solar designers claim that solar radiation on an east exposure can be just as intense as on a west exposures, it is the duration (amount of time) of this exposure that makes a critical difference. During a typical midsummer day the sun will rise about 6:00 a.m. and start to become intense at 8:00 a.m.

Then temperatures will escalate some 20° between 11:00 a.m. and 11:30 a.m. Direct sun will be leaving the southern boundary of Zone B about 11:00 a.m. and by 3:00 p.m. the majority of Zone B will be in shade. Tropicals such as Sago Palms, Split-Leaf Philodendrons, and Bird-of-Paradise do quite will in Zone B but often perish in Zone A.

Zone C encompasses the structure's northern and northeast exposure. It receives the least amount of solar radiation and the most hours of shade. Designers often make the mistake of thinking that this is the most protected zone. While this is true in terms of summer protection, it should be remembered that this will be the coldest zone in winter and the most likely area to experience freezing temperatures to plant materials. Zone C often appeals to exotics and tropicals as well as some sensitive ground covers. When introducing these types of plant materials into the design it will be necessary to locate them under overhangs or the canopies of evergreen trees to prevent frost from coming into contact with foilage.

I would add to Johnson and Harbison' zones **Zone D** (introduced shade) and **Zone E** (deep shade). Introduced shade occurs underneath trellises or within enclosed courtyards or atriums. The level of shade can be expressed as a percentage when an overhang is involved. A certain percent of shade is provided under a mesh screen or trellis with a certain number of boards per foot. In enclosed courtyards where building and wall heights vary and overhangs fall at different angles of pitch, it is difficult to calculate the amount of shade and where it will fall. It is wise to have options for plant selection and to be flexible in their use so that a planting approach can be determined after the space is constructed and the shadow pattern can be observed. Introduced shade can offer numerous planting opportunities and allow for the planting of some species in areas not initially suitable for their use.

Deep shade is a unique condition that occurs in tight areas under stair wells or as a result of architecture with deeply recessed facades or in underground areas. Overhead environmental protection may or may not occur in deep shade conditions and some of the freezing problems attendant to north exposures may also occur here. Some plants like Algerian Ivy or Cast-Iron Plant are marvelously adapted to deep shade. Area F is not to be taken lightly, as it comes into play quite often in arid-region style architecture. Some plants can be gradually acclimated to deep shade, but this can be an expensive undertaking.

Macro-Planting Zones

Macro planting zones relate to very large regions with average temperatures, average moisture levels, and average number of growing days being used to define the zone. The major limiting factor in these planting zones is hardiness. Hardiness is determined by a plant's tolerance to low temperature, or more specifically, a plant is considered hardy until subjected to a temperature at which it will freeze. Contrary to popular belief, high temperature is not the main limiting factor in introducing plant material to the desert — cold temperature is.

The "bible," *Sunset's Western Garden Book*, defines four desert zones. Mary Rose Duffield and Warren D. Jones, in *Plants for Dry Climates,* address three zones, while noting that arid grasslands which surround deserts have some characteristics and plant species which cross over. Arid grasslands are attendant primarily to the Great Basin Desert and other areas that can typically depend on 10 or more inches of rain a year. Arid grasslands resemble the savannahs of Africa or steppes of Asia in another striking example of parallel evolution.

The *Sunset's Western Garden Book* discusses high desert (Zone 10), medium to high desert (Zone 11), Arizona's intermediate desert (Zone 12), and low or subtropical desert (Zone13). This reference manual probably has the best breakdown of planting zones and the most useful information available anywhere. The U.S. Department of Agriculture (U.S.D.A.) presents 11 national plant hardiness zones based on wide ranges of mean annual temperatures. All desert zones described herein fall predominately within their Zone 9. The reader is cautioned to consult other references besides this classification system, as the U.S.D.A. zones are so broad as to be ineffective for everyday consultation. *Plants for Dry Climates* describes three desert zones and is similar to the breakdown we will use here and in the plant compendium.

The four desert zones we will concern ourselves with are low desert, transitional zone, intermediate desert, and high desert.

Low Desert: This area lies below 1,500 feet and can extend downward to 200 feet below sea level. Temperatures can average over 100°F for over 100 days, primarily in June, July, and August. Days ranging over 100°F are not uncommon as early as April or as late as

October. Coldest months are January and February when freezes frequently occur. October and March freezes can catch maintenance personnel and gardeners off-guard. For the purposes of this book, freezing will be defined as 32°F and a hard freeze occurs at 20°F or below. While many plants can survive an occasional freeze, a hard freeze can be devastating. In the low desert, planting seasons are defined by the rotation of summer Bermuda Grass to Winter Rye Grass. The rotation of seasonal color (annuals) is often planned to coincide with these events. March 21 is considered optimum seeding time for Bermuda, while September 21 is the cut-off date for Bermuda and is the optimum seeding time for Rye Grass. The low desert can have up to 300 growing days and offers the extremely high temperatures needed to produce citrus and melon crops. Fruits such as apples do not do well here as there are not enough chilling days to trigger adequate flower production. The predominate indicator plant is Creosote (*Larrea tridenta*). Environments within the low desert can vary greatly. In the Sonoran Desert, for example, Phoenix, Arizona can experience up to 10 inches of rain a year while the Coachella Valley in the Colorado subdesert frequently receives less than 3 inches. The Coachella Valley is lower in elevation, hotter in summer, and freezes more often in winter. Remember that because of the temperature extremes (high to low) in this macro zone the impact of introduced microclimatic conditions are the most pronounced here.

Transitional Zone. This macro zone starts at 1,500 feet and rises to 2,000 feet in elevation. It is an area that typically occurs at the mid-bajada level or, more accurately, at the toe of the upper bajada. When this zone occurs on steep hillsides or within alluvial fans, it is surprising to note that this is where most of the healthier and denser California Fan Palm oases occur in the Colorado subdesert. It also represents the upper reaches of the Saguaro's characteristic range in the Sonoran Desert. While more ideally suited to low desert plant materials, the transitional zone can protect tropicals and exotics during periods of winter freezing becuase it receives warm air updrafts from the valley floor. Being such a vague and narrowly recognized zone, it is not a part of the matrix of plant descriptions. The transitional zone is a place for observation and experimentation being slightly cooler in summer and warmer in winter than the low-desert zone.

Intermediate Desert. This macro zone starts at about 2,000 feet and tails off at about 3,500 feet. In general, it is cooler and frequently wetter than the low desert. In the Sonoran Desert it is represented by the side slopes of mountain ranges and low level plateaus. Indicator plants are Foothill Palo Verde *(Cercidium microphylla*), Greasewood (*Sareobatus vermiculatus*), and Sugar Bush (*Rhus ovata*). The growing season varies between 200 to 250 days. Winter temperatures can fall to -10°F. Rainfall can be as high as 15 inches per year in some areas, although 6 inches would be a generous estimate for rain-shadow areas of the leeward and desert-facing slopes of mountain ranges. The low end of the Mohave Desert is considered to be at 2,500 feet. While 100°F days are commonplace at the height of the summer months, there are less than 90 annually, and spring and fall nights can drop to 60°F followed by 80 to 90°F days. While natives of the intermediate desert can be planted successfully in the low desert, they frequently require more water and, often, some degree of sun protection.

High Desert. This macro zone starts at 3,500 feet and extends to a little over 5,000 feet. A typical representation of the high desert is considered to be at 4,000 feet, and in the Mohave, this is the ideal growing elevation for the Joshua Tree (*Yucca brevifolia*) which is a well-recognized indicator plant. The growing season lasts an average of 200 days and there is sufficient chilling to offer ideal fruit (Apples, Cherries) growing conditions. Rainfall can occasionally approach 15 inches in the higher areas of the Mohave, but is more often about 10 inches in the highest areas of the Colorado Desert. Indicator plants are *Juniper (Juniperus californica*), Manzanita species (*Arctostaphylos*), and Jojoba (*Simmondsia chinensis).* Occasionally Oak species will be encountered in association with riparian communities. Piñon Pine (*Pinus edulis*) will occasionally get a foothold in plateau areas, especially on windward facing slopes. Ponderosa Pine (*Pinus ponderosa*) occurs at the highest elevations and marks the departure from the high desert into conifer forest zones. The windward sides of barrier mountain ranges, are classified as Chapparral/Desert Plant Communities. While in elevation these areas fall into the desert zone classification, they are likely to receive more rainfall and occasional fog. All the plants indicated in the compendium can be grown in the Chaparral at the appropriate elevation, but they will probably require less supplemental irrigation. Chaparral materials can be used in most low-elevation desert designs but they frequently require solar protection, more irrigation, and an acclimation period.

Before examining the plant lists and plant compendium, let's look at how typical planting plans are developed and drawn in the landscape architect's office.

Planting Plans

Sometimes when the palette is simple, say 20 plants or less, graphic conventions can be used and called out on a simple legend. Often, especially on larger projects with several microclimatic conditions, a special language will need to be utilized. This language will be described.

As noted earlier in this chapter, in the practice of landscape architecture, plants are usually grouped into five major categories: (1) trees, (2) shrubs, (3) vines and espaliers, (4) ground covers, and (5) turf grasses. There are specialty plants such as cacti and succulents, but they are usually shown on legends as trees or shrubs. Likewise, water plants are usually shown as shrubs for simplicity.

Trees are indicated by a circle split in half. In the upper part of the circle are three letters. The first letter calls out the genus. The second letter calls out the species. The third letter notes that the tree has either a single (S) or multiple (M) trunk(s). In instances where call outs may duplicate themselves, as *in Platanus acerfolia* vs. *Prosopis alba*, select the first two letters of the genus for one or the other. In the case of palms, use a P for the third letter. Use a C for cacti. The bottom part of the circle always gives the quantity of trees connected by a line to that circle.

Shrubs are indicated by a hexagon split in two. The top part of the hexagon has two letters. The first letter indicates the genus. The second letter indicates species. Again, in the event of duplication, use the first two letters of the genus. Vines and espaliers are usually separated into their own category (under the shrub heading) on the plant legend. This is good, because they will require special staking, wiring, espaliering, and other methods of attachment to architectural elements or even on to trees.

Ground covers and turf grasses are indicated by an open square with one letter inside. The letter usually is the first letter of the genus. In cases of duplication use the first letter of the common name. Quantities are not given for ground covers because they are usually planted from one-gallon containers or flats at predetermined centers. Quantities are usually not given for turf grasses, either, although the overall square footage of turf areas is sometimes calculated and noted.

A complete plant legend will include key, botanical name, common name, size, quantity, and remarks. The key lets anyone reviewing the plan know where specific plant material is located. The botanical name is the most important item on the legend. It lets the supplier know exactly what plant is desired. It ensures that there will be no mistakes in ordering from region to region. In short, it provides uniformity and clarity in an otherwise diverse industry. The common name is how local people refer to a plant. The name may be different from region to region and this sometimes causes confusion. Common names are shown on the plant legend as a courtesy to local suppliers and plan reviewers more than anything else. Sometimes common names give meaning to a theme. For instance, a meditation garden at a church facility may have Palms, Olives, Crown of Thorns, and Our Lord's Candle. The botanical name does nothing, while the common names have the desired religious connotation.

Size usually means container size or box size. Containers come in sizes of 4 inches, 1 gallon, 5 gallon, and 15 gallon. Boxes range from 16 to 104 inches to larger. When looking at the unit costs of plant material, you will notice that prices sometimes double from a smaller to the next size larger container or box. This should be kept in mind when specifying plant material. Palms are usually called out by brown trunk height. This is the height from the top of the root ball (grade) to the bottom of the first frond (canopy). Specialty plants are called out by height, spread, or other factors. Saguaro cacti are called out by their overall height and number of arms while Ocotillos are called out by height and number of canes (branches). Whatever method of sizing plant material is used, it is important to be consistent with call outs. When using different sizes of the same species make sure you note on the plans where these differences occur.

Whether or not to give quantities on a plant legend has been a point of argument among landscape architects. I favor it. Many landscape architects do not like the criticism or liability when discrepancies occur between the quantity on the legend and what is shown on the plans. If this is the case, a simple note on the plans stating that the plan takes precedence over the legend should suffice. The reason I like to give quantities is two-fold. First, it aids in developing an in-house cost estimate to see if the design meets the owner's budget. Second, it does aid contractors bidding the job and, when done accurately, gains their respect. Another thing that gains their respect is checking with nurserymen and growers to assure species availability before specifying.

The "remarks" heading allows for special call-outs or notes such as to leave palm trunks natural or to prune or peel them. Staking, trunk height to first branch, required root barriers, etc., are the types of items that are usually included in the legend under remarks.

In closing, planting plans themselves should be clear, concise, and, above all, understandable. Before embarking on this endeavor, consider the level of comprehension of the construction estimator and the eventual end installer. Often the education and experience level of these two individuals is quite different. Try to design to the lowest acceptable common denominator. A high-end residential contractor can usually be depended upon to be more sensitive to and knowledgeable about planting than a low-bid public works contractor. Both may be very good contractors for what they do, but it is the responsibility of the landscape architect to know who will be doing what and to tailor his drawings to their eventual audience.

The Plant Compendium

Organization of the Compendium

The Plant Compendium at the end of this chapter (p. 243), separates plants into eleven different categories:

1. Trees and Palms
2. Shrubs
3. Espaliers
4. Vines
5. Ground Covers
6. Turf Grasses
7. Cacti, Succulents, Yuccas, Desert Grasses, and Spoons
8. Bulbs, Corms, Tubers, and Rhizomes
9. Aquatic Plants
10. Annuals
11. Wildflowers

Within the first 10 categories, there is an overall classification matrix which identifies plants with some or all of these ten major headings:

1. Environmental Grouping
2. Size
3. Macro Zone
4. Micro Zone
5. Design Use
6. Water Requirements
7. Leaf Habit
8. Flower Show
9. Fall Color
10. Star Performer

Also, on a category-by-category basis, following the classification matrix, the Plant Compendium provides brief descriptions and explanatory line drawings of selected species. Plants selected to be addressed in greater detail were chosen because of frequent use, client popularity, or environmental suitability. There are far more plants noted within the matrixes than are described.

The focus of the descriptions is more on design application rather than horticultural interest. For this reason, the descriptions will, for the most part, differ greatly from other planting texts that you may have read.

The first five plant types in the plant categories are adequately defined within the body of this planting chapter. The remaining six categories, however, will require a more lengthy explanation.

Turfgrasses are fairly self-explanatory. Remember that turf is the largest water-using dry-land plant type. All desert turfs have a winter or summer dormancy period and must be rotated with other species to maintain a constant green surface.

Cacti, succulents, yuccas, desert grasses and desert spoons include native, naturalized, or introduced, desert-type plant materials. All, with the exception of the grasses, have a fleshy cellular structure which enables the plant to shrink and swell or open and close in response to the availability of moisture. The cacti, succulents, and yuccas possess CAM. The grasses and spoons are desert adapted and use leaf curling as a protection device against sun exposure and to reduce transpiration rates. This is a broad category that could invite a lot of argument. The common denominator among the plants in this category is that they are desert specific and none easily fits into any other category.

Bulbs, corms, tubers, and rhizomes are all specialized reproductive tissues which have evolved to guarantee faster, more efficient plant propagation, and thus enhance the chances for survival of the species. Bulbs are specialized leaf tissue, while corms, tubers, and rhizomes are specialized stems or branches in one form or another. All set at or just below the soil surface and are capable of root and top growth formation when they receive the proper environmental conditions. What is important to note is that these plants, by and large, require seasonal or biseasonal lifting from the soil and some method of dividing. This type of plant material has not been frequently used in the desert. They require generally moist soils at specific times of the year to trigger their growth and flower production cycles. Most of the species mentioned in this section are grown for their floral display.

Aquatic plants include in-water and lake-edge, bog-type species. Given the number of lakes, ponds, and water features used as oases in desert design, it is my opinion that this category of plant material is grossly underused.

The annuals described were primarily chosen for their floral show. Rotation of annual color in the desert usually occurs biannually. Annuals are given a place of great importance for the entry definition of most developments. Annuals are also used frequently to provide spot color in pots and planters. An attempt is made to not only include the usual favorites, but also to recommend some newcomers that can provide some variety and, quite possibly, renew the viewer's attention.

Wildflowers are perhaps the most ambiguous category. These include primarily annuals sown from seed for the purposes of providing seasonal color and some ground plane stabilization. The mixes are not depicted within the classification matrixes because several of the categories do not apply. An explanation of the purpose of each mix is provided. In most cases the mix is structured to overall size in terms of height and bulk. Species are selected to provide as much year round color rotation as possible. Although these mixes, when established, could survive on seasonal rain, they fare better with occasional irrigation just prior to their most prolific bloom periods. They also need some supplemental irrigation at the time of their initial sowing to assure germination and establishment.

The Plant Classification Matrix

The classification matrix, for the most part, is self-explanatory. Most of the categories are well defined through the course of the chapter. Sizes indicated relate to average mature growth. Individual specimens can be larger or smaller due to site-specific cultural and environmental conditions. The sizes given, however, are an accurate reflection of what can be expected under normal circumstances. To round out definitions for the Plant Compendium, the terms "oasis," "transitional," and "desert" are used to describe where plants may best be employed in the planting plan. This coincides with the feather-to-desert concept mentioned in the design chapter, and gives the reader a brief insight into environmental requirements and planting composition by cultural and watering demands.

Recommending plant placement in the oasis, transition, or desert zones is often a matter of personal opinion and taste. The reader and other designers may have valid reasons to question these opinions based on criteria or tastes that I am unaware of. It should be noted, however, that the placements recommended are also based on what is believed to be the area(s) that best guarantees the prosperity and survival of any given species.

Water requirements fall into the general categories of low, moderate, or high. It will aid irrigation design if plants with similar water requirements are grouped together. Notice that these groupings usually follow the break out of the plant's macro zone preferences when using natives and micro zone preferences when using introduced material. Generally, more water is available at a higher macro zone elevation or a shadier micro zone classification.

The leaf habit category pertains to the tendency of a plant to either stay in leaf year round or to be barren for a certain period of time. Evergreen means the plant is in leaf throughout its lifetime. Semievergreen, as it applies to this text, means that the plant is normally in leaf except during periods of cold or drought stress, during which time it will drop its leaves. Deciduous means that a plant under discussion will definitely lose its leaves for a specific period during each and every year. The most unpredictable plants in this category are the semievergreens because their changes are weather dependent, and the weather itself cannot be predicted.

Flower show pertains to what time of year a plant predictably will flower. Spring equates to late February to mid-May. Summer encompasses mid-May to late August. Fall equates to mid-September through November. Winter includes December, January, and early February. Note that all angiosperms flower in one form or another. The plants shown under this category in the matrixes are only those that have a flower show that is significant enough to be considered as a factor in design application.

Fall color is another ambiguous heading. Most deciduous material, in the desert setting, turns color in December, which has previously been defined as winter. The reason the category is termed 'fall color' is because colorful displays of leaf color usually occurs in autumn in eastern and midwestern states. Large numbers of people subconsciously think of leaves turning color and eventually dying as something that happens in fall. Suffice it to say that if a plant is in this category, it can frequently be relied upon to come into fall color right before the Christmas holidays. As with flower show, some trees that are deciduous do not necessarily display a colorful fall leaf show. Those trees not deemed to have a significant fall color show are not indicated in the matrixes.

The star performer category should be examined closely. The plants grouped herein are not to be viewed as being indestructible. The intent of this grouping is to single out plants that will yield the greatest chance of success if utilized in conjunction with their proper macro and micro zones while receiving the appropriate amount of irrigation. Star performers are selected based on experience and observation. In planting areas that cause concern, they are the best possible selection for the situation. There are many plants not chosen as star performers that could possibly do equally as well.

No plant list or compendium will ever be complete or be to the liking of any given reviewer. One helpful hint to remember when researching other texts, nurseries, or botanic gardens is to look for new or previously unknown plants within a genus that has provided useful selections in the past. Also, new hybrids and cultivars are constantly being developed from the more popular species.

The Plant Compendium Summary

This compendium is intended to act as a point of departure for desert designers. It is doubtful that this, or any other plant reference resource, will ever be complete. To try to keep them all in mind at one time would be mind boggling and cause enough indecision to immobilize a designer. Good references are a must. Charts and well-organized matrixes help tremendously. But in the final analysis, it will be the designer's dedication and conscientious effort to provide the best possible planting scheme that will improve and advance the cause of planting design.

Tree Physiology

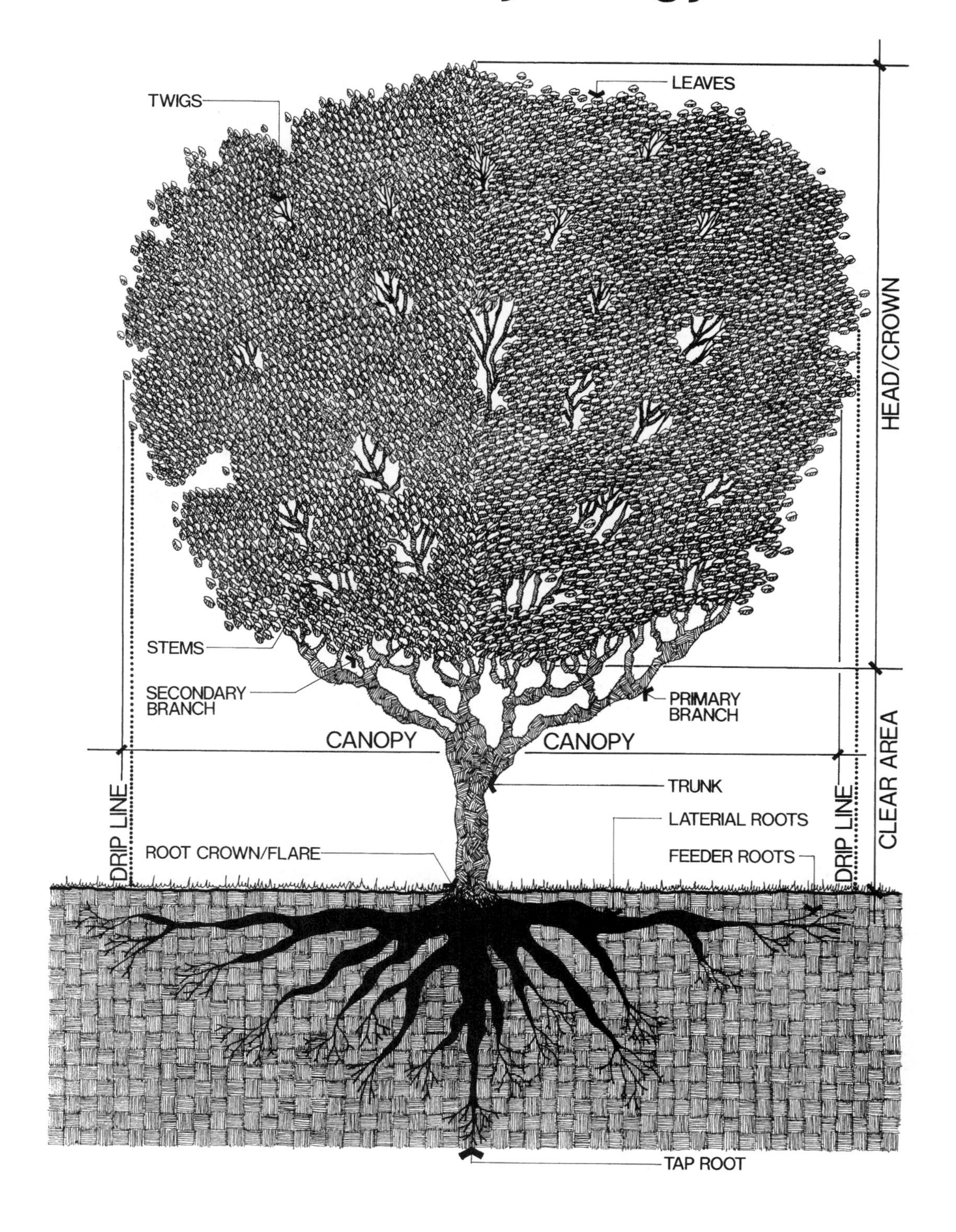

Plant Physiology

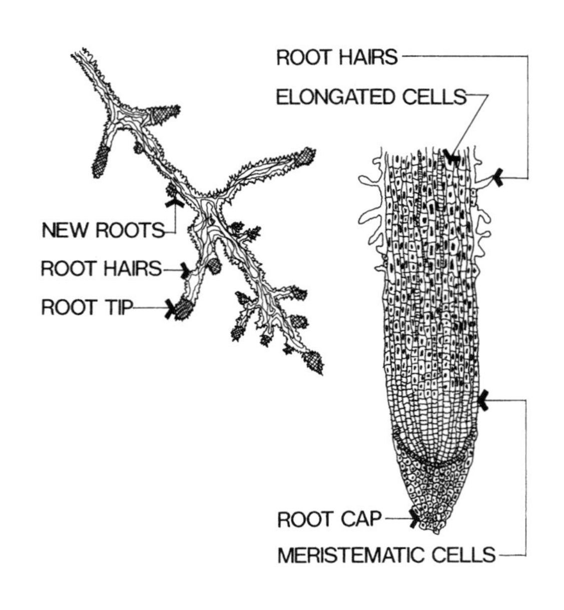
ROOT HAIRS
ELONGATED CELLS
NEW ROOTS
ROOT HAIRS
ROOT TIP
ROOT CAP
MERISTEMATIC CELLS
ROOTS

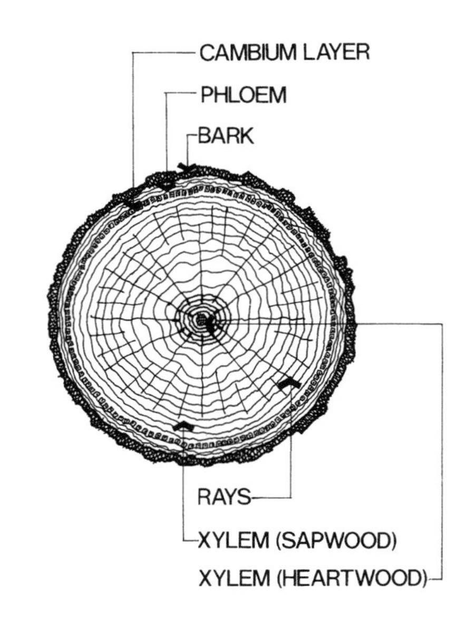
CAMBIUM LAYER
PHLOEM
BARK
RAYS
XYLEM (SAPWOOD)
XYLEM (HEARTWOOD)
DICOT STEM

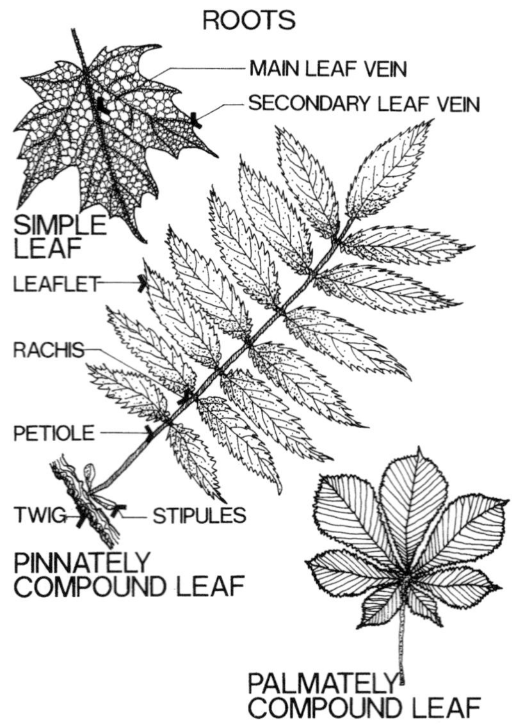
MAIN LEAF VEIN
SECONDARY LEAF VEIN
SIMPLE LEAF
LEAFLET
RACHIS
PETIOLE
TWIG
STIPULES
PINNATELY COMPOUND LEAF
PALMATELY COMPOUND LEAF

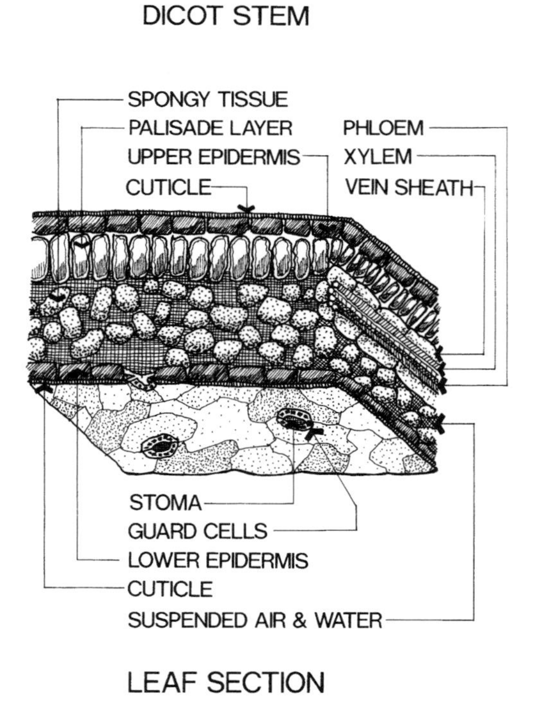
SPONGY TISSUE
PALISADE LAYER
UPPER EPIDERMIS
CUTICLE
PHLOEM
XYLEM
VEIN SHEATH
STOMA
GUARD CELLS
LOWER EPIDERMIS
CUTICLE
SUSPENDED AIR & WATER
LEAF SECTION

Plant Reproduction

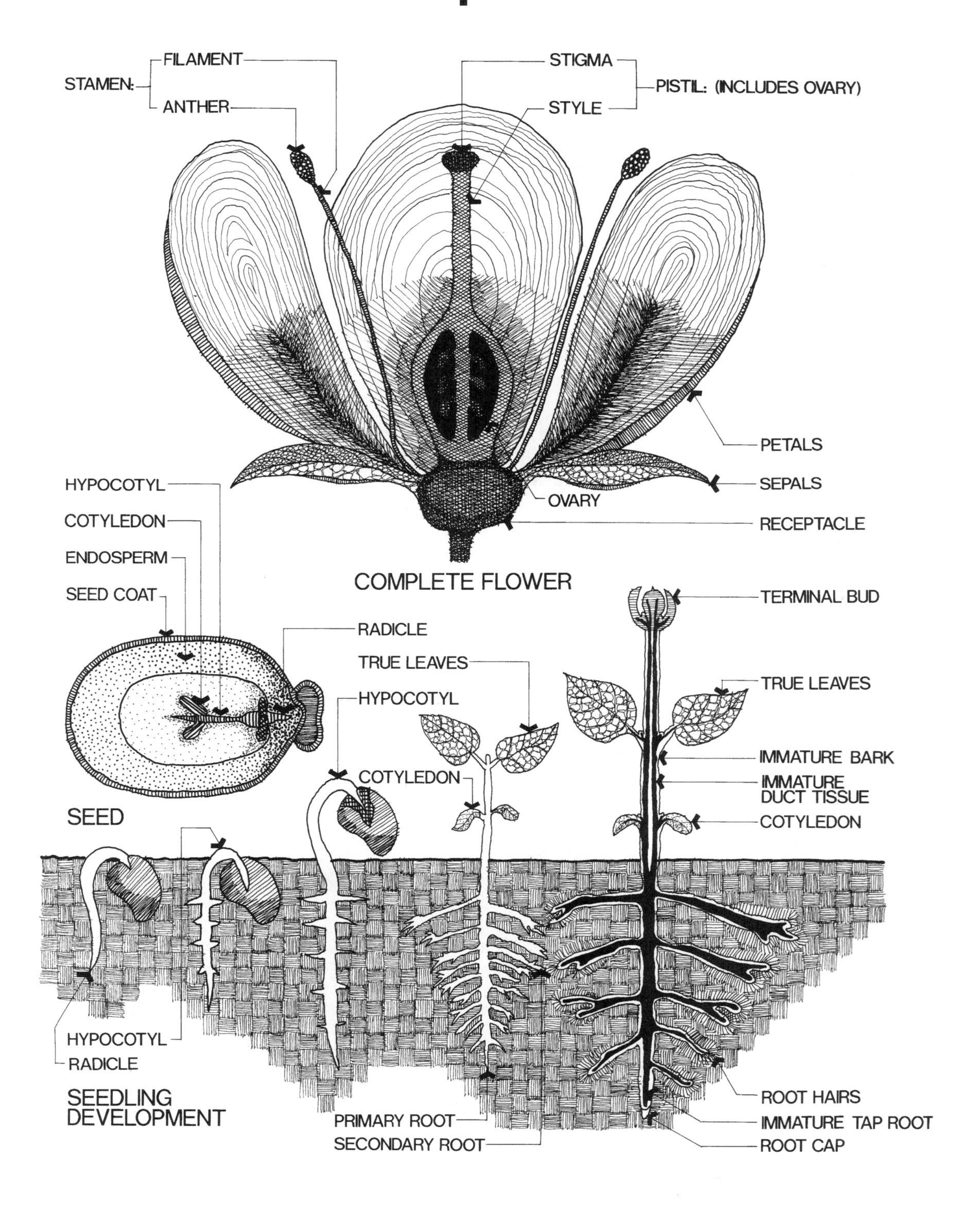
STAMEN:
FILAMENT
ANTHER
STIGMA
STYLE
PISTIL: (INCLUDES OVARY)
PETALS
SEPALS
OVARY
RECEPTACLE
COMPLETE FLOWER
HYPOCOTYL
COTYLEDON
ENDOSPERM
SEED COAT
RADICLE
SEED
TRUE LEAVES
HYPOCOTYL
COTYLEDON
TERMINAL BUD
TRUE LEAVES
IMMATURE BARK
IMMATURE DUCT TISSUE
COTYLEDON
HYPOCOTYL
RADICLE
SEEDLING DEVELOPMENT
PRIMARY ROOT
SECONDARY ROOT
ROOT HAIRS
IMMATURE TAP ROOT
ROOT CAP

Plant Orders

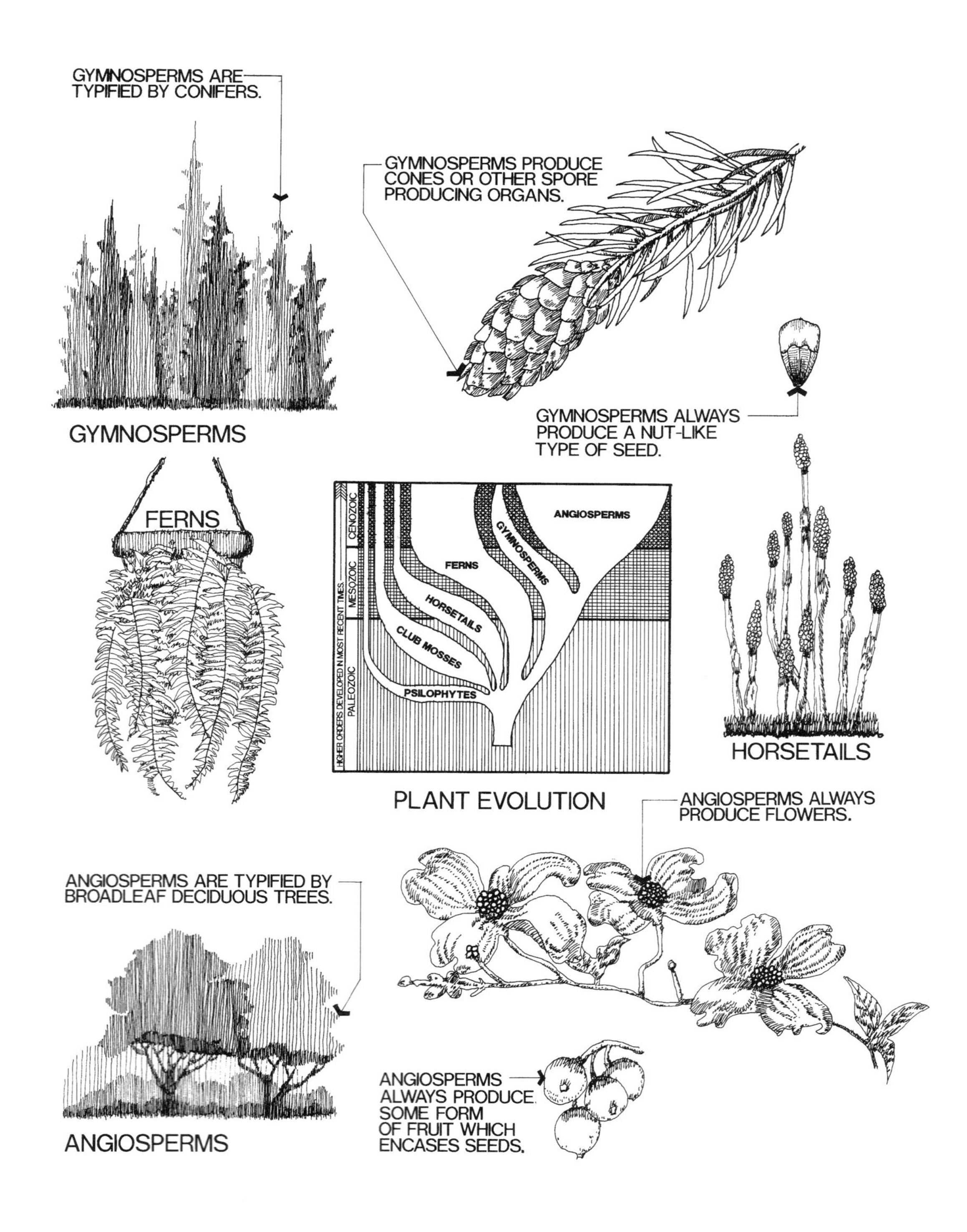
GYMNOSPERMS ARE TYPIFIED BY CONIFERS.
GYMNOSPERMS PRODUCE CONES OR OTHER SPORE PRODUCING ORGANS.
GYMNOSPERMS
GYMNOSPERMS ALWAYS PRODUCE A NUT-LIKE TYPE OF SEED.
FERNS
CENOZOIC
MESOZOIC
PALEOZOIC
HIGHER ORDERS DEVELOPED IN MOST RECENT TIMES
ANGIOSPERMS
GYMNOSPERMS
FERNS
HORSETAILS
CLUB MOSSES
PSILOPHYTES
PLANT EVOLUTION
HORSETAILS
ANGIOSPERMS ALWAYS PRODUCE FLOWERS.
ANGIOSPERMS ARE TYPIFIED BY BROADLEAF DECIDUOUS TREES.
ANGIOSPERMS
ANGIOSPERMS ALWAYS PRODUCE SOME FORM OF FRUIT WHICH ENCASES SEEDS.

Micro-Planting Zones

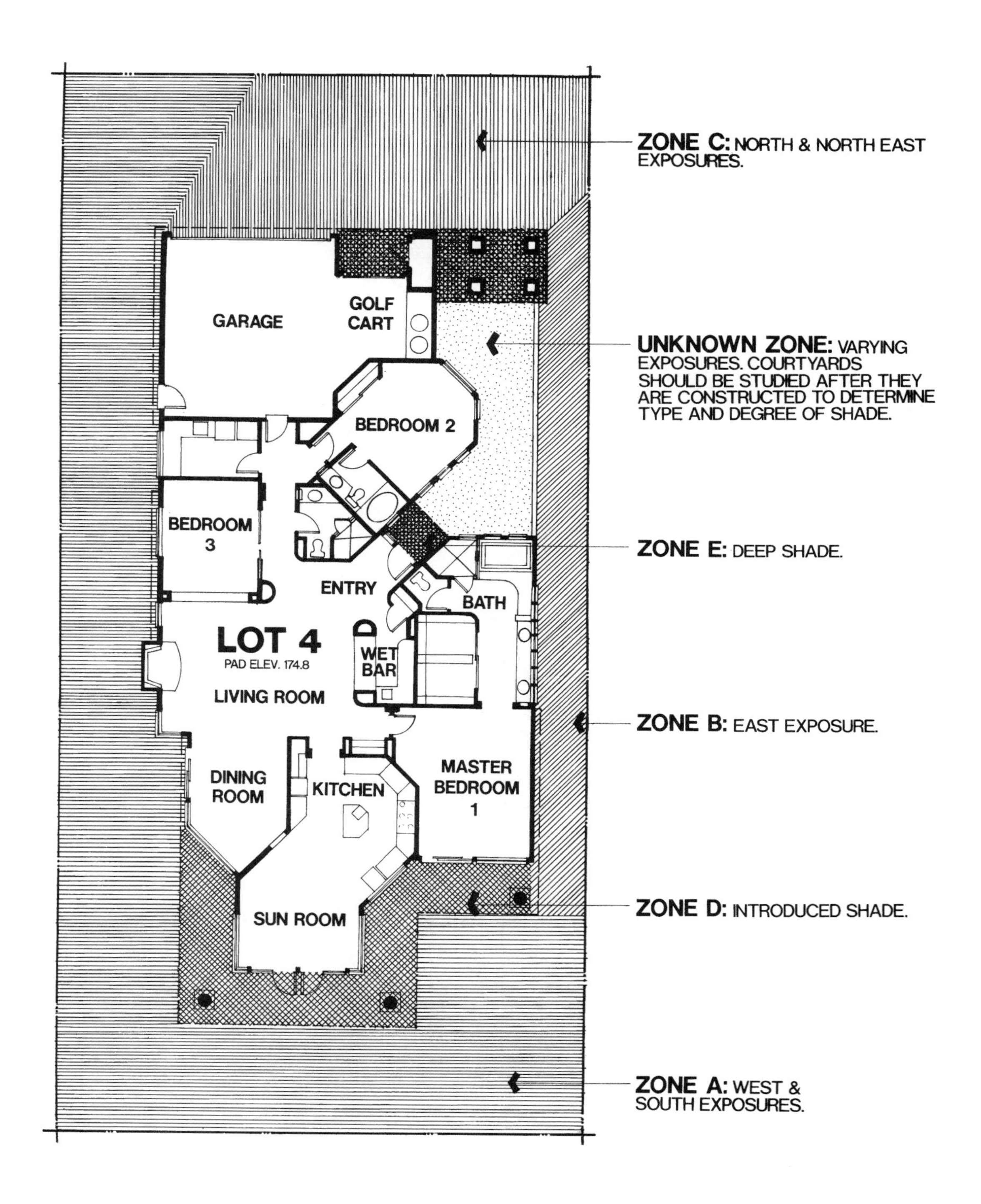
ZONE C: NORTH & NORTH EAST EXPOSURES.
UNKNOWN ZONE: VARYING EXPOSURES. COURTYARDS SHOULD BE STUDIED AFTER THEY ARE CONSTRUCTED TO DETERMINE TYPE AND DEGREE OF SHADE.
ZONE E: DEEP SHADE.
ZONE B: EAST EXPOSURE.
ZONE D: INTRODUCED SHADE.
ZONE A: WEST & SOUTH EXPOSURES.
GARAGE
GOLF CART
BEDROOM 2
BEDROOM 3
ENTRY
BATH
LOT 4
PAD ELEV. 174.8
WET BAR
LIVING ROOM
DINING ROOM
KITCHEN
MASTER BEDROOM 1
SUN ROOM

Macro-Planting Zones/Native Vegetation

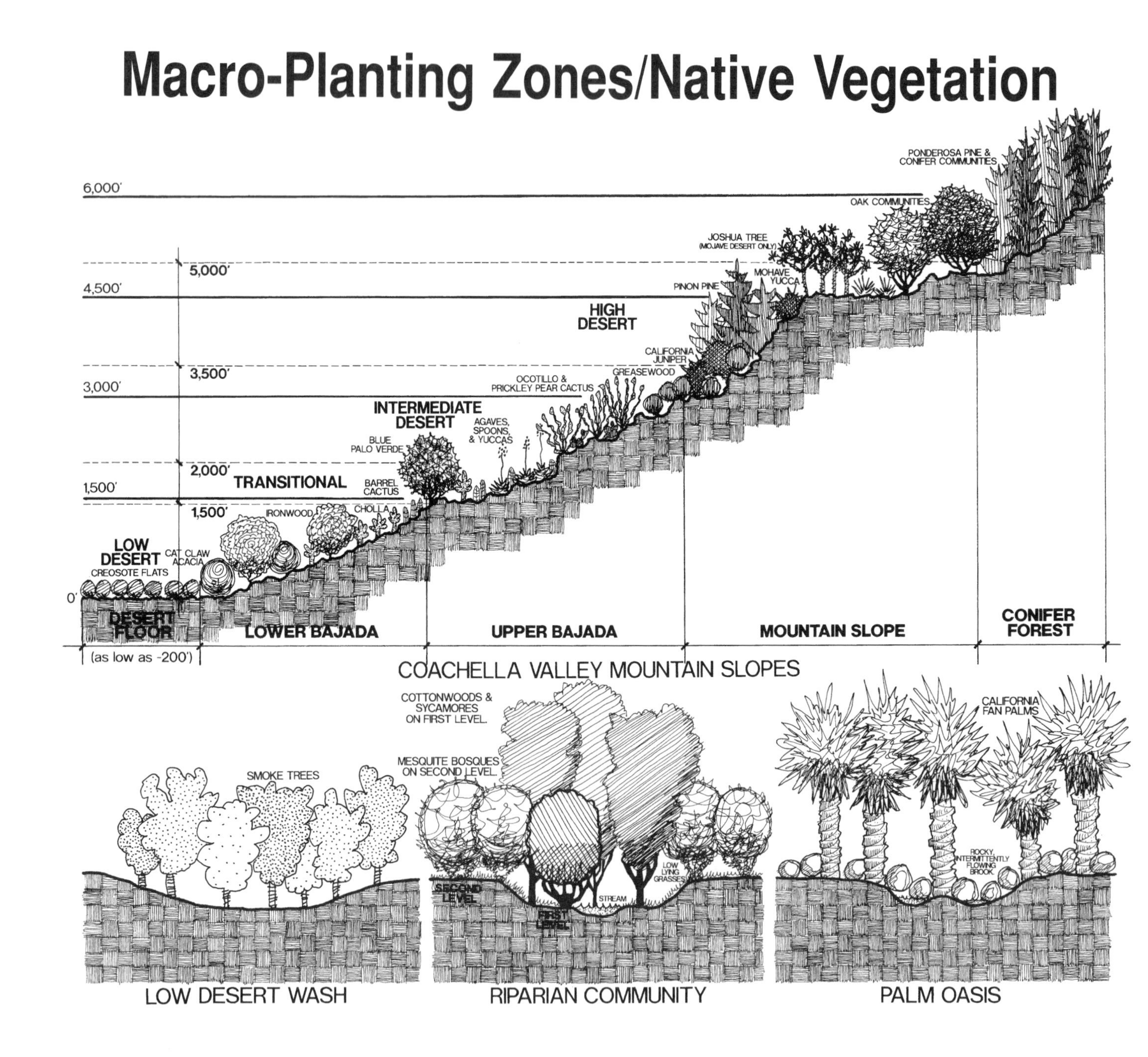

PONDEROSA PINE & CONIFER COMMUNITIES
6,000'
OAK COMMUNITIES
JOSHUA TREE (MOJAVE DESERT ONLY)
5,000'
4,500'
PINON PINE
MOHAVE YUCCA
HIGH DESERT
CALIFORNIA JUNIPER
3,500'
GREASEWOOD
OCOTILLO & PRICKLEY PEAR CACTUS
3,000'
INTERMEDIATE DESERT
AGAVES, SPOONS, & YUCCAS
BLUE PALO VERDE
2,000'
TRANSITIONAL
BARREL CACTUS
1,500'
1,500'
IRONWOOD
CHOLLA
LOW DESERT
CAT CLAW ACACIA
CREOSOTE FLATS
0'
DESERT FLOOR
LOWER BAJADA
UPPER BAJADA
MOUNTAIN SLOPE
CONIFER FOREST
(as low as -200')
COACHELLA VALLEY MOUNTAIN SLOPES
COTTONWOODS & SYCAMORES ON FIRST LEVEL
MESQUITE BOSQUES ON SECOND LEVEL
SMOKE TREES
CALIFORNIA FAN PALMS
ROCKY, INTERMITTENTLY FLOWING BROOK
LOW LYING GRASSES
SECOND LEVEL
FIRST LEVEL
STREAM
LOW DESERT WASH
RIPARIAN COMMUNITY
PALM OASIS

Graphic Legend-Type Planting Plan

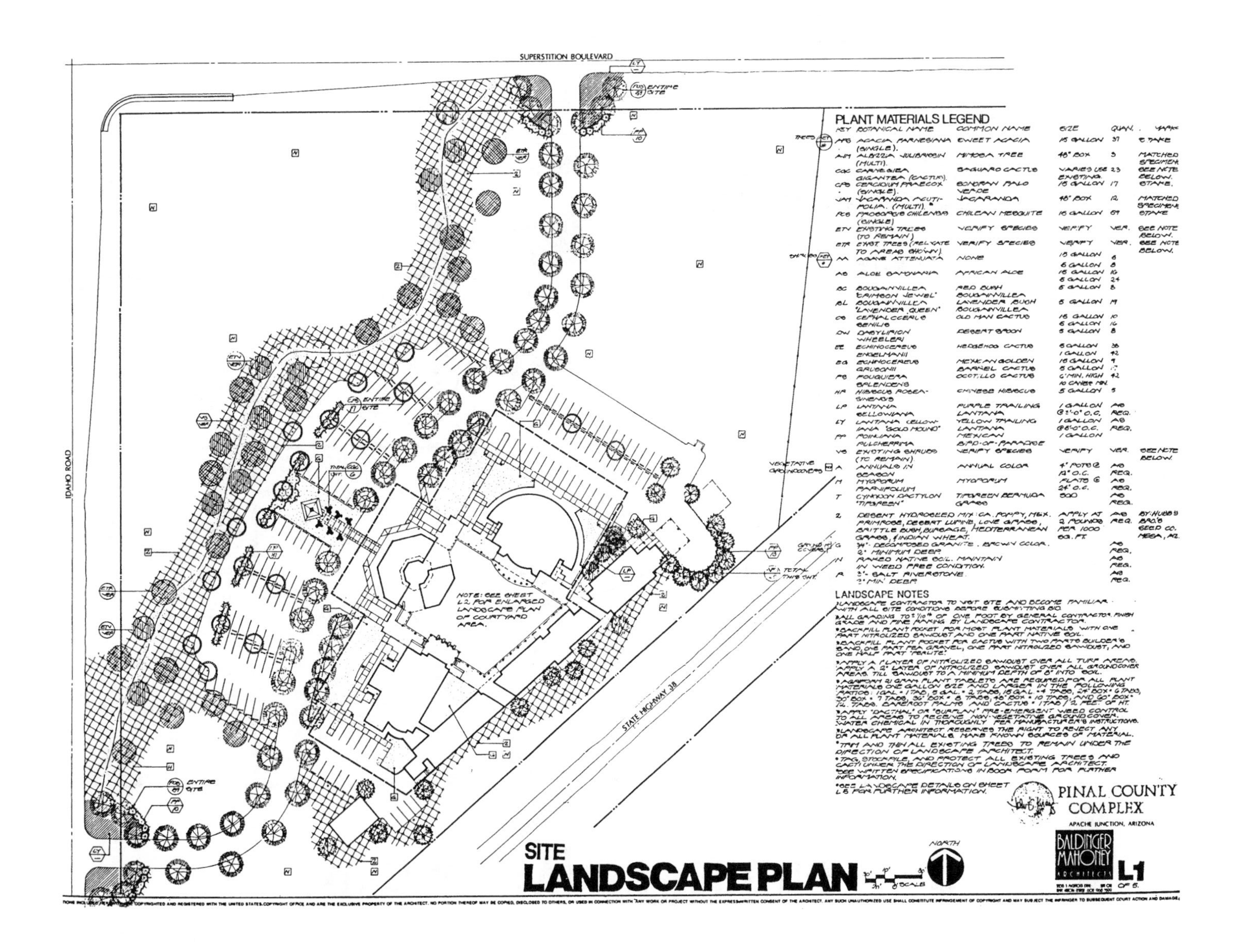

Symbol-Type Planting Plan

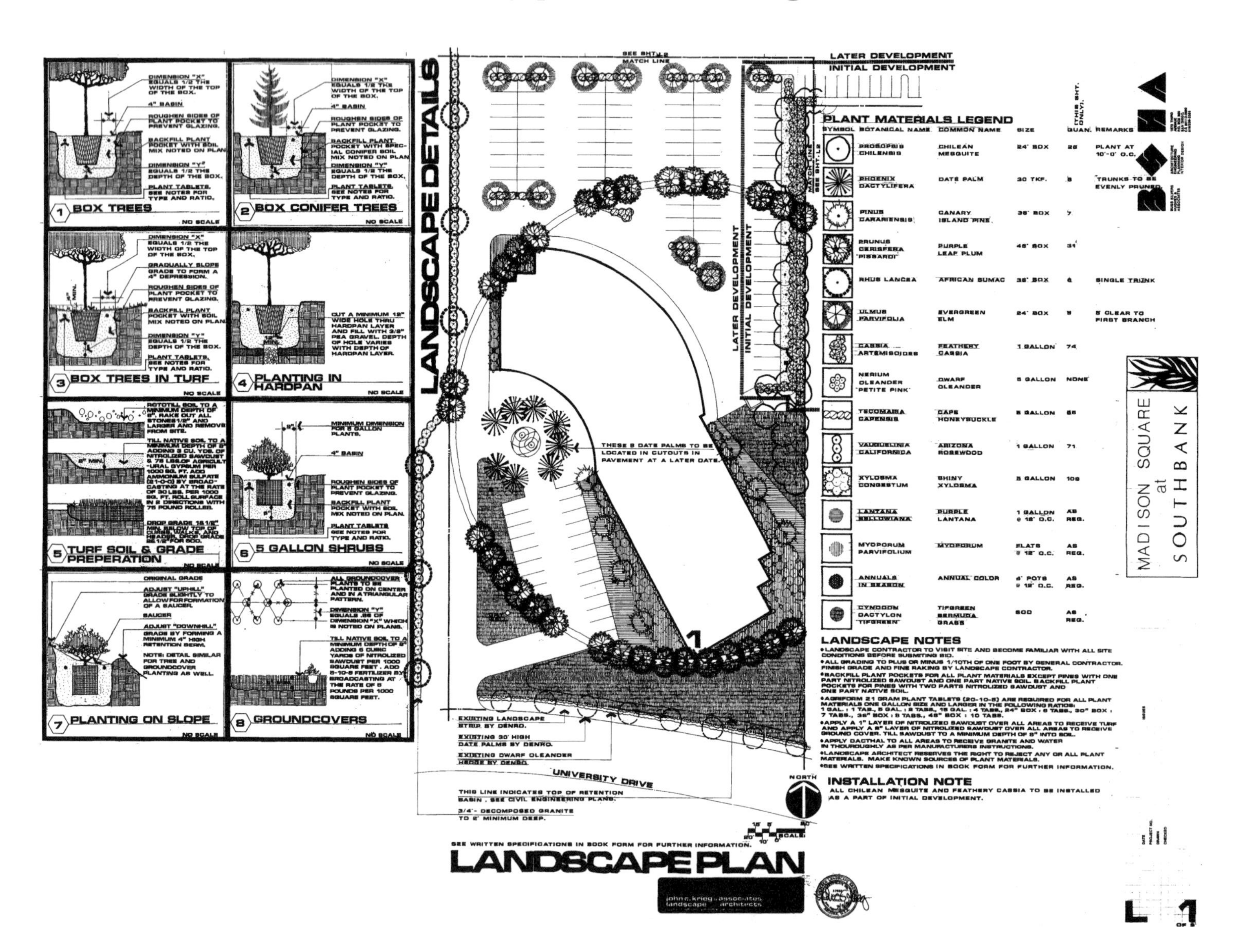

Plant Materials

Morea Lily

Hibiscus

Confetti Lantana

Dwarf Zinnias

Plant Materials

Staked Bougainvilleas

Bush Bougainvilleas

Plumbago and Texas Ranger

Russian Sage

Jacaranda in summer

Ornamental Cacti and Succulents

Cacti on nursery bench

Hanging cacti and succulents

Variegated Euphorbia

Euphorbia

Cactus in Bloom

Fishhook Barrel Cactus

Glossary

Abiotic: Nonbiotic factors: wind, rain, sun exposure, temperature, gravity.

Acidic soil: Soil that ranges from 0 to 6.9 on the pH scale.

Aeration: Degree to which air pockets exist in soil.

Age distribution (demographics): The ranges of ages within plant or animal populations. This will show whether the population is on the rise, at a steady state, or on the decline.

Alkaline soil: Soil that ranges from 7.1 to 14 on the pH scale.

Amendments: Organic or inorganic matter and materials added to a soil to improve its plant growing capability.

Angiosperms: The highest group of plant materials and the most recent to appear on the evolutionary scale. Most notable characteristics are method of flower production and seed development within enclosed ovaries.

Annual: A plant that completes its entire life cycle within one growing season.

Antidesiccants (antitranspirants): Oils and other chemicals sprayed on plant materials to reduce moisture loss due to transpiration. Used frequently during transplanting and installation operations, especially in hot or windy weather.

Anther: The uppermost segment of a stamen that contains the pollen. Part of the male sex organs in the flower structure of an angiosperm.

Apical dominance: The characteristic inherent in a terminal (end) bud to repress the growth rate of lateral (downstream) buds. Because it grows first and fastest it is dominant. Apical dominance is especially important to the main vertical stem of a tree as this stem determines the overall height and shape of the tree's canopy.

Areole: Specialized growth nodes on the ribs and pads of cactus species giving rise to thorns.

Avoiders: That group of plants whose primary survival strategy is to simply avoid adverse climatic conditions (temperature and moisture) through the process of winter or summer deciduousness or, most frequently, annualism.

Bark: Technically refers to all trunk branch or stem tissue that lies outside the phloem. Colloquially refers to the outermost "seen" portions of a plant that are not leaves, flowers, or fruit.

Biennual: A plant that completes its entire life cycle within two growing seasons.

Biosphere: The earth and all the environmental and biological processes that occur within its atmosphere.

Biotic: Life or life conditions of living organisms.

Blade: The flattest, widest, and largest part of a leaf.

Blowsand: Fine sand particles transported by wind to foreign areas. Blowsand is frequently unwanted and of little to no nutrient value.

Botanist: An individual who by education and training is adept at some phase of plant biology, including plant identification and plant morphology.

Botany: The science of plants and plant life.

Branches: Conductive and support organs. Usually of an angled or horizontal disposition. Smaller than the trunk and larger than stems or twigs. Likewise, occurs after the trunk and before the twigs in a tree's crown. Branches often give the head of a tree its visual character.

Bud: Fleshy outgrowth from a stem which can give rise to leaf, flower, or additional stem tissue.

Bulb: Modified leaf tissue formed into fleshy, conical underground storage structures. Bulbs represent that given species most efficient propagative strategy.

Cacti: Usually leafless, succulent plants which frequently possess spines (modified leaves) that originate from areoles. Contain a pronounced cortex, significant inner pith tissue, and the ability to shrink and swell their girth rapidly, as a method of storing available moisture. Utilize crassulacean acid metabolism to manufacture food.

Calcium: A micronutrient utilized in the growth and functioning of plants.

Caliche (calcium carbonate): Layer of soil (stratum) that is extremely dense and impermeable to moisture. Formed due to high concentrations of calcium carbonate. A layer of caliche must be carved or broken through to more permeable soil layers so that drainage can be provided for adequate plant growth.

Calyx: Starting at the base of a flower, this is the collective name given to all the sepals. The calyx is most frequently green and leaf-like in appearance.

Canopy: Term used to describe the underside of a tree's crown or head. Often used interchangeably with crown.

Cambium: Thin layer of meristematic (growth initiating) cells. The cambium lies between the xylem and phloem and forms the growth cells for both these critical conductive tissues. Since the plant cannot live without functioning xylem and phloem, a severed (girdled) cambium that does not come in contact with a growing medium (soil/water) will result in the death of the plant. Plant propagation by cuttings is performed by cutting and exposing as many young cambium cells as possible to a growing medium.

Carbohydrates: Food manufactured by plants as a result of the process of photosynthesis.

Carnivore: An animal that eats herbivores, omnivores, and other carnivores for food. Carnivores occupy the highest and smallest level in the food chain.

Carpellate: Consisting of carpels — e.g., female pine cones.

Carrying capacity: The amount of plant and animal life an ecosystem can adequately sustain.

Cell: The basic unit of life. Contains protoplasm (living matter), which in the case of plants, is surrounded by a cell wall.

Cellulose: Nonliving component that comprises the majority of the cell wall. As such, it comprises most of the woody tissue in plant materials.

Chelated fertilizer: A fertilizer in water soluble form.

Chlorophyll: Green pigment in plant cells that is essential in the absorption of light to aid the process of photosynthesis. The photosynthetic process also produces chlorophyll so the cell and the process perpetuate one another.

Chlorosis: Yellowing of leaf margins that indicates an absence of usable iron.

Class: Level of plant and animal classification. Occurs below kingdom and above family.

Climate: Average (mean) weather conditions of a regional or area that can normally be expected to occur over a specific period of time.

Climax: The highest plant community in an ecosystem arrived at through the process of succession.

Complete fertilizer: A fertilizer with measurable amounts of all three macronutrients — nitrogen (N), phosphorus (P), and potassium (K).

Complete flower: A flower containing both male (stamens) and female (pistil) parts in conjunction with petals and sepals.

Cohesion: The force that causes molecules to join (stick) together.

Community: Grouping of different populations within a defined area.

Composting: Stockpiling nutrient rich organic material and allowing it to decompose. The resulting mixture of materials is used as a soil amendment.

Compound leaf: A leaf comprised of two or more leaflets.

Cones: Sexual structures of the conifers that can be likened to male and female flowers. The male (staminate) cone eventually produces pollen which fertilizes the female (carpellate) cone. Male cones are small and fall quickly from the tree. Female cones are larger, take a long time to ripen and open to disperse seeds before eventually falling from the tree.

Conifers: Plants belonging to the gymnosperm class. Typified by modified leaves called needles. Most but not all are evergreen. Pines are the most recognizable conifers.

Controlled-release fertilizer: Pelleted fertilizer that is oil-coated so that it will decompose over a predictable period of time.

Corm: Modified stem tissue formed into fleshy underground storage structures. Most efficient method of propagation in species having them.

Corolla: Occurs above the calyx. Term used to jointly describe all the petals. Term is frequently used to describe ray flowers. (See Ray flower.)

Cortex: That tissue of a stem or root lying immediately inside the epidermis. In cacti and succulents the cortex is thick and serves as the primary layer of outer tissue which contains the inner pith.

Cotyledon(s): Embryonic leaves. The first leaves to appear after germination. Cotyledons are not true leaves. Plants with one cotyledon are become monocots and plants with two or more cotyledons are become dicots.

Crown: Refers to the size and shape of a tree's head, when in leaf.

Cuticle: A waxlike covering over the epidermis.

Cultivar: A hybrid plant material that can be reproduced (usually vegetatively) with its special characteristics kept intact.

Deciduous: Plants that lose their leaves for a predictable period during each growing season.

Density: In terms of plant or animal populations, this defines the number of individuals located within a specific area.

Dicots: Flowering plants which produce two or more seed leaves at germination.

Dioecious: Plants that produce separate male and female flowers on separate plants.

Disclimax: A plant environment that is not allowed to attain its climax plant community is said to be held in a state of disclimax. This is most frequently done with agricultural and timber crops for economic reasons.

Drip line: The area of ground lying directly underneath the outermost edges of a tree's crown. This area will receive the most rainwater in the natural state and will logically contain the largest concentration of subsurface feeder roots.

Edaphic: Pertaining to soil and soil characteristics.

Endosperm: Food storage tissue which occurs in seeds. Surrounds the seed embryo and supplies energy at germination until the seedling has grown to the capacity to start manufacturing its own food.

Energy: Strength or power in action. The capacity of doing or being converted to do work. Energy can be solar, chemical, electrical, etc.

Entire (simple) leaf: Independent leaf blades arising from a single petiole.

Epidermis: The outermost cellular layer in roots, stems, and leaves.

Espalier: Trees or shrubs pruned and trained to lie flat against a wall.

Eutropy: The natural process of aging.

Evergreen: Plants that do not predictably lose their leaves during any given growing season.

Eury: Describing organisms that are tolerant of a wide spectrum of environmental conditions.

Exotic: Technically, any plant that is introduced into any area that would not have the ability to naturalize in that area if left to its own devices. In southwest landscape trades, the term frequently implies tender and tropical plant material.

Family: Plant classification category lower than order and higher than genus. Includes plants that are related by a broad range of characteristics.

Fibrous root system: Plants that have a wide spreading root system and an insignificant or absent taproot.

Field capacity: The maximum volume of water soil can hold by cohesion before releasing it to drainage.

Filament: Stalk like part of the floral male sex organ. The filament of the stamen supports the anther.

Flower: The reproductive organs of plants within the angiosperms.

Food pyramid: A graphic depiction illustrating that higher organisms require more energy than lower organisms and, therefore, are fewer in number. Less sophisticated organisms (e.g., Algae), capable of manufacturing their own food, comprise the base of the pyramid. Also referred to as a food chain.

Fruit: A ripened ovary encasing seeds.

Gametophyte: The sexual generation in a plant's live cycle.

Genus: Plant classification category lower than family and higher than species. Genus characteristics are so recognizable that narrow groups of plants can be identified.

Geotropism: An organism's response to the forces of gravity.

Germination: The process by which an embryonic plant breaks out of the seed coat and commences its individual life span.

Girdling: Any process that completely severs the cambium layer in the trunk of a tree causing it to die.

Ground cover: Low-lying, wide-spreading plant material under 18 inches in height.

Growth form (rate): Rate at which a population increases.

Guaranteed analysis: The actual percentage or amount of macronutrients (N,P,K) in any given bag of fertilizer. Usually clearly indicated on the label.

Guard cells: Small cells within the leaf epidermis that occur in direct association with the stomata. The guard cells determine the size of the opening in the stomata at any given point in time under varying sets of circumstances.

Gymnosperms: Second highest group of plant materials. Occurring just before the angiosperms on the evolutionary scale. Plants produce seeds (usually in conjunction with pine cones) but do not produce true fruit.

Habitat: The specific region an organism inhabits.

Hardiness: Term used to define a plant's degree of tolerance to cold.

Herbivore: An animal that eats plants exclusively for food. Occupies a lower level on the food chain. Thus there will always be more herbivores than carnivores.

Hermaphrodite: A plant that produces perfect flowers. All hermaphrodites are monoecious.

High desert zone: Macro planting zone which occurs at 3500 feet in elevation and exists to 5000 feet. Lies between the intermediate desert zone and the conifer forest zone, which comes into being above 5000 feet.

Hybridization: Breeding of individuals within a species to take advantage of superior gene characteristics. A hybrid will often exceed the parent plants in one or more areas.

Hydrotropism: An organism's response to the presence of water.

Hypocotyl: An embryonic stem that appears after germination and supports the seedling until more mature stem tissue begins to form.

Intermediate desert zone: Macro planting zone which occurs at 1500 feet in elevation and exists to 3500 feet. Lies between the transitional zone and the high desert zone.

Internode: Branch or stem area that lies between two nodes.

Iron: Micronutrient utilized in the growth and functioning of plants.

Kingdom: Highest classification category for all life on earth. An organism is placed in a kingdom, as the point of departure to its scientific identification.

Lamella: Same as a leaf blade. The largest flattened part of a leaf.

Landscape architect: An individual who by training, experience, and licensing is capable of designing outdoor spaces, doing environmental studies, and selecting plant materials suitable for a specific region. A landscape architect is primarily concerned with resource conservation and stewardship of the land so that it serves its highest and best purpose.

Lateral bud: Buds that occur on a branch or stem below the apical or terminal buds.

Leader: Shoot that terminates a trunk, branch, or stem which is the point of continuation for the next season's growth.

Leaf habit: As it applies to this book, a Compendium category that defines a plant as being deciduous, semievergreen, or evergreen.

Leaf stalk: Specialized stem which supports a leaf. (See Petiole.)

Leaf veins: Noticeable round lines that occur in geometric patterns across the leaf blade. These veins are conductors, consisting of xylem and of phloem tissue.

Leaves: Flattened tissue arising from stems that typically houses the cellular structures that perform the process of photosynthesis.

Lignin: Aside from cellulose, the principal components of cell walls and a major component of wood.

Limiting factor: That climatic, edaphic, or biotic factor that is limited or missing and thus will inhibit plant growth.

Limits of tolerance: Degree to which an organism can survive with or without certain climatic, edaphic, or biotic conditions.

Linnaeus: Individual who developed the system of plant and animal classification in use today.

Loam: A soil containing equal or near equal parts of silt, sand, and clay. Loam is a fine planting soil which, with the addition of organic matter, can rate as exceptional soil.

Lobed leaf: A simple leaf with noticeable indentations.

Low desert zone: Macro planting zone which occurs at sea level or the desert floor and exists to 1,500 in elevation. Abuts the transitional zone.

Lower epidermis: Outermost layer of leaf tissue occurring on the underside (bottom) of a leaf. Contains guard cells and stomata.

Macrogametophyte: In gymnosperms, an ovary-like structure at the base of a scale on a carpelate cone that receives pollination from male cones. This gametophyte eventually matures into a seed that is dispersed when the female (carpelate) cone opens.

Macronutrients: Nitrogen (N), phosphorous (P), and potassium (K).

Macro planting zones: Low desert, transition zone, intermediate desert, and high desert.

Magnesium: A micronutrient utilized in the growth and functioning of plants.

Mechanical analysis: Describes the various percentages of silt, sand, and clay particles in any given soil type.

Megasporophyll: In the gymnosperms, these occur at the underside of scales on carpellate (female) cones and mature into one or more megaspores which ripen into mega-gametophytes. See mega-gametophyte.

Meristematic cells: Cells which initiate elongated types of growth. The tips of roots and stems are pushed along further due to the growth of meristematic cells.

Meristematic tip: Outermost of the meristematic cells and the most actively splitting (growing) cells.

Micronutrients: For the purposes of this chapter, all nutrients with the exception of nitrogen, phosphorous, and potassium (N, P, K), which are macronutrients.

Micropyle: Opeing of ovule tube through which pollen can grow to reach and fertilize an egg.

Micro planting zones: Zones which occur as a result of being in direct proximity to a structure. See zones A through F.

Microsporangium: In gymnosperms these are pollen sacs produced on the underside of the scales on a staminate (male) cone. These sacs contain spores which mature into male winged pollen which developes the male gametophyte.

Monocots: Flowering plants which produce one seed leaf at germination.

Monoecious: Plants that produce both male and female organs either as separate flowers or as complete flowers on one plant.

Morphology: The science concerned with the cellular structure and overall physical makeup of plants and animals.

Mortality: Death rate within a population.

Mycorrhiza: Soil borne fungi that grow in association with and share a symbiotic relationship with root hairs.

Natality: Birth rate within a population.

Native: Refers to plant material that is indigenous to an area or region.

Naturalized: Refers to plant material that was foreign to an area or region, which has been introduced there. Due to inherent characteristics that enable the plant to adapt to the new environment, it is capable of surviving, reproducing, and spreading in its new home. Therefore, the plant has become naturalized.

Natural selection: Theory developed by Charles Darwin which postulates that the strongest members of any given species will survive, mate and produce superior offspring that will assure the survival of the species.

Nectar: Sweet, sugary substance secreted at the base of flowers through glands called nectaries that attract pollinators such as bees, hummingbirds, and flies. Bees make honey from nectar.

Nectaries: Glands which secrete nectar.

Neutral soil: Soil that tests at 7.0 on the pH scale.

Niche: The area within an ecosystem that an organism occupies and to which it is best adapted. This is called niche selection. This process lessens competition between species and contributes diversity to the ecosystem.

Nitrogen (N): A macronutrient. Promotes overall growth, but in particular, affects green (leaf) growth.

Nodes: Areas occurring at intervals along a stem where leaves and/or buds arise.

Nutrient levels: The measurable amounts of macro- and micronutrients with any given area of soil.

Organ: Discreet structure composed of tissues. The organ performs one or more specific functions within the organism.

Organic matter: Material derived from living organisms such as manure or leaf mold that is usually in a state of decomposition. Organic matter greatly enhances soil structure and fertility.

Organism: Any genetically uniform living individual. Term is most often used to refer to individual plant or animal species.

Ovary: Female reproductive structure. Ovaries ripen into some form of fruit which encases seeds.

Palisade tissue: Row of vertically arranged leaf cells that occur immediately inside the upper epidermis. Most carbohydrate production occurs in the palisade tissue.

Palmately compound leaf: Consists of separate leaflets (compound) that join very near a common leaf stalk (petiole) giving the leaves a hand-like (palm) appearance.

Perennial: A plant that lives for over teo or more growing seasons.

Perfect fllower: A flower containing both male (stamens) and female (pistil) part, but lacking petals and sepals.

Perianth: Term used to describe the calyx and corolla of a flower as a unit. Description is most frequently used when these two floral parts are the same color.

Permanent wilting point: The point at which a plant cannot draw up water fast enough to meet the rate at which it is transpiring. Unless drastic, immediate measures are taken, a plant that has reached its permanent wilting point will soon die.

Petals: Leaf-like, usually very colorful appendages of a flower occurring at the base of the ovary. This is often, but not always, the showy part of the flower.

Petiole: Specialized stem which acts a leaf stalk.

pH value: Term used to describe the level of acidity or alkalinity in soil. The pH scale ranges from 0 to 14, with 7 being neutral. 0 to 6.9 is acidic while 7.1 to 14 is alkaline.

Phloem: Conductive stem tissue which occurs inside the bark before the cambium. Phloem primarily transports manufactured nutrients to other growing parts of the plant.

Phosphorous (P): A macronutrient. Primarily aids conductive tissue (roots and stem) growth.

Photosynthesis: The process by which green plants produce sugar from carbon dioxide and water in the presence of chlorophyll while giving off oxygen as a waste product.

Phototropism: An organism's response to the presence of light.

Phreatophytes: Plants that are commonly referred to as "water spenders". In the desert, these plants grow in proximity to riparian environments. The plants simply sink their roots into a permanent water source, take up massive quantities of water, and transpire rapidly.

Pinnately compound leaf: Leaf with smaller leaflets located along a common axis (modified petiole or rachis).

Pistil: Collective term used to describe the female sex organs in angiosperms. The pistil consists of an ovary at the base, a vase-like style, and is tipped with a sticky circular structure called the stigma.

Pollen: The mass of microspores that are produced by the anther at the end of the male stamens. Pollen can be likened to animal sperm in that it serves essentially the same function in the plant kingdom. Pollen eventually fertilizes the female ovary.

Pollination: When a pollen grain sticks to the stigma at the top of the style and then develops a pollen tube which grows through the micropyle and into an ovule, pollination occurs.

Population: A grouping of the same organism type within a given area.

Potassium (K): A macronutrient. Primarily aids top growth, especially new leaf and flower production.

Rachis: A specialized petiole. The segments of a leaf stalk that occur between leaflets are collectively called a rachis.

Radicle: An embryonic root. The first growth tissue to emerge from the seed coat.

Riparian: Of or near a body of water.

Ray flower: One of the outer petaled flowers of the daisy-like heads of the composite family. The inner disk is composed of fertile flowers.

Receptacle: That part of the flower that fuses the specialized flower stem to the floral parts.

Respiration: Cellular process in plants whereby manufactured food (sugars) is oxidized to release the energy needed for cellular functioning (work). For the purposes of this chapter, how manufactured food is used within the plant.

Rhizome: A specialized stem that grows horizontally at grade or underground. Often, rhizomes are thickened and fleshy, holding food stores. When rhizomes surface they give rise to new plants. Vegetative propagation can be performed simply by separating rhizomes from the parent plant.

Root: Usually underground portion of a plant, composed of conductive tissue containing xylem, cambium, and phloem. Roots are distinguished from stems in that they do not have nodes. Roots are able to draw in water and nutrients quickly through their cellular structure. Roots also act to firmly anchor plants into their soil base.

Root cap: A protective coating at the very ends of roots (root apex) that prevents injury as the root penetrates through soil.

Salinity: As it applies to this chapter, the level of measurable soluble salts in a given soil area is referred to as the soil's level of salinity.

Seed: Embryonic plant housed in a hard protective seed coat. Often a seed will have a store of food called an endosperm that the seedling can draw nourishment from until it has matured enough to produce its own food.

Semi-evergreen: Plants that are predominately evergreen but will be either winter or drought deciduous in the event of atypical climatic conditions.

Sepals: Leaf-like appendages that occur between the receptacle and the petals. Usually green and insignificant in comparison to the petals, but not always. Bougainvilleas, for example, get their brilliant colors from sepals and the actual flower is insignificant.**Sessile:** Describes leaves that grow out directly from a stem. Leaves with no petioles.

Shrubs: For the purposes of this chapter, plants that are under 15 feet in height and comprised of many stems.

Simple fertilizer: A fertilizer that contains only one or two of the three macronutrients (N, P, K).

Slow-release fertilizer: Similar to a controlled-release fertilizer but covered with even more oil so that it will take a longer period of time to decompose.

Soil fertility: Amount of macronutrients, micronutrients, and organic matter in any given soil will determine its fertility.

Soil reaction: A soil's pH. See pH.

Soil texture: Similar to a soil's mechanical analysis but also refers to organic matter content and how a soil looks and feels to the touch.

Soils testing laboratory: A facility that performs tests on soils for mechanical analysis and fertility. Most laboratories furnish written reports as to existing soil characteristics and make recommendations as how to best improve the soil for planting.

Species: Very specific plant classification category. Defines unique individuals with definite identifiable characteristics.

Spongy tissue: Comprised of large, highly expandable cells that lie directly underneath the palisade tissue in leaves. Spongy tissue stores high amounts of water and some nutrients and makes them available to the palisade tissue for use during the process of photosynthesis.

Spores: Tiny reproductive bodies produced by plants. Pollen is a type of spore. Gymnosperms rely heavily on both male and female type spores in their reproductive processes.

Stamen: Male sex organ of angiosperms. A stamen is stalk-like and contains two main parts. The stalk itself is called a filament. The filament is topped with a rounded growth called the anther. The anther will produce pollen which is usually granular and golden yellow, and rests on the outer surface of the anther.

Staminate: Producing stamens.

Steady state: When a climax plant community is at the height of its reign, it is said to have reached a condition of steady state.

Stems: Conductive and support organs. Occur as an angled or horizontal, smaller scale extension of the trunk. Stems and twigs eventually form stalks for leaves, flowers, or fruit. In smaller sized plants, especially annuals, the term stem is frequently used to refer to the main leader(s) which directly supports leaf stalks.

Steno-: Describing organisms that can tolerate only a narrow range (spectrum) of environmental conditions.

Stigma: Uppermost part of the pistil, the female sex organ in angiosperms. Frequently sticky to aid in catching pollen grains.

Stipules: Paired, blade-like appendages at the base of the petiole. Stipules look like tiny leaves but they are not. Their real purpose is not entirely understood. Stipules do aid in plant identification.

Stoma (plural, stomata): Found on the underside of leaves. Name given to the opening or pore that allows air and gases to enter and leave the leaf to aid the processes of respiration and transpiration. Stomata are opened and closed by the guard cells.

Style: Middle part of the pistil, the female sex organ in angiosperms. Pollen grows down the style by means of a pollen tube to fertilize an ovule within the ovary.

Subspecies: See variety.

Succession: Process whereby various plant communities succeed one another (seral vegetation) until the utmost or most environmentally suited climax plant community occurs.

Succulents: Leafless plants that perform the process of photosynthesis with modified, thick, green fleshy stems. Succulents utilize crassulacean acid metabolism (CAM) to aid in the manufacture of food. Most have very waxy cuticles, a pronounced cortex, and significant inner pith tissue.

Sulfur: A micronutrient utilized in the growth and functioning of a plant.

Symbiotic relationship: As it applies to this chapter, an ecological relationship between two or more biologically different organisms in which all affected organisms derive a benefit (mutualism). As an example, roots and mycorrhiza exhibit a symbiotic relationship.

System: Specialized organ or group of organs, in conjunction with specialized tissues, that perform a specific function within an organism.

Taproot: The main root of a plant which extends vertically downward immediately below the above ground trunk. The taproot can grow very deep to locate water in an underground water table. Several desert plants (e.g., smoke tree) have pronounced taproots. Taproots also firmly anchor plants in soil.

Taxonomy: The science of plant and animal classification. Taxonomy relies on Latin which is the universal language of science.

Terminal bud: Any bud which occurs at the apex (outermost portion) of a branch, stem or twig. Terminal buds give rise to the next season's growth.

Tissue: An aggregation of similar cells have the same physiological function.

Transitional zone: Macro planting zone which occurs at 1500 to 2000 feet in elevation. Lies between the low desert zone and the intermediate desert zone.

Transpiration: Loss of water through the leaves of plants in the form of a vapor.

Tolerators: That group of plants which have developed survival strategies that allow them to cope with year-round adverse climatic conditions.

Trees: Vertically upright plant material over 15 feet in height.

Trophic level: An organism's position on the food pyramid or within the food chain.

Trunk: A plant's largest conductive organ. Supports all branches, stems, and twigs associated with the leaf crown. Trunks are typified by hardened outer bark and house the largest volume of xylem, cambium, and phloem tissue.

Tuber: Modified, fleshy, underground stems. Develops buds or eyes (e.g., potato) that can be used in vegetative propagation. Many tubers are important sources of edible food.

Turgor pressure: Pressure created within a cell when it swells with water intake. Turgor pressure stimulates guard cells to open or close stomata.

Twig: Smallest conductive organ in a plant. Arises from branches or stems and gives rise to leaf, flower, and fruit stalks.

Upper epidermis: Outermost layer of a leaf tissue occurring on the upperside (top) of a leaf. Does not contain guard cells and stomata.

Variety: A hybrid. Similar to a cultivar. Technically, a subdivision (subspecies) of a species. Varieties contain the main characteristics of the species but will differ in some noticeable way (color, size, growth rate, etc.).

Vines: Plants that climb by utilizing twining, tendrils, or suckers. Typically, vines lie flat against a vertical surface and spread flat over a horizontal surface. Vines fit into a variety of small, tight, or narrow planting situations.

Water spenders: See Phreatophytes.

Wildflowers: Annuals not typically cultivated for the domestic garden. Useful for revegetation of disturbed desert floor and hillside areas. Frequently incorporated into native hydroseed mixtures.

Xylem: Innermost conductive tissue in roots, trunks, branches, stems, twigs, and leaf veins. Used primarily to transport water. Proportionately, the largest amount of conductive tissue, as it takes approximately 20 units of water to manufacture one unit of food.

Zinc: A micro nutrient utilized in the growth and functioning of plants.

Zone A: A microzone. A structure's west and south exposures.

Zone B: A microzone. A structure's east exposure.

Zone C: A microzone. A structure's north and northeast exposures.

Zone D: A microzone. Introduced shade that can be expressed as a percentage of filtered light.

Zone E: A microzone. Deep shade caused by solid building overhangs.

Zygote: The cell produced by the fusion of gametes.

Plant Compendium

Matrix Charts

Descriptions

Trees and Palms

	MASTER PLANT MATERIALS MATRIX		ENVIRON. GROUPING				SIZE		MACRO ZONE			MICRO ZONE					DESIGN USE			WATER REQ.			LEAF HABIT			FLOWER SHOW				F. C.	★
DESCRIBED	BOTANICAL NAME	COMMON NAME	NATIVE	NATURALIZED	EXOTIC	TROPICAL	HEIGHT	WIDTH	LOW DESERT	INTERMEDIATE DESERT	HIGH DESERT	A — SUNNY	B — PART SUNNY	C — LITTLE SUNNY	D — INTRO. SHADE	E — DEEP SHADE	OASIS	TRANSITION	DESERT	LOW WATER	MODERATE WATER	HIGH WATER	EVERGREEN	SEMI EVERGREEN	DECIDUOUS	SPRING FLOWERS	SUMMER FLOWERS	FALL FLOWERS	WINTER FLOWERS	FALL COLOR	STAR PERFORMER
✔	*Acacia abyssinica*	Abyssinian Acacia			✔		30'	20'	✔	✔		✔	✔			✔		✔		✔				✔		✔					
	Acacia aneura	Mulga			✔		20'	15'		✔	✔		✔	✔			✔		✔		✔				✔		✔				
	Acacia craspedocarpa	Leather Leaf Acacia			✔		20'	15'	✔			✔	✔					✔	✔	✔				✔		✔					
	Acacia cultiformis	Knife Acacia			✔		15'	10'	✔			✔	✔					✔		✔	✔			✔		✔					
✔	*Acacia farnesiana*	Sweet Acacia		✔			25'	20'	✔			✔	✔					✔	✔		✔			✔		✔		✔			★
✔	*Acacia greggii*	Catclaw Acacia	✔				20'	15'	✔			✔							✔	✔				✔		✔					★
	Acacia pendula	Weeping Myall			✔		20'	15'	✔	✔		✔	✔				✔	✔	✔	✔	✔			✔		✔					
	Acacia salicina	Weeping Acacia			✔		25'	15'	✔	✔		✔	✔					✔	✔	✔				✔		✔					
	Acacia saligna	Weeping Wattle			✔		30'	20'	✔	✔		✔	✔					✔	✔	✔	✔			✔		✔					
	Acacia schaffneri	Wheat's Acacia			✔		20'	20'	✔	✔		✔	✔		✔		✔	✔	✔	✔	✔			✔		✔					
✔	*Acacia smallii*	Sweet Acacia		✔			25'	20'	✔			✔	✔					✔	✔		✔			✔		✔		✔			★
✔	*Acacia stenophylla*	Shoestring Acacia			✔		20'	15'	✔			✔	✔				✔	✔			✔		✔			✔		✔	✔		
✔	*Ailanthus altissima*	Tree-of-Heaven		✔			50'	30'	✔	✔	✔	✔	✔	✔	✔	✔	✔	✔		✔	✔				✔					✔	
✔	*Albizia julibrissin*	Mimosa Tree			✔		30'	40'	✔	✔	✔	✔	✔	✔	✔		✔	✔			✔				✔	✔	✔			✔	★
	Alnus rhombifolia	Alder			✔		70'	40'		✔	✔		✔	✔	✔		✔					✔			✔					✔	
	Araucaria bidwillii	Bunya Bunya			✔		80'	60'	✔				✔	✔	✔		✔			✔			✔								
✔	*Arbutus unedo*	Strawberry Tree			✔		25'	20'	✔	✔			✔	✔	✔		✔	✔		✔	✔		✔					✔			
✔	*Arecastrum romanzoffianum*	Queen Palm			✔	✔	40'	20'	✔			✔	✔		✔		✔					✔	✔								★
	Bauhinia congesta	White Orchid Tree			✔		20'	15'	✔				✔	✔	✔		✔				✔	✔			✔	✔				✔	
	Bauhinia variegata 'Candida'	White Orchid Tree			✔		20'	15'		✔			✔	✔		✔		✔				✔	✔	✔		✔	✔			✔	
	Bauhinia variegata purpurea	Purple Orchid Tree			✔		30'	20'	✔			✔	✔				✔				✔	✔			✔	✔				✔	
✔	*Beaucarnea recurvata*	Ponytail Palm			✔	✔	12'	4'	✔	✔			✔		✔		✔				✔	✔	✔								

Trees and Palms

MASTER PLANT MATERIALS MATRIX

DESCRIBED	BOTANICAL NAME	COMMON NAME	NATIVE	NATURALIZED	EXOTIC	TROPICAL	HEIGHT	WIDTH	LOW DESERT	INTERMEDIATE DESERT	HIGH DESERT	A — SUNNY	B — PART SUNNY	C — LITTLE SUNNY	D — INTRO. SHADE	E — DEEP SHADE	OASIS	TRANSITION	DESERT	LOW WATER	MODERATE WATER	HIGH WATER	EVERGREEN	SEMI EVERGREEN	DECIDUOUS	SPRING FLOWERS	SUMMER FLOWERS	FALL FLOWERS	WINTER FLOWERS	FALL COLOR	STAR PERFORMER
			ENVIRON. GROUPING				SIZE		MACRO ZONE			MICRO ZONE					DESIGN USE			WATER REQ.			LEAF HABIT			FLOWER SHOW				F. C.	★
✔	*Brachychiton populneus*	Australian Bottle Tree			✔		40'	25'	✔	✔		✔	✔	✔	✔		✔	✔			✔		✔								★
	Brahea armata	Mexican Blue Palm			✔		25'	10'	✔	✔		✔	✔				✔	✔		✔	✔		✔								
	Brahea edulis	Guadalupe Palm			✔		25'	10'	✔			✔	✔				✔	✔		✔	✔		✔								
	Butia capitata	Pindo Palm			✔		18'	12'	✔	✔		✔	✔		✔		✔	✔			✔	✔	✔								
✔	*Busera microphylla*	Elephant Tree	✔				18'	28'	✔			✔	✔						✔	✔	✔			✔							
✔	*Caesalpinia cacalaco*	Crown of Gold		✔			20'	25'		✔			✔	✔					✔	✔	✔	✔		✔			✔				
✔	*Callistemon citrinus*	Lemon Bottlebrush			✔		18'	10'	✔	✔		✔	✔					✔		✔	✔		✔			✔					
✔	*Callistemon viminalis*	Weeping Bottlebrush			✔		30'	20'	✔	✔		✔	✔					✔			✔		✔			✔					
	Catalpa speciosa	Catalpa			✔		50'	30'	✔	✔	✔	✔	✔	✔	✔		✔				✔	✔			✔	✔	✔			✔	
	Carya illinoensis	Pecan			✔		70'	40'	✔	✔		✔	✔		✔		✔					✔			✔					✔	
	Casuarina cunninghamiana	River She-Oak			✔		70'	35'	✔	✔		✔	✔					✔		✔	✔		✔								
✔	*Celtis occidentalis*	Common Hackberry			✔		50'	40'	✔	✔	✔	✔	✔	✔			✔	✔		✔					✔						
✔	*Ceratonia siliqua*	Carob Tree			✔		40'	35'	✔	✔		✔	✔	✔				✔		✔	✔		✔								
✔	*Cercidium floridum*	Blue Palo Verde	✔				25'	25'	✔			✔	✔						✔	✔				✔		✔					
✔	*Cercidium microphyllum*	Foothill Palo Verde	✔				20'	20'	✔	✔		✔	✔						✔	✔				✔		✔					★
✔	*Cercidium praecox*	Sonoran Palo Verde	✔				18'	18'	✔		✔	✔						✔	✔	✔				✔		✔					
	Cercis occidentalis	Western Redbud			✔		18'	12'	✔	✔	✔	✔	✔	✔	✔		✔				✔	✔			✔	✔					
	Chamaedorea seifrizii	Seifrizii Palm			✔		10'	6'	✔					✔	✔	✔	✔					✔	✔							✔	
✔	*Chamaerops humilis*	Mediterranean Fan Palm			✔		15'	15'	✔	✔		✔	✔	✔	✔		✔	✔			✔		✔								★
✔	*Chilopsis linearis*	Desert Willow	✔				25'	20'	✔	✔		✔	✔	✔			✔	✔	✔		✔				✔	✔	✔				★
	Chitalpa tashkentensis	Chitalpa			✔		30'	20'→		✔	✔		✔	✔	✔			✔	✔			✔				✔	✔				★
✔	*Chorisia speciosa*	Floss Silk Tree			✔	✔	50'	30'	✔				✔				✔	✔			✔				✔	✔			✔		

Trees and Palms

MASTER PLANT MATERIALS MATRIX

			Environ. Grouping				Size		Macro Zone			Micro Zone					Design Use			Water Req.			Leaf Habit			Flower Show				F. C.	★
DESCRIBED	BOTANICAL NAME	COMMON NAME	NATIVE	NATURALIZED	EXOTIC	TROPICAL	HEIGHT	WIDTH	LOW DESERT	INTERMEDIATE DESERT	HIGH DESERT	A — SUNNY	B — PART SUNNY	C — LITTLE SUNNY	D — INTRO. SHADE	E — DEEP SHADE	OASIS	TRANSITION	DESERT	LOW WATER	MODERATE WATER	HIGH WATER	EVERGREEN	SEMI EVERGREEN	DECIDUOUS	SPRING FLOWERS	SUMMER FLOWERS	FALL FLOWERS	WINTER FLOWERS	FALL COLOR	STAR PERFORMER
✔	*Cinnamomum camphora*	Camphor Tree			✔		50'	30'	✔	✔		✔	✔				✔	✔			✔			✔							
✔	*Citrus* 'Marsh Seedless'	Citrus - Grapefruit			✔		25'	25'	✔	✔		✔	✔				✔				✔		✔			✔					
✔	*Citrus* 'Ruby Pink'	Citrus - Pink Grapefruit			✔		20'	20'	✔			✔	✔				✔				✔		✔			✔					
	Citrus 'Dwarf Meyer'	Citrus - Lemon			✔		10'	5'	✔			✔	✔				✔				✔		✔			✔					
✔	*Citrus* 'Eureka'	Citrus - Lemon			✔		20'	25'	✔	✔		✔	✔				✔				✔		✔			✔					
✔	*Citrus* 'Bearss'	Citrus - Lime			✔		15'	15'	✔	✔		✔	✔				✔				✔		✔			✔					
	Citrus 'Rangpur'	Citrus - Lime			✔		15'	15'	✔			✔	✔				✔				✔		✔			✔					
✔	*Citrus* 'Kinnow'	Citrus - Mandarin Orange			✔		20'	25'	✔			✔	✔				✔				✔		✔			✔					
	Citrus 'Blood'	Citrus - Orange			✔		15'	15'	✔	✔		✔	✔				✔				✔		✔			✔					
✔	*Citrus* 'Navel'	Citrus - Orange			✔		20'	20'	✔			✔	✔				✔				✔		✔			✔					
✔	*Citrus* 'Valencia'	Citrus - Orange			✔		20'	20'	✔	✔		✔	✔				✔				✔		✔			✔					
	Citrus 'Fortune'	Citrus - Tangelo			✔		15'	15'	✔			✔	✔				✔				✔		✔			✔					
✔	*Citrus* 'Dancy'	Citrus - Tangerine			✔		15'	10'	✔	✔		✔	✔				✔				✔		✔			✔					
	Citrus 'Temple'	Citrus - Tangor			✔		15'	15'	✔			✔	✔				✔				✔		✔			✔					
✔	*Cupressus arizonica*	Arizona Cypress	✔				40'	20'	✔	✔	✔	✔	✔	✔				✔	✔	✔			✔								★
	Cupressus sempervirens	Italian Cypress			✔		80'	10'	✔	✔	✔	✔	✔	✔			✔			✔	✔		✔								
✔	*Cycas revoluta*	Sago Palm			✔	✔	8'	10'	✔	✔	✔		✔	✔	✔		✔				✔	✔	✔								★
✔	*Dalbergia sissoo*	Sissoo			✔		20'	25'	✔			✔						✔	✔	✔	✔			✔		✔	✔				
✔	*Dalea spinosa*	Smoke Tree	✔				20'	20'	✔			✔							✔	✔				✔		✔	✔				
	Dracaena draco	Dragon Tree			✔	✔	20'	15'	✔				✔	✔	✔		✔	✔			✔		✔			✔	✔				
✔	*Elaeagnus angustifolia*	Russian Olive			✔		20'	15'	✔	✔	✔	✔	✔		✔			✔	✔		✔				✔		✔				★
✔	*Eriobotrya japonica*	Loquat			✔	✔	20'	15'	✔	✔	✔	✔	✔	✔	✔		✔				✔	✔	✔					✔	✔		

Trees and Palms

MASTER PLANT MATERIALS MATRIX

	BOTANICAL NAME	COMMON NAME	ENVIRON. GROUPING				SIZE		MACRO ZONE			MICRO ZONE					DESIGN USE			WATER REQ.			LEAF HABIT			FLOWER SHOW				F. C.	★
DESCRIBED			NATIVE	NATURALIZED	EXOTIC	TROPICAL	HEIGHT	WIDTH	LOW DESERT	INTERMEDIATE DESERT	HIGH DESERT	A — SUNNY	B — PART SUNNY	C — LITTLE SUNNY	D — INTRO. SHADE	E — DEEP SHADE	OASIS	TRANSITION	DESERT	LOW WATER	MODERATE WATER	HIGH WATER	EVERGREEN	SEMI EVERGREEN	DECIDUOUS	SPRING FLOWERS	SUMMER FLOWERS	FALL FLOWERS	WINTER FLOWERS	FALL COLOR	STAR PERFORMER
	Erythrina coralloides	Naked Coral Tree			✔		30'	40'	✔	✔		✔	✔				✔	✔			✔				✔	✔	✔			✔	
	Erythrina humeana	Natal Coral Tree			✔		30'	30'	✔	✔		✔	✔				✔	✔			✔				✔	✔	✔			✔	
✔	*Erythrina lysistemon*	NCN (Coral Tree)			✔		40'	60'	✔			✔	✔					✔		✔	✔				✔	✔	✔			✔	
	Eucalyptus citriodora	Lemon-Scented Gum			✔		80'	25'	✔			✔	✔	✔				✔			✔	✔	✔								
	Eucalyptus erythrocorys	Red-Cap Gum			✔		20'	15'	✔	✔		✔	✔	✔			✔	✔		✔	✔		✔			✔	✔				
	Eucalyptus ficifolia	Red-Flowering Gum			✔		40'	25'	✔			✔	✔	✔			✔	✔		✔	✔		✔			✔	✔				
	Eucalyptus lehmannii	Bushy Yate			✔		20'	20'	✔			✔	✔	✔				✔		✔	✔		✔								
	Eucalyptus leucoxylon	White Ironbark			✔		50'	30'	✔	✔		✔	✔	✔				✔		✔	✔		✔								
✔	*Eucalyptus microtheca*	Coolibah Tree			✔		50'	25'	✔	✔	✔	✔	✔	✔				✔	✔	✔	✔		✔								★
✔	*Eucalyptus polyanthemos*	Silver Dollar Gum			✔		30'	20'	✔	✔		✔	✔	✔			✔	✔		✔	✔		✔								
	Eucayptus rostrata	Red Gum			✔		70'	35'	✔	✔		✔	✔	✔				✔		✔	✔		✔								
✔	*Eucalyptus rudis*	Desert Gum			✔		35'	20'	✔	✔		✔	✔	✔				✔	✔	✔	✔		✔								
✔	*Eucalyptus sideroxylon* 'Rosea'	Red Ironbark			✔		50'	25'	✔	✔		✔	✔	✔				✔		✔	✔		✔			✔			✔		
✔	*Eucalyptus spathulata*	Narrow-Leafed Gimlet			✔		25'	15'	✔	✔		✔	✔	✔				✔	✔	✔	✔		✔								
	Eucalyptus torquata	Coral Gum			✔		20'	15'	✔			✔	✔	✔			✔	✔		✔	✔		✔			✔	✔				
	Eucalyptus viminalis	Manna Gum			✔		150'	100'	✔	✔		✔	✔	✔				✔		✔	✔		✔								
✔	*Feijoa sellowiana*	Pineapple Guava			✔		20'	15'	✔	✔		✔	✔		✔		✔	✔			✔	✔	✔			✔					★
✔	*Ficus benjamina*	Chinese Weeping Banyan			✔	✔	30'	20'	✔				✔	✔	✔		✔					✔	✔								
	Ficus carica	Edible Fig			✔		30'	20	✔	✔		✔	✔				✔					✔			✔						
	Ficus elastica 'Decora'	Rubber Tree			✔	✔	25'	20'	✔					✔	✔	✔	✔					✔	✔								
	Ficus florida	NCN			✔	✔	50'	30'	✔				✔	✔	✔	✔	✔					✔	✔								
	Ficus microcarpa	Weeping Indian Laurel Fig			✔		30'	20'	✔				✔	✔	✔		✔					✔	✔								

Trees and Palms

MASTER PLANT MATERIALS MATRIX

	BOTANICAL NAME	COMMON NAME	ENVIRON. GROUPING				SIZE		MACRO ZONE			MICRO ZONE					DESIGN USE			WATER REQ.			LEAF HABIT			FLOWER SHOW				F. C.	★
DESCRIBED			NATIVE	NATURALIZED	EXOTIC	TROPICAL	HEIGHT	WIDTH	LOW DESERT	INTERMEDIATE DESERT	HIGH DESERT	A — SUNNY	B — PART SUNNY	C — LITTLE SUNNY	D — INTRO. SHADE	E — DEEP SHADE	OASIS	TRANSITION	DESERT	LOW WATER	MODERATE WATER	HIGH WATER	EVERGREEN	SEMI EVERGREEN	DECIDUOUS	SPRING FLOWERS	SUMMER FLOWERS	FALL FLOWERS	WINTER FLOWERS	FALL COLOR	STAR PERFORMER
✔	*Ficus microcarpa nitida*	Indian Laurel			✔		30'	20'	✔				✔	✔	✔		✔					✔	✔								
	Fortunella margarita	Kumquat			✔		18'	18'	✔	✔		✔	✔				✔				✔		✔			✔					
✔	*Fraxinus uhdei*	Evergreen Ash		✔			70'	35'	✔	✔		✔	✔	✔			✔	✔			✔	✔			✔					✔	
	Fraxinus uhdei 'Majestic Beauty'	Evergreen Ash		✔			70'	35'	✔	✔		✔	✔				✔	✔			✔	✔			✔					✔	
✔	*Fraxinus velutina*	Arizona Ash	✔				50'	30'	✔	✔	✔	✔	✔	✔			✔	✔			✔				✔					✔	
	Fraxinus velutina 'Modesto'	Modesto Ash		✔			50'	30'	✔	✔	✔	✔	✔	✔			✔	✔			✔				✔					✔	
✔	*Fraxinus velutina* 'Rio Grande'	Fan-Tex Ash		✔			40'	25'	✔	✔	✔	✔	✔	✔			✔	✔		✔	✔				✔					✔	★
✔	*Geijera parviflora*	Australian Willow			✔		25'	20'	✔	✔		✔	✔				✔	✔			✔	✔		✔							★
✔	*Ginkgo biloba*	Maidenhair Tree			✔		75'	40'	✔	✔	✔	✔	✔	✔			✔	✔			✔				✔					✔	
✔	*Gleditsia triacanthos inermis*	Thornless Honey Locust			✔		60'	35'	✔	✔	✔	✔	✔	✔	✔		✔	✔		✔	✔				✔					✔	
	Grevillea robusta	Silk Oak			✔		60'	30'	✔	✔		✔	✔	✔	✔		✔	✔			✔		✔			✔					
	Gymnocladus dioica	Kentucky Coffee Tree			✔		50'	30'		✔	✔	✔	✔	✔	✔			✔	✔			✔				✔					✔
✔	*Jacaranda acutifolia*	Jacaranda			✔		40'	30'	✔	✔		✔	✔				✔	✔			✔				✔	✔	✔			✔	★
	Juglans major	Arizona Walnut	✔	✔			50'	30'	✔	✔		✔	✔				✔					✔			✔					✔	
✔	*Koelreuteria bipinnata*	Chinese Flame Tree			✔		40'	30'	✔	✔	✔	✔	✔				✔					✔			✔	✔				✔	
✔	*Lagerstroemia indica*	Crape Myrtle			✔		25'	15'	✔	✔		✔	✔				✔	✔			✔				✔	✔	✔	✔			★
✔	*Ligustrum japonicum* 'Texanum'	Waxleaf Privet			✔		20'	12'	✔	✔	✔	✔	✔	✔	✔		✔				✔		✔								
✔	*Ligustrum lucidum*	Glossy Privet			✔		25'	15'	✔	✔	✔	✔	✔	✔	✔		✔				✔		✔								
✔	*Liquidambar styraciflua*	American Sweet Gum			✔		60'	25'	✔	✔	✔	✔	✔				✔					✔			✔					✔	★
	Liriodendron tulipifera	Tulip Tree			✔		80'	40'	✔	✔	✔	✔	✔				✔					✔			✔	✔				✔	
	Livistona chinensis	Chinese Fountain Palm			✔		15'	10→	✔			✔	✔	✔			✔				✔	✔	✔								
✔	*Lysiloma thornberi*	Fern-of-the-Desert	✔				20'	20'	✔			✔	✔		✔			✔	✔	✔					✔						

Trees and Palms

MASTER PLANT MATERIALS MATRIX

	BOTANICAL NAME	COMMON NAME	ENVIRON. GROUPING				SIZE		MACRO ZONE			MICRO ZONE					DESIGN USE			WATER REQ.			LEAF HABIT			FLOWER SHOW				F. C.	★
DESCRIBED			NATIVE	NATURALIZED	EXOTIC	TROPICAL	HEIGHT	WIDTH	LOW DESERT	INTERMEDIATE DESERT	HIGH DESERT	A — SUNNY	B — PART SUNNY	C — LITTLE SUNNY	D — INTRO. SHADE	E — DEEP SHADE	OASIS	TRANSITION	DESERT	LOW WATER	MODERATE WATER	HIGH WATER	EVERGREEN	SEMI EVERGREEN	DECIDUOUS	SPRING FLOWERS	SUMMER FLOWERS	FALL FLOWERS	WINTER FLOWERS	FALL COLOR	STAR PERFORMER
✔	*Magnolia grandiflora*	Southern Magnolia			✔		80'	40'	✔	✔		✔	✔				✔					✔	✔			✔	✔				
	Melaleuca linariifolia	Flaxleaf Paperbark																													
✔	*Melaleuca quinquenervia*	Cajeput Tree			✔		40'	30'	✔			✔	✔				✔	✔			✔		✔			✔		✔			
	Melia azedarach	Chinaberry		✔			40'	30'	✔	✔	✔	✔	✔	✔	✔		✔	✔			✔				✔					✔	
	Morus alba	White Mulberry		✔			60'	40'	✔	✔	✔	✔	✔	✔	✔		✔	✔			✔				✔					✔	
	Musa paradisiaca	Edible Banana			✔	✔	18'	8'	✔				✔	✔	✔		✔					✔	✔								
	Nerium oleander	Common Oleander			✔		20'	20'	✔	✔	✔	✔	✔				✔				✔	✔	✔			✔	✔	✔			
✔	*Nyssa sylvatica*	Tupelo			✔		50'	30'			✔	✔	✔	✔			✔	✔			✔				✔					✔	
✔	*Olea europaea*	Common Olive			✔		30'	25'	✔	✔		✔	✔				✔	✔			✔		✔								★
✔	*Olea europaea* 'Swan Hill'	Fruitless Olive			✔		25'	20'	✔	✔		✔	✔				✔	✔			✔		✔								
✔	*Olneya tesota*	Desert Ironwood	✔				30'	30'	✔	✔		✔	✔					✔	✔	✔				✔							
✔	*Parkinsonia aculeata*	Jerusalem Thorn	✔				30'	30'	✔	✔		✔	✔					✔	✔	✔	✔			✔		✔	✔				
	Persea americana	Avocado			✔		25'	20'	✔			✔	✔				✔					✔	✔								
	Phoenix canariensis	Canary Island Date Palm			✔		30'	30'	✔	✔		✔	✔				✔				✔	✔	✔								
✔	*Phoenix dactylifera*	Date Palm			✔		60'	30'	✔	✔		✔	✔				✔				✔	✔	✔								★
✔	*Phoenix roebelinii*	Pigmy Date Palm			✔		8'	6'	✔	✔		✔	✔				✔					✔	✔								
	Photinia serrulata	Chinese Photinia			✔		25'	15'	✔	✔	✔	✔	✔	✔	✔		✔				✔		✔			✔					
✔	*Phyllostacis aurea*	Golden Bamboo			✔		20'	8'	✔	✔		✔	✔	✔	✔		✔	✔			✔		✔								
✔	*Phyllostacis bambusoides*	Giant Timber Bamboo			✔		40'	12'	✔	✔		✔	✔	✔	✔		✔	✔			✔		✔								
✔	*Phyllostacis nigra*	Black Bamboo			✔		12'	6'	✔	✔			✔	✔	✔		✔	✔			✔		✔								
	Pinus brutia	Brutia Pine			✔		60'	40'	✔	✔	✔	✔	✔	✔				✔	✔	✔	✔		✔								
✔	*Pinus canariensis*	Canary Island Pine			✔		75'	25'	✔	✔		✔	✔	✔			✔	✔			✔	✔	✔								

Trees and Palms

MASTER PLANT MATERIALS MATRIX

	BOTANICAL NAME	COMMON NAME	ENVIRON. GROUPING				SIZE		MACRO ZONE			MICRO ZONE					DESIGN USE			WATER REQ.			LEAF HABIT			FLOWER SHOW				F. C.	★
DESCRIBED			NATIVE	NATURALIZED	EXOTIC	TROPICAL	HEIGHT	WIDTH	LOW DESERT	INTERMEDIATE DESERT	HIGH DESERT	A — SUNNY	B — PART SUNNY	C — LITTLE SUNNY	D — INTRO. SHADE	E — DEEP SHADE	OASIS	TRANSITION	DESERT	LOW WATER	MODERATE WATER	HIGH WATER	EVERGREEN	SEMI EVERGREEN	DECIDUOUS	SPRING FLOWERS	SUMMER FLOWERS	FALL FLOWERS	WINTER FLOWERS	FALL COLOR	STAR PERFORMER
✔	*Pinus eldarica*	Mondell Pine			✔		60'	40'	✔	✔	✔	✔	✔	✔				✔	✔	✔	✔		✔								★
✔	*Pinus halepensis*	Aleppo Pine			✔		60'	45'	✔	✔	✔	✔	✔	✔				✔	✔		✔		✔								
✔	*Pinus pinea*	Italian Stone Pine			✔		50'	40'	✔	✔	✔	✔	✔	✔				✔	✔		✔		✔								
	Pinus roxburghii	Chir Pine			✔		60'	30'	✔	✔		✔	✔	✔			✔	✔			✔	✔	✔								
✔	*Pistacia chinensis*	Chinese Pistache			✔		60'	50'	✔	✔	✔	✔	✔	✔			✔	✔		✔	✔				✔					✔	
	Pistacia vera	Pistachio Nut			✔		30'	25'		✔	✔	✔	✔				✔			✔	✔				✔					✔	
✔	*Pithecellobium flexicaule*	Texas Ebony	✔				25'	15'	✔	✔	✔	✔	✔					✔	✔	✔				✔							★
	Platanus racemosa	California Sycamore		✔	✔		80'	60'	✔	✔	✔	✔	✔	✔			✔	✔				✔			✔					✔	
✔	*Platanus wrightii*	Arizona Sycamore	✔				60'	40'	✔	✔	✔	✔	✔	✔			✔	✔				✔			✔					✔	★
	Podocarpus gracilior	Fern Pine			✔	✔	40'	20'	✔	✔			✔	✔	✔		✔					✔	✔								
	Podocarpus macrophyllus	Yew Pine			✔	✔	40'	20'	✔	✔			✔	✔	✔		✔					✔	✔								
	Populus canadensis	Balm-of-Gilead		✔			80'	40'	✔	✔	✔	✔	✔	✔			✔	✔				✔			✔					✔	
	Populus canadensis "Mohave Hybrid"	Cottonless Cottonwood		✔			80'	40'	✔	✔	✔	✔	✔	✔			✔	✔				✔			✔					✔	
✔	*Populus fremontii*	Western Cottonwood	✔				100'	50'	✔	✔	✔	✔	✔	✔			✔	✔				✔			✔					✔	
✔	*Prosopis alba*	Argentine Mesquite		✔	✔		35'	30'	✔	✔		✔	✔					✔	✔	✔	✔			✔							★
✔	*Prosopis chilensis*	Chilean Mesquite		✔	✔		30'	25'	✔	✔		✔	✔					✔	✔	✔	✔			✔							★
✔	*Prosopis glandulosa*	Honey Mesquite	✔				40'	40'	✔	✔	✔	✔	✔					✔	✔	✔	✔			✔							
✔	*Prosopis pubescens*	Screwbean Mesquite	✔				20'	15'	✔	✔		✔	✔					✔	✔	✔	✔			✔							
✔	*Prosopis velutina*	Velvet Mesquite	✔				35'	35'	✔	✔		✔	✔					✔	✔	✔	✔			✔							
	Prunus americana	Fruiting Plum			✔		20'	15'	✔	✔		✔	✔				✔					✔			✔	✔				✔	
✔	*Prunus caroliniana*	Carolina Laurel Cherry			✔		20'	15'	✔	✔	✔	✔	✔				✔			✔	✔		✔			✔					★
✔	*Prunus cerasifera* 'Atropurpurea'	Purple-Leaf Plum			✔		30'	20'	✔	✔		✔	✔				✔				✔	✔			✔	✔					

Trees and Palms

MASTER PLANT MATERIALS MATRIX

	BOTANICAL NAME	COMMON NAME	ENVIRON. GROUPING				SIZE		MACRO ZONE			MICRO ZONE					DESIGN USE			WATER REQ.			LEAF HABIT			FLOWER SHOW				F. C.	★
DESCRIBED			NATIVE	NATURALIZED	EXOTIC	TROPICAL	HEIGHT	WIDTH	LOW DESERT	INTERMEDIATE DESERT	HIGH DESERT	A — SUNNY	B — PART SUNNY	C — LITTLE SUNNY	D — INTRO. SHADE	E — DEEP SHADE	OASIS	TRANSITION	DESERT	LOW WATER	MODERATE WATER	HIGH WATER	EVERGREEN	SEMI EVERGREEN	DECIDUOUS	SPRING FLOWERS	SUMMER FLOWERS	FALL FLOWERS	WINTER FLOWERS	FALL COLOR	STAR PERFORMER
✔	*Prunus c.* 'Krauter Vesuvius'	Krauter Purple Plum			✔		20'	15'	✔	✔		✔	✔				✔				✔	✔			✔	✔					
	Prunus lyonii	Catalina Cherry			✔		45'	30'	✔	✔		✔	✔				✔	✔		✔	✔		✔								
	Prunus persica	Flowering Peach			✔		25'	15'	✔	✔	✔	✔	✔				✔				✔	✔			✔	✔				✔	
✔	*Punica granatum*	Pomegranate			✔		20'	10'	✔	✔	✔	✔	✔				✔			✔					✔	✔				✔	
	Pyrus aristocrat	Aristocrat Pear			✔		40'	25'	✔	✔	✔	✔	✔	✔			✔					✔			✔	✔				✔	
✔	*Pyrus calleryana*	Bradford Pear			✔		35'	20'	✔	✔	✔	✔	✔	✔			✔				✔	✔			✔	✔				✔	★
✔	*Pyrus kawakamii*	Evergreen Pear			✔		40'	30'	✔	✔		✔	✔	✔			✔				✔	✔			✔	✔				✔	
✔	*Quercus agrifolia*	Coast Live Oak		✔			70'	70'		✔	✔	✔	✔				✔	✔			✔		✔								
✔	*Quercus engelmannii*	Englemann Oak		✔			60'	40'	✔	✔	✔	✔	✔				✔	✔			✔				✔					✔	
✔	*Quercus ilex*	Holly Oak	✔	✔			50'	30'	✔	✔	✔	✔	✔				✔	✔			✔		✔								★
✔	*Quercus lobata*	California White Oak		✔			80'	80'	✔	✔	✔	✔	✔				✔	✔			✔				✔					✔	
✔	*Quercus suber*	Cork Oak	✔	✔			60'	40'	✔	✔	✔	✔	✔				✔	✔			✔				✔					✔	
✔	*Rhapis excelsa*	Lady Palm			✔		12'	8'	✔	✔				✔	✔		✔					✔	✔								
✔	*Rhus lancea*	African Sumac			✔		30'	30'	✔	✔		✔	✔				✔	✔		✔	✔		✔								★
	Robinia pseudoacacia	Black Locust			✔		75'	40'	✔	✔	✔	✔	✔				✔	✔		✔	✔				✔	✔				✔	
	Sabal palmetto	Cabbage Palm			✔		20'	10'	✔	✔		✔	✔				✔	✔			✔		✔								
	Sabal uresana	Sonoran Palmetto	✔	✔			30'	15'	✔	✔		✔	✔				✔	✔	✔		✔		✔								
✔	*Salix babylonica*	Weeping Willow			✔		50'	40'	✔	✔	✔	✔	✔				✔					✔			✔					✔	
✔	*Sambucus mexicana*	Mexican Elderberry	✔				20'	15'	✔	✔		✔	✔					✔	✔	✔	✔				✔	✔					
✔	*Schinus molle*	California Pepper Tree			✔		40'	40'	✔	✔		✔	✔				✔	✔	✔	✔	✔		✔								★
✔	*Schinus terebinthifolius*	Brazilian Pepper Tree			✔		30'	25'	✔	✔		✔	✔				✔	✔		✔	✔		✔								★
✔	*Tamarix aphylla*	Tamarisk		✔	✔		60'	50'	✔	✔	✔	✔	✔					✔		✔	✔		✔								

Trees and Palms

MASTER PLANT MATERIALS MATRIX

DESCRIBED	BOTANICAL NAME	COMMON NAME	ENVIRON. GROUPING				SIZE		MACRO ZONE			MICRO ZONE					DESIGN USE			WATER REQ.			LEAF HABIT			FLOWER SHOW				F. C.	★
			NATIVE	NATURALIZED	EXOTIC	TROPICAL	HEIGHT	WIDTH	LOW DESERT	INTERMEDIATE DESERT	HIGH DESERT	A — SUNNY	B — PART SUNNY	C — LITTLE SUNNY	D — INTRO. SHADE	E — DEEP SHADE	OASIS	TRANSITION	DESERT	LOW WATER	MODERATE WATER	HIGH WATER	EVERGREEN	SEMI EVERGREEN	DECIDUOUS	SPRING FLOWERS	SUMMER FLOWERS	FALL FLOWERS	WINTER FLOWERS	FALL COLOR	STAR PERFORMER
	Thevetia thevetioides	Giant Thevetia			✔		18'	18'	✔	✔		✔	✔	✔			✔				✔		✔				✔	✔			
	Tilia cordata	Little-Leaf Linden			✔		50'	30'	✔	✔	✔	✔	✔				✔					✔			✔					✔	
	Tipuanu tipu	Tipu Tree			✔		50'	35'	✔			✔	✔				✔	✔				✔			✔		✔			✔	
✔	*Trachycarpus fortunei*	Windmill Palm			✔	✔	15'	20'	✔	✔		✔	✔				✔				✔	✔	✔								
✔	*Tupidanthus calypatrus*	Tupidanthus			✔	✔	12'	8'	✔	✔			✔	✔	✔		✔					✔	✔								
✔	*Ulmus parvifolia*	Evergreen Elm			✔		40'	60'	✔	✔	✔	✔	✔	✔			✔				✔				✔						★
	Ulmus parvifolia 'Drake'	Evergreen Elm			✔		40'	60'	✔	✔	✔	✔	✔	✔			✔				✔				✔						
	Ulmus parvifolia 'True Green'	Evergreen Elm			✔		40'	60'	✔	✔	✔	✔	✔	✔			✔				✔				✔						
	Vitex angus-castus	Chaste Tree			✔		25'	30'	✔	✔	✔	✔	✔					✔		✔	✔				✔						
✔	*Washingtonia filifera*	California Fan Palm	✔				40'	16'	✔	✔		✔	✔				✔	✔	✔	✔	✔		✔								★
✔	*Washingtonia robusta*	Mexican Fan Palm		✔			60'	16'	✔	✔		✔	✔				✔	✔		✔	✔		✔								★
	Zelkova serrata	Sawleaf Zelkova			✔		60"	40'	✔	✔	✔	✔	✔				✔					✔			✔					✔	
	Ziziphus jujuba	Chinese Jujube			✔		30'	20'	✔	✔	✔	✔	✔				✔			✔	✔				✔					✔	

Shrubs

MASTER PLANT MATERIALS MATRIX

DESCRIBED	BOTANICAL NAME	COMMON NAME	NATIVE	NATURALIZED	EXOTIC	TROPICAL	HEIGHT	WIDTH	LOW DESERT	INTERMEDIATE DESERT	HIGH DESERT	A — SUNNY	B — PART SUNNY	C — LITTLE SUNNY	D — INTRO. SHADE	E — DEEP SHADE	OASIS	TRANSITION	DESERT	LOW WATER	MODERATE WATER	HIGH WATER	EVERGREEN	SEMI EVERGREEN	DECIDUOUS	SPRING FLOWERS	SUMMER FLOWERS	FALL FLOWERS	WINTER FLOWERS	FALL COLOR	STAR PERFORMER
✔	*Abelia grandiflora*	Glossy Abelia			✔		8'	6'	✔	✔	✔	✔	✔	✔	✔		✔				✔			✔		✔	✔				
	Acacia notabilis	NCN		✔			10'	10'	✔	✔		✔	✔		✔			✔	✔		✔			✔		✔		✔			
✔	*Acanthus mollis*	Acanthus			✔	✔	4'	6'	✔	✔	✔		✔	✔	✔		✔				✔	✔	✔				✔				
✔	*Agapanthus africanus*	Lily-of-the-Nile			✔	✔	3'	2'	✔	✔			✔	✔	✔		✔				✔	✔	✔				✔				
✔	*Agapanthus a.* 'Peter Pan'	Dwarf Lily-of-the Nile			✔	✔	18"	12"	✔	✔			✔	✔	✔		✔				✔	✔	✔				✔				
✔	*Alyogyne huegelii*	Blue Hibiscus			✔		6'	4'	✔			✔						✔			✔		✔			✔	✔	✔	✔		
	Anisacanthus thurberi	Desert Honeysuckle	✔				5'	5'	✔	✔	✔	✔							✔	✔				✔		✔	✔				
	Aralia elegantissima	False Aralia			✔	✔	6'	4'	✔						✔		✔					✔	✔								
	Artemisia caucasica	Silver Spreader		✔			3'	3'	✔	✔	✔	✔	✔		✔			✔	✔	✔				✔							
	Artemisia pycnocephala	Coast Sagebrush		✔			2'	4'	✔	✔	✔	✔	✔		✔			✔	✔	✔				✔							
	Arundo donax	Carrizo		✔	✔		15'	10'	✔	✔	✔	✔	✔	✔	✔			✔			✔	✔	✔								
✔	*Aspidistra elatior*	Cast-Iron Plant			✔		3'	3'	✔	✔				✔	✔	✔		✔			✔		✔								★
✔	*Atriplex canescens*	Four-Wing Saltbush	✔				3'	4'	✔	✔	✔	✔	✔						✔	✔				✔							★
	Atriplex glauca	NCN	✔	✔			1'	10'	✔	✔	✔	✔	✔						✔	✔				✔							
	Atriplex polycarpa	Desert Saltbush	✔				1'	8'	✔	✔	✔	✔	✔						✔	✔				✔							
✔	*Atriplex semibaccata*	Australian Saltbush		✔	✔		12"	5'	✔	✔		✔							✔	✔				✔							
	Aucuba japonica 'Variegata'	Gold Dust Plant			✔	✔	6'	6'	✔	✔	✔		✔	✔	✔	✔	✔					✔	✔								
	Azalea indica	Sun Azalea			✔		4'	4'	✔	✔	✔		✔		✔		✔					✔	✔			✔					
	Azalea 'Southern Indica'	Fielder's White Azalea			✔		4'	4'	✔	✔	✔		✔		✔		✔					✔	✔			✔					
	Azalea rutherfordiana 'Alaska'	Alaska Azalea			✔		4'	4'	✔	✔	✔		✔		✔		✔					✔	✔			✔					
	Azalea rutherfordiana 'Rose Queen'	Rose Queen Azalea			✔		4'	4'	✔	✔	✔		✔		✔		✔					✔	✔			✔					
✔	*Baccharis* 'Centennial'	Hybrid Desert Broom		✔			2'	6'		✔	✔	✔	✔		✔		✔	✔		✔	✔		✔				✔				★
	BOTANICAL NAME	COMMON NAME	ENVIRON. GROUPING				SIZE		MACRO ZONE			MICRO ZONE					DESIGN USE			WATER REQ.			LEAF HABIT			FLOWER SHOW				F. C.	★

Shrubs

MASTER PLANT MATERIALS MATRIX

DESCRIBED	BOTANICAL NAME	COMMON NAME	ENVIRON. GROUPING				SIZE		MACRO ZONE			MICRO ZONE					DESIGN USE			WATER REQ.			LEAF HABIT			FLOWER SHOW				F. C.	★
			NATIVE	NATURALIZED	EXOTIC	TROPICAL	HEIGHT	WIDTH	LOW DESERT	INTERMEDIATE DESERT	HIGH DESERT	A — SUNNY	B — PART SUNNY	C — LITTLE SUNNY	D — INTRO. SHADE	E — DEEP SHADE	OASIS	TRANSITION	DESERT	LOW WATER	MODERATE WATER	HIGH WATER	EVERGREEN	SEMI EVERGREEN	DECIDUOUS	SPRING FLOWERS	SUMMER FLOWERS	FALL FLOWERS	WINTER FLOWERS	FALL COLOR	STAR PERFORMER
	Baccharis pilularis	Dwarf Coyote Bush		✔			2'	6'		✔	✔	✔	✔		✔		✔	✔		✔	✔		✔				✔				
	Baccharis 'Warrens Hybrid'	Coyote Bush		✔			2'	5'		✔	✔	✔	✔		✔		✔	✔		✔	✔		✔								
✔	*Baccharis sarothroides*	Desert Broom	✔				8'	8'	✔	✔	✔	✔	✔						✔	✔				✔			✔				
	Baileya multiradiata	Desert Marigold	✔				8"	12"	✔			✔	✔						✔	✔				✔		✔					
	Bambusa g. 'Alphonse Karr'	NCN			✔		10'	6'	✔	✔		✔	✔		✔		✔				✔		✔								
	Bambusa oldhamii	Oldham Bamboo			✔		15'	10'	✔	✔		✔	✔		✔		✔				✔		✔								
	Bauhinia galpinii	Red Bauhinia			✔		15'	15'	✔				✔		✔		✔	✔			✔	✔		✔		✔					
✔	*Bougainvillea* 'Crimson Jewel'	Red Bush Bougainvillea			3		3'	3'	✔	✔		✔	✔		✔		✔	✔		✔	✔			✔		✔	✔				★
	Bougainvillea 'Convent'	Purple Bush Bougainvillea			✔		3'	6'	✔			✔	✔		✔		✔	✔			✔			✔		✔	✔				
	Bougainvillea 'Hawaii'	Golden Bush Bougainvillea			✔		3'	6'	✔			✔	✔		✔		✔	✔			✔			✔		✔	✔				
	Bougainvillea 'La Jolla'	La Jolla Bougainvillea			✔		3'	6'	✔			✔	✔		✔		✔	✔			✔			✔		✔	✔				
✔	*Bougainvillea* 'Lavender Queen'	Lavender Bush Bougainvillea			✔		3'	6'	✔			✔	✔		✔		✔	✔			✔			✔		✔	✔				
	Bougainvillea 'Pink Calabra'	Pink Bush Bougainvillea			✔		3'	6'	✔			✔	✔		✔		✔	✔			✔			✔		✔	✔				
✔	*Bougainvillea* 'Rosenka'	Gold/Pink Bougainvillea			✔		6'	6'	✔	✔		✔	✔		✔		✔	✔		✔	✔			✔		✔	✔		✔		
✔	*Bougainvillea* 'Texas Dawn'	Texas Dawn Bougainvillea			✔		4'	4'	✔			✔	✔		✔		✔	✔			✔			✔		✔	✔				
✔	*Bougainvillea* 'White Madonna'	White Bush Bougainvillea			✔		2'	4'	✔			✔	✔		✔		✔	✔			✔			✔		✔	✔				
✔	*Buxus microphylla japonica*	Japanese Boxwood			✔		5'	5'	✔	✔	✔	✔	✔		✔	✔	✔	✔			✔		✔								
	Calliandra californica	Baja Fairy Duster		✔			4'	6'	✔	✔		✔						✔	✔	✔				✔		✔	✔				
✔	*Calliandra eriophylla*	Fairy Duster	✔	✔			3'	5'	✔	✔		✔						✔	✔	✔				✔		✔	✔				★
	Calliandra inaequilatera	Pink Powder Puff		✔			4'	6'	✔	✔		✔	✔		✔		✔	✔		✔	✔			✔		✔	✔				
	Camellia japonica 'Swan Lake'	Camellia			✔		8'	8'	✔	✔			✔		✔		✔					✔	✔			✔			✔		
	Camellia sasanqua	Camellia			✔		6'	4'	✔	✔			✔		✔		✔					✔	✔			✔			✔		

Shrubs

MASTER PLANT MATERIALS MATRIX

DESCRIBED	BOTANICAL NAME	COMMON NAME	NATIVE	NATURALIZED	EXOTIC	TROPICAL	HEIGHT	WIDTH	LOW DESERT	INTERMEDIATE DESERT	HIGH DESERT	A — SUNNY	B — PART SUNNY	C — LITTLE SUNNY	D — INTRO. SHADE	E — DEEP SHADE	OASIS	TRANSITION	DESERT	LOW WATER	MODERATE WATER	HIGH WATER	EVERGREEN	SEMI EVERGREEN	DECIDUOUS	SPRING FLOWERS	SUMMER FLOWERS	FALL FLOWERS	WINTER FLOWERS	FALL COLOR	STAR PERFORMER
✔	*Carissa grandiflora*	Natal Plum			✔		5'	5'	✔	✔		✔	✔		✔		✔				✔	✔	✔			✔	✔				
	Carissa g. 'Boxwood Beauty'	Natal Plum			✔		2'	2'	✔	✔		✔	✔		✔		✔				✔	✔	✔			✔	✔				
	Carissa g. 'Fancy'	Fancy Natal Plum			✔		6'	6'	✔	✔		✔	✔		✔		✔				✔	✔	✔			✔	✔				
✔	*Carissa* g. 'Green Carpet'	Natal Plum			✔		2'	4'	✔	✔		✔	✔		✔		✔				✔	✔	✔			✔	✔				
	Carissa g. 'Prostrata'	Prostrate Natal Plum			✔		2'	6'	✔	✔		✔	✔		✔		✔				✔	✔	✔			✔	✔				
	Carissa g. 'Tuttle'	Tuttle's Natal Plum			✔		2'	5'	✔	✔		✔	✔		✔		✔			✔				✔		✔		✔	✔		
✔	*Cassia artemisioides*	Feathery Cassia		✔			6'	6'	✔	✔		✔	✔					✔	✔	✔				✔		✔		✔	✔		★
	Cassia candolleana	Green Senna		✔			5'	5'	✔	✔		✔	✔					✔	✔	✔				✔		✔		✔	✔		
✔	*Cassia nemophila*	Bushy Senna		✔			6'	6'	✔	✔		✔	✔					✔	✔	✔				✔		✔		✔	✔		
✔	*Cassia phyllodenia*	Desert Cassia		✔			10'	8'	✔	✔		✔	✔					✔	✔	✔				✔		✔		✔	✔		
	Cassia tomentosa	Woolly Senna		✔			8'	8'	✔	✔		✔	✔					✔	✔	✔				✔		✔		✔	✔		
	Cassia wislizeni	Shrubby Senna		✔			4'	4'	✔	✔		✔	✔					✔	✔	✔				✔		✔		✔	✔		
	Casuarina helmsii	Helmsii She-Oak		✔			15'	15'	✔	✔		✔	✔					✔		✔	✔		✔								
	Centaurea cineraria	Dusty Miller		✔			2'	2'	✔	✔	✔	✔	✔		✔			✔	✔	✔				✔		✔					
✔	*Chaenomeles japonica*	Japanese Flowering Quince		✔			6'	4'	✔	✔	✔	✔	✔				✔	✔			✔				✔	✔				✔	
	Chamelaucium uncinatum 'Vista'	Geraldton Wax Flower		✔	✔		6'	6'	✔	✔		✔	✔		✔			✔	✔	✔	✔		✔			✔			✔		
	Choisya ternata	Mexican Orange			✔		8'	8'	✔	✔			✔		✔		✔	✔			✔		✔						✔		
	Cistus corbariensis	White Rockrose		✔			4'	6'	✔	✔		✔	✔		✔		✔	✔		✔	✔			✔		✔	✔				
	Cistus purpureus	Orchid Rockrose			✔		4'	6'	✔	✔		✔	✔		✔		✔	✔		✔	✔		✔			✔					
	Cistus villosus	Desert Rockrose			✔		4'	4'	✔	✔		✔	✔		✔		✔	✔		✔	✔		✔			✔					
	Citrus 'Dwarf'	Dwarf Citrus (See Cat.)			✔		6'	6'	✔	✔		✔	✔		✔		✔				✔	✔	✔			✔					
	Clivia miniata	Kaffir Lily			✔		2'	2'	✔				✔	✔	✔		✔					✔	✔						✔		
	BOTANICAL NAME	COMMON NAME	ENVIRON. GROUPING				SIZE		MACRO ZONE			MICRO ZONE					DESIGN USE			WATER REQ.			LEAF HABIT			FLOWER SHOW				F. C.	★

Shrubs

MASTER PLANT MATERIALS MATRIX

DESCRIBED	BOTANICAL NAME	COMMON NAME	ENVIRON. GROUPING				SIZE		MACRO ZONE			MICRO ZONE					DESIGN USE			WATER REQ.			LEAF HABIT			FLOWER SHOW				F. C.	★
			NATIVE	NATURALIZED	EXOTIC	TROPICAL	HEIGHT	WIDTH	LOW DESERT	INTERMEDIATE DESERT	HIGH DESERT	A — SUNNY	B — PART SUNNY	C — LITTLE SUNNY	D — INTRO. SHADE	E — DEEP SHADE	OASIS	TRANSITION	DESERT	LOW WATER	MODERATE WATER	HIGH WATER	EVERGREEN	SEMI EVERGREEN	DECIDUOUS	SPRING FLOWERS	SUMMER FLOWERS	FALL FLOWERS	WINTER FLOWERS	FALL COLOR	STAR PERFORMER
	Cocculus laurifolius	Laurel Leaf Cocculus			✔		20'	20'	✔	✔		✔	✔	✔	✔	✔	✔					✔	✔								
✔	*Convolvulus cneorum*	Bush Morning Glory			✔		4'	4'	✔	✔		✔	✔		✔			✔	✔	✔	✔		✔			✔	✔				
✔	*Convolvulus mauritanicus*	Ground Morning Glory			✔		2'	6'	✔	✔		✔	✔		✔			✔	✔	✔	✔		✔			✔	✔				★
✔	*Convolvulus tricolor*	Dwarf Morning Glory			✔		12"	24"	✔			✔	✔		✔			✔	✔	✔	✔		✔			✔	✔				
✔	*Cordia boissieri*	Anacahuita		✔	✔		10'	8'	✔	✔	✔	✔	✔					✔	✔	✔				✔		✔		✔			
	Cordia parvifolia	Little Leaf Cordia			✔		6'	4'	✔	✔	✔	✔	✔					✔	✔	✔			✔			✔					
	Cordyline stricta	NCN			✔		10'	8'	✔				✔	✔	✔		✔				✔	✔	✔								
✔	*Cortaderia selloana*	Pampas Grass			✔		16'	16'	✔	✔	✔	✔	✔		✔			✔			✔		✔					✔	✔		
✔	*Cortaderia selloana* 'Pumila'	Dwarf Pampas Grass			✔		4'	4'	✔	✔		✔	✔		✔		✔	✔			✔		✔					✔	✔		★
	Cotinus coggyglia	Smoke Tree			✔		15'	20'			✔	✔	✔						✔	✔					✔	✔					
	Cotoneaster buxifolius	Bright Bead Cotoneaster			✔		2'	6'	✔	✔	✔	✔	✔		✔		✔	✔			✔			✔		✔					
	Cotoneaster lacteus	Red Clusterberry			✔		6'	8'	✔	✔	✔	✔	✔		✔		✔	✔			✔		✔			✔					
✔	*Dalea greggi*	Prostrate Indigo Bush	✔	✔			2'	5'	✔	✔		✔							✔	✔					✔	✔					
	Dalea capitata "Sierra Gold"	Yellow Dalea	✔	✔			4'	5'	✔			✔	✔						✔	✔			✔			✔					
	Dictamus albus	Gas Plant			✔		4'	4'			✔	✔	✔						✔	✔			✔			✔					
✔	*Dalea pulchra*	Indigo Bush	✔				5'	5'	✔			✔							✔	✔			✔			✔					
	Dalea wizlizenii	NCN	✔	✔			2'	4'	✔	✔		✔							✔	✔					✔	✔					
✔	*Dodonaea viscosa*	Hop Bush	✔	✔			12'	10'	✔	✔		✔	✔				✔	✔	✔	✔			✔								
✔	*Dodonaea viscosa* "Purpurea"	Purple Hop Bush	✔	✔			10'	8'	✔	✔		✔	✔				✔	✔	✔	✔			✔								
	Elaeagnus ebbingei	Ebbing Silverberry			✔		10'	10'	✔	✔	✔		✔		✔		✔	✔			✔		✔					✔			
	Elaeagnus pungens	Silverberry			✔		6'	6'	✔	✔	✔		✔		✔			✔			✔		✔					✔			
	Encelia californica	NCN	✔				4'	4'	✔	✔	✔	✔							✔	✔				✔		✔					

Shrubs

MASTER PLANT MATERIALS MATRIX

DESCRIBED	BOTANICAL NAME	COMMON NAME	NATIVE	NATURALIZED	EXOTIC	TROPICAL	HEIGHT	WIDTH	LOW DESERT	INTERMEDIATE DESERT	HIGH DESERT	A — SUNNY	B — PART SUNNY	C — LITTLE SUNNY	D — INTRO. SHADE	E — DEEP SHADE	OASIS	TRANSITION	DESERT	LOW WATER	MODERATE WATER	HIGH WATER	EVERGREEN	SEMI EVERGREEN	DECIDUOUS	SPRING FLOWERS	SUMMER FLOWERS	FALL FLOWERS	WINTER FLOWERS	FALL COLOR	STAR PERFORMER
			ENVIRON. GROUPING				SIZE		MACRO ZONE			MICRO ZONE					DESIGN USE			WATER REQ.			LEAF HABIT			FLOWER SHOW				F.C.	★
✔	*Encelia farinosa*	Brittle Bush	✔				4'	4'	✔	✔	✔	✔							✔	✔				✔		✔					★
	Encelia virginensis	Virginia River Encelia	✔	✔			3'	3'	✔	✔	✔	✔							✔	✔				✔		✔					
✔	*Ensete ventricosum*	Abyssinian Banana			✔	✔	18'	10'	✔	✔	✔		✔	✔	✔		✔					✔	✔			✔					★
✔	*Ericameria laricifolia*	Turpentine Bush	✔	✔			4'	5'		✔	✔	✔	✔		✔				✔	✔			✔								
✔	*Eriogonum fasciculatum*	California Buckwheat	✔				4'	4'	✔	✔	✔	✔							✔	✔				✔			✔				
✔	*Euonymus japonica*	Evergreen Euonymus			✔		8'	6'	✔	✔	✔	✔	✔		✔		✔			✔	✔		✔								
	Euonymus japonica "Microphylla"	Box-Leaf Euonymus			✔		6'	6'	✔	✔	✔	✔	✔		✔		✔			✔	✔		✔								
	Euryops athanasiae	Euryops			✔		6'	6'	✔	✔		✔	✔		✔		✔				✔		✔			✔		✔	✔		
✔	*Euryops pectinatus*	Common Euryops			✔		6'	4'	✔	✔		✔	✔		✔		✔				✔		✔			✔		✔	✔		
	Euryops P. "Emerald Green"	Euryops			✔		5'	4'	✔	✔	✔	✔		✔		✔					✔		✔			✔		✔	✔		
	Euryops P. "Green Gold"	Euryops			✔		5'	4'	✔	✔		✔	✔		✔		✔				✔		✔			✔		✔	✔		
	Euryops virides	Green Euryops			✔		6'	4'	✔	✔		✔	✔		✔		✔				✔		✔			✔		✔	✔		
	Fallugia paradoxa	Apache Plume	✔	✔			6'	6'	✔	✔	✔	✔	✔		✔			✔	✔	✔				✔		✔					
✔	*Fatsia japonica*	Japanese Aralia			✔	✔	5'	4'	✔	✔			✔	✔	✔		✔				✔	✔	✔								
✔	*Felicia amelloides*	Blue Marguerite			✔		2'	4'	✔			✔	✔		✔		✔	✔			✔	✔	✔				✔				★
	Ficus lyrata	Fiddleleaf Fig			✔		12'	8'	✔				✔	✔	✔		✔					✔	✔								
	Franseria deltoidea	Triangle Bursage	✔	✔			6'	6'	✔	✔		✔	✔		✔			✔	✔	✔				✔							
	Franseria dumosa	White Bursage	✔	✔			4'	4'	✔	✔		✔	✔		✔				✔	✔				✔							
✔	*Fremontodendron mexicanum*	Southern Flannel Bush	✔	✔			10'	8'	✔	✔		✔							✔	✔	✔		✔			✔	✔				
	Gardenia jasminoides	Gardenia			✔	✔	6'	6'	✔	✔			✔	✔	✔		✔					✔	✔			✔			✔		
	Gardenia "August Moon"	Gardenia			✔	✔	3'	3'	✔	✔			✔	✔	✔		✔					✔	✔			✔			✔		
✔	*Gardenia* "Radicans"	Gardenia			✔	✔	2'	3'	✔	✔			✔	✔	✔		✔					✔	✔			✔			✔		

Shrubs

MASTER PLANT MATERIALS MATRIX

DESCRIBED	BOTANICAL NAME	COMMON NAME	ENVIRON. GROUPING				SIZE		MACRO ZONE			MICRO ZONE					DESIGN USE			WATER REQ.			LEAF HABIT			FLOWER SHOW				F. C.	★
			NATIVE	NATURALIZED	EXOTIC	TROPICAL	HEIGHT	WIDTH	LOW DESERT	INTERMEDIATE DESERT	HIGH DESERT	A — SUNNY	B — PART SUNNY	C — LITTLE SUNNY	D — INTRO. SHADE	E — DEEP SHADE	OASIS	TRANSITION	DESERT	LOW WATER	MODERATE WATER	HIGH WATER	EVERGREEN	SEMI EVERGREEN	DECIDUOUS	SPRING FLOWERS	SUMMER FLOWERS	FALL FLOWERS	WINTER FLOWERS	FALL COLOR	STAR PERFORMER
✔	*Gardenia* "Veitchii Improved"	Gardenia			✔	✔	5'	5'	✔	✔			✔	✔	✔		✔					✔	✔			✔			✔		
	Grayia spinosa	Spiny Hopsage	✔	✔			8'	6'	✔	✔		✔	✔		✔				✔	✔				✔							
✔	*Grevillea* "Noellii"	NCN			✔		4'	4'	✔	✔		✔						✔		✔	✔		✔			✔					
	Hakea suavelolens	Sweet Hakea			✔		15'	15'	✔	✔		✔	✔		✔			✔	✔	✔			✔					✔	✔		
✔	*Helictotrichon sempervirens*	Blue Oat Grass		✔	✔		3'	3'	✔	✔	✔	✔	✔		✔		✔	✔	✔			✔	✔								
✔	*Hemerocallis fulva*	Daylily		✔	✔		5'	5'	✔	✔	✔	✔	✔	✔	✔		✔	✔			✔		✔			✔	✔				★
✔	*Hibiscus rosa-sinensis*	Chinese Hibiscus (See Cat.)			✔		8'	6'	✔			✔	✔		✔		✔					✔	✔			✔			✔		
	Hibiscus R-S "Bride"	Chinese Hibiscus (White)			✔		4'	4'	✔			✔	✔		✔		✔					✔	✔			✔			✔		
	Hibiscus R-S "Brilliant"	Chinese Hibiscus (Red)			✔		12'	2'	✔			✔	✔		✔		✔					✔	✔			✔			✔		
	Hibiscus R-S "Ecstasy"	Chinese Hibiscus (Red)			✔		4'	4'	✔			✔	✔		✔		✔					✔	✔			✔			✔		
	Hibiscus R-S "Hula Girl"	Chinese Hibiscus (Yellow)			✔		6'	6'	✔			✔	✔		✔		✔					✔	✔			✔			✔		
	Hibiscus R-S "President"	Chinese Hibiscus (Pink)			✔		7'	7'	✔			✔	✔		✔		✔					✔	✔			✔			✔		
	Hibiscus R-S "Red Dragon"	Chinese Hibiscus (Red)			✔		6'	6'	✔			✔	✔		✔		✔					✔	✔			✔			✔		
	Hibiscus R-S "Rosea"	Chinese Hibiscus (Red)			✔		6'	6'	✔			✔	✔		✔		✔					✔	✔			✔			✔		
	Hibiscus R-S "Ross Estey"	Chinese Hibiscus (Pink)			✔		8'	8'	✔			✔	✔		✔		✔					✔	✔			✔			✔		
	Ilex altaclarensis "Wilsonii"	Wilson Holly			✔		6'	6'	✔	✔	✔	✔	✔		✔		✔				✔	✔	✔			✔			✔	✔	
	Ilex cornuta "Burfordii"	Burford Holly			✔		6'	4'	✔	✔	✔	✔	✔		✔		✔				✔	✔	✔			✔				✔	
	Ilex cornuta "Rotunda"	Dwarf Chinese Holly			✔		2'	2'	✔	✔	✔	✔	✔		✔		✔				✔	✔	✔			✔				✔	
	Ilex vomitoria	Yaupon			✔		15'	15'	✔	✔	✔	✔	✔		✔		✔				✔	✔	✔			✔				✔	
	Ilex vomitoria "Stoke's"	Stoke's Yaupon			✔		2'	2'	✔	✔	✔	✔	✔		✔		✔				✔	✔	✔			✔				✔	
✔	*Isomeris arborea*	Bladderpod	✔	✔			4'	4'	✔	✔	✔	✔	✔		✔			✔	✔	✔				✔		✔				✔	
✔	*Jasminum sambac*	Arabian Jasmine			✔		5'	5'	✔				✔		✔		✔				✔		✔			✔					

Shrubs

MASTER PLANT MATERIALS MATRIX

DESCRIBED	BOTANICAL NAME	COMMON NAME	NATIVE	NATURALIZED	EXOTIC	TROPICAL	HEIGHT	WIDTH	LOW DESERT	INTERMEDIATE DESERT	HIGH DESERT	A — SUNNY	B — PART SUNNY	C — LITTLE SUNNY	D — INTRO. SHADE	E — DEEP SHADE	OASIS	TRANSITION	DESERT	LOW WATER	MODERATE WATER	HIGH WATER	EVERGREEN	SEMI EVERGREEN	DECIDUOUS	SPRING FLOWERS	SUMMER FLOWERS	FALL FLOWERS	WINTER FLOWERS	FALL COLOR	STAR PERFORMER
✔	*Juniperus chinensis* "Pfitzerana"	Pfitzer Juniper			✔		6'	12'	✔	✔	✔	✔	✔		✔		✔			✔	✔		✔								
	Juniperus chinensis prostrata	Prostrate Juniper			✔		2'	8'	✔	✔	✔	✔	✔		✔		✔			✔	✔		✔								
	Juniperus chinensis "Torulosa"	Hollywood Juniper			✔		10'	12'	✔	✔	✔	✔	✔		✔		✔			✔	✔		✔								
✔	*Juniperus sabina* "Arcadia"	Arcadia Juniper			✔		12"	10'	✔	✔	✔	✔	✔		✔		✔			✔	✔		✔								
✔	*Juniperus sabina* "Tamariscifolia"	Tam Juniper			✔		18"	12'	✔	✔	✔	✔	✔		✔		✔			✔	✔		✔								
	Juniperus "Seagreen"	Seagreen Juniper			✔		5'	5'	✔	✔	✔	✔	✔		✔		✔			✔	✔		✔								
	Justicia brandegeana	Shrimp Plant		✔			3'	2'	✔	✔	✔	✔							✔	✔				✔		✔					
✔	*Justicia californica*	Chauparosa	✔				4'	3'	✔	✔	✔	✔							✔	✔				✔		✔					
	Justicia spicigera	Mexican Honeysuckle		✔			5'	5'	✔	✔	✔	✔							✔	✔				✔		✔					
✔	*Lantana camara*	Bush Lantana			✔		6'	8'	✔	✔		✔	✔					✔		✔	✔		✔			✔	✔	✔	✔		★
✔	*Lantana sellowiana*	Trailing Purple Lantana			✔		2'	6'	✔	✔		✔	✔					✔		✔	✔		✔			✔	✔	✔	✔		★
✔	*Lantana sellowiana* "Confetti"	Confetti Lantana			✔		2'	5'	✔	✔		✔	✔					✔		✔	✔		✔			✔	✔	✔	✔		★
✔	*Lantana sellowiana* "Gold Mound"	Trailing Gold Lantana			✔		2'	5'	✔	✔		✔	✔					✔		✔	✔		✔			✔	✔	✔	✔		★
✔	*Lantana sellowiana* "Radiation"	Radiation Lantana			✔		4'	6'	✔	✔		✔	✔					✔		✔	✔		✔			✔	✔	✔	✔		★
✔	*Lantana sellowiana* "Sunburst"	Trailing Yellow Lantana			✔		3'	6'	✔	✔		✔	✔					✔		✔	✔		✔			✔	✔	✔	✔		★
✔	*Lantana sellowiana* "White"	Trailing White Lantana			✔		2'	5'	✔	✔		✔	✔					✔		✔	✔		✔			✔	✔	✔	✔		★
✔	*Larrea tridentata*	Creosote Bush	✔				10'	8'	✔	✔	✔	✔							✔	✔				✔		✔					
✔	*Laurus nobilis*	Sweet Bay			✔		15'	20'	✔	✔			✔		✔		✔	✔		✔	✔		✔								
	Lavandula dentata	English Lavender			✔		3'	3'	✔	✔		✔	✔		✔		✔	✔			✔		✔				✔	✔			
	Leucophyllum candidum "Silver Cloud"	Silver Cloud Texas Ranger	✔	✔			4'	4'	✔	✔		✔	✔					✔	✔	✔				✔		✔		✔			
	Leucophyllum candidum "Thunder Cloud"	Thunder Cloud Texas Ranger	✔	✔			3'	3'	✔	✔		✔	✔					✔	✔	✔				✔		✔		✔			
✔	*Leucophyllum frutescens*	Texas Ranger	✔	✔			7'	7'	✔	✔		✔	✔					✔	✔	✔	✔			✔		✔		✔			★
	BOTANICAL NAME	COMMON NAME	ENVIRON. GROUPING				SIZE		MACRO ZONE			MICRO ZONE					DESIGN USE			WATER REQ.			LEAF HABIT			FLOWER SHOW				F. C.	★

Shrubs

MASTER PLANT MATERIALS MATRIX

	BOTANICAL NAME	COMMON NAME	ENVIRON. GROUPING				SIZE		MACRO ZONE			MICRO ZONE					DESIGN USE			WATER REQ.			LEAF HABIT			FLOWER SHOW				F. C.	★
DESCRIBED			NATIVE	NATURALIZED	EXOTIC	TROPICAL	HEIGHT	WIDTH	LOW DESERT	INTERMEDIATE DESERT	HIGH DESERT	A — SUNNY	B — PART SUNNY	C — LITTLE SUNNY	D — INTRO. SHADE	E — DEEP SHADE	OASIS	TRANSITION	DESERT	LOW WATER	MODERATE WATER	HIGH WATER	EVERGREEN	SEMI EVERGREEN	DECIDUOUS	SPRING FLOWERS	SUMMER FLOWERS	FALL FLOWERS	WINTER FLOWERS	FALL COLOR	STAR PERFORMER
	Leucophyllum F. "Compacta"	Dwarf Texas Ranger	✔	✔			5'	5'	✔	✔	✔	✔	✔					✔	✔	✔				✔		✔		✔			
✔	*Leucophyllum F.* "Green Cloud"	Green Cloud Texas Ranger	✔	✔			6'	6'	✔	✔	✔	✔	✔					✔	✔	✔	✔			✔		✔		✔			★
	Leucophyllum F. "White Cloud"	White Cloud Texas Ranger	✔	✔			7'	7'	✔	✔	✔	✔	✔					✔	✔	✔				✔		✔		✔			
✔	*Leucophyllum langmaniae* "Rio Bravo"	Dwarf Green Texas Ranger	✔	✔			4'	4'	✔	✔		✔	✔					✔	✔	✔	✔			✔		✔		✔			★
✔	*Leucophyllum laevigatum*	Chihuahuan Sage	✔	✔			4'	5'	✔	✔		✔	✔					✔	✔	✔				✔		✔		✔			
✔	*Leucophyllum zygophyllum*	Blue Ranger	✔	✔			3'	3'	✔	✔		✔	✔					✔	✔	✔				✔		✔		✔			
✔	*Ligustrum japonicum* "Texanum"	Waxleaf Privet			✔		10'	6'	✔	✔	✔	✔	✔		✔		✔				✔	✔	✔								★
	Liriope gigantea	Large Lily Turf			✔	✔	3'	3'	✔	✔			✔	✔	✔	✔	✔					✔	✔					✔			
✔	*Liriope muscari*	Big Blue Lily Turf			✔	✔	18"	12"	✔	✔			✔	✔	✔	✔	✔					✔	✔					✔			★
	Lycium cooperi	Copper Wolfberry	✔	✔			6'	6'	✔	✔		✔							✔	✔				✔		✔					
	Mahonia aquifolium	Oregon Grape			✔		6'	5'	✔	✔	✔		✔		✔		✔	✔			✔		✔			✔					
	Mahonia bealei	Leatherleaf Mahonia			✔		10'	10'	✔	✔	✔	✔	✔		✔		✔	✔			✔		✔			✔					
	Mahonia fremontii	Desert Mahonia		✔	✔		6'	6'	✔	✔	✔	✔	✔		✔		✔	✔			✔		✔			✔					
	Moraea bicolor	Fortnight Lily			✔		4'	3'	✔	✔			✔	✔	✔		✔					✔	✔			✔	✔	✔			
✔	*Moraea iridioides*	Morea Lily			✔		3'	2'	✔	✔			✔	✔	✔		✔					✔	✔			✔	✔	✔			★
✔	*Murraya paniculata*	Orange Jessamine			✔		6'	5'	✔	✔			✔	✔	✔		✔					✔	✔			✔		✔	✔		
	Murraya exotica	Dwarf Orange Jessamine			✔		4'	3'	✔	✔			✔	✔	✔		✔					✔	✔			✔		✔	✔		
✔	*Myrtus communis* "Compacta"	Dwarf Myrtle			✔		4'	4'	✔	✔	✔	✔	✔	✔	✔		✔	✔			✔		✔				✔				★
✔	*Nandina domestica*	Heavenly Bamboo			✔		6'	4'	✔	✔		✔	✔	✔	✔		✔	✔		✔	✔		✔			✔		✔		✔	★
✔	*Nandina domestica* "Compacta"	Dwarf Heavenly Bamboo			✔		4'	4'	✔	✔		✔	✔	✔	✔		✔	✔		✔			✔			✔				✔	
✔	*Nandina domestica* "Harbour Dwarf"	Heavenly Bamboo			✔		2'	2'	✔	✔		✔	✔	✔	✔		✔	✔		✔			✔			✔				✔	
✔	*Nandina domestica* "Nana"	Small Heavenly Bamboo			✔		12"	12"	✔	✔		✔	✔	✔	✔		✔	✔		✔			✔			✔				✔	

Shrubs

MASTER PLANT MATERIALS MATRIX

DESCRIBED	BOTANICAL NAME	COMMON NAME	NATIVE	NATURALIZED	EXOTIC	TROPICAL	HEIGHT	WIDTH	LOW DESERT	INTERMEDIATE DESERT	HIGH DESERT	A — SUNNY	B — PART SUNNY	C — LITTLE SUNNY	D — INTRO. SHADE	E — DEEP SHADE	OASIS	TRANSITION	DESERT	LOW WATER	MODERATE WATER	HIGH WATER	EVERGREEN	SEMI EVERGREEN	DECIDUOUS	SPRING FLOWERS	SUMMER FLOWERS	FALL FLOWERS	WINTER FLOWERS	FALL COLOR	STAR PERFORMER
✔	*Nandina domestica* "Pygmae"	Pygmy Heavenly Bamboo			✔		10"	8"	✔	✔		✔	✔	✔	✔		✔	✔		✔			✔			✔				✔	
✔	*Nephroleps cordifolia*	Sword Fern			✔		3'	2'	✔	✔				✔	✔	✔	✔					✔	✔								
✔	*Nerium oleander*	Common Oleander			✔		20'	20'	✔	✔	✔	✔	✔		✔		✔	✔		✔	✔		✔			✔	✔		✔		
✔	*Nerium oleander* "Algiers"	Medium Red Oleander			✔		12'	12'	✔	✔	✔	✔	✔		✔		✔	✔		✔	✔		✔			✔	✔		✔		
✔	*Nerium oleander* "Casablanca"	Medium White Oleander			✔		12'	12'	✔	✔	✔	✔	✔		✔		✔	✔		✔	✔		✔			✔	✔		✔		
✔	*Nerium oleander* "Mrs. Roeding"	Medium Pink Oleander			✔		8'	8'	✔	✔	✔	✔	✔		✔		✔	✔		✔	✔		✔			✔	✔		✔		
✔	*Nerium oleander* "Little Red"	Dwarf Red Oleander			✔		5'	5'	✔	✔	✔	✔	✔		✔		✔	✔		✔	✔		✔			✔	✔		✔		
✔	*Nerium oleander* "Petite Pink"	Dwarf Pink Oleander			✔		6'	6'	✔	✔	✔	✔	✔		✔		✔	✔		✔	✔		✔			✔	✔		✔		★
✔	*Nerium oleander* "Petite Salmon"	Dwarf Salmon Oleander			✔		4'	6'	✔	✔	✔	✔	✔		✔		✔	✔		✔	✔		✔			✔	✔		✔		
	Olea europaea "Little Ollie"	Dwarf Olive			✔		4'	6'	✔	✔	✔	✔	✔		✔		✔	✔			✔		✔								
✔	*Osmanthus fragrans*	Sweet Olive			✔		10'	8'	✔	✔	✔		✔	✔	✔		✔	✔		✔			✔			✔	✔				
	Parthenium argentatum	Guayule	✔	✔			3'	3'	✔	✔	✔	✔						✔	✔	✔				✔			✔	✔			
✔	*Pennisetum setaceum*	Fountain Grass		✔			4'	4'	✔	✔	✔	✔	✔				✔	✔	✔	✔				✔				✔	✔		
✔	*Pennisetum setaceum* "Cupreum"	Red Fountain Grass			✔		6'	4'	✔	✔	✔	✔	✔					✔		✔				✔				✔	✔		★
	Penstemon antirrhinoides	Yellow Penstemon		✔			4'	4'	✔	✔		✔	✔					✔	✔	✔				✔		✔					
	Penstemon centranthifolius	Scarlet Bugler		✔			3'	3'	✔	✔		✔	✔					✔	✔	✔				✔		✔					
	Penstemon heterophyllus purdyi	Blue Penstemon		✔			3'	3'	✔	✔		✔	✔					✔	✔	✔				✔		✔					
✔	*Penstemon spectalilis*	Showy Penstemon		✔			4'	2'	✔	✔		✔	✔					✔	✔	✔				✔		✔					
	Penstemon wrightii			✔			3'	2'	✔	✔		✔	✔					✔	✔	✔				✔		✔					
	Philadelphus coronarius	Sweet Mock Orange			✔		8'	10'	✔	✔	✔		✔		✔		✔				✔				✔		✔				
	Philadelphus lewisii	Wild Mock Orange		✔	✔		6'	6'	✔	✔	✔		✔		✔		✔			✔	✔				✔		✔				
✔	*Philodendron selloum*	Split-Leaf Philodendron			✔	✔	8'	10'	✔	✔			✔	✔	✔		✔					✔	✔								★
	BOTANICAL NAME	COMMON NAME	ENVIRON. GROUPING				SIZE		MACRO ZONE			MICRO ZONE					DESIGN USE			WATER REQ.			LEAF HABIT			FLOWER SHOW				F. C.	★

Shrubs

MASTER PLANT MATERIALS MATRIX

DESCRIBED	BOTANICAL NAME	COMMON NAME	NATIVE	NATURALIZED	EXOTIC	TROPICAL	HEIGHT	WIDTH	LOW DESERT	INTERMEDIATE DESERT	HIGH DESERT	A — SUNNY	B — PART SUNNY	C — LITTLE SUNNY	D — INTRO. SHADE	E — DEEP SHADE	OASIS	TRANSITION	DESERT	LOW WATER	MODERATE WATER	HIGH WATER	EVERGREEN	SEMI EVERGREEN	DECIDUOUS	SPRING FLOWERS	SUMMER FLOWERS	FALL FLOWERS	WINTER FLOWERS	FALL COLOR	STAR PERFORMER
✔	*Phormium tenax*	New Zealand Flax			✔		10'	8'	✔	✔	✔	✔	✔		✔			✔			✔		✔			✔	✔				
✔	*Photinia fraseri*	Fraser's Photinia			✔		10'	10'	✔	✔	✔	✔	✔		✔		✔	✔			✔		✔			✔					★
	Pittosporum phillyraeoides	Willow Pittosporum			✔		20'	15'	✔	✔			✔		✔		✔				✔		✔			✔					
✔	*Pittosporum tobria*	Mock Orange			✔		8'	8'	✔	✔			✔		✔		✔				✔		✔			✔					
	Pittosporum T. "Variegata"	Variegated Mock Orange			✔		6'	6'	✔	✔			✔		✔		✔				✔		✔			✔					
✔	*Pittosporum T.* "Wheeler's Dwarf"	Dwarf Mock Orange			✔		18"	3'	✔	✔			✔		✔		✔				✔	✔	✔			✔					
	Platycladus orientalis	Globe Arborvitae			✔		25'	25'	✔	✔	✔	✔	✔		✔		✔				✔		✔								
✔	*Plumbago auriculata*	Cape Plumbago			✔		4'	6'	✔	✔		✔	✔					✔			✔			✔		✔	✔	✔			
	Plumbago scandens "Summer Snow"	White Plumbago			✔		2'	4'	✔	✔			✔	✔	✔		✔	✔			✔	✔		✔		✔	✔	✔			
✔	*Plumeria rubra*	Fragipani			✔		8'	8'	✔	✔			✔		✔		✔				✔		✔				✔	✔			
	Poinciana gilliesii	Yellow Bird-of-Paradise	✔	✔			12'	12'	✔	✔		✔						✔	✔		✔	✔			✔	✔	✔	✔			
✔	*Poinciana pulcherrima*	Mexican Bird-of-Paradise	✔	✔			8'	8'	✔	✔		✔						✔	✔		✔	✔			✔	✔	✔	✔			★
✔	*Pyracantha* species	Firethorn			✔		—	—	✔	✔	✔	✔	✔					✔		✔	✔		✔			✔				✔	★
✔	*Pyracantha coccinea* "Lalandei"	Firethorn			✔		10'	10'	✔	✔	✔	✔	✔					✔		✔	✔		✔			✔				✔	★
✔	*Pyracantha fortuneana* "Graberi"	Firethorn			✔		8'	8'	✔	✔	✔	✔	✔					✔		✔	✔		✔			✔					★
✔	*Pyracantha* "Santa Cruz"	Firethorn			✔		4'	4'	✔	✔	✔	✔	✔					✔		✔	✔		✔			✔					★
✔	*Pyracantha* "Tiny Tim"	Dwarf Firethorn			✔		2'	3'	✔	✔	✔	✔	✔					✔		✔	✔		✔			✔					★
	Rhamnus californica	California Coffeeberry		✔			8'	8'	✔	✔	✔	✔	✔		✔			✔		✔	✔			✔		✔					
	Rhamnus crocea	Redberry		✔			4'	4'	✔			✔	✔		✔			✔		✔	✔			✔		✔					
✔	*Rhaphiolepsis indica*	India Hawthorn			✔		5'	5'	✔	✔			✔		✔		✔				✔	✔	✔			✔		✔			★
✔	*Rhaphiolepsis indica* "Clara"	White India Hawthorn			✔		4'	4'	✔	✔			✔		✔		✔				✔	✔	✔			✔		✔			★
✔	*Rhaphiolepsis indica* "Coates Crimson"	Red India Hawthorn			✔		2'	2'	✔	✔			✔		✔		✔				✔	✔	✔			✔		✔			★
	BOTANICAL NAME	COMMON NAME	ENVIRON. GROUPING				SIZE		MACRO ZONE			MICRO ZONE					DESIGN USE			WATER REQ.			LEAF HABIT			FLOWER SHOW				F. C.	★

Shrubs

MASTER PLANT MATERIALS MATRIX

DESCRIBED	BOTANICAL NAME	COMMON NAME	NATIVE	NATURALIZED	EXOTIC	TROPICAL	HEIGHT	WIDTH	LOW DESERT	INTERMEDIATE DESERT	HIGH DESERT	A — SUNNY	B — PART SUNNY	C — LITTLE SUNNY	D — INTRO. SHADE	E — DEEP SHADE	OASIS	TRANSITION	DESERT	LOW WATER	MODERATE WATER	HIGH WATER	EVERGREEN	SEMI EVERGREEN	DECIDUOUS	SPRING FLOWERS	SUMMER FLOWERS	FALL FLOWERS	WINTER FLOWERS	FALL COLOR	STAR PERFORMER
✔	*Rhaphiolepsis indica* "Rosea"	Pink India Hawthorn			✔		3'	3'	✔	✔			✔		✔		✔				✔	✔	✔			✔		✔			★
✔	*Rhaphiolepsis indica* "Springtime"	India Hawthorn			✔		6'	6'	✔	✔			✔		✔		✔				✔	✔	✔			✔		✔			★
✔	*Rhaphiolepsis indica* "Majestic Beauty"	NCN (Large Hawthorn)			✔		12'	12'	✔	✔			✔		✔		✔				✔	✔	✔			✔		✔			
✔	*Rhus ovata*	Sugar Bush	✔				12'	12'	✔	✔	✔	✔	✔		✔			✔	✔	✔			✔			✔				✔	
✔	*Romneya coulteri*	Matilija Poppy		✔			8'	4'	✔	✔	✔	✔	✔		✔			✔	✔	✔				✔		✔	✔				
✔	*Rosa* species	Rose (See Cat.)			✔		—	—	✔	✔	✔	✔	✔		✔		✔	✔			✔				✔	✔		✔			
	Rosa species "Climbing"	Climbing Roses (See Cat.)			✔		—	—	✔	✔	✔	✔	✔		✔		✔	✔			✔	✔			✔	✔		✔			
	Rosa species "Minature"	Minature Roses (See Cat.)			✔		—	—	✔	✔	✔	✔	✔		✔		✔	✔			✔	✔			✔	✔		✔			
	Rosa species "Standard"	Tree Roses (See Cat.)			✔		—	—	✔	✔	✔	✔	✔		✔		✔	✔			✔	✔			✔	✔		✔			
	Rosa "Floribunda"	Floribundas (See Cat.)			✔		—	—	✔	✔	✔	✔	✔		✔		✔	✔			✔	✔			✔	✔		✔			
	Rosa "Grandiflora"	Grandifloras (See Cat.)			✔		—	—	✔	✔	✔	✔	✔		✔		✔	✔			✔	✔			✔	✔		✔			
	Rosa "Hybrid Tea"	Hybrid Teas (See Cat.)			✔		—	—	✔	✔	✔	✔	✔		✔		✔	✔			✔	✔			✔	✔		✔			
	Rosa "Polyanthas"	Spray Roses (See Cat.)			✔		—	—	✔	✔	✔	✔	✔		✔		✔	✔			✔	✔			✔	✔		✔			
✔	*Rosmarinus officinalis*	Rosemary			✔		4'	6'	✔	✔		✔	✔		✔		✔	✔		✔			✔			✔	✔				
✔	*Rosmarinus officinalis* "Prostratus"	Prostrate Rosemary			✔		6'	8'	✔	✔		✔	✔		✔		✔	✔		✔			✔			✔	✔				
	Ruellia californica	Ruellia	✔	✔			6'	6'	✔	✔		✔	✔					✔	✔	✔	✔			✔		✔	✔				
✔	*Ruellia peninsularis*	Ruellia	✔	✔			4'	4'	✔	✔		✔	✔					✔	✔	✔				✔		✔	✔				
	Salazaria mexicana	Common Bladdersage	✔	✔			2'	3'	✔	✔	✔	✔	✔		✔			✔	✔	✔				✔		✔	✔				
	Salvia clevelandii	Chaparrel Salvia		✔			3'	3'	✔	✔	✔	✔						✔	✔	✔				✔		✔	✔				
	Salvia coccinea	Texas Sage		✔			4'	4'	✔	✔	✔	✔						✔	✔	✔				✔		✔	✔				
✔	*Salvia greggii*	Autumn Sage	✔	✔			4'	4'	✔	✔	✔	✔							✔	✔				✔		✔	✔				★
	Salvia leucantha	Mexican Bush Sage	✔	✔			6'	6'	✔	✔	✔	✔						✔	✔	✔				✔		✔	✔				
	BOTANICAL NAME	COMMON NAME	ENVIRON. GROUPING				SIZE		MACRO ZONE			MICRO ZONE					DESIGN USE			WATER REQ.			LEAF HABIT			FLOWER SHOW				F. C.	★

Shrubs

MASTER PLANT MATERIALS MATRIX

			ENVIRON. GROUPING				SIZE		MACRO ZONE			MICRO ZONE					DESIGN USE			WATER REQ.			LEAF HABIT			FLOWER SHOW				F. C.	★
DESCRIBED	BOTANICAL NAME	COMMON NAME	NATIVE	NATURALIZED	EXOTIC	TROPICAL	HEIGHT	WIDTH	LOW DESERT	INTERMEDIATE DESERT	HIGH DESERT	A — SUNNY	B — PART SUNNY	C — LITTLE SUNNY	D — INTRO. SHADE	E — DEEP SHADE	OASIS	TRANSITION	DESERT	LOW WATER	MODERATE WATER	HIGH WATER	EVERGREEN	SEMI EVERGREEN	DECIDUOUS	SPRING FLOWERS	SUMMER FLOWERS	FALL FLOWERS	WINTER FLOWERS	FALL COLOR	STAR PERFORMER
✔	*Salvia leucophylla*	Purple Sage		✔			6'	6'	✔	✔	✔	✔						✔	✔	✔				✔		✔	✔				★
	Salvia superba "Blue Hills"	Blue Spike Salvia		✔			3'	3'	✔	✔	✔	✔						✔	✔	✔				✔		✔	✔				
✔	*Santolina chamaecyparissus*	Lavender Cotton	✔				18"	3'	✔	✔	✔	✔	✔					✔	✔	✔			✔			✔	✔				★
✔	*Santolina virens*	Green Lavender Cotton	✔				12"	2'	✔	✔	✔	✔	✔		✔		✔	✔	✔	✔			✔			✔	✔				★
✔	*Sarobatus vermiculatus*	Greasewood	✔	✔			15'	12'	✔	✔	✔	✔	✔					✔	✔	✔				✔			✔				
✔	*Senecio cineraria*	Dusty Miller		✔	✔		2'	2'	✔	✔	✔	✔	✔		✔			✔	✔	✔				✔		✔	✔	✔	✔		
✔	*Simmondsia chinensis*	Jojoba	✔	✔			6'	6'	✔	✔	✔	✔	✔		✔			✔	✔	✔			✔			✔					
✔	*Solanum rantonnetii* "Royal Robe"	Potato Bush			✔		6'	4'	✔	✔			✔		✔			✔			✔			✔		✔	✔				
✔	*Sophora secundiflora*	Mescal Bean	✔	✔			10'	10'	✔	✔		✔					✔	✔	✔	✔			✔			✔	✔				
	Strelitzia nicolai	Giant Bird-of-Paradise			✔	✔	18'	10'	✔	✔			✔		✔		✔					✔	✔			✔		✔	✔		
✔	*Strelitzia reginae*	Bird-of-Paradise			✔	✔	6'	6'	✔	✔			✔		✔		✔					✔	✔			✔		✔	✔		★
	Syringa persica	Persian Lilac			✔		6'	6'	✔	✔			✔		✔		✔	✔			✔	✔			✔					✔	
	Tagetes lemmoni	Mountain Marigold	✔	✔			3'	3'	✔	✔		✔	✔		✔			✔	✔	✔	✔			✔		✔			✔		
✔	*Tecoma stans*	Yellow Bells		✔	✔		12'	12'	✔	✔		✔	✔		✔			✔		✔	✔		✔				✔	✔			★
✔	*Tecomaria capensis*	Cape Honeysuckle			✔		8'	12'	✔	✔		✔	✔		✔		✔	✔			✔	✔	✔				✔	✔	✔		
	Ternstroemia gymnanthera	Ternstroemia			✔		4'	4'	✔	✔		✔	✔		✔		✔	✔					✔				✔				
	Teucrium chamaedrys	Germander			✔		2'	4'	✔	✔	✔	✔	✔		✔		✔	✔			✔		✔			✔	✔				
	Teucrium fruticans	Bush Germander			✔		4'	6'	✔	✔	✔	✔	✔		✔		✔	✔			✔		✔			✔	✔				
✔	*Thevetia neriifolia*	Yellow Oleander			✔		8'	10'	✔	✔		✔	✔		✔		✔	✔			✔	✔	✔			✔	✔	✔	✔		★
✔	*Vauquelinia californica*	Arizona Rosewood	✔	✔			8'	6'	✔	✔		✔						✔	✔	✔			✔			✔	✔				★
	Viburnum burkwoodii	Burkwood Viburnum			✔		6'	6'	✔				✔		✔		✔	✔			✔	✔			✔	✔		✔	✔		
	Viburnum suspensum	Sandankwa Viburnum			✔		8'	10'	✔				✔		✔		✔	✔			✔	✔	✔			✔		✔	✔		

Shrubs

MASTER PLANT MATERIALS MATRIX

DESCRIBED	BOTANICAL NAME	COMMON NAME	ENVIRON. GROUPING				SIZE		MACRO ZONE			MICRO ZONE					DESIGN USE			WATER REQ.			LEAF HABIT			FLOWER SHOW				F. C.	★
			NATIVE	NATURALIZED	EXOTIC	TROPICAL	HEIGHT	WIDTH	LOW DESERT	INTERMEDIATE DESERT	HIGH DESERT	A — SUNNY	B — PART SUNNY	C — LITTLE SUNNY	D — INTRO. SHADE	E — DEEP SHADE	OASIS	TRANSITION	DESERT	LOW WATER	MODERATE WATER	HIGH WATER	EVERGREEN	SEMI EVERGREEN	DECIDUOUS	SPRING FLOWERS	SUMMER FLOWERS	FALL FLOWERS	WINTER FLOWERS	FALL COLOR	STAR PERFORMER
	Viburnum tinus "Compacta"	Dwarf Laurustinus			✔		5'	3'	✔				✔		✔		✔	✔			✔	✔	✔			✔		✔	✔		
	Viburnum tinus "Lucidum"	Shining Laurustinus			✔		10'	8'	4✔	✔	✔		✔		✔		✔	✔			✔	✔	✔			✔		✔	✔		
✔	*Viburnum tinus* "Spring Bouquet"	Laurustinus			✔		10'	8'	✔	✔	✔		✔		✔		✔	✔			✔	✔	✔			✔		✔	✔		★
	Viguiera deltoidea	Goldeneye	✔	✔			4'	4'	✔			✔							✔	✔				✔		✔					
	Xanthosma violaceum	Elephant's Ear			✔	✔	2'	2'	✔	✔				✔	✔	✔	✔					✔	✔								
✔	*Xylosma congestum*	Shiny Xylosma			✔		10'	10'	✔	✔	✔	✔	✔		✔		✔	✔		✔	✔		✔								★
✔	*Xylosma congestum* "Compacta"	Dwarf Xylosma			✔		6'	6'	✔	✔	✔	✔	✔		✔		✔	✔		✔	✔		✔								★
✔	*Zauschneria californica*	Hummingbird Flower	✔				3'	3'	✔	✔		✔	✔		✔			✔	✔	✔				✔		✔	✔				

Espaliers

MASTER PLANT MATERIALS MATRIX

	BOTANICAL NAME	COMMON NAME	ENVIRON. GROUPING				SIZE		MACRO ZONE			MICRO ZONE					DESIGN USE			WATER REQ.			LEAF HABIT			FLOWER SHOW				F. C.	★
DESCRIBED			NATIVE	NATURALIZED	EXOTIC	TROPICAL	HEIGHT	WIDTH	LOW DESERT	INTERMEDIATE DESERT	HIGH DESERT	A — SUNNY	B — PART SUNNY	C — LITTLE SUNNY	D — INTRO. SHADE	E — DEEP SHADE	OASIS	TRANSITION	DESERT	LOW WATER	MODERATE WATER	HIGH WATER	EVERGREEN	SEMI EVERGREEN	DECIDUOUS	SPRING FLOWERS	SUMMER FLOWERS	FALL FLOWERS	WINTER FLOWERS	FALL COLOR	STAR PERFORMER
	Bauhinia variegata purpurea	Orchid Tree			✔		8'	3'	✔	✔			✔		✔		✔				✔	✔			✔	✔			✔		
✔	*Beaumontia grandiflora*	Easter Lily Vine			✔		8'	3'	✔					✔	✔		✔				✔		✔				✔				
	Camellia species	Camellia			✔		6'	3'	✔	✔				✔	✔		✔					✔	✔			✔					
✔	*Citrus* species	Citrus			✔		12'	3'	✔	✔			✔		✔		✔	✔			✔	✔	✔			✔					
✔	*Eriobotrya japonica*	Loquat			✔		15'	5'	✔	✔	✔		✔	✔	✔		✔	✔			✔	✔	✔					✔	✔		★
✔	*Feijoa sellowiana*	Pineapple Guava			✔		12'	3'	✔	✔		✔	✔		✔		✔	✔		✔	✔		✔			✔					★
	Ficus benjamina	Chinese Weeping Banyan			✔	✔	8'	2'	✔				✔	✔	✔		✔					✔	✔								
✔	*Grewia caffra*	Lavender Starflower			✔		12'	3'	✔	✔		✔	✔		✔		✔	✔			✔		✔			✔			✔		★
	Hibiscus rosa sinensis	Chinese Hibiscus			✔		8'	3'	✔			✔	✔		✔		✔				✔		✔			✔			✔		
✔	*Magnolia grandiflora*	Southern Magnolia			✔	✔	15'	5'	✔	✔			✔		✔		✔				✔		✔			✔	✔				
	Murraya paniculata	Satinwood			✔		8'	2'	✔	✔			✔	✔	✔		✔					✔	✔			✔			✔		
	Photinia fraseri	Fraser's Photinia			✔		12'	3'	✔	✔	✔		✔	✔	✔		✔				✔		✔			✔					
	Plumbago auriculata	Cape Plumbago			✔		6'	3'	✔			✔	✔					✔			✔		✔			✔					
	Podocarpus gracilior	Fern Pine			✔	✔	8'	2'	✔	✔			✔	✔	✔		✔					✔	✔								
✔	*Pyracantha fortuneana* "Graberi"	Pyracantha			✔		12'	8'	✔	✔	✔	✔	✔				✔	✔		✔	✔		✔			✔					★
	Pyracantha "Santa Cruz"	Pyracantha			✔		12'	8'	✔	✔	✔	✔	✔				✔	✔		✔	✔		✔			✔					
✔	*Pyrus kawakamii*	Evergreen Pear			✔		12'	3'	✔	✔			✔	✔	✔		✔				✔	✔			✔	✔				✔	
	Tecomaria capensis	Cape Honeysuckle			✔		12'	3'	✔	✔			✔		✔		✔	✔			✔	✔	✔				✔	✔	✔		
	Tecoma stans	Yellow Bells			✔		18'	4'	✔	✔	✔	✔	✔					✔			✔		✔			✔	✔				
✔	*Vitis labrusca*	Edible Grape (Slip Skin)			✔		6'	8'	✔	✔		✔	✔		✔		✔					✔			✔					✔	
✔	*Vitis vinifera*	Edible Grape (Tight Skin)			✔		6'	8'	✔	✔		✔	✔		✔		✔					✔			✔					✔	

Vines

MASTER PLANT MATERIALS MATRIX

	BOTANICAL NAME	COMMON NAME	ENVIRON. GROUPING				MACRO ZONE			MICRO ZONE					DESIGN USE			WATER REQ.			LEAF HABIT			FLOWER SHOW				F. C.	★
DESCRIBED			NATIVE	NATURALIZED	EXOTIC	TROPICAL	LOW DESERT	INTERMEDIATE DESERT	HIGH DESERT	A — SUNNY	B — PART SUNNY	C — LITTLE SUNNY	D — INTRO. SHADE	E — DEEP SHADE	OASIS	TRANSITION	DESERT	LOW WATER	MODERATE WATER	HIGH WATER	EVERGREEN	SEMI EVERGREEN	DECIDUOUS	SPRING FLOWERS	SUMMER FLOWERS	FALL FLOWERS	WINTER FLOWERS	FALL COLOR	STAR PERFORMER
	Akebia quinata	Fiveleaf Akebia			✓		✓	✓	✓		✓	✓			✓				✓			✓		✓					
	Ampelopsis brevipedunculata	Blueberry Climber			✓		✓	✓	✓		✓	✓			✓				✓				✓	✓					
✓	*Antigonon leptopus*	Coral Vine			✓		✓	✓		✓	✓	✓	✓		✓	✓		✓	✓			✓		✓		✓	✓		★
	Bougainvillea species	Bougainvillea			✓		✓	✓		✓	✓				✓	✓		✓	✓			✓		✓			✓		
✓	*Bougainvillea* "Barbara Karst"	Red Vine Bougainvillea			✓		✓	✓		✓	✓				✓	✓		✓	✓			✓		✓			✓		★
	Bougainvillea brasilensis	Purple Vine Bougainvillea			✓		✓	✓		✓	✓				✓	✓	✓	✓				✓		✓			✓		
✓	*Calliandra inaequilaera*	Pink Powder Puff		✓			✓	✓		✓	✓		✓		✓	✓		✓	✓			✓		✓	✓				
	Calliandra tweedii	Trinidad Flame Bush		✓			✓	✓		✓	✓		✓			✓	✓	✓	✓			✓		✓	✓				
	Campsis radicans	Trumpet Vine			✓		✓	✓	✓	✓	✓		✓			✓			✓				✓			✓			
✓	*Clematis* species	Clematis (See Cat)			✓		✓	✓	✓		✓		✓		✓				✓	✓			✓	✓	✓	✓	✓		
✓	*Clytostoma callistegioides*	Violet Trumpet Vine			✓		✓				✓	✓	✓		✓	✓			✓			✓		✓	✓	✓			★
	Distictis species	Trumpet Vines			✓		✓			✓	✓				✓	✓			✓		✓			✓	✓				
✓	*Doxantha cati*	Cat's Claw Vine			✓		✓	✓		✓	✓		✓		✓	✓	✓	✓	✓			✓		✓	✓				★
	Euonymus fortunei	Euonymus			✓		✓	✓	✓	✓	✓	✓	✓		✓				✓	✓	✓			✓					
✓	*Ficus pumila*	Creeping Fig			✓		✓	✓				✓	✓	✓	✓					✓	✓								★
✓	*Gelsemium sempervirens*	Carolina Jessamine			✓		✓	✓		✓	✓		✓		✓				✓	✓	✓			✓			✓		★
✓	*Hardenbergia violacea*	Vine Lilac			✓		✓	✓	✓	✓	✓		✓		✓	✓		✓	✓		✓			✓			✓		
	Jasminum grandiflorum	Spanish Jasmine			✓		✓	✓			✓	✓	✓		✓					✓		✓		✓	✓				
✓	*Jasminum nitidum*	Angelwing Jasmine			✓		✓	✓			✓		✓		✓					✓		✓		✓	✓				
	Lonicera japonica "Halliana"	Hall's Honeysuckle			✓		✓	✓	✓	✓	✓	✓	✓	✓	✓	✓			✓	✓	✓			✓	✓				
✓	*Mandevilla* "Alice Du Pont"	NCN			✓	✓	✓				✓		✓		✓					✓	✓					✓	✓		
	Mascagnia lilacina	Mexican Purple Orchid Vine		✓			✓			✓	✓					✓			✓				✓	✓					

Vines

MASTER PLANT MATERIALS MATRIX

	BOTANICAL NAME	COMMON NAME	ENVIRON. GROUPING				MACRO ZONE			MICRO ZONE					DESIGN USE			WATER REQ.			LEAF HABIT			FLOWER SHOW				F. C.	★
DESCRIBED			NATIVE	NATURALIZED	EXOTIC	TROPICAL	LOW DESERT	INTERMEDIATE DESERT	HIGH DESERT	A — SUNNY	B — PART SUNNY	C — LITTLE SUNNY	D — INTRO. SHADE	E — DEEP SHADE	OASIS	TRANSITION	DESERT	LOW WATER	MODERATE WATER	HIGH WATER	EVERGREEN	SEMI EVERGREEN	DECIDUOUS	SPRING FLOWERS	SUMMER FLOWERS	FALL FLOWERS	WINTER FLOWERS	FALL COLOR	STAR PERFORMER
	Mascagnia macuoptena	Yellow Orchid Vine		✔			✔			✔	✔					✔			✔				✔	✔					
	Muehlenbeckia complexa	Mattress Vine			✔		✔			✔						✔			✔				✔	✔					
✔	*Parthenocissus tricuspidata*	Boston Ivy			✔		✔	✔	✔		✔	✔	✔		✔					✔			✔					✔	
✔	*Passiflora alatocaerulea*	Passion Vine			✔		✔	✔		✔	✔		✔		✔				✔			✔		✔	✔				
	Phaedranthus buccinatorius	Blood-Red Trumpet Vine			✔		✔				✔	✔	✔		✔					✔	✔			✔	✔				
	Podrenea vicasoliana	Pink Trumpet Vine			✔		✔	✔		✔	✔				✔	✔			✔		✔			✔	✔				
	Polygonum aubertii	Silver Lace Vine			✔			✔	✔	✔	✔	✔			✔	✔			✔				✔	✔					
✔	*Pyrostegia venusta*	Flame Vine			✔		✔			✔						✔	✔	✔	✔		✔					✔	✔		★
✔	*Rosa banksiae "Alba Plena"*	Lady Bank's Rose (White)			✔		✔	✔	✔	✔	✔		✔		✔	✔			✔				✔	✔	✔				★
✔	*Rosa banksiae "Lutea"*	Lady Bank's Rose (Yellow)			✔		✔	✔	✔	✔	✔		✔		✔	✔			✔				✔	✔	✔				★
	Rosa species	Climbing Roses			✔		✔	✔	✔	✔	✔				✔	✔			✔				✔	✔	✔	✔			
✔	*Solanum jasminoides*	Potato Vine			✔		✔			✔	✔		✔		✔	✔			✔			✔		✔	✔	✔	✔		
	Tetrastigma voinieranum	NCN			✔		✔					✔	✔	✔	✔				✔		✔								
	Thunbergia alata	Black-Eyed Susan Vine			✔		✔			✔	✔				✔	✔			✔				✔	✔	✔				
	Thunbergia gregarli	Orange Clock Vine			✔		✔			✔	✔				✔	✔			✔				✔	✔	✔				
	Thunbergia mysorersis	NCN			✔		✔			✔	✔				✔	✔			✔				✔	✔	✔				
✔	*Trachelospermum jasminoides*	Star Jasmine			✔		✔					✔	✔		✔					✔	✔			✔					
	Vitis girdiana	Wild Grape		✔	✔		✔	✔		✔	✔		✔		✔					✔			✔	✔				✔	
	Wisteria sinensis	Wisteria (Blue)			✔		✔	✔	✔	✔	✔		✔		✔					✔			✔	✔				✔	
	Wisteria sinensis "Alba"	Wisteria (White)			✔		✔	✔	✔	✔	✔		✔		✔					✔			✔	✔				✔	

Ground Covers

MASTER PLANT MATERIALS MATRIX

DESCRIBED	BOTANICAL NAME	COMMON NAME	ENVIRON. GROUPING				SIZE		MACRO ZONE			MICRO ZONE					DESIGN USE			WATER REQ.			LEAF HABIT			FLOWER SHOW				F. C.	★
			NATIVE	NATURALIZED	EXOTIC	TROPICAL	HEIGHT	WIDTH	LOW DESERT	INTERMEDIATE DESERT	HIGH DESERT	A — SUNNY	B — PART SUNNY	C — LITTLE SUNNY	D — INTRO. SHADE	E — DEEP SHADE	OASIS	TRANSITION	DESERT	LOW WATER	MODERATE WATER	HIGH WATER	EVERGREEN	SEMI EVERGREEN	DECIDUOUS	SPRING FLOWERS	SUMMER FLOWERS	FALL FLOWERS	WINTER FLOWERS	FALL COLOR	STAR PERFORMER
✔	*Acacia redolens* "Desert Carpet"	NCN			✔		2'	12'	✔	✔		✔	✔					✔	✔	✔			✔			✔			✔		★
✔	*Acacia redolens*	Prostrate Acacia		✔	✔		4'	12"	✔	✔		✔	✔					✔	✔	✔			✔			✔			✔		★
✔	*Ajuga reptans*	Carpet Bugle			✔		6"	12"	✔	✔	✔		✔		✔		✔					✔	✔			✔	✔				
✔	*Ajuga reptens* "Purpurea"	Bronze Ajuga			✔		6"	12"	✔	✔	✔		✔		✔		✔					✔	✔			✔	✔				
✔	*Aptenia cordifolia*	Candy Apple			✔		6"	24"	✔				✔		✔		✔				✔	✔	✔			✔	✔				
✔	*Arctotheca calendula*	Cape Weed		✔	✔		6"	18"	✔			✔	✔		✔			✔			✔		✔			✔					
✔	*Arundinaria pygmaea*	Pygmy Bamboo			✔	✔	6"	12"	✔				✔	✔	✔		✔					✔	✔								
✔	*Asparagus meyeri*	Meyer's Asparagus Fern			✔	✔	16"	24"	✔	✔		✔	✔		✔		✔				✔	✔	✔			✔				✔	
✔	*Asparagus sprengeri*	Asparagus Fern			✔		24"	36"	✔	✔		✔	✔		✔		✔				✔		✔			✔				✔	★
✔	*Baccharis pilularis* "Twin Peaks"	Hybrid Dwarf Coyote Bush	✔	✔			2'	6'	✔	✔	✔	✔	✔		✔		✔			✔	✔	✔	✔	✔		✔					
	Calylophus hartweggi	Calylophus	✔				2'	4'	✔	✔	✔	✔	✔					✔	✔	✔				✔		✔	✔	✔			
	Campanula elatines garganica	Adriatic Bellflower			✔		6"	18"	✔	✔	✔		✔		✔		✔					✔	✔			✔	✔				
	Carissa grandiflora prostrata	Prostrate Natal Plum			✔		2'	6'	✔	✔			✔		✔		✔					✔	✔			✔			✔		
	Carissa G. "Boxwood Beauty"	Natal Plum			✔		2'	2'	✔	✔			✔		✔		✔					✔	✔			✔			✔		
	Carissa G. "Green Carpet"	Natal Plum			✔		18"	4'	✔	✔			✔		✔		✔					✔	✔								
	Carpobrotus chilensis	Baja Ice Plant		✔	✔		4"	24"	✔	✔		✔	✔		✔			✔		✔	✔		✔				✔				
	Carpobrotus edulis	South African Ice Plant			✔		4"	24"	✔			✔	✔		✔			✔		✔	✔	4✔	✔				✔				
✔	*Cerastium tomentosum*	Snow-in-Summer		✔	✔		8"	3'		✔	✔	✔	✔		✔			✔	✔		✔		✔			✔	✔				
	Chamaemelum nobile	Chamomile			✔		8"	12"	✔	✔	✔	✔	✔		✔		✔				✔	✔	✔			✔	✔				
✔	*Cissus antarctica*	Kangaroo Treebine			✔	✔	6"	18"	✔	✔			✔	✔	✔		✔				✔		✔								
✔	*Cistus salvifolius*	Sageleaf Rockrose		✔	✔		2'	4'	✔	✔		✔	✔					✔			✔		✔			✔	✔				
✔	*Dichondra repens*	Dichondra			✔	✔	6"	6"	✔	✔			✔		✔		✔				✔	✔	✔								

Ground Covers

MASTER PLANT MATERIALS MATRIX

	BOTANICAL NAME	COMMON NAME	ENVIRON. GROUPING				SIZE		MACRO ZONE			MICRO ZONE					DESIGN USE			WATER REQ.			LEAF HABIT			FLOWER SHOW				F. C.	★
DESCRIBED			NATIVE	NATURALIZED	EXOTIC	TROPICAL	HEIGHT	WIDTH	LOW DESERT	INTERMEDIATE DESERT	HIGH DESERT	A — SUNNY	B — PART SUNNY	C — LITTLE SUNNY	D — INTRO. SHADE	E — DEEP SHADE	OASIS	TRANSITION	DESERT	LOW WATER	MODERATE WATER	HIGH WATER	EVERGREEN	SEMI EVERGREEN	DECIDUOUS	SPRING FLOWERS	SUMMER FLOWERS	FALL FLOWERS	WINTER FLOWERS	FALL COLOR	STAR PERFORMER
✔	*Drosanthemum speciosum*	Arizona Ice Plant		✔	✔		8"	3'	✔	✔		✔	✔		✔			✔		✔	✔		✔			✔	✔				
✔	*Duchesnea indica*	Indian Mock Strawberry			✔		6"	24"	✔	✔	✔	✔	✔	✔			✔	✔			✔	✔	✔							✔	★
✔	*Euonymus fortunei radicans*	Common Winter Creeper			✔		6"	24"	✔	✔	✔	✔	✔	✔	✔		✔				✔		✔								
✔	*Festuca ovina glauca*	Blue Fescue			✔	✔	8"	10"	✔	✔			✔		✔		✔				✔		✔								
✔	*Fragaria chiloensis*	Ornamental Strawberry			✔		10"	3'	✔	✔	✔		✔		✔		✔				✔		✔								
	Fragaria species	Fruiting Strawberry			✔		12"	3'	✔	✔	✔		✔		✔		✔				✔		✔								
✔	*Fragaria* #25	Strawberry			✔		12"	3'	✔	✔	✔		✔		✔		✔				✔		✔								
✔	*Fragaria* "Lassen"	Strawberry			✔		12"	3'	✔	✔	✔		✔		✔		✔				✔		✔								
✔	*Fragaria* "Tioga"	Strawberry			✔		12"	3'	✔	✔	✔	✔					✔				✔		✔								
	Francoa ramosa	Maiden's Wreath			✔		12"	12"	✔				✔		✔		✔				✔		✔				✔				
✔	*Gazania uniflora*	Trailing Yellow Gazania			✔		12"	3'	✔	✔		✔						✔	✔	✔	✔		✔			✔			✔		★
	Gazania U "Aztec Queen"	Multi-Colored Gazania			✔		6"	24"	✔	✔	✔		✔		✔			✔			✔		✔			✔			✔		
	Gazania U "Colorama"	White-Colored Gazania			✔		6"	24"	✔	✔	✔	✔	✔		✔			✔			✔		✔			✔			✔		
	Gazania U "Copper King"	Copper-Colored Gazania			✔		6"	24"	✔	✔	✔	✔	✔		✔			✔			✔		✔			✔			✔		
	Gazania U "Fiesta Red"	Red-Colored Gazania			✔		6"	24"	✔	✔	✔	✔	✔		✔			✔			✔		✔			✔			✔		
	Gazania U "Moonglow"	Yellow-Colored Gazania			✔		6"	214"	✔	✔	✔	✔	✔		✔			✔			✔		✔			✔			✔		
	Gazania U "Sunburst"	Orange-Colored Gazania			✔		6"	24"	✔	✔	✔	✔	✔		✔			✔			✔		✔			✔			✔		
	Gazania U "Sunglow"	Yellow-Colored Gazania			✔		6"	24"	✔	✔	✔	✔	✔		✔			✔			✔		✔			✔			✔		
	Gazania splendens	Clumping Gazania		✔	✔		6"	24"	✔	✔	✔	✔	✔		✔			✔	✔	✔	✔		✔			✔			✔		
	Halimum species	Halimum		✔	✔		2'	4'	✔	✔		✔	✔					✔	✔	✔			✔			✔	✔				
✔	*Hedera canariensis*	Algerian Ivy			✔		12"	4'	✔	✔	✔			✔	✔	✔	✔					✔	✔								★
✔	*Hedera helix*	English Ivy			✔		8"	3'	✔	✔	✔			✔	✔	✔	✔					✔	✔								

Ground Covers

MASTER PLANT MATERIALS MATRIX

DESCRIBED	BOTANICAL NAME	COMMON NAME	ENVIRON. GROUPING				SIZE		MACRO ZONE			MICRO ZONE					DESIGN USE			WATER REQ.			LEAF HABIT			FLOWER SHOW				F. C.	★
			NATIVE	NATURALIZED	EXOTIC	TROPICAL	HEIGHT	WIDTH	LOW DESERT	INTERMEDIATE DESERT	HIGH DESERT	A — SUNNY	B — PART SUNNY	C — LITTLE SUNNY	D — INTRO. SHADE	E — DEEP SHADE	OASIS	TRANSITION	DESERT	LOW WATER	MODERATE WATER	HIGH WATER	EVERGREEN	SEMI EVERGREEN	DECIDUOUS	SPRING FLOWERS	SUMMER FLOWERS	FALL FLOWERS	WINTER FLOWERS	FALL COLOR	STAR PERFORMER
	Hedera helix "Hanii"	Hahn's English Ivy			✔		6"	2'	✔	✔	✔			✔	✔	✔	✔					✔	✔								
	Helianthemum nummularium	Sunrose		✔	✔		8″	3′	✔	✔	✔	✔	✔					✔		✔			✔			✔					
	Herniaria glabra	Rupture Wort			✔	✔	3"	6"	✔	✔	✔	✔	✔	✔	✔		✔				✔	✔	✔							✔	
	Hypericum calycinum	Creeping St. Johnswort			✔		12"	36"	✔	✔	✔		✔		✔		✔				✔	✔		✔		✔	✔				
	Imperata cylindrica "Rubra"	Japanese Blood Grass			✔		2′	2′	✔	✔	✔	✔	✔		✔		✔				✔	✔	✔								
	Juniperus horizontalis (variety)	Prostrate Juniper			✔		18"	8'	✔	✔	✔	✔	✔	✔	✔		✔				✔		✔								
	Lampranthus aurantiacus	Orange Ice Plant		✔	✔		15"	18"	✔			✔	✔					✔			✔		✔			✔	✔				
	Lampranthus spectabilis	Trailing Ice Plant		✔	✔		12"	24"	✔			✔	✔					✔			✔		✔			✔	✔				
✔	*Lippia repens*	Lippia			✔		4"	12"	✔	✔		✔	✔		✔		✔	✔			✔			✔		✔		✔			
✔	*Liriope muscari* "Silvery Sunproof"	Silver Lily Turf			✔		12"	8"	✔	✔			✔	✔	✔		✔				✔		✔			✔	✔				
✔	*Liriope spicata*	Creeping Lily Turf			✔		12"	✔	✔				✔	✔	✔		✔				✔		✔			✔	✔				
✔	*Loniceria japonica* "Halliana"	Hall's Japanese Honeysuckle		✔	✔		3'	15'	✔	✔	✔	✔	✔	✔	✔		✔				✔		✔			✔	✔				
	Malephora crocea	Ice Plant		✔	✔		6"	18"	✔	✔	✔	✔						✔	✔	✔			✔			✔	✔				
✔	*Melampodium eucanthum*	Blackfoot Daisy	✔	✔			12"	12"	✔	✔		✔						✔	✔	✔					✔	✔	✔				
✔	*Myoporum parvifolium*	Myoporum			✔		4"	6'	✔	✔		✔	✔		✔		✔	✔			✔		✔								★
	Nepeta catavia	Catnip			✔		2′	3′	✔	✔	✔	✔	✔				✔	✔			✔										
	Nepeta faassenii	Catmint			✔		2′	2→	✔	✔	✔	✔	✔				✔	✔			✔										
✔	*Oenothera berlandieri*	Mexican Primrose	✔	✔			6"	24"	✔	✔	✔	✔						✔	✔	✔	✔				✔	✔	✔				
✔	*Ophiopogon japonicus*	Mondo Grass			✔		8"	6"	✔	✔			✔	✔	✔		✔				✔		✔								
✔	*Osteospermum fruticosum*	Trailing African Daisy		✔	✔		12"	3'	✔	✔		✔	✔		✔		✔	✔			✔				✔	✔		✔	✔		
✔	*Pachysandra terminalis*	Japanese Spurge			✔		8"	10"	✔	✔	✔		✔	✔	✔	✔	✔				✔		✔			✔					
✔	*Parthenocissus quinquefolia*	Virginia Creeper			✔		12"	24"	✔	✔	✔		✔		✔		✔	✔							✔					✔	

Ground Covers

MASTER PLANT MATERIALS MATRIX

DESCRIBED	BOTANICAL NAME	COMMON NAME	NATIVE	NATURALIZED	EXOTIC	TROPICAL	HEIGHT	WIDTH	LOW DESERT	INTERMEDIATE DESERT	HIGH DESERT	A — SUNNY	B — PART SUNNY	C — LITTLE SUNNY	D — INTRO. SHADE	E — DEEP SHADE	OASIS	TRANSITION	DESERT	LOW WATER	MODERATE WATER	HIGH WATER	EVERGREEN	SEMI EVERGREEN	DECIDUOUS	SPRING FLOWERS	SUMMER FLOWERS	FALL FLOWERS	WINTER FLOWERS	FALL COLOR	STAR PERFORMER
✔	*Polygonum capitatum*	Pink Clover Blossom			✔		6"	20"	✔	✔		✔	✔					✔			✔		✔			✔	✔	✔	✔		★
✔	*Potentilla verna*	Spring Cinquefoil			✔		4"	10"	✔	✔	✔		✔		✔		✔	✔		✔	✔		✔			✔	✔	✔	✔		★
✔	*Psilostrophe cooperi*	Paper Flower	✔	✔			18"	24"	✔	✔	✔	✔	✔		✔			✔	✔	✔				✔		✔	✔	✔			
	Ranunculus repens "Pleniflorus"	Creeping Buttercup		✔	✔		12"	24'	✔	✔	✔	✔	✔		✔			✔	✔	✔			✔			✔	✔				
	Salvia chionophylla "Quicksilver"	Quicksilver Salvia		✔	✔		12"	24"	✔	✔		✔	✔		✔			✔	✔	✔			✔			✔					
✔	*Soleirolia soleirolii*	Baby's Tears			✔	✔	2"	6"	✔	✔				✔	✔		✔					✔	✔								
✔	*Teucrium chamaedrys*	Germander			✔		12"	24"	✔	✔		✔	✔		✔		✔	✔		✔	✔		✔			✔	✔	✔	✔		
✔	*Thymus praecox arcticus*	Creeping Thyme		✔	✔		6"	24"	✔	✔	✔	✔	✔		✔			✔		✔	✔		✔			✔	✔				
	Thymus pseudolanuginosus	Woolly Thyme		✔	✔		3"	12"	✔	✔	✔	✔	✔		✔			✔		✔	✔		✔			✔	✔				
	Trachelospermum asiaticum	Asiatic Jasmine			✔	✔	12"	3'	✔	✔	✔		✔	✔	✔		✔					✔	✔			✔					
✔	*Trachelospermum jasminoides*	Star Jasmine			✔	✔	18"	4'	✔	✔	✔		✔	✔	✔		✔					✔	✔			✔	✔				★
	Tradescantia fluminensis	Wandering Jew			✔		8"	12"	✔	✔			✔	✔	✔		✔					✔	✔								
✔	*Trifolium fragiferium*	O'Connor's Legume		✔	✔		6"	5'	✔	✔	✔	✔	✔		✔			✔		✔	✔		✔								
✔	*Verbena peruviana* "Cherry Pink"	Pink Verbena		✔	✔		6"	24"	✔	✔	✔	✔	✔		✔			✔		✔	✔			✔		✔	✔				
✔	*Verbena peruviana* "Starfire"	Red Verbena		✔	✔		6"	24"	✔	✔	✔	✔	✔		✔			✔		✔	✔			✔		✔	✔				
✔	*Vinca major*	Periwinkle			✔	✔	12"	24"	✔	✔	✔		✔	✔	✔		✔				✔	✔	✔			✔	✔				
✔	*Vinca minor*	Dwarf Periwinkle			✔	✔	6"	18'	✔	✔	✔		✔	✔	✔		✔				✔	✔	✔			✔	✔				★
✔	*Vitis girdiana*	Wolfberry or Wild Grape		✔			18"	4'	✔				✔		✔		✔				✔	✔			✔					4,	
	BOTANICAL NAME	COMMON NAME	ENVIRON. GROUPING				SIZE		MACRO ZONE			MICRO ZONE					DESIGN USE			WATER REQ.			LEAF HABIT			FLOWER SHOW				F. C.	★

Turf Grasses

MASTER PLANT MATERIALS MATRIX

DESCRIBED	BOTANICAL NAME	COMMON NAME	NATIVE	NATURALIZED	EXOTIC	TROPICAL	HEIGHT	WIDTH	LOW DESERT	INTERMEDIATE DESERT	HIGH DESERT	A — SUNNY	B — PART SUNNY	C — LITTLE SUNNY	D — INTRO. SHADE	E — DEEP SHADE	OASIS	TRANSITION	DESERT	LOW WATER	MODERATE WATER	HIGH WATER	EVERGREEN	SEMI EVERGREEN	DECIDUOUS	STAR PERFORMER
			ENVIRON. GROUPING				SIZE		MACRO ZONE			MICRO ZONE					DESIGN USE			WATER REQ.			LEAF HABIT			★
	Agrostis stolonifera	Creeping Bentgrass (Seed/Sod)			✔		˘"	—		✔	✔		✔	✔	✔		✔					✔		✔		
	Buchloe dactyloides	Buffalo Grass (Sod)			✔		2"	—		✔	✔	✔	✔		✔		✔				✔	✔		✔		
✔	*Cynodon dactylon*	Common Bermuda Grass (Seed)		✔	✔		1°"	—	✔	✔	✔	✔					✔					✔		✔		★
	Cynodon dactylon "Santa Ana"	Bermuda Grass (Sod)			✔		1"	—	✔	✔		✔	✔	✔	✔		✔					✔		✔		
	Cynodon dactylon "Tifdwarf"	Bermuda Grass (Sod)			✔		˘"	—	✔	✔		✔	✔	✔	✔		✔					✔		✔		
✔	*Cynodon dactylon* "Tifgreen"	Hybrid Bermuda (Sod)			✔		1"	—	✔	✔		✔	✔				✔					✔		✔		★
✔	*Cynodon dactylon* "Tifway"	Hybrid Bermuda (Sod)			✔		°"	—	✔	✔		✔	✔				✔					✔		✔		★
	Festuca elatior	Tall Fescue (Seed)			✔		3"	—		✔	✔		✔	✔	✔		✔					✔		✔		
	Festuca rubra	Red Fescue (Seed)					2"																			
✔	*Lolium multiflorum*	Annual Ryegrass (Seed)			✔		2"	—	✔	✔	✔	✔	✔		✔		✔					✔		✔		★
	Lolium perenne	Perennial Ryegrass (Seed)																								
	Poa pratensis	Kentucky Bluegrass (Seed/Sod)			✔		2°"	—			✔		✔	✔	✔		✔					✔		✔		
✔	*Stenotaphrum secundatum*	Saint Augustine Grass (Plugs)			✔		2°"	—	✔	✔		✔	✔	✔	✔		✔					✔		✔		
✔	*Zoysia tenuifolia*	Korean Grass (Plugs)			✔		ʃ"	—	✔	✔		✔	✔	✔	✔		✔					✔		✔		
	LAWN SUBSTITUTES																									
	Dichondra repens	Dichondra																								
	Lippia repens	Lippia																								
	Myoporum parvifolium	Myoporum																								
	Potentilla verna	Spring Cinquefoil																								
	Thymus praecox arcticus	Creeping Thyme																								

Cacti, Succulents, Yuccas, Desert Grasses, and Spoons

MASTER PLANT MATERIALS MATRIX

DESCRIBED	BOTANICAL NAME	COMMON NAME	NATIVE	NATURALIZED	EXOTIC	TROPICAL	HEIGHT	WIDTH	LOW DESERT	INTERMEDIATE DESERT	HIGH DESERT	A — SUNNY	B — PART SUNNY	C — LITTLE SUNNY	D — INTRO. SHADE	E — DEEP SHADE	OASIS	TRANSITION	DESERT	LOW WATER	MODERATE WATER	HIGH WATER	EVERGREEN	SEMI EVERGREEN	DECIDUOUS	SPRING FLOWERS	SUMMER FLOWERS	FALL FLOWERS	WINTER FLOWERS	STAR PERFORMER
	Adromischus festivus	Plover Eggs			✔		8"	18"	✔				✔		✔			✔		✔			✔							
✔	*Agave americana*	Century Plant	✔	✔			6'	10'	✔	✔		✔	✔					✔	✔	✔			✔							
	Agave americana "Marginata"	Variegated Century Plant	✔	✔			5'	8'	✔	✔		✔	✔					✔		✔			✔							
✔	*Agave angustifolia* "variegata"	Variegated Agave	✔	✔			4'	4'	✔	✔		✔	✔					✔		✔			✔							★
✔	*Agave attenuata*	Dragon Tree Agave	✔	✔		✔	2'	4'	✔	✔			✔		✔		✔	✔		✔			✔							★
	Agave deserti	NCN	✔	✔			2'	3'	✔	✔		✔	✔					✔	✔	✔			✔							
	Agave filifera	Needle and Thread Agave	✔	✔			2'	3'	✔	✔		✔	✔					✔	✔	✔			✔							
✔	*Agave parryi*	NCN	✔	✔			2'	3'	✔	✔		✔	✔				✔	✔	✔	✔			✔							
	Agave parryi hauchucensis	Blue Agave	✔	✔			2'	3'	✔	✔		✔	✔					✔	✔	✔			✔							
✔	*Agave parviflora*	Green Agave	✔	✔			2'	3'	✔	✔		✔	✔				✔	✔	✔	✔			✔							
✔	*Agave victoriae reginae*	NCN	✔	✔			16"	16"	✔	✔		✔	✔				✔	✔		✔			✔							
✔	*Agave vilmoriniana*	Octopus Agave	✔	✔			4'	6'	✔	✔		✔	✔		✔		✔	✔		✔			✔							
	Agave weberi	Smooth-Edged Agave	✔	✔			6'	10'	✔	✔		✔	✔					✔	✔	✔			✔							
	Aloe arborescens	Giant Aloe		✔	✔		14'	12'	✔	✔		✔	✔		✔			✔		✔	✔		✔			✔			✔	
✔	*Aloe barbadensis*	Aloe Vera		✔	✔		18"	24"	✔	✔		✔	✔		✔			✔		✔	✔		✔			✔			✔	★
	Aloe brevifolia	NCN		✔	✔		8"	6"	✔	✔		✔	✔		✔			✔		✔	✔		✔			✔			✔	
✔	*Aloe ferox*	Fire Flower Aloe		✔	✔		15'	5'	✔	✔		✔	✔		✔			✔		✔	✔		✔			✔			✔	
	Aloe multiformis	Purple Crown		✔	✔		12"	24"	✔	✔		✔	✔		✔			✔		✔	✔		✔			✔			✔	
✔	*Aloe nobilis*	Dwarf Aloe		✔	✔		6"	12"	✔	✔		✔	✔		✔			✔		✔	✔		✔			✔			✔	★
✔	*Aloe saponaria*	African Aloe		✔	✔		12"	24"	✔	✔		✔	✔		✔			✔		✔	✔		✔			✔			✔	★
✔	*Aloe variegata*	Partridge Breast Aloe		✔	✔		5'	12"	✔	✔		✔	✔		✔			✔		✔	✔		✔			✔			✔	
	Aeonium urbicum	NCN			✔	✔	6"	10"	✔			✔	✔		✔			✔		✔	✔		✔							
	BOTANICAL NAME	COMMON NAME	ENVIRON. GROUPING				SIZE		MACRO ZONE			MICRO ZONE					DESIGN USE			WATER REQ.			LEAF HABIT			FLOWER SHOW				★

Cacti, Succulents, Yuccas, Desert Grasses, and Spoons

MASTER PLANT MATERIALS MATRIX

DESCRIBED	BOTANICAL NAME	COMMON NAME	NATIVE	NATURALIZED	EXOTIC	TROPICAL	HEIGHT	WIDTH	LOW DESERT	INTERMEDIATE DESERT	HIGH DESERT	A — SUNNY	B — PART SUNNY	C — LITTLE SUNNY	D — INTRO. SHADE	E — DEEP SHADE	OASIS	TRANSITION	DESERT	LOW WATER	MODERATE WATER	HIGH WATER	EVERGREEN	SEMI EVERGREEN	DECIDUOUS	SPRING FLOWERS	SUMMER FLOWERS	FALL FLOWERS	WINTER FLOWERS	STAR PERFORMER
	Aeonium urbicum "Atropurpureum"	NCN			✔	✔	6"	10"	✔			✔	✔		✔			✔		✔	✔		✔						✔	
	Astrophytum myriostigma	Bishop's Cap			✔		4"	4"	✔	✔			✔		✔			✔		✔			✔			✔				
✔	*Carnegiea gigantea*	Saguaro Cactus	✔	✔			40'	3'	✔	✔		✔	✔						✔	✔			✔			✔				★
✔	*Cephalocereus senilis*	Old Man Cactus			✔		15'	12"	✔	✔			✔		✔			✔	✔	✔			✔							
	Cereus peruvianus	Peruvian Apple			✔		12'	8'	✔			✔	✔		✔			✔	✔	✔			✔			✔				
	Cereus peruvianus "Monstrosus"	Giant-Club			✔		10'	6'	✔			✔	✔		✔			✔	✔	✔			✔			✔				
	Cleistocactus strausii	Silver Torch			✔		6'	8"	✔			✔	✔		✔			✔	✔	✔			✔			✔			✔	
	Conophytum pearsonii	Living Stone			✔		2"	4"	✔				✔		✔			✔		✔			✔							
	Corphyantha vivipara bisbeeana	Golf Ball Cactus			✔		2"	2"	✔				✔		✔			✔		✔			✔			✔				
✔	*Crassula argentea*	Jade Plant			✔	✔	4'	6'	✔	✔			✔	✔	✔		✔			✔	✔		✔			✔			✔	
	Crassula falcata	Flat-Leaf Jade Plant			✔	✔	5'	6'	✔	✔			✔	✔	✔			✔		✔	✔		✔			✔			✔	
	Crassula socialis	Creeping Crassula			✔	✔	2"	8"	✔	✔			✔	✔	✔			✔		✔	✔		✔			✔			✔	
	Cylindropuntia fulgida "Mannillata Monstrosa"	Boxing Glove Cactus	✔	✔			10'	6'	✔	✔		✔	✔		✔			✔	✔	✔			✔			✔				
	Dasylirion acrotriche	Green Desert Spoon	✔	✔			5′	6′	✔	✔		✔	✔		✔				✔	✔			✔							
	Dasylirion longissima	Grass Tree		✔	✔		6'	8'	✔	✔		✔	✔		✔				✔	✔			✔							
✔	*Dasylirion wheeleri*	Desert Spoon		✔	✔		5'	6'	✔	✔		✔	✔		✔				✔	✔			✔							★
✔	*Dracaena draco*	Dragon Tree			✔		20'	6'	✔	✔			✔		✔		✔	✔		✔	✔		✔							
	Dudleya brittonii	NCN			✔		12"	24"	✔	✔				✔	✔		✔	✔			✔		✔							
	Echeveria agavoides	Molded Wax			✔	✔	4"	6"	✔				✔		✔			✔		✔	✔		✔							
✔	*Echeveria imbricata*	Hen and Chicks			✔		8"	6"	✔	✔			✔		✔		✔	✔		✔	✔		✔			✔				★
✔	*Echinocactus grusonii*	Golden Barrel Cactus		✔	✔		4'	3'	✔	✔		✔	✔		✔			✔	✔	✔			✔			✔				★
	Echinocactus polycephalus	Woolly-Headed Barrel	✔				2'	3'	✔	✔		✔	✔		✔				✔	✔			✔			✔				
	BOTANICAL NAME	COMMON NAME	ENVIRON. GROUPING				SIZE		MACRO ZONE			MICRO ZONE					DESIGN USE			WATER REQ.			LEAF HABIT			FLOWER SHOW				★

Cacti, Succulents, Yuccas, Desert Grasses, and Spoons

MASTER PLANT MATERIALS MATRIX

	BOTANICAL NAME	COMMON NAME	ENVIRON. GROUPING				SIZE		MACRO ZONE			MICRO ZONE					DESIGN USE			WATER REQ.			LEAF HABIT			FLOWER SHOW				★
DESCRIBED			NATIVE	NATURALIZED	EXOTIC	TROPICAL	HEIGHT	WIDTH	LOW DESERT	INTERMEDIATE DESERT	HIGH DESERT	A — SUNNY	B — PART SUNNY	C — LITTLE SUNNY	D — INTRO. SHADE	E — DEEP SHADE	OASIS	TRANSITION	DESERT	LOW WATER	MODERATE WATER	HIGH WATER	EVERGREEN	SEMI EVERGREEN	DECIDUOUS	SPRING FLOWERS	SUMMER FLOWERS	FALL FLOWERS	WINTER FLOWERS	STAR PERFORMER
✔	*Echinocereus engelmannii*	Hedgehog Cactus	✔				18"	24"	✔	✔		✔	✔		✔				✔	✔			✔			✔				★
	Echinopsis multiplex	Easter Lily Cactus			✔		8"	2"	✔				✔		✔			✔		✔			✔			✔	✔			
✔	*Epiphyllum* species	Christmas Cactus			✔		—	—	✔				✔		✔		✔	✔			✔		✔	✔					✔	
	Epiphyllum hybrid	Pink Epiphytic Cactus			✔		—	—	✔				✔		✔		✔	✔			✔		✔	✔					✔	
	Epiphyllum hybrid "Cinco de Mayo"	Red Epiphytic Cactus			✔		—	—	✔				✔		✔		✔	✔			✔		✔	✔					✔	
	Epiphyllum hybrid "Clara Ann"	Yellow Epiphytic Cactus			✔		—	—	✔				✔		✔		✔	✔			✔		✔	✔					✔	
	Epiphyllum hybrid "Concerto"	Purple Epiphytic Cactus			✔		—	—	✔				✔		✔		✔	✔			✔		✔	✔					✔	
	Epiphyllum anguliger	Fishbone Cactus			✔		—	—	✔				✔		✔			✔			✔		✔	✔					✔	
	Epiphyllum oxypetalum	Dutchman's Pipe			✔		—	—	✔				✔		✔			✔			✔		✔	✔					✔	
	Epiphyllum bupleurifolia	Pineapple Euphorbia			✔		—	—	✔				✔		✔			✔			✔		✔	✔					✔	
✔	*Epithelantha bokei*	Button Cactus			✔		3"	3"	✔	✔		✔	✔		✔			✔	✔	✔			✔			✔	✔			
	Espostoa lanata	Peruvian Old Man Cactus			✔		8′	2′	✔	✔		✔	✔		✔			✔	✔	✔			✔			✔	✔			
	Euphorbia bupleurifolia	Pineapple Euphorbia			✔		4"	8"	✔	✔			✔		✔			✔		✔	✔			✔		✔	✔			
	Euphorbia "Bojeri"	Crown of Thorns			✔		3'	3'	✔	✔			✔		✔			✔		✔	✔			✔		✔	✔			
	Euphorbia canarirnsis	Candelabra Euphorbia			✔		10'	12'	✔	✔			✔		✔			✔		✔	✔			✔		✔	✔			
	Euphorbia "Chocolate Drop"	NCN			✔		3'	3'	✔	✔			✔		✔			✔		✔	✔			✔		✔	✔			
	Euphorbia ingens	African Milk Tree			✔		10'	12"	✔	✔			✔		✔			✔		✔	✔			✔		✔	✔			
	Euphorbia lactea cristata	Elk's Horn Euphorbia			✔		12"	18"	✔	✔			✔		✔			✔		✔	✔			✔		✔	✔			
✔	*Euphorbia milii*	Crown of Thorns			✔		4'	4'	✔	✔			✔		✔			✔		✔	✔			✔		✔	✔	✔	✔	
	Euphorbia obesa	Baseball Plant			✔		6"	2"	✔	✔			✔		✔			✔		✔	✔			✔						
✔	*Euphorbia pulcherrima*	Poinsettia			✔		10'	6'	✔	✔			✔	✔	✔		✔	✔			✔			✔					✔	
	Euphorbia spendens	Pink Crown of Thorns			✔		3'	3'	✔	✔			✔	✔	✔			✔		✔	✔			✔		✔			✔	

Cacti, Succulents, Yuccas, Desert Grasses, and Spoons

MASTER PLANT MATERIALS MATRIX

DESCRIBED	BOTANICAL NAME	COMMON NAME	NATIVE	NATURALIZED	EXOTIC	TROPICAL	HEIGHT	WIDTH	LOW DESERT	INTERMEDIATE DESERT	HIGH DESERT	A — SUNNY	B — PART SUNNY	C — LITTLE SUNNY	D — INTRO. SHADE	E — DEEP SHADE	OASIS	TRANSITION	DESERT	LOW WATER	MODERATE WATER	HIGH WATER	EVERGREEN	SEMI EVERGREEN	DECIDUOUS	SPRING FLOWERS	SUMMER FLOWERS	FALL FLOWERS	WINTER FLOWERS	STAR PERFORMER
			ENVIRON. GROUPING				SIZE		MACRO ZONE			MICRO ZONE					DESIGN USE			WATER REQ.			LEAF HABIT			FLOWER SHOW				★
	Euphorbia tirucalli	Pencilbush			✔		12"	18"	✔	✔		✔	✔		✔			✔			✔			✔						
	Euphorbia zantii	Shrubby Euphorbia			✔		4'	4'	✔	✔		✔	✔		✔			✔			✔			✔						
✔	*Ferocactus acanthodes*	Compass Barrel Cactus	✔				9'	2'	✔	✔		✔							✔	✔			✔			✔	✔			
✔	*Ferocactus wislizenii*	Fishhook Barrel Cactus	✔				6'	2'	✔	✔		✔							✔	✔			✔			✔	✔			★
✔	*Fouquieria columnaris*	Boojum Tree			✔		20'	4'	✔	✔		✔	✔						✔	✔				✔		✔			✔	
✔	*Fouquieria splendens*	Ocotillo	✔				22'	16'	✔	✔		✔	✔						✔	✔				✔		✔			✔	★
	Gymnocalycinum michanovichii	Plaid Cactus			✔		4"	6"	✔				✔		✔			✔		✔			✔			✔	✔			
	Gymnocalcinum quehlianum	Dwarf Chin Cactus			✔		4"	6"	✔				✔		✔			✔		✔			✔			✔	✔			
	Gymnocalycinum saglione	Giant Chin Cactus			✔		10"	12"	✔				✔		✔			✔		✔			✔			✔	✔			
	Gymnocalycinum schicknedantzii	White Chin Cactus			✔		4"	6"	✔				✔		✔			✔		✔			✔			✔	✔			
✔	*Haworthia attenyata*	White Wart Haworthia			✔		12"	8"	✔	✔		✔	✔		✔			✔		✔			✔			✔				
✔	*Haworthia fasciata*	Fairy Washboard			✔		6"	6"	✔	✔		✔	✔		✔			✔		✔			✔			✔				
	Haworthia retusa	NCN			✔		6"	6"	✔	✔		✔	✔		✔			✔		✔			✔			✔				
	Haworthia setata	Lace Haworthia			✔		6"	6"	✔	✔		✔	✔		✔			✔		✔			✔			✔				
✔	*Hesperaloe fumifera*	White Yucca	✔	✔			6'	4'	✔	✔	✔	✔	✔		✔			✔		✔			✔			✔	✔			
✔	*Hesperaloe parviflora*	Red Yucca	✔	✔			4'	4'	✔	✔	✔	✔	✔		✔			✔	✔	✔			✔			✔	✔			★
	Huernia confusa	Lifesaver Plant			✔		4"	6"	✔				✔		✔			✔		✔	✔		✔			✔			✔	
	Huernia zebrina	Zebra Flower			✔		6"	8"	✔				✔		✔			✔		✔	✔		✔			✔			✔	
✔	*Lemaireocereus marginatus*	Mexican Fence Post	✔	✔			10'	12'	✔	✔		✔	✔		✔				✔	✔			✔			✔				
✔	*Lemaireocereus thurberi*	Pipeorgan Cactus	✔	✔			22'	30'	✔	✔		✔	✔		✔				✔	✔			✔			✔				
	Lithops dinteri	Stoneface			✔		2"	4"	✔				✔		✔			✔		✔			✔			✔				
	Lobivia species	NCN			✔		8"	4"	✔				✔		✔			✔	✔	✔			✔			✔				

Cacti, Succulents, Yuccas, Desert Grasses, and Spoons

MASTER PLANT MATERIALS MATRIX

	BOTANICAL NAME	COMMON NAME	ENVIRON. GROUPING				SIZE		MACRO ZONE			MICRO ZONE					DESIGN USE			WATER REQ.			LEAF HABIT			FLOWER SHOW				★
DESCRIBED			NATIVE	NATURALIZED	EXOTIC	TROPICAL	HEIGHT	WIDTH	LOW DESERT	INTERMEDIATE DESERT	HIGH DESERT	A — SUNNY	B — PART SUNNY	C — LITTLE SUNNY	D — INTRO. SHADE	E — DEEP SHADE	OASIS	TRANSITION	DESERT	LOW WATER	MODERATE WATER	HIGH WATER	EVERGREEN	SEMI EVERGREEN	DECIDUOUS	SPRING FLOWERS	SUMMER FLOWERS	FALL FLOWERS	WINTER FLOWERS	STAR PERFORMER
	Lobivopsis species	NCN			✔		16"	8"	✔				✔		✔			✔	✔	✔			✔			✔				
	Lophocereus schottii	Totem Pole Cactus			✔		10'	4'	✔	✔		✔	✔		✔			✔	✔	✔			✔			✔				
	Mammillaria elongata	Lace Cactus		✔			24"	12"	✔	✔		✔	✔		✔			✔	✔	✔			✔			✔	✔			
	Mammillaria fragilis	Thimble Cactus		✔			4"	4"	✔	✔		✔	✔		✔			✔	✔	✔			✔			✔	✔			
	Mammillaria hahniana	Old Lady Cactus		✔			18"	8"	✔	✔		✔	✔		✔			✔	✔	✔			✔			✔	✔			
	Mammilaria microcarpa	Fishhook Cactus	✔	✔			6"	12"	✔	✔		✔	✔		✔			✔	✔	✔			✔			✔	✔			
	Mammillaria prolifera	Little Candles		✔			8"	2"	✔	✔		✔	✔		✔			✔	✔	✔			✔			✔	✔			
✔	*Mammillaria spinosissima*	Red Headed Irishman		✔			12"	6"	✔	✔		✔	✔		✔				✔	✔			✔			✔	✔			
✔	*Mammillaria tetrancistra*	Fishhook Cactus	✔				18"	10"	✔	✔		✔	✔		✔				✔	✔			✔			✔	✔			
	Muhlenbergia capillaris "Regal Mist"	Red Deer Grass	✔	✔			3'	4'	✔	✔		✔	✔		✔		✔	✔	✔	✔	✔		✔			✔				
	Muhlenbergia dumosa	Giant Mullee	✔	✔			4'	5'	✔	✔		✔	✔		✔		✔	✔	✔	✔	✔		✔			✔				
	Muhlenbergia lindheimeri "Autumn Glow"	Yellow Deer Grass	✔	✔			4'	5'	✔	✔		✔	✔		✔		✔	✔	✔	✔	✔		✔			✔				
✔	*Muhlenbergia rigens*	Dwarf Mullee	✔	✔			2'	5'	✔	✔		✔	✔		✔		✔	✔	✔	✔	✔		✔			✔				
	Nolina bigelovii	Mexican Grasstree		✔			10'	6'	✔	✔		✔	✔		✔		✔	✔	✔	✔	✔		✔							
	Nolina microcarpa	Beargrass		✔			4'	6'	✔	✔		✔	✔		✔		✔	✔	✔	✔	✔		✔							
✔	*Nolina parryi*	Beargrass		✔			3'	6'	✔	✔		✔	✔		✔		✔	✔	✔	✔	✔		✔							★
✔	*Opuntia acanthocarpa*	Buckhorn Cholla	✔				5'	4'	✔	✔		✔							✔	✔			✔			✔			✔	
✔	*Opuntia basilaris*	Prickly Pear or Beavertail Cactus	✔				4'	6'	✔	✔		✔							✔	✔			✔			✔			✔	
✔	*Opuntia bigelovii*	Teddybear Cholla	✔				4'	3'	✔	✔		✔							✔	✔			✔			✔			✔	★
	Opuntia echinocarpa	Golden Cholla	✔				3'	2'	✔	✔		✔							✔	✔			✔			✔			✔	
✔	*Opuntia microdasys*	Bunny Ears	✔				18"	2'	✔	✔		✔							✔	✔			✔			✔			✔	
	Opuntia phaeacantha	Engelmann's Prickly Pear		✔	✔		4'	6'	✔	✔		✔	✔		✔				✔	✔			✔			✔			✔	

Cacti, Succulents, Yuccas, Desert Grasses, and Spoons

DESCRIBED	MASTER PLANT MATERIALS MATRIX		ENVIRON. GROUPING				SIZE		MACRO ZONE			MICRO ZONE					DESIGN USE			WATER REQ.			LEAF HABIT			FLOWER SHOW				★
	BOTANICAL NAME	COMMON NAME	NATIVE	NATURALIZED	EXOTIC	TROPICAL	HEIGHT	WIDTH	LOW DESERT	INTERMEDIATE DESERT	HIGH DESERT	A — SUNNY	B — PART SUNNY	C — LITTLE SUNNY	D — INTRO. SHADE	E — DEEP SHADE	OASIS	TRANSITION	DESERT	LOW WATER	MODERATE WATER	HIGH WATER	EVERGREEN	SEMI EVERGREEN	DECIDUOUS	SPRING FLOWERS	SUMMER FLOWERS	FALL FLOWERS	WINTER FLOWERS	STAR PERFORMER
	Opuntia ramosissima	Pencil Cholla		✔	✔		6'	4'	✔	✔		✔							✔	✔			✔			✔			✔	
✔	*Opuntia violacea* "Santa Rita"	Blue-Blade		✔	✔		2'	4'	✔	✔		✔						✔	✔	✔			✔			✔			✔	★
✔	*Opuntia vulgaris*	Prickly Pear Cactus		✔	✔		20'	20'	✔	✔		✔							✔	✔			✔			✔			✔	
	Opuntia vulgaris "Variegata"	Joseph's Coat		✔	✔		20'	20'	✔	✔		✔							✔	✔			✔			✔			✔	
	Pachypodium lamerei	Club Foot			✔	✔	4'	2'	✔				✔		✔			✔		✔	✔		✔							
	Pleiospilos bolusi	African Living Rock			✔		2"	4"	✔				✔		✔			✔		✔			✔			✔				
	Pleiospilos nelii	Split Rock			✔		3"	5"	✔				✔		✔			✔		✔			✔			✔				
✔	*Portulacaria afra*	Elephant's Food			✔		4'	6'	✔			✔	✔		✔		✔	✔			✔		✔							★
	Puya berteroniana	Desert Bromeliad			✔	✔	4'	2'	✔			✔	✔		✔		✔	✔		✔	✔		✔			✔			✔	
✔	*Sansevieria trifasciata*	Mother-in-Law's Tongue			✔		4'	2'	✔	✔			✔	✔	✔		✔	✔			✔		✔							
	Sansevieria trifasciata "Hahnii"	Bird's Nest Sansevieria			✔		8"	24"	✔	✔			✔	✔	✔		✔	✔			✔		✔							
	Schlumbergera bridgesii	Christmas Cactus			✔		—	—	✔				✔		✔			✔			✔		✔			✔			✔	
✔	*Sedum acre*	Goldmoss Sedum			✔		4"	20"	✔	✔			✔		✔		✔			✔	✔		✔							
	Sedum morganianum	Donkey Tail			✔	✔	—	—					✔		✔		✔	✔			✔		✔							
	Sedum sieboldii	NCN			✔		8"	8"	✔	✔			✔		✔		✔			✔	✔		✔							
	Sedum spathulifolium	NCN			✔		6"	10"	✔	✔			✔		✔		✔			✔	✔		✔							
	Sempervivum arachnoideum	Cobweb Houseleek			✔		2'	2'	✔	✔	✔		✔		✔		✔	✔			✔		✔				✔			
✔	*Sempervivum tectorum*	Hen and Chicks			✔		6"	8"	✔	✔	✔		✔		✔		✔	✔			✔		✔				✔			
	Stapelia gigantea	Starfish Flower			✔		8"	18"	✔	✔			✔		✔			✔			✔		✔				✔	✔		
	Stapelia variegata	Toad Cactus			✔		4"	10"	✔	✔			✔		✔			✔			✔		✔				✔	✔		
	Stenocereus marginatus	Mexican Pipe Organ			✔		10'	10'	✔	✔		✔	✔		✔			✔	✔	✔			✔			✔				
	Trichocereus peruvianus	Peruvian Torch			✔		15'	6'	✔			✔	✔		✔			✔	✔	✔			✔			✔				

Cacti, Succulents, Yuccas, Desert Grasses, and Spoons

MASTER PLANT MATERIALS MATRIX

			Environ. Grouping				Size		Macro Zone			Micro Zone					Design Use			Water Req.			Leaf Habit			Flower Show				★
Described	Botanical Name	Common Name	Native	Naturalized	Exotic	Tropical	Height	Width	Low Desert	Intermediate Desert	High Desert	A — Sunny	B — Part Sunny	C — Little Sunny	D — Intro. Shade	E — Deep Shade	Oasis	Transition	Desert	Low Water	Moderate Water	High Water	Evergreen	Semi Evergreen	Deciduous	Spring Flowers	Summer Flowers	Fall Flowers	Winter Flowers	Star Performer
	Trichocereus schickendantzii	NCN			✔		4'	2'	✔			✔	✔		✔			✔	✔	✔			✔			✔				
	Trichocereus spachianus	Golden Torch			✔		7'	3'	✔			✔	✔		✔			✔	✔	✔			✔			✔				
	Yucca aloifolia	Spanish Bayonet		✔			10'	10'	✔	✔		✔						✔	✔	✔			✔			✔	✔			
	Yucca baccata	Datil Yucca		✔			3'	6'	✔	✔		✔							✔	✔			✔			✔	✔			
✔	*Yucca brevifolia*	Joshua Tree		✔			30'	20'	✔	✔	✔	✔							✔	✔			✔			✔	✔			
✔	*Yucca elata*	Soaptree Yucca	✔				6'	6'	✔	✔		✔						✔	✔	✔			✔			✔	✔			★
	Yucca elephantipes	Giant Yucca	✔				8'	6'	✔	✔		✔							✔	✔			✔			✔	✔			
	Yucca glauca	Small Soapweed	✔				3'	4'	✔	✔		✔						✔	✔	✔			✔			✔	✔			
✔	*Yucca gloriosa*	Spanish Dagger		✔			12'	10'	✔	✔		✔					✔	✔	✔	✔	✔		✔			✔	✔			★
✔	*Yucca mohavensis*	Mohave Yucca		✔			8'	6'	✔	✔	✔	✔							✔	✔			✔			✔	✔			
✔	*Yucca pendula*	Pendulous Yucca		✔			3'	4'	✔	✔		✔					✔	✔	✔	✔	✔		✔			✔	✔			★
	Yucca rigida	Blue Yucca	✔				8'	3'	✔	✔		✔						✔	✔	✔			✔			✔	✔			
✔	*Yucca rostrata*	NCN		✔			8'	4'	✔	✔		✔						✔	✔	✔			✔			✔	✔			
✔	*Yucca whipplei*	Our Lord's Cradle	✔				6'	10'	✔	✔	✔	✔							✔	✔			✔				✔	✔		

Bulbs, Corms, Tubers, and Rhizomes

MASTER PLANT MATERIALS MATRIX

	BOTANICAL NAME	COMMON NAME	ENVIRON. GROUPING				SIZE		MACRO ZONE			MICRO ZONE					DESIGN USE			WATER REQ.			FLOWER SHOW				★
DESCRIBED			NATIVE	NATURALIZED	EXOTIC	TROPICAL	HEIGHT	WIDTH	LOW DESERT	INTERMEDIATE DESERT	HIGH DESERT	A — SUNNY	B — PART SUNNY	C — LITTLE SUNNY	D — INTRO. SHADE	E — DEEP SHADE	OASIS	TRANSITION	DESERT	LOW WATER	MODERATE WATER	HIGH WATER	SPRING FLOWERS	SUMMER FLOWERS	FALL FLOWERS	WINTER FLOWERS	STAR PERFORMER
✔	*Allium giganteum*	Giant Allium			✔		5'	2'	✔	✔	✔	✔	✔		✔		✔				✔			✔			
	Amarcrinum memoria-corsii	NCN			✔		4'	2'	✔	✔	✔	✔	✔		✔		✔	✔				✔		✔			
	Amaryllis belladonna	Naked Lady			✔		3'	3'	✔	✔	✔	✔	✔		✔		✔			✔	✔			✔	✔		
	Babiana stricta	Baboon Flower			✔		12"	12"	✔	✔	✔	✔	✔		✔		✔	✔				✔	✔				
✔	*Brodiaea pulchella*	Blue Dicks		✔	✔		8"	6"	✔	✔		✔	✔		✔		✔	✔			✔		✔				
✔	*Canna species*	Canna Lily (See Cat.)			✔		5'	3'	✔	✔		✔	✔	✔	✔		✔	✔				✔	✔			✔	★
	Colchicum autumnale	NCN			✔		12"	12"	✔	✔	✔	✔	✔		✔		✔	✔	✔		✔		✔	✔			
	Crinum moorei	Pink Crinum			✔		3'	3'	✔	✔		✔	✔		✔		✔	✔				✔	✔	✔			
	Crinum powellii	Rose Crinum			✔		12"	12"	✔	✔		✔	✔		✔		✔	✔				✔	✔	✔			
	Crinum powellii "Album"	White Crinum			✔		18"	18"	✔	✔		✔	✔		✔		✔	✔				✔	✔	✔			
✔	*Crocosmia crocosmiiflora*	Montbretia		✔	✔		3'	2'	✔	✔			✔	✔	✔		✔	✔			✔		✔				
	Crocosmia masoniorum	NCN			✔		30"	30"	✔	✔			✔	✔	✔		✔	✔			✔		✔				
	Crocus angustifolius	Cloth of Gold Crocus			✔		6"	4"	✔	✔	✔	✔	✔		✔		✔	✔			✔		✔			✔	
	Crocus goulmeyii	NCN			✔		6"	4"	✔	✔	✔	✔	✔		✔		✔	✔			✔		✔			✔	
	Crocus imperati	NCN			✔		6"	4"	✔	✔	✔	✔	✔		✔		✔	✔			✔		✔			✔	
	Crocus sativus	Saffron Crocus			✔		6"	4"	✔	✔	✔	✔	✔		✔		✔	✔			✔		✔			✔	
✔	*Crocus vernus*	Dutch Crocus			✔		6"	4"	✔	✔	✔	✔	✔		✔		✔	✔			✔		✔			✔	
	Cyrtanthus mackenii	NCN			✔		12"	12"	✔				✔		✔		✔					✔	✔				
✔	*Freesia armstrongii*	Freesia		✔	✔		18"	12"	✔	✔			✔	✔	✔		✔	✔			✔		✔				★
	Freesia refracta	Freesia		✔	✔		18"	12'	✔	✔			✔	✔	✔		✔	✔			✔		✔				
✔	*Fritillaria imperialis*	Crown Imperial			✔	✔	3'	2'	✔	✔		✔	✔		✔		✔	✔				✔		✔			
	Gladiolus callianthus	Abyssinian Sword Lily			✔		2'	2'	✔	✔	✔	✔	✔		✔		✔	✔				✔	✔				

Bulbs, Corms, Tubers, and Rhizomes

DESCRIBED	MASTER PLANT MATERIALS MATRIX		NATIVE	NATURALIZED	EXOTIC	TROPICAL	HEIGHT	WIDTH	LOW DESERT	INTERMEDIATE DESERT	HIGH DESERT	A — SUNNY	B — PART SUNNY	C — LITTLE SUNNY	D — INTRO. SHADE	E — DEEP SHADE	OASIS	TRANSITION	DESERT	LOW WATER	MODERATE WATER	HIGH WATER	SPRING FLOWERS	SUMMER FLOWERS	FALL FLOWERS	WINTER FLOWERS	STAR PERFORMER
	Gladiolus colvillei	Baby Gladiolus			✔		18"	18"	✔	✔	✔	✔	✔		✔		✔	✔				✔	✔				
✔	*Gladiolus hortulanus*	Garden Gladiolus			✔		4'	2'	✔	✔	✔	✔	✔		✔		✔	✔				✔	✔				
	Gladiolus primulinus	South African Gladiolus			✔		3'	2'	✔	✔	✔	✔	✔		✔		✔	✔				✔	✔				
	Gladiolus tristis	Dainty Gladiolus			✔		14"	14"	✔	✔	✔	✔	✔		✔		✔	✔				✔	✔				
✔	*Hippeastrum* species	Amaryllis			✔		2'	2'	✔	✔			✔	✔	✔		✔					✔	✔				
	Homeria breyniana aurantiaca	Apricot-Colored Homeria		✔	✔		18"	18"	✔	✔	✔	✔	✔		✔			✔			✔		✔				
	Homeria lilacina	Lilac-Colored Homeria		✔	✔		18"	18"	✔	✔	✔	✔	✔		✔			✔			✔		✔				
	Homeria ochroleuca	Gold-Colored Homeria		✔	✔		18"	18"	✔	✔	✔	✔	✔		✔			✔			✔		✔				
	Ipheion uniflorum	Spring Starflower		✔	✔		8"	18"	✔	✔	✔	✔						✔			✔		✔				
✔	*Iris douglasiana*	Santa Barbara Iris		✔	✔		18"	12"	✔	✔		✔	✔		✔			✔	✔	✔	✔		✔				
	Iris ensata	Japanese Iris			✔		4'	3'	✔	✔		✔	✔		✔			✔			✔		✔	✔			
	Iris foetidissima	Gladwin Iris			✔		2'	2'	✔	✔	✔	✔	✔		✔		✔				✔		✔	✔			
	Iris innominata	Oregon Iris		✔	✔		12"	10"	✔	✔	✔	✔	✔		✔		✔				✔		✔	✔			
✔	*Iris missouriensis*	Western Blue Flag		✔	✔		18"	18"	✔	✔	✔	✔	✔		✔		✔				✔		✔	✔			
	Iris reticulata	Violet Scented Iris			✔		8"	6"	✔	✔	✔	✔	✔		✔			✔			✔	✔	✔	✔			
	Iris sibirica	Siberian Iris			✔		30"	30"	✔	✔	✔	✔	✔		✔		✔				✔		✔	✔			
✔	*Iris* species	Tall Bearded Iris (See Cat.)			✔		4'	2'	✔	✔	✔	✔	✔		✔		✔				✔		✔	✔			★
	Iris tingitana	Moroccan Iris			✔		18"	18"	✔	✔	✔	✔	✔				✔	✔			✔	✔	✔	✔			
	Iris tenax	Washington Iris			✔		12"	12"	✔	✔	✔	✔	✔				✔				✔		✔	✔			
	Iris unguicularis	Winter Iris			✔		2'	2'	✔	✔	✔	✔	✔				✔				✔		✔			✔	
	Ixia viridiflora	Green-Colored Ixia			✔		18"	18"	✔	✔	✔	✔	✔		✔			✔	✔	✔			✔	✔			
	Lachenalia pearsonii	NCN		✔	✔		12"	12"	✔	✔		✔						✔	✔	✔			✔			✔	
	BOTANICAL NAME	COMMON NAME	ENVIRON. GROUPING				SIZE		MACRO ZONE			MICRO ZONE					DESIGN USE			WATER REQ.			FLOWER SHOW				★

Bulbs, Corms, Tubers, and Rhizomes

MASTER PLANT MATERIALS MATRIX

DESCRIBED	BOTANICAL NAME	COMMON NAME	NATIVE	NATURALIZED	EXOTIC	TROPICAL	HEIGHT	WIDTH	LOW DESERT	INTERMEDIATE DESERT	HIGH DESERT	A — SUNNY	B — PART SUNNY	C — LITTLE SUNNY	D — INTRO. SHADE	E — DEEP SHADE	OASIS	TRANSITION	DESERT	LOW WATER	MODERATE WATER	HIGH WATER	SPRING FLOWERS	SUMMER FLOWERS	FALL FLOWERS	WINTER FLOWERS	STAR PERFORMER
	Lapeirousia alba	White Lapeirousia		✔	✔		12"	12"	✔	✔	✔	✔						✔	✔	✔	✔		✔				
	Morea villosa	Peacock Feather		✔	✔		12"	18"	✔	✔	✔	✔	✔		✔			✔	✔		✔		✔				
✔	*Muscari armeniacum*	Grape Hyacinths			✔		8"	4"	✔	✔			✔	✔	✔		✔	✔			✔		✔				
	Narcissus bulbocodium	Hoop Petticoat Daffodil			✔		8"	8"	✔	✔	✔		✔	✔	✔		✔	✔			✔		✔			✔	
✔	*Narcissus cyclamineus* "Feb. Gold"	Daffodil			✔		12"	8"	✔	✔	✔		✔	✔	✔		✔	✔			✔		✔			✔	★
✔	*Narcissus jonquilla*	Jonquil Daffodil			✔		10"	10"	✔	✔	✔		✔	✔	✔		✔	✔			✔		✔			✔	
	Narcissus poeticus "Actaea"	Poet's Narcissus			✔		12"	12"	✔	✔	✔		✔	✔	✔		✔	✔			✔		✔			✔	
	Narcissus species "Unsurpassable"	Daffodil			✔		12"	12"	✔	✔	✔		✔	✔	✔		✔	✔			✔		✔			✔	
	Narcissus species "Windblown"	Daffodil			✔		10"	10"	✔	✔	✔		✔	✔	✔		✔	✔			✔		✔			✔	
	Narcissus tazetta "Cragford"	Scarlet Cup Daffodil			✔		8"	8"	✔	✔	✔		✔	✔	✔		✔	✔			✔		✔			✔	
	Narcissus triandrus	Angel's Tears Daffodil			✔		6"	6"	✔	✔	✔		✔	✔	✔		✔				✔		✔			✔	
	Nerine bowdenii	NCN			✔		12"	12"	✔				✔	✔	✔		✔					✔			✔	✔	
	Ornithogalum thyrsoides	NCN			✔		12"	12"	✔	✔	✔	✔	✔		✔		✔	✔				✔	✔				
✔	*Ranunculus asiaticus*	Persian Ranunculus			✔		18"	12"	✔	✔	✔	✔	✔		✔		✔	✔			✔		✔				★
	Ranunculus repens "Plentiflorus"	Creeping Buttercup			✔		12"	12"	✔	✔	✔	✔	✔		✔		✔	✔			✔		✔				
✔	*Sparaxis tricolor*	Harlequin Lily		✔	✔		8"	4"	✔			✔	✔		✔		✔	✔			✔		✔	✔			★
✔	*Sprekelia formosissima*	Aztec Lily		✔	✔		12"	6"	✔	✔		✔	✔		✔		✔	✔			✔		✔		✔		
	Sternbergia lutea	NCN			✔		9"	9"	✔	✔	✔	✔	✔		✔			✔	✔		✔		✔		✔		
	Streptanthera cuprea	NCN		✔	✔		10"	10"	✔	✔		✔	✔		✔		✔	✔			✔		✔		✔		
	Tritonia crocata	Flame Freesia		✔	✔		18"	18"	✔	✔		✔						✔	✔	✔	✔		✔				
	Tritonia hyalina	Dwarf Freesia		✔	✔		12"	12"	✔	✔		✔						✔	✔	✔	✔		✔				
	Tulipa clusiana	Lady Tulip			✔		16"	16"	✔	✔	✔		✔		✔		✔	✔			✔		✔				
	BOTANICAL NAME	COMMON NAME	ENVIRON. GROUPING				SIZE		MACRO ZONE			MICRO ZONE					DESIGN USE			WATER REQ.			FLOWER SHOW				★

Bulbs, Corms, Tubers, and Rhizomes

	MASTER PLANT MATERIALS MATRIX		ENVIRON. GROUPING				SIZE		MACRO ZONE			MICRO ZONE					DESIGN USE			WATER REQ.			FLOWER SHOW				★
DESCRIBED	BOTANICAL NAME	COMMON NAME	NATIVE	NATURALIZED	EXOTIC	TROPICAL	HEIGHT	WIDTH	LOW DESERT	INTERMEDIATE DESERT	HIGH DESERT	A — SUNNY	B — PART SUNNY	C — LITTLE SUNNY	D — INTRO. SHADE	E — DEEP SHADE	OASIS	TRANSITION	DESERT	LOW WATER	MODERATE WATER	HIGH WATER	SPRING FLOWERS	SUMMER FLOWERS	FALL FLOWERS	WINTER FLOWERS	STAR PERFORMER
	Tulipa kaufmanniana	Water Lily Tulip			✔		18"	18"	✔	✔	✔		✔		✔		✔	✔			✔		✔				
✔	*Tulipa* species "Cottage"	Cottage Tulip			✔		36"	12"	✔	✔	✔		✔		✔		✔	✔			✔		✔				★
✔	*Tulipa* species "Darwin"	Darwin Tulip			✔		36"	12"	✔	✔	✔		✔		✔		✔	✔			✔		✔				★
✔	*Tulipa* species "Mendell"	Mendell Tulip			✔		24"	10"	✔	✔	✔		✔		✔		✔	✔			✔		✔				★
	Tulipa sylvestris	Wild Tulip			✔		12"	12"	✔	✔	✔		✔		✔		✔	✔			✔		✔				
✔	*Veltheimia bracteata*	NCN			✔	✔	3'	2'	✔	✔		✔	✔		✔		✔	✔				✔	✔				
✔	*Watsonia beatricis*	NCN			✔		6'	4'	✔	✔		✔	✔		✔		✔	✔				✔		✔	✔		
	Watsonia pyramidata	NCN			✔		6'	4'	✔	✔		✔	✔		✔		✔	✔				✔		✔	✔		

Aquatic Plants

MASTER PLANT MATERIALS MATRIX

DESCRIBED	BOTANICAL NAME	COMMON NAME	ENVIRON. GROUPING				SIZE		MACRO ZONE			MICRO ZONE					DESIGN USE			LEAF HABIT			FLOWER SHOW				★
			NATIVE	NATURALIZED	EXOTIC	TROPICAL	HEIGHT	WIDTH	LOW DESERT	INTERMEDIATE DESERT	HIGH DESERT	A — SUNNY	B — PART SUNNY	C — LITTLE SUNNY	D — INTRO. SHADE	E — DEEP SHADE	OASIS	TRANSITION	DESERT	EVERGREEN	SEMI EVERGREEN	DECIDUOUS	SPRING FLOWERS	SUMMER FLOWERS	FALL FLOWERS	WINTER FLOWERS	STAR PERFORMER
	Acorus calamus	Sweet Flag			✔		18"	6"	✔	✔	✔	✔	✔		✔		✔	✔		✔			✔				
	Alisma plantago	Water Plantain			✔		6"	12"	✔	✔	✔	✔	✔		✔		✔			✔			✔	✔			
	Aponogeton distachyus	Water Hawthorn			✔		8"	48"	✔	✔	✔	✔	✔	✔	✔	✔	✔				✔						
	Calla arum	Water Arum			✔		12"	12"	✔	✔	✔	✔	✔		✔		✔			✔			✔	✔			
	Caltha palustris	Marsh Marigold			✔		2'	2'	✔	✔	✔	✔	✔		✔		✔	✔		✔			✔	✔			
	Colocasia antiquorum illustris	Splotched Taro			✔	✔	2'	2'	✔			✔	✔		✔		✔				✔						
✔	*Colocasia esculenta*	Elephant Ear's			✔	✔	6'	4'	✔			✔	✔		✔		✔	✔			✔						★
✔	*Colocasia indica*	Green Taro			✔	✔	2'	2'	✔			✔	✔		✔		✔	✔			✔						
✔	*Colocasia violacea*	Violet-Stemmed Taro			✔	✔	2'	1'	✔			✔	✔		✔		✔	✔			✔						
✔	*Cyperus alternifolius*	Umbrella Plant		✔	✔	✔	4'	3'	✔	✔		✔	✔	✔	✔		✔	✔		✔			✔				★
	Cyperus papyrus	Egyptian Paper Plant		✔	✔	✔	10'	6'	✔	✔		✔	✔	✔	✔		✔	✔		✔			✔				
	Eichhornia crassipes	Hyacinth		✔	✔	✔	12"	12"	✔			✔	✔		✔		✔			✔			✔	✔			
✔	*Eleocharis tuberosa*	Chinese Water Chestnut			✔	✔	12"	24"	✔	✔	✔	✔	✔		✔		✔			✔							
✔	*Equisetum hyemale*	Horsetail		✔	✔	✔	4'	2'	✔	✔	✔	✔	✔		✔		✔	✔		✔							★
✔	*Gunnera chilensis*	NCN			✔	✔	8'	8'	✔				✔	✔	✔		✔			✔				✔			
	Gunnera manicata	NCN			✔	✔	8'	8'	✔				✔	✔	✔		✔			✔				✔			
	Hosta plantaginea	Plantain Lily			✔		2'	2'	✔	✔			✔	✔	✔		✔	✔		✔				✔			
	Hottonia palustris	Water Violet			✔		6"	2"	✔	✔	✔	✔	✔		✔		✔				✔		✔	✔			
	Hydrocleis nymphaeoides	Water Poppy			✔		2"	24"	✔	✔	✔	✔	✔		✔		✔			✔			✔	✔			
	Hydrocotyle umbellata	Pennywort			✔		–	–	✔	✔	✔	✔	✔		✔		✔					✔					
	Iris pseudacorus	Yellow Water Iris		✔	✔		5'	3'	✔	✔	✔	✔	✔		✔		✔	✔		✔			✔	✔			
	Iris versicolor	Purple Water Iris		✔	✔		3'	2'	✔	✔	✔	✔	✔		✔		✔	✔		✔			✔	✔			

Aquatic Plants

MASTER PLANT MATERIALS MATRIX

DESCRIBED	BOTANICAL NAME	COMMON NAME	NATIVE	NATURALIZED	EXOTIC	TROPICAL	HEIGHT	WIDTH	LOW DESERT	INTERMEDIATE DESERT	HIGH DESERT	A — SUNNY	B — PART SUNNY	C — LITTLE SUNNY	D — INTRO. SHADE	E — DEEP SHADE	OASIS	TRANSITION	DESERT	EVERGREEN	SEMI EVERGREEN	DECIDUOUS	SPRING FLOWERS	SUMMER FLOWERS	FALL FLOWERS	WINTER FLOWERS	STAR PERFORMER
✔	*Lemna minor*	Duckweed			✔	✔	–	–	✔	✔		✔	✔		✔		✔			✔							
	Marsillea quadrifolia	Water Clover			✔	✔	–	–	✔	✔		✔	✔		✔		✔				✔						
✔	*Myriophyllum aquaticum*	Parrot Feather			✔	✔	8"	4"	✔	✔		✔	✔		✔		✔			✔							
✔	*Nelumbo lutea*	American Water Lotus (See Cat.)			✔	✔	3'	6'	✔	✔		✔	✔		✔		✔			✔			✔	✔			
✔	*Nelumbo nucifera*	Asiatic Water Lotus (See Cat.)			✔	✔	3'	6'	✔	✔		✔	✔		✔		✔			✔			✔	✔			
✔	*Nymphaea* species	Water Lily (See Cat.)			✔	✔	4'	48"	✔	✔		✔	✔		✔		✔			✔			✔	✔	✔		★
	Nymphoides indicum	Water Snowflake			✔	✔	1"	2"	✔	✔	✔	✔	✔		✔		✔			✔			✔	✔			
	Nymphoides peltatum	Floating Hearts			✔	✔	1"	2"	✔	✔	✔	✔	✔		✔		✔			✔			✔	✔			
	Pistia stratiodes	Water Lettuce			✔	✔	1"	4"	✔	✔	✔	✔	✔		✔		✔			✔							
	Pontederia paniculata	Azure Pickerel			✔	✔	4'	4'	✔	✔	✔	✔	✔		✔		✔			✔	✔		✔	✔			
	Roripppa nasturtium-aquaticum	Water Cress			✔	✔	–	–	✔	✔		✔	✔		✔		✔			✔							
✔	*Sagittaria latifolia*	Common Arrowhead			✔	✔	18"	18"	✔		✔	✔	✔		✔		✔			✔			✔	✔			
	Sagittaria sagittifolia	Giant Arrowhead			✔	✔	3'	3'	✔	✔	✔	✔	✔		✔		✔			✔			✔	✔			
	Thalia dealbata	Water Canna			✔		4'	4'	✔	✔	✔	✔	✔		✔		✔			✔			✔	✔			
	Trapa natans	Water Chestnut			✔		4"	4'	✔	✔	✔	✔	✔		✔		✔			✔			✔	✔			
✔	*Typha angustifolia*	Graceful Cattail		✔	✔		6'	4'	✔	✔	✔	✔	✔		✔		✔			✔			✔	✔			
✔	*Typha latifolia*	Cattail		✔	✔		4'	3'	✔	✔	✔	✔	✔		✔		✔			✔			✔	✔			★
✔	*Typha minima*	Pigmy Cattail		✔	✔		12"	12"	✔	✔	✔	✔	✔		✔		✔			✔			✔	✔			
	BOTANICAL NAME	COMMON NAME	ENVIRON. GROUPING				SIZE		MACRO ZONE			MICRO ZONE					DESIGN USE			LEAF HABIT			FLOWER SHOW				★

Annuals

MASTER PLANT MATERIALS MATRIX

DESCRIBED	BOTANICAL NAME	COMMON NAME	ENVIRON. GROUPING				SIZE		MACRO ZONE			MICRO ZONE					DESIGN USE			WATER REQ.			FLOWER SHOW				★
			NATIVE	NATURALIZED	EXOTIC	TROPICAL	HEIGHT	WIDTH	LOW DESERT	INTERMEDIATE DESERT	HIGH DESERT	A — SUNNY	B — PART SUNNY	C — LITTLE SUNNY	D — INTRO. SHADE	E — DEEP SHADE	OASIS	TRANSITION	DESERT	LOW WATER	MODERATE WATER	HIGH WATER	SPRING FLOWERS	SUMMER FLOWERS	FALL FLOWERS	WINTER FLOWERS	STAR PERFORMER
✓	*Abronia villosa*	Sand Verbena	✓				6"	18"	✓	✓		✓							✓	✓			✓				★
	Achillea ageratifolia	Greek Yarrow			✓		10"	12"	✓	✓	✓	✓	✓					✓	✓		✓			✓			
	Achillea millefolium	Common Yarrow			✓		3'	3'	✓	✓	✓	✓	✓					✓	✓		✓			✓			
✓	*Achillea tomentosa*	Woolly Yarrow		✓	✓		10"	18"	✓	✓	✓	✓	✓					✓	✓		✓			✓			
	Alcea rosea	Hollyhock			✓		6'	2'	✓	✓	✓	✓	✓		✓		✓	✓			✓			✓			
	Alpinia zerumbet	Shell Ginger			✓		8'	3'	✓	✓	✓		✓		✓		✓					✓	✓	✓			
	Amaranthus caudatus	Love-Lies-Bleeding			✓		4'	2'	✓	✓	✓	✓	✓	✓	✓		✓	✓		✓	✓			✓			
✓	*Antirrhinum majus*	Snapdragon (See Cat.)			✓		3'	3'	✓	✓	✓	✓	✓				✓	✓			✓		✓			✓	
	Arctotis hybrid	Annual African Daisy		✓	✓		4"	36"	✓	✓		✓						✓	✓	✓	✓		✓				
✓	*Astilbe hybrid*	False Spiraea			✓		3'	2'	✓	✓	✓	✓	✓	✓	✓		✓					✓		✓			★
	Begonia "Erythrophylla"	Beefsteak Begonia			✓		12"	18"	✓	✓	✓		✓	✓	✓		✓					✓	✓	✓	✓		
	Begonia masoniana	Iron Cross Begonia			✓		18"	18"	✓	✓	✓		✓	✓	✓		✓					✓	✓	✓	✓		
✓	*Begonia semperflorens*	Bedding Begonia			✓		12"	20"	✓	✓	✓		✓	✓	✓		✓					✓	✓	✓	✓		
✓	*Begonia tuberhybrida*	Tuberous Begonia			✓		18"	18"	✓	✓	✓		✓	✓	✓		✓					✓		✓	✓		★
	Bellis perennis	English Daisy			✓		6"	6"	✓	✓	✓		✓		✓			✓			✓		✓			✓	
	Brachycome iberidifolia	Swan River Daisy			✓		12"	18"	✓	✓	✓	✓						✓			✓		✓	✓			
✓	*Caladium bicolor*	Fancy-Leafed Caladium (See Cat.)			✓	✓	2'	2'	✓	✓				✓	✓			✓				✓					
✓	*Calendula officinalis*	Calendula			✓		2'	2'	✓	✓	✓	✓					✓	✓			✓		✓		✓	✓	★
	Callistephus chinensis	China Aster			✓		3'	2'	✓	✓	✓	✓						✓	✓	✓	✓			✓			
	Campanula isophylla	Bellflower			✓		30"	18"	✓	✓	✓		✓		✓		✓				✓		✓	✓			
✓	*Campanula medium*	Canterbury Bells			✓		30"	18"	✓	✓	✓		✓		✓		✓				✓		✓	✓			
✓	*Catharanthus roseus*	Madagascar Periwinkle			✓		18"	18"	✓	✓	✓	✓	✓		✓		✓				✓		✓	✓	✓		★

Annuals

MASTER PLANT MATERIALS MATRIX

	BOTANICAL NAME	COMMON NAME	ENVIRON. GROUPING				SIZE		MACRO ZONE			MICRO ZONE					DESIGN USE			WATER REQ.			FLOWER SHOW				★
DESCRIBED			NATIVE	NATURALIZED	EXOTIC	TROPICAL	HEIGHT	WIDTH	LOW DESERT	INTERMEDIATE DESERT	HIGH DESERT	A — SUNNY	B — PART SUNNY	C — LITTLE SUNNY	D — INTRO. SHADE	E — DEEP SHADE	OASIS	TRANSITION	DESERT	LOW WATER	MODERATE WATER	HIGH WATER	SPRING FLOWERS	SUMMER FLOWERS	FALL FLOWERS	WINTER FLOWERS	STAR PERFORMER
✔	*Celosia plumosa*	Cockscomb			✔		2'	3'	✔	✔	✔	✔					✔			✔			✔	✔			
	Centaurea cyanus	Bachelor's Button (See Cat.)			✔		2'	2'	✔	✔	✔	✔	✔					✔	✔	✔	✔		✔	✔			
✔	*Chrysanthemum frutescens*	Marguerite			✔		3'	4'	✔			✔	✔				✔	✔			✔		✔				★
	Chrysanthemum maximum	Shasta Daisy			✔		3'	3'	✔	✔		✔	✔				✔	✔			✔	✔	✔				
	Chrysanthemum morifolium	Florist's Chrysanthemum			✔		3'	3'	✔			✔	✔				✔	✔			✔	✔	✔				
	Chrysanthemum paludosum	NCN			✔		10"	14"	✔			✔	✔				✔	✔			✔		✔				
	Clarkia concinna	Red Ribbons	✔	✔			18"	18"	✔	✔	✔	✔	✔					✔	✔	✔	✔		✔				
✔	*Coleus hybridus*	Coleus			✔		18"	18"	✔	✔	✔		✔	✔	✔		✔					✔					
	Consolida ambigua	Larkspur			✔		4'	2'	✔	✔	✔	✔	✔					✔	✔	✔	✔		✔	✔			
	Coreopsis tinctoria	Calliopsis		✔			3'	2'	✔	✔	✔	✔	✔					✔	✔	✔			✔	✔			
✔	*Cosmos bipinnatus*	Cosmos		✔	✔		5'	4'	✔	✔	✔	✔					✔	✔			✔			✔			
	Cosmos sulphureus	Yellow Cosmos		✔	✔		6'	4'	✔	✔	✔	✔					✔	✔			✔			✔			
	Cyclamen species	Cyclamen (See Cat.)			✔	✔	8"	12"	✔	✔	✔	✔	✔		✔		✔					✔	✔	✔			
✔	*Dianthus barbatus*	Sweet William			✔		20"	10"	✔	✔	✔	✔		✔		✔	✔				✔			✔	✔		
	Dianthus caryophyllus "Border"	Border Carnation (See Cat.)			✔		12"	12"	✔	✔	✔		✔		✔		✔	✔			✔			✔	✔		
	Dianthus caryophyllus "Florist"	Florist Carnation (See Cat.)			✔		4'	3'	✔	✔	✔		✔		✔		✔	✔				✔	✔	✔	✔	✔	
	Diascia barberae	Twinspur			✔		6"	6"	✔	✔	✔			✔	✔		✔	✔			✔		✔	✔			
	Dimorphotheca sinuata	Cape Marigold			✔		12"	18"	✔	✔	✔	✔						✔	✔	✔			✔				
✔	*Eschscholzia californica*	California Poppy	✔	✔			16"	16"	✔	✔	✔	✔						✔	✔	✔			✔				★
	Fuchsia hybrida	Hybrid Fuchsia (See Cat.)			✔		3'	3'	✔	✔	✔		✔		✔		✔	✔			✔	✔	✔	✔	✔		
	Gaillardia pulchella	Blanket Flower	✔	✔			4'	2'	✔	✔	✔	✔						✔	✔	✔	✔			✔	✔		
✔	*Gazania splendens*	Clumping Gazania		✔	✔		4"	18"	✔	✔	✔	✔	✔					✔	✔	✔	✔		✔			✔	★

Annuals

MASTER PLANT MATERIALS MATRIX

DESCRIBED	BOTANICAL NAME	COMMON NAME	NATIVE	NATURALIZED	EXOTIC	TROPICAL	HEIGHT	WIDTH	LOW DESERT	INTERMEDIATE DESERT	HIGH DESERT	A — SUNNY	B — PART SUNNY	C — LITTLE SUNNY	D — INTRO. SHADE	E — DEEP SHADE	OASIS	TRANSITION	DESERT	LOW WATER	MODERATE WATER	HIGH WATER	SPRING FLOWERS	SUMMER FLOWERS	FALL FLOWERS	WINTER FLOWERS	STAR PERFORMER
	Gyosophila elegans	NCN			✔		18"	18"	✔	✔	✔	✔					✔	✔			✔	✔	✔	✔			
	Gypsophila paniculata	Baby's Breath			✔		2'	2'	✔	✔	✔	✔	✔				✔	✔			✔	✔		✔	✔		
✔	*Helianthus annuus*	Common Sunflower		✔			10'	2'	✔	✔	✔	✔						✔				✔		✔	✔		★
	Helichrysum bracteatum	Strawflower			✔		3'	3'	✔	✔	✔	✔						✔	✔	✔				✔			
✔	*Heuchera sanguinea*	Coral Bells		✔			2'	2'	✔	✔	✔		✔	✔	✔		✔	✔					✔	✔			
	Hyssopus officinalis	Hyssop			✔		18"	18"	✔	✔	✔	✔	✔		✔			✔	✔	✔	✔			✔	✔		
	Iberis umbellata	Globe Candytuft			✔		12"	12"	✔	✔	✔	✔	✔		✔		✔	✔				✔	✔	✔			
✔	*Impatiens wallerana*	Impatiens (See Cat.)			✔		24"	18"	✔	✔			✔		✔		✔					✔	✔		✔	✔	★
	Kniphofia uvaria	Red-Hot Poker			✔		4'	2'	✔	✔	✔	✔	✔		✔		✔	✔			✔			✔			
✔	*Lathyrus odoratus*	Sweet Pea (See Cat.)			✔		8'	2'	✔	✔	✔	✔	✔		✔		✔	✔				✔	✔	✔			
	Linum flavum	Golden Flax	✔	✔			15"	15"	✔			✔						✔	✔	✔			✔				
✔	*Linum grandiflorum* "Rubrum"	Scarlet Flax	✔	✔			18"	10"	✔			✔						✔	✔	✔			✔				
✔	*Linum perenne*	Perennial Blue Flax	✔	✔			2'	2'	✔			✔						✔	✔	✔			✔				
✔	*Lobularia maritima*	Sweet Alyssum	✔	✔	✔		4"	12"	✔	✔	✔	✔	✔	✔	✔		✔	✔			✔	✔	✔		✔		★
	Malcolmia maritima	Virginian Stock		✔	✔		10"	10"	✔	✔	✔	✔	✔		✔		✔	✔			✔	✔	✔		✔		
	Matthiola incana	Stock			✔		3'	3'	✔	✔		✔	✔		✔		✔	✔			✔		✔			✔	
	Nemesia strumosa	False Snapdragon			✔		16"	16"	✔	✔		✔	✔		✔		✔	✔			✔		✔				
	Nicotiana alata	NCN			✔		3'	3'	✔	✔	✔	✔	✔		✔		✔	✔				✔		✔			
	Nierembergia repens	Cup Flower (See Cat.)			✔		12"	12"	✔	✔	✔	✔	✔		✔		✔	✔			✔			✔			
	Paeonia species	Peony (See Cat.)			✔		3'	3'	✔	✔	✔	✔	✔		✔		✔	✔			✔	✔		✔	✔		
✔	*Papaver nudicaule*	Iceland Poppy (See Cat.)		✔	✔		24"	10"	✔	✔	✔	✔	✔		✔		✔	✔			✔		✔	✔			★
✔	*Pelargonium hortorum*	Common Geranium (See Cat.)			✔		3'	2'	✔	✔	✔	✔	✔		✔		✔				✔	✔	✔		✔	✔	★
	BOTANICAL NAME	COMMON NAME	ENVIRON. GROUPING				SIZE		MACRO ZONE			MICRO ZONE					DESIGN USE			WATER REQ.			FLOWER SHOW				★

Annuals

MASTER PLANT MATERIALS MATRIX

	Botanical Name	Common Name	Environ. Grouping				Size		Macro Zone			Micro Zone					Design Use			Water Req.			Flower Show				★
DESCRIBED	BOTANICAL NAME	COMMON NAME	NATIVE	NATURALIZED	EXOTIC	TROPICAL	HEIGHT	WIDTH	LOW DESERT	INTERMEDIATE DESERT	HIGH DESERT	A — SUNNY	B — PART SUNNY	C — LITTLE SUNNY	D — INTRO. SHADE	E — DEEP SHADE	OASIS	TRANSITION	DESERT	LOW WATER	MODERATE WATER	HIGH WATER	SPRING FLOWERS	SUMMER FLOWERS	FALL FLOWERS	WINTER FLOWERS	STAR PERFORMER
✔	*Perovskia atriplicifolia*	Russian sage			✔		3'	5'	✔	✔	✔	✔	✔	✔		✔	✔		✔	✔				✔			
✔	*Petunia hybrida*	Common Petunia (See Cat.)			✔		18"	24"	✔	✔	✔	✔	✔		✔		✔					✔	✔		✔		★
✔	*Petunia hybrida* "Grandiflora"	Petunia (See Cat.)			✔		18"	24"	✔	✔	✔	✔	✔		✔		✔					✔	✔		✔		★
✔	*Petunia hybrida* "Multiflora"	Petunia (See Cat.)			✔		18"	24"	✔	✔	✔	✔	✔		✔		✔					✔	✔		✔		★
	Phacelia campanularia	Desert Bluebells	✔				12"	12"	✔	✔		✔							✔	✔			✔		✔		
✔	*Phlox drummondii*	Annual Phlox (See Cat.)	✔	✔			18"	12"	✔	✔	✔	✔	✔				✔				✔		✔	✔			
	Phlox paniculata	Summer Phlox (See Cat.)	✔	✔			3'	3'	✔	✔	✔	✔	✔				✔				✔		✔	✔			
	Physalis alkekengi	Chinese Lantern Plant			✔		2'	2'	✔	✔	✔	✔	✔					✔		✔	✔		✔	✔			
	Primula vulgaris	Primrose (See Cat.)			✔		12"	12"	✔	✔	✔			✔	✔		✔	✔			✔		✔				
	Reseda odorata	Mignonette			✔		18"	30"	✔	✔	✔		✔	✔	✔		✔	✔				✔		✔	✔		
✔	*Rudbeckia hirta*	Black-Eyed Susan	✔	✔			4'	2'	✔	✔	✔	✔	✔					✔		✔	✔			✔			
✔	*Salvia officinalis*	Garden Sage		✔	✔		2'	2'	✔	✔	✔	✔	✔		✔		✔	✔		✔	✔			✔	✔		★
	Scabiosa atropurpurea	Pincushion Flower			✔		2'	2'	✔	✔	✔	✔	✔		✔			✔	✔	✔			✔	✔			
✔	*Tagetes erecta*	American Marigold (See Cat.)		✔			36"	18"	✔	✔	✔	✔	✔		✔			✔					✔	✔			★
	Trollius ledebouri	Globeflower	✔				24"	12"	✔			✔						✔	✔	✔	✔		✔	✔			
✔	*Tropaeolum majus*	Common Nasturtium			✔		2'	3'	✔	✔	✔	✔	✔		✔			✔		✔	✔				✔	✔	★
✔	*Viola wittrockiana*	Pansy (See Cat.)			✔		4"	8"	✔	✔	✔	✔	✔		✔		✔				✔	✔	✔			✔	
✔	*Zinnia elegans*	Zinnia			✔		3'	2'	✔	✔	✔	✔					✔	✔				✔		✔			★

Trees and Palms

Valley Oak

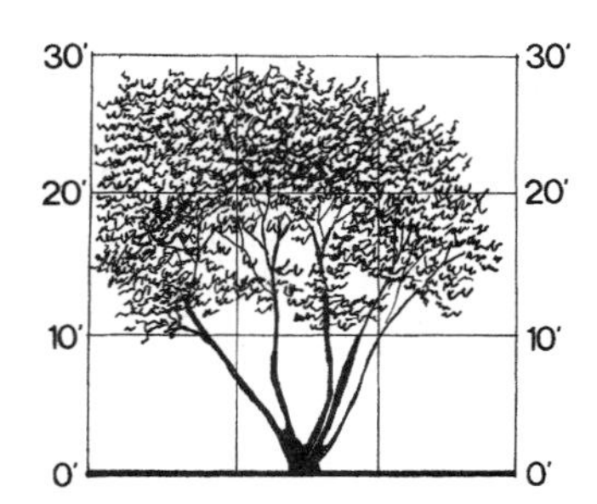

Acacia abyssinica **Semi-evergreen**
Abyssinian Acacia

Exotic from Africa. Flat topped at maturity. Multiple trunk trees are more interesting. Like all Acacias, it has round (puffball-like) yellow flowers. Flowers appear in midspring. Grows relatively fast. Darker green foliage than the rest of the genus.

Acacia aneura **Evergreen**
Mulga

There is some botanical misunderstanding as to what tree is actually aneura. Do not specify trees in the needle-leaf form for they are inferior. Undivided, small, silvery gray leaves typify the desirable tree. Very dense head, spreading 12 to 15 feet wide and 20 feet high from the base. Good visual screen tree. Rod-shaped yellow flowers occur in spring and summer. Branches are arched and sweeping in the direction of the wind. This tree looks especially nice in informal masses. Sometimes hard to establish, they exhibit fast growth on moderate irrigation once they gain a foothold.

Acacia farnesiana* or *Acacia smalli **Semi-evergreen**
Sweet Acacia

Horticultural debate occurs as to whether these are the same tree. *Smalli* is probably a hybrid of *farnesiana* and is believed to be a little hardier. From the tropics of South America. An easy tree to prune for nice multi-trunk effect. Yellow, very fragrant, round, ball-like flowers in late winter to early spring and occasionally in fall. Fast growth. Gray-green foliage.

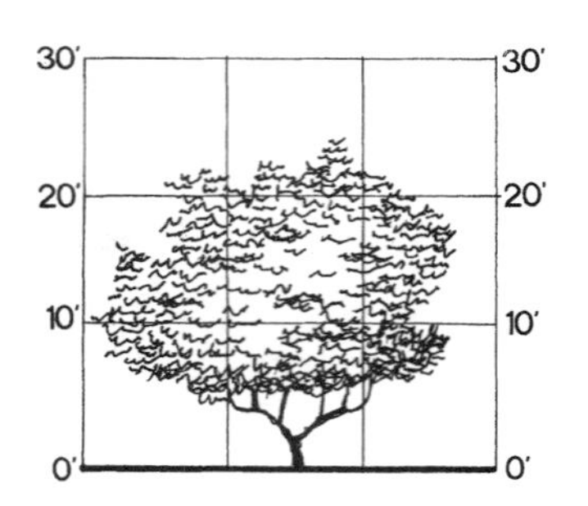

★ *Acacia greggii* **Semi-evergreen**
Cat's Claw Acacia

Native to the Sonoran Desert, found naturally at outer edges of riparian communities. A fine, small scale, desert tree. Drought-deciduous if not watered. Will lose leaves briefly in very cold winters. Extremely fine bipinnate foliage. Tiny yellow puffball flowers in early through late spring. Fast growth. Tough tree. Good screen tree to prevent unwanted intrusion due to numerous 1/4 inch needle-sharp thorns (cat claws).

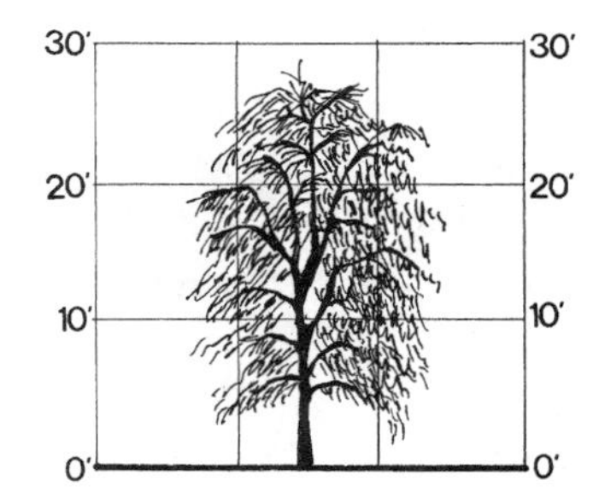

Acacia stenophylla **Semi-evergreen**
Shoestring Acacia

Adapted leaves, one-foot long green threads (shoestrings) hang from horizontal to drooping stems which protrude from upright spreading main branches. A native to Australia. A very clean tree with an extremely light head. Good to use around pools or in front of objects you want filtered but not completely screened out. I use this tree in extremely tight areas between walks and decking adjacent to walls or close to overhangs. The rather flexible branches bend and compress into small spaces while the tree itself does not look cramped. Fast growth. Fall, winter, spring flowers of no major significance. Moderate to low water use at maturity.

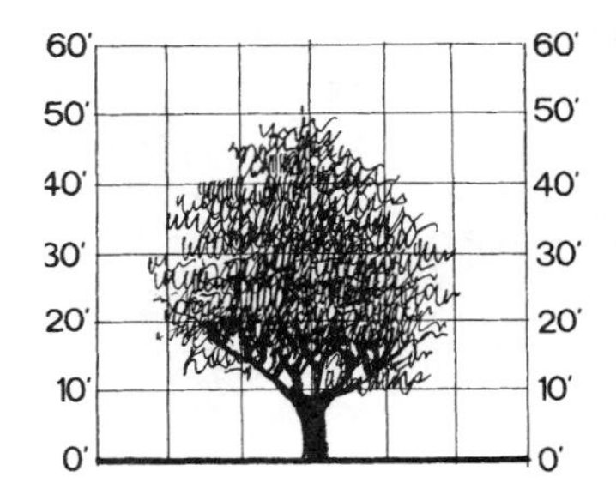

Ailanthus altissima **Deciduous**
Tree-of-Heaven

A junk tree in my estimation, mentioned here only because you will encounter it frequently. Weak-stemmed and suckers profusely. Larger trees on existing projects may need to be incorporated into the design scheme. Grows under extremely poor conditions and will tolerate excessive air pollution. Fast growth. Messy fruit and frequent wind damage. This tree in will, however, withstand drought and tolerate any soil, including saline.

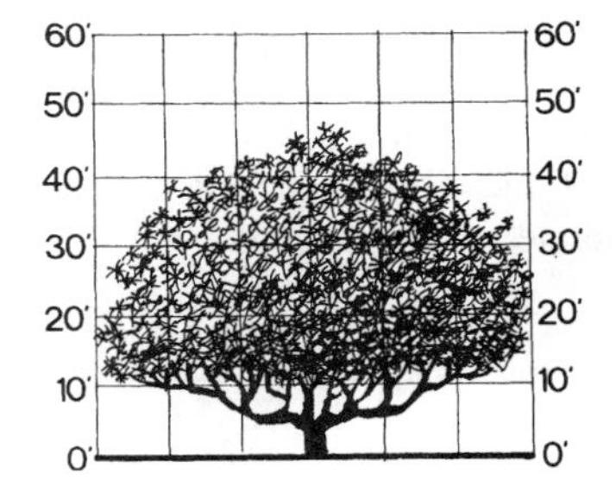

★ ***Albizia julibrissin*** **Deciduous**
Mimosa Tree

Very wide-spreading, low-canopy tree from Asia. It is quite exotic. Light, airy foliage. Multi-trunk specimens seem to be more proportionate and somehow healthier. A great tree to view from above if looking into a courtyard or from the second or third floor of a building as flowers congregate at the top of the canopy. Feather-light, pink flowers resembling pincushions, occur in late spring through late summer. Flower litter can be significant as can litter from seed pods. Foliage is light enough to grow turf under. In this application I suggest using root barriers to encourage downward development of the root system. Will tolerate low water, but grows faster with more watering. The tree will stay deciduous three months out of the year. Interesting growth structure tempers leaf loss. I rate this as one of my Top Ten Desert Trees, although the design programs of the majority of my clientele rarely allow for its use.

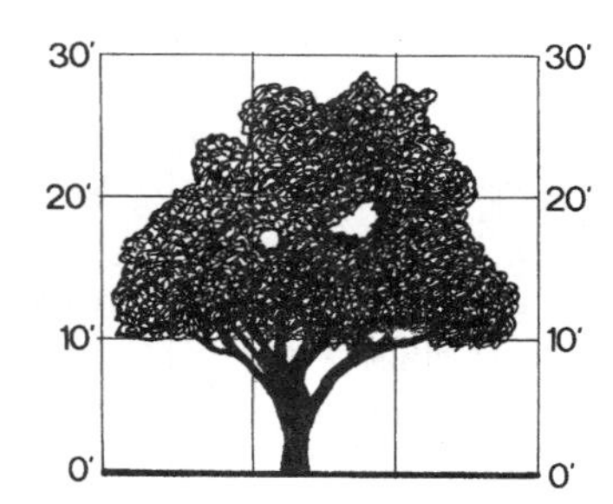

Arbutus unedo **Evergreen**
Strawberry Tree

Needs some sun protection, but an extremely interesting tree. Leathery foliage. Interesting twisted, reddish bark at maturity. Edible, tasteless red fruit resembles strawberries. A very good small patio tree. Slow growth, but little water usage.

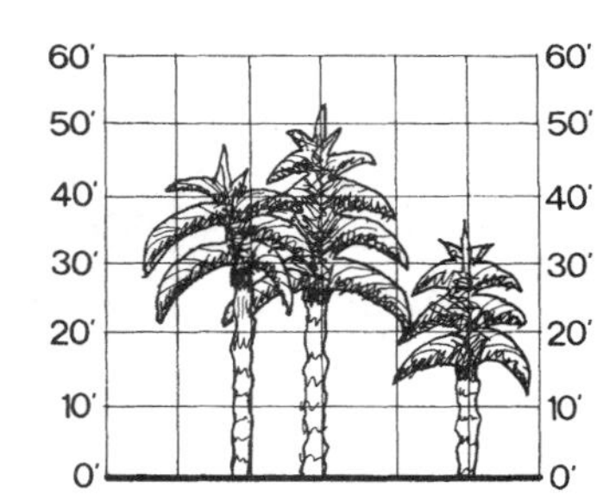

★ ***Arecastrum romanzoffianum*** **Evergreen**
Queen Palm

Smallest of the three "big palm" species used in the desert. Very clean palm, used frequently around pools and spas. Insignificant flowers and fruit. Dark green fronds give refined, almost tropical effect. Smooth trunks look elegant and are easy to mount lighting fixtures onto. Star performer in an oasis setting where its graceful appearance can set the stage for other exotics and tropicals. Not my favorite as a street or lawn tree in the desert, although it is frequently used as such. Fast growth with ample water.

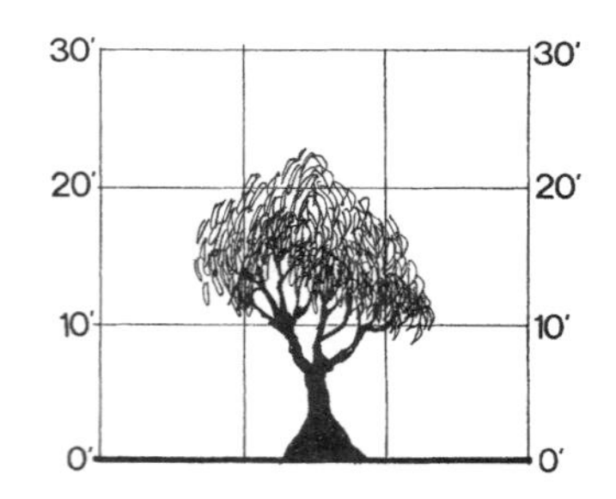

Beaucarnea recurvata **Evergreen**
Ponytail Palm

A horticultural oddity. Sometimes called Bottle Palm or Elephant's Foot due to huge basal proportions. Useful as an accent, as it draws attention with a base that can spread 4 feet across at maturity on a 12-foot-high palm. The base tapers rapidly to a few branches that support 3-foot long by 3/4 in. wide pendulous leaves. Not a favorite of mine, but client's seem to be absolutely enthralled with this plant. Moderate to slow growth.

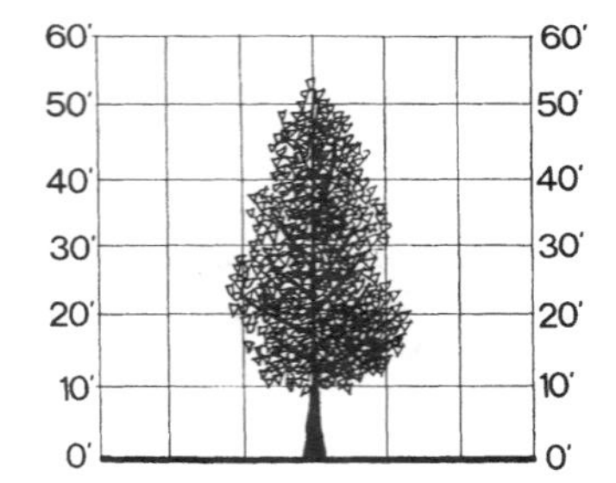

★ ***Brachychiton populneus*** **Evergreen**
Australian Bottle Tree

Tall vertical tree with pyramidal shape. Good substitute for Eucalyptus in high wind areas or in soils where iron availability is a problem. Medium green leaves are light green, sometimes bronzy at growing tips. Trees are quite variable at maturity. Easiest way to assure uniformity is to specify a single leader (main trunk). Trees that branch off or "Y" at the base of the crown are bushy in youth, but irregular with age. Called "Bottle Tree" due to the shape of its trunk, which is wide at grade and tapers quickly to about 3 feet above grade. Cultivar 'Rio Salado' being grown in Arizona offers widest leaf, straight leader, and fuller habit. Fast growth with moderate water. Will withstand drought at maturity.

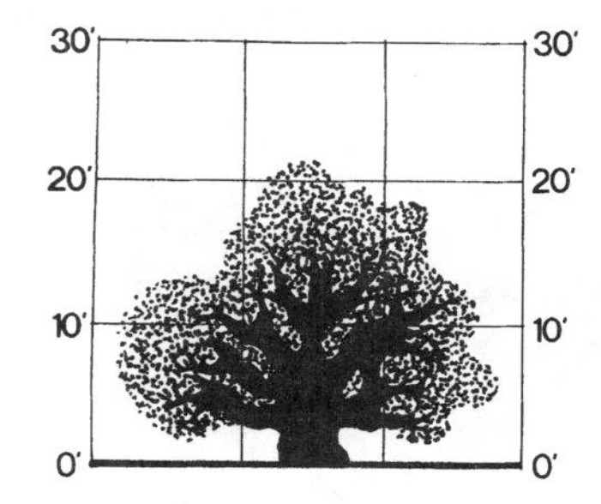

Busera microphylla **Semi-evergreen**
Elephant Tree

Never a particularly abundant species, this southern Sonoran Desert native should receive more use. Currently, availability is a problem, as is finding the right design application for a tree that draws immediate visual attention. Called "Elephant Tree" because of its thick trunk which gives way to thick fast-tapering branches. Truly an exotic look. Whitish bark bleeds red sap when cut. Indians believed sap was a powerful medicine and guarded the whereabouts of these trees with extreme secrecy. Grows naturally on rocky hillsides and, due to its frost-tender nature, should be grown on hillsides when introduced, as these areas receive warm updrafts during cold winter nights. Slow growth.

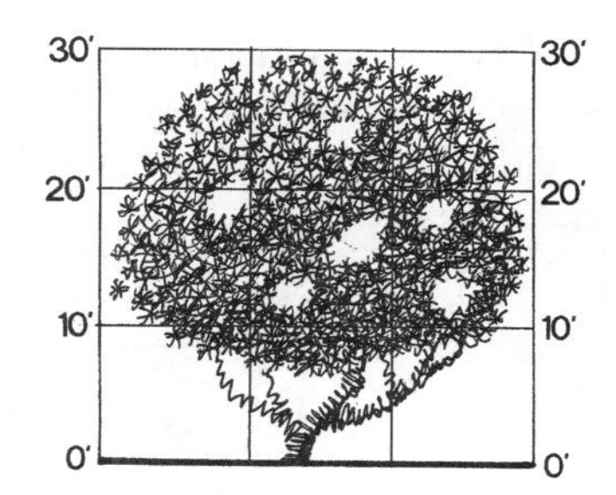

Caesalpinia cacalaco **Evergreen**
Cascalote

This is one of the new miracle trees in the desert. Its one drawback is that it can be somewhat frost-tender, especially in its youth. Do not plant in lower valley floor areas. Does best on sunny south facing slopes. Lush foliage similar to Lysiloma and Jacaranda. This tree would do well mixed in with these two desert stalwarts, especially since its evergreen and could carry the composition in winter. Most prized for its brilliant yellow floral show displayed at the outer edges of its canopy and occurring late winter to early spring. Showy brown seed pods sometimes persist until spring. The thorny trunk thwarts intruders. A good small scale evergreen canopy tree is hard to find in arid regions thus making this species all the more valuable. Fast growth with ample watering.

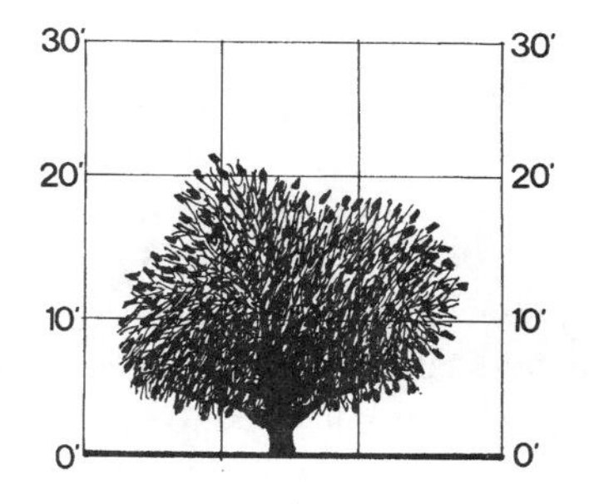

Callistemon citrinus **Evergreen**
Lemon Bottle Brush

Will need some training to appear as a stand-alone, single-stem tree. Better used when drooping foliage and flowers are allowed to extend to the ground. Great to look up at from below, making it useful in raised planters. Spectacular red, brush-like flowers blooms midspring extending into summer. Use away from pedestrian traffic, as bees are attracted in masses. Can be chlorotic (iron deficiency) in deserts, especially in alkaline soils. Tolerates saline soils. Called "Lemon Bottlebrush" due to odor of flowers. Fast growth.

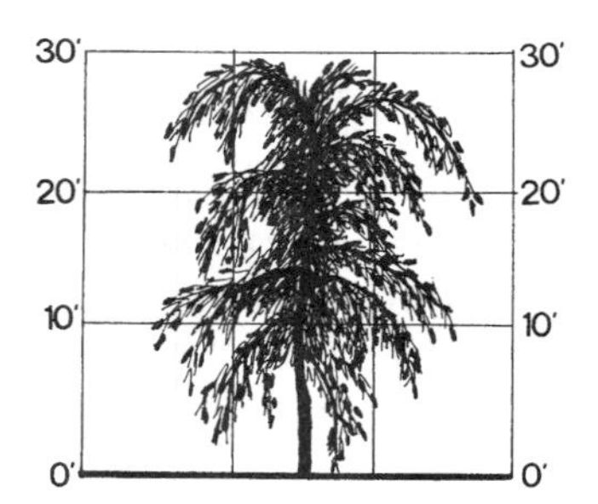

Callistemon viminalis **Evergreen**
Weeping Bottle Brush Tree

Taller and more vertical in character than *Callistemon citrinus*. Weeping effect gives rise to the common name. The 6 inch deep red, bottlebrush-like flowers are attractive, but draw bees. This tree can look extremely chlorotic in iron poor soils. Fast growth with moderate irrigation.

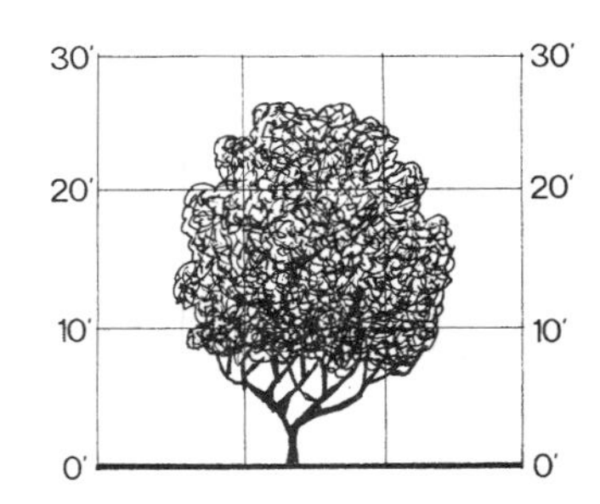

Cassia excelsa **Semi-evergreen**
Crown of Gold

A good, small-scale tree that is ideal for the desert transition garden. Looks good when grouped with other members of the genus. Evergreen in all but the coldest winters. Primary advantage is its spectacular floral show that occurs in spring and fall. A good selection for a south-facing side slope as the tree is somewhat frost-tender. Masses of 12-inch-plus yellow blossoms hang on for 3 to 4 weeks. Fast growth with medium watering. A tree that is beginning to enjoy more widespread use in the low desert.

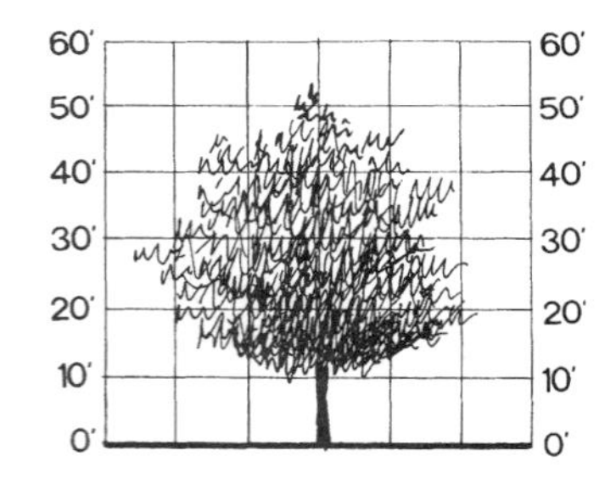

Celtis occidentalis **Deciduous**
Common Hackberry

A very durable tree that should be used more often. Somewhat loosely pyramidal crown. Noted for deep, noninvasive root system, making it a good parking-lot selection. Stays deciduous a long time before leafing out in mid- to late spring, which may invite use in strip shopping centers where the visibility of building-mounted signage is of utmost importance during tourist season. Moderate growth rate.

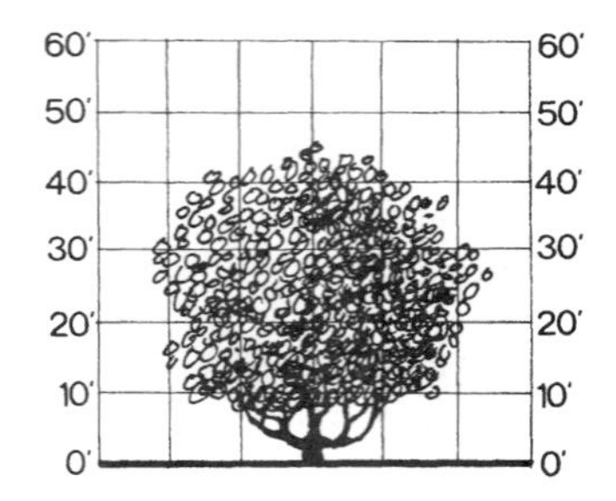

Ceratonia siliqua **Evergreen**
Carob Tree

One of the widest-spreading evergreen trees in the desert. Dense growth. Allowed to grow on open ground, this tree can become massive. Natural growth tendency is to spread out from base, so it will need to be shaped to become a single-trunk tree. Buttressing root system dictates root barriers anywhere pavement, curbs, or walls are near. Can be planted on 15-foot centers for a dense, impenetrable, large-scale hedge. Leathery foliage is deep green to evergreen in color. Specify female trees, as males produce foul-smelling flowers. Dense shade. Forget about planting turf underneath its canopy. Moderate growth rate. Tree has biblical significance, and agriculturally, fruit is used as a chocolate substitute.

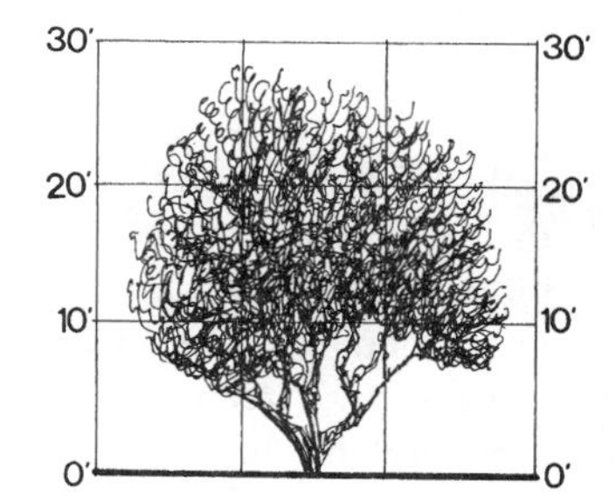

Cercidium floridum **Semi-evergreen**
Blue Palo Verde

True native. The largest of the Palo Verdes and the first of the genus to bloom, signaling the arrival of spring in the desert. As with all Palo Verdes, this tree is drought-deciduous. When the tree drops its leaves, carbohydrates and chlorophyll are manufactured in the green trunk. The Palo Verde is a study of marvelous adaptation to the stresses of desert conditions. Fast growing with little water consumption. Tree is subject to infestations of mistletoe, a parasite. It is also short-lived, having an average life span of 30 years. Despite these disadvantages (new trees can be planted and mistletoe can be controlled), this is a fine desert tree.

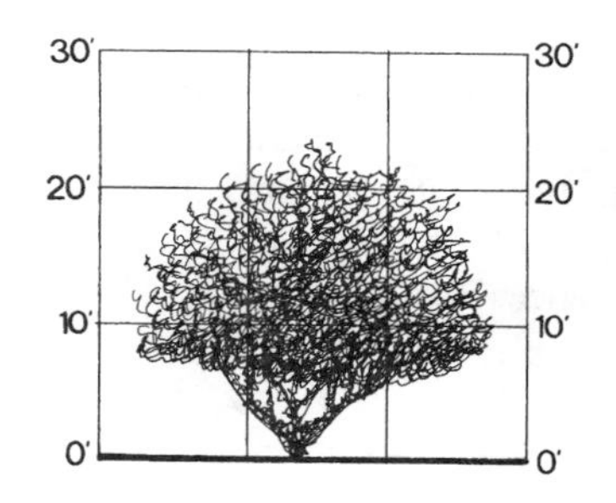

★ *Cercidium microphyllum* **Semi-evergreen**
Foothill Palo Verde

This is the Palo Verde mentioned in previous chapters that shares in the ongoing process of succession with the Saguaro Cactus. Unfortunately for the Palo Verde, in the wild, the Saguaro always wins. In the designed landscape this can be a breath-taking specimen. Branching somewhat horizontally above beefy, twisted main trunks. Nice, yellow flower show at midspring extending into late summer. Slow to moderate growth is actually a plus, as younger and smaller trees have a better appearance.

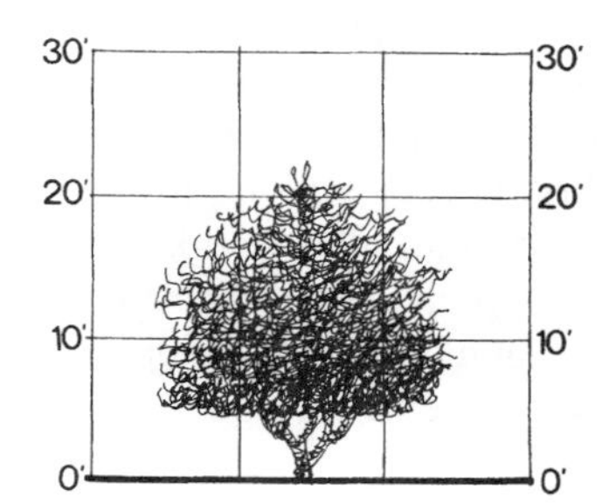

Cercidium praecox **Semi-evergreen**
Sonoran Palo Verde

Gaining in popularity. Smallest of the Palo Verdes. Most consistent in form, which is upright branching with a rounded habit. Bears the familiar yellow blossoms in spring. Rounded crown becomes more umbrella-like at the upper edges with maturity. Upward-reaching branches are sculptural in effect. Many landscape architects consider this tree to be the ultimate Palo Verde. Fast growing.

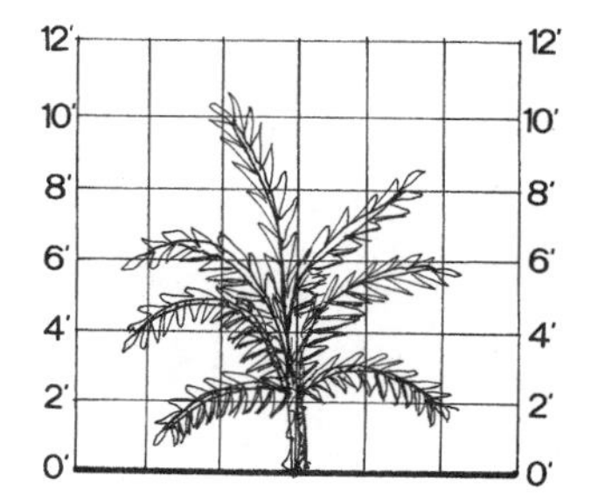

Chamaedorea seifrizii **Evergreen**
Seifrizii Palm

Very popular, small, fern-like palm with multiple trunks. Needs shade and winter frost protection. Popular indoor plant frequently sold in grocery stores. Drinks ample water. Definitely an oasis/tropical plant. Used primarily for high-end residential projects. Slow growth.

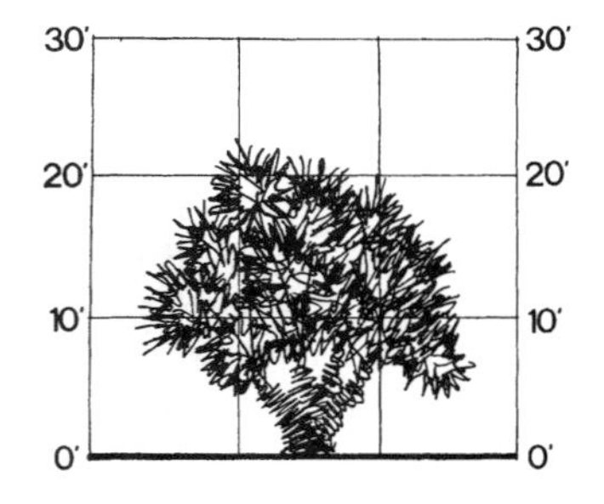

★ *Chamaerops humilis* **Evergreen**
Mediterranean Fan Palm

As the common name implies, an import from the Mediterranean region of Europe. Where height is not a factor, this is the hardiest palm you can select. Light-green, upright, spikey fronds on multiple trunks. A good understory selection to use with the *Washingtonia* genus. Good container and raised planter plant. Slow growth can be helped along with fertilizer and additional watering. This palm will live with low water, but prefers a moderate amount of irrigation.

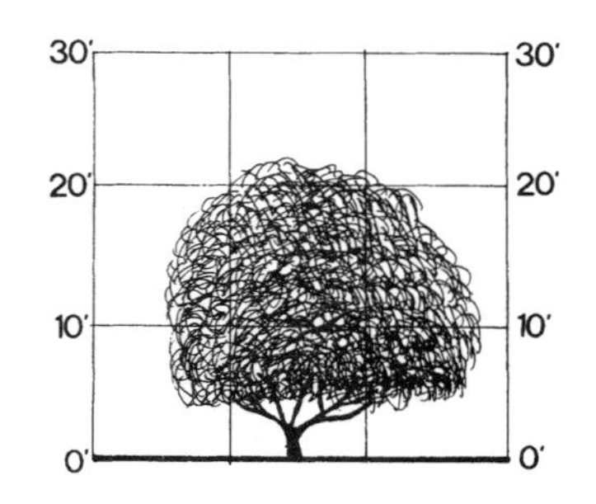

★ *Chilopsis linearis* **Deciduous**
Desert Willow

Not a true willow (genus *Salix*), but reminiscent of some because of its weeping habit and its propensity to grow close to or in riparian environments. Pinkish flowers appear mid-spring and occur intermittently throughout the summer. May need some pruning, especially thinning of the head and removal of suckers, to obtain best appearance. Rapid growth.

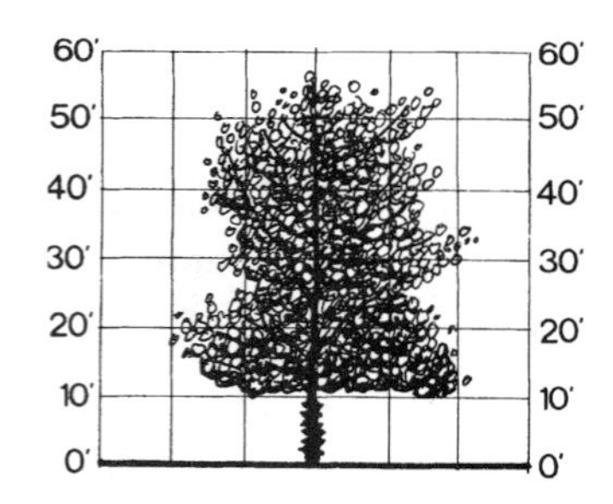

Chorisia speciosa **Deciduous**
Floss Silk Tree

Tree needs protection in the desert as it will freeze at 28°F. Not a good selection for open areas. In areas offering solar radiation, or on hillsides, this tree survives adequately. Frequently used for its magnificent flower show which occurs anytime between mid-November through February at the height of the tourist season. Tree is briefly deciduous during its blooming period. Flowers are pink to medium purple, hibiscus-like, only with narrower petals. Thorns to 3/4 inch long on trunk of tree, particularly at the base, are unusual and lend an exotic appearance. Tree's canopy becomes woody with age. Moderate growth. A nice tree in the right situation, but care should be exercised in its selection.

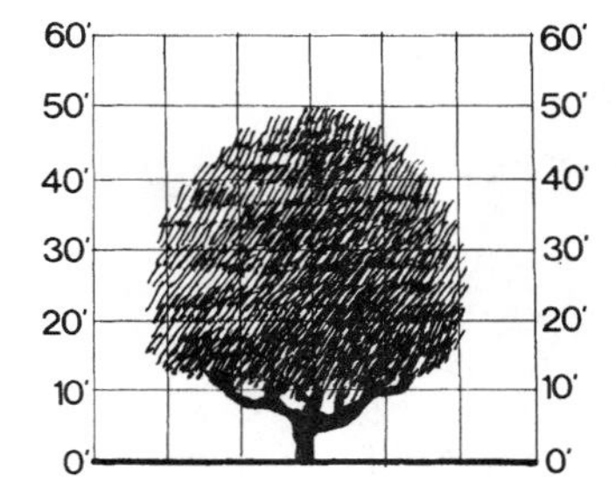

Cinnamomum camphora **Semi-evergreen**
Camphor Tree

Large scale round-headed trees. Most books rate this tree an evergreen while I rate it a Semi-evergreen for two reasons. First, leaves yellow and go dormant in winter and second, there is a predictable heavy leaf drop in midspring (March) that is followed by flower and fruit drop. Not a good tree in heavily used pedestrian areas or parking lots because of all the litter. Foliage is handsome and the tree is quite pest free. Invasive roots can be controlled by planting with root barriers. Fast growth.

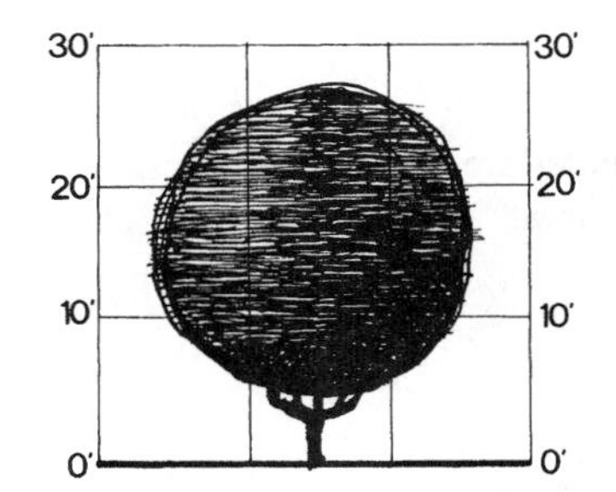

Citrus species **Evergreen**
Citrus (consult grower's catalogues)

Several desert climates are ideal for growing citrus trees. Extended periods of high temperatures allow for the formation of full-flavored, juicy fruit. Sandy soil also provides for fast drainage — another requirement of Citrus. In other soils, add admendments to improve drainage. These trees offer the familiar grapefruit, oranges, lemons, limes, tangerines, and various hybrid fruits. Citrus are round-headed, deep-green trees that provide a fragrant aroma in the spring of each year. The trees are easily grown, needing some frost protection during the coldest winter nights and not wishing to be left in standing water. This is not a particularly good selection for turf areas as the root system is excessively greedy and will compete with the grass for all surface moisture. When using Citrus in turf, do so using root barriers. Another feature common to Citrus is that they are almost always grafted onto a hardy root stock of another species. Cut all sucker growth below the grafted bud union as this growth will be from the undesirable plant. Trunks of young, newly planted Citrus need protection from sun scald. Wrap trees or paint with a latex paint. The perceived necessity to use only white paint is an old wives' tale. Paint the same color as the trunk; this looks more natural and serves the same purpose. *Lush and Efficient* by Eric Johnson and David Harbison provides an excellent section describing the cultural requirements of Citrus and is recommended reading. Note that Citrus can be easily grown as espaliers and is available in dwarf varieties for property with limited space. Following is listing of a few of the varieties:

★ ***Citrus 'Marsh Seedless'***
Citrus Grapefruit

The most commonly planted grapefruit in southern California. Extremely large size, crown to thirty feet round if allowed to branch to ground. Trimmed into a tree shape, it is 25 feet by 25 feet. Fast growth.

★ ***Citrus 'Ruby Pink'***
Citrus Pink Grapefruit

The best variety of pink grapefruit. Moderate growth.

★ ***Citrus 'Eureka'***
Citrus Lemon

Most common lemon available. The lemon most often found in supermarkets. Fruit occurs on the trees year round. Twenty-foot round tree. Lemons are the fastest growing species of Citrus.

★ ***Citrus 'Bearss'***
Citrus Lime

Best California lime. Fifteen-foot rounded tree. Grows in the same conditions that are favorable to oranges. Moderate growth rate.

★ ***Citrus 'Kinnow'***
Citrus Mandarin Orange

Mandarin orange of exceptional flavor. Atypical of the genus, it grows in a somewhat columnar habit. Twenty-feet high by 15-feet wide. Moderate growth rate.

★ ***Citrus 'Navel'***
Citrus Orange

A meat orange more for eating than juicing. Produces fruit December to February. Twenty-foot rounded tree. Moderate growth rate.

★ ***Citrus 'Valencia'***
Citrus Orange

A juice orange. The species most commercial orange juice is produced from. Fruit matures in summer months and will stay on tree and be edible through the fall.

★ ***Citrus 'Dancy'***
Citrus Tangerine

Upright, spreading, small tree 15 feet high and 10 feet wide. This Christmas tangerine is available in December. Excellent taste. Somewhat frost-tender. Slow growth.

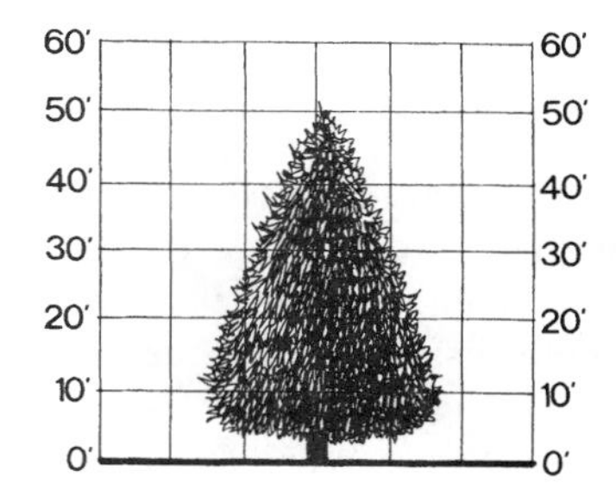

★ ***Cupressus arizonica*** **Evergreen**
Arizona Cypress

Pyramidal evergreen that serves as an excellent visual screen or windbreak. A short lifespan (30 years) and occasional attacks from beetles are its drawbacks. A good alternative screen tree to Tamarind although slower growing. Moderate growth rate. A tree that should be grown and used more often.

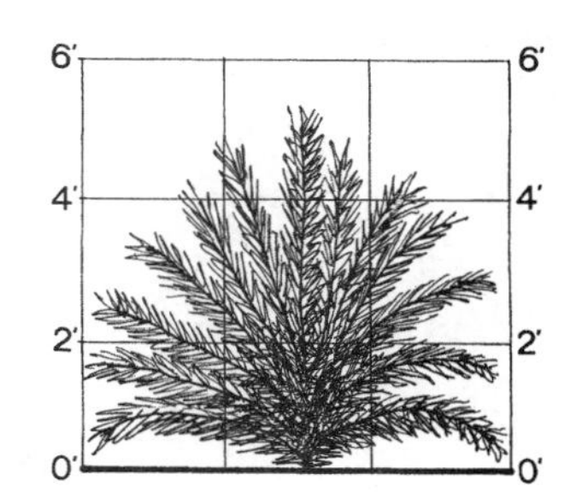

★ ***Cycas revoluta*** **Evergreen**
Sago Palm

Makes the star-performer list because it is so frequently used and, by all appearances, will continue to be. Plant is not really a palm, but rather a gymnosperm and is botanically more closely allied with the conifers. It is truly bizarre and beautiful. Keep out of full sun in low desert and protected from winter elements in high desert. Bright-green, fern-like leaves and hairy brown trunks. Multiple trunks common. Very maintenance-free, just hose dust off the fronds. A fine entry or atrium specimen.

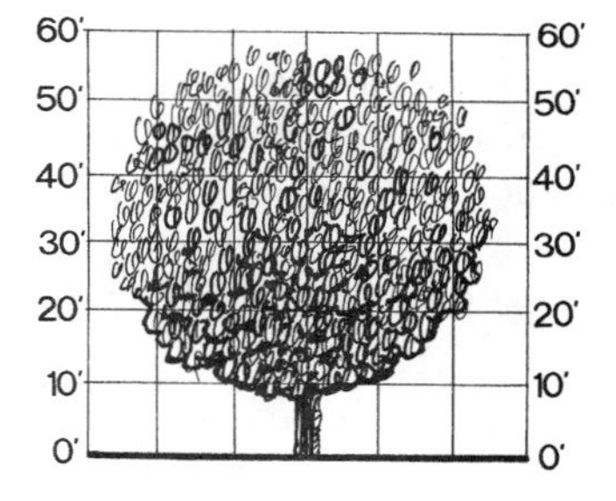

Dalbergia sissoo **Evergreen**
Sissoo

Native to the Napal region of the Indian peninsula. Grows in secondary riparian bench areas in association with Acacia species. Like Acacia, it exhibits the ability to withstand arid conditions and develop drought tolerance. A recent U.S. Southwest deserts introduction, the tree comes with some high hopes. First, it is a broadleaf evergren tree of considerable scale (60 feet high by 40 feet wide). This feature is a rarity among desert tree selections. It could become a major street and park type specimen. Leaves are bright green, offering a nice contrast to the gray-greens of most desert materials. Easterners will note that the shape and vaination of the leaves are reminiscent of European Beech (*Fagus sylvatica*). Upright, spreading branches form a loose open canopy. Use box specimens as younger trees are frost tender. A tree with enough inherent potential to become a star performer with increased use. Moderate growth on moderate water.

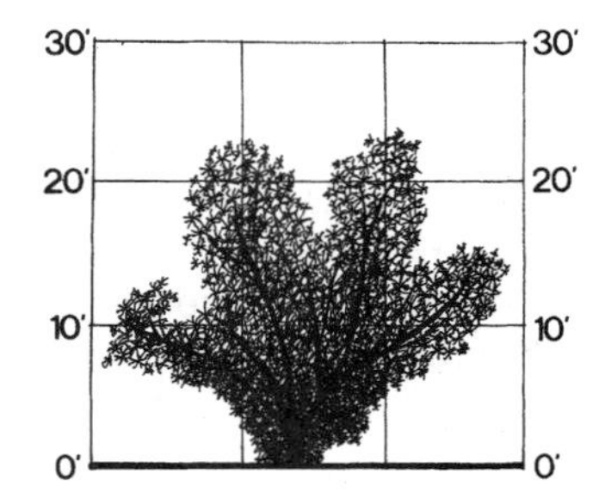

Dalea spinosa **Semi-evergreen**

Smoke Tree

I disagree with the common name and view this Colorado Desert native more as a large unruly shrub rather than a tree. I would not give it the importance of a tree in the landscape, because its growth habit is irregular and undependable. However, others vehemently disagree, so it is presented here as a tree. This is the spectacular purple-blooming plant depicted in paintings found in every notable art gallery in the Southwest. When *Dalea spinosa* is in bloom it is certainly a show stopper. Flower show, mostly in June, is often followed by long periods of drought deciduousness and winter deciduous behavior. It is this extremely long out-of-leaf period that makes it hard to place Smoke Tree in the ornamental landscape. Use this plant as a backdrop, or an occasional vertical accent, or as it occurs in nature, at the bottom of natural or emulated desert washes. Slow growth.

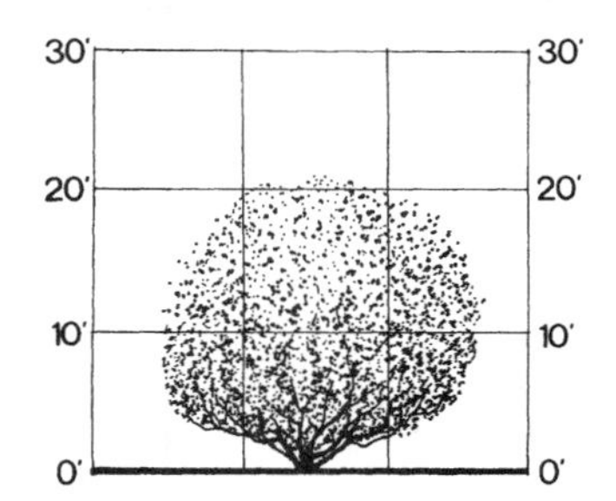

Elaeagnus angustifolia **Deciduous**

Russian Olive

A tree that is not frequently used in the low desert. Heavily relied upon at other elevations. As its common name implies, it looks similar to an Olive (*Olea europaea*) in appearance. It is deciduous and decidedly smaller. Foliage is longer, looser, more willow-like, and its underside appears silvery in the wind. Excellent windbreak selection. Known for tolerating all types of soil conditions, even wet clays. Small, yellow flowers are insignificant except to say they put out a strongly pleasing fragrance. Fast growing on minimal water, it offers itself as a very good selection for the tight budget project.

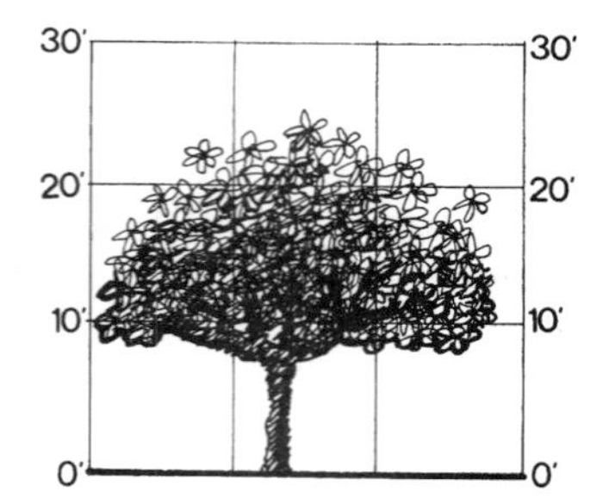

Eriobotrya japonica **Evergreen**

Loquat

Loquat is winter-blooming and has striking foliage. Fruit is edible. Must be shaped at youth to take on a tree-like appearance. Dramatic foliage is the plant's best feature. Leaves that are over 2 inches wide and 6 inches long (or more) thrust out and downward from the tree's crown. Loquat makes an excellent espalier, however, o not use against walls with reflected heat. Likes afternoon shade in the low desert. Moderate growth rate.

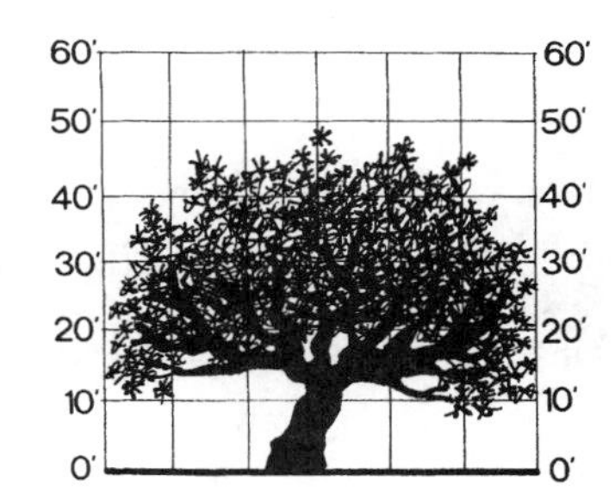

Erythrina lysistemon **Deciduous**
N.C.N. (Coral Tree)

Very large and striking in size and branch structure. Compares with the Kaffirboom Coral Tree (*Erythrina caffra*), which is a show stopper on the coast. This Coral Tree takes desert conditions. Deciduous. Orange blossoms through winter into early spring when leaves are off the tree. Like all Erythrinas, it has vicious thorns. Be careful where you use it. Moderate growth on low summer water.

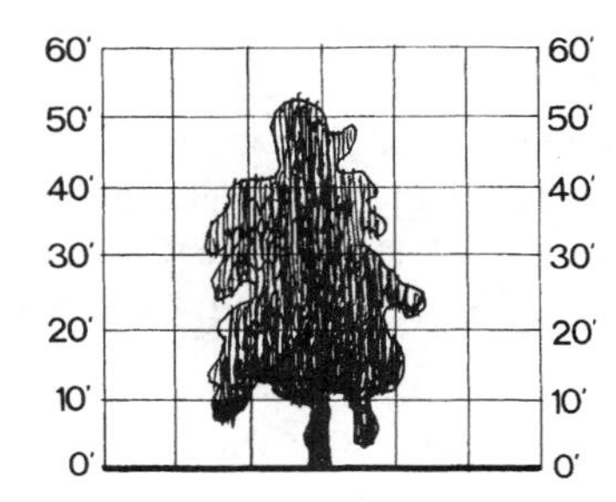

★ ***Eucalyptus microtheca*** **Evergreen**
Coolibah Tree

From Australia. If you were to use only one Eucalyptus in the desert, this would be the tree. It is the most dependable in growth habit and the most wind resistant. Wind breakage is the most prominent drawback to using Eucalyptus in the desert. Extremely fast-growing trees. At initial installation, smaller trees are better than larger ones, as they adapt to local cultural conditions and adjust growth rate accordingly. Good screen tree, visually speaking. Although it is used as a windbreak, I personally would not recommend it. Character of the tree gives it stature in the transitional garden.

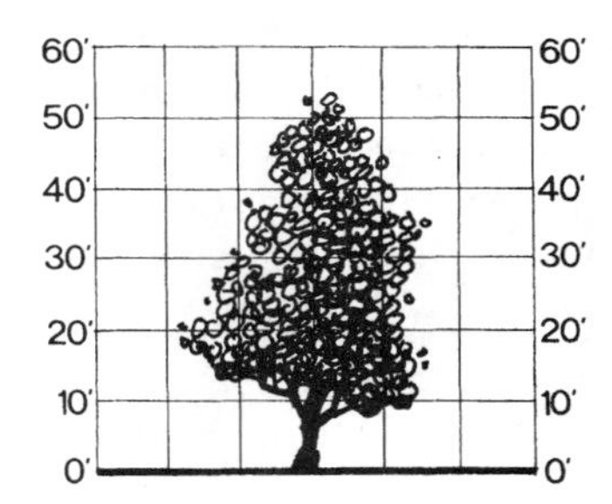

Eucalyptus polyanthmos **Evergreen**
Silver Dollar Gum

Weak stemmed; keep it out of windy areas. Primary feature of the tree, as its common name implies, is its silver gray, rounded (silver dollar) leaves. Used in the right setting, the trees can be strikingly beautiful. As with all Eucalyptus, extremely fast growth.

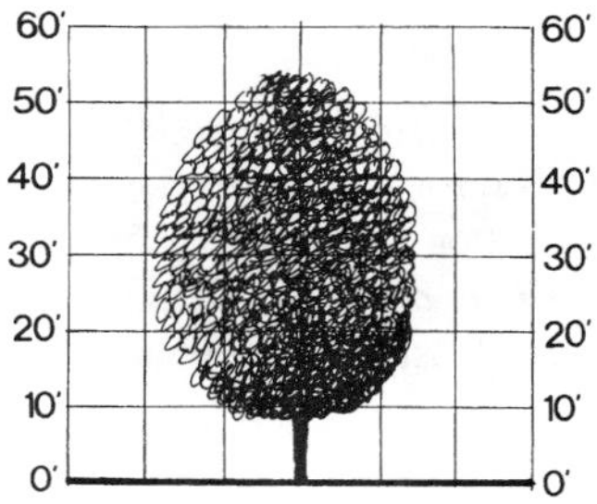

60' 50' 40' 30' 20' 10' 0'

Eucalyptus rudis **Evergreen**
Desert Gum

Upright oval head to go with oblong oval leaves. Medium size. Takes desert conditions. Good hedge row tree. Best cultivars are out of Arizona. The tree has been in use in the Phoenix area for some time. Fast growth.

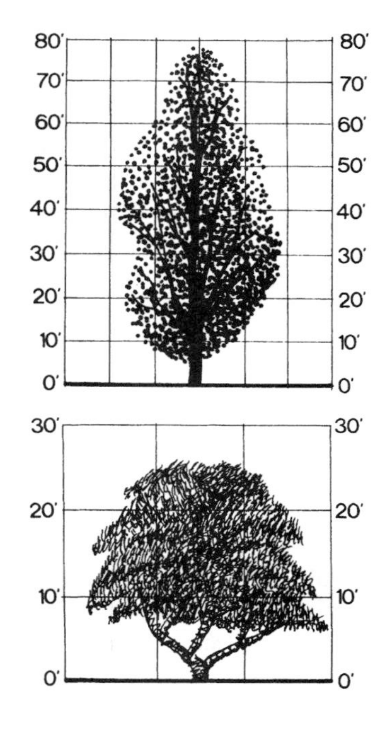

Eucalyptus sideroxylon 'Rosa' **Evergreen**
Red Ironbark

Common name refers to fissures in the bark which are deep and rust (iron) colored in comparison to the lighter brown outer bark. Gray-green foliage. Try to use in areas protected from wind. Dark pink fluffy flowers in clusters through the winter season. The casual observer will often miss the flower show. Frost-tender in youth.

Eucalyptus spathulata **Evergreen**
Narrow-Leafed Gimlet

Atypical of the Eucalyptus genus. This tree is small with a wide spreading head. Resembles an African sumac (*Rhus lancea*) but it is smaller, has grayer leaves, and a more open habit. Interesting trunk structure and bark color. Can get nipped by hard frosts. Good, small-scale, transition desert tree. Fast growth.

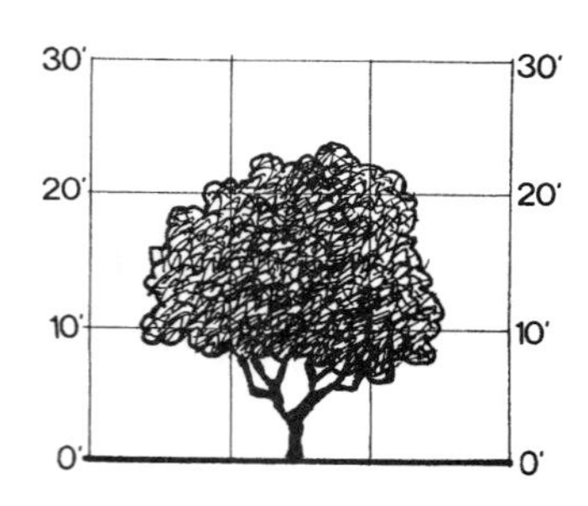

★ ***Feijoa sellowiana*** **Evergreen**
Pineapple Guava

A true gem for the small-scale garden. From South America, its red centered, pink and white-petaled flowers are quite exotic. The petals are edible and good to use in salads. The fruit is also edible once it falls from the tree. Small tree does better as a multistemmed specimen. Also does nicely as an espalier. Gray-green foliage. Flowers in late spring and fruit ripens early fall. While it will take full sun it prefers some afternoon shade. Moderate growth.

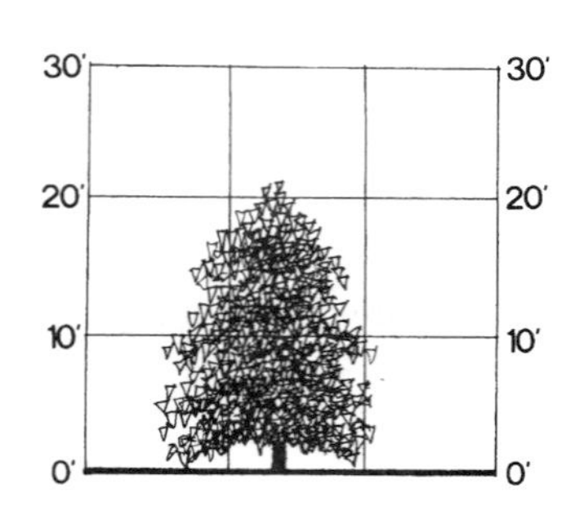

Ficus benjamina **Evergreen**
Weeping Fig or Chinese Weeping Banyan

Heavily used in low-lying desert cities and heavily damaged by frost in occasional cold winters. Not the best selection for a street or lawn tree. Receives use due to beautiful foliage displayed on a weeping habit. Tropical effect. Fast growth. Carolina Cherry (*Prunus caroliniana*) is a much hardier and more dependable selection in open, frost susceptible areas.

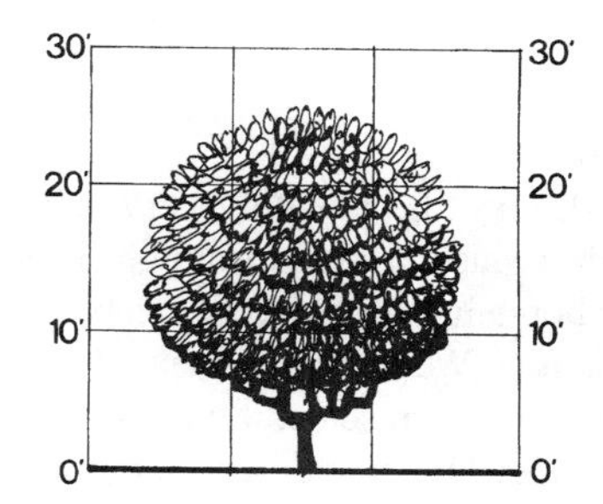

***Ficus microcarpa* 'Nitida'** **Evergreen**
Indian Laurel

Same freezing problems as the Weeping Fig (*Ficus benjamina*). Nice foliage is oblong and medium green. Often pruned into a lollipop tree which does not really enhance its beautiful foliage, which is most noticeable at the edges of the crown. Give this tree courtyard type protection. As with *Ficus benjamina*, Carolina Cherry (*Prunus caroliniana*) is a good alternate, as is Glossy Privet (*Ligustrum lucidum* 'Texanum') in frost areas.

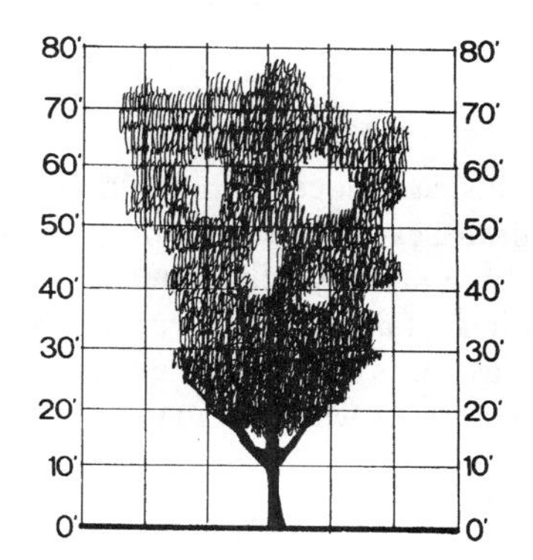

Fraxinus uhdei **Deciduous**
Evergreen Ash

Forget the common name. In the desert, this tree is definitely deciduous. Striking late fall to early winter (November, December) yellow leaf show. Large vase-shaped tree. One of my personal favorites but I cannot call it a star performer because it is relatively short-lived (60 years). When the crown starts dying out, removing the tree can constitute a major expense. A more practical tree than cottonwood (*Populus fremontii*) if trying to emulate a desert riparian environment. High branching towering canopy leaves plenty of room for smaller understory trees. Fast growth.

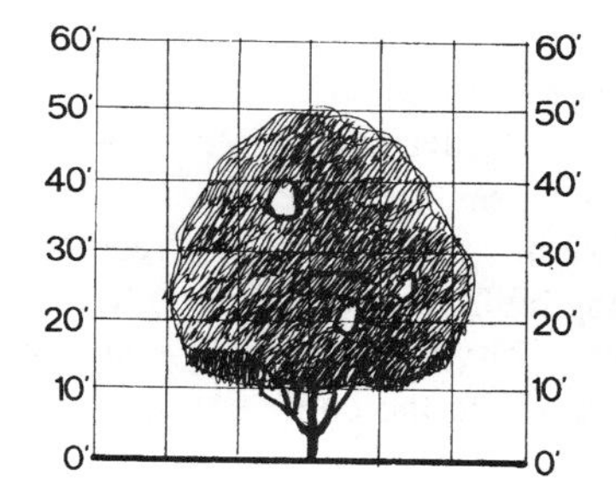

Fraxinus velutina **Deciduous**
Arizona Ash

Nice tree. Upright oval canopy of medium density. Looks nice, inviting in a breeze. Medium-to-large-scale lawn or street tree. Late fall leaf show is not as impressive as its cousin *uhdeii*, but longer lived. Several cultivars, the most common of which is 'Modesto' have improved growth rate and disease resistance. Moderate growth.

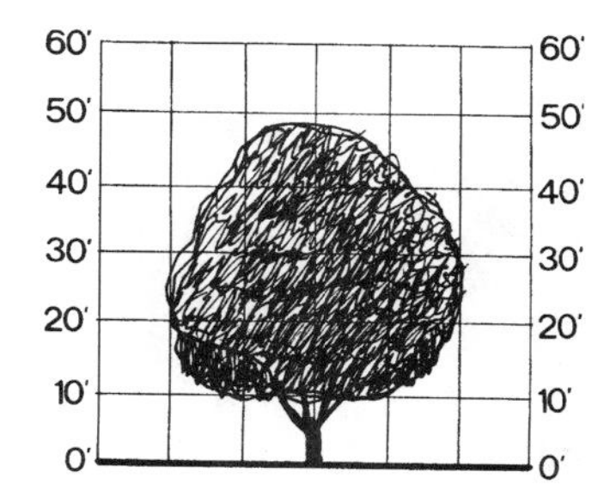

★ ***Fraxinus velutina* 'Rio Grande'** **Deciduous**
Fan-Tex Ash

Cultivar of Arizona Ash (*Fraxinus velutina*). Smaller, denser canopy, with beefier leaves. Drought resistant at maturity and, a plus in the desert, the most wind resistant ash with thick branch and stem structures. Orange to yellow fall leaf show. A fine tree that is growing in popularity in the Southwest. Moderate growth.

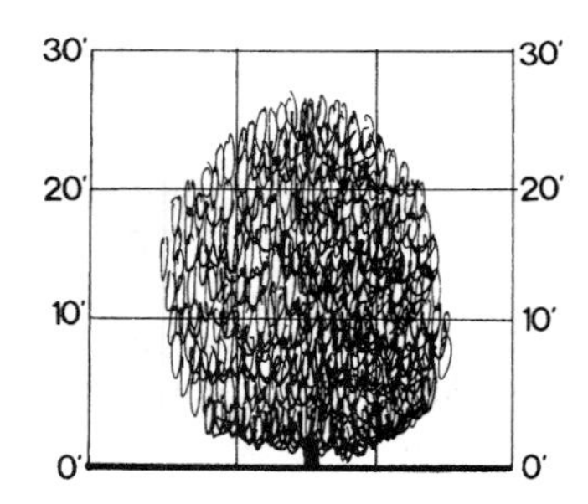

★ ***Geijera parviflora*** **Evergreen**
Australian Willow

A great tree. Does a lot of things well. Looks like a Willow (*Salix*), but does not act like a Willow. Can be quite drought-resistant, although it requires moderate watering to look its best. At home in the lawn or it can be grouped with desert natives. A suburb transition tree. Weeping habit and airy canopy make it ideal by water features. Small to medium scale, it will not approach the size of a willow. Moderate growth rate. This tree deserves more play.

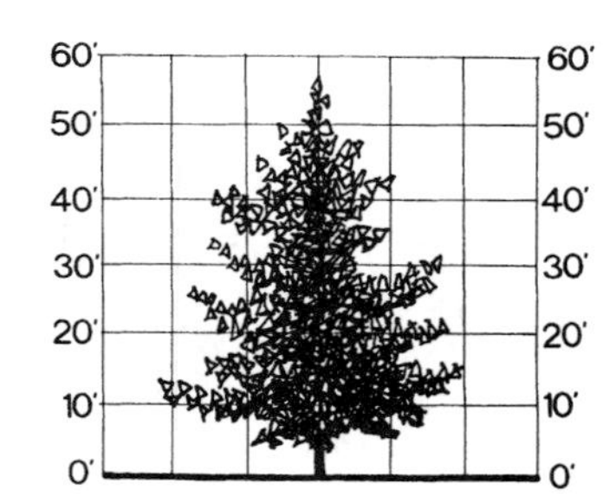

Ginkgo biloba **Deciduous**
Maidenhair Tree

Grand old man of the plant kingdom, this deciduous gymnosperm has been around since the paleozoic era. If you have a back fairway or forgotten space, give this tree a break. Slow-growing. Irregular in youth, matures to an oval to open pyramidal shaped canopy. Delicate fan-shaped leaves turn brilliant yellow in late fall. Specify male trees as fruit of female smells bad and its litter is a nuisance. Good city tree that can take whatever man dishes out.

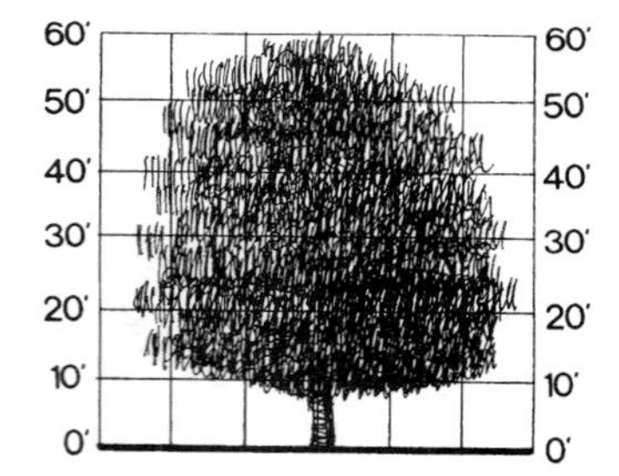

Gleditsia triacanthos inermis **Deciduous**
Thornless Honey Locust

Nice tree. Medium to large scale. Horizontal branching, light airy canopy. Extensively used on eastern campuses as a mall or plaza tree. Not for those with "deciduo-phobia" (fear of deciduous trees) as it is leafless 3 to 4 months out of the year. Appeals to those with "sign-o-phobia" (fear of trees blocking business signs) as it is deciduous during bulk of tourist season. No diseases and shuns air pollution, making it a good city tree. Drought-resistant with age. Moderate growth. Resist the urge to use the cultivar 'Sunburst' as it looks chlorotic in a desert setting.

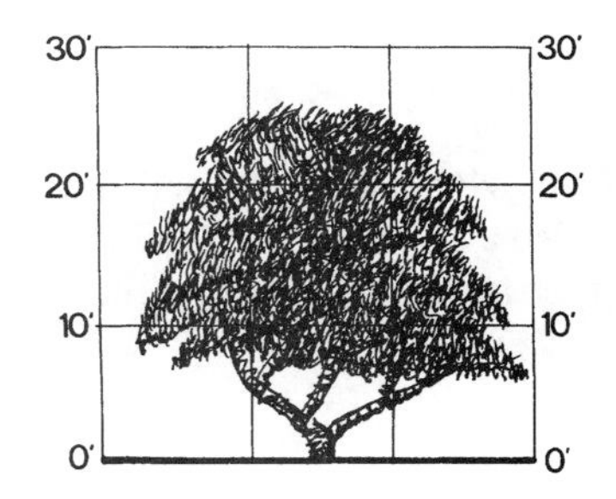

★ ***Jacaranda acutifolia*** **Deciduous**
Jacaranda

Exotic from Brazil widely used and enjoyed in the low desert. Purple to deep blue, spiked sprays of flowers appear in March and April here and 2 months later on the coast. Once you see a Jacaranda in full bloom against the open desert sky you will never forget the tree. Listed as a star performer, but should be protected in its youth as it is frost-tender. Trees smaller than 36-inch box run the risk of freezing in winter. Larger trees get nipped but come back quickly. Growers suggest cutting back on irrigation in late summer to harden off new shoots prior to winter. Spreading, irregular canopy supports feathery light green foliage that follows blooming and turns to medium green by midsummer. Multi-trunk trees show good character. A great tree but sometimes overused, particularly when crammed into smaller areas. Crape Myrtle (*Lagerstroemia indica*) may be a better selection in this situation. Moderate growth with moderate irrigation. Will not display bloom in extremely windy areas.

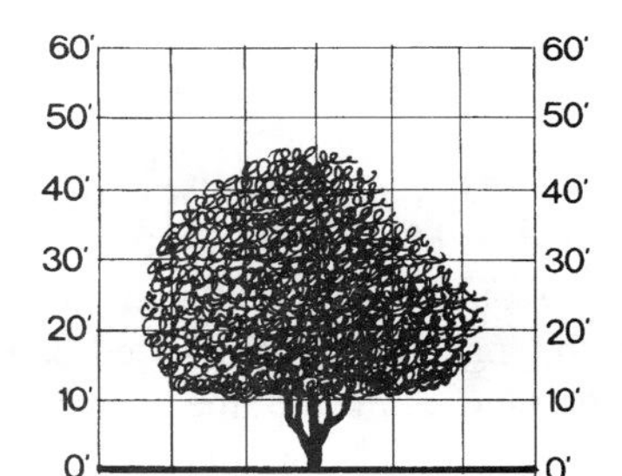

Koelreuteria bipinnata **Deciduous**
Chinese Flame Tree

Flat-topped tree. Profusion of yellow-panicled flowers in late spring to early summer followed by very attractive, cinnamon-red, papery seedpods which persist until late fall before turning yellow with foliage and dropping by December. A good tree with few cultural problems. Should receive more use. Biggest problem apparently is slow growth. Consider using larger box sizes (48 inch box and up). Would make a nice alternative to the much-used Jacaranda.

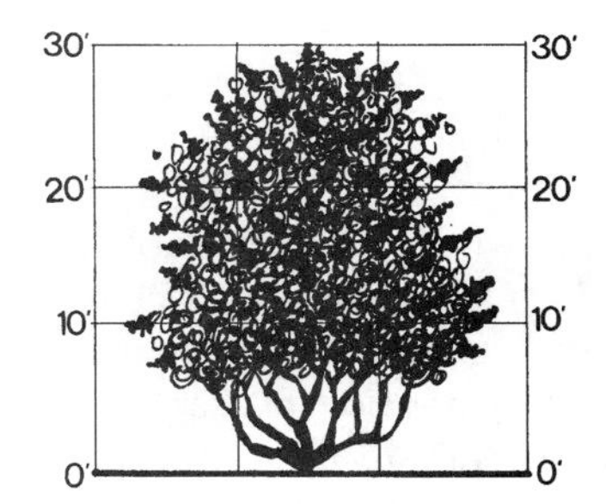

★ ***Lagerstroemia indica*** **Deciduous**
Crape Myrtle

Summer and fall flower show is unrivaled by any other tree. Most common color is deep pink but cultivars in red, lavender, even white are readily available. Briefly deciduous in winter. Tough, small-scale tree. Loose, upright vase- shaped. Likes full sun and is cold hardy. White to tan, flakey bark adds winter interest. Fast growth with few pests. A hard tree to beat. Lagerstroemias are beginning to receive wider use in the deserts. A reliable grower is: Monrovia Nursery Co., 18331 E. Foothill Boulevard, Azusa, CA 91702-1336; Tel: 800-999-9321.

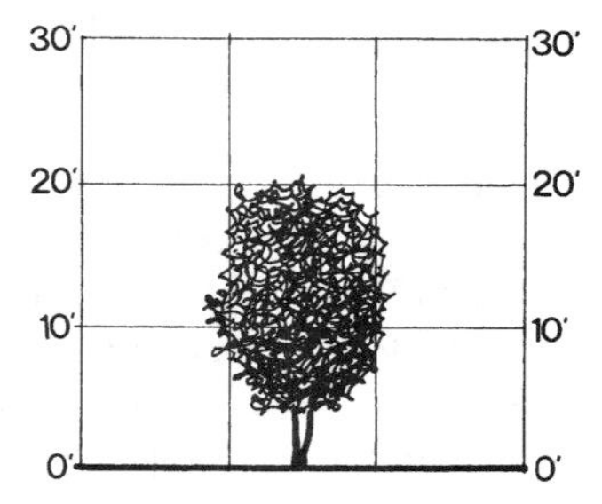

Ligustrum japonicum 'Texanum' **Evergreen**
Waxleaf Privet or Texas Privet

Small trees somewhat hardier than the species lucidum. Smaller than *lucidum*, takes heat better, requires less water. Also a good alternate to Ficus. With pruning, it is an excellent 10- to 12-foot high hedge row selection. Fast growth.

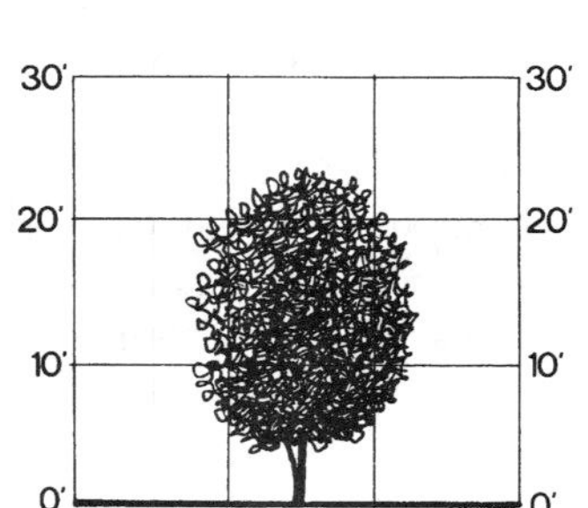

Ligustrum lucidum **Evergreen**
Glossy Privet

Small tree that some would classify as a shrub. When frequently pruned from above it becomes a shrub, but if left to its own devices or with lower branch pruning it acquires tree-like characteristics. Good substitute for ficus as it is more cold hardy and requires less water. Fast growth.

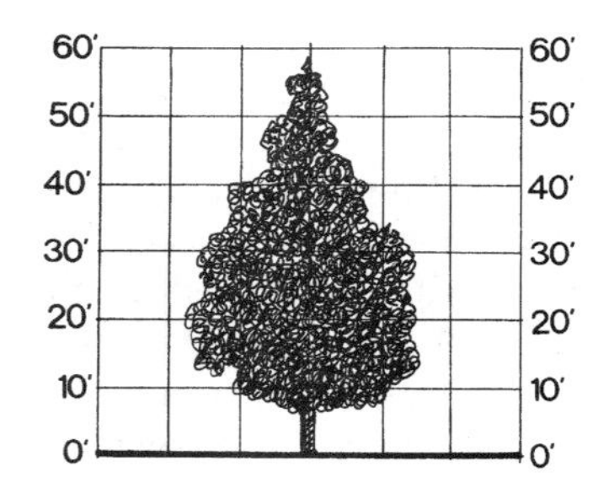

★ ***Liquidamber styraciflua*** **Deciduous**
American Sweet Gum

Not a reliable low desert performer. Sweet Gum is a true star performer in the high desert areas where soil alkalinity does not dip below 5.5%. In cases where it does, Tupelo (*Nyssa sylvatica*) would be a better selection. This tree is valued for its -inch wide by 3-inch long, five-pointed, lobed, star-like foliage display. Yellows and oranges are standard fare. Some reds are available from varieties. Check with growers. Will take urban conditions and poor draining soils. A solid selection that will not disappoint where conditions are right.

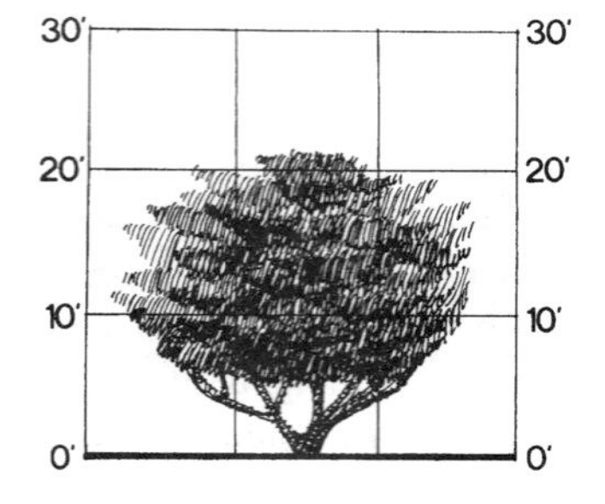

Lysiloma thornberi **Deciduous**
Fern-of-the-Desert

Small-scale Sonoran Desert native. Grows wild in the foothills of the Rincon Mountains east of Tucson, Arizona. The tree's major drawback is that it is frost tender. When protected, it makes a fine multitrunk specimen. Trunk structure is attractive, especially when located in a raised planter where canopy can be looked up into. Reminds me of a dwarf *Jacaranda acutifolia* with finer textured leaves. Same general shape and branching characteristics. Drought tolerant when <%0>established. Fast growing if it doesn't encounter a freeze; if frost damaged it is best to cut tree to ground and start over.

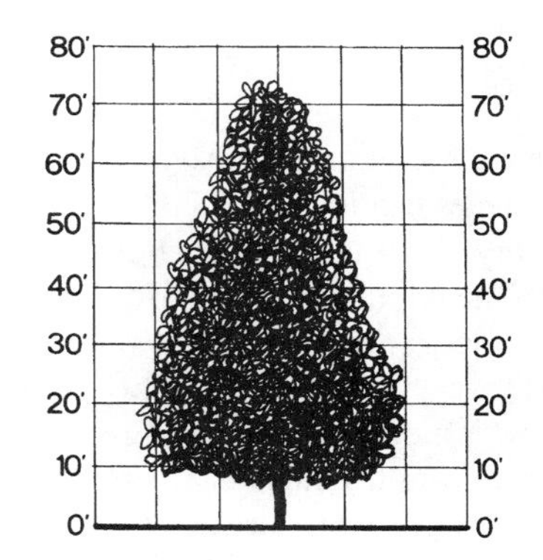

Magnolia grandiflora **Evergreen**
Southern Magnolia

Very dense pyramidal tree native to southeastern U.S. Sentimental favorite. Flower show is from May to August, here. Flowers are white, 8 inches across and set at the outer edges of the tree's canopy. Tree drops long leathery leaves constantly which creates a maintenance problem. Best growth with some afternoon sun protection in summer. Very large, dark green, rough-textured tree that visually dominates the landscape. Moderate growth rate. Keep out of wind to prevent excessive drying of the leaves. Several varieties are available that are significantly smaller than the species. Consult with growers.

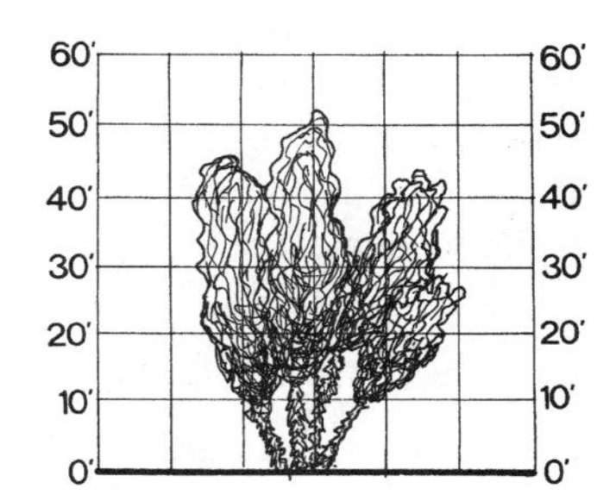

Melaleuca quinquenervia **Evergreen**
Flaxleaf Paperbark

Low desert use only. Prefers sandy soil but will tolerate alkalinity and salt conditions. The tree is most frequently employed in its multiturnk form as a substitute for Eucalyptus. Shorter (40 feet high) than most of the larger Eucalyptus varieties, its 4-inch long oblong foliage is supported on loosely spreading upreaching branches. Bark is creamy white and characteristically flaky. The tree is a good selection for high wind conditions. Moderate growth on moderate irrigation, it becomes increasingly more drought tolerant with age and requires less water.

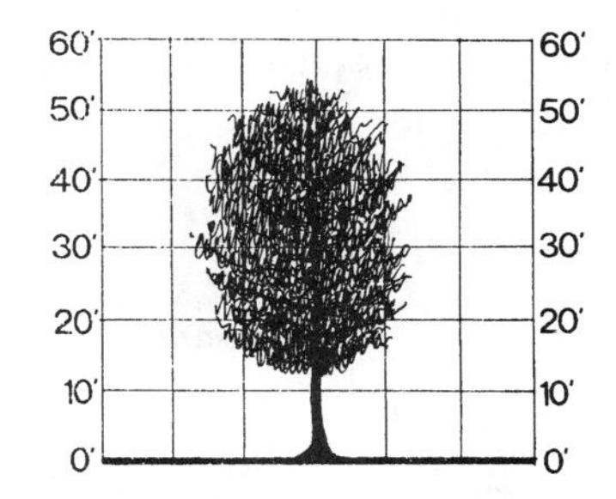

Nyssa sylvatica **Evergreen**
Tupelo

Large scale tree maturing to an upright irregular oval crown. This tree has a dependable fall leaf show which, besides Chinese Pistache (*Pistacia chinesis*), is one of the few reds you will find in the desert. A good reliable substitute for American Sweet Gum (*Liquidambar styraciflua*) where soils may be alkaline or otherwise infertile. Like Sweet Gum, it will tolerate poor draining or wet soils. Glossy oval green leaves are up to five inches long. Flowers are of no consequence, but birds find the bluish black small olive-like fruit to their liking. Moderate growth with adequate watering. A tree that deserves more widespread use in the high desert.

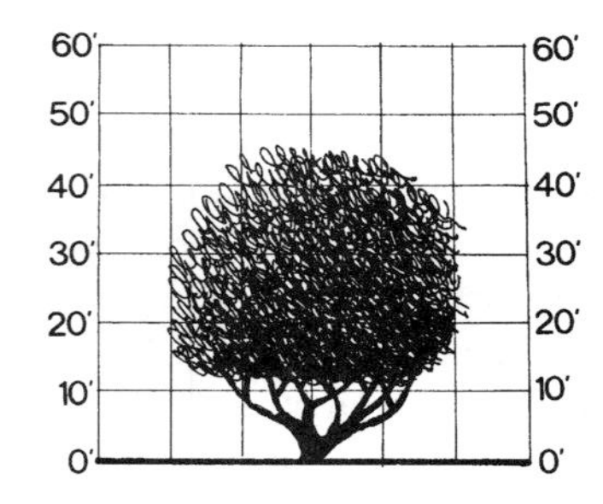

★ ***Olea europaea*** **Evergreen**
Common Olive

A link to the past, this tree is native to the Mediterranean region of Europe, probably having its origins in Greece. Trees can live up to 200 years. Thin, oval, gray-green foliage is tough, leathery, and 2 inches long. Foliage sometimes appears silvery when blowing in the wind. Horizontal oval head sets on top of familiar multiple trunks. Single-trunk trees are uncommon and difficult to keep in that condition. The Olive will sucker constantly and try to revert to its natural condition. Fruit, which occurs after spring flowering, ripens through summer and blackens in mid-fall. When it starts falling from the trees it is ready for harvest. Fruit freshly picked is hard and bitter tasting. It must be soaked in a brine solution to become edible. Plant olives away from pedestrian pathways as fruit litter constitutes a big problem. Spring blossoming produces an abundance of pollen which aggravates several allergy sufferers. If your clientele does not want to deal with the fruit problem, the flowering trees can be sprayed with hormones to control fruiting. If pollen, as well as fruit are a problem, select a fruitless variety. The best fruitless variety is 'Swan Hill.' Common Olive grows quickly to its mature height. Canopy fills out later. Moderate growth with moderate water. Drought resistant with age.

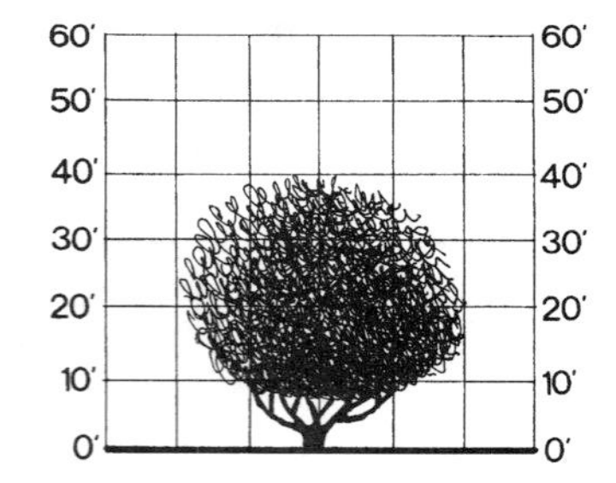

Olea europaea 'Swan Hill' **Evergreen**
Fruitless Olive

This is the most dependably fruitless Olive variety. A genetic mutation of the flowers renders them infertile — thus no pollen and no olives. Tree is produced from cuttings. In my opinion, Swan Hill's canopy looks less dense and somewhat lighter in foliar color than the species. Growth does not appear to be as vigorous. Slow to moderate growth.

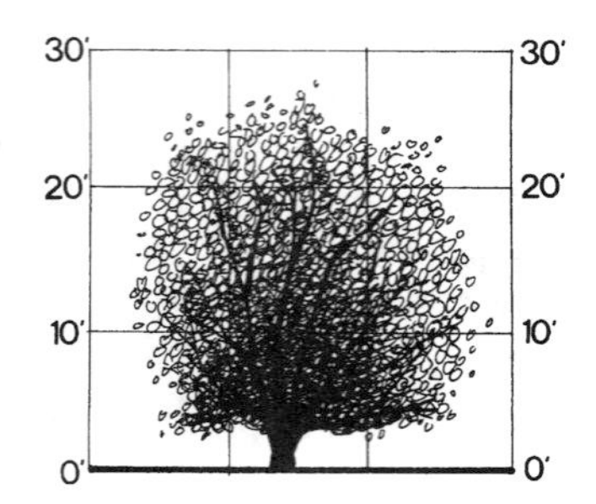

Olneya tesota **Semi-evergreen**
Desert Ironwood

Viewed from a distance, this tree looks the same in shape, color, and size as the Common Olive. With the exception of a lighter canopy, you could confuse the two. I rate the tree Semi-evergreen as it will keep its leaves year round except in hard frosts when it becomes winter deciduous or in extreme drought when it becomes drought deciduous. Insignificant orchid flowers in spring produce 2-inch seed pods which ripen through summer and fall from tree in early fall. Called Ironwood because of its extremely hard heartwood. Only real drawback to this tree is its extremely slow growth rate and the fact that smaller trees will freeze to the ground and have to start the whole growth process over the following spring. Some growers are starting to offer boxed trees up to 30 inches in size. Hopefully, trees in 48-inch boxes and above will soon become readily available as this tree deserves more use, especially in desert and xeriscape-type designs. Better availability should move Ironwood into star performer status.

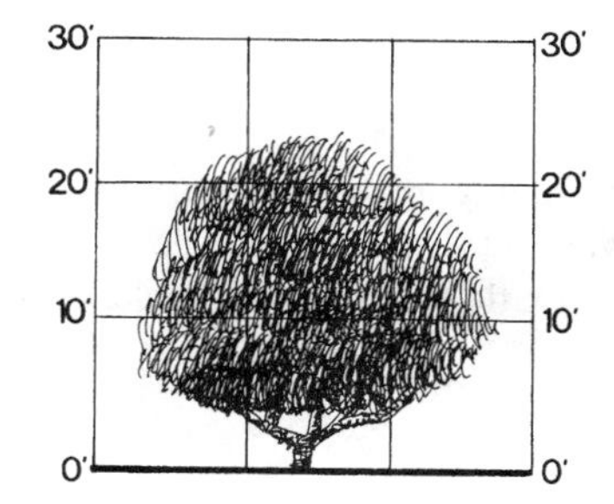

Parkinsonia aculeata **Semi-evergreen**
Jerusalem Thorn or Mexican Palo Verde

Not a true Palo Verde. Tree grows extremely fast but is weak stemmed and short-lived. Used extensively throughout the Southwest, but I prefer the true Cercidiums. This tree's main feature is a heavy yellow flower show in late spring and occurring intermittently through summer and fall. You pay dearly for the flowers with excessive leaf and stem litter. Do not use adjacent to pedestrian or vehicular circulation. Thorns can easily penetrate a car tire. This tree belongs on the horizon line, not in the backyard. Religious significance should not be overlooked in theme gardens.

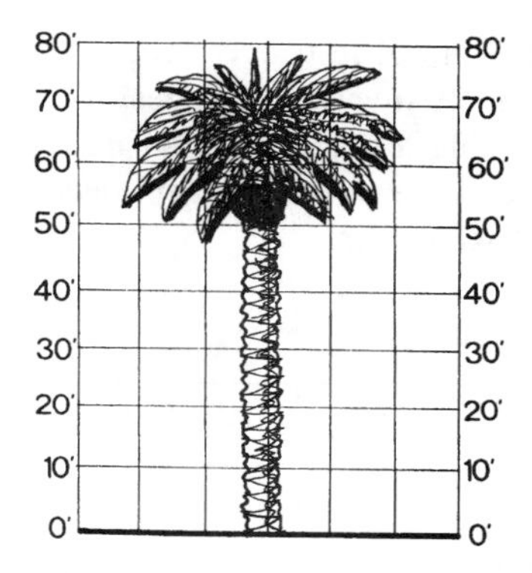

★ ***Phoenix dactylifera*** **Evergreen**
Date Palm

This is the calling card tree of the Coachella Valley in Southern California. One of the first things visitors there see as they fly into the valley are huge blocks of these trees arranged in a grid pattern on the ground plane. These blocks are called date gardens and are of economic importance. Many of the taller gardens in existence today were established in the World War II era in the hope that date crystals could be used as a sugar substitute. Dates planted from offshoots form trees that produce edible fruit in 5 years and live for over 200 years. The trees produce harvestable fruit for 70 years, so the World War II-era trees are still going strong. Water to many of these groves, however, has been shut off and these magnificent palms are dying where they stand. The problem is economic. These trees are 40 to 50 feet high. While the fruit is just as good as that of shorter, younger trees, the labor involved in managing and harvesting a crop is much greater. Workers have to performing necessary tasks, up to 11 times a year, such as cross-pollinating the flowers, putting protective bags over the fruits, and harvesting the crop. It is a lot easier to work from a stable step ladder or the back of a pickup truck than to hang 50 feet in the air from a ladder. Land owners simply cannot afford the labor costs and shut off the tap so they don't have to pay for the water. This is sad for two reasons. First, the trees have ornamental landscape design value as large-scale courtyard, boulevard, and entry definers. If healthy, they are relatively easy to transplant. Taller trees actually cost much less than shorter trees. There are independent growers available who will work the groves under contract in exchange for the profit from the harvest — less water costs. While an owner makes nothing initially, he will turn a profit when he is able to sell healthy trees for commercial landscape purposes. This avenue needs to become further explored to save and reuse these magnificent trees. The second reason is historic. These trees were first brought to the valley from the Mideast in 1890 and agricultural production became a viable industry in 1913. It's a shame to see history die on the vine, so to speak. Several varieties are available, the two most common being 'Deglet Noor' and 'Medjool.' 'Medjools' are gaining popularity, agriculturally, as they are the heaviest producers of fruit. When using a large quantity of Date Palms on a project, it is wise to buy all the trees from one block as they will likely be of the same species, height, and age.

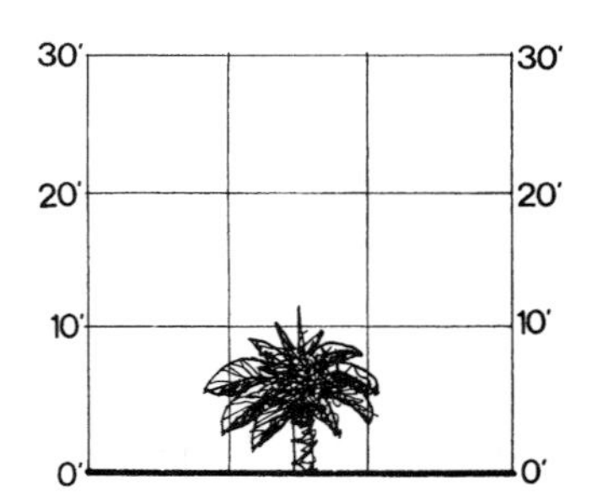

Phoenix roebelerii **Evergreen**
Pigmy Date Palm

Nothing like its cousin *dactylifera*. Ornamental plant that requires protection with a capital P. Be careful where you use it. Do not expose to full sun. Fine-leaved fronds make it an attractive small-scale palm. It makes a good tropical accent. Slow growth.

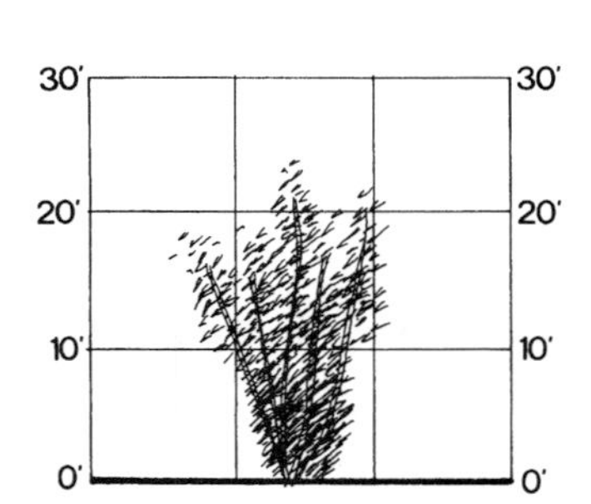

Phyllostancys aurea **Evergreen**
Golden Bamboo

Limited use for bamboo in the desert. Helpful in tropical courtyard type settings and near water features. Extremely invasive. Suggest planting it inside 6-foot-deep root barriers or not using it at all. Yellowish to golden canes to 20 feet tall. Light, airy foliage. All exposures except deep shade (Zone E); grows best in filtered light. Fast growth.

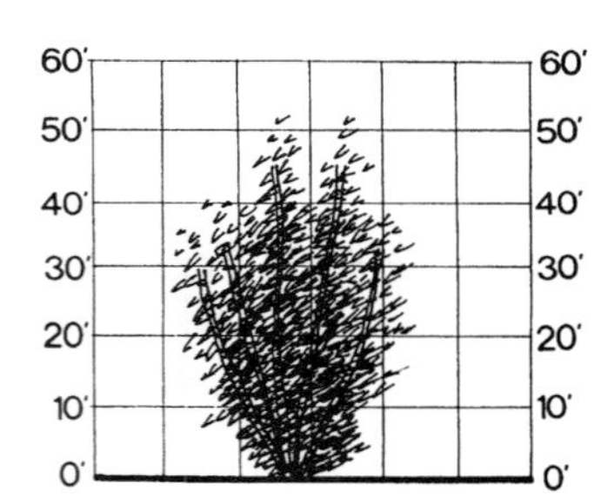

Phyllostancys bambosoides **Evergreen**
Giant Timber Bamboo

This is the bamboo of movie sets and zoos. Very large and very invasive. Sometimes hard to get. Use root barriers, but it is even better if bamboo is completely enclosed in some form of hardscape. A beautiful plant that prefers filtered light. Fast growth. Use caution when planting. If in doubt, leave it out.

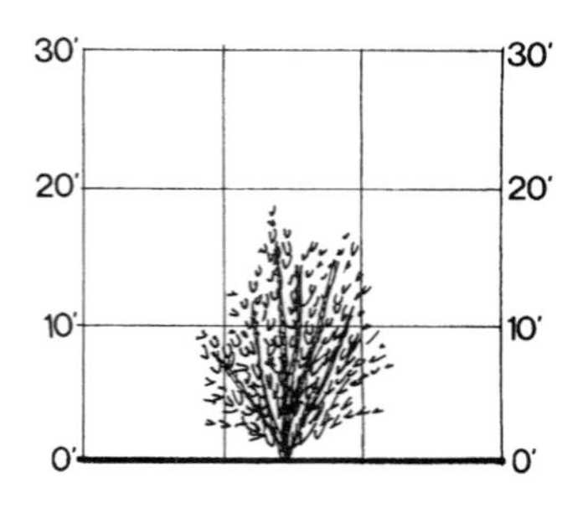

Phyllostancys nigra **Evergreen**
Black Bamboo

Whenever I feel compelled to use a bamboo, after much wailing and gnashing of teeth, this is the one I usually choose. Although it is smaller and less invasive than its cousins, I still use a root barrier with this plant. Prefers afternoon shade. Some black on the canes gives rise to the common name. A pretty bamboo. Fast growth.

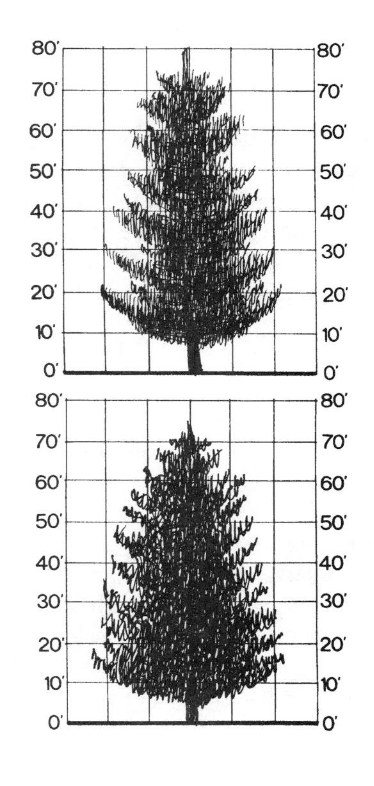

Pinus canariensis **Evergreen**
Canary Island Pine

Thinnest and tallest of the desert pines. Most delicate in appearance. From the Canary Islands, it is quite handsome and exotic. Tiered branches with long graceful needles. Good tree in tight spaces. Fastest growing.

★ ***Pinus eldarica*** **Evergreen**
Mondell Pine

Once believed to be a cultivar of the Aleppo Pine (*Pinus halepensis*), this tree is more pyramidal in growth habit, more dependable in form, greener, and faster growing. It is also about 20% smaller at maturity. Good looking tree that makes an immediate impact on a project, even from 15 gallon containers. Few pests or diseases. Fast growth.

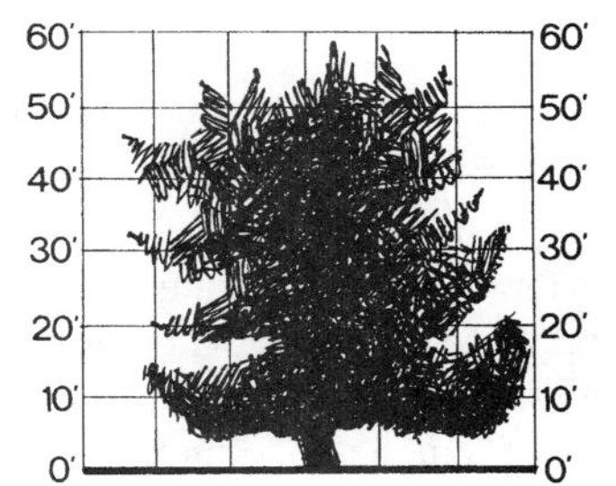

Pinus halepensis **Evergreen**
Aleppo Pine

Before *P. eldarica* came to the fore, this was considered the best pine for the desert. It is a fine tree which reaches massive proportions at maturity. Rugged, irregular crown is striking against the skyline. This is no downstream tree. Use it where you have plenty of room for it to spread out. Dependable windbreak. Moderate growth.

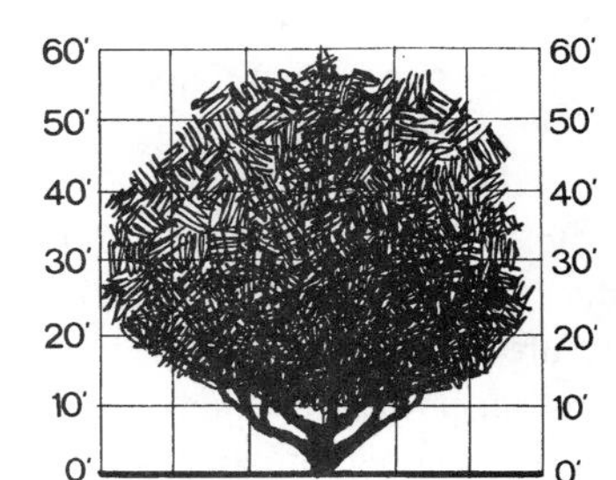

Pinus pinea **Evergreen**
Italian Stone Pine

From the Mediterranean. Distinctive, flat-topped canopy give this tree a distinctive character. Large tree approaching the proportions of an Aleppo (*Pinus halepensis*) at maturity, but with a more uniform crown. Needles look more yellow-green than the other pines, giving it a dryer appearance. This allows it to be used further out towards the desert in a transition area. Slow growth.

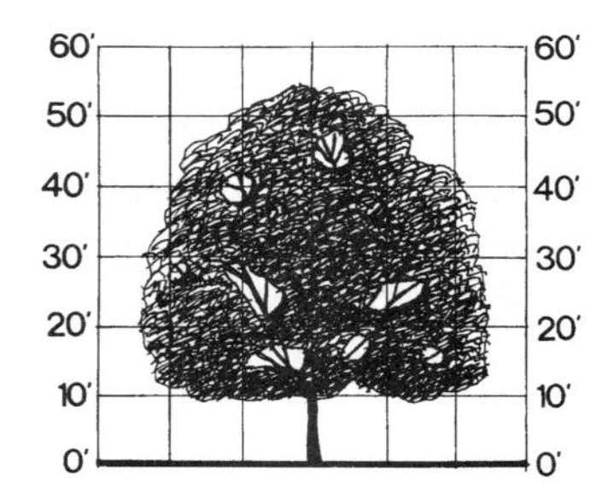

Pistacia chinensis **Deciduous**
Chinese Pistache

An excellent deciduous tree for the desert which deserves more widespread use. Brilliant red fall color show is rare among low desert plant materials. Needs well-drained soil. Rounded or domed-shaped canopy can extend nearly to ground. Young trees can be gawky in appearance and need staking and selective pruning to enhance development. Withstands air pollution and drought. Grows at a somewhat slow rate into a fine lawn or street tree specimen.

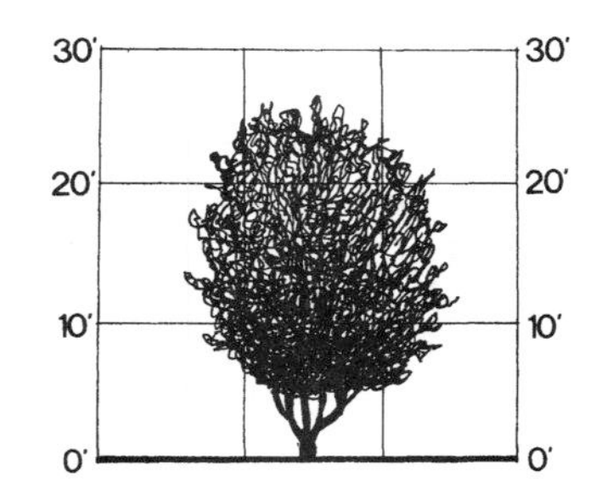

★ ***Pithecellobium flexicaule*** **Semi-evergreen**
Texas Ebony

Small-scale tree, with a unique branching habit. Needs shaping to take on a tree-like appearance. Sometimes used as a large shrub. Dark green foliage is rarity among desert plant materials. Recent introduction from Texas and New Mexico whose popularity is spreading westward. Yellow spring flower show and attractive smooth gray bark are bonuses. Specify in larger box sizes and check availability as this tree can be hard to obtain and is a slow grower.

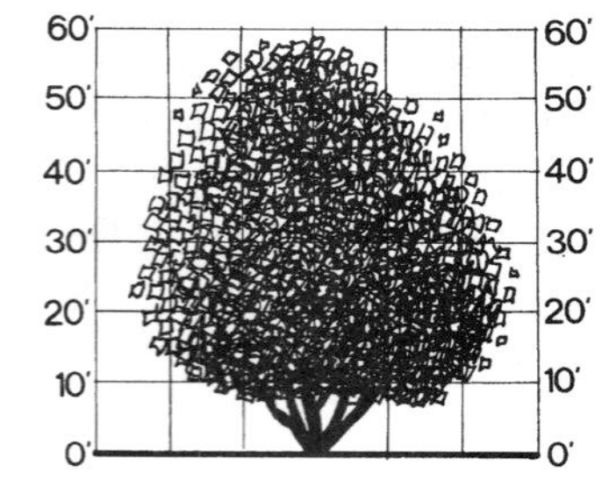

★ ***Platanus wrightii*** **Deciduous**
Arizona Sycamore

Very closely related to *Platanus racemosa* the California Sycamore. In fact, many botanists classify *wrightii* as a variety of *racemosa*. There are some notable differences which justify a separate species classification. *P.wrightii* is found native in riparian communities throughout the Sonoran Desert. This tree resists high heat and wind more readily than *racemosa*. Like all Sycamores, it has the familiar flaky white, cream, and tan bark at the base of its trunk. A deciduous tree, its yellow fall color show can be quite nice. As a phreatophyte, Sycamores can use a lot of water and, if used in association with turf, they should be planted with root barriers to avoid surface roots. One special feature of all Sycamores is that they accommodate heavy pruning to control canopy size. In a process called pollarding, Sycamores can be cut back at the same branch node season after season. Large scars or "knees" develop which create a grotesque character or even an Old World flavor. I have used this tree successfully in courtyards and in bosque or geometric settings. Sycamores tolerate a great deal of air pollution which, along with the ancient Ginkgo (*Ginkgo biloba*), makes it the consummate city tree. Fast growth.

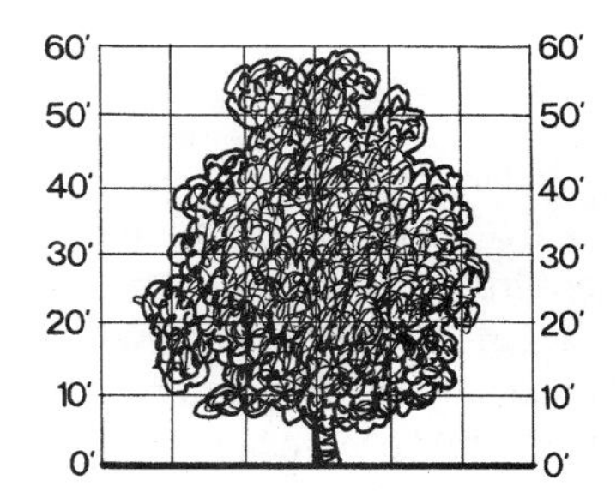

Populus fremontii **Deciduous**
Western Cottonwood

Massive signal tree of the west. In the native condition, it is the ultimate phreatophyte, being found and consistently seen along water courses and older riparian type environments. Utilized by man as a single-file windbreak and/or property line definer. Extremely fast growth rate makes it a voracious consumer of water. Susceptible to wind breakage, especially when older. Do not use adjacent to structures. Glistening bright green leaves in spring turn to dull green in summer and give way to an impressive golden yellow late fall show. Triangular shaped leaves are up to 4 inches across and are gray-green on their undersides. Trees look silvery in the breeze. Specify male cuttings or one of the new "cottonless" cultivars to avoid annoying cottony fruit in early summer. When using to simulate a natural riparian environment, consider grouping it with *Fraxinus* and *Platanus*, which are its neighbors in nature and they also use less water.

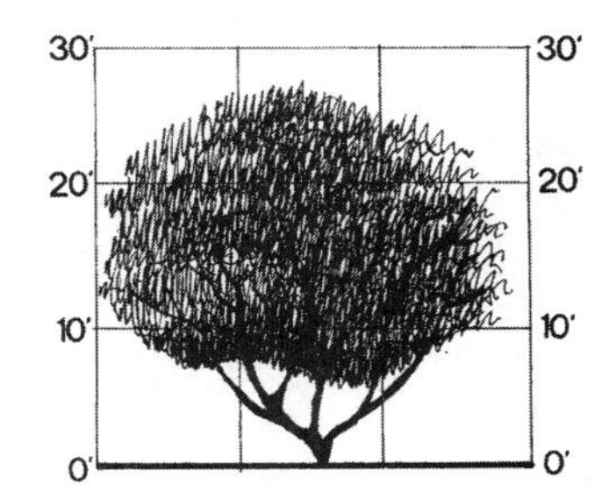

★ ***Prosopis alba*** **Semi-evergreen**
Argentine Mesquite

Probably has the largest canopy of all the Mesquites. Lower branches are usually removed, making for a tree with a wide-spreading umbrella-like top. Blue-green foliage makes the most dense canopy within the genus. Evergreen in all but the coldest winters when it will drop its leaves. This is the most popular Mesquite in the California desert and gets a lot of use. The variety "Colorado" is thornless. With moderate watering the tree exhibits extremely fast growth. Young trees need to have their heads thinned frequently to prevent toppling over in windy areas.

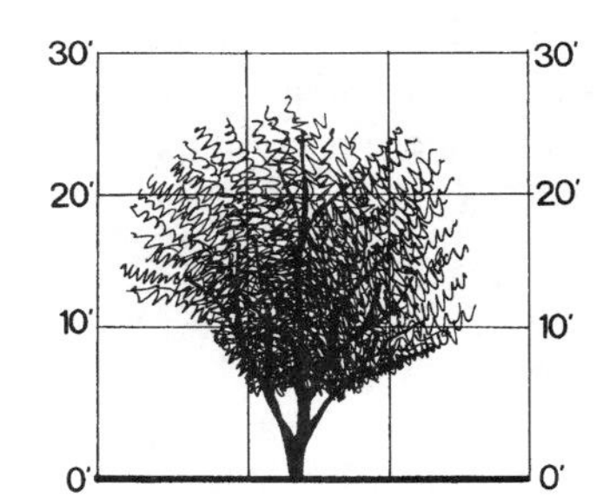

★ ***Prosopis chilensis*** **Semi-evergreen**
Chilean Mesquite

Always a star performer in my estimation. This tree has not been frequently used in California. Widely used in Arizona where it is more readily available. Lack of use stems from unreliable identification of the tree. In past years, several trees of varying characteristics were collectively called Chilean Mesquite. The true Chilean Mesquite, and the one most frequently available from Arizona growers, is a beautiful tree. *Prosopis chilensis* has light green foliage, an upright vase shape, and cinnamon-brown bark. Like *Prosopis alba*, it is evergreen except in the coldest winters. I prefer this mesquite as it requires less pruning to shape and is easier to walk and plant under. Fast growth.

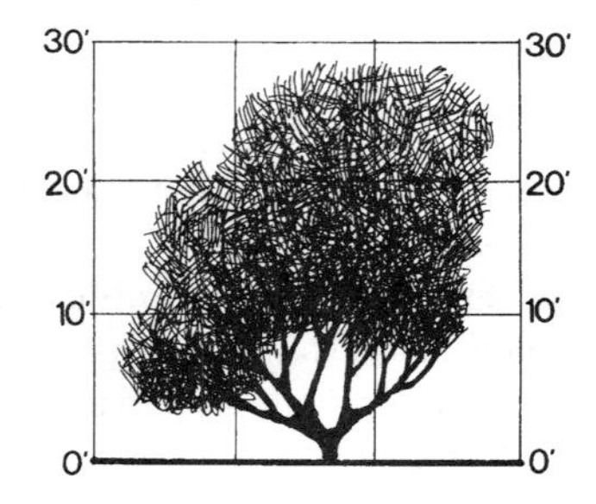

Prosopis glandulosa **Semi-evergreen**
Honey Mesquite

This is the largest mesquite. It has an irregular open, almost weeping habit. Foliage is light green. Some compare the tree in appearance to the California pepper (*Schinus molle*), but it is more irregular and open. The tree is becoming more widespread in the open desert as it volunteers itself further and further westward from its native Chihuahuan Desert habitat. The common name is derived from the excellent honey that bees make from the tree's blossoms. Biggest drawback is that it is decidedly deciduous and leaf litter can be a problem. Fast growth.

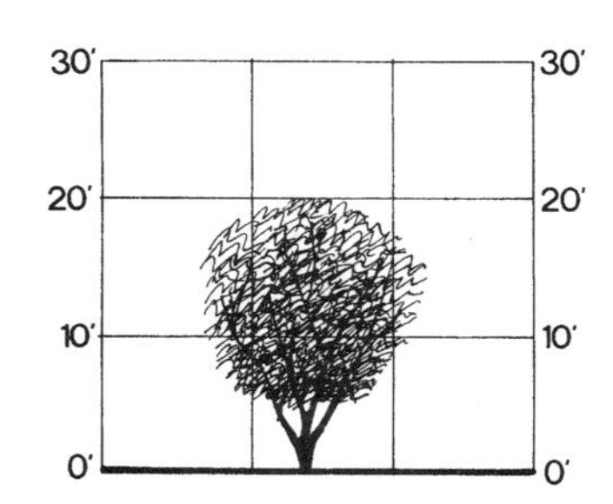

Prosopis pubescens **Semi-evergreen**
Screwbean Mesquite

A horticultural novelty. Small tree that could be called a shrub. Two-inch long fruit is tightly coiled into pods that are edible. Good tree for a theme or interpretive garden. Not an especially attractive ornamental landscape tree. Fast growth.

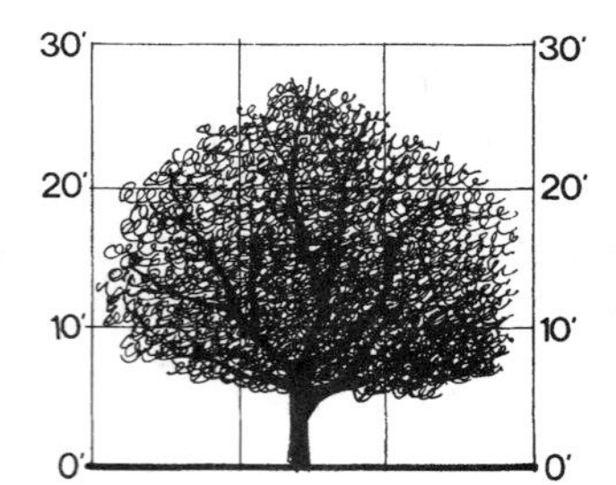

Prosopis velutina **Semi-evergreen**
Velvet Mesquite

Light green tree with an open rounded habit. Common name comes from soft gray-green foliage. Tree is widespread throughout the Sonoran Desert. Velvet mesquite is similar in many ways to *Prosopis glandulosa*, except in shape. Fast growth. As with all mesquites, it should be remembered that this tree prefers a secondary riparian environment and, with a deep taproot, is more a water spender than a drought tolerant tree. Mesquites will accept dry conditions but remain small and grow much slower. The best compromise is to use Mesquites in the transitional design and allow them to have moderate water. With this type of application, mesquites fill a lot of desert design voids.

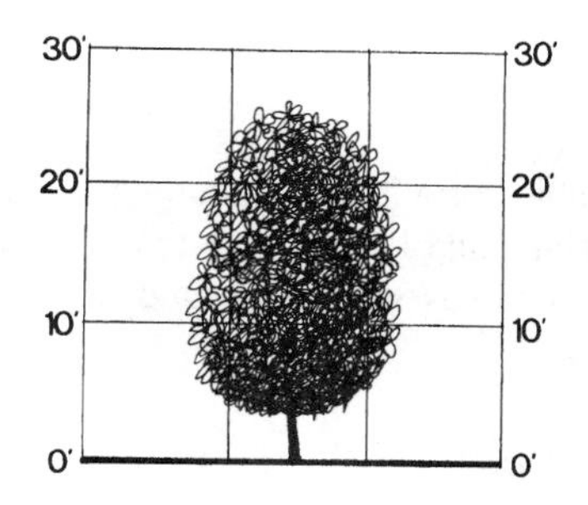

★ ***Prunus caroliniana*** **Evergreen**

Carolina Laurel Cherry

A very useful tree that is beginning to receive use as an excellent replacement for *Ficus nitida*. The Carolina Laurel Cherry is frost hardy and will take all but reflected heat. These two elements are banes to the Ficus. Upright rounded habit. Must be shaped to encourage a tree-like appearance. Pleasant white flower clusters in spring. Moderate growth rate. A tree that should get more use and replace *Ficus nitida* in all but the most protected areas.

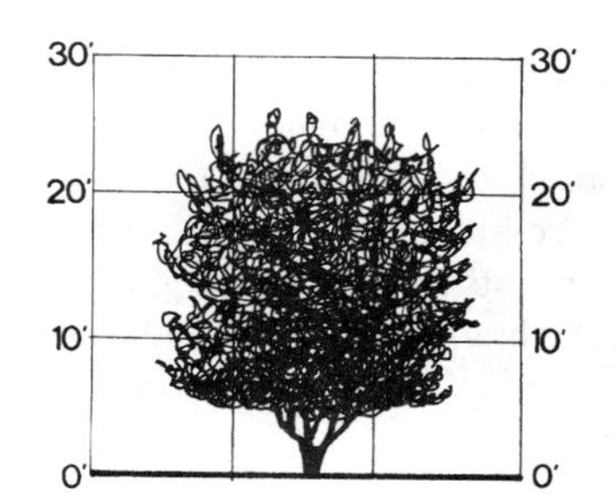

Prunus cerasifera 'Atropurpurea' **Deciduous**

Purple-lLeaf Plum

Truly an exotic tree with red-purple foliage. Leaf color and pinkish-white spring flowers are the tree's primary attributes. Very dependable small-scale garden tree. Visually, it is very dominant in the landscape so use it with care or in special situations. Deciduous with insignificant fall show. Moderate growth rate.

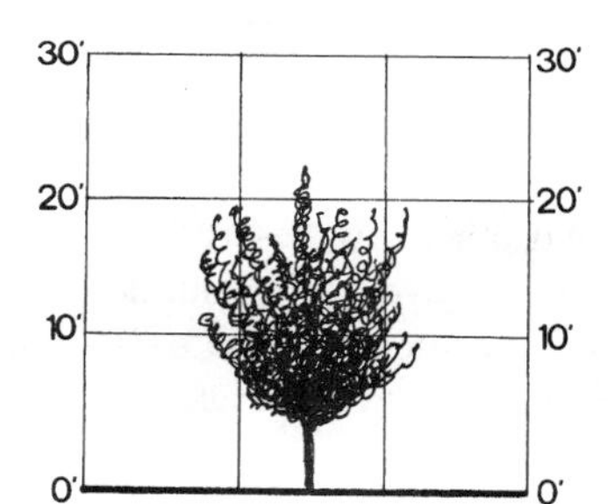

Prunus cerasifera 'Krauter Vesuvius' **Deciduous**

Krauter Purple Plum

A cultivar of 'Atropurpurea' that is more widely used in the desert than the parent plant. 'Krauter Vesuvius' has the deepest purple foliage of any *cerasifera* hybrid. The purple borders on black. The tree is smaller in overall stature and the flowers are a deeper, more intense pink than 'Atropurpurea'. A nice small tree. Moderate to slow growth.

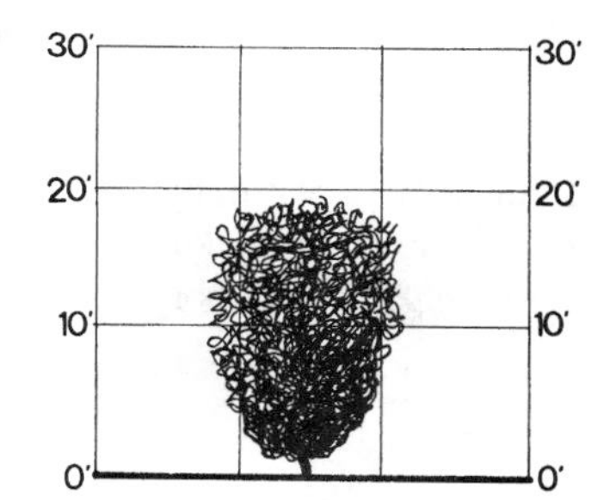

Punica granatum **Deciduous**

Pomegranate

Small deciduous tree to large shrub. Spring flower show of red blossoms. Fall leaf show is yellow. Plant is noted for its fruit and its ability to withstand high heat. Fruit appears in autumn and is orange-red, maturing to deep red. Seeds are flavorful and used in jams. Left unpruned, it makes a good screen or windbreak when planted on 10 foot centers. Fast growth and quite drought resistant.

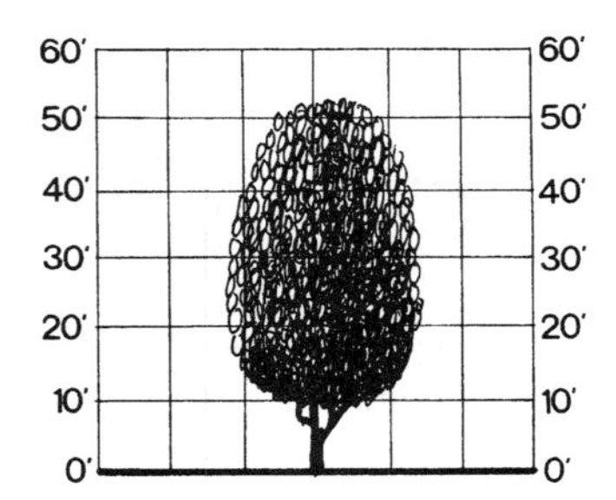

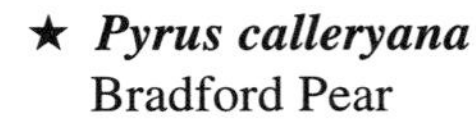

★ ***Pyrus calleryana*** **Deciduous**
Bradford Pear

A fine medium-sized tree with a predictable upright oval habit. A handsome deciduous tree that flowers white in spring and offers orange to orange-red foliage in fall. Well behaved in lawn areas as well as around the patio. Moderate growth.

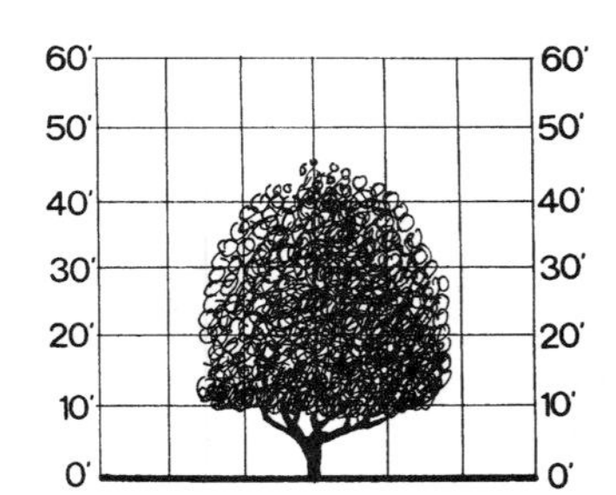

Pyrus kawakamii **Deciduous**
Evergreen Pear

The most frequently used of the ornamental pears in the Southwest. Canopy is wide-spreading rounded to weeping in habit. No two canopies are the same. Brilliant white flower show in spring. In the desert, the tree is not evergreen as its common name implies. Yellow to orange to an occasional red fall leaf show. Tree requires pruning in its interior to maintain a good habit. This is best done in winter when the branch structure can be studied. Light green foliage, turning to deeper green by midsummer. An attractive tree but it takes some work. Fast growth.

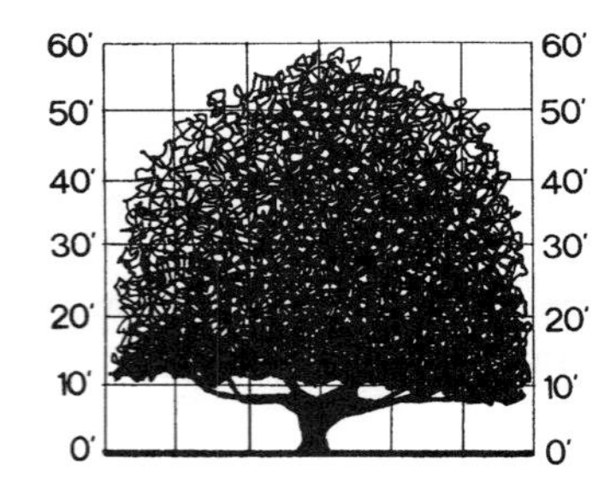

Quercus agrifolia "Heritage" **Evergreen**
Coast Live Oak

Can be grown in the California desert and other low desert locations but prefers it a little higher and a little cooler. An evergreen with deep green foliage with a predictable leaf drop in spring. An important tree to California's history and worth planting above 1500 feet. Slow to moderate growth.

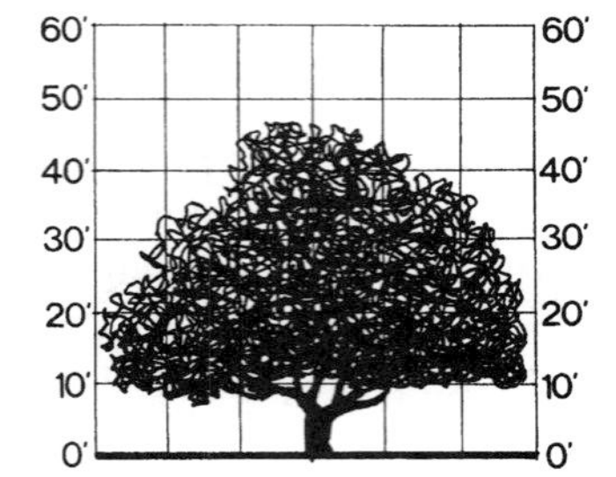

Quercus engelmannii **Deciduous**
Mesa Oak

Large tree that is briefly deciduous. Not frequently grown in the desert but it is adaptable to this region. Reddish fall leaf show. Native to California foothills and frequently intermixed with *Quercus agrifolia*. Umbrella canopy. Slow to moderate growth.

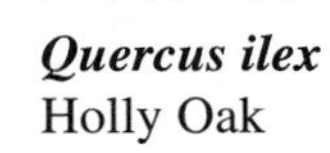

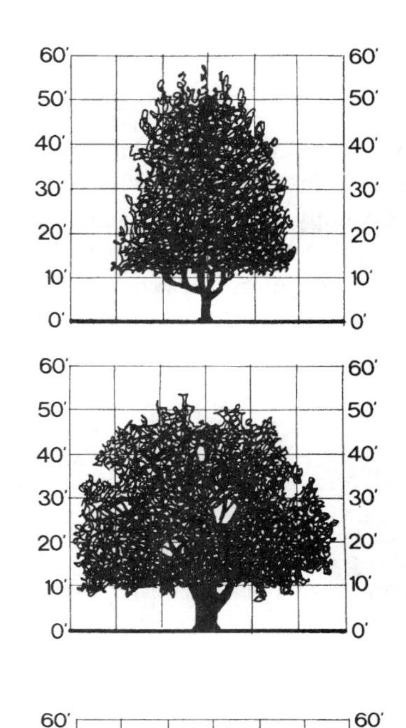

Quercus ilex **Evergreen**
Holly Oak

Upright, loosely pyramidal head. Tree accepts more water than other oaks. Will even tolerate being planted in lawn areas. Not as horizontally open in habit as most oaks, which is its only drawback. Slow to moderate growth.

Quercus lobata **Deciduous**
California White Oak

A tree of massive proportions. Rounded crown with horizontally spreading branches, especially closer to the ground. A tree that needs a large area and looks better when allowed to stand alone. Deciduousness of growth is its major drawback. Moderate growth. In a large-scale throw-away area it is certainly worth a try.

Quercus suber **Deciduous**
Cork Oak

Yes, this is the famous oak that cork is garnered from. A large evergreen tree that does well in desert conditions. Somewhat upright rounded habit. Slow growth.

Rhapis excelsa **Evergreen**
Lady Palm

Tropical effect. Small multitrunk palm which requires sun and frost protection. Very popular in high-end residential areas but better avoided in commercial applications. Slow growth.

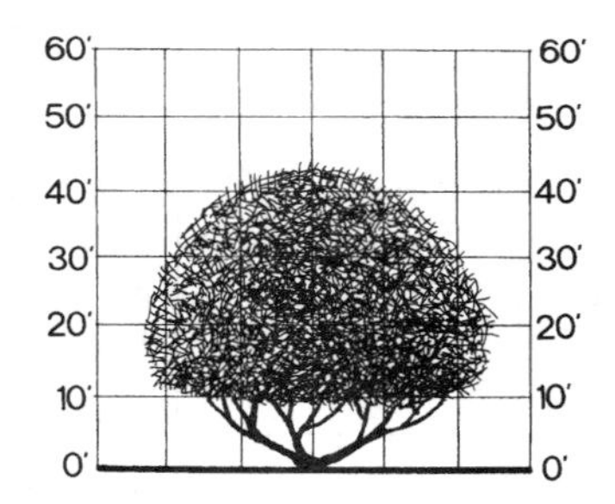

★ ***Rhus lancea*** **Evergreen**

African Sumac

In the desert, this tree is a star performer of immense importance. Bright army-green foliage is a departure from the gray-green and blue-greens of several desert trees. Dense evergreen canopy has a fine visual texture. Rounded to horizontal oval form. Red-brown bark is very attractive. Can be used as a single or multiple-trunk tree. Small yellow flowers are messy in late spring. Can be grown in lawn conditions or can be quite drought tolerant. Moderate growth rate.

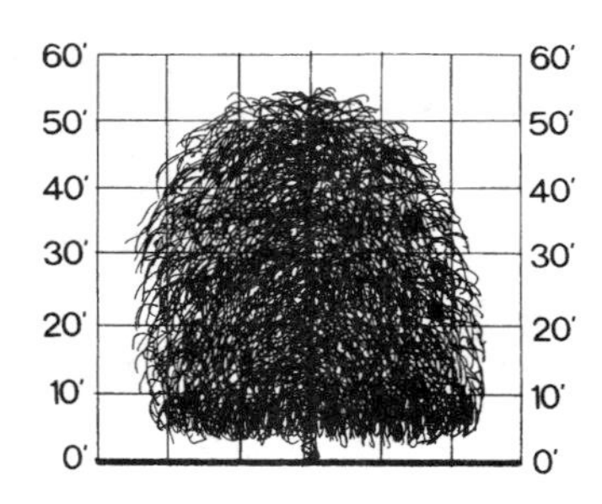

Salix babylonica **Deciduous**

Weeping Willow

A distinctive tree known across America for its weeping habit. Weak stemmed and the ultimate phreatophyte, this is a tree to be chosen carefully. It does have some applications, however. Salix can withstand, indeed flourish with, wet feet. That is, they will grow in standing water — even in heavy clay soils. Always plant Weeping Willows out of the wind as branches break easily. Yellow fall leaf show is pleasant. An extremely fast growing tree. Requires ample water.

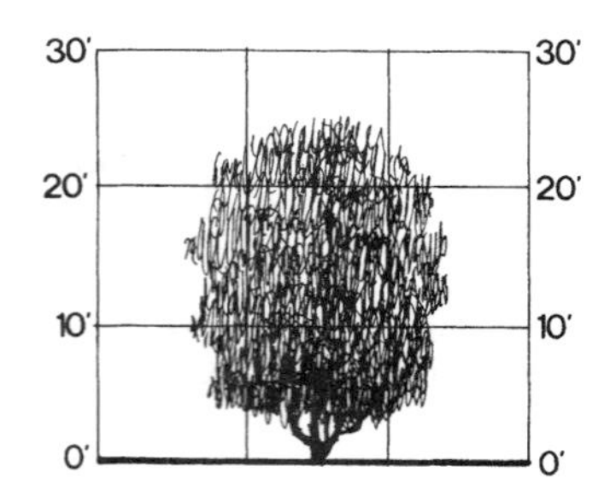

Sambucus mexicana **Deciduous**

Mexican Elderberry

Small tree with upright oval habit. This is the plant seen blooming in profusion at 4000 feet. Flat clusters of creamy yellow flowers in mid-spring to early summer. Tolerates tough growing conditions. Edible fruit in late summer. Can be drought deciduous. Fast growth.

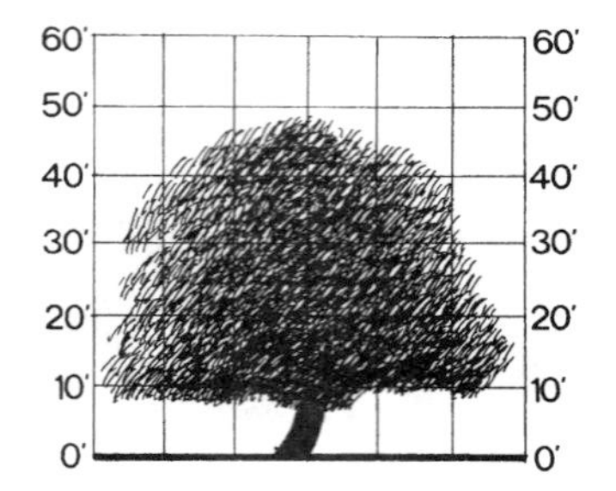

★ ***Schinus molle*** **Evergreen**

California Pepper Tree

Wide-spreading and resembles the Weeping Willow (*Salix babylonica*) when allowed to grow to the ground. Light yellow-green foliage. Extremely invasive root system. It is a good idea to use root barriers wherever it is planted in the proximity of agriculture fields, sidewalks, roads, and highways. Can suffer wind breakage. Stronger as a multi-trunk tree. Fast growth.

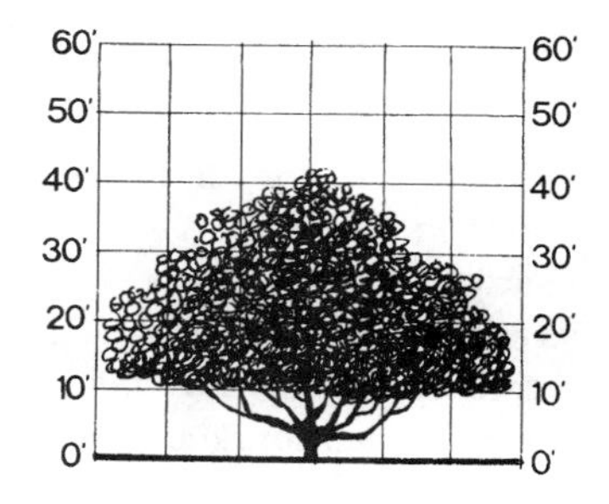

★ *Schinus terebinthifolius* **Evergreen**
Brazilian Pepper Tree

Quite a bit different than its cousin *Schinus molle*. Dark green, coarse foliage. Upright horizontal umbrella shaped canopy. In my opinion, better as a single-trunked tree. Dense crown. Withstands drought conditions with maturity. Good windbreak and can be grown in lawn areas. Fast growth rate. Note that this tree requires frequent thinning prior to maturity.

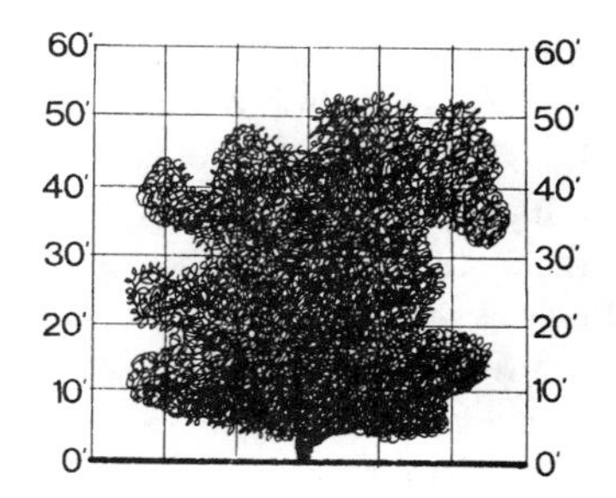

Tamarix aphylla **Evergreen**
Tamarisk

A tree to be used with caution as Tamarisk volunteers readily and has a root system that seeks available water with a vengence. This tree is extremely invasive and will crowd out anything in its path by utilizing two methods. First, it attains immense size rapidly. Second, it literally drips salt deposits from its leaves, ultimately killing anything below it — even Oleander. Tree does serve a purpose, however, as a large-scale windbreak and/or visual screen. Used along railway lines for this very purpose. Gray-green foliage is a familiar sight along property lines in agricultural areas. Very fast (10 feet a year) growth.

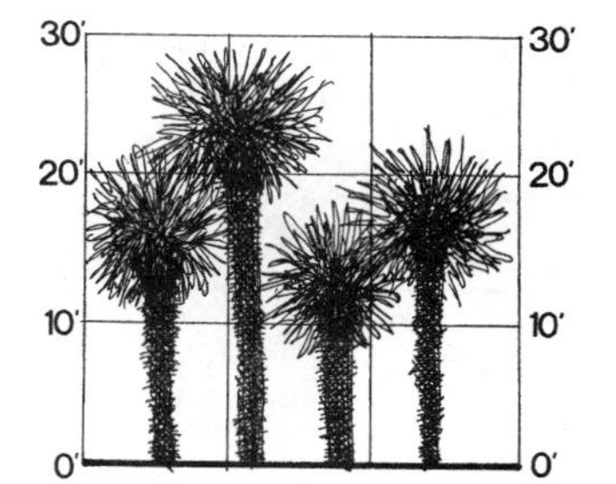

Trachycarpus fortunei **Evergreen**
Windmill Palm

Small palm that resembles the *Washingtonia* genus but displays darker green fronds. Also more frost tender than Washingtonia. Attractive tropical feel. Trunk gets thicker from the base of, or just below, the fronds, giving it a top-heavy look. Keep it out of the wind. Slow growth rate.

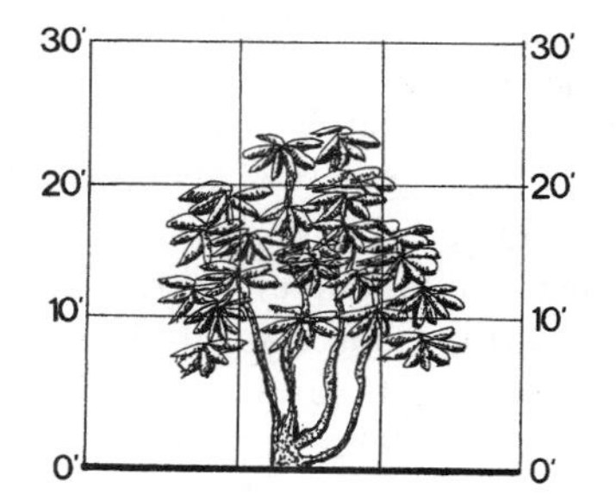

Tupidanthus calyptratus **Evergreen**
Tupidanthus

Definitely the plant for the exotic or tropical garden. Bright green, whorled, drooping foliage similar to Schefflera. Needs sun, wind, and above all, frost protection. Excellent container plant. Looks good with Bird-of-Paradise (*Strelitzia reginae*) and Split-leaf Philodendron (*Philodendron selloum*) in a shady atrium. Fast growth.

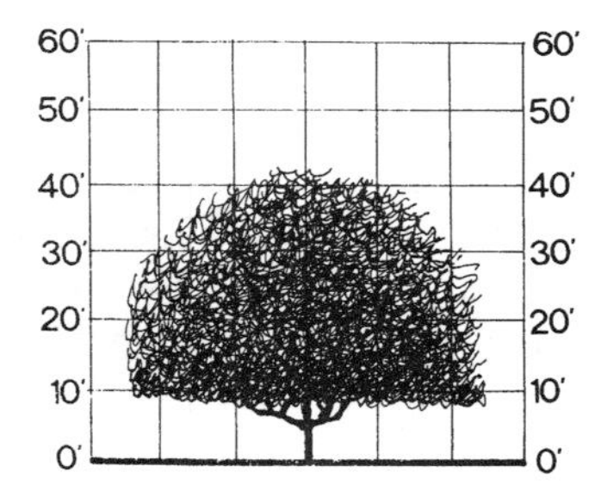

★ ***Ulmus parvifolia*** **Deciduous**
Evergreen Elm

Like the Evergreen Ash (*Fraxinus uhdei*) and the Evergreen Pear (*Pyrus kawakamii*) this tree is anything but evergreen in the desert. Known for its dependable, large-scale, weeping, umbrella-shaped canopy. An excellent low-canopy tree where it has the room to spread out. Flakey bark at maturity. An absolutely beautiful tree. Variety 'Drake' is more weeping in habit with smaller darker green leaves. True Green' stays evergreen later into the fall season. Fast growth.

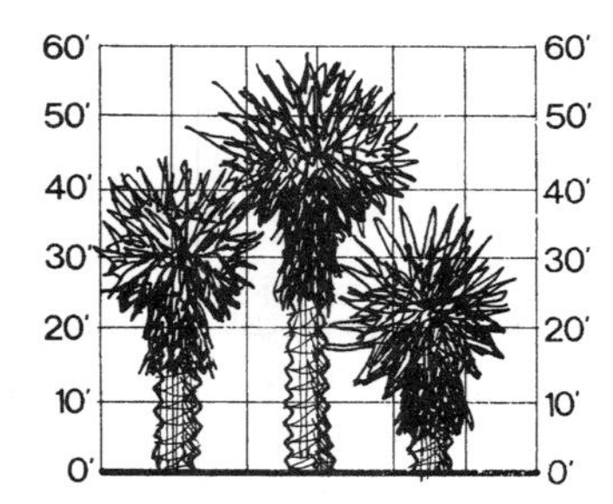

★ ***Washingtonia filifera*** **Evergreen**
California Fan Palm

The real palm in Palm Springs. This is what early-day vacationers saw when they came to use the area's hot mineral waters. The symbiotic relationship between the Cahuilla Indians and the palm is of particular interest. The tree rarely exceeds 40 feet in height, although specimens to 80 feet do exist. Light yellow-green fronds occupy ab areaabout 16 feet in circumference. Fronds turn down to trunk and die as palm grows in height. If left untrimmed the dead fronds overlap and form an inward spiraling petticoat. Note that trees left with the petticoat attached or unpeeled should be used carefully around structures as the petticoat is extremely flammable. With the leaf stalk (collars) peeled, the bark takes on a red-brown, skin-like appearance fading to buff-brown. The trunk of this palm can be massive, measuring 6 to 8 feet in diameter. Although the root system is fibrous and well-behaved (palms are monocots) the trunks will heave walls if planted too close. In my opinion, this tree is frequently used for the wrong applications. In the residential landscape it is dominant and sometimes overpowering. I prefer to use *Washingtonia filifera* in simulated desert canyon scenes, as it occurs in nature. It serves as a good street tree if correctly positioned so that the trunks do not block the vision of motorists. They also make a fine living wall. Moderate growth rate.

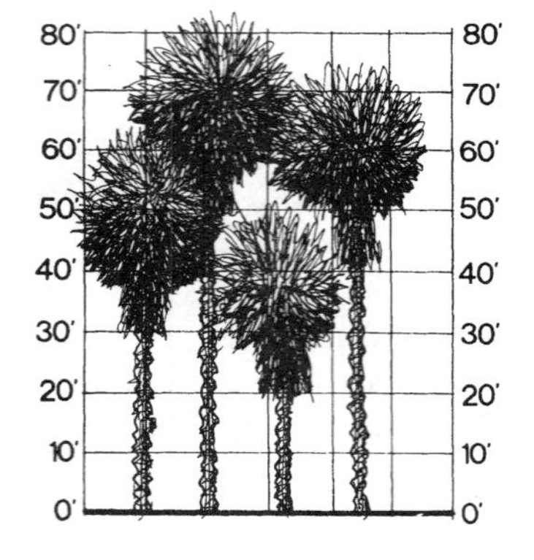

★ ***Washingtonia robusta*** **Evergreen**
Mexican Fan Palm

This palm is native to Mexico, particularly the Baja peninsula. This is the palm featured along boulevards in Beverly Hills. Similar to the California Fan Palm (*Washingtonia filifera*) in all aspects except it has a radically thinner trunk and grows much taller. Trunk diameter at the base is 18 to 24 inches. Averages 60 feet in height with 100 feet not being uncommon. You can tell the different species apart in younger trees by noting that *robusta* has a reddish streak on the underside of its leaf stalk (petiole) where it adjoins the trunk. Like its cousin, *filifera, robusta* fronds have a stalk laden with short stout thorns. These thorns can be vicious, cutting the skin like a saw blade, so care should be exercised in maintenance. Fast growth rate is probably the major contributing factor to the species name: *robusta*.

Shrubs

Mexican Bird-of-Paradise

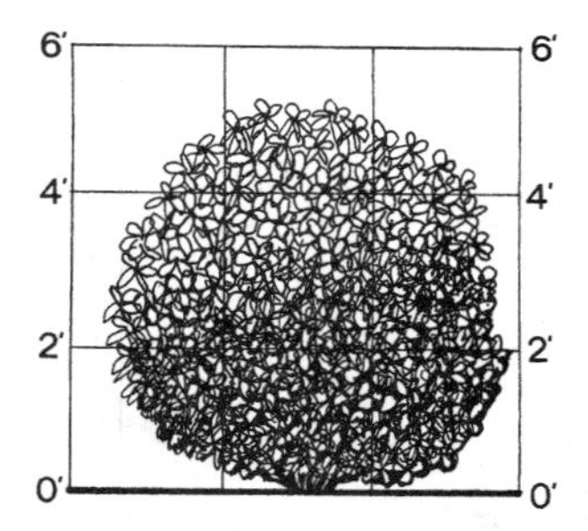

Abelia grandiflora **Semi-evergreen**
Glossy Abelia

Glossy dark-green leaves are quite attractive. Whitish pink flowers appear in late spring and continue through summer. Smaller-growing (4-feet high) cultivar 'Edward Goucher' is frequently specified. Freezes to ground at 0°F, but will come back the same season, but takes a couple of seasons to recover to full size. Rated as a semi-evergreen, this shrub will drop its leaves at 32°F. Not as much a risk in the low desert in protected areas as it would be in middle and high desert. Fast growth.

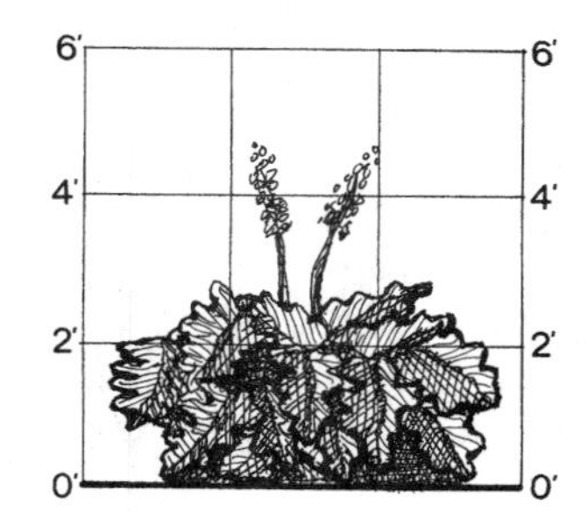

Acanthus mollis **Evergreen**
Acanthus

Definitely a plant to be used for tropical effect in atriums and other protected areas. Grown for its large, 6-inch wide by 8-inch long, deeply lobed, dark-green leaves. Rated a semi-evergreen because it will die to ground during the hottest summers. Spreads by invasive rhizomes so it must be contained. Variety 'Latifolia' is hardy and widely used. Use with other tropicals such as Split-Leaf Philodendron (*Philodendron selloum*), Bird-of-Paradise (*Strelitzia reginae*), or Japanese Aralia (*Fatsia japonica*) as these plants will act as filler plants when Acanthus dies down in summer. Exotic flower spikes appear in early summer; some gardeners remove them to enhance foliage appearance. Fast growth.

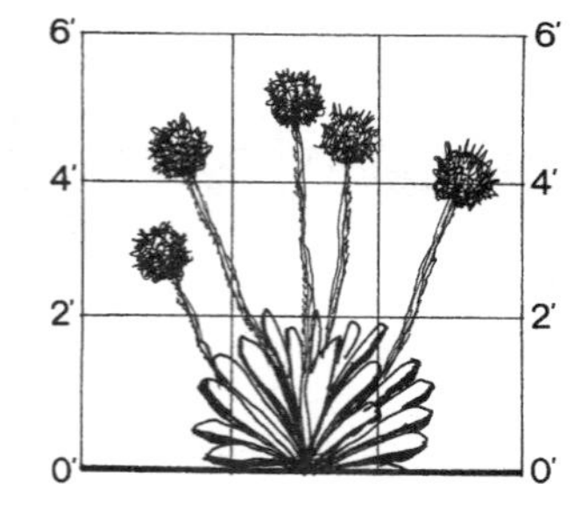

Agapanthus africanus **Evergreen**
Lily-of-the-Nile

Summer blooming exotic. A perennial that can be reliably grown with shrubs if divided every 5 years. Globe-like, 4-inch round flowers are supported on stiff stalks and hover above 2-foot-long strap-like leaves. Purple is the predominate flower color although a white variety is also available. Despite what other references say, do not keep in full sun in the desert. Fast growth.

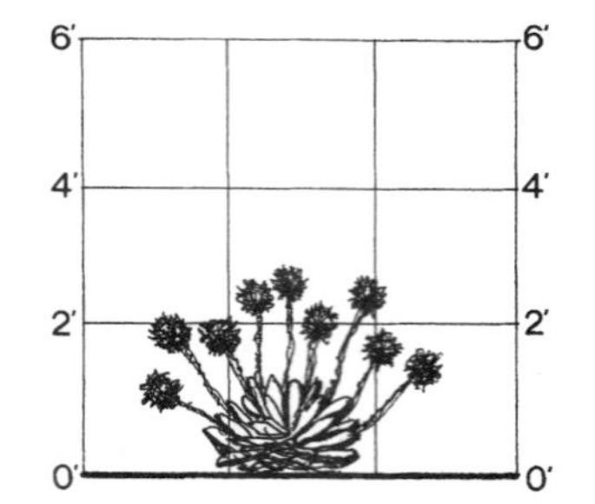

Agapanthus africanus 'Peter Pan' **Evergreen**
Dwarf Lily-of-the-Nile

Smaller variety of the Agapanthus mentioned above. Flowers 18-inch high with 12-inch long leaves. Looks good mixed with the larger Agapanthus for a tiered effect. Purple summer flowers with whites available. Surprisingly, it is tougher than the species, especially to sun exposure. Filtered sun to shade. Fast growth.

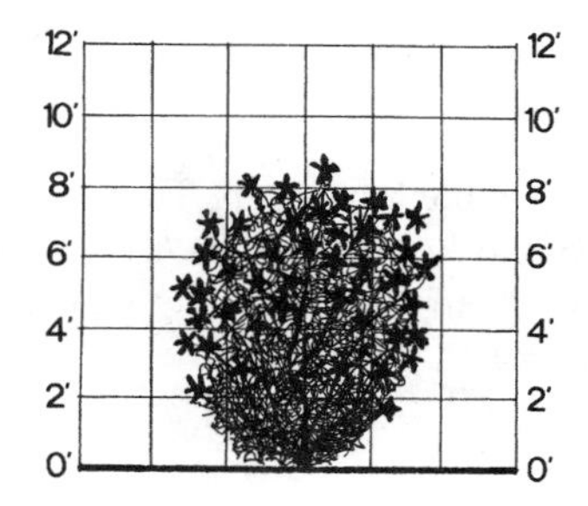

Alyogyne huegelii **Evergreen**

Blue Hibiscus

Needs protection from frost and full to nearly full sun in the desert. Worth the effort required as blue flowers appear intermittently year round. Foliage is deeply lobed, dark-green and, for the most part, is insignificant. Flowers of lilac blue are 5 inches across and shiny. Very showy. Use smaller foreground plants at the base of Blue Hibiscus to draw attention to plant's upper regions where it blossoms heaviest. Moderate growth.

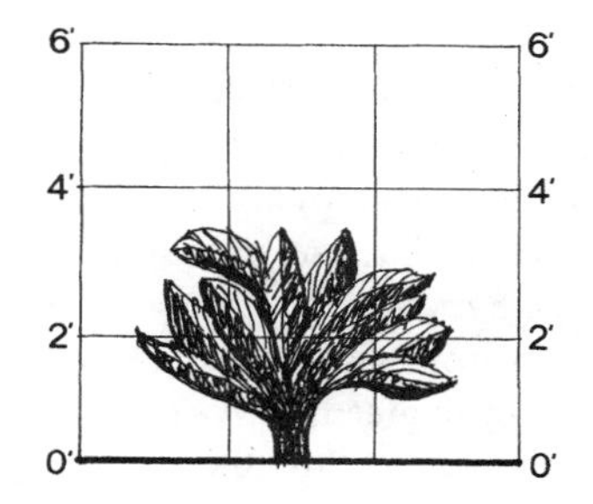

★ ***Aspidistra elatior*** **Evergreen**

Cast-Iron Plant

A plant with one specific purpose — to survive, even flourish, in deep shade. Leaves 3-feet long by 3 inches wide, corn-like, deep-green leaves. Takes abuse that would kill most other plants. Likes friable, well-drained soil, but can take any soil, even clay. Because it gets put in throw away areas under stairwells and in deep crevices it is frequently forgotten. Simply hosing the dust off its leaves will remarkably improve its appearance. Moderate growth rate.

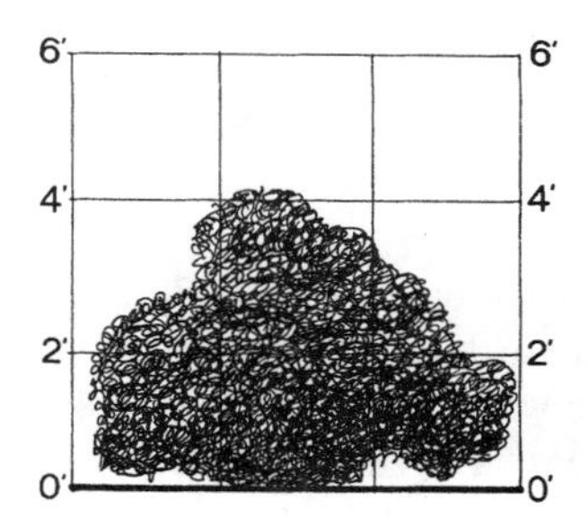

★ ***Atriplex canescens*** **Semi-evergreen**

Four-Wing Saltbush

Tough native found in all North American deserts. Common name derived from the ability of the genus to secrete salt through its leaves, making them quite tolerant of saline soils. Cattle do not find their leaves objectionable and several agricultural experiments are under way for the use of saltbush as a forage plant. Exhibits drought deciduousness in hottest parts of summer. Grown predominately for grayish foliage. Flowers are insignificant, but do attract desert birds. Moderate growth.

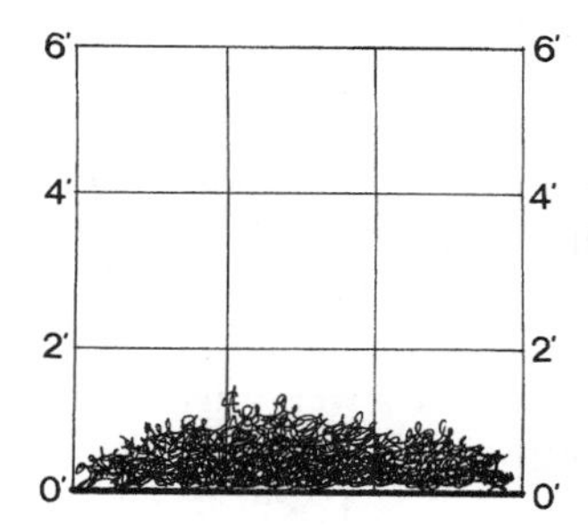

Atriplex semibaccata **Semi-evergreen**

Australian Saltbush

Could be classified as a ground cover, but it is very uneven in habit. Many of the same characteristics of *Atriplex canescens* except much lower and more wide-spreading. Highly fire retardant. Slow growth.

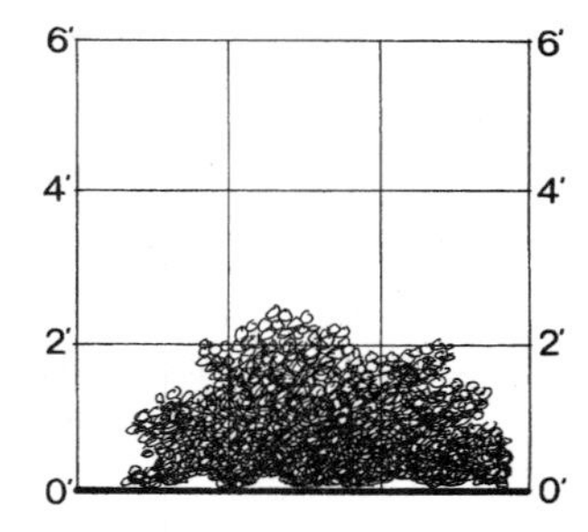

★ *Baccharis 'Centennial'* **Evergreen**
Hybrid Desert Broom

Most dependable Baccharis species for use in the low desert. This is apparently a hybrid between *Baccharis pilularis* and *Baccharis sarothroides*. It is deep green and mounding.The plant's ability to resist freezing makes it a good, if somewhat unkempt, alternate to Carissa. Moderate growth rate.

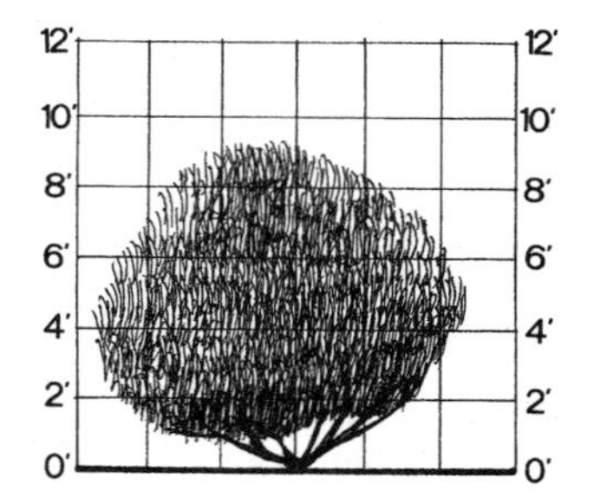

Baccharis sarothroides **Semi-evergreen**
Desert Broom

Native to the Sonoran Desert. Grows in association with desert washes or on the outskirts of agricultural areas where it can pick up some irrigation runoff. Use this plant with care as females produce an annoying cottony bloom in the fall. You can try to specify male plants only, but a reliable source is yet to be found. Desert Broom will get leggy with too much water and is short-lived. Plant is invasive due to immense number of seeds. Desert broom does have some advantages, however. It is the brightest green, native desert shrub. Its extremely fast growth will knit soils and slopes while the shade it provides allows other species to germinate and get a foothold. For this reason, it is frequently incorporated in desert hydroseed mixes.

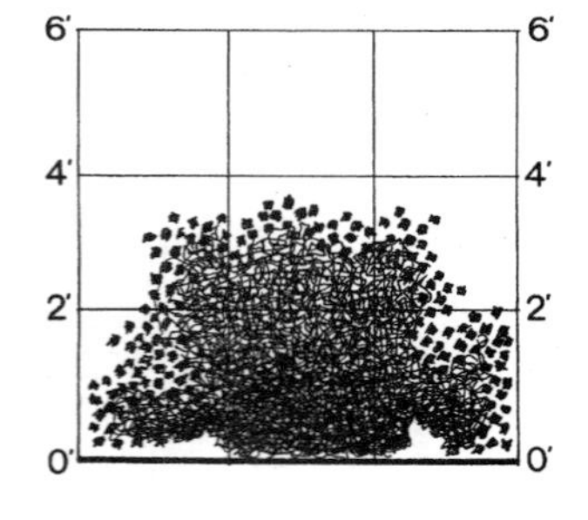

★ *Bougainvillea 'Crimson Jewel'* **Semi-evergreen**
Red Bush Bougainvillea

A true Bush Bougainvillea. As the others listed on the Master Shrub Matrix, can be trained as vines or espaliers or kept as loose shrubs or bank covers. This one is a true 36-inch high by 36-inch wide bright-red blooming shrub. Watch around children as all Bougainvilleas have vicious thorns. Also great care should always be exercised when transplanting Bougainvilleas from containers. Do not disturb rootball. If root ball is cracked or broken — forget it; the plant's chances of survival are minimal. Once established,however, Bougainvilleas are rampant growers. Used in the wrong setting, they will need to be cut back a half dozen times a summer. They will take over and crowd out other plants. Needs water to become established, then they are fairly drought-tolerant. In fact, if irrigation is cut back in late summer, winter flower color becomes more intense. Blooms are, in actuality, sepals held in bracts encasing tiny yellow flowers. The only drawback to Bougainvilleas is freezing, but once established they will often freeze to ground and then recover all their growth the following season. In addition to introduced annual color, Bougainvilleas, especially 'Crimson Jewel,'provide the most striking and massive color show in the desert. Rapid growth.

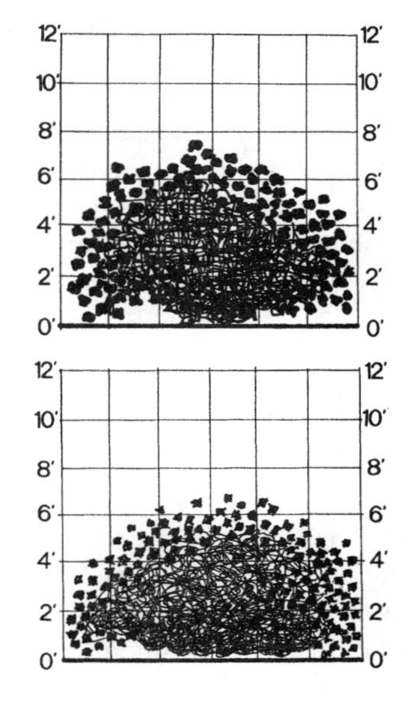

***Bougainvillea* 'Lavender Queen'** **Semi-evergreen**
Lavender Bush Bougainvillea

Nearly pure purple. Can be either a shrub or espalier. Espaliers will freeze more readily, owing to less insulating leaf mess. Fast growth.

***Bougainvillea* 'Rosenka'** **Semi-evergreen**
Gold/Pink Bougainvillea

Horticultural oddity. Light golden blossoms age to faint pink. Next to 'Crimson Jewel' it is the most popular Bush Bougainvillea and is used heavily. It is also nearly a true shrubs, needing only occasional pruning of wayward shoots. Dead blossoms hang on the plant a long time so use in an area where attention can be drawn to other things or where maintenance personnel can easily shake them of. Fast growth.

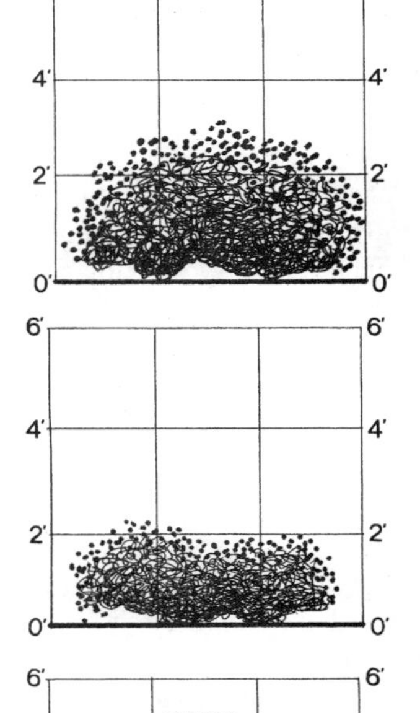

***Bougainvillea* 'Texas Dawn'** **Semi-evergreen**
Texas Dawn Bougainvillea

Deep pink and the most dependable shade of pink among the Bougainvilleas. Fast growth.

***Bougainvillea* 'White Madonna'** **Semi-evergreen**
White Bush Bougainvillea

Closest to white of all Bougainvilleas. Also the most frost-tender. Use in protected areas. Hardest to establish with slowest growth rate.

Buxus microphylla japonica **Evergreen**
Japanese Boxwood

A good formal shrub from Japan. I use this plant on projects where I know the maintenance personnel will clip everything in sight into balls or squares. This shrub readily adapts to a number of geometric configurations. Dark-green, tight foliage. Moderate growth rate.

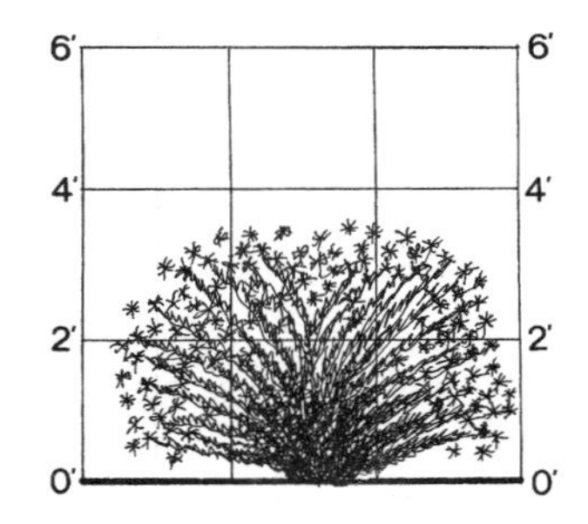

★ ***Calliandra eriophylla*** **Semi-evergreen**
Fairy Duster

Native to chaparral areas outside San Diego and introduced to the California desert to the point where it has naturalized. Will drop its leaves in a severe drought or during a very cold winter but, for the most part, remains evergreen. (I list as a semi-evergreen.) Pincushion flowers are pink/red with deep red centers. Blooms late spring through summer. Fast growth.

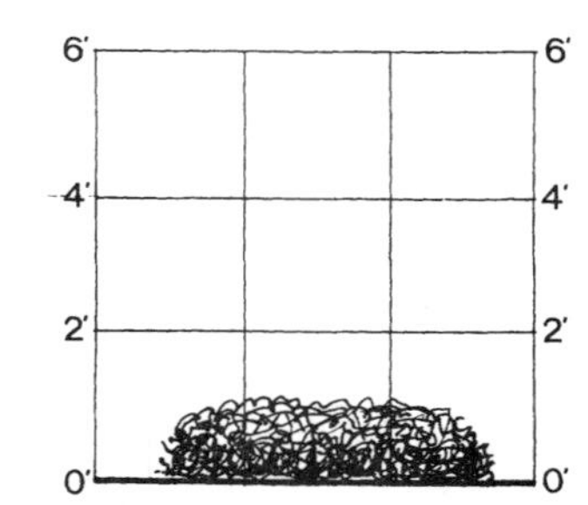

Carissa grandiflora ***Evergreen***
Natal Plum

South African native introduced to hot-weather climates around the world. Dark, tight, glossy-green foliage. Beautiful white, star-shaped flowers appear late spring and occur intermittently throughout summer, sometimes into fall. Will take full sun, but likes some late afternoon summer shade. Limiting factor is hardiness as the plant will freeze during periods of extended frost. Needs winter protection. Moderate growth rate.

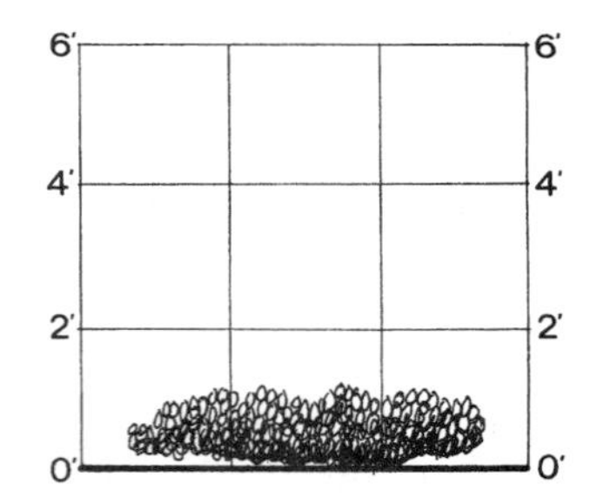

Carissa grandiflora 'Green Carpet' **Evergreen**
Natal Plum

Although heavily used here and in Arizona, I cannot classify this shrub a star performer because of its propensity to freeze. Smaller and more well-behaved than the species, 'Green Carpet' needs winter protection and is better off out of direct sun. Moderate growth rate.

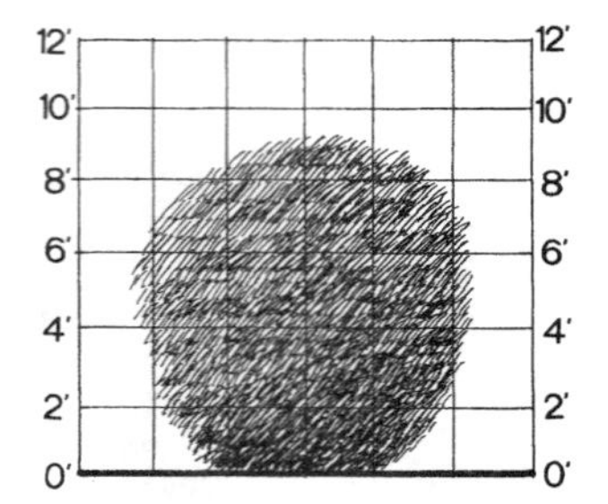

★ ***Cassia artemisioides*** **Semi-evergreen**
Feathery Cassia

From Australia, this is one of my all-time favorites. Light, airy, gray-green foliage and a profusion of yellow blossoms February through June. A tough, dependable shrub especially suited as a backdrop or filtered screen. Its soft, springy branches can be compressed and they return to form. This makes it an excellent parking lot selection where cars can actually be allowed to hit it, indicating where to stop. Grows to maturity within a year's time of planting from one-gallon containers. Can be damaged in an extremely cold winter but recovers quickly. Use it where there is room for it to spread to its natural size. Does not like to be sheared and will get leggy if it isn't. If you need to reduce its size or if you inherit a pruned plant, simply cut it to the ground and it will regrow to its natural form. One of the best design selections available for the transitional garden.

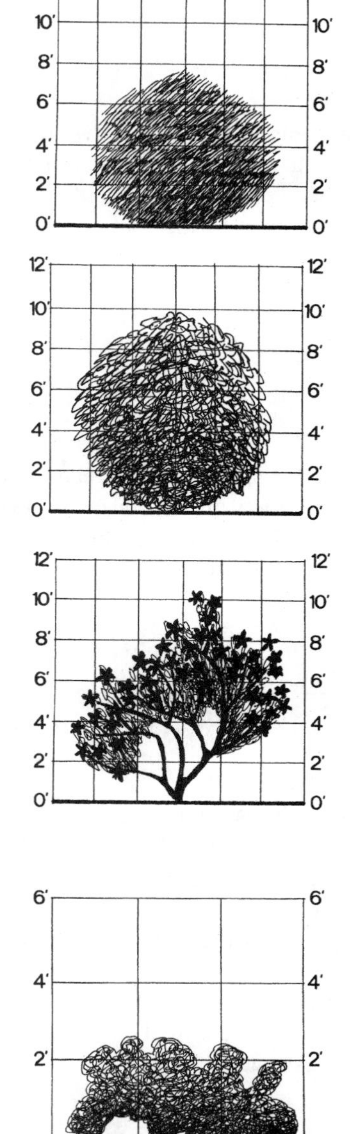

Cassia nemophilla **Semi-evergreen**
Bushy Senna

Similar in every way to *Cassia artemisioides* except it has green foliage and is more winter-hardy. Because of the difference in foliage color, the flowers appear to be a deeper yellow than *Cassia artemisoides*. Fast growth.

Cassia phyllodinea **Semi-evergreen**
Desert Cassia

Same foliage color as *Cassia artemsioides,* but leaf blades are bigger and more noticeable. Bloom period is December into June, which is somewhat longer than *artemisioides*. Also, matures to be more drought-resistant. A good selection, but not as profuse a flower show. Fast growth.

Chaenomeles japonica **Deciduous**
Japanese Flowering Quince

Deciduous shrubs with interesting branch structure when out of leaf. First shrub to flower in spring in the high desert. Number of varieties in pinks, reds, white, and orange. A good shrub to use in difficult situations because they tolerate wide temperature ranges from freezing to severe heat. Moderate growth.

Convolvulus cneorum **Evergreen**
Bush Morning Glory

Silvery-gray foliage. White flowers in midspring to late summer. Very delicate look. Works well with the Cassias and Leucophyllums. Fast growth. Trim to ground to remove leggy growth and rejuvenate plant.

★ ***Convolvulus mauritanicus*** **Evergreen**
Ground Morning Glory

Similar to *Convolvulus cneorum* except foliage is smaller and greener and the overall size of the plant is smaller. Flowers are a lovely shade of pale blue; about one inch in diameter. Unlike most species seen in the desert. Takes heat and wind well and should get more use. Fast growth from one-gallon containers. Excellent transition plant.

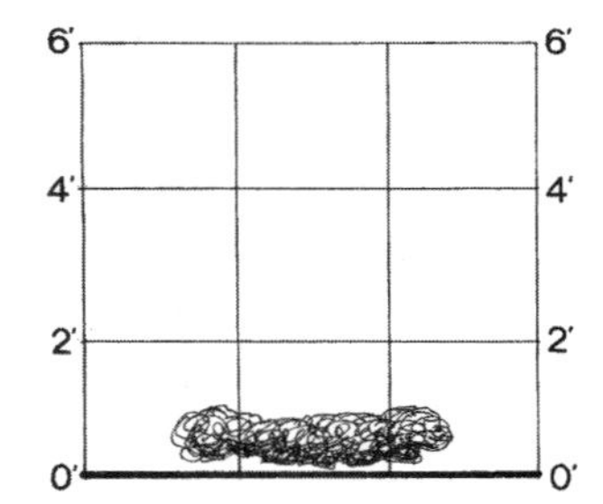

Convolvulus tricolor **Evergreen**
Dwarf Morning Glory

Hard to classify as a ground cover although it is small, because plantings do not cover the ground uniformly. For this reason, it is presented here as a shrub. Some botanists place it with annuals, but in a warm winter it lives through the seasons. Mentioned here because of its foliage value and its blue flowers are a treat. Acts as a nice foreground plant in front of either of its two cousins, *C. cneorum* or *C. mauritanicus*. Fast growth. Bloom is heaviest in summer. Looks nice as a potted plant.

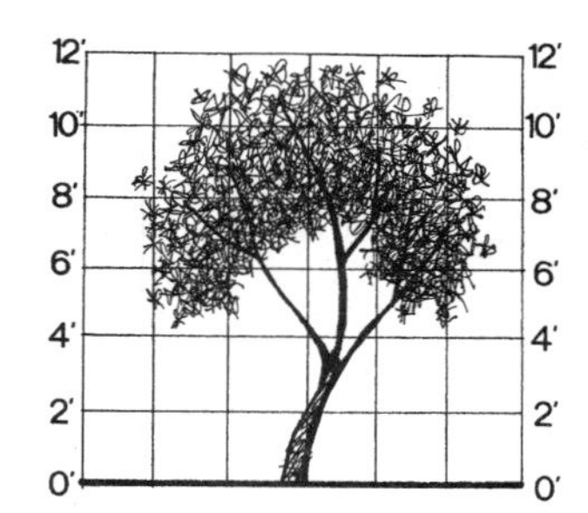

Cordia boissieri **Semi-evergreen**
Anacahuita

Introduction from the Chihuahuan Desert. Large shrub that can be pruned into a small tree. Large white flowers with yellow throats appear in late spring and may reappear in fall. Will lose leaves in severe frost, but comes back rapidly. Moderate growth rate. Deserves to be used more frequently in the low desert.

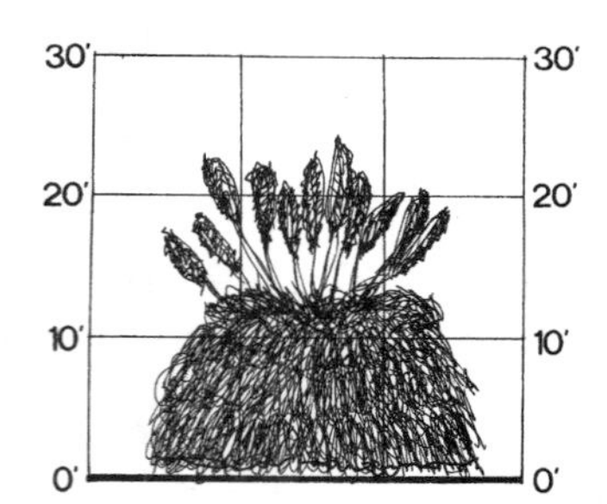

Cortaderia selloana **Evergreen**
Pampas Grass

Massive grass, so care needs to be taken in its use and placement. Can reach its mature size within a year's time of initial planting from one-gallon containers. Leaf edges are very sharp so keep away from pedestrians. Good windbreak. Excellent water-effect plant. Invasive root system — use root barriers. Plant is prized for its fluffy plumes which extend vertically to as high as 16 feet into the air. Plumes appear in September and hang on until December/January. Varieties with pink plumes are available from select growers. Avoid *Cortaderia jubata* which can become a freely seeding nuisance weed. Properly applied, *C.selloana*, is a spectacular plant.

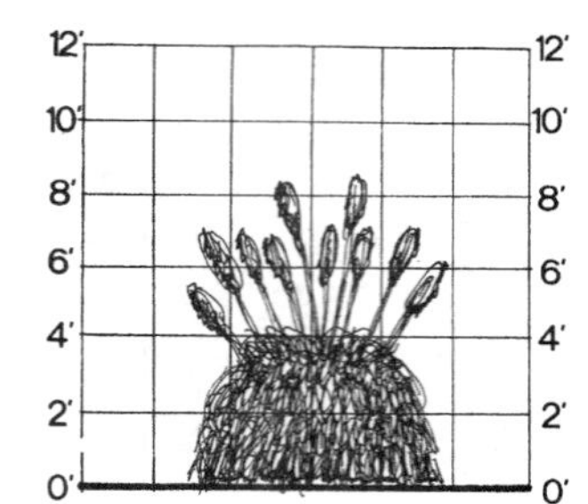

★ ***Cortaderia selloana* 'Pumila'** **Evergreen**
Dwarf Pampas Grass

Roughly half the size of *selloana* and not nearly as invasive. Recently introduced. Rave reviews are in and 'Pumila' rates star performer status. May be the grass to replace the invasive Fountain Grass (*Pennisetum setaceum*) in small-scale water feature plantings. Fast growth.

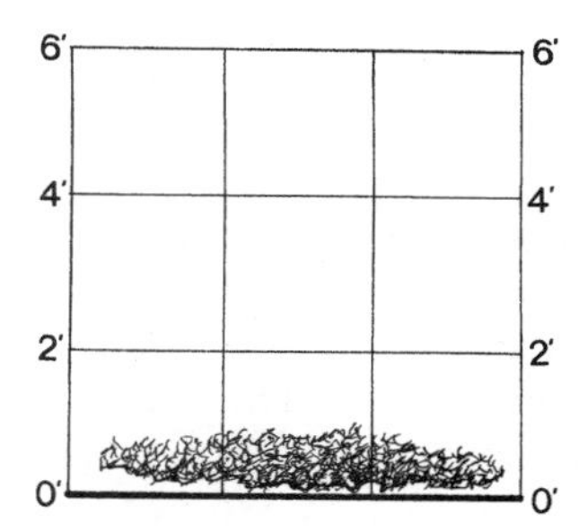

Dalea greggii **Semi-evergreen**
Prostrate Indigo Bush

Gray-foliaged, spreading shrub or ground cover. Suggest application as a shrub, as growth pattern does not make it a dependable uniform ground cover. Purple flowers in midspring are seen by the trained observer but may go unnoticed by the general populace. Fast growth.

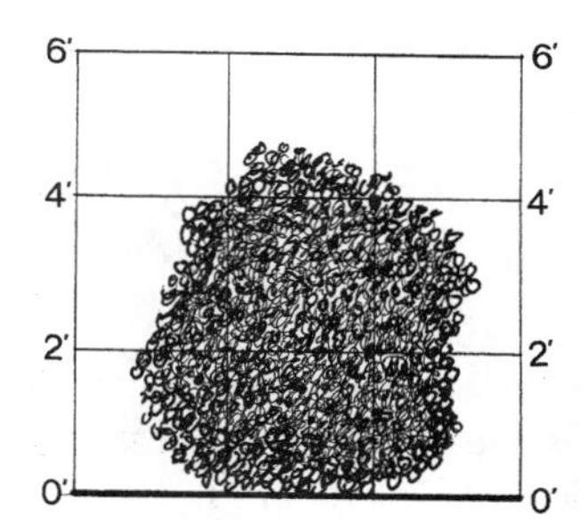

Dalea pulchra **Semi-evergreen**
Indigo Bush

Medium-scale shrub that is partially drought deciduous unless it receives supplemental summer irrigation. Flowers are a light lavender and occur in spring prior to *D.spinosa*'s floral show. A good selection for tough desert conditions. In the late 1980s, it was the Lencophyllums; in the early 1990s, it was Salvias; now the Daleas are the new superstar genus. Expect several important introductions and hybrids before the end of the century. Mountain States Nursery in Phoenix (602-247-6354) offers *Dalea capitata*, which is similar to *pulchra* except it has yellow flowers. Fast growth on low water.

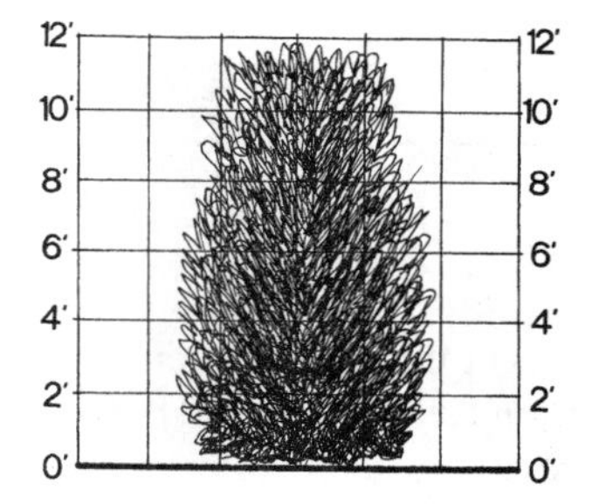

Dodonaea viscosa **Evergreen**
Hop Bush

Very large shrub native to southwest and Mexico. Can be an alternative to the widely used Common Oleander (*Nerium oleander*) hedge. It exhibits better and faster growth with water but will accept considerable drought. Major drawback is that it will freeze, especially younger plants. Can be planted at 6 foot on center and trimmed into a formal hedge but, in my opinion, looks better and much more natural untrimmed. Fast growth.

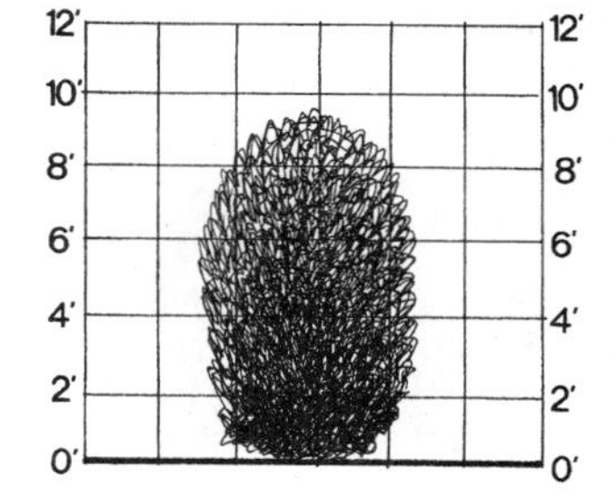

Dodonaea viscosa 'Purpurea' **Evergreen**
Purple Hop Bush

Same characteristics as *Dodonaea viscosa* except it has bronze to purple foliage. Purple Hop Bush is also slightly smaller and more frost tender than the species. Variety 'Saratoga' is the most purple of all and has the most dependable upright oval form. Fast growth.

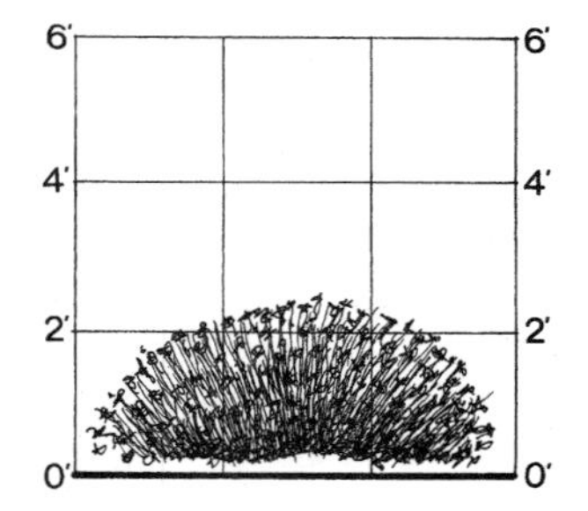

★ *Encelia farinosa* **Semi-evergreen**
Brittle Bush

What a tremendous midspring flower show this native shrub puts on. Travel on Interstate 10 around Banning or the south-facing slopes of the Little San Bernardino Mountains outside Palm Springs, California, in late March and the ground is pure yellow with brilliant Encelia in full bloom. Gray foliage. Plant will become drought or frost deciduous, but remains evergreen if not exposed to either of these conditions. Used frequently in wildflower seed mixes. Fast growth.

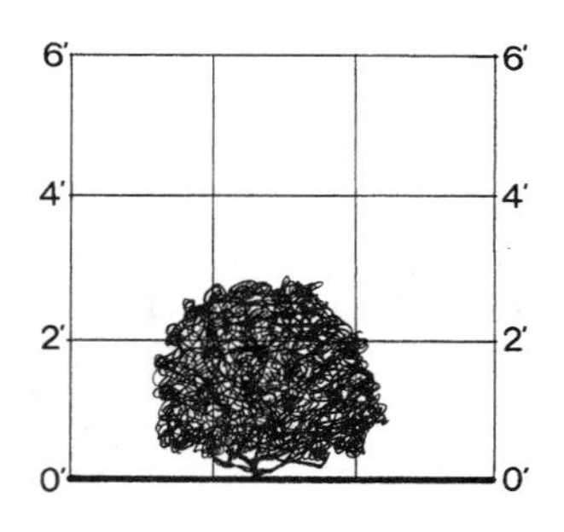

★ *Ericameria laricifolia* **Evergreen**
Turpentine Bush

Sonaran Desert native that is one of the few true, deep-green desert shrubs. Found on the side slopes of bajadas, it is one of the first volunteers to revegetate damaged soils. A very good choice in areas requiring fire restoration. Three feet high in the wild it can get to 6 feet with artificial irrigation. Prized for its massive golden-yellow fall floral display. Foliage takes on a golden tint during late fall and winter months. The common name derives from the odor produced when the leaves are crushed. An excellent choice for the native garden. Fast growth.

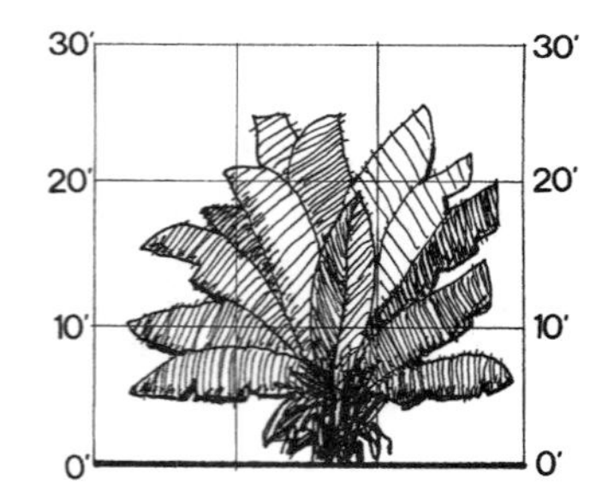

Ensete ventricosum **Evergreen**
Abyssinian Banana

Novelty plant grown for the tropical effect of its bright green 12-inch-wide translucent leaves. Keep it protected from full sun and frost and out of the wind. Plants die out every 3 years or so immediately after flowering. This plant does not send out offshoots, so replacements are necessary if it blooms or is killed by frost. Replacements can fill a void within 3 months. If this need for occasional replacement is an undesirable feature, consider the true edible Banana (*Musa paradisiaca*) or Giant Bird of Paradise (*Strelitzia nicolai*). Good selection if you have the room and need a bold, tropical, vertical accent. Extremely fast growth.

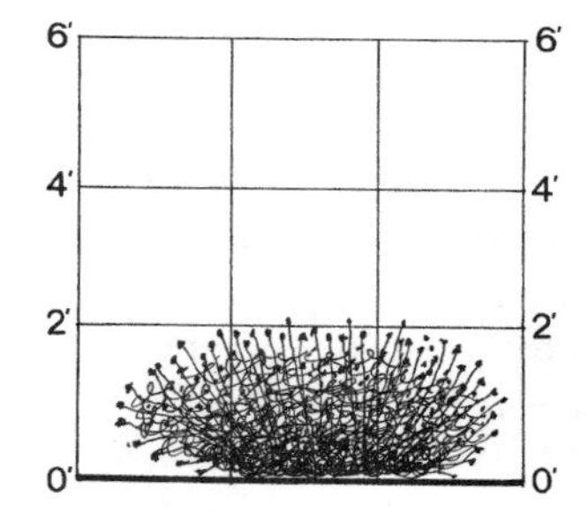

Eriogonum fasciculatum **Semi-evergreen**
California Buckwheat

Definitely for the desert scene or native garden. Not a well-kept ornamental landscape plant. Irregular shaped, semi-evergreen (drought deciduous) plant that blooms white to pink flowers throughout the summer months. Flowers die and brown on the plant, giving it a dried flower appearance. Very tough. Used in a lot of native seed mixes for erosion control and bank stabilization. Fast growth.

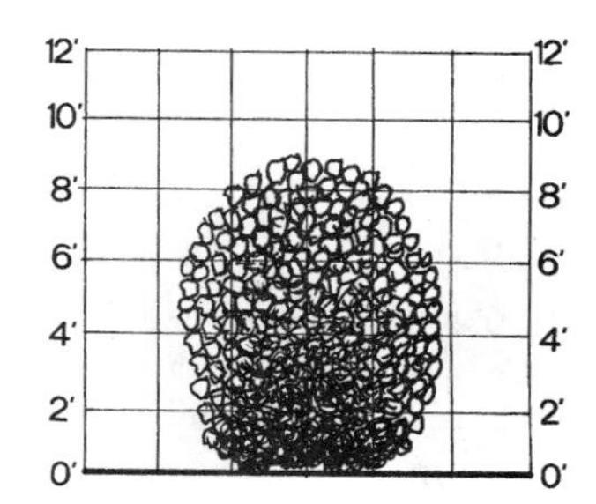

Euonymus japonica **Evergreen**
Evergreen Euonymus

Useful shrub that is often overlooked. Six to 8-foot-high upright, bright-green shrub. Several varieties are grown with variegated and/or silver foliage. Not a plant for wet, shady areas because it contacts mildew easily. Mildew is seldom a problem in the desert, but cases do occur. Moderate growth.

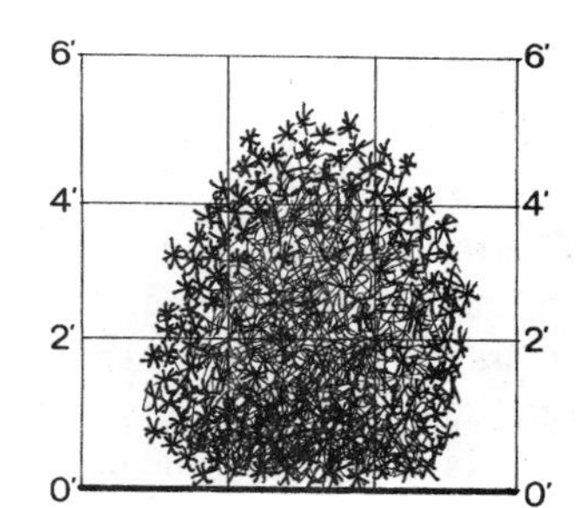

Euryops pectinatus **Evergreen**
Common Euryops

Very popular Southern California plant. I personally do not rate it a star performer because it freezes easily. Valued for its yellow flowers and long blooming period of late fall through early spring. Species *E.viridis* is exactly the same except its foliage is bright green instead of the familiar dark blue green. Fast growth.

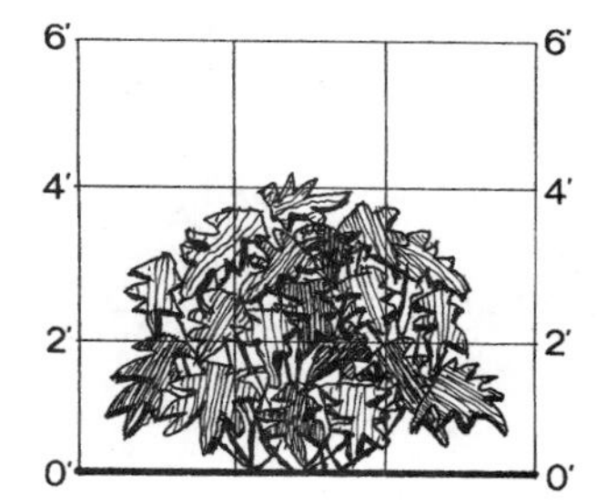

***Fatsia japonic*a** **Evergreen**
Japanese Aralia

Definitely a plant for the protected oasis garden. Cooks in bright sun and will freeze in the open winter air. Primary advantage is its light-green foliage and well-behaved character. Will grow under the same conditions as a Split-Leaf Philodendron (*Philodendron selloum*) but will not get nearly as unruly and will accept even less light. Moderate growth.

★ *Felicia amelloides* **Evergreen**
Blue Marguerite

Several improved varieties are available besides the light sky blue species with golden-yellow centered flowers. The species is valued for its agressive growth and profuse late spring through summer blooming. This can be enhanced by picking spent flowers from the plant. Looks exceptional as a foreground planting to Blue Hibiscus (*Alyogyne huegelii*) or consider mixing it with Blackfoot Daisy (*Melampodium leucanthum*). Cut back seasonally to avoid leggy growth. Fast growth with low water requirement.

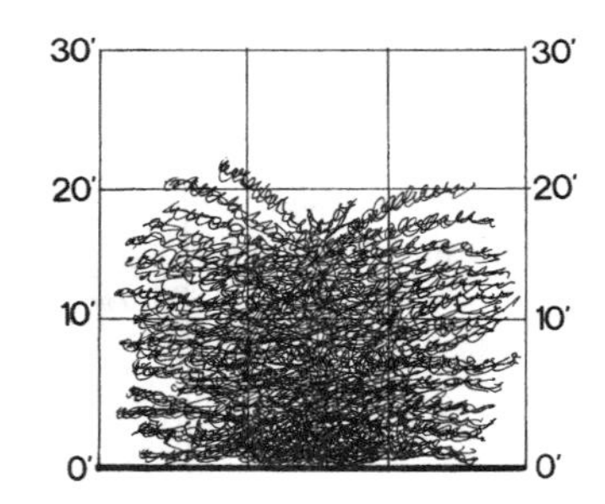

***Fremontodendron mexican*um** **Evergreen**
Southern Flannel Bush

Native to chaparral communities of San Diego County and is beginning to naturalize into the Colorado Desert. Glossy green foliage with yellow blossoms interspersed on branches. Attractive when in bloom from April through June. Likes sandy soil and becomes drought resistant with age. Fast growth. With more use, it could become a Star Performer.

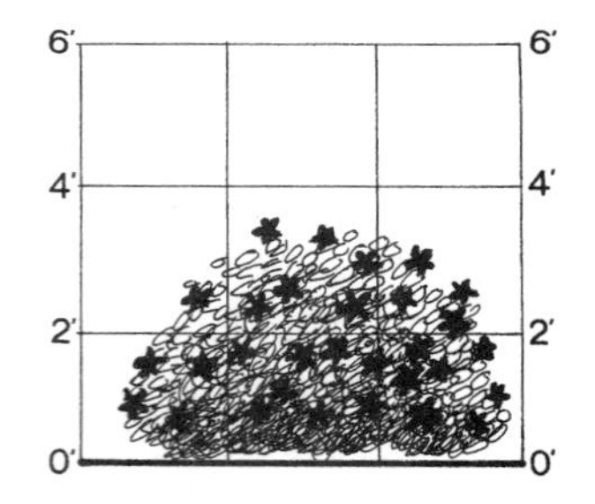

Gardenia jasminoides 'Veitchii Improved' **Evergreen**
Gardenia

Most commonly used Gardenia in the desert. Gardenias need an acid soil to thrive and cannot take full sun. Grown more in the clay soil. Clay soil adapts more readily to mixing with peat moss and other amendments to make soil acidic. In nonclay areas it is better to use gardenias in very small areas or in pots or raised planters where the soil mix can be controlled. Gardeners will go to the effort to obtain the blossom and fragrance of the 3-inch white flowers in April and May. Slow growth. Acid-loving companion plants to gardenias include Azaleas, Camellias, and Rhododendrons. All need sun protection and require a lot of maintenance but some clients consider these plants worth the trouble. Moderate growth.

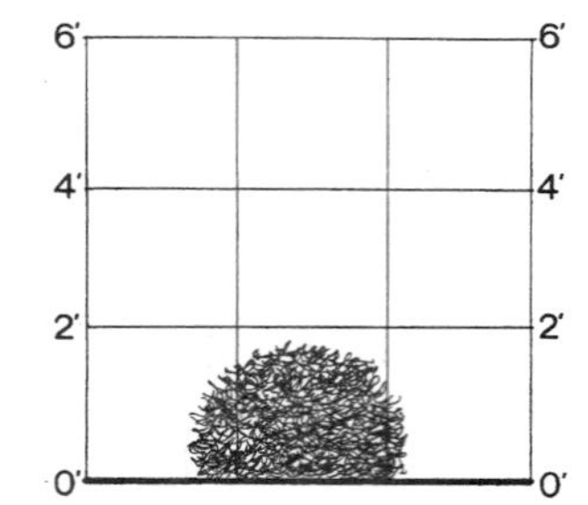

Gardenia radicans **Evergreen**
(No common name)

Much smaller than *Gardenia jasminoides* and valued as a foreground plant to the larger species in the acid soil and/or scent garden. Inch wide white flowers in late spring to early summer are fragrant and attractive. Similar care and cultural requirements to jasminoides. Slow growth.

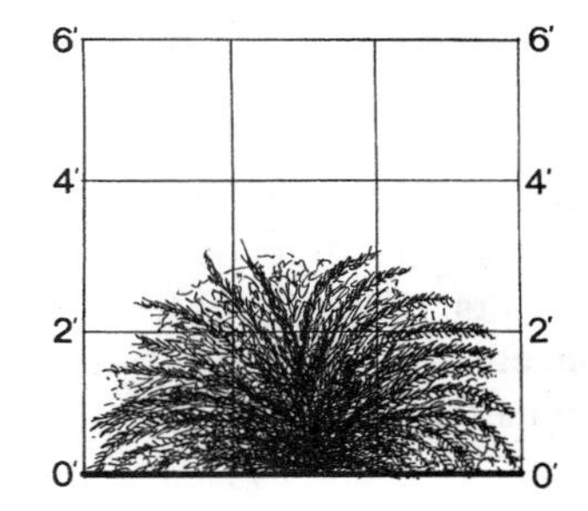

***Grevillea* 'Noellii'** **Evergreen**

Grevillea

A shrub that is beginning to receive more use. Stringy, pendulous habit makes it somewhat irregular. Not for the formal garden and definitely not to be used as a clipped hedge. Good selection in varied height planters or for slopes. Pink flowers occur in late spring. Green needle-like foliage. Fast growth.

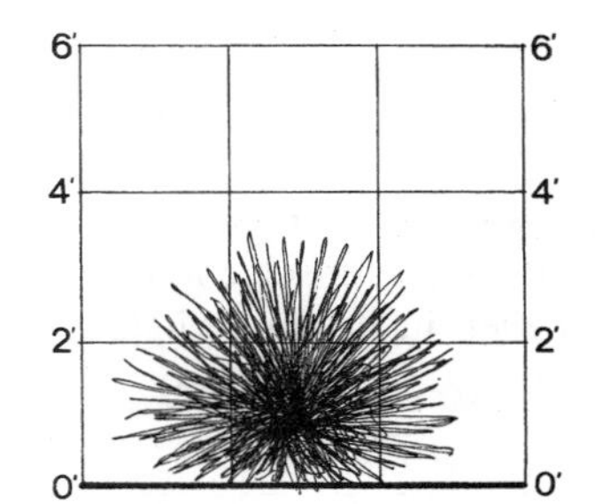

Helictotrichon sempervirens **Evergreen**

Blue Oat Grass

Not frequently used in the low desert and often not easy to obtain, this plant is worth experimenting with. Looks a lot like Blue Fescue (*Festuca ovina glauca*) but is larger (3 feet vs. 10 inches) and leaf blades are gracefully arching. Looks good as a background plant to smaller grasses, especially the aforementioned Blue Fescue. Slow growth with moderate water.

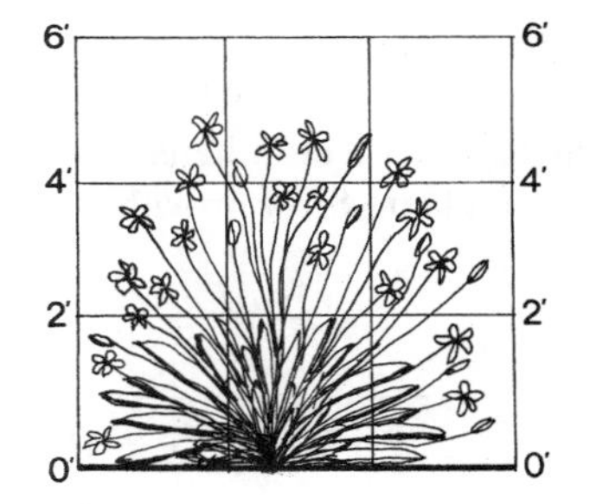

★ *Hemerocallis fulva* **Evergreen**

Daylily (consult grower's catalogues)

One of the toughest late spring, early summer flowering perennials you will ever find. Green grass-like foliage. Lily-like flowers most commonly seen in shades of yellow, orange, and red. Pinks and even a white are now on the market. Will take full sun but appreciates some afternoon shade. Excellent effect when used at a lake or simulated stream edge. Dwarf varieties are gaining popularity. Fast growth.

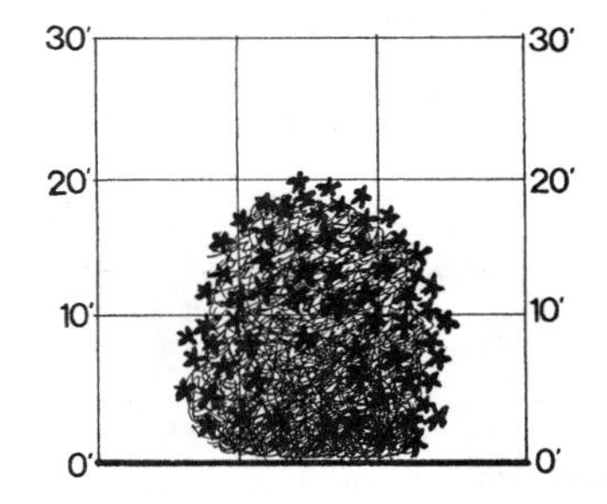

Hibiscus rosa-sinensis **Evergreen**

Chinese Hibiscus

A big favorite with a big problem. All hibiscus will freeze if left out in the open. This is something you can depend on. In narrow sideyards between houses or under deep roof overhangs Hibiscus will usually survive the on-slaught of winter. Hibiscus displays dark green foliage and 3- to 4-inch-wide flowers in every color of the rainbow. Relishes sandy soil, heat, and ample applications of fertilizer. If placed in the right location and given a moderate amount of maintenance, hibiscus will reward you with winter and spring color of an assortment and intensity unlike that of any other desert shrub. It is a good selection for containers if the containers can be moved to protected areas. Fast growth.

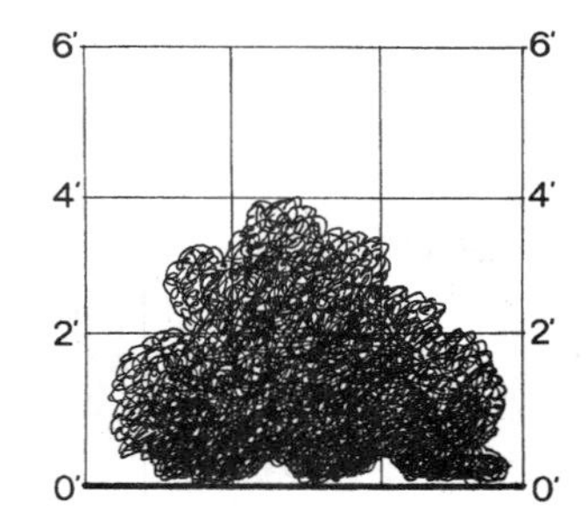

Isomeris arborea **Semi-evergreen**
Bladder Pod

Medium-sized evergreen native. Intense yellow bloomer January, February, and March. Resembles Cassia in a lot of ways. Would be a good selection to use in seed mixes for natural revegetation of the desert floor. Common name refers to fattened, downward pointed, bullet-like, seed pods that occur in profusion. Pods brown through summer months. Occasionally drought deciduous. Fast growth with little water.

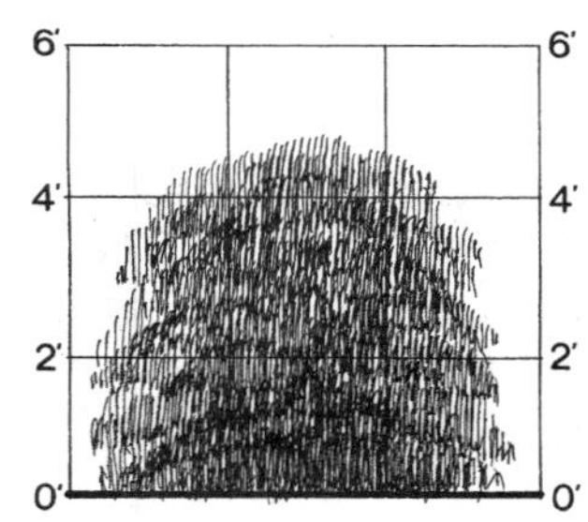

Jasminum sambac **Evergreen**
Arabian Jasmine

Grown for flowers and its especially pleasing scent. Frost tender and needs protection. Do not plant in full sun. Good atrium selection. Flowers are quite showy and frequently used to make leis in Hawaii. Moderate growth.

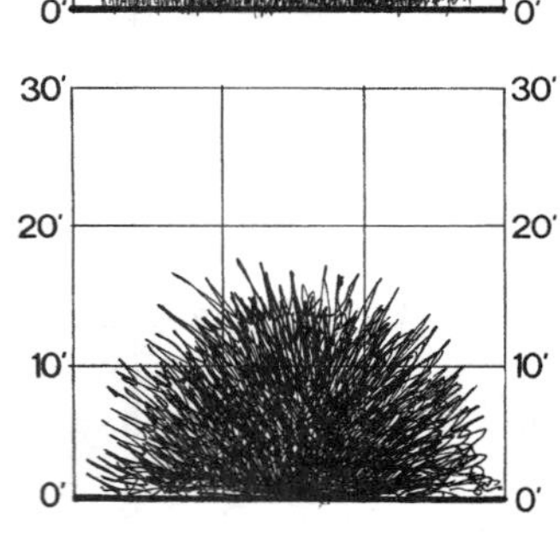

Juniperus chinensis 'Pfitzerana' **Evergreen**
Pfitzer's Juniper

Evergreen conifer. Probably one of the most commonly used junipers in the U.S. Deep green upright arching branches to 6 feet in height. Extremely tough. Good dense visual- or wind-screen plant. Slow growth.

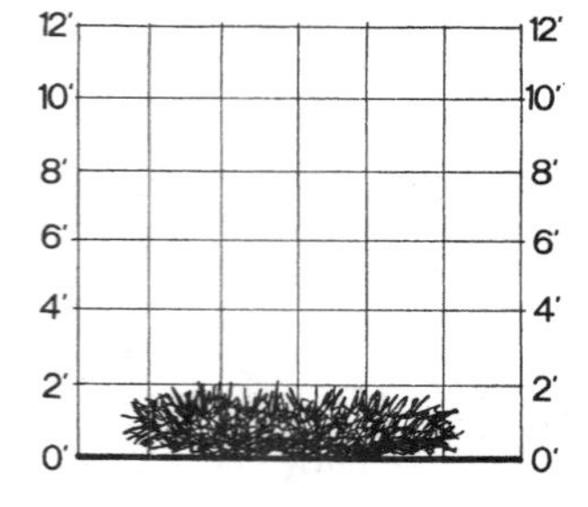

Juniperus sabina 'Arcadia' **Evergreen**
Arcadia Juniper

Very low growing. Hard to classify as a ground cover because very slow growth requires some ground plane treatment between newly planted shrubs. Bright green foliage. Slow growth.

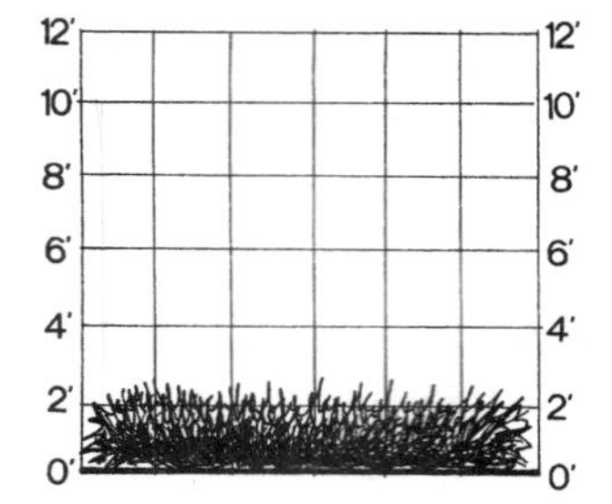

Juniperus sabina 'Tamariscifolia' **Evergreen**
Tam Juniper

Higher than 'Arcadia' but still much lower and wide-spreading than 'Pfitzerana'. Good choice as a bank cover as its moderate growth rate is probably the fastest among junipers. Blue green foliage forms a dense mat. Slow growth.

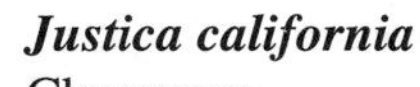

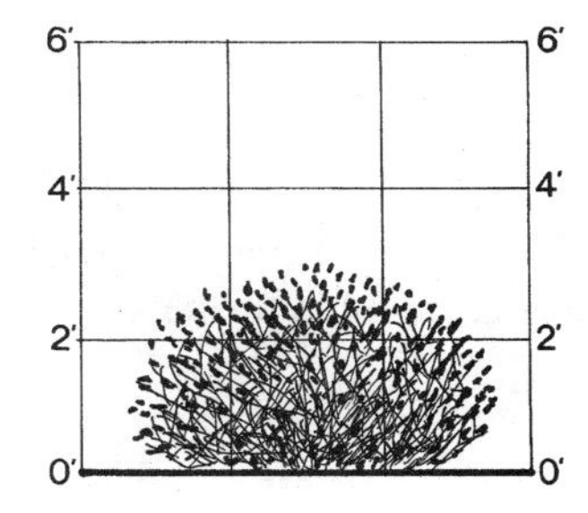

Justica california **Semi-evergreen**
Chuparosa

Mounding shrub with an irregular habit. Desert native. Foliage is not as dependable as flowers, which are bright red to orange and tubular shaped. Flowers attract hummingbirds. Foliage, when it is on the plant, is light green and oval. Plant is drought deciduous and will freeze to ground in a cold winter but recovers quickly. Not a stand alone plant but has uses when other material is placed behind it for visual depth. Fast growth.

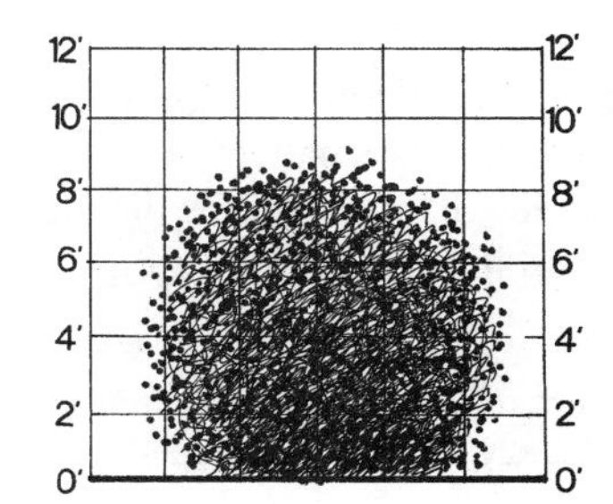

Lantana camara **Evergreen**
Bush Lantana

The large scale, shrub form of Lantana. If kept in frost free conditions, this plant can get huge. Six foot height with 8, 10, and even wider spreads is not uncommon. The species has multicolored flowers that are yellow gold in the center and ringed with cerise pink. Sometimes a lavender third ring appears, usually on older plants with older blooms. Will freeze to the ground in winter in open areas but recovers quickly. In extreme drought conditions it will exhibit drought deciduousness but, for the most part, it is evergreen. I like to use this and other Lantanas in conjunction with Bougainvillea as they have similar cultural requirements and both will produce more intense winter blossoms if watering is cut back in late summer. Fast growth.

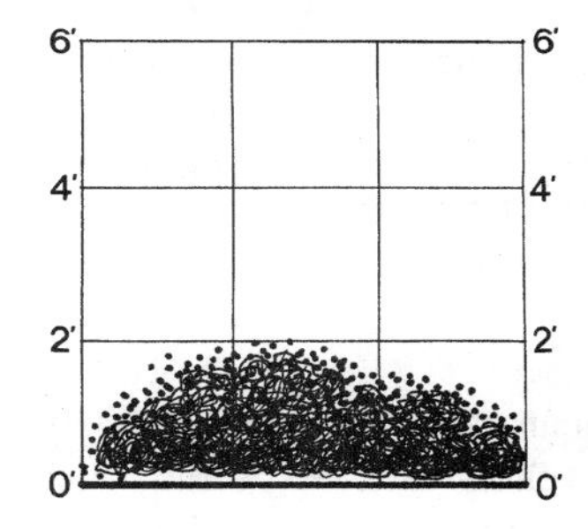

★ ***Lantana sellowiana (Lantana montevidensis)*** **Evergreen**
Trailing Lantana

The ultimate transition plant material for the desert. Green enough to border the oasis garden and colorful enough to lead the eye out and transition into the desert garden or even open desert. Legitimate debate occurs over whether this plant should be classified as a shrub or a ground cover. It is used frequently as a large scale, loose, rambling ground cover. It is also used for spot color and is excellent in pots or raised planters. I classify it with the shrubs as it is difficult to keep any Lantana below 18 inches. Disagreement also occurs as to the origins and correct classification of the myriad of cultivars. Some say *camara* while others insist *sellowiana* (most recently *montevidensis*) and some suspect hybridization between the two. I suspect cultivars originate from all three sources and once found they are vegetatively propagated to insure trueness of desirable characteristics. For this reason specify Lantana and then the cultivar and don't bother with the actual species. Reputable nurserymen will supply the correct plant. The most popular *Lantana sellowiana*, by far, is the common purple variety which grows at about 2 feet high and spreads 6 feet easily. It is a very prolific bloomer and is not fussy about soil. It becomes more drought hardy as it matures but newly established plants should receive a moderate amount of water. Refrain from using in direct proximity to agricultural areas as the plant is known to attract whiteflies. All Lantanas exhibit fast growth. Other Lantana cultivars of note follow.

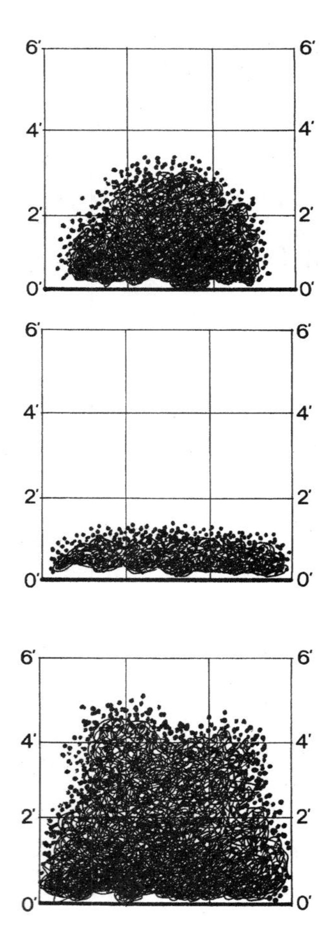

Lantana sellowiana '_Confetti_' **Evergreen**

A riot of color. Blossoms very similar to *Lantana camara* so be sure container plants are tagged and from a reliable grower. Three feet high by 8 feet wide. Yellow, pink, and lavender colors occur within the blossoms.

Lantana sellowiana '_Gold Mound_' **Evergreen**

Smaller in size than 'Sunburst' to be described below. Has the goldest blossoms of the yellow varieties and the blossoms are smaller in circumference. Perhaps, because more of the foliage is seen, it appears to be the greenest of the Lantanas. Well-behaved plant. Good in pots. Two feet high by 5 feet wide.

Lantana sellowiana '_Radiation_' **Evergreen**

Brilliant orange blossoms with golden pumpkin centers. Very tough. Probably the hardiest Lantana and always the quickest to recover from a severe frost. Gets very large — 4 feet high by a minimum of 8 feet wide. Also the fastest growing Lantana. Looks good with Mexican bird-of-paradise (*Poinciana pulcherrima*) as the blossoms are in the same color range.

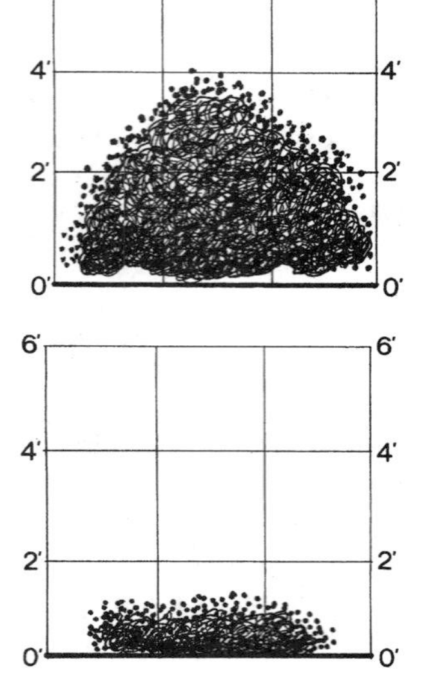

Lantana sellowiana '_Sunburst_' **Evergreen**

Largest and hardiest of the yellow Lantanas. Yellow fades as blossoms mature to faint yellow. Looks good with yellow varieties of Lady Bank's Rose (*Rosea banksiae*) and Cassia as flowers are in the same color spectrum.

Lantana sellowiana '_White_' **Evergreen**

Little is known about some of the pure white varieties becoming available in limited quantities from a few growers. Listed here to make note of the fact the white does exist. White varieties are the most frost tender of the lantanas.

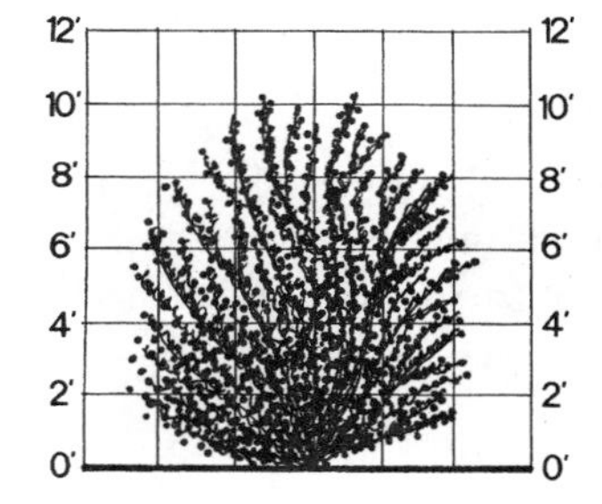

Larrea tridentata **Semi-evergreen**
Creosote Bush

Primary indicator plant of the Mojave Desert. Also occurs with frequency on the desert floor of the Sonoran, Chihuahuan, and Great Basin Deserts. Suffice it to say, if you see a creosote bush, you are somewhere within a desert environment. Plant can be, and often is, drought deciduous. When in leaf, tiny leaflets are bright green with new growth being light yellow-green. Creosote blooms intermittently year-round with the heaviest blooms following the infrequent desert rains. Small yellow blossoms are succeeded by tiny whitish-gray Pussy Willow-type fruit. Leaves are crushed commercially for creosote oil, the preservative used in railroad ties and other woods. Several botanists believe the Creosote secretes a root toxin that discourages other plants, especially other Creosotes from rooting within a specific radius (± 10 feet) of it. This would help to explain the somewhat random geometric spacing of the plants in the Creosote Flat parts of the open desert. Scientific evidence is not conclusive on this issue at this time. Desert dwellers become well aware of the pungent odor of creosote after a desert cloudburst. The odor comes from the high oil content in the leaves. Slow, methodical growth.

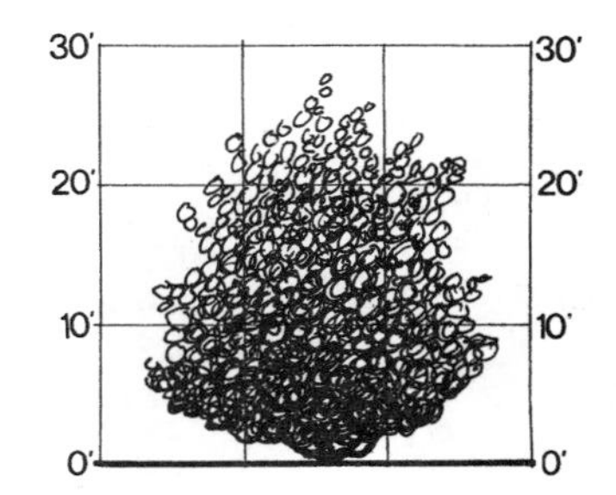

Laurus nobilis **Evergreen**
Sweet Bay Laurel

Large shrub, bordering on a tree. I classify it as a shrub because the plant wants to grow full to the ground and suckers profusely at its base. Thus, although it can be trimmed as a tree, its natural tendency is to remain a shrub. Good large scale screen. Could be used as a substitute to *Nerium oleander* in a protected situation such as under existing large-scale trees. This plant's biggest drawback is that it prefers some afternoon shade and younger plants will freeze in a hard frost. This is the shrub that provides bay leaves for cooking. Moderate growth with water, it becomes drought tolerant with maturity.

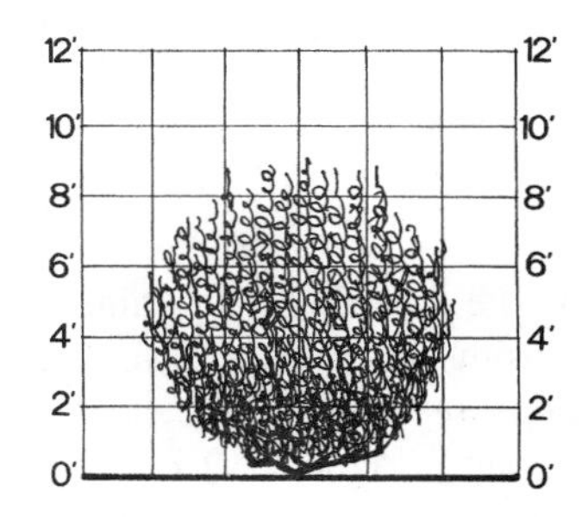

★ *Leucophyllum frutescens* **Semi-evergreen**
Texas Ranger

Native to the Chihuahuan Desert of Texas, and thus the common name. Gray-leafed shrub that sports a profusion of lavender flowers in mid-spring and early summer when hotter weather triggers their appearance. When climatic conditions are right, the plant will oftentimes offer a fall floral display. Plant has a leaf structure that swells when water is present and shrinks and repels sunlight in times of drought. Moderately watered specimens look better than less watered plants. Therefore, even though the plant is drought tolerant, it needs more water to look its best. Fast growth. Texas Ranger makes the star performer list because it fulfills a variety of needs and its flower show can be spectacular.

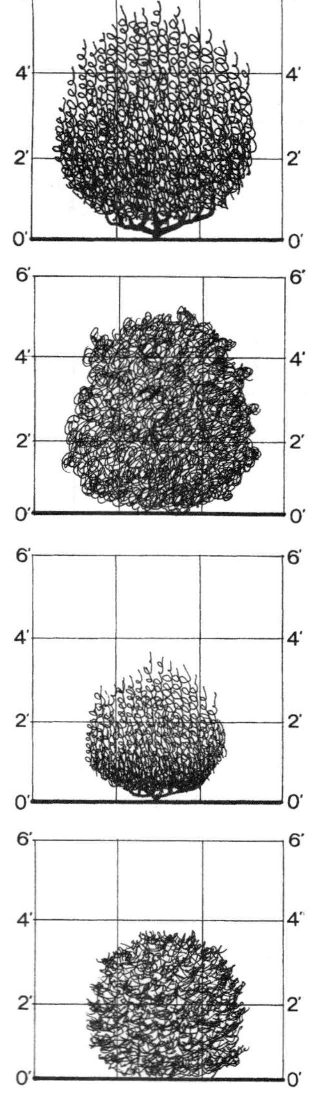

★ Leucophyllum frutescens 'Green Cloud' **Semi-evergreen**
Green Cloud Texas Ranger

Has all the attributes of the species but is slightly smaller and its foliage is green. Flower color and blooming period are the same. Check availability before specifying large quantities, as 'Green Cloud' is somewhat hard to get. Fast growth.

Leucophyllum laevigatum **Semi-evergreen**
Chihuahuan Sage

Bluer flowers than the other tall species of *Leucophyllum*. Looser, rangier habit and sparser foliage makes it a poor selection for up-close viewing. This heavy bloomer is employed frequently in median and roadway design where what it lacks in foliage is made up for in color show. Fast growth.

★ ***Leucophyllum langmaniae 'Rio Bravo'*** **Semi-evergreen**
Dwarf Green Texas Ranger

Valued for its floral extravaganza. Somewhat smaller and denser than 'Green Cloud.' Looks good as a backdrop for Purple Lantana. Verify availability before specifying. Fast growth.

Leucophyllum zygophyllum 'Cimarron' **Semi-evergreen**
Blue Ranger

Hats off, once again, to Mountain States Nursery for introducing this cultivar. Blue Ranger is a floral show stopper in every sense of the word. It is giving 'Thundercloud' a real run for its money. Same height as 'Thunder Cloud' with looser habit and ever more profuse blossoms. A terrific little shrub. Fast growth.

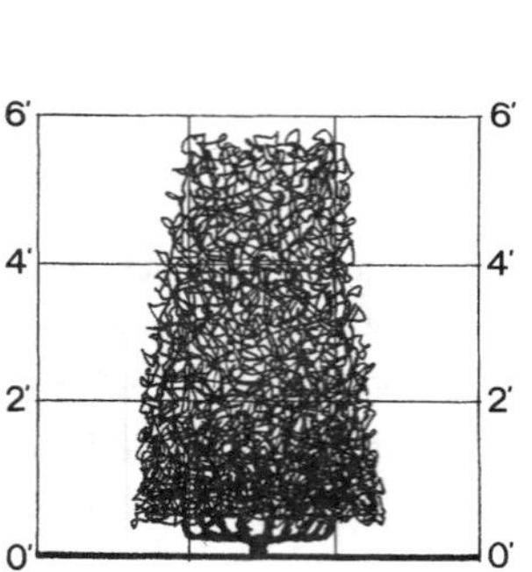

Ligustrum japonicum "Texanum" **Evergreen**
Waxleaf Privet

Can develop into a medium size tree in the open and if so trained. For the purposes of this discussion, I suggest using this plant as a formal clipped shrub or hedge plant. Will sunburn against reflective surfaces. Berries produced from insignificant flowers will stain pavement. It is better to keep this shrub out in the open or in a planter bed. Can be severely pruned even to the point of topiary. Very good choice for hedge or medium size screen. Fast growth.

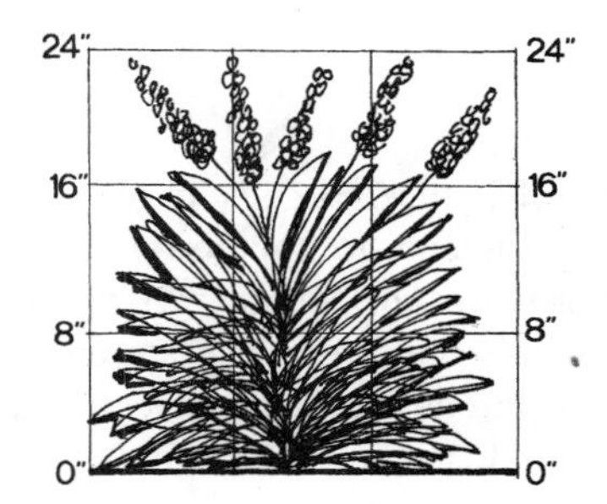

★ *Liriope muscari* **Evergreen**
Big Blue Lily Turf

Twelve- to 18-inch-high, grass-like plant. Foliage is dark green. Common name is derived from blue flower spikes that jut out above foliage. Needs protection from the west sun. An excellent, small-scale, water effect plant. Good for the atrium or courtyard. Works well with Dwarf Pampas Grass, Nolina, *Moraea iridioides*, and Mondo Grass (*Ophiopogon japonicus*). Moderate growth rate.

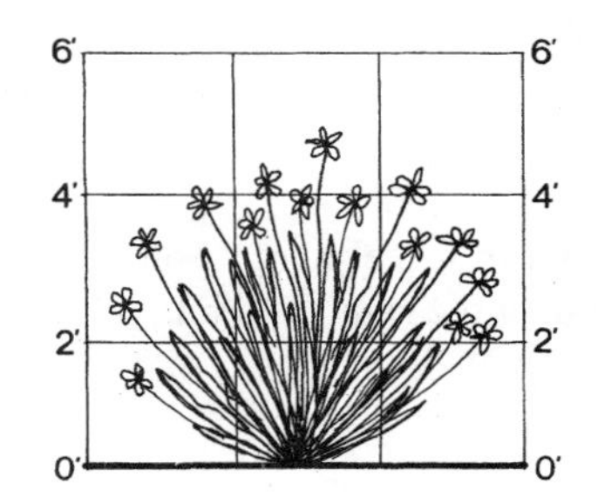

★ *Moraea iridioides (Dietes vegata)* **Evergreen**
Fortnight Lily

Intensively used 3-foot high, grass-like plant. Does best in the low desert. Needs winter protection in middle elevation desert and is risky in the high desert. Beloved for its long lasting bloom period. Flowers are iris-like, white with dark splotches about 2 inches in diameter. Plant sets out a profusion of blooms every 2 or 3 weeks. Will tolerate full sun but prefers some afternoon shade. Fast growth.

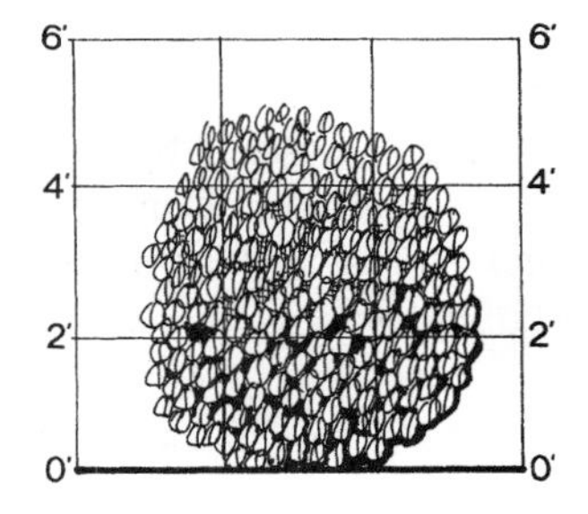

Murraya paniculata **Evergreen**
Orange Jessamine

First and foremost — this plant needs protection. Would not suggest using it except that it is frequently requested on high-end residential projects. Keep out of south and west sun and protect it from frost. Prized by homeowners for its glossy, pendulous branches and white, jasmine scented flowers which bloom throughout the fall and winter months. Slow growth. Specify larger plants for any immediate impact.

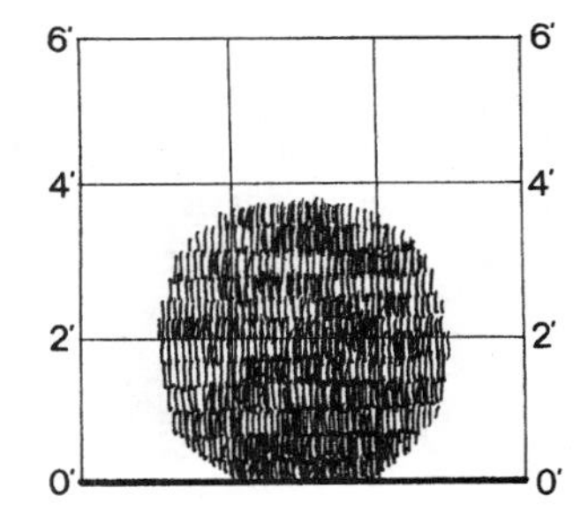

★ *Myrtus communis 'Compacta'* **Evergreen**
Dwarf Myrtle

All the attributes of the species but smaller. Probably grows larger in sandy soils than anywhere else. Four feet wide and as round although it is sometimes larger. The species (*M. communis*) will get 10 to 12 feet round, and although it can be maintained at 6 to 8 feet, it would require a constant pruning effort. The value of 'Compacta' is its toughness, dependable habit, dense dark green foliage, and minimal maintenance requirements when properly used. Moderate growth rate.

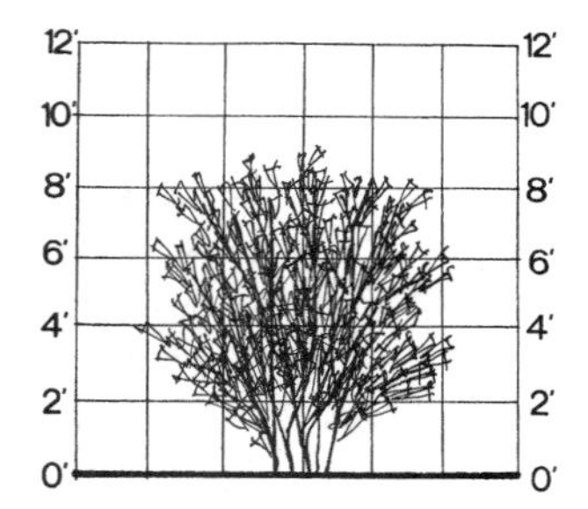

★ *Nandina domestica* **Evergreen**
Heavenly Bamboo

Not a true bamboo. A plant with a lot of virtues. Biggest drawback is that although it will take full sun, this condition tends to stunt its overall growth. Species is the largest *Nandina* which usually tops out at 6 feet high but 8 to 10 feet is not uncommon. New growth is pinkish red. Mature growth is light green. In winter sun and frost conditions foliage can become brilliant red for 2 or 3 months. Foliage itself is quite lacy on upright multiple stems. With cultural needs met, all *Nandinas* are fast growers. This is a beautiful plant with a number of useful cultivars, some of which are listed below.

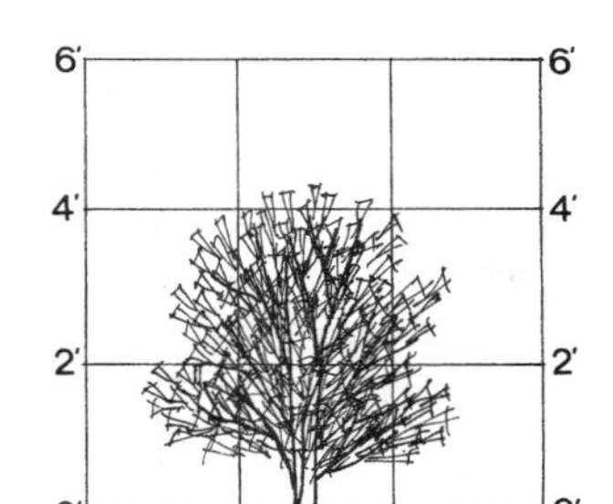

***Nandina domestica* 'Compacta'** **Evergreen**
Dwarf Heavenly Bamboo

Smaller than the species to a maximum of 4 feet high. Somewhat tighter foliage characteristics. Fast growth under the right cultural conditions.

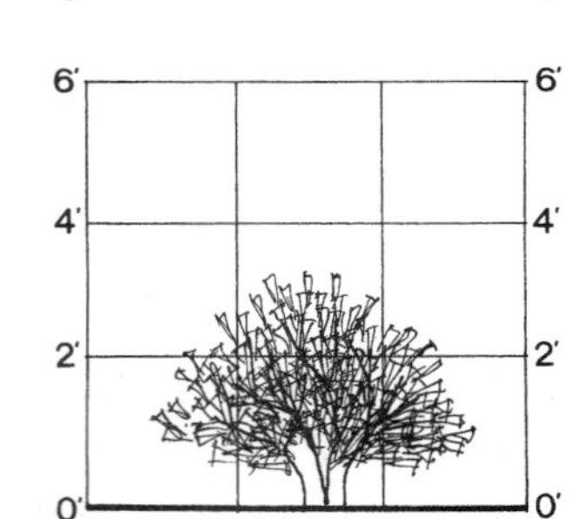

***Nandina domestica* 'Harbour Dwarf'** **Evergreen**
Heavenly Bamboo

More of a tall ground cover to 24 inches high. Spreads by underground rhizomes to roughly half the width (2 feet) of parent plant. Coppery to bronze red in winter. Looks good as a foreground planting to *Photinia fraseri* and with *Duchesnea indica* as an understory ground plane element. Fast to moderate growth rate.

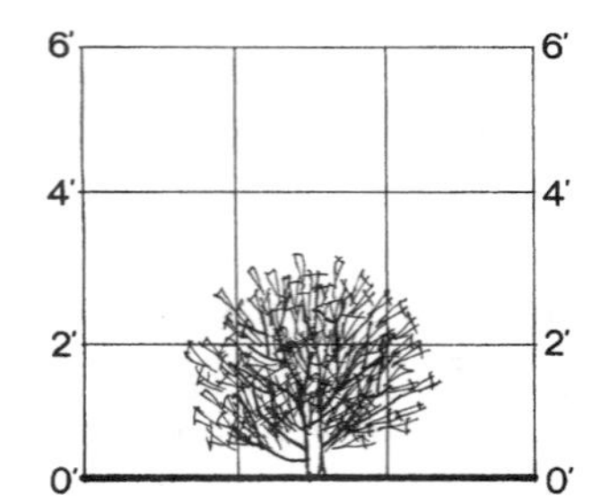

***Nandina domestica* 'Nana'** **Evergreen**
Small Heavenly Bamboo

Twelve inches tall with dome-like growth. Unpredictable growth makes it a poor ground cover selection. Best as a stand alone accent or container plant. A similar variety is 'Gulf Stream' offered by Monrovia Nursery (800-999-9321).

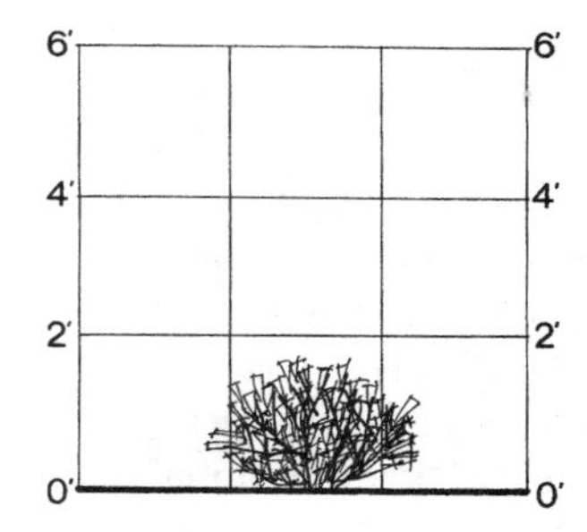

Nandina domestica 'Pygmaea' **Evergreen**
Pygmy Heavenly Bamboo

Dense, clumping, and grassy. Ten inches high with an occasional taller shoot. Brilliant red in winter. Plant at 12 inches on center. Excellent ground cover.

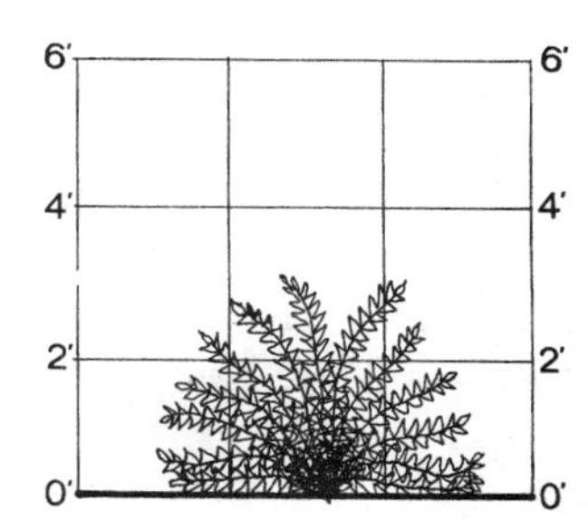

Nephrolepis cordifolia **Evergreen**
Sword Fern

Only ground plane fern with broad leaves that can confidently be grown in the desert. Light, bright green fronds are tufted vertically to three feet high. Needs sun and frost protection. East exposure with a deep overhang is a good location as are atriums and courtyards. Plant at 12 to 18 inches on center for loose ground cover. Good water effect plant. Moderate growth rate. Fertilize periodically with high nitrogen fertilizer for best frond color.

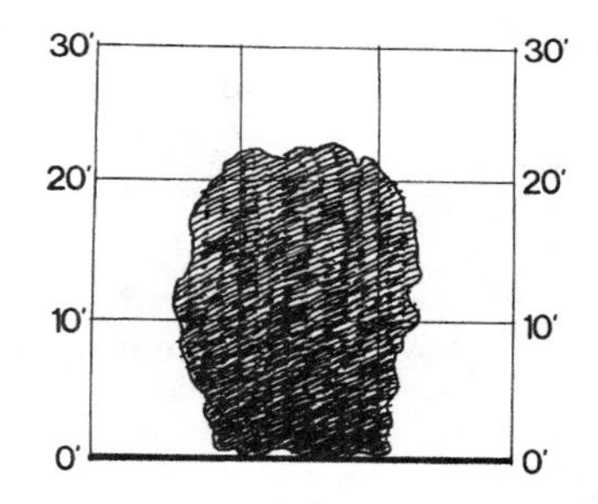

Nerium oleander **Evergreen**
Common Oleander

Perhaps no plant in the desert is more loved or despised depending on where it is used and the observer's point of view. Deep blue-green foliage. Extremely fast growing. All parts of the Oleander, and especially the leaves, are poisonous. Not a good selection for children's play areas or around livestock enclosures. Common variety can get 12 to 20 feet high depending on location. As hedges, they grow somewhat smaller if planted on 4, 5, or 6foot centers. Under no circumstances will it be an easy task to keep Common Oleander under 10 feet. Aside from wind and vision screen capabilities, the color show of the familiar white or pink blossoms goes on all spring into early fall. Be sure to specify white or pink blossoms if you only want one color. Common Oleander is frequently trained on standards as a tree. This is a nice effect but requires lots of maintenance as the trunk standard is floppy and suckers profusely from its base. Can't beat the color, however. In my opinion, *Lagerstroemia* would be a better choice for this application. Largest Oleander is the white 'Sister Agnes'. Less vigorous white is 'Casablanca.' 'Algiers' is a medium sized red. 'Mrs. Roeding' is a dependable 6- to 8-foot-high, excellent pink and one I frequently use. Larger Oleanders exhibit extremely fast growth. Smaller or dwarf varieties are described below.

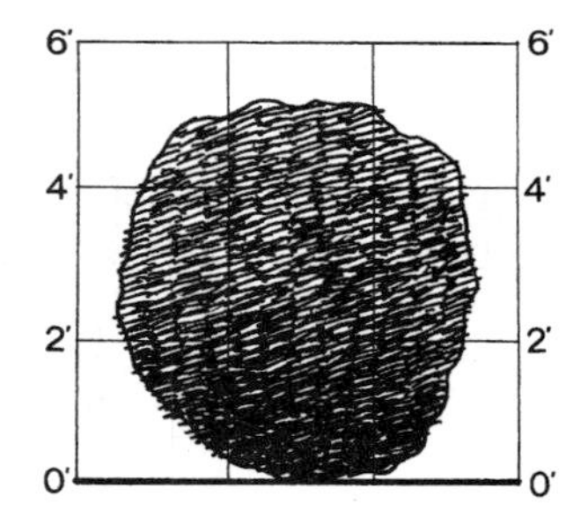

★ *Nerium oleander 'Petite Pink'* **Evergreen**
Dwarf Oleander

This is, by far, the most popular and commonly used Oleander in most desert communities. Brilliant light pink flowers in masses throughout spring and summer and on into winter. Like the species it is extremely tough and grows in all soil conditions. The plant accepts all levels of watering. The only real drawback, besides being poisonous, is that the outer edges of the plant will get nipped in a frost, but it recovers quickly. 'Petite Salmon' is smaller than 'Petite Pink' and has a rounded looser habit. 'Petite Salmon' also stands up a little better in a severe frost. Little is known about 'Little Red' except that it is available and is somewhat smaller than 'Petite Pink'. Fast growth with moderate irrigation for all Dwarf Oleanders.

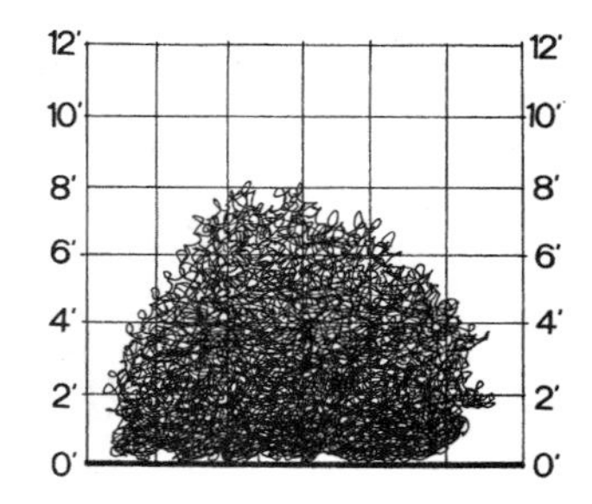

Osmanthus fragrans **Evergreen**
Sweet Olive

A nice, large scale, loose habit shrub that should get more use. Looks something like a *Xylosma* except the leaves are a dull light green versus shiny. Spring and summer flowers are inconspicuous but very fragrant. Needs some shade. Will tolerate a variety of soils including acidic. Looks good as a backdrop to *Gardenia* in the scented garden. Drought tolerant at maturity. Moderate growth rate.

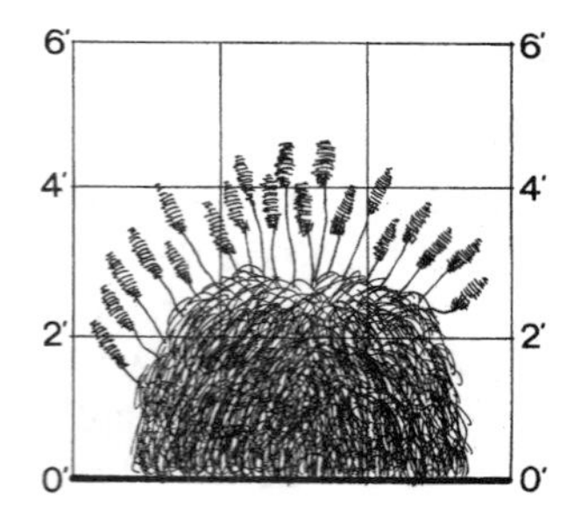

Pennisetum setaceum **Semi-evergreen**
Fountain Grass

Frequently used grass plant 18 inches to 4 feet high with attractive seed plumes. Seeds are viable and the plant is quite invasive. If you are going to use it, count on it to spread — it's that simple. Nice water effect and accent plant. Drought tolerant from the outset. Fast growth.

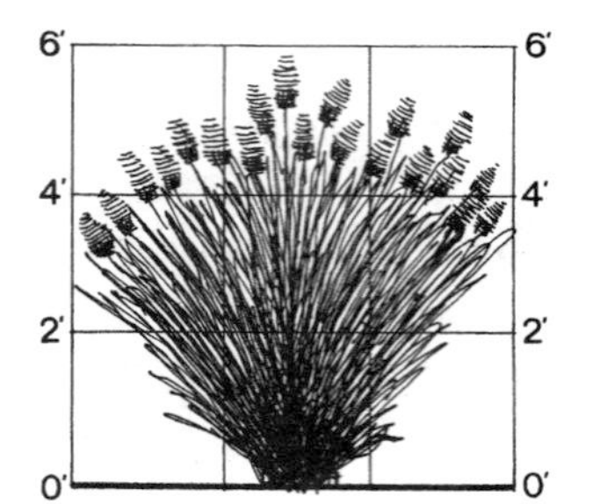

★ *Pennisetum setaceum 'Cupreum'* **Semi-evergreen**
Red Fountain Grass

Larger and coarser than the species. Be advised that it can look quite brown instead of red, especially if kept dry. Becoming more popular as seeds are sterile and it is not as invasive as the species. It does, however, spread by clumping and will take over smaller planting areas. Fast growth.

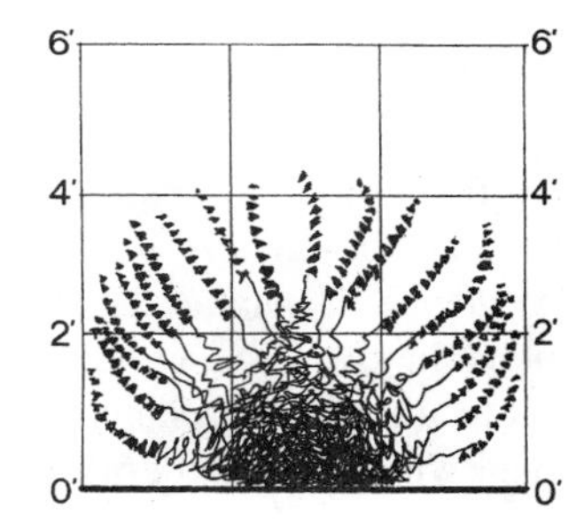

Penstemon spectalilis **Semi-evergreen**
Showy Penstemon

The genus *Penstemon* is quite widespread with over 150 species on the North American continent. Many are native to the western U.S. *Penstemon spectalbilis* grows wild in the chaparral plant communities of San Diego County and is beginning to naturalize inland, being introduced through wildflower and native shrub hydroseed mixes. Rose to purple flowers with an occasional blue. Like most plants with tubular flowers, they readily attract hummingbirds. Likes to be dry — do not overwater. Fast growth and short-lived (3 to 5 years).

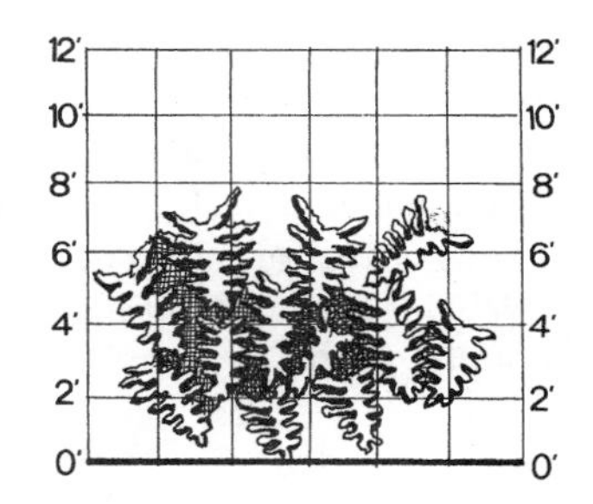

★ *Philodendron selloum* **Evergreen**
Split-leaf Philodendron

In the shady tropical garden, this is indeed a star performer. Do not use in deep shade as the plant will reach for (grow out towards) any available light. Great plant to use under a centrally located skylight. Dark green, heart-shaped leaves are deeply cut, 3 feet long by 18 inches wide. Wash leaves occasionally with a garden hose as clean foliage gives it a far better appearance. A plant can outgrow the smaller space and needs to be cut back to the ground, in which case it quickly begins to reestablish itself. Extremely fast growth rate can be easily accelerated with a high nitrogen liquid fertilizer. Certainly a plant for the tropical oasis type garden.

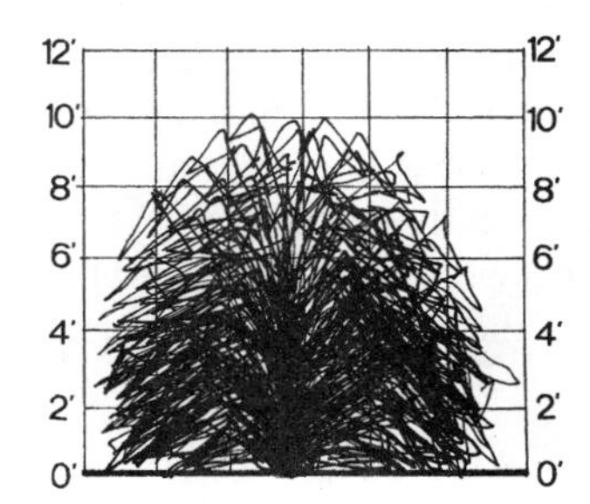

Phormium tenax **Evergreen**
New Zealand Flax

Large, somewhat grass-like plants. Strap-like leaves are 5 inches wide and 6 to 10 feet long. Foliage is always some variety of red or purple. All exposures and soils. Massive at maturity — could be a good complement to Pampas grass (big foliage vs. thin foliage; Dark red vs. light green). Red and yellow flower stalks extend out of bent leaves for 2 feet. Fast growth.

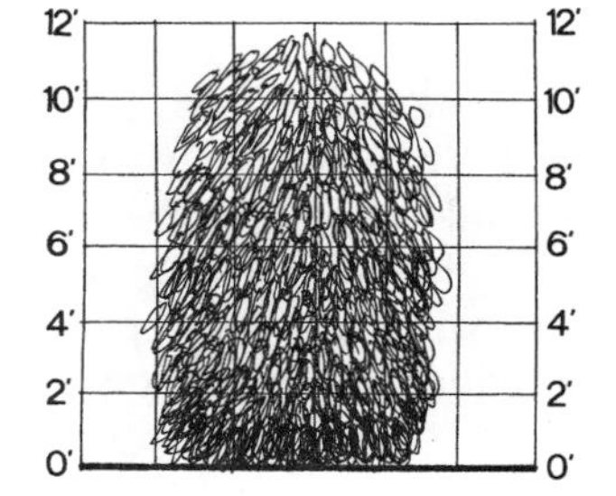

★ *Photinia fraseri* **Evergreen**
Fraser's Photinia

Large shrub that is purple-red on its growing tips and will turn entirely that color in cold weather. Nice spring flower show of creamy white flowers. Takes all exposures but will cook in reflected heat of west glass. Can be used as a formal or informal hedge and can be kept smaller with tighter spacing. Five inch long, oblong, serrated leaves offer a thick contrast as a backdrop to Nandinas, while being in the same color spectrum. Fast growth.

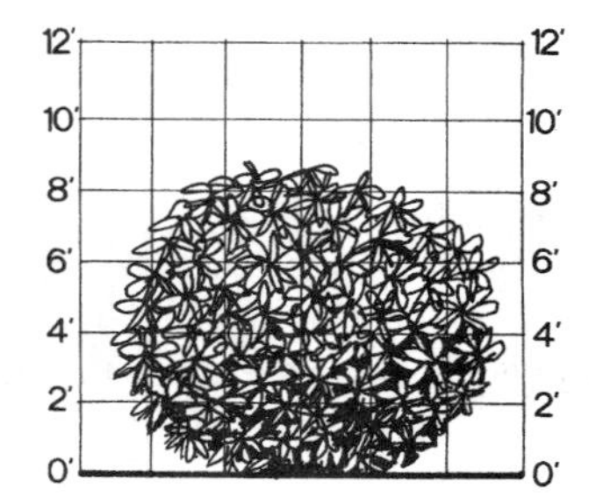

Pittosporum tobira **Evergreen**
Mock Orange

Dark green, whorled foliage. White flat flower masses in spring are quite aromatic. Can get huge, so watch where you put it. Clean rounded character defies the need for pruning. Variety 'Variegata' is smaller, has light green with cream edged foliage, and is not quite as hardy. Use all Pittosporums on east exposures or in filtered light for best results. Young plants will burn in direct summer sunlight. Drought resistant with age. Well drained soil is a must. Moderate growth rate.

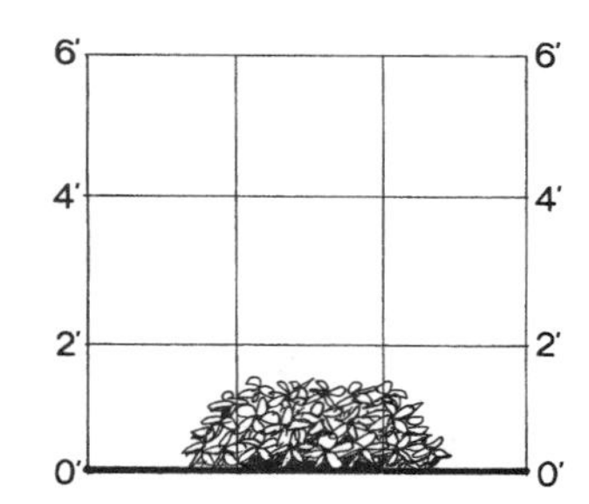

Pittosporum tobira 'Wheeler's Dwarf' ***Evergreen***
Dwarf Mock Orange

Extremely popular in the low desert cities. I do not list it as a star performer because of its slow growth rate and its sun tenderness. In protected locations, it is quite handsome. Dense growing leaves are the same shape as species but thinner and a little shorter. New leaves are an attractive, glossy light green. Has a flower show but nothing on the scale of the species. Moderate growth rate.

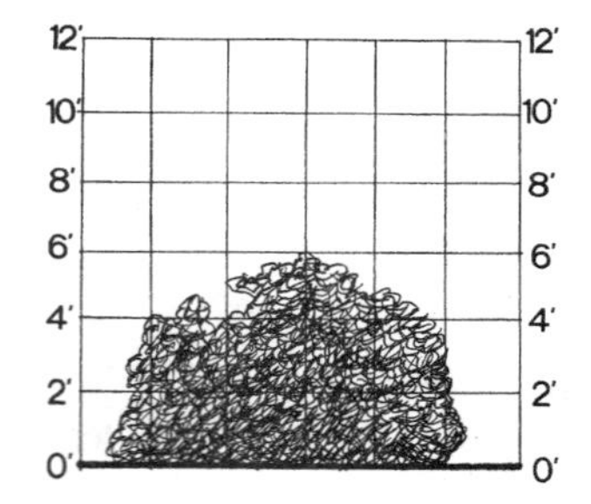

Plumbago auriculata **Semi-evergreen**
Cape Plumbago

Massive light blue flower show from March to Christmas makes this loose low-growing shrub very popular. Its primary disadvantage is that it will die back to the ground in a cold winter. It comes back from a hard frost rather quickly with the onslaught of hot weather. Plumbago takes full sun, although the blue flowers literally bleach in this exposure. If this is the desired effect it is better to use the variety 'Alba' which has white flowers. East exposures are good and south is the best for flower production and color. Fast growth.

Plumeria rubra **Evergreen**
Frangipani

This deciduous shrub is valued for its exotic leaves and showy late spring to early fall floral display. The 10- to 15-inch-long leaves are whorled, bright green, leathery, and pointed at the tips. Floral clusters appear at the center of the whorls. Several colors are available (red, yellow, white, pink, purple),s so be sure to specify desired hue. Prefers afternoon shade, frost protection, and dry winter soil. Fast growth.

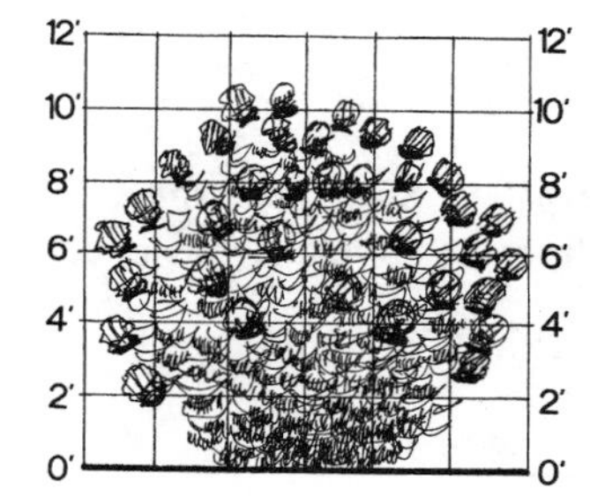

★ ***Poinciana pulcherrima***
(Caesalpinia pulcherrima)
Mexican Bird-of-Paradise

Deciduous

A large scale summer all star. Brilliant, 8-inch round balls of golden orange flowers with deep red protruding stamens. In the swelter of late August this is truly a refreshing sight to see. You can count on it to freeze to the ground nearly every winter. In fact, it is the ultimate plant to use in open throw away areas. In this application you can cut it to the ground in November and it will be back by May and 6 to 8 feet high by the end of July. Extremely fast growth. Needs very little water. Botanists have changed the genus to *Caesalpinia*, but to me this will always be *Poinciana*— the flower of romance.

★ ***Pyracantha species***
Firethorn

Evergreen

This is one of the toughest groups of shrubs the landscape architect will ever have at his disposal. Once established, they prefer dry soils. They dislike being sprayed and prolonged periods of exposing their foliage to water should be avoided. If the design and budget allow, it is better to irrigate this plant with bubblers or emitters so as to keep the application of water close to the ground and off the plant's leaves. The only disease problem Pyracantha has with any regularity is fire blight which is rarely a problem in the desert. If kept in full sun with the soil left on the dry side, Pyracantha will never let you down. All varieties have thorns to some degree or another. Espaliers seem to have the most wicked thorns while lower growing types have the least. All Pyracanthas function as great barrier plants. All put out a heavy display of creamy white blossoms in spring which are eventually followed by a profusion of clusters of orange or red berries. The berries start out green and mature slowly achieving their brilliant colors in fall. The berries often remain on the plant through winter and birds love them. Foliage is 2 inches long, oval to oblong, and glossy green. All Pyracanthas are moderate to fast growers. Listed below are some of the more commonly used Pyracanthas in the desert.

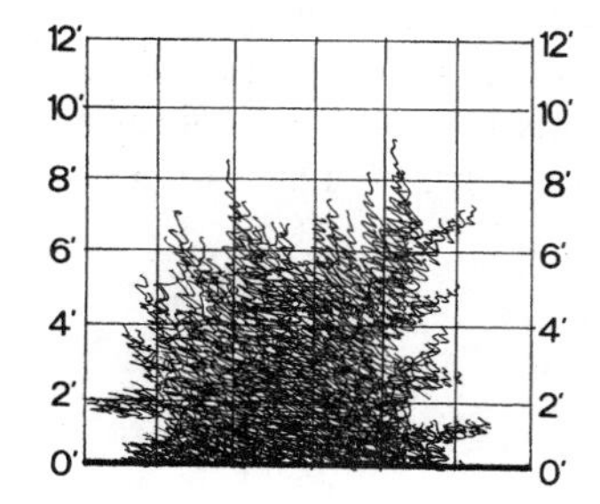

★ ***Pyracantha coccinea 'Lalandei'***

Evergreen

Very hardy, tall shrub or espalier. Orange berries in fall. Flowers appear in March and berries attain mature color in October.

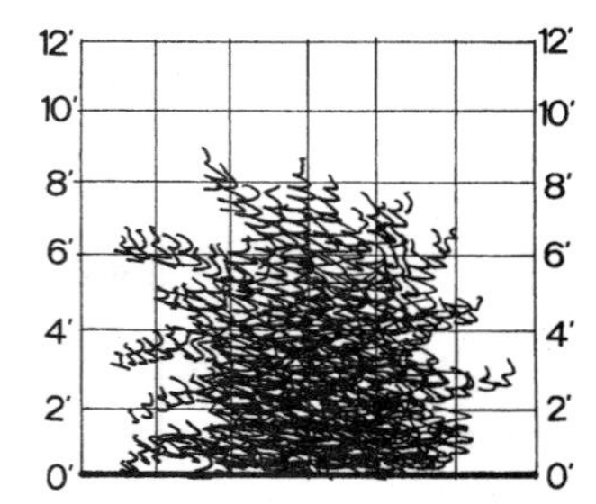

★ *Pyracantha fortuneana* 'Graberi' **Evergreen**

Upright shrub used frequently as an espalier. Spring blossoms. Red berries in late fall persist through winter. The most popular Pyracantha for desert use.

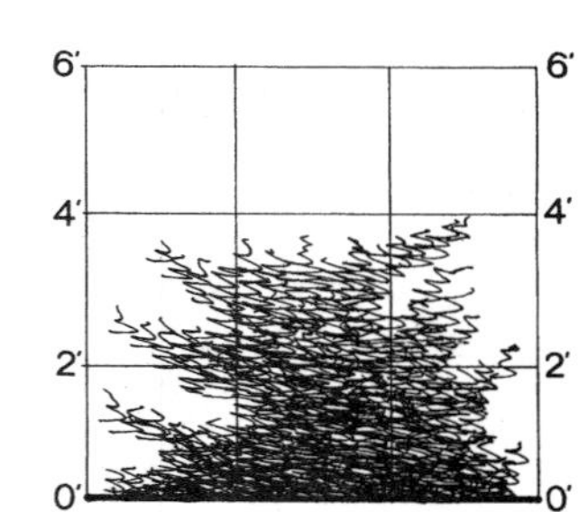

★ *Pyracantha* 'Santa Cruz' **Evergreen**

Actual species origin is debated so specify as noted above. Five foot rounded shrub which can be trimmed to 3 feet high. Plant on 5-foot centers. Red berries.

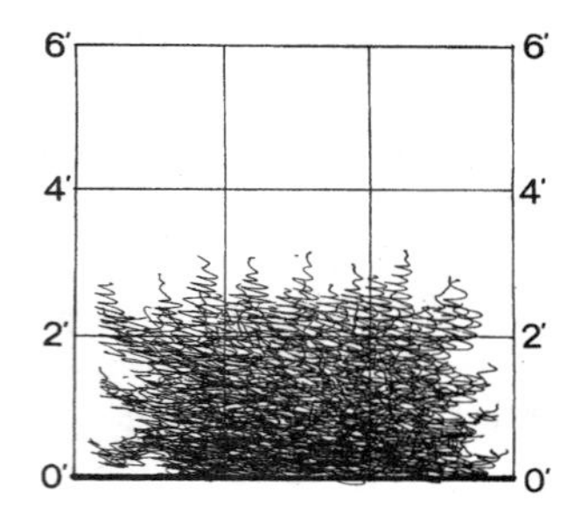

★ *Pyracantha* 'Tiny Tim' **Evergreen**

Very popular, low growing shrub or high ground cover. To 3 feet tall but can be easily kept at 18 inches high by sweeping with automatic hedge shears. Plant on 3-foot centers. Red berries. Tighter foliage than 'Santa Cruz' makes it look fuller. Smallest thorns of all the Pyracanthas. Thorns are still intimidating enough to make 'Tiny Tim' an excellent barrier type planting. Especially useful in parking lot planters.

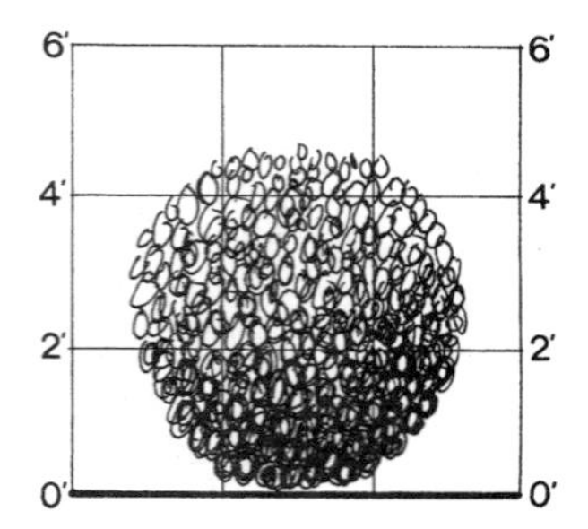

★ *Rhaphiolepis indica* **Evergreen**
India Hawthorn

Shrubs prized for their dependably neat habit and flowering characteristics. Often used as a foundation planting on east and north exposures or in other protected areas. Rhapiolepis, especially younger plants, will cook in full summer sun. *Indica* is a medium shrub to 5 feet high with dark green, whorled, leathery foliage. Magnificent white flower show in spring followed by insignificant dark blue berries. Occasionally exhibits a flower show in fall but it is of less intensity than spring's. Indian Hawthorn looks good as a foreground plant to Frangipani or Pittosporum. All Rhapiolepis grow at a moderate rate. Listed below are some of the more popular varieties.

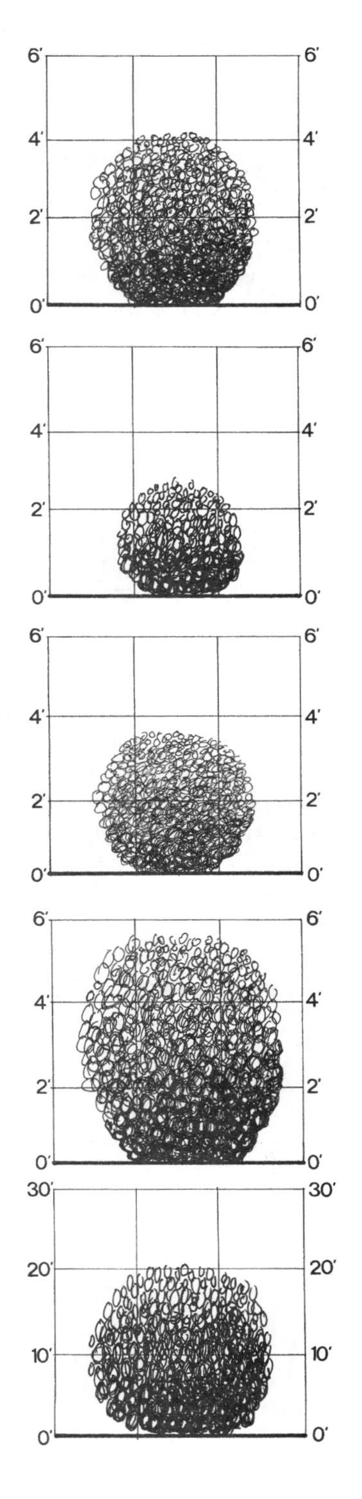

★ ***Rhaphiolepis indica 'Clara'*** **Evergreen**
White India Hawthorne

One of my favorites. White flowers. Four feet high. Coppery new growth makes plant a good choice to use in the foreground of a planting of Photinia fraseri.

★ ***Rhaphiolepis indica 'Coates Crimson'*** **Evergreen**
Red India Hawthorne

AS the name implies, this is the reddest blossoming Rhapiolepis, but flowers are still more reddish pink than true red. Smaller than the species, it can be kept at 2 feet high.

★ ***Rhaphiolepis indica 'Rosea'*** **Evergreen**
Pink India Hawthorne

One of the older varieties. Light-to-medium-pink flowers. Looser growth than the species. Accepts more shade and blooms better there than other varieties.

★ ***Rhaphiolepis indica 'Springtime'*** **Evergreen**
India Hawthorne

As large as or larger than the species. Deep pink blossoms. Probably the hardiest variety to date.

Rhaphiolepis indica 'Majestic Beauty' **Evergreen**
NCN (Large Hawthorne)

The species origin of this plant is unknown. Some growers believe that this plant is a hybrid between the *Eriobotrya* and *Rhapiolepis* genera. In truth, no one knows for sure. In appearance it looks like *Rhapiolepis indica* except it is larger in every aspect — leaves, flowers, and overall size. 'Majestic Beauty' is dependably 10 feet by 10 feet but is often 15 feet high or larger. Spring and fall bring light pink flowers that are more fragrant than *indica*. Used as a backdrop to smaller plant material or sometimes trained as a small tree. Being a large-scale flowering shrub that will behave in a confined area are its biggest attributes. Moderate growth rate.

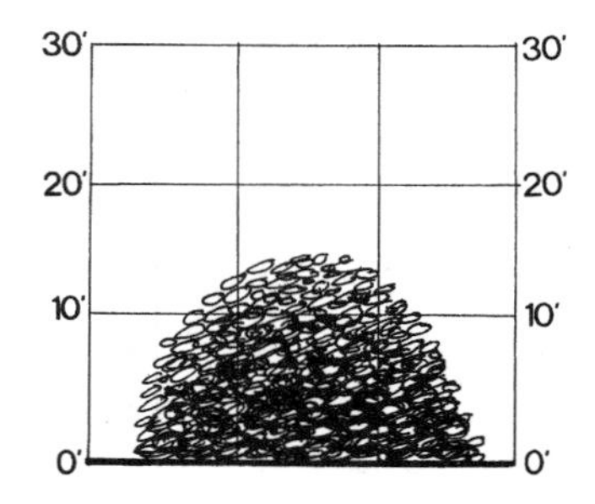

Rhus ovata **Evergreen**
Sugar Bush

Large-scale, wide spreading native shrub. Seen frequently in the middle elevations of the Colorado Desert. Atypical of most other desert species in that it looks deep green. Gives a very lush appearance while being very drought tolerant. A massive shrub to 12 feet, it could be a good substitute for *Nerium oleander*. Shape is that of an informal sprawling mound. Does not look good sheared so it would not be a good choice for a formal screen. Deep red, 1-inch buds form in fall and give way to whitish pink flowers in spring. Flowers develope small hairy, reddish fruit that is coated with a sugary substance (thus the common name). The only real problem is that it will not establish in hot weather so it needs to be planted in spring or fall. Moderate growth rate. With more use, *Rhus ovata* could become a star performer.

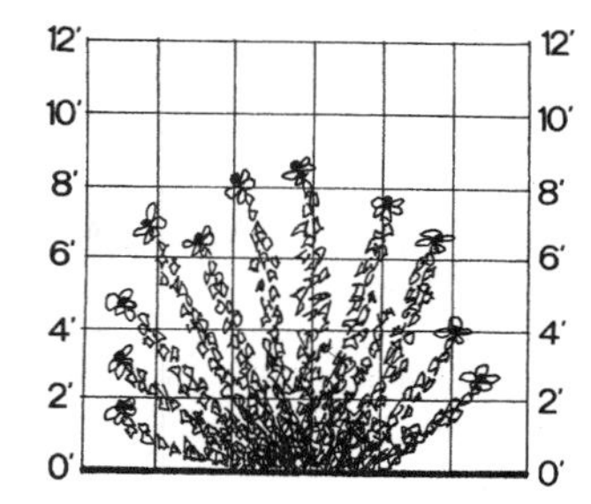

Romneya coulteri **Semi-evergreen**
Matilija Poppy

Spectacular spring blooming, perennial shrub. Gray-green foliage lines upright spreading and thorny branches that fan out at the ground. Vase-shaped plant to 8 feet tall. Two factors inhibit its use. First, *R. coulteri* is very hard to propagate and establish. If you specify it, be sure it's available well in advance of installation. Second, the plant spreads by rhizomes and is extremely invasive. Must be used in contained areas or with root barriers. The huge 8-inch-wide flat white flowers with golden ball-like centers make it worth the trouble. A plant that could be used in throw away areas much like *Poinciana pulcherrima* and can easily be cut to the ground in winter. Once it becomes established it grows rapidly. Remove rhizomes and choke off summer irrigation to retard growth.

Rosa species **Deciduous**

Rose (Consult grower's catalogues.)

This flowering shrub, beloved the world over, would take volumes to adequately describe. I would be remiss if I did not mention it here as roses are always popular and are the most frequently requested plants by residential clients. Because of the cultural requirements and the immense variations between species and the fact that the large majority of roses blossom better when severely pruned, a design that uses any quantity of roses should locate them in a separate rose garden. Broad cultural requirements for garden roses are slightly acid (pH < or > 6.0) soil and filtered light to some afternoon shade. Better rose gardens are the product of one main factor — frequent and ample fertilization. The American Rose Society rates roses on a scale of one to ten, and this system can be used when buying plants. The higher the rating, the better the plant and,correspondingly,the more expensive. Roses bloom extremely fast in the desert so choose varieties with larger (more petals) blossoms as they take longer to develop, open, and fade. The Lady Bank's Rose (*Rosea banksiae*) is a climbing rose that will be described under vines. It is a desert favorite. For garden species any of the numerous grower catalogues will be helpful. One suggestion is: Jackson & Perkins, One Rose Lane, Medford, Oregon 97501-0701, 1-800-292-4769. Growth rate of roses varies, but with fertilization on a regular basis and proper pruning techniques, it is usually quite fast.

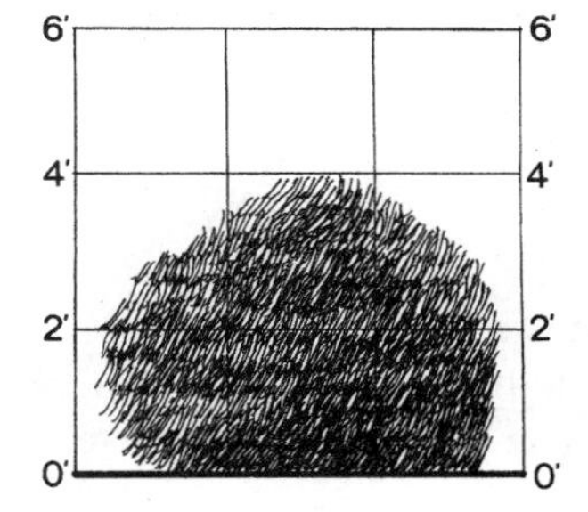

Rosmarinus officinalis **Evergreen**

Rosemary

Gray-green foliaged shrub that will take extremely poor soil conditions and city smog. Only real drawbacks are that mature plants get woody and need thinning and the aromatic pale blue flowers attract bees. Needs some water but gets leggy and unattractive with too much. Foliage used in cooking. Fast growth.

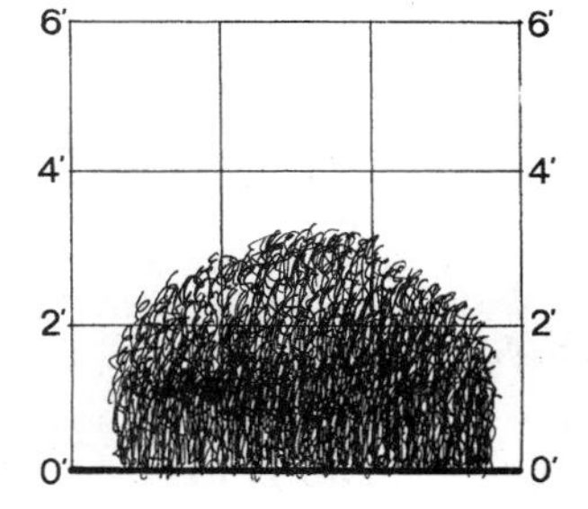

Rosmarinus officinalis 'Prostratus' **Evergreen**

Prostate Rosemary

Smaller than the species (3 feet high) and foliage appears grayer. Excellent when used to cascade over walls or down the face of raised planters. Tough as the species. Fast growth.

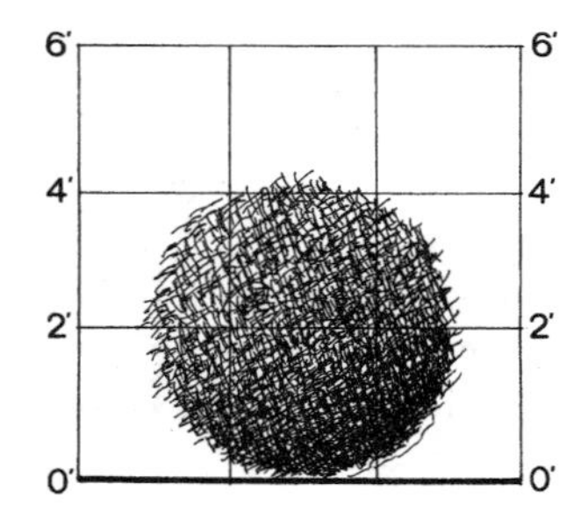

Ruellia pennisularis **Semi-evergreen**
No Common Name

A medium-sized Sonoran Desert native. Unlike most desert shrubs, Ruellia has bright green foliage. Will drop its leaves in winter if temperatures drop below 20° F but it recovers quickly in spring. Medium blue, 1-inch, 4-petaled flowers in spring and summer. Becomes increasingly more drought tolerant as it matures. Fast growth. Ruellia is just beginning to receive widespread use.

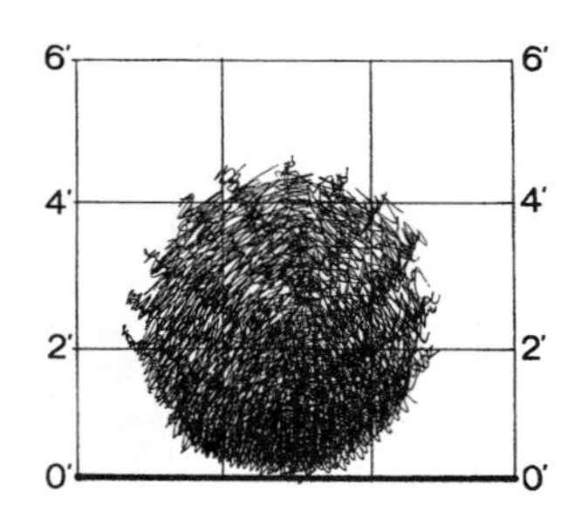

★ ***Salvia greggii*** **Semi-evergreen**
Autumn Sage

Salvia greggii is getting increased use in the Southwest. Native to Mexico and the southern Sonoran Desert, it is beginning to naturalize westward and is being used more and more in native hydroseed mixes. Four feet tall and graceful. It has the greenest foliage of the available Salvias. Flowers ranging from red to rose-pink appear in late spring and last through July. Plant will hold its leaves with occasional deep watering. Does not like a lot of water or irrigation from spray heads. It is perfectly happy to go drought deciduous and this is the best way to treat the plant. Because of its preference to be very dry, this Salvia is exclusively for desert use as even the transitional landscape may be too wet for it. Fast growth.

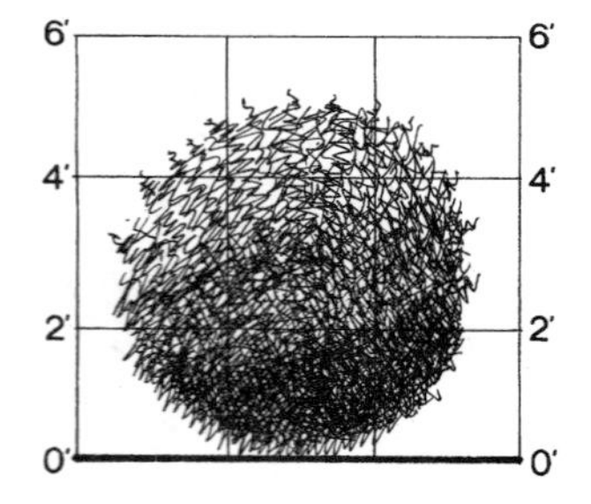

★ ***Salvia leucophylla*** **Semi-evergreen**
Purple Sage

Similar cultural requirements to its cousin *S. leucantha* except it will tolerate a little more summer water and can thus be moved into the transitional garden. Foliage color is gray to whitish-gray. Flowers in late spring are light purple. Larger than *S. greggii*, to 6 feet high. Fast growth. Good in native hydroseed mixes.

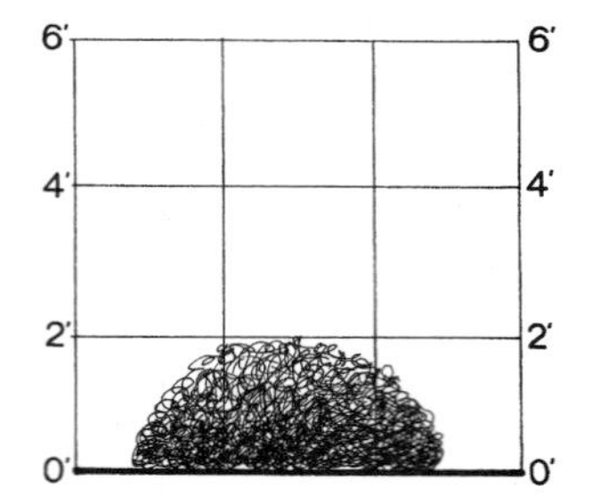

★ ***Santolina chamaecyparissus*** **Evergreen**
Lavender Cotton

Low-growing, gently-mounding shrubs with a stiff habit. Gray-green, fine textured foliage. Yellow, 3/4-inch balled flowers supported on stout stalks rise 4 inches above the foliage crown. Plant does better if occasionally trimmed to 12 inches high. Lavender Cotton will freeze to ground in severe frost but comes back to full size the following spring. Snip off dead blossoms for better flower production. Fast growth.

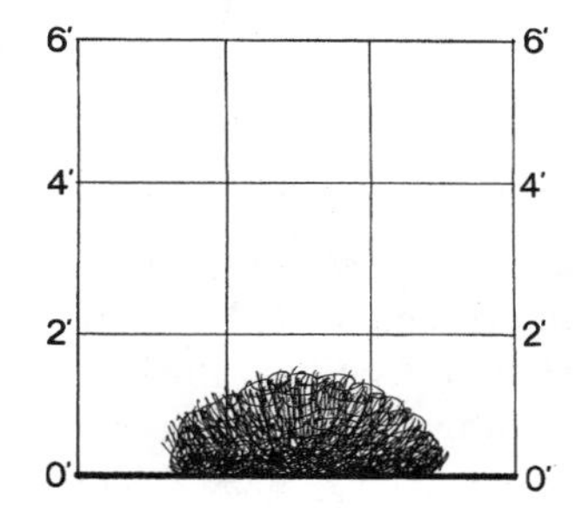

★ *Santolina virens* **Evergreen**
Green Lavender Cotton

Needs well-drained soil and occasional clipping to look its best. Very similar to *S. chamaecyparissus* except a little smaller and foliage is green. Same yellow ball-like flowers. Fast growth. Green foliage gives it a place in the transitional garden bordering the oasis garden.

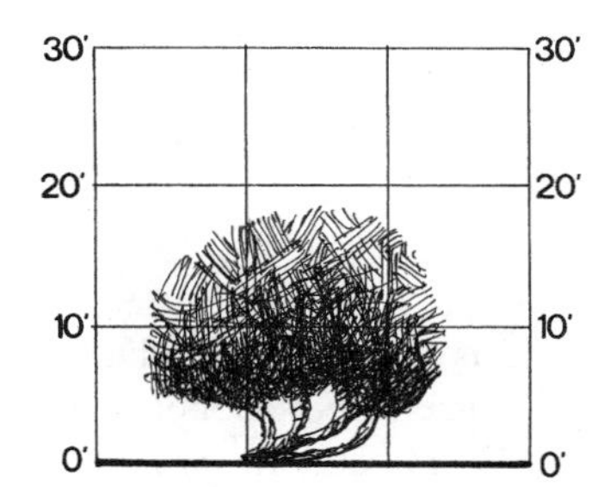

Sarobatus vermiculatus **Semi-evergreen**
Greasewood or Ribbonwood

Large stands or Ribbonwood flats of this shrub can be found at 4000 to 4500 feet throughout the Southwest. Not commonly offered by growers. It is a large-scale shrub you will occasionally come across. Will accept saline soils. Light green in spring to dull green in summer, foliage is supported on twisted orangish brown to cream trunks. Better to use this plant above 1000 feet. It is adaptable to the desert floor and grows well in alkaline soils. Flowers in spring are cottony white puffs with a soft appearance.

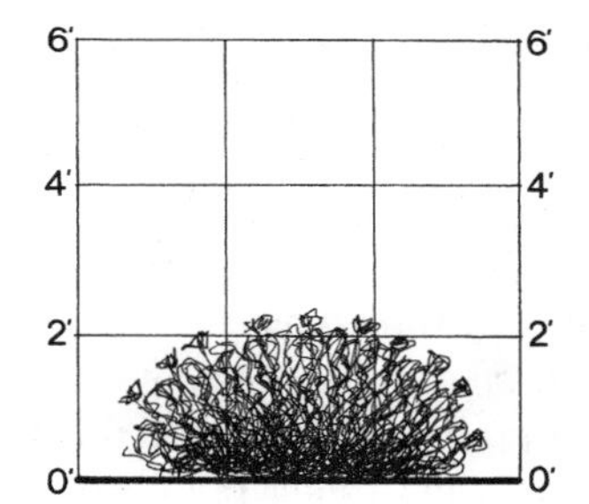

Senecio cineraria **Semi-evergreen**
Dusty Miller

Clumping perennial to 2 1/2 feet high. Valued for its whitish-gray foliage. Yellow, spring and summer appearing, daisy-like flowers are nice. Plant freezes readily. If you want more permanence, *Encelia farinosa* would be a better selection. Often grouped with annuals, where foliage offers color contrast. Foliage is very attractive when downlighted at night. Fast growth.

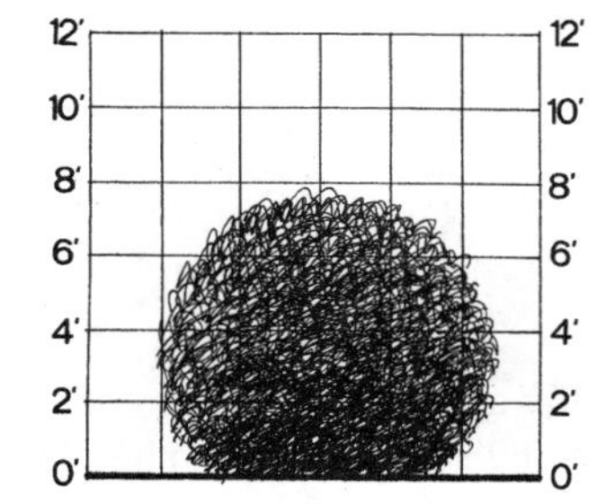

Simmondsia chinensis **Evergreen**
Jojoba

Sonoran Desert native of growing commercial value. Oil garnered from crushed beans is used in ointments and shampoos. The plants are dioecious so male plants need to be spaced throughout commercial stands to guarantee female flowering (insignificant flowers) and fruit production. While more at home above 1500 feet, jojoba can be grown with success on the desert floor. Surprisingly, this shrub takes to clipping and can look quite neat. (It is a member of the Boxwood Family.) Grayish 2-inch-long oval leaves look leathery on informal plants. Two drawbacks are that it is frost tender when young and grows slowly its first 2 seasons. Both these problems are starting to be overcome as some growers are starting to offer 5- and 15-gallon container sizes. Jojoba is a much faster grower from containers. A shrub that is destined to become a star performer with more ornamental landscape use.

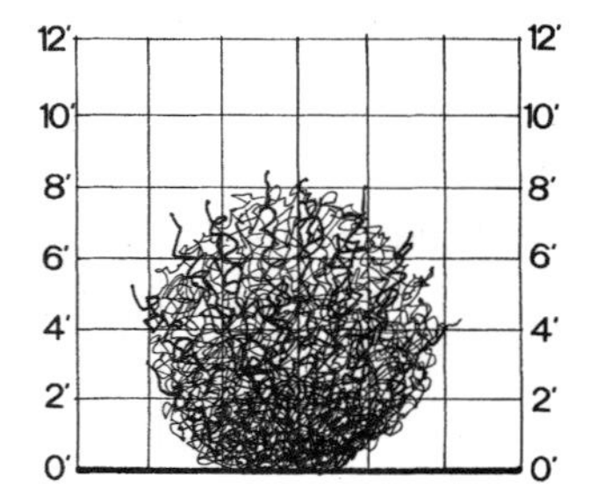

***Solanum rantonnetii* 'Royal Rube'** **Semi-evergreen**
(Lycianthes rantonnetii)
Potato Bush

Often sold as *Lycianthes rantonnetii*, so verify selection with local growers. A rambling shrub that will freeze to the ground in cold winters but comes back fast. Bright green foliage. Beautiful deep blue flowers are 1 inch across with yellow anthers. They occur throughout the hot months (May to September). Needs pruning to avoid getting a leggy look. Many gardeners consider the floral show worth the extra work. Fast growth with some afternoon sun protection.

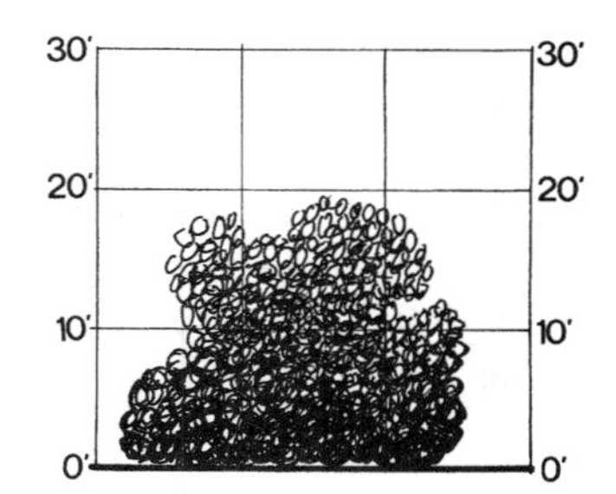

Sophora secundiflora **Evergreen**
Mescal Bean

A very large shrub that can even be trained as a tree. Lots of advantages with one big disadvantage — the seeds it produces are poisonous. Be careful where you use it. Deep green foliage on silvery bark. In spring, 8-inch long pendulous violet aromatic flowers appear. Very attractive. Slow to start, this drought tolerant shrub becomes a moderate grower.

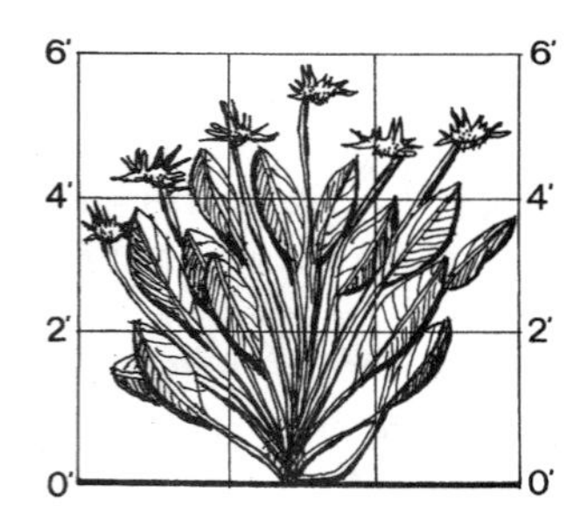

★ *Strelitzia reginae* **Evergreen**
Bird-of-Paradise

For the tropical oasis garden only. Applied correctly, it is a magnificent star performer. Two-foot-long banana-like cupped leaves are supported on long stalks. Thick green flower stalks support exotic orange, yellow, and blue "bird-like" flowers. Five feet high and spreading as wide on whorled multiple leaf stalks. Flower show is most profuse in late fall through winter. Appreciates early fall fertilization to drive the winter floral extravaganza. This plant is the official flower of the City of Los Angeles. While some say it's overused, it rarely disappoints. Moderate growth. Cut flower stalks at base when flowers fade for a neater appearance.

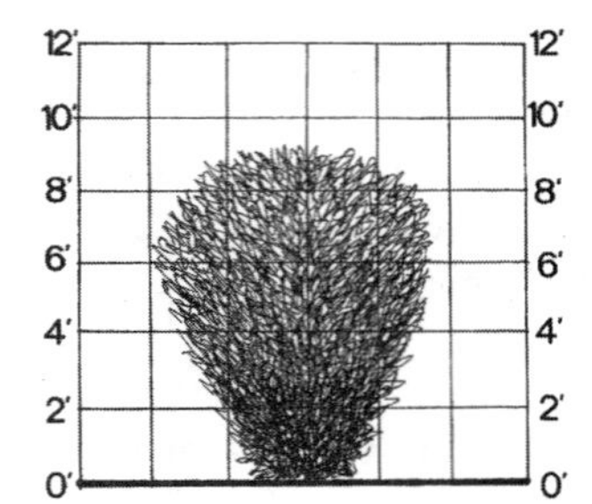

★ *Tecoma stans* **Evergreen**
Yellow Bells

Large scale, sprawling shrub occasionally trained as a small tree or espalier. Blue-green foliage is deeply divided. Showy yellow floral mass from June through January if a frost does not occur or plant is protected from frost. Variety 'Smithii' has orange flowers. Flowers are 2 inches wide and bell-shaped. Young plants die to the ground in frost while mature plants get nipped 12 inches into their canopy. Remove dead wood. Blossoming more intense with liberal applications of high phosphorous fertilizer. Cut fading flowers to prolong bloom period. Fast growth.

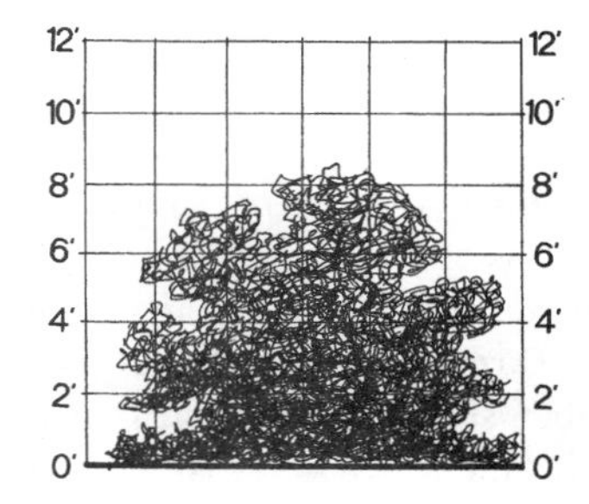

Tecomaria capensis **Evergreen**
Cape Honeysuckle

From the Cape Horn region of South Africa. Luxuriant, glossy, deep green, finely cut foliage. Sprawling habit and rampant growth make this plant an excellent selection for steep bank soil erosion control. Drawbacks are that it will freeze and it takes a moderate amount of water to look its best. It looks its best when producing brilliant orange trumpet-like flowers to 2 inches long throughout fall and winter months. Plant can become massive in fertile soil so give it room to spread out.

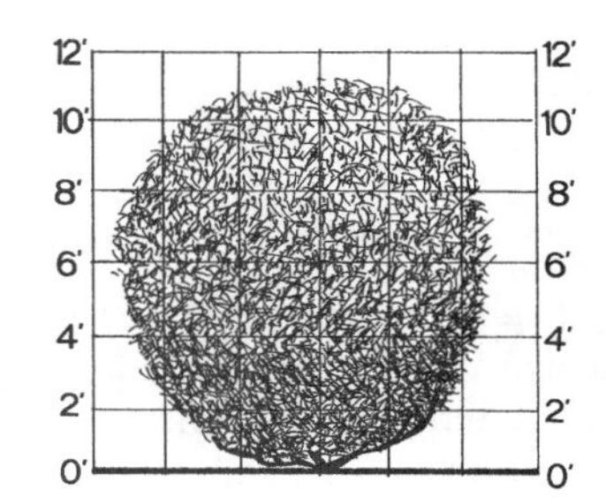

★ *Thevetia neriifolia* **Evergreen**
Yellow Oleander

Graceful, medium green, lacy foliage and an extended bloom period are this plant's biggest attributes. Can be held as a 6-foot-high shrub but requires constant top pruning up to six times a summer. Better to let it go to 12 feet. Often pruned into a small multistemmed tree. Yellow blossoms are tubular and appear year round but are bountiful when the weather is hot. Give this plant frost protection. It will survive in the open but will die back severely (sometimes to ground) and is sometimes slow to recover. Not a true Oleander but is similar in that all parts of the plant are poisonous. Revels in heat, even reflected heat against a west wall. A star performer because it is beloved by many and it is a good selection when used in the right situation.

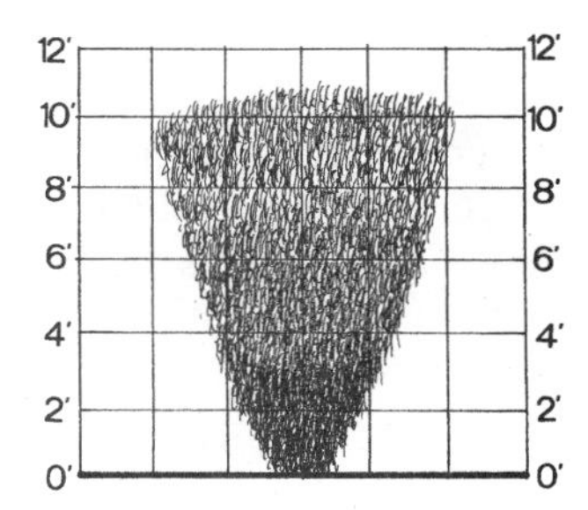

★ *Vauquelinia californica* **Evergreen**
Arizona Rosewood

Here is a shrub whose popularity is going to skyrocket in the next five years. Very similar to *Nerium oleander* except it stays 8 feet high without much pruning and foliage is a lighter, more appealing, green. Also, this plant is not poisonous. Flat white flower clusters in summer months do not rival Oleander's show but they are attractive. As an informal screen, Vauquelinia is unmatched. About the only disadvantage is that it grows at a slow to moderate rate.

★ *Viburnum tinus 'Spring Bouquet'* **Evergreen**
Laurustinus

An evergreen Viburnum that has dark green, oval leaves supported on reddish stems. Sweet Viburnum fragrance is emitted from white flower clusters that occur late fall to early summer. Fragrance is fainter than other members of the genus but noticeable. Dark buds are nearly as attractive as the ensuing flowers. Laurustinus needs sun protection but is frost hardy. 'Spring Bouquet' is the best variety for the low desert. Slow to moderate growth but worth the wait. Acts as a nice backdrop to *Rhaphiolepis indica*. Grows well anywhere star jasmine (*Trachelospermum jasminoides*) grows and looks good when used in conjunction with this ground cover.

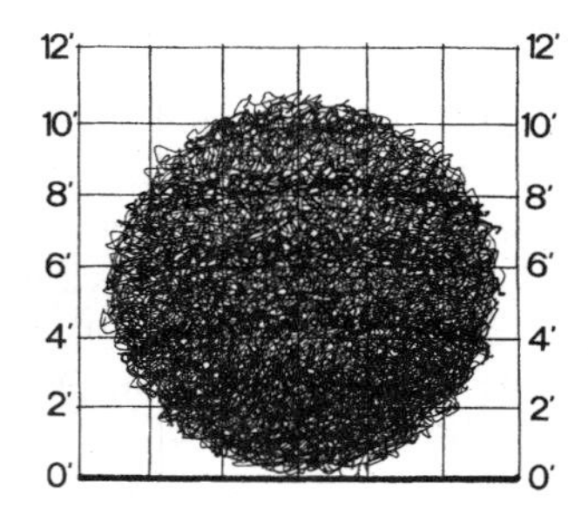

★ *Xylosma congestum* **Evergreen**
Shiny Xylosma

An allstar performer. Beautiful triangular, light green foliage is coppery-red at the growing tips. Floral show is insignificant. This is a foliage plant all the way. Can become a massive shrub in fertile sandy soils reaching 12 to 15 foot proportions. Sometimes pruned up into a small tree. Takes any exposure and becomes drought tolerant with age. Graceful arching stems form irregular mound. Fast growth.

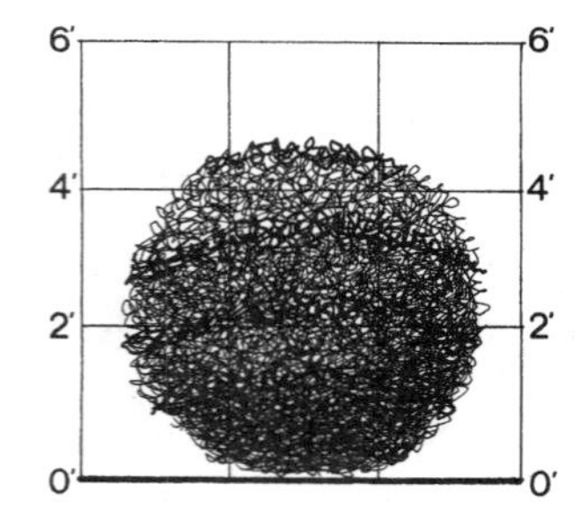

★ *Xylosma congestum 'Compacta'* **Evergreen**
Dwarf Xylosma

For foundation planting and placement in smaller planters, this is a better selection than the species as it can be relied upon to stay significantly smaller. 'Compacta' has all the attributes of the species. The only drawback is it is too graceful to really work well with natives and, as such, is only useful in oasis and transitional settings. All plants should have this problem! Fast growth.

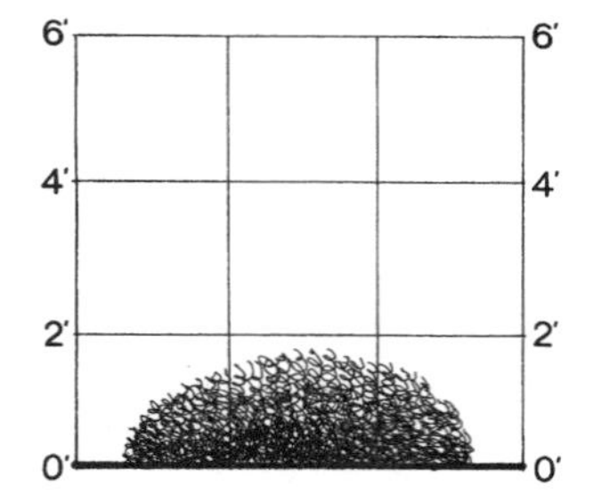

Zauschneria californica **Deciduous**
Hummingbird Flower

Foliage is sparse and unattractive and has no real importance. This plant is used in native seed mixes for fast growth and spot color. Summer and fall blooming, 2-inch-long, red tubular flowers, attract hummingbirds in droves which makes it useful in the natural garden. Fast growth.

Espaliers

Lavender Starflower

Beaumontia grandiflora **Evergreen**
Easter Lily Vine

A plant that deserves more use in the low desert. A massive twining vine to 25 feet in height, it is listed as an espalier because its sheer weight will require ample support. Everything about Beaumontia is large-scale. The funnel-like 4- to 5-inch-long white flowers resemble an actual Easter Lily — thus the common name. The deep-green leaves are 8 inches long, deeply veined, and luxuriant. Needs moist, rich soil, some sun protection, and generous fertilization to look its best. Fast growth.

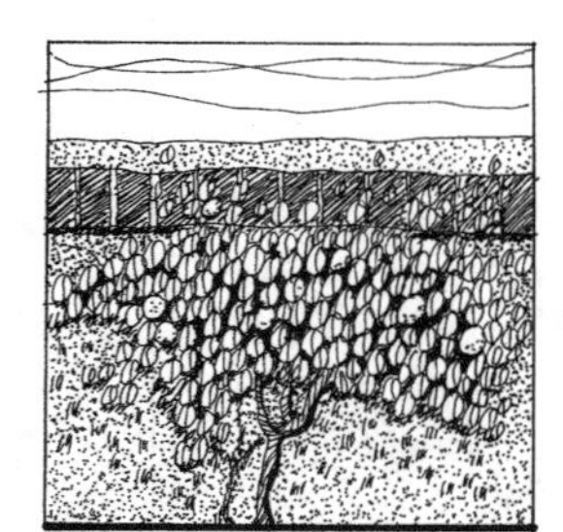

Citrus species **Evergreen**
Citrus (consult growers' catalogues)

Virtually all Citrus can be trained as espaliers. On the small property with limited planting area, this is an excellent way to get eye-level green and some fruit production. Do not espalier citrus on exposed west walls where reflected heat will burn the plant. Citrus, in an espaliered state, are not afforded the same growing conditions as Citrus found on open ground. For this reason, additional fertilization and close attention to watering are very important. In addition, espaliered citrus often do not attain the trunk and branching girth of other citrus. Tie to supports, brace side branches with vertical supports, or remove immature fruit that is not needed (rarely do homeowners eat all the fruit their Citrus produces) as weight reduction measures. With glossy, bright-green foliage, springtime floral scent, and delicious fruit, espaliered Citrus is a welcome addition to any garden. Fast growth.

★ ***Eriobotrya japonica*** **Evergreen**
Loquat

Used frequently in the desert as an espalier. Needs minimal bracing or support as trunk attains girth in an espaliered state and smaller fruit (2 inches long) are not heavy enough to weigh side branches down. An added bonus is that Loquat is a fall bloomer. While creamy-white flower clusters are only somewhat noticeable, their fragrance is very pleasant.The miniature, yellow-orange, pear-like fruit appears in spring. Fruit is fleshy with large seeds and is acidic tasting. Not everyone likes the taste so you should try it before installing the plant. The main attraction of Loquat is its exotic 8- to 12-inch-long foliage: green above, bronze below. Moderate growth rate.

★ *Feijoa sellowiana* **Evergreen**
Pineapple Guava

This is a plant of many virtues. In its natural state, this is a small tree or large shrub (like most espaliers). Espaliered, it takes on a refined character. Try to keep flattened crown at least 3 feet thick. If it is any thinner, you might not get any of the exotic red and white flowers with the edible petals that appear in spring. Oval, grayish-green fruit ripens in fall. Fruit is edible when it falls from the plant. Fruit production is not as good in the desert as in other areas. Moderate growth rate.

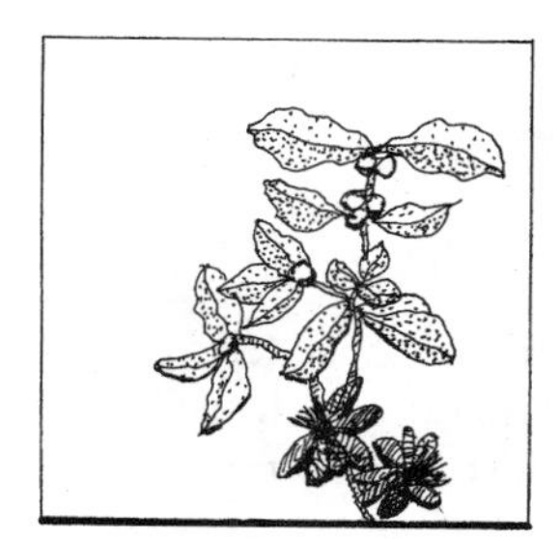

★ *Grewia caffra* **Evergreen**
Lavender Starflower

An excellent espalier beginning to receive more use in the desert. Advantages are that it tends to grow in a naturally flat pattern and will take hot south and west exposures. Dark-green foliage and heavy branches need minimal support. Common name derived from star-shaped, one-inch wide, lavender flowers with noticeable yellow centers. Flowers in late spring through summer, and frequently into midwinter. A tough espalier that will perform better than all others noted here in windy locations. Fast growth.

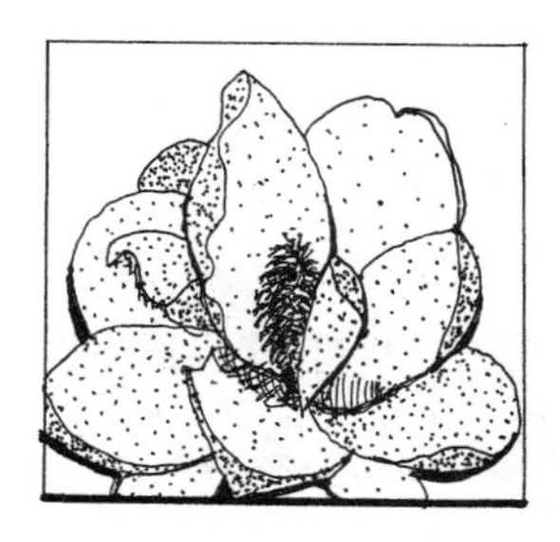

Magnolia grandiflora **Evergreen**
Southern Magnolia

Not an espalier for all exposures or purposes. Use only in filtered light to intermediate shade. Does not provide a profusion of blooms, but in a small area all you need is a half dozen. Flowers are white turning to cream, 10 inches in diameter and fragrant. Southern Magnolia flowers in spring and summer. Looks especially good in combination with Gardenia. It takes Magnolias up to 15 years to first set bloom, so be sure to specify only plants that have previously flowered. Eight-inch-long, dark green, leathery leaves make a fine backdrop to the atrium or tropical garden.

Murraya paniculata **Evergreen**
Satinwood

This is a favorite among high-end residential clients. Plant needs shade to deep shade and frost protection. Bright-green glossy leaves that lie flat and droop downward give plant an elegant appearance. White flowers to about 1 inch in circumference are bell-shaped and appear on the plant in late summer, winter, and early spring. Timing is perfect for the Southwest's country club season which gives this somewhat fussy espalier more play than it would otherwise deserve. Slow growth.

★ ***Pyracantha fortuneana 'Graberi'*** **Evergreen**
Firethorn

This is the most widely used Pyracantha in the desert. Very tough and dependable. Needs full sun to perform and look its best. Masses of white flowers in spring are followed by red berries in fall that hang on the plant throughout the winter months. Very showy during the winter tourist season. Do not irrigate with spray heads unless you have no other options and, at that, let it be a west wall where the plant will dry quickly. Vicious thorns make it a poor selection for heavily traveled pedestrian areas. Moderate growth rate as an espalier.

Pyrus kawakamii **Deciduous**
Evergreen Pear

As an espalier, this deciduous plant is grown for its deep-green leaves and brilliant orange-red fall foliage show. White flowers, which are a prime feature on the tree, are few and far between on a heavily pruned espalier. Good plant, readily available in espaliered form, but has no really outstanding features. Widely grown here because it is widely grown elsewhere. Slow growth.

Vitis labrusca (*slip skin*) **Deciduous**
Vitis vinifera (*tight skin*)
Edible Grape (consult growers' catalogs)

Large-scale overhead plant material for the sturdy arbor. A profusion of cultivars and varieties are available so research will be necessary to select the best plant for your situation. *Vitis vinifera* is considered a wine grape while *V. labrusca* is a table/jelly-type grape. The wine grape takes desert heat better. A dedicated winter pruning effort will need to be undertaken to get the plant to look and produce its best. Major shaping takes 3 years; thereafter the job gets easier. One of the few vine-like plants that has a noticeable and usable (in a design sense) trunk structure. Moderate growth to maturity and fast yearly foliage fill out after that. Moderate water requirement.

Vines

Blue Dawnflower

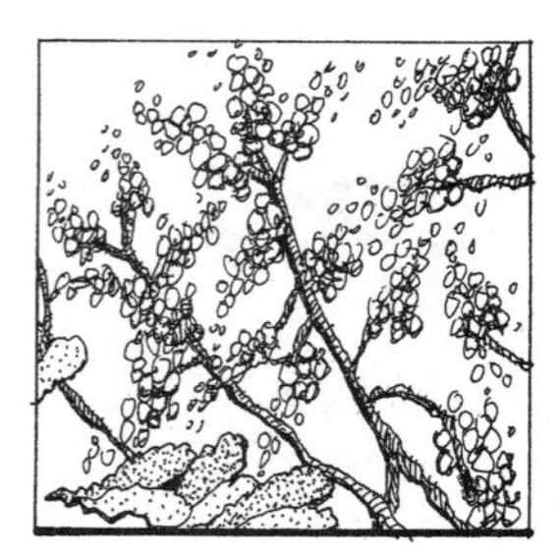

★ ***Antigonon leptopus*** **Semi-evergreen**
Coral Vine

Frequently used and widely admired. In the desert, its biggest drawback is that it is deciduous during the coldest winters. Often used in conjunction with unpeeled California or Mexican Fan Palms as the vine climbs up and circles the cut trunk collars — a nice effect. Green, lance-shaped leaves to 4 inches long are almost delicate. This plant likes heat and will perform best on a west exposure but will take all exposures, including north. Vine climbs by tendrils. Sprays of pink, pea-shaped blossoms, occur from June to November. Fast growth.

★ ***Bougainvillea 'Barbara Karst'*** **Semi-evergreen**
Red Vine Bougainvillea

Most prolific blooming of the red Bougainvilleas. It gets large and, if confined to too small a space will require constant pruning during the summer months. Brilliant red blooms with a hint of purple (bloom color is actually from sepals. Flowers are contained inside the sepal bracts and are white/yellow and insignificant). All Bougainvilleas will freeze to the ground in a cold winter if left unprotected. They recover quickly often attaining their pre-frost size in one growing season. Plant all Bougainvilleas with care as they are sensitive to minimal root disturbance. Plants do not have a natural climbing tendency so they need to be twined through or attached to lattice work and other garden structures. With their cultural requirements met, Bougainvilleas grow extremely fast.

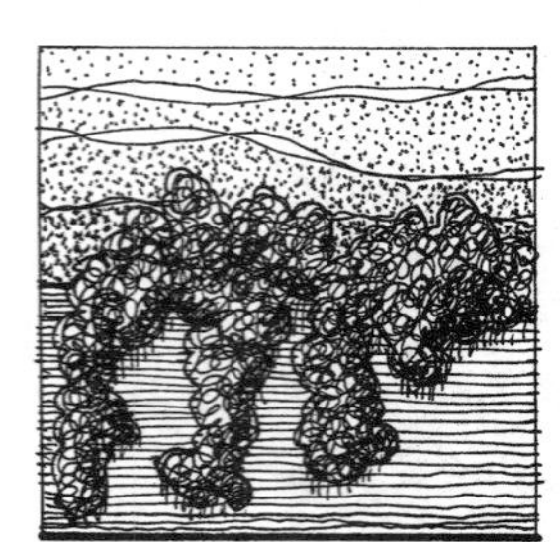

Bougainvillea brasiliensis **Semi-evergreen**
Purple Vine Bougainvillea

Hardiest of the desert Bougainvilleas. A little more dependable in frost-prone areas than 'Barbara Karst.' Light purple blossoms are a welcome visual relief to the all-too-familiar red. Naturally more clumping than other Vine Bougainvilleas. Give it room to spread out. Fast growth.

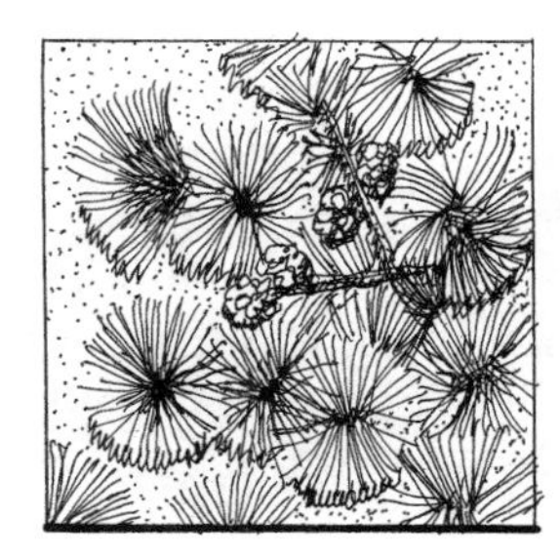

Calliandra inaequilatera **Semi-evergreen**
Pink Powder Puff

Despite its frequent use, this Calliandra cannot be rated a star performer because it is very frost-tender and it must have protection. Best use is on a west wall under an overhang. Many consider it well worth the risk because of its 3-inch-diameter deep-pink flowers that occur from November to April, making it a good tourist season selection. Tall, slender natural form makes it an easy plant to espalier by removing the plant's front face. Tie to supports to stabilize. It does not recover quickly, if at all, from a frost. Moderate growth rate.

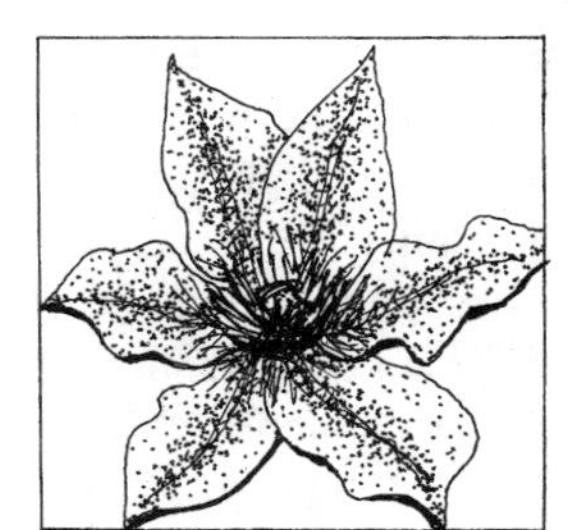

Clematis species **Deciduous**
Clematis (consult growers' catalogues)

For the private home garden or the horticultural enthusiast, this is a vine to make note of. The vine's biggest disadvantage, in the eyes of many observers, is that they are winter deciduous. Dark-green leaves are irregularly lance shaped. Plant climbs by use of twining leaf stalks and stems. Stems break easily, so keep plant in wind free atriums and courtyards and provide as much support as possible. Clematis will reward you with absolutely spectacular flowers in every color imaginable — even light and deep blues. There are spring-flowering varieties, fall-flowering varieties, some that bloom over both seasons, and even some that bloom in winter. Flowers are flat, star shaped, 2 inches to 9 inches across, according to variety, and look good displayed floating in water. Flowers are followed by attractive seed pods which look visually pleasant on the plant or in dried flower arrangements. An excellent plant to treat as an annual or even as a backdrop to an annual garden. Clematis species like well-drained, predominately sandy, soil. Mixing in some soil amendments and fertilizers will aid the vine in establishment. One quirk of Clematis culture is that they like their roots shaded and their top growth in 4 or 5 hours of daily sunlight. This make them a good selection for tiny pavement cutouts as the pavement shades their roots. East and south exposures are best; west is too hot. It would be impossible to describe the some 200-plus varieties available. One of the better catalogue sources is: Wayside Gardens, One Garden Lane, Hodges, SC 92595-0001; Tel: 800/345-1124. Clematis deserves more widespread use in the desert and, with some degree of exposure, will more than likely get it.

★ ***Clytostoma callistegioides*** **Semi-evergreen**
Lavender Trumpet Vine

Wavy, dark-green, downward drooping leaves suggest a cooling effect and, indeed, this vine needs shade or partial shade to look and perform its best. A magnificent late spring bloomer with 3-inch-long, trumpet-shaped, lavender flowers in profusion. Picking spent blossoms increases floral production and bloom period. Fast growth with moderate water.

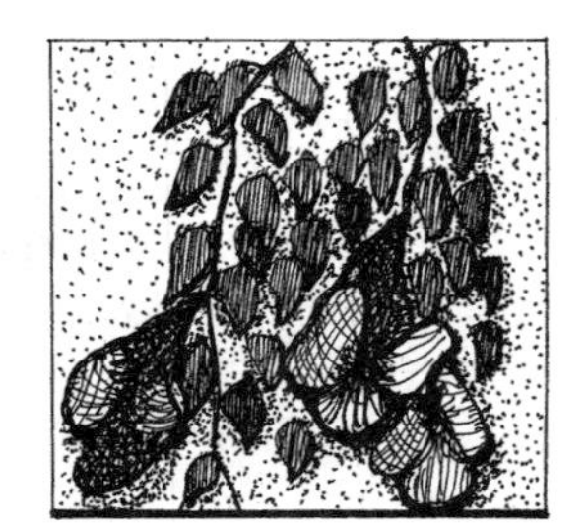

★ ***Doxantha cati (Macfadyena unguis-cati)*** **Semi-evergreen**
Cat's Claw Vine

In my opinion, the ultimate desert vine. Will take most exposures, with north and deep shade being the exceptions. It prefers the hot, west side of a structure. Vine climbs by utilizing hooked, needle-thin tendrils, thus the common name Cat's Claw. Vigorous climber that does not really do any damage to the structure it climbs upon. The natural tendency of the vine is to bolt upward two or three stories, or even higher until it reaches an apex. When it cannot climb any further, it then begins to spread out. This tendency makes it a good selection for tall vertical architectural elements like fireplaces and columns. Cut to the ground to control. I have climbed onto two-story roofs and simply dumped the vine off the roof and to the ground, cut it there, and removed it. Be careful to plant it facing the wind; not with the wind, or it will blow off its support. Light-green, 2-inch long, lance-shaped, glossy leaves. Three- to 4-inch long, trumpet-shaped, yellow flowers appear in late spring to early summer and are quite showy. The only drawback is that it will drop its leaves during an extremely cold winter. Extremely fast growth. A great vine.

★ ***Ficus pumila*** **Evergreen**
Creeping Fig

This is the vine frequently used on north exposures where Cat's Claw Vine (*Doxantha cati*) cannot be used. Tiny, oval, deep green leaves in youth create a delicate tracery against surfaces. As they mature, these leaves become longer, glossier, and denser. Be careful where you use this vine. Under the right conditions it can become huge and rampant. Creeping Fig climbs by sending aerial rootlets into walls and posts. Removal means structural damage and almost certain repainting. Do not use on wood surfaces. Good desert vine for shady conditions and where it can be controlled. Moderate growth rate when young gives way to a fast growth rate at maturity.

Gelsemium sempervirens **Evergreen**
Carolina Jessamine

Fast growing vine or sprawling ground cover which has a natural tendency to climb by twining. Good sprawling character has a cascading effect. Very showy, 2-inch-deep by 2-inch-round, bright yellow masses of tubular flowers appear in late winter to July. Deep green, glossy leaves. This vine will freeze in extreme winters but this is usually not a problem. It recovers quickly. Drawbacks are that flowers attract bees and all parts of the plant are poisonous. Not a good selection for children's play areas. Moderate growth rate with moderate watering.

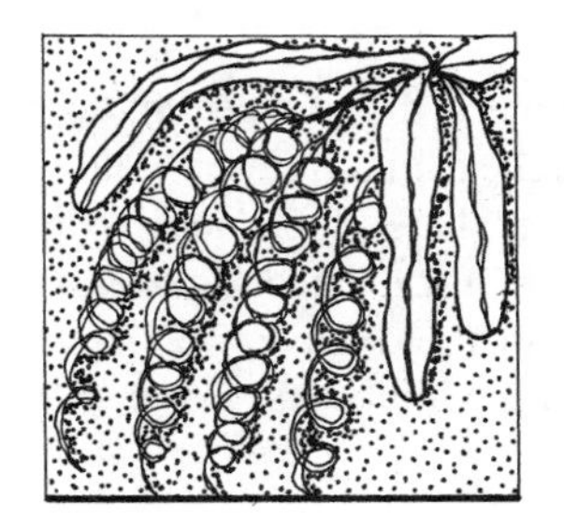

Hardenbergia vislacea **Evergreen**
Lilac Vine

A newcomer from Australia, it has not received a lot of use to date. Will not tolerate wet feet, which precludes its use in clay soils. Does best when pampered with fertilizers and occasional adding of new organic matter. Two- to 4-inch-long, lance-shaped, narrow leaves with rounded tops. Spiraled flowers about 1/2 inch wide, are long as the leaves, and occur in sprays or clusters — very attractive. North and east exposure only. Moderate growth rate.

Jasminum nitidum **Evergreen**
Angelwing Jasmine

Plant grown for lovely scent and one-inch wide, white, pinwheel-shaped flowers that appear in late spring and continue through summer. Plant climbs by twining. Heart-shaped leathery green foliage is glossy and attractive. Plant needs frost protection and sun protection. Slow to moderate growth rate. Need for ample water limits it to the oasis garden

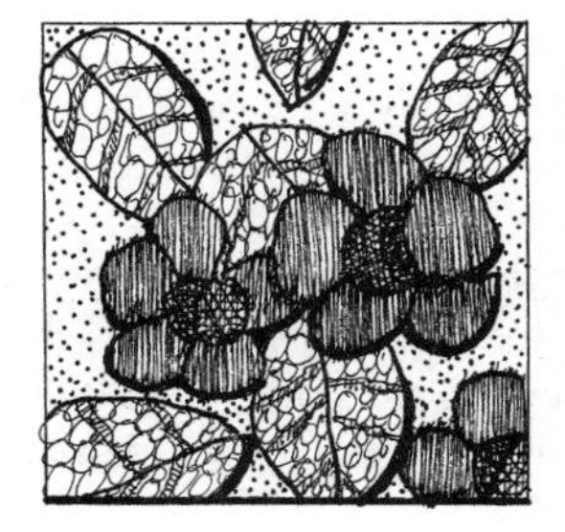

Mandevilla 'Alice Du Pont' **Evergreen**
Mandevilla

A plant not really suited to desert areas, but is frequently planted here. The reason for its popularity is its spectacular pink flowers from November to April (the tourist season). I suggest viewing the plant as an annual because, in all but the most protected locations, it is going to freeze sooner or later. It is mentioned here because it is frequently requested by clients, especially those in the residential sector. Slow growth by twining.

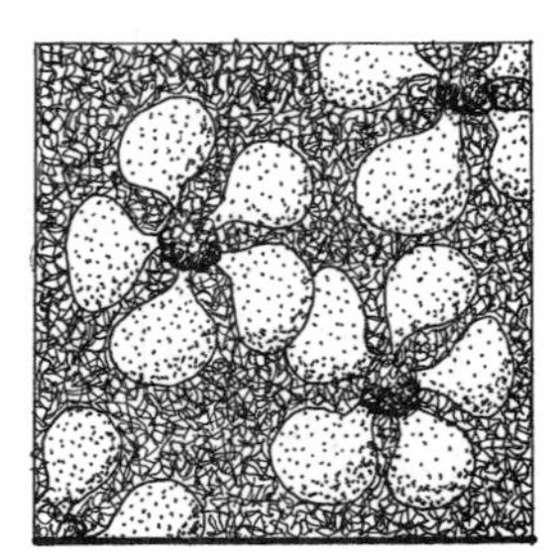

Mascagnia lilacaena **Deciduous**
Mexican Purple Orchid Vine

From south of the border, this is a festive introduction that is sure to increase in popularity. Medium-green leaves are reminiscent of Honeysuckle. Flowers are 5-lobed and up to 3 inches round in clusters. Another nice feature is that its unusual seed pods look good in flower arrangements. A hot weather, summer-blooming vine, it will appreciate some afternoon shade nevertheless. Fast growth on low to moderate water.

Parthenocissus tricuspidata **Deciduous**
Boston Ivy

The major drawback to this beautiful vine is that it's deciduous and out of leaf in January, February, and March in the event of a very cold winter. It is a north exposure vine of graceful character. Three-lobed leaves droop downward. Plant climbs by use of tendrils with disk-shaped suckers at their ends. Vine turns a deep-maroon red in December and leaves persist at this color until January or sometimes longer in mild winters. Moderate growth rate.

Passiflora alatocaerulea **Semi-evergreen**
Passion Vine

Not the best for desert use but, because of its legendary religious significance, it does have a place in the religious theme garden. Climbs by use of aerial rootlets that form suction cups. Because of its rambling character, the vine could use some additional support. Best appearance occurs when it is pruned back yearly after second year of growth. Medium-green, smooth, 3-lobed leaves. Flowers from spring through summer usually have 10 petals (10 faithful apostles), 5 stamens (5 wounds), and a lacy purple crown (crown of thorns). Moderate growth rate with moderate water.

★ ***Pyrostegia venusta*** **Evergreen**
Flame Vine

An evergreen vine, with 3-inch-long, bright orange, tubular flowers that appear in late fall and last through most of the winter. Fast grower in hot locations. Three-inch oval green leaves. Likes full sun. Grows to 20 feet, climbing by twining tendrils. Becomes more drought-resistant with maturity.

★ *Rosa banksiae* **Deciduous**
Lady Bank's Rose

Rampant, somewhat loose-growing, sprawling vine. Not for the refined, close-up garden. Needs space to spread out and support to climb. With its needs met, the Lady's Bank's Rose will reward you with a profusion of miniature rose blossoms from April into July. Predominantly evergreen, but it will drop its yellow-green glossy leaves in a cold winter. A good informal bank cover. Train over the distant trellis or gazebo. Variety 'Alba Plena' has white flowers, while 'Lutea' has soft-yellow flowers. Fast growth rate with moderate irrigation.

Solanum jasminoides **Semi-evergreen**
Potato Vine

Twining grower to 30 feet high although usually much less (15 feet) in the desert. One-inch white flowers with a blue tinge occur intermittently year-round with the greatest profusion in spring. Will drop its 3-inch purplish-green leaves in a hard frost but recovers quickly. Needs a severe yearly pruning to look its best. Fast growth.

Trachelospermum jasminoides ***Evergreen***
Star Jasmine

This plant is used more often as a ground cover than a vine in the desert. Star Jasmine provides lush green foliage and bright, white, star-shaped flowers in late spring. Fragrance is very pleasing. Although the plant has a twining habit, it needs some training and a method of support to act as a true climbing vine. It is worth the effort to get the plant to window height so that flowers and aroma can be truly appreciated. Moderate growth rate with ample watering.

Ground Covers

Candy Apple

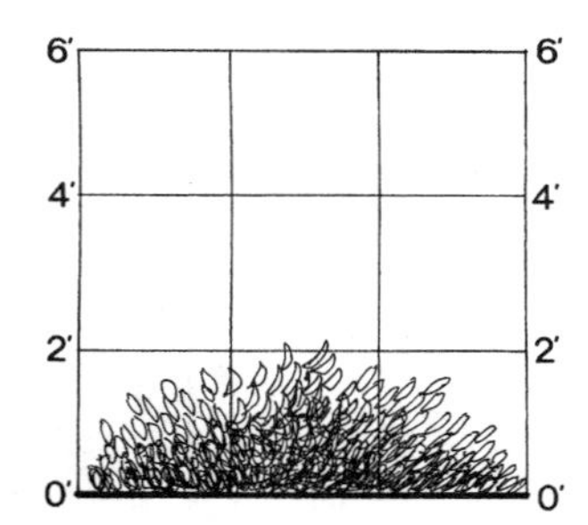

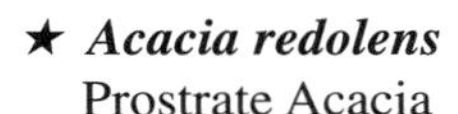

★ *Acacia redolens* **Evergreen**
Prostrate Acacia

A large area is required to accommodate the rampant growth of this wide-spreading Australian ground cover. Oblong-shaped, gray-green, 1 1/2-inch long leaves spring upright from arching stems. Familiar Acacia-yellow flower balls appear late winter (February) and last into April. No particular cultural requirements, except it prefers well-drained soil. Not for a formal or refined planting, as its habit is too irregular. Rather, it is a good selection as a bank cover or highway median planting. Drought tolerant. Plant on 6-foot minimum centers. Fast growth with minimal irrigation. Variety 'Desert Carpet' stays consistently lower (2 feet high) and more uniform.

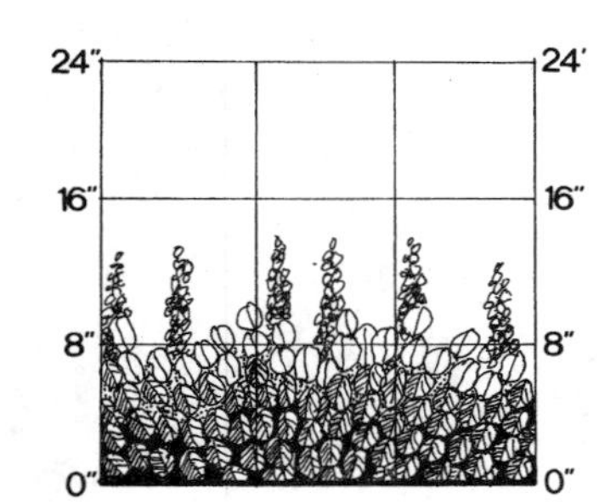

Ajuga reptans **Evergreen**
Carpet Bugle

Plant is 6 inches high and spreading to 1 foot wide. Blue flower spikes extend above the plant an additional 6 inches. Flowers occur spring through summer and are noticeable, but not spectacular. Needs sun protection and is better suited to somewhat shady locations. Four-inch deep green leaves form a dense mat. Plant on 6-inch minimum centers. Moderate growth rate with ample water.

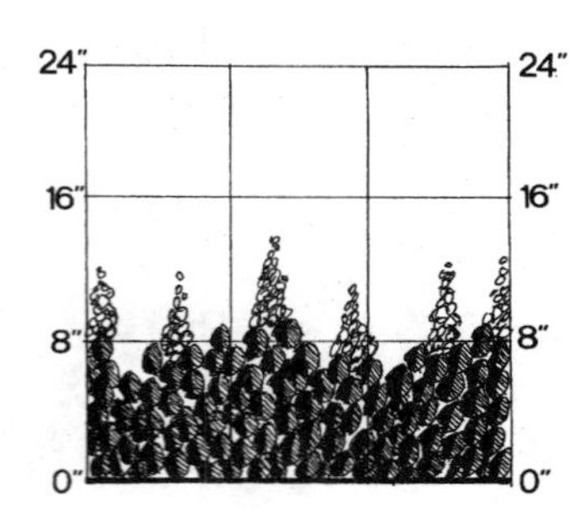

Ajuga reptans 'Purpurea' **Evergreen**
Bronze Ajuga

Similar in all aspects to the species described above except the leaves are bronze and slightly larger. Looks good as an understory plant to Nandina, Photinia, or Purple Leaf Plum (*Prunus cerasifera* 'Atropurpurea'). Moderate growth rate. Leaves will not get as bronze in shady locations and plant must be grown in locations that receive afternoon shade.

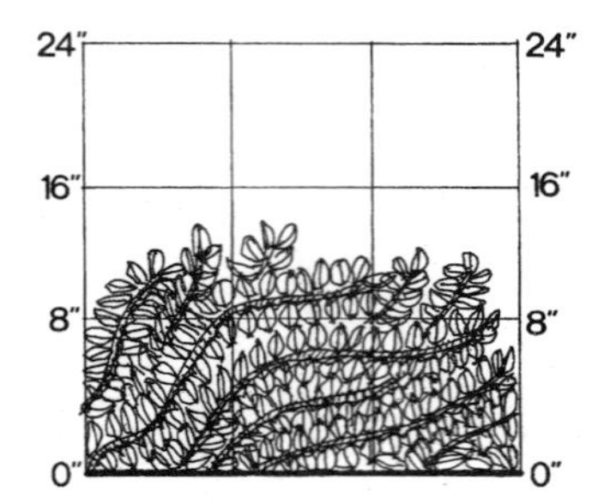

Aptenia cordifolia **Evergreen**
Candy Apple

Fleshy, deep-green, glossy, heart-shaped leaves about 1-inch long and 3/4 inches across. Leaves are supported on fleshy deep green stalks. This ground cover is beginning to get more use in the desert although, most other rsources don't rate it as suitable for this region. Does need some sun protection. East exposure is the best. Will go virtually dormant in a frost, but recovers quickly. One-inch diameter bright-red flowers in spring and summer. Plant on 12-inch or 18-inch centers. Fast growth with ample water; slower growth with moderate water.

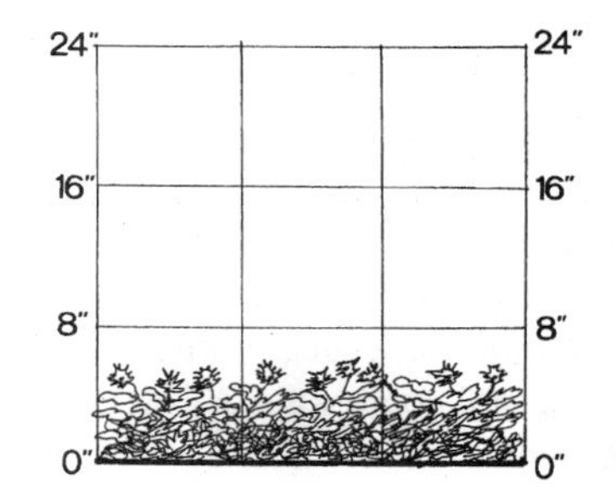

Arctotheca calendula **Evergreen**
Cape Weed

A loose ground cover that is not frequently used here because Gazania is more popular and widely known. Leaves are greener than Gazania and wider. Yellow, daisy-like flowers occur March through June. Covers a larger area faster than Gazania and is just as drought tolerant once established. Not a ground cover for refined areas but Cape Weed has its uses. Plant on 12-inch centers. Extremely fast growth.

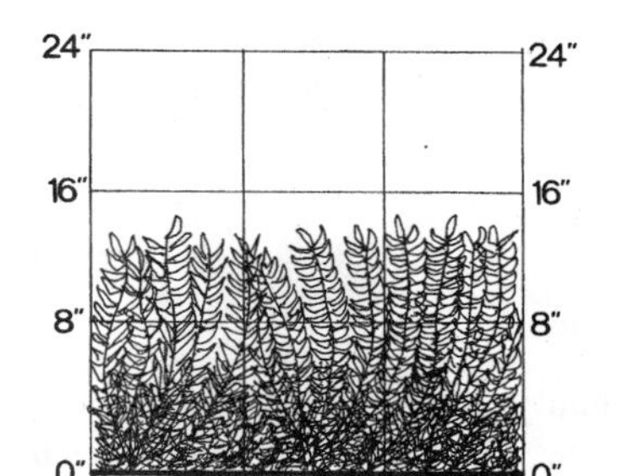

Arundinaria pygmaea **Evergreen**
Pygmy Bamboo

A true bamboo that spreads rapidly. It is 6 to 12 inches high, light green, and airy. Can take some foot traffic. Mow to 3 or 4 inches once a year to control height and encourage new and lusher green growth. Provide some sun and frost protection. Plant on 12-inch centers. Fast growth.

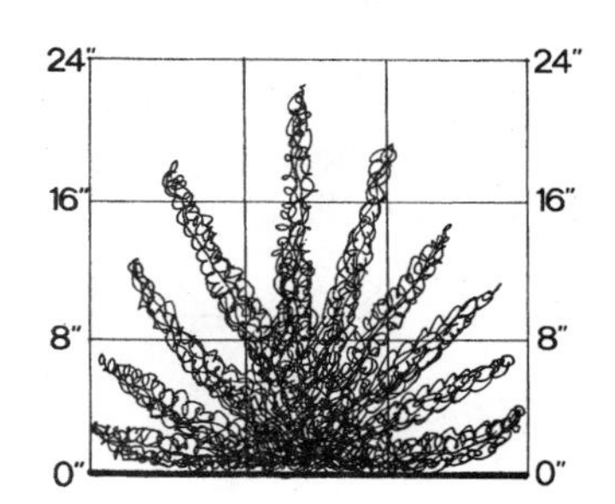

Asparagus meyeri **Evergreen**
Meyer's Asparagus Fern

Not quite as hardy as *Asparagus sprengeri* described below, but an attractive ground cover just the same. Tight-leaved, upright fronds have a plume-like appearance. Leaves are thin, stiff, and needle-like. Foliage color is always light green to yellow-green (chartreuse). Good accent-bedding plant or dramatic foreground plant to larger exotics. Accepts any exposure but prefers some afternoon shade. Will freeze to the ground at 20°F, but recovers quickly from its fleshy roots. Plant on 18-inch centers. Moderate growth rate.

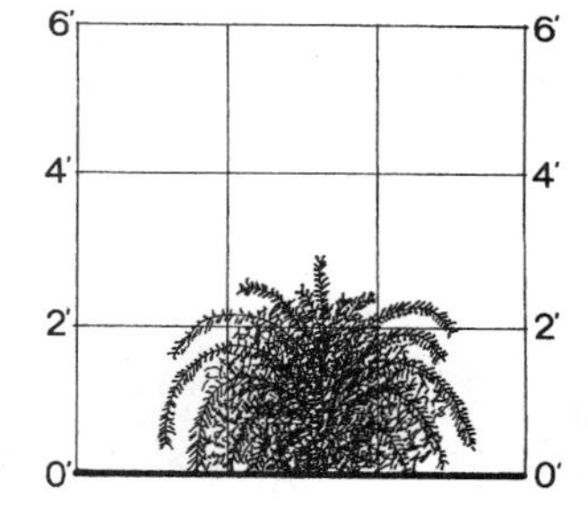

★ ***Asparagus sprengeri*** **Evergreen**
Asparagus Fern

Arching stems (fronds) are thinner and sparser than *Asparagus meyeri*. Stems will cascade over pots and planters and down walls for 3 or 4 feet. Lacy effect. Insignificant white flowers in spring produce bright red berries in summer and fall. Entire plant has a loose, billowing effect. Looks very nice as a base for Mediterranean Fan Palms (*Chamaerops humilis*) or *Yucca gloriosa*. An excellent, stand-alone ground cover acting as a base plane plant material for a stand of trees. Will take any exposure, including the west side of structures, but will yellow in deeply shaded areas. Fast growth with moderate irrigation. Plant 1-gallon containers on 18-inch centers or from flats at 6-inches on center. Becomes somewhat drought tolerant with age. Will freeze in hard winters, but recovers quickly.

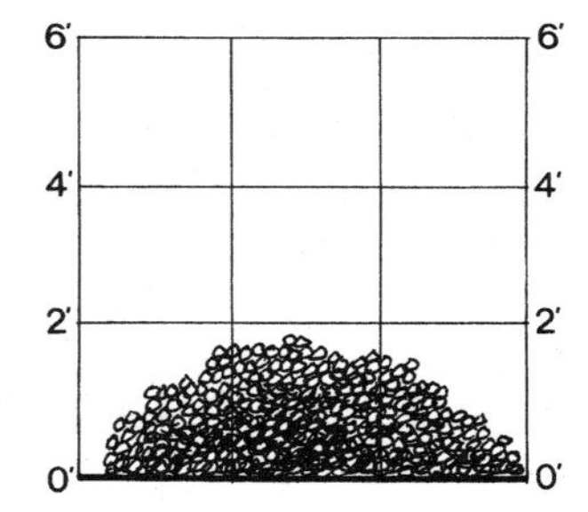

Baccharis pilularis 'Twin Peaks' **Evergreen**
Hybrid Dwarf Coyote Bush

The best low-growing *Baccharis*. 'Twin Peaks' is grown from male cuttings. This is important as *Baccharis* is dioecious (male and female flowers on separate plants) and female plants from the species produce a cottony and messy unattractive flower. *Baccharis pilularis* is a species known to have a wide range of tolerance to a variety of cultural conditions. All types of soils, including saline, are accepted, although sandy well-drained soil is preferred. Any level of soil moisture is acceptable from very wet (swampy) to very dry. Plants are fairly drought tolerant with age, but like an infrequent deep watering in the desert. Excellent bank cover as the wide-spreading root system knits soil firmly. Plant on 2-foot minimum centers. Moderate growth rate.

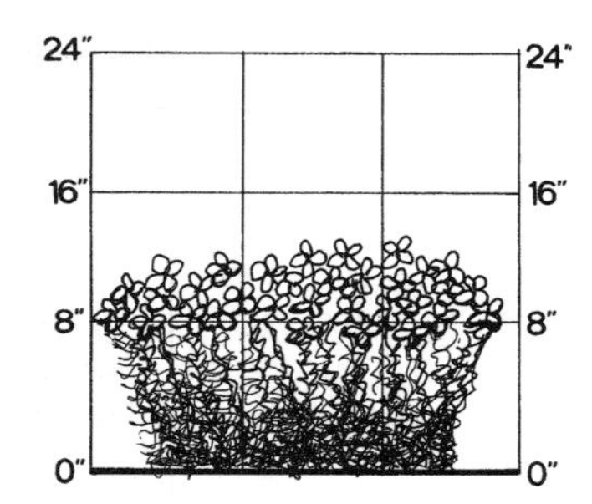

Calylophus hartweggi **Deciduous**
Calylophus

A plant noted for its toughness, especially to high-desert conditions. Similar to yellow flowering species of Mexican Primrose (*Oenothera stubbei*). It is superior due to hardiness and the length of its yellow bloom period, which extends from March until November. Essentially dormant during the winter months, it apparently takes a well-deserved rest. Its appearance for the following season will be greatly enhanced by shearing it to the ground with a string trimmer when it is dormant. Fast growth.

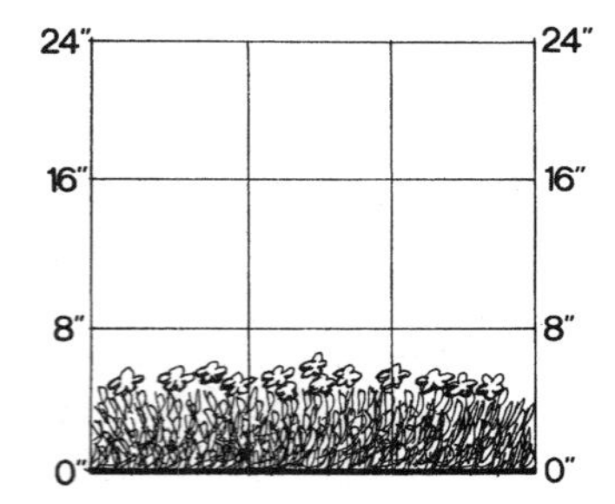

Cerastium tomentosum **Evergreen**
Snow-in-Summer

Tough, low-growing (8 inches high) ground cover with silvery-gray foliage. Fast growing, it will spread to 3 feet wide in one year. Needs moderate watering to look its best. Produces masses of tiny white blossoms in late spring and through summer. Primary reason it is not used more often is that it looks "ratty" during December and January at the start of the Southwest's tourist season. Plant on 9-inch minimum centers.

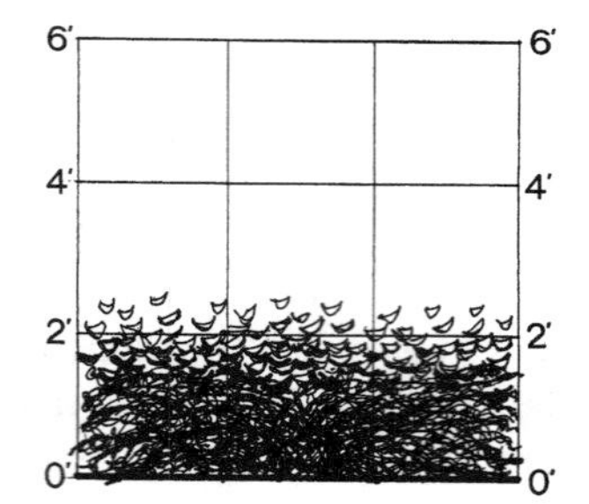

Cistus salvifolius **Evergreen**
Sageleaf Rock Rose

Cistus, as a genus, warrants more research in desert environments. Sageleaf Rock Rose has small, gray-green leaves and 1 1/2-inch wide white flowers with orange/yellow centers. Tough with a capital "T." Achieves 2 feet in height and spreads to 6 feet. Very fast growth with low to moderate irrigation.

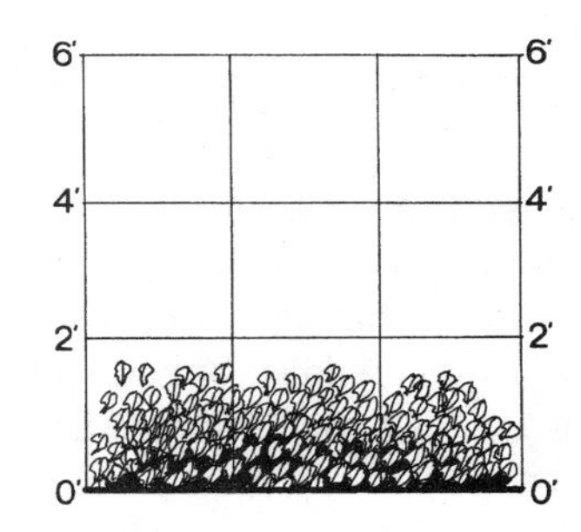

Cissus antarctica **Evergreen**
Kangaroo Treebine

A ground cover with a clean and refined character. Kangaroo Treebine is not usually recommended for this region. It does have 1 good application however — it grows nicely under deep overhangs that provide intermediate to deep shade. Oval to triangular, 1 1/2-inch-long, light green leaves are graceful and attractive and the primary feature of the plant. Must be protected from south and west sun and frost exposure. Plant on 12 inch centers. Moderate growth rate.

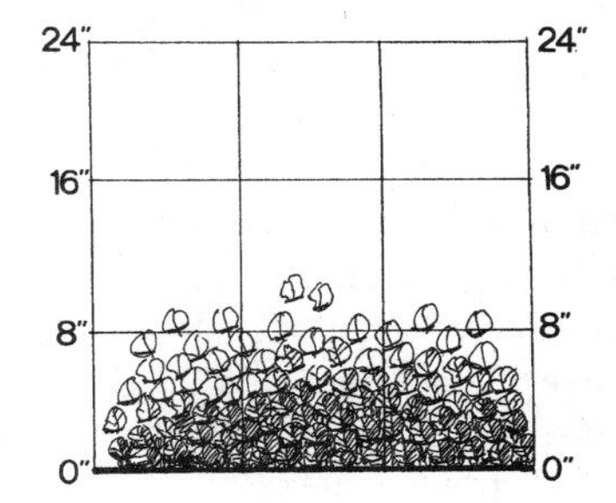

Dichondra repens **Evergreen**
Dichondra

Used as a substitute for turf grass in many locales. I wouldn't recommend it for such in all but seldom used traffice areas of the desert. It will cook with extended sun exposure in open areas. When frequently walked on or mowed, its lily pad-like leaves become tiny and compact. Allowed to grow as a ground cover, Dichondra takes on a graceful undulating appearance and the light green "lily pads" can get up to 1/2-inch across on 6- to 12-inch stalks. Nice watery effect. Good between stepping stones or pavers in protected areas. Mow down with string trimmers twice a year to improve growth. Can be seeded or planted from 4-inch plugs at 12 inches on center. Moderate growth rate with ample water. Appreciates an occasional application of high nitrogen fertilizer.

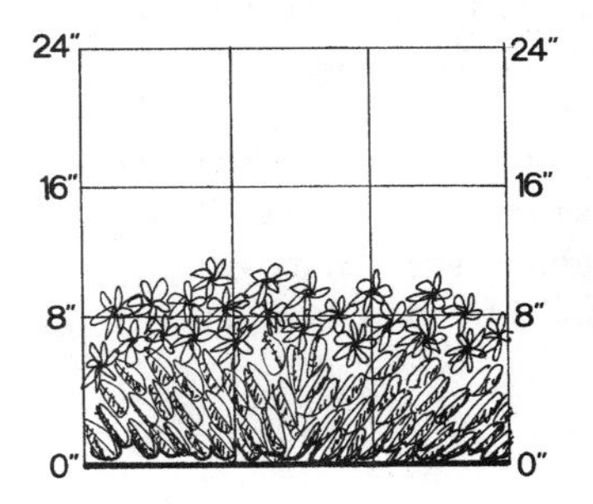

Drosanthemum speciosum **Evergreen**
Arizona Ice Plant

A cultivar of unknown origin (probably *Drosanthemum hispidum*) offered by Mountain States Nursery in Phoenix, Arizona (602-247-6354). Like all ice plants it has fleshy, completely rounded leaves. Makes a dense mat 8 inches deep. In late spring, masses of 2-inch round, rose colored, daisy-like flowers appear. Will take full sun but appreciates a little shade. Tends to go dormant in winter months. If using as a bank cover, be sure soils are stable. Ice plants have been known to literally slide off a bank due to their sheer weight. Plant on 12-inch centers. Fast growth with moderate water.

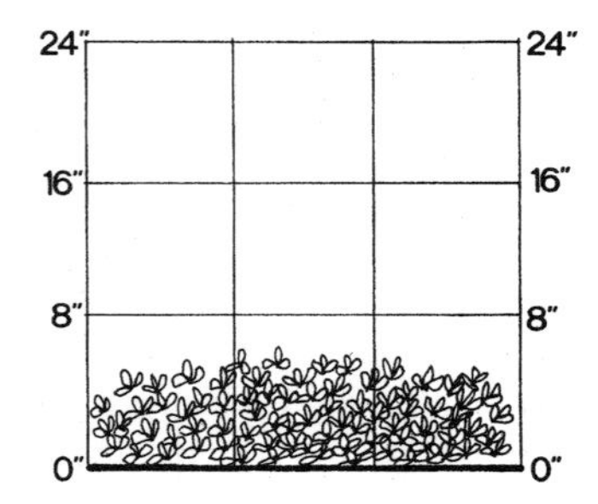

★ ***Duchesnea indica*** **Evergreen**

Indian Mock Strawberry

Not a true strawberry. Bears its 1/2-inch, red fruit above its 3-lobed, strawberry-like leaves. True strawberries always bear their fruit below their leaves. Mock strawberry also has an insignificant yellow blossom as opposed to the typical white of true strawberries. Foliage turns reddish bronze in winter. Plant acts as a nice base for Nandina or Photinia which are reddish-tinted shrubs. Edible, but nearly tasteless fruit appears early summer. This ground cover needs some sun protection in the desert. Plant on 12-inch centers. Fast growth with ample water.

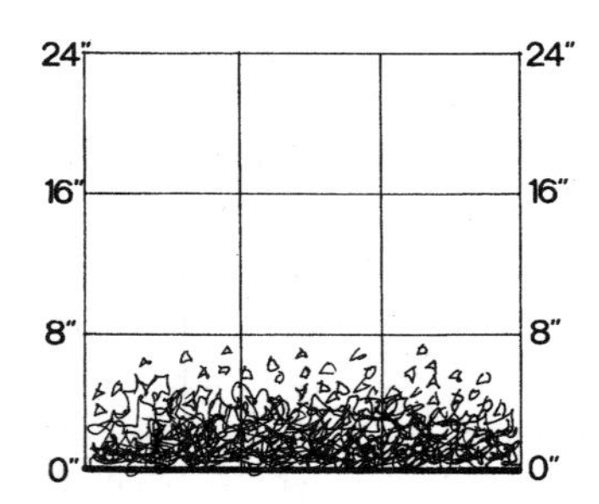

Euonymus fortunei radicans **Evergreen**

Common Winter Creeper

Very tough ground cover taking all exposures, but prefers some afternoon shade in the desert. It has evergreen, rounded leaves with a tiny point. This plant is under used in the desert. It will survive the hardest freeze. Primary drawback is that it can become invasive if not controlled and, if left untrimmed, can appear stringy. It also displays no significant flower show. Plant on 24-inch centers. Fast growth with ample water.

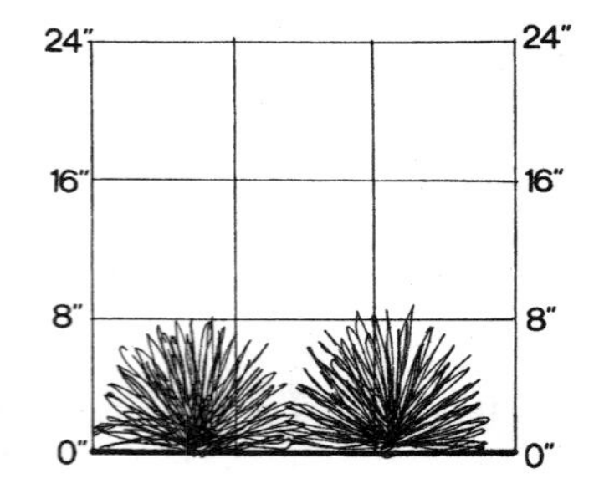

Festuca ovina 'Glauca' **Evergreen**

Blue Fescue

A horticultural oddity for the theme or view garden. Grassy balls 8 inches high by 10 inches wide. Blue-gray leaf blades. Must be massed for striking visual effect. Looks good planted by Mondo Grass (*Ophiopogon japonicum*) which is same size and character, but deep green in color. Consider as a foreground plant to Blue Oat Grass (*Helictotrichon sempervivens*). Needs sun protection. Plant on 6-inch centers to connect foliage. Slow growth with moderate water. Requires constant maintenance to remove unsightly leaves but it is worth the work when this plant is fitted to the right application.

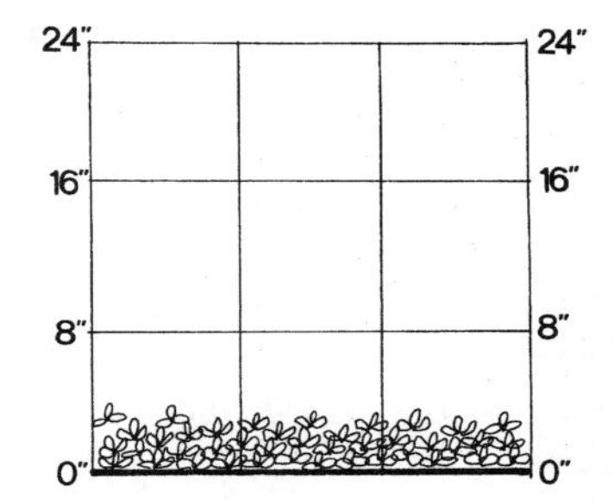

Fragaria chiloensis **Evergreen**
Ornamental Strawberry

The familiar wild strawberry of fields and pastures across the country. Tiny summer fruit is tart and tasteful. In the ornamental garden, 3-toothed bright green leaflets make an airy, low ground cover. This plant needs shade and moist, but well-drained soil. Heavy, early spring fertilizing is quite helpful. Not really a first-choice ground cover, but does have a use in the wild or natural theme garden. Plant on 6-inch centers. Moderate growth rate with moderate water.

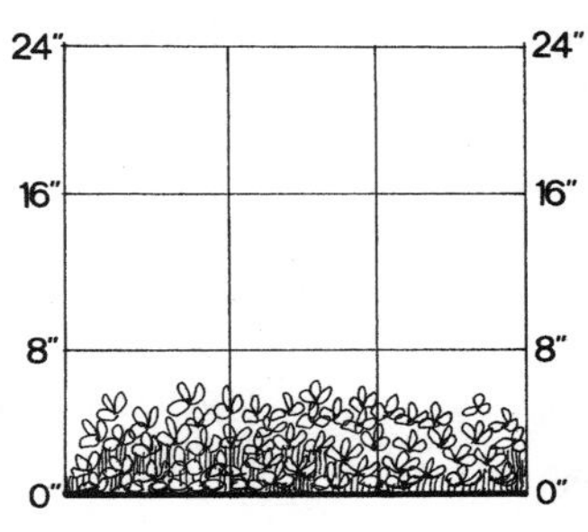

Fragaria species **Evergreen**
Fruiting Strawberry

It is not a well-known fact among designers, but edible strawberries do quite well in the desert, particularly in sandy soil areas. All Strawberry plants need an east exposure or introduced shade to be productive. All fruiting strawberries grow fast with ample water. All appreciate heavy early spring fertilization. Plant on 18-inch centers for best fruit production. Listed below are three of the most commonly used varieties:

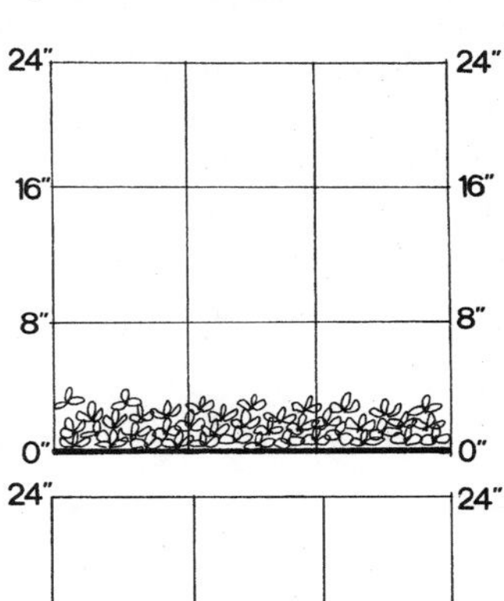

Fragaria #25
A recent introduction. Takes more sunlight and heat than other varieties.

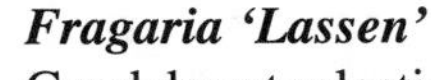

Fragaria 'Lassen'
Good desert selection. Takes heat well. Medium-sized fruit is quite tasty and freezes well. An added advantage is that it produces two crops of berries — one in spring the other in fall.

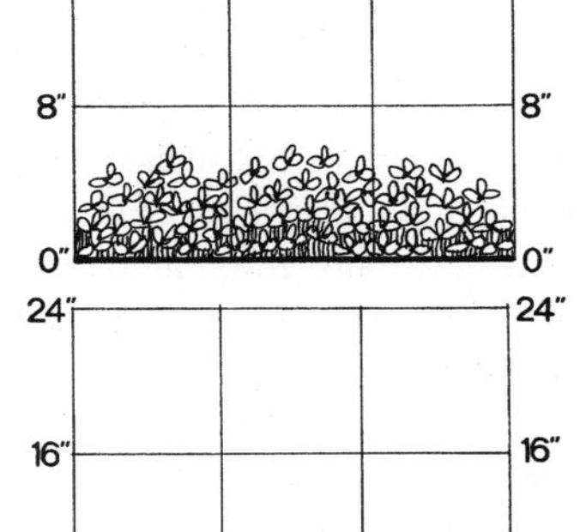

Fragaria 'Tioga'
Better yield and larger size than 'Lassen' above. Needs a little more shade. Only one crop of spring/summer berries.

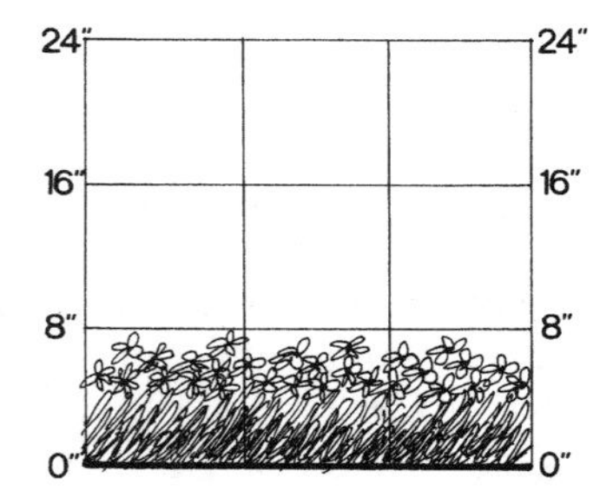

Gazania uniflora **Evergreen**
Trailing Yellow Gazania (consult growers' catalogues)

An immensely popular ground cover imported from South Africa. It is not as widely used in California as in Arizona because sandy soils allow for greater selection of other ground covers as opposed to the alkaline Arizona soils. Gray-green, fleshy foliage forms a dense mat. Yellow, daisy-like flowers hover 3 inches above the 8-inch-high mat. Bloom period starts in February and lasts through June. Numerous varieties in a wide array of colors have been hybridized from the species. See Ground Cover Matrix Chart for a brief listing. None of the hybrids are as healthy or as prolific blooming as the species but all have a purpose. Very fast growth with moderate watering. Plants become drought tolerant with maturity. Plant on 12- or 18-inch centers.

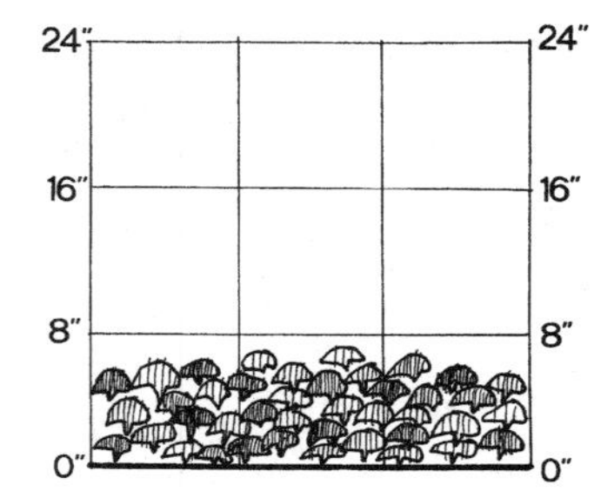

★ *Hedera canariensis* **Evergreen**
Algerian Ivy

Related by genus to the familiar English ivy (*Hedera helix*) but has some noticeable differences. Leaves are 3-lobed, not 5-lobed. Leaves are also deep green, quite large (8 inches across) and not noticeably veined. This plant is a great ground cover selection for intermediate to deep shade areas. Once established, it grows quickly. Flowers are not noticeable. The primary feature of the plant is the glossy leaves. *H. canariensis* will climb but is not an invasive climber and should be given support if this is the desired effect. A high nitrogen fertilizer will help leaf growth and gloss. Takes ample water to look its best. Plant on 12-inch centers.

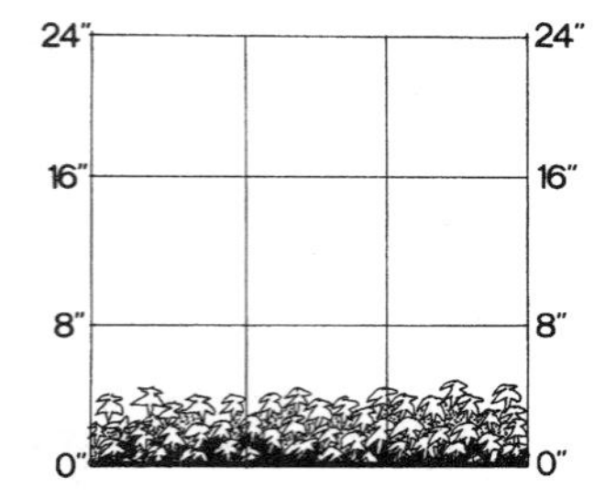

Hedera helix **Evergreen**
English Ivy

Although more well known and preferred nationally, this ground cover does not perform as well in the desert as its cousin *Hedera canariensis*. It is a clean, refined plant. The leaves are a medium-green to 2 inches across, 5-lobed, and sycamore-like. New leaves are a shiny, bright green. It is an excellent climber, utilizing aerial rootlets. It will damage painted structures and penetrate into stucco. A good ground cover for shady areas or spaces with filtered light. It roots as it grows along the soil surface and will form a dense, soil retentive, mat. The cultivar 'Hahnii' has brighter, somewhat smaller, green leaves than the species and looks even more elegant. It is often preferred over the species in a tropical garden setting. Moderate growth with ample water. Plant on 6- or 9-inch centers.

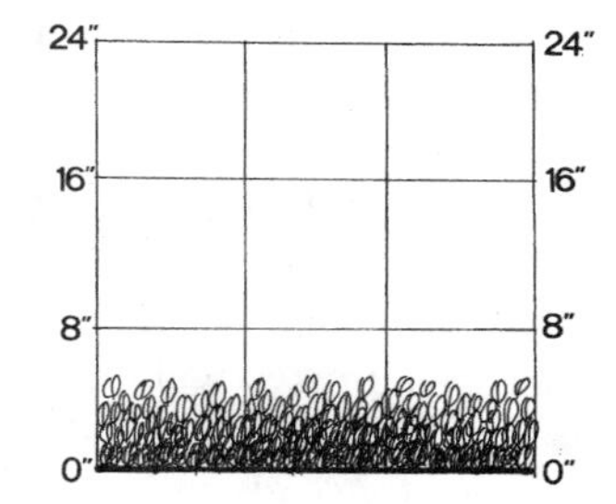

Lippia repens ***Semi-evergreen***
Lippia

A very nice ground cover that has the one major disadvantage of going dormant in the winter months of December, January, and most of February. Not a ground cover to be used in a feature planting of a seasonal home. Gray-green leaves, 1/8 inch wide by 1 inch in length, make a 4-inch mat over the soil surface. Will put out nice, round, lilac flower balls in spring and sometimes fall. Bees like the flowers, but they are easy to mow or remove with a string trimmer in high-traffic areas. Very useful ground cover for very narrow areas such as the usual 4 to 6 inches that are provided between stepping stones. Plant from 4-inch plugs at 12 inches on center. Fast growth with moderate water and ample early spring applications of high-nitrogen fertilization.

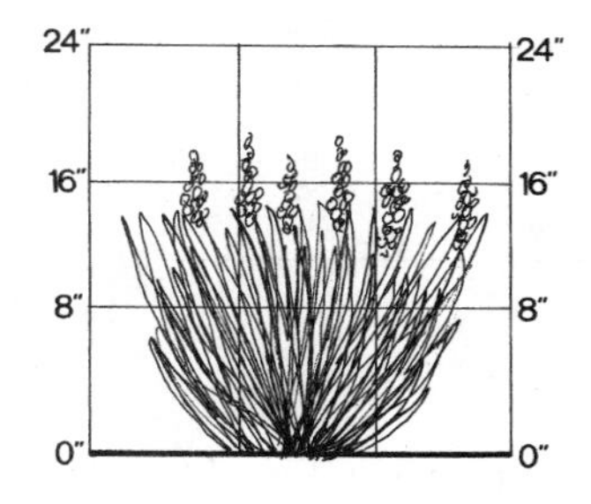

Liriope muscari 'Silvery Sunproof' **Evergreen**
Silver Lily Turf

Slightly over 12 inches high, this cultivar differs from the species (described in shrub section) in that leaves are gold striped, turning to a complete silvery-white. Looks good massed and particularly attractive when downlit at night. Purple-blue flower spikes in spring rise higher above this cultivar than the species which, in turn, makes them showier. Plant on 8-inch centers. Moderate growth rate.

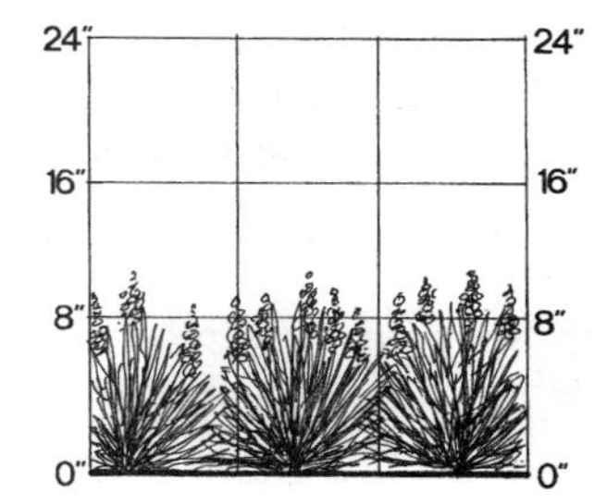

Liriope spicata **Evergreen**
Creeping Lily Turf

Smallest and the most ground cover-like of the Liriopes. Not widely used and deserves more attention. It is 8 inches high and 12 inches wide, spreading by rhizomes. Grassy foliage is looser than *Liriope muscari* giving it more rambling appearance. Toughest of the Liriopes, also, but not particularly attractive in winter. Mow or trim to the ground once a year. The best time for mowing is early December. Light blue to white flowers appear in spring and extend to 12 inches above the ground. Plant on 9- to 12-inch centers. Nice ground cover for the right location. Moderate growth rate with moderate watering.

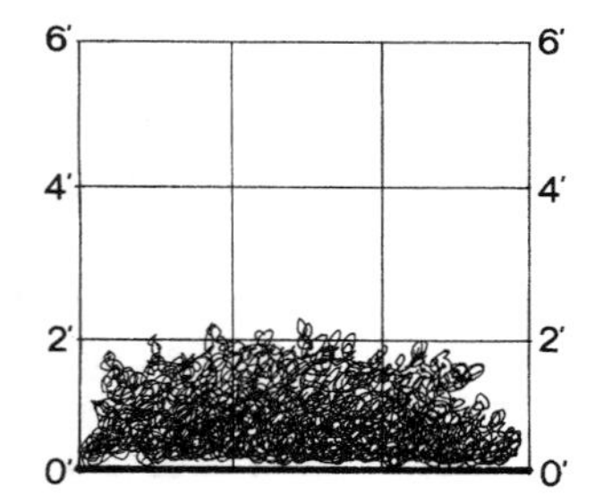

Lonicera japonica 'Halliana' **Evergreen**
Hall's Japanese Honeysuckle

A word of warning from the outset. This is an extremely aggressive ground cover. It can take over an entire planting bed in a single growing season. Use a lot of forethought before you specify it. Two main criteria for its use are a large area and that there be no shrubbery intermixed with it. You will never win the battle of trying to prevent its growing into shrubs and eventually killing them. I have used it as a base planting for single smooth-trunked trees such as Australian Bottle Tree (*Brachychiton populneus*) with great success, but, even in this instance, the ground cover has to be removed from the trunks every 3 months. Whenever Honeysuckle is used, it is best used alone. When it hits a wall, it climbs, so factor this into your space selection. One-inch, asymmetric, white flowers in spring are sweetly aromatic and attract bees and hummingbirds. Deep-green, 3/4-inch, oval foliage spreads by runners and does it ever spread! Takes all exposures and becomes quite drought tolerant at maturity. Excellent, large-scale, bank cover for erosion protection. Plant on 3-foot minimum centers. With moderate watering in its youth this is a lightening-fast grower.

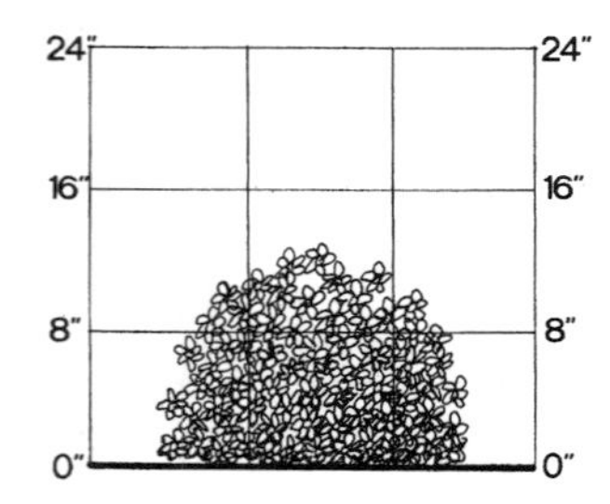

Melampodium leucanthum **Deciduous**
Blackfoot Daisy

Nice little plant that is frequently used as an annual. Listed here because it will return season after season. Blackfoot Diasy will drop all its leaves in a mild frost and die to the ground in a hard frost. It exhibits a profuse flower show of white daisy-like blossoms. Plant's main use is as a spring annual and for soil stabilization. Foliage is dark green. Better establishment will occur when it is seeded, but if planted as a liner or from one-gallon containers, plant on 12-inch centers. Fast growth with a low-water requirement.

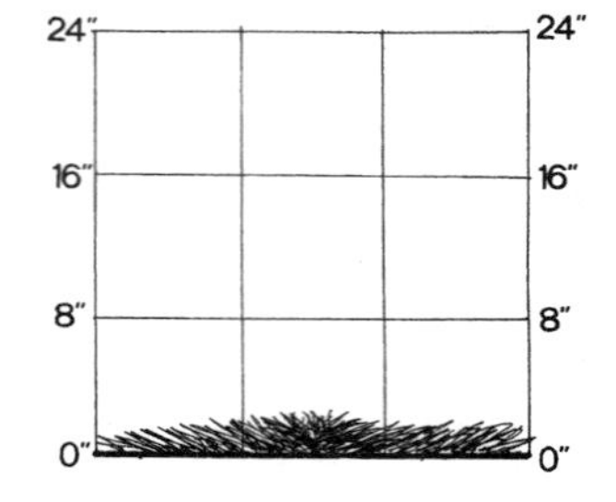

★ ***Myoporum parvifolium*** **Evergreen**
Myoporum

A ground cover rapidly gaining widespread popularity in the desert. Although several references do not rate it hardy enough for the desert zones, the plant has survived the hard freezes in 1990 and 1991 better than most other ground covers. Medium-green, coarse-textured, and low lying. It forms a dense mat in a single growing season. Plant on 3-foot minimum centers. Is somewhat drought resistant at maturity, but prefers moderate water throughout its life span. Myoporum is one of the true miracle plants of the desert.

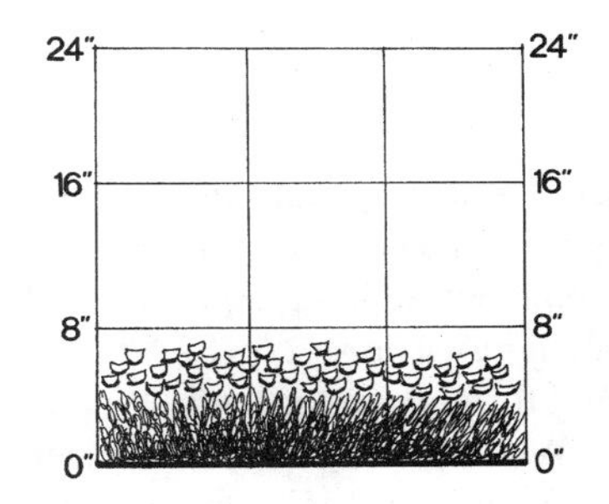

Oenothera berlandieri **Deciduous**
Mexican Primrose

Lovely, small-scale, clumping ground cover. Foliage stays green the greater part of the year but is dormant and unattractive in December and January. Loose, airy, rambling habit. Is not a plant for close-up viewing. Brilliant 1 1/ 2- inch, cupped, light pink flowers with faint yellow centers from late February into June. Plant is often included in native hydroseed mixes. Plant on 18-inch minimum centers. Fast growth with moderate water. Quite drought resistant once established. Trim with a string trimmer once a year for a better, fuller appearance and improved blooming.

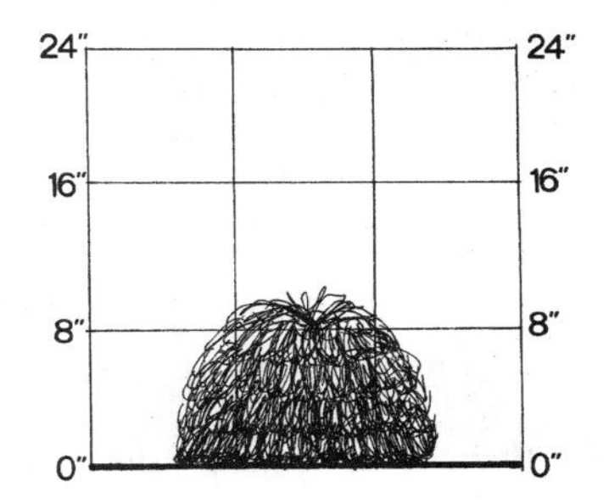

Ophiopogon japonicus **Evergreen**
Mondo Grass

Similar in shape, size, and character to Blue Fescue (*Festuca ovina* 'Glauca') except foliage is deep green. It looks nice intermixed with or adjacent to Blue Fescue and has the same cultural requirements except it can take a little more sun and needs a little more water to look its best. Needs constant maintenance to look neat. Plant on 6-inch centers. Slow growth.

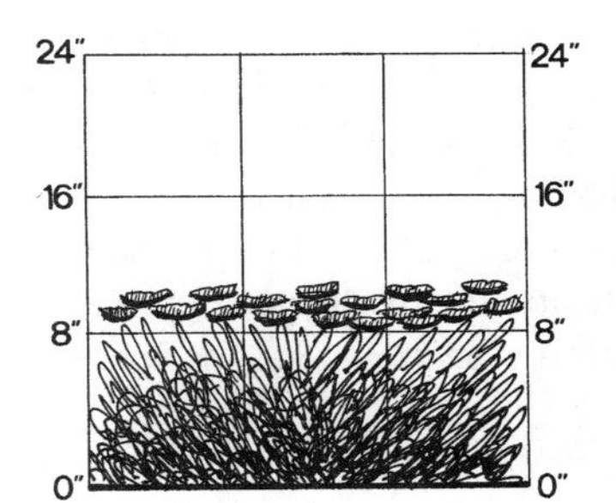

Osteospermum fruticosum **Semi-evergreen**
Trailing African Daisy

Perennial in most Southern California zones, it is frequently planted as an annual in arid areas. If winters are mild, it will survive 2 or 3 seasons. If there is a hard frost it will struggle and is better off pulled and replanted. Nicest feature of this ground cover is the 2-inch round, daisy-like white or purple blossoms that occur during the height of the tourist season — November to March. Medium-green foliage. Loose ground cover. Plant on 12- or 18-inch centers. Fast growth with moderate irrigation

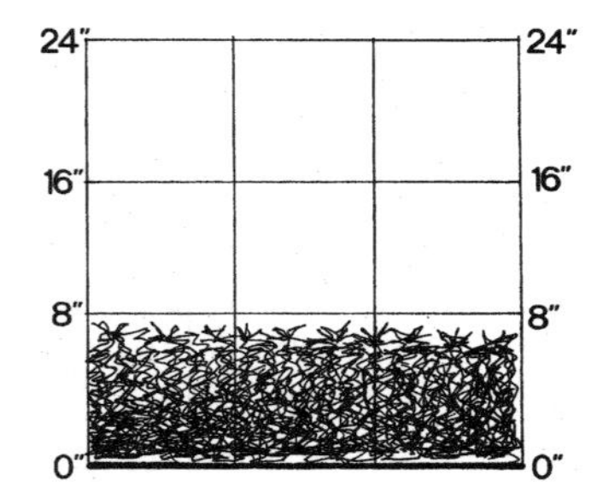

Pachysandra terminalis **Evergreen**
Japanese Spurge

Definitely a plant for the oasis garden. Used frequently in more northern zones, this is as clean and as appealing a ground cover as you will ever find. In the desert, frost is not the limiting factor, but sunlight, especially reflected glare, is. Because of its preference for slightly acid soil (pH 5.5 to 6.5) special soil amendments would be required for optimum growth. Would be an excellent selection as a soil cover under Azalea,Gardenia, or Rhododendron, which are often cultivated in protected gardens. Light-green, oval, saw-toothed leaves project horizontally from stiff, succulent, 8-inch-high stems. Four-inch-high, vertical, white flower spikes occur at terminus of stems in spring. Will take just about any amount of shade, including deep shade, but does better in filtered light. Not a star performer because of its infrequent use, but could be in the right situation. Plant on 6-inch centers. Slow growth can be helped along slightly with doses of high nitrogen fertilizer.

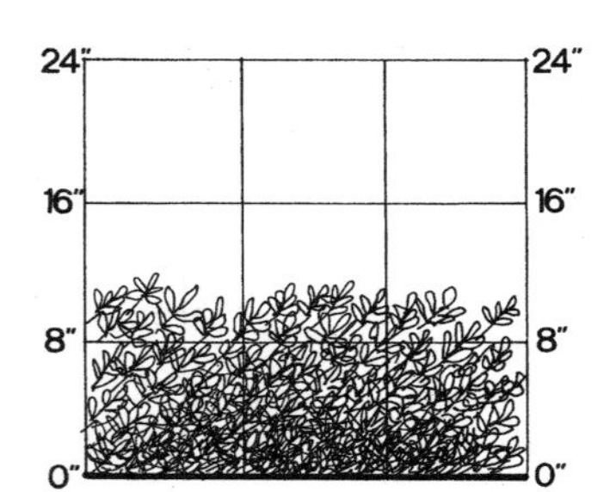

Parthenocissus quinquefolia **Deciduous**
Virginia Creeper

Very similar to its cousin Boston Ivy (*Parthenocissus tricuspidata*) which is described in the vine section. While Boston Ivy is tight and has a 3-lobed simple leaf, Virginia Creeper is loose and rambling with a palmately (5 points) compound leaf. Virginia Creeper is deep green, turning to a copper-crimson in cold weather. It does not achieve the deep maroon of Boston Ivy nor is it as vigorous a climber. What it lacks in climbing ability, it makes up for in spreading proficiency. Needs some shade; do not plant in full sun — east exposure is as far as you should test it. Looks good on the ground plane for a woodsy effect. Try butting it up to Boston ivy on the vertical plane for an especially nice winter appearance. Plant on 18 inch centers. Moderate growth with moderate water.

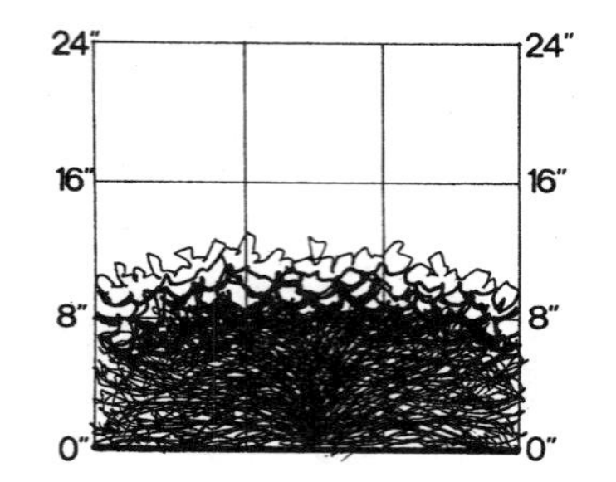

Philostrophe cooperi **Semi-evergreen**
Paper Flower

Native to the high and intermediate deserts of the Southwest, this ground cover has been introduced to the low desert where it readily naturalizes. Spectacular and long lived (March to September) flower show. Masses of 1-inch yellow blossoms completely cover the plant in such abundance that the foliage cannot be seen. Fast growth with low watering.

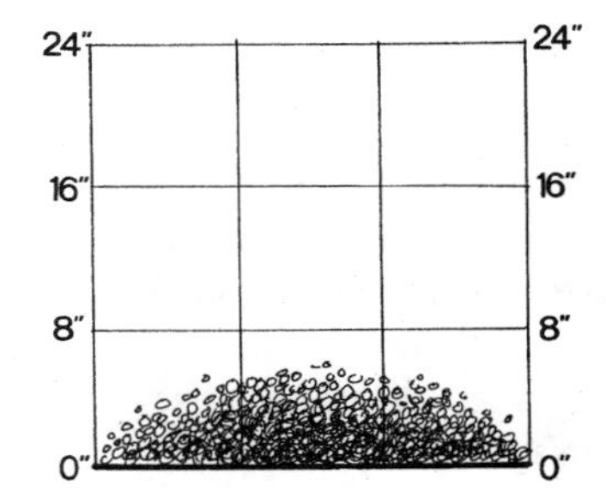

★ *Polygonum capitatum* **Semi-evergreen**
Pink Clover Blossom

Not a refined ground cover. Very invasive, so use it in areas where curbs and walls can contain it or in large throw-away type areas. Dark-green, 1 1/2-inch-long, oval, lance-tipped leaves. Leaves take on a pinkish tinge at maturity. Blooms year round, but heaviest flower show comes with the heat of late spring and summer. Appealing 1-inch sprays of small, round, pink flowers. Plant on 12-inch minimum centers. Will become drought tolerant, to a degree, with age but prefers moderate irrigation. Given moderate water, it is a fast grower.

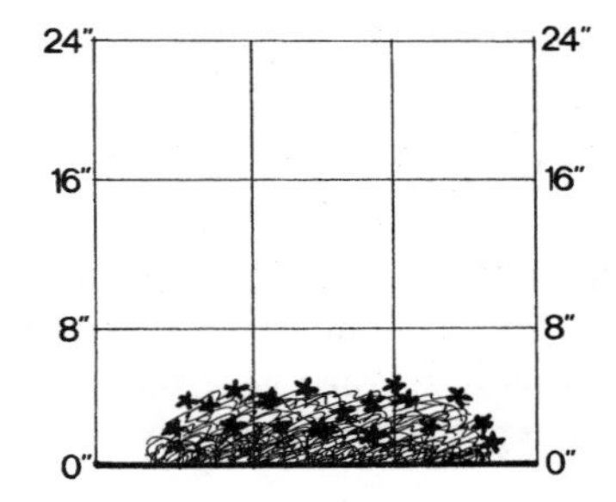

★ *Potentilla verna* **Evergreen**
Spring Cinquefoil

This tiny ground cover is beginning to make a big impact in the desert. Needs some afternoon shade to be effective. Do not use it in the open or on west exposures. One-eighth-inch, bright green, oval leaves are tightly grouped on 4-inch-high stems. Buttercup-shaped, bright yellow, 1/4 inch round, flowers appear in late spring and persist through summer. Becomes more drought tolerant with age but does best with moderate irrigation. Good substitute for *Dichondra repens* in nontraffic areas. Plant on 4-inch minimum centers. Fast growth.

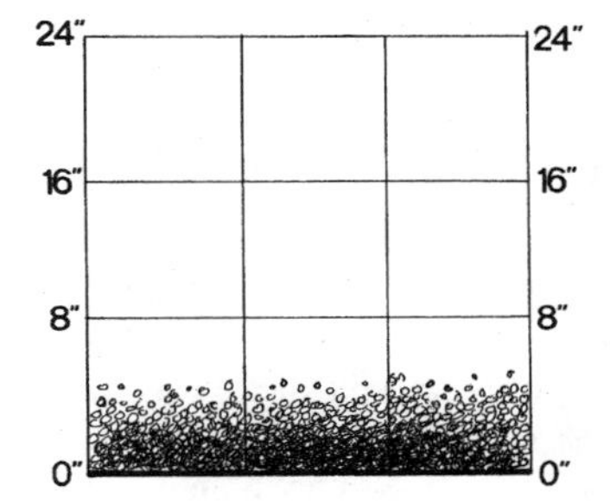

Soleirolia soleirolii (Helxine soleirolli) **Evergreen**
Baby's Tears

This low, dense, delicately leaved ground cover makes an excellent soil cover in the atrium or tropical garden. Prefers shade, but will accept filtered light. Will freeze in winter if left exposed but recovers quickly. A fine plant to use between pavers and in other tight areas. A rapid grower when subjected to ample waterings. Appreciates a high-nitrogen fertilizer in spring to get it off to a quick start. Plant from 4-inch plugs at 6 to 12 inches on center.

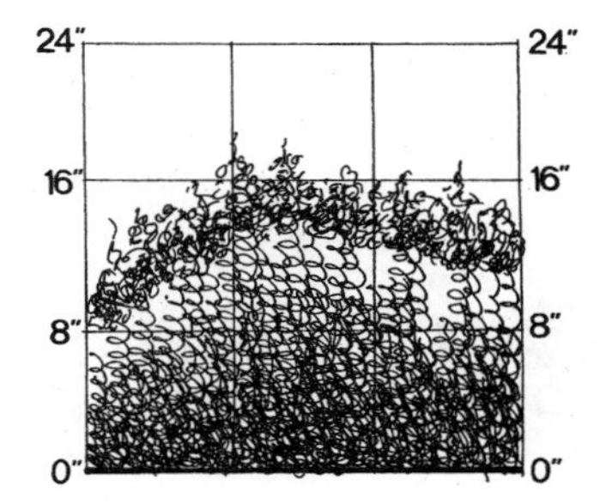

Teucrium chamaedrys **Evergreen**
Germander

Not frequently used in arid areas, this ground cover deserves more consideration. Very upright character. Bright-green, 3/4-inch-long, holly-like leaves with rounded edges. Needs some top shearing with a string trimmer to encourage even growth. Pink-lavender flowers occur in late spring and by summer's end are light pink to white. Germander, being a member of the mint family, is somewhat aromatic. Needs fast draining soil. Will withstand drought and prefers low watering. Moderate growth rate.

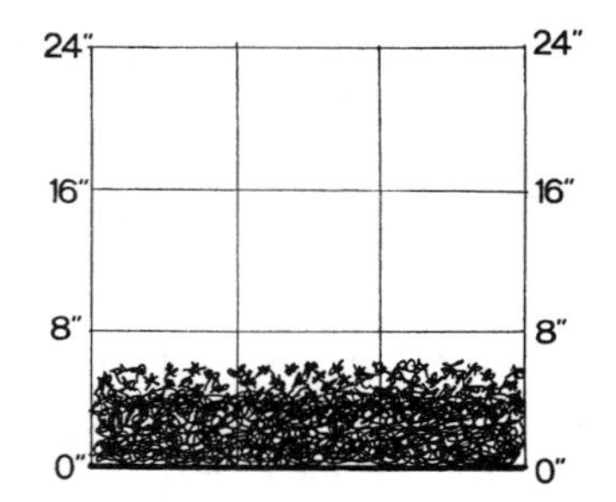

Thymus praecox arcticus **Evergreen**
Creeping Thyme

Good open-area, high-desert selection where other ground covers will either cook or freeze. Creeping Thyme can take the climate swing with ease. Small 1/4-inch-long leaves mound up to 6 inches high, good between steppers. Plant on 9-inch centers. Light purple fading to white flowers in clusters from late spring into September. Can be used for food seasoning. Fast growing with low to moderate water usage.

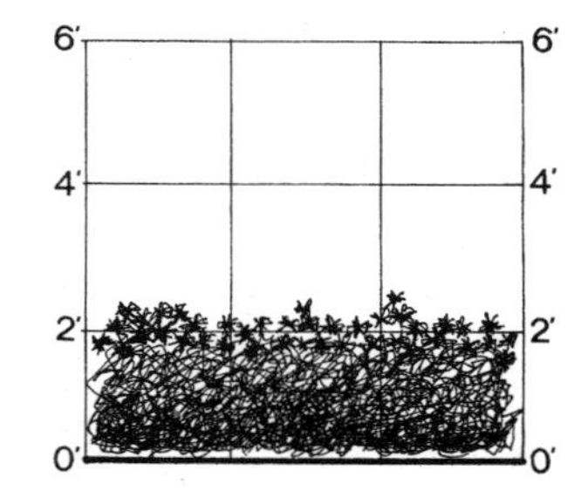

★ ***Trachelospermum jasminoides*** **Evergreen**
Star Jasmine

Described in the vine section where it is not listed as a star performer. While it makes an adequate vine, in the desert it is more highly prized as a ground cover. As a ground cover it needs filtered light to intermediate shade. Will not tolerate full sun or deep shade. Pinch runners for denser growth. Deep green foliage. Bright-white, star-shaped flowers, famous for their fragrance, show up in late spring. Plant on 18-inch centers. Water generously for moderate growth rate which can be helped along with ample, early spring fertilization.

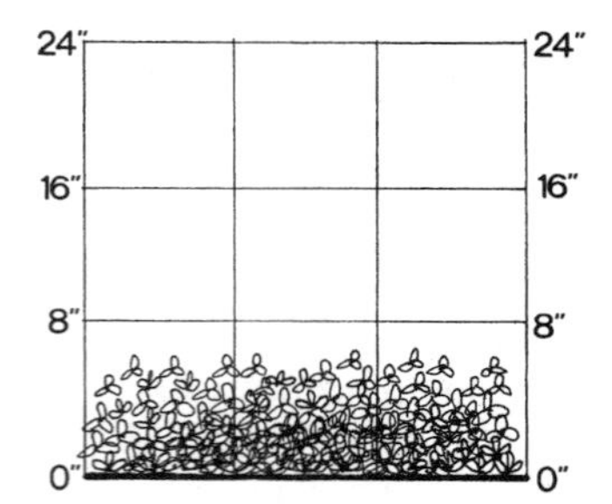

Trifolium fragiferum **Evergreen**
O'Connor's Legume

A plant worth experimenting with as a low-traffic area turf alternative. This is a clover from Australia which is getting increased use in California's interior valleys and chaparral communities. It has exhibited fast growth and a good degree of drought tolerance. Tripartite, bright-blue-green growth leaves, whose leaflets are more oval than other clovers. Six inches seems to be its optitum height, although it can be encouraged to go up to 12 inches with ample watering. Takes trimming and looks better with it. Is being considered in some areas as a lawn substitute, but the suspicion is that it will sunburn if cut lower than 2 inches in the desert. Can be grown from seed or planted from 4-inch plugs at 12 inches on center. Fast growth.

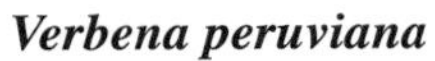

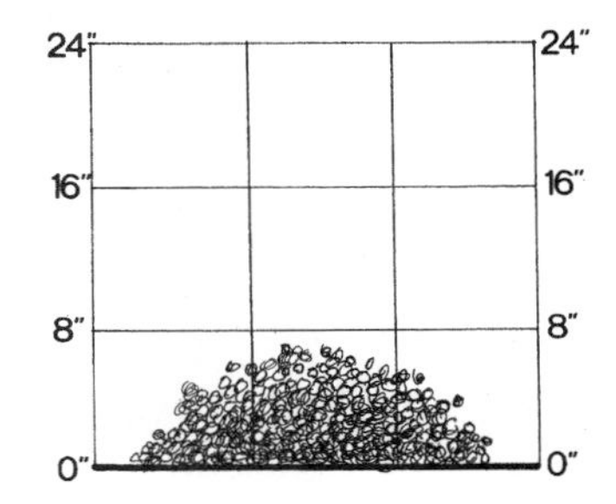

Verbena peruviana — **Semi-evergreen**

Verbena (consult growers' catalogues)

Dull-green, flat-matted foliage is of little consequence: this plant is grown for its massive bloom. Flowers as abundantly as *Lantana sellowiana* but stays lower. It looks very nice as a foreground plant to Lantana. Does not look good in winter and will burn in full summer sun. Most landscape architects treat it as an annual or as a throw-away plant that will brown out in summer and winter but bloom in periods of moderate temperatures. It is drought tolerant but grows and blooms better with moderate irrigation. Flower show is heaviest in spring. Variety 'Cherry Pink' is the hardiest, blooming deep pink, and easiest to obtain. Variety 'Starfire' has brilliant red flowers and is a real eye catcher. Purple and white varieties are avaiable. Fast growth.

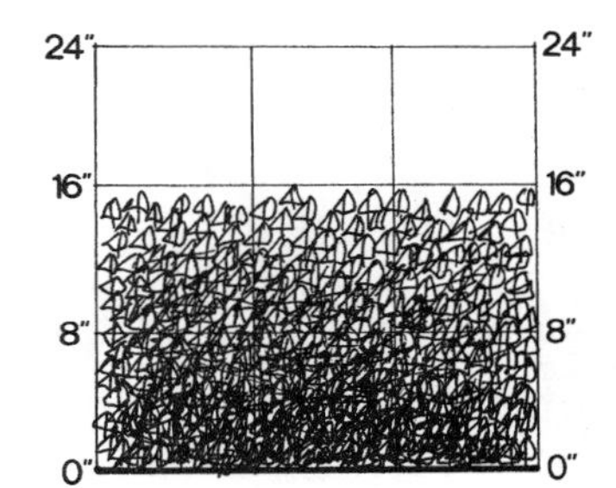

Vinca major — **Evergreen**

Periwinkle

Similar in all aspects to *Vinca minor* below, except it is taller, with more rounded leaves, and a looser habit; it appreciates a little more sun. Flowers also lean more towards a lavender hue and are larger. Same cultural requirements as *V. minor*. Nice plant, just not quite as nice as its cousin. Use where there is filtered light, but exposure is questionable for *V. minor*.

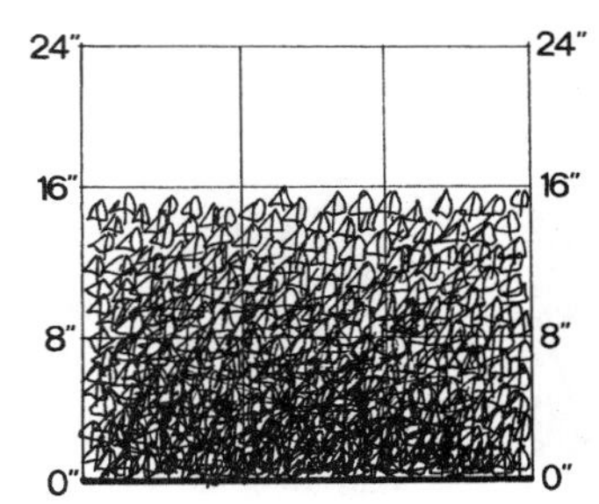

★ **Vinca minor** — **Evergreen**

Dwarf Periwinkle

If grown in shade, this elegant little ground cover is a star performer in every sense of the word. Use it in the tropical oasis garden as an understory plant to exotics like Bird-of-Paradise (*Strelitzia reginae*) or Split-leaf Philodendron (*Philodendron selloum*) where it fits right in. Deep-green, 1/2-inch-long leaves are closely spaced on loose trailing stalks. Pinch stalk tips occasionally to encourage denser growth and fuller appearance. Five-petaled, short, 3/4-inch, star-shaped blue to violet flowers appear in spring and are quite dainty. The deeper the shade the plant is in, the more blue the flower hue. Plant on 6-inch centers. Moderate growth with ample water. Appreciates ample fertilization.

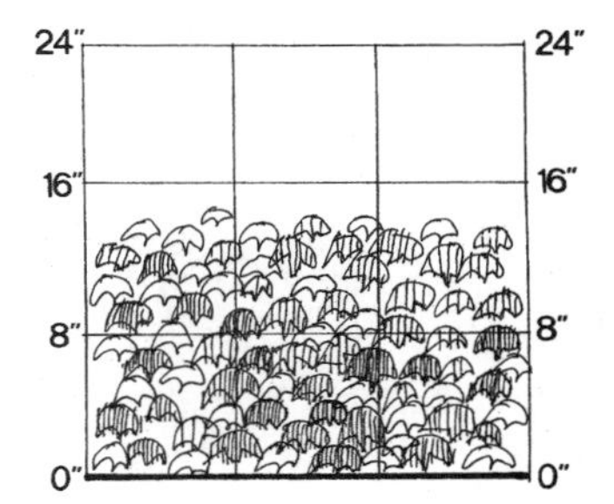

Vitis girdiana — **Deciduous**

Wolfberry (Wild Grape)

This deep-green, rambling ground cover fills the wash running below the famous Palm Springs Aerial Tramway. As such, it is probably the most frequently viewed natural ground cover in Southern California. Its culture and form are similar to the edible grapes, but its foliage is a darker green. Hopefully, it will become propagated for ornamental use. Would be a good selection for a naturalistic design that emulates a Palm Canyon effect in conjunction with *Washingtonia filifera* and other plants unique to the California desert.

Turf Grasses

Rolled sod

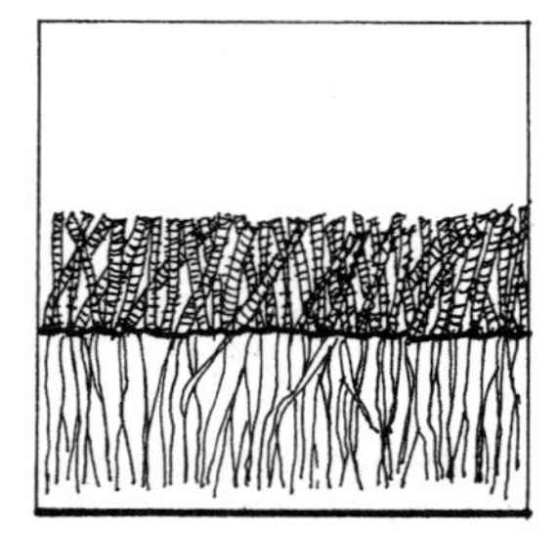

★ ***Cynodon dactylon*** **Semi-evergreen**
Common Bermuda Grass

The most prevalent lawn in Southwest desert gardens. Consistently a star performer if given good drainage and full sun. Medium green, fine textured leaves spread by utilizing underground runners. Common Bermuda is referred to as a warm weather or summer grass. It will go dormant in winter, turning brown from November to March. It is frequently overseeded with Annual Rye Grass (described below) but it should be remembered that if your personal taste can tolerate it — Bermuda Grass does not have to be overseeded. That is, it can be left in its dormant state and it frequently is in middle class residential neighborhoods. When leaving Bermuda Grass in a winter dormant, state remember that although the grass is brown the roots are still growing and appreciate a deep water soaking about once a month. Common Bermuda is the only Bermuda variety that can be propagated from seed. All the other varieties have to be planted from sod, plugs, or stolons. While the hybrids will set seed, the seed is sterile. Due to the fact that most Bermudas are mowed between 1/2 inch and 1 1/2 inch high, the seed heads are rarely seen. This is a good thing as pollen from Bermuda Grass flowers, which precede the seed, can be very tough on pollen sufferers. Common Bermuda is almost always established from seed because if sod or other propagation methods are chosen then a hybrid with better growth or shade tolerance characteristics would be selected as a justification for the additional expense. The start date for seeded common Bermuda grass is March 21, and the cutoff date is September 21. Seeding before or after these dates means running the risk of an early or late season frost destroying a new stand of turf. All Bermudas, and especially the species, like monthly applications of a high nitrogen fertilizer. In alkaline soils, applications of iron are extremely beneficial. Seed at the rate of 2 pounds per 1,000 square feet of area. Mow at 1 1/2 inches high. All Bermudas perform better if mowed with a reel mower, especially the hybrids listed below, which are two of the most commonly used Bermuda Grass hybrids.

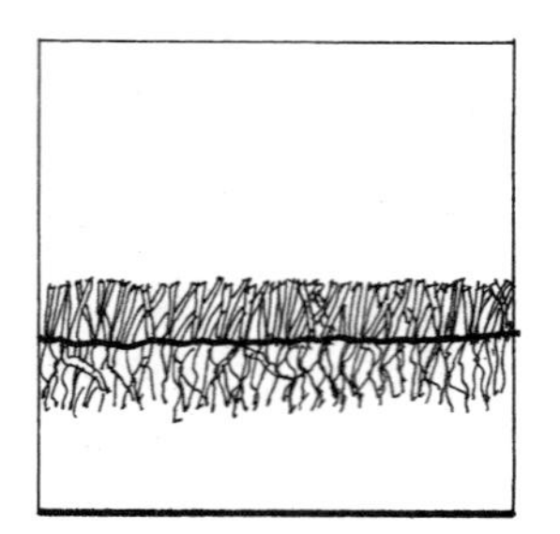

★ ***Cynodon dactylon 'Tifgreen'*** **Semi-evergreen**

Finer textured are darker green than the species. Will tolerate partial shade, where it presents its darkest shade of green. From sod, plugs, or stolons. Mow at 1 inch high with a reel mower.

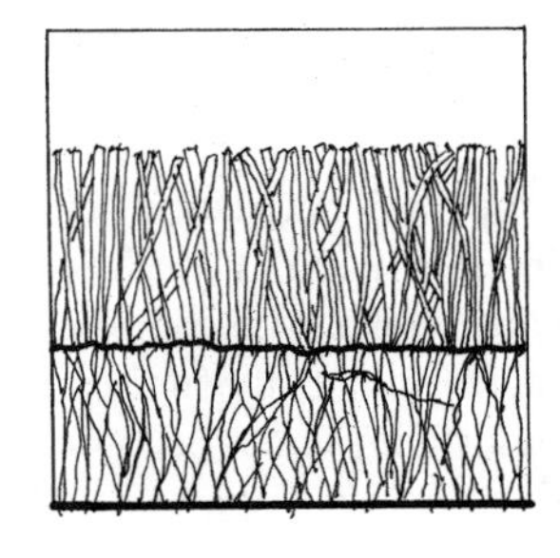

★ ***Cynodon dactylon 'Tifway'*** **Semi-evergreen**

Finer textured than the species. Can be mowed (with a reel mower) in excess of 2 inches high making it a favorite for residential lawn construction as it requires less frequent cuttings than other varietie,s. From sod, plugs, or stolons. Sod is definitely the best method of establishment for this Bermuda variety.

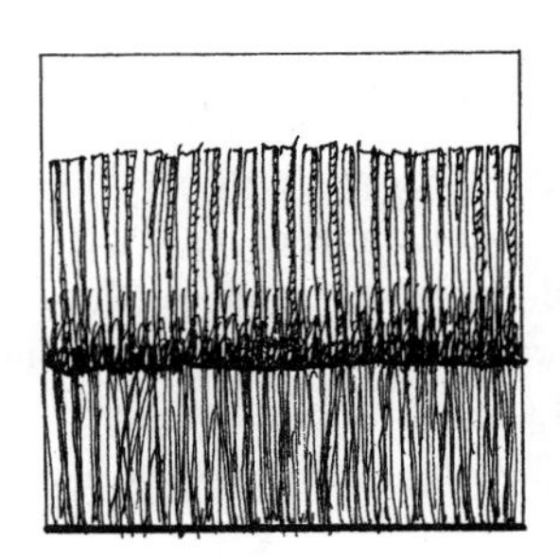

★ ***Lolium multiflorum*** **Semi-evergreen**
Annual Rye Grass

The only green winter lawn for the desert. Very popular for over-seeding Bermuda Grass lawns. (It is not recommended to overseed the remaining 2 grasses described below.) Start date for seeding of Rye Grass is September 21, although a warm fall may allow perfect conditions for seeding of rye all the way into late November. After November it is risky to seed as the chances of a frost kill are high. It is advisable to mow Bermuda to the ground (scalp) and power rake the grass at grade (de-thatch). Rye is then overseeded at the rate of 10 pounds per 1000 sq. ft. of area. Rye is an extremely fast grower, appearing in 7 to 10 days. The new Rye should be mowed with a rotary mower 3 weeks after germination. Rye needs fertilization with a high nitrogen fertilizer on a monthly basis during the winter months to look its best. Leaves are coarse when compared to Bermuda grass, shiny and light green, turning to bright green about a month after establishment. In March, the Rye Grass is scalped and the Bermuda grass take over for the warm season. Where water conservation is an issue and the property users are present only during the Rye Grass season, it is conceivable to have only Rye and simply let it die out while dust and erosion are controlled by the established root system. When fall comes, simply re-seed with the coming season's new Rye Grass planting. Since turf is the highest water user (especially a summer lawn) and the most maintenance-intensive plant material in the landscape, this is not as absurd as it may sound, especially if the stand of turf is behind a wall and out of the public's view.

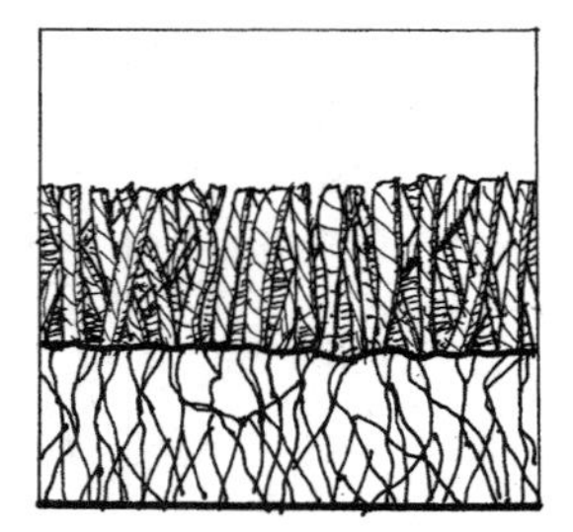

Stenotaphrum secundatum **Semi-evergreen**
Saint Augustine Grass

So named because it was developed in the Saint Augustine area of Florida. The grass will remain green in mild winters although it is virtually dormant during this period. Blades of this grass are wide, stiff, and lie very flat. This light bluish-green grass of a coarse texture spreads by surface runners that root freely as they fan out over the soil's surface. Grass becomes quite thick and thatch-like, having a somewhat springy or buoyant feeling when walked on. Saint Augustine, despite its spring, is not a particularly good play or sport surface. The coarse leaves scrape skin when slid across and the grass thins with heavy foot traffic. Two advantages of Saint Augustine are that it will tolerate shade and it can be flood irrigated with ease. It does not seem to mind being underneath standing water as much as other lawns do. A good choice for small shady areas. Establish from sod or plugs. Plugs cover soil in one growing season if spaced no more than 12 inches on center. Sod is better for more of an immediate effect. Mow at 2 inches high with a rotary mower. Power rake (de-thatch) once a year as the procedure greatly enhances the health and appearance of the turf.

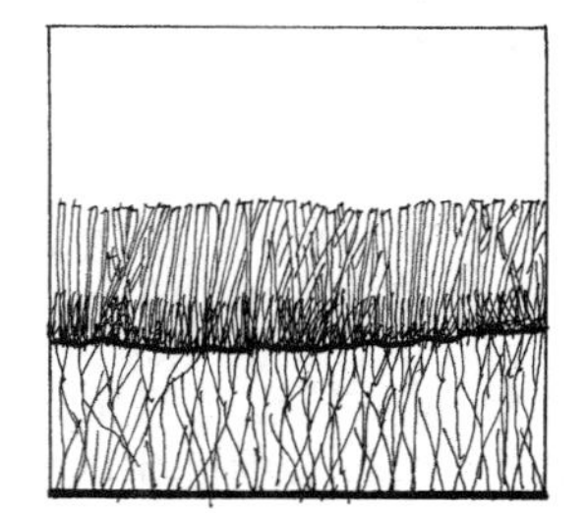

Zoysia tenuifolia **Semi-evergreen**
Korean Grass

A grass not frequently grown in the desert and, realistically speaking, should probably be your last choice. The grass does have its uses, however. The grass tolerates shady conditions. Zoysia also is the most salt tolerant of the turf grasses, which would make it a good selection in areas adjacent to the playas. The informal bumpy appearance of the grass is quite natural looking and appealing. This effect could be put to good use in areas that are hard to mow or only need occasional mowing. Similar to Bermuda grass in color and texture. Goes winter dormant sooner than and stays browner longer than Bermuda Grass. Zoysia grass is also more susceptible to pests and diseases than either Bermuda or Saint Augustine grass. Besides its shade tolerance, Zoysia's biggest advantage is that it can take a lot of foot traffic. Most effective desert planting is from sod. Cut at 3/4 inches high.

Cacti, Succulents, Yuccas, Desert Grasses, and Spoons

Cacti & Succulent Garden

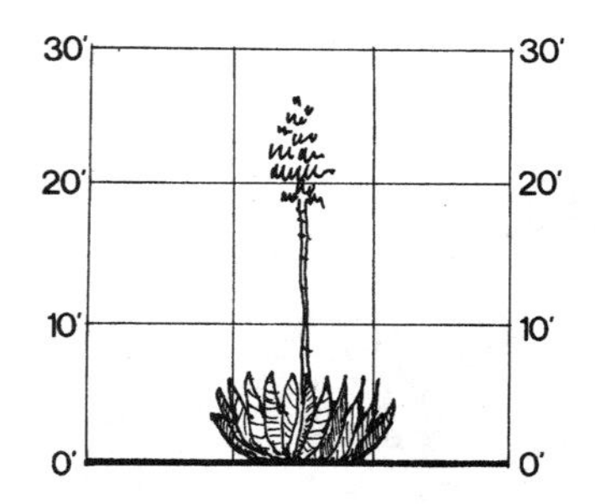

Agave americana **Evergreen**
Century Plant

The largest plant in this bizarre genus: the scale of this bluish-green succulent is massive. All Agaves die after blooming. That's the bad news — the good news is that, if planted small, *Agave americana* will probably live a minimum of 10 years before sending forth a 20- to 30-foot-high flower stalk upon which flat, hairy yellow flowers horizontally perch. Any Agave in bloom is a wonder of nature and something you will never forget. *Americana*, having the tallest flower stalk of the genus, is perhaps the most unforgettable Agave. Most Agaves that have been established at 1 location for a while develop offshoots or pups which replace the original plant after it dies. Fleshy leaves arranged in a tight circular pattern have vicious points and teeth along their margins, so this is not a plant to be placed adjacent to heavily traveled pedestrian circulation patterns. Very tough — takes full outdoor exposure. Slow growth with minimal water. Do not overwater — even moderate irrigation is too much, and will rot the plant.

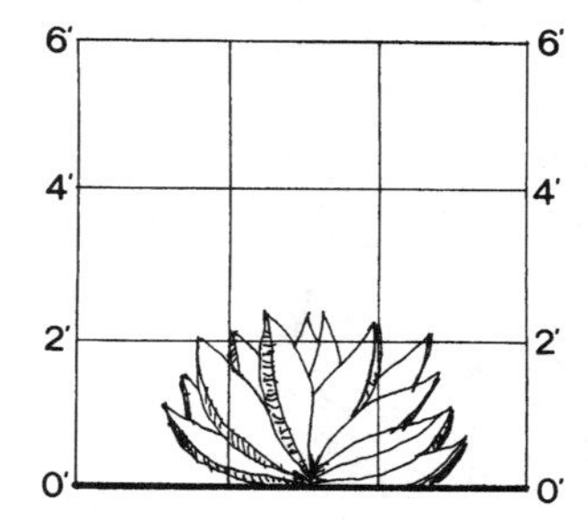

★ ***Agave attenuata*** **Evergreen**
Dragon Tree Agave

Chalky light green leaves are a hue not usually found in nature. This Agave tolerates shade, and conversely, will cook in bright sunlight. Do not use *A. attenuata* on south or west exposures. A plant that fits well into all design use planting zones. Its beautiful leaf rosettes are quite exotic and the light foliage color boldly contrasts the normal dark greens of a shady tropical garden. It carries itself well through the transitional garden mixing and matching with the blue-gray of Cassias, Leucophyllums, Salvias, and the like. Its membership in the Cacti family holds it in good stead when combined with Cacti, Aloes, and other Agave species in the desert garden. Leaf tips are relatively soft and there are no teeth on the leaf margins, making this Agave user friendly. Slow growth with moderate (but no more) irrigation.

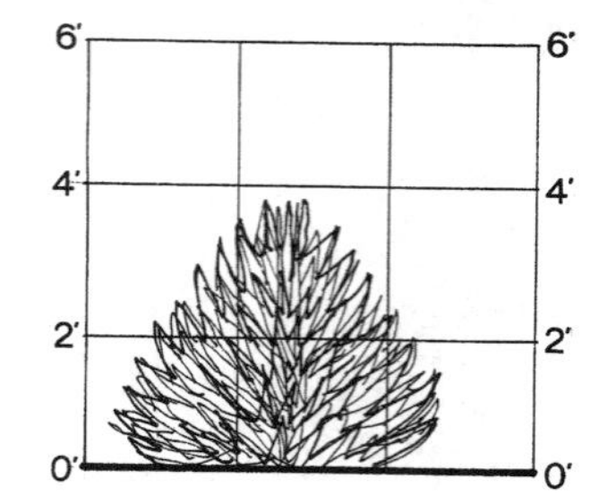

★ ***Agave angustifolia "variegata"*** **Evergreen**
Varigated Agave

An extremely popular Agave in the westernmost deserts. Relatively small size (3-foot rounded clump) makes it ideal for the home garden. Good plant to set out in varying container sizes at initial planting as this will emulate the plant's natural tendency to set out pups in the wild. Very tight rosettes of sharp-tipped upward-cupped 1 1/2-inch-wide sword-like leaves, green on the inside and yellow along the entire margin, for which this Agave is most valued. The plant is also appreciated for its attractive, relatively neat appearance and overall hardiness. Moderate growth with moderate to low water.

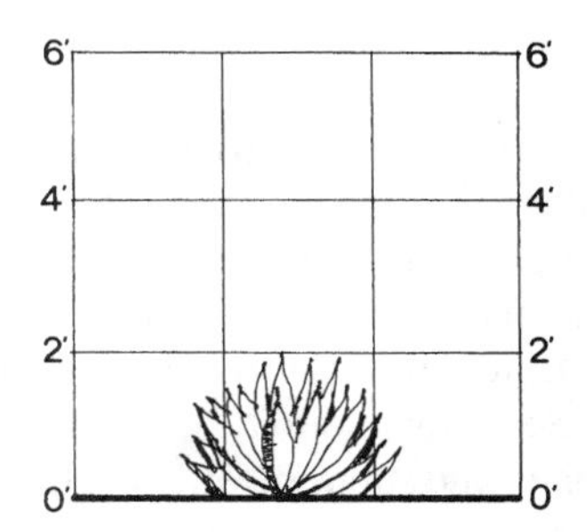

Agave parryi **Evergreen**
(No common name)

Smaller agave whose extremely tight leaf rosettes are said to resemble huge artichokes. Gray-green foliage color. Leaves have vicious tips and the plant sets out numerous pups, so use it where it has room to spread or can definitely be contained. Moderate growth on minimal water.

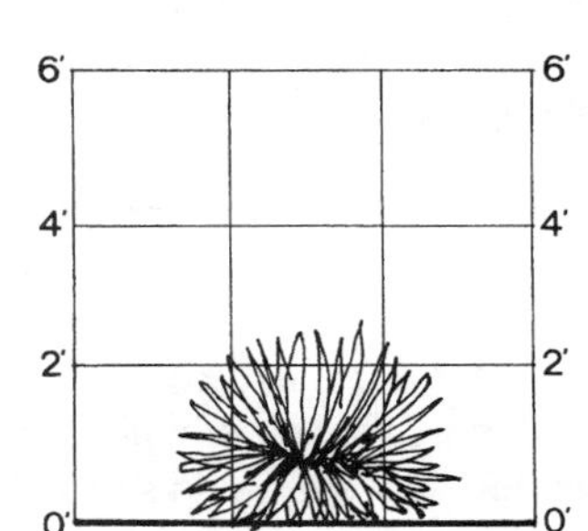

Agave parviflora **Evergreen**
Green Agave

Beautiful bright green, tightly whorled leaves with thin white edges running the length of the margins. Sharp points and wicked teeth. The greenest of the Agaves, lends itself well in helping the planting plan flow from the oasis garden to the transitional garden and beyond. Moderate growth rate with low irrigation.

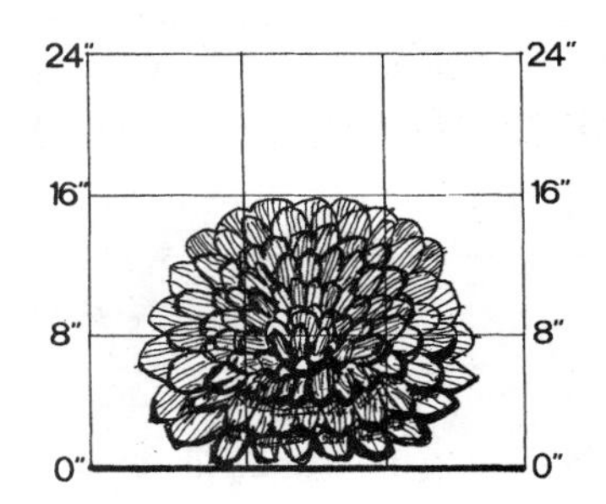

Agave victoriae - reginae **Evergreen**
(No common name)

The smallest of the Agaves, usually being a 12-inch to 18-inch round with a 24-inch clump being uncommon. Leaves are fleshy, triangular, dark green in color and packed into a very tight rosette. Although very small, this Agave will send out a 12-foot long flower spike after about 20 years of life. Atypical of the genus, *A.victoriae-reginae* does not set out pups and dead plants must be replaced. Slow growth with little water. A very good selection for smaller scale gardens.

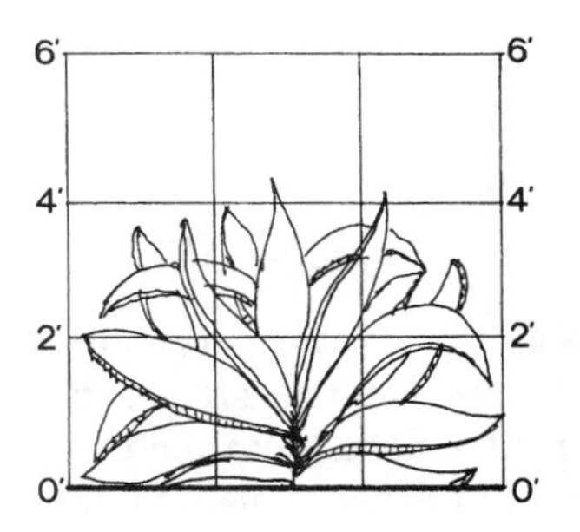

Agave vilmoriniana **Evergreen**
Octopus Agave

A plant that gets heavy use. Primary feature of this medium sized Agave are its twisted, undulating leaves. Foliage is a light green-gray and most similar to *Agave attenuata*. Like *attenuata*, it does not like full sun but is a little tougher, taking south exposures. Looks very nice as a background plant to *attenuata*. While some feel that this is the most uniquely beautiful Agave, others feel it is grotesque. Use Octopus Agave only when the eventual site users seem to have an appreciation for the plant. Slow growth with moderate (no more) water.

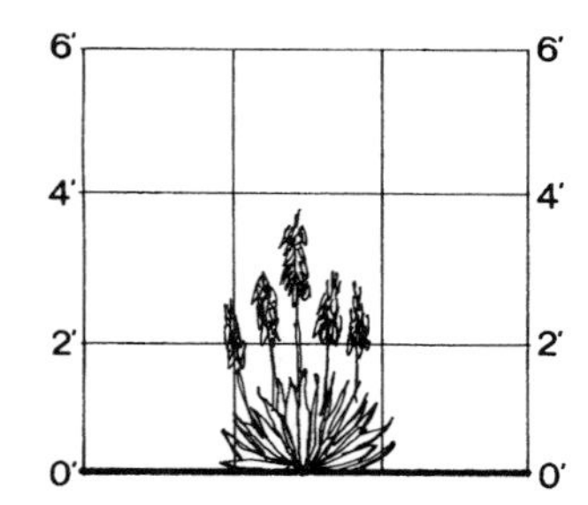

Aloe barbadensis **Evergreen**
Aloe Vera

A plant with a rich history. Originally from North Africa, Spanish padres brought it to the New World for medicinal use. Aloe Vera oil produced by crushing the leaves is used as a skin ointment to treat burns. Dark, gray-green leaves are sharp-tipped and the margins possess reddish teeth. Like most Aloes, *barbadensis* blooms intermittently year round, but its heaviest floral production is from February to September. Stout, fleshy flower stalks rise 3 to 3 feet above the base of the plant and support vertical, almost cone-shaped, yellow flowers. Extremely drought-resistant, but grows and looks better with minimal irrigation. Use in large areas because, like Agaves, Aloes (especially this one) set out many pups. Moderate growth rate.

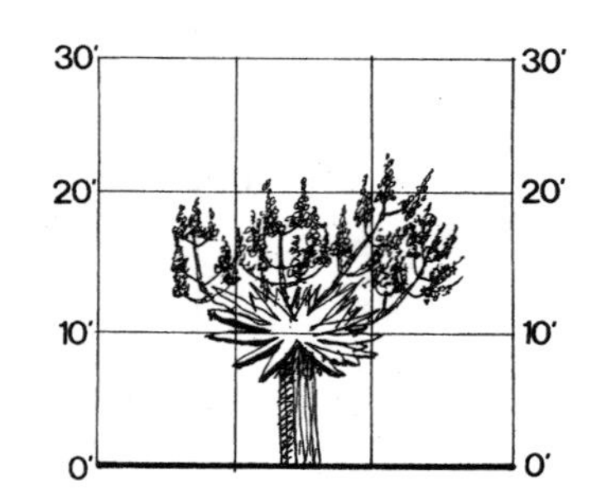

Aloe ferox **Evergreen**
Fire Flower Aloe

Tree-type Aloe to 15 feet high with clumping foliage mounted on a thick trunk. Dull-green, three-foot long leaves are very spiny and spread horizontally outward from the trunk. Red flower clusters reminiscent of candelabra occur primarily in early spring (February and March), but are capable of occurring anytime. An exotic that you don't see everyday in the desert, but worth a try, especially when viewing from second floor areas where the plant presents its flowers at or near eye level. Moderate growth rate with low water requirements.

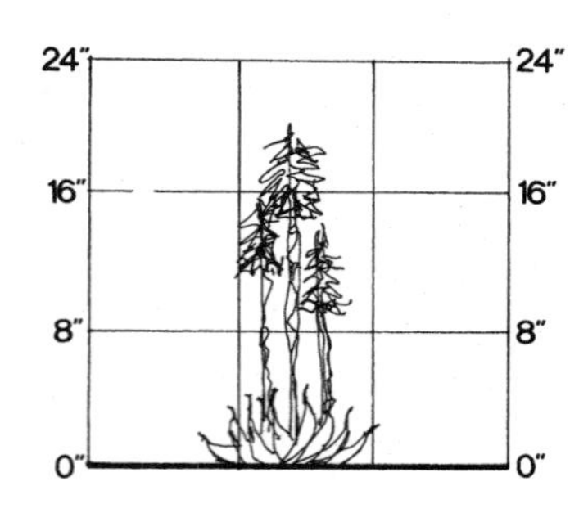

★***Aloe nobilis*** **Evergreen**
Dwarf Aloe

A great little plant for tight areas or in shallow pots and planters. Roots can be crowded over long periods of time. Dark-green, 12-inch-long leaves are lined with tiny, hooked teeth. Jutting dramatically from the tight rosettes of foliage are 2-foot long, stiff, flower stalks bearing reddish-orange blossoms. Flowers year round, heaviest in late spring to early summer. Moderate growth rate on low water.

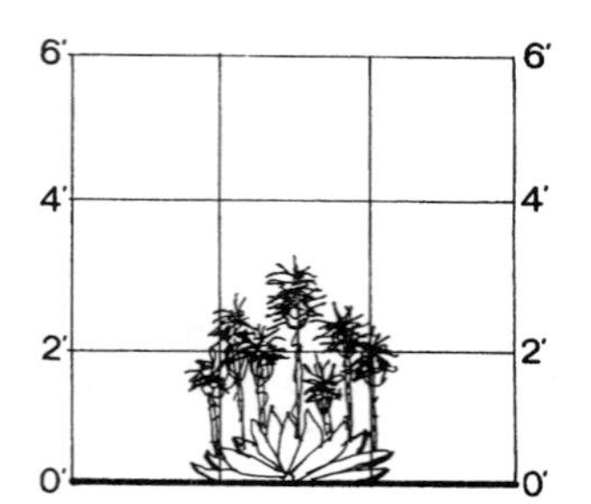

Aloe saponaria **Evergreen**
African Aloe

Differs from the majority of the genus as its leaves are very short and flower stalks, proportionally, are very high. Leaves are light-green and variegated with white bands and spots. They extend 8 inches out from the center of a small rosette. Fleshy, vertical flower stalks extend roughly three times the width of the plant. Rising from the plant's base to a height of 2 1/2 to 3 feet, these stalks support flat masses of orange-red, whorled, tubular flowers. Flowers persist on the plant for up to 6 weeks. Fast growth with moderate watering. The plant sets off pups with regularity.

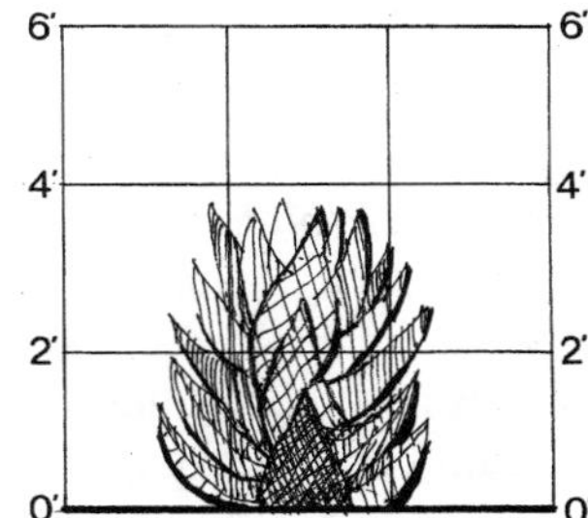
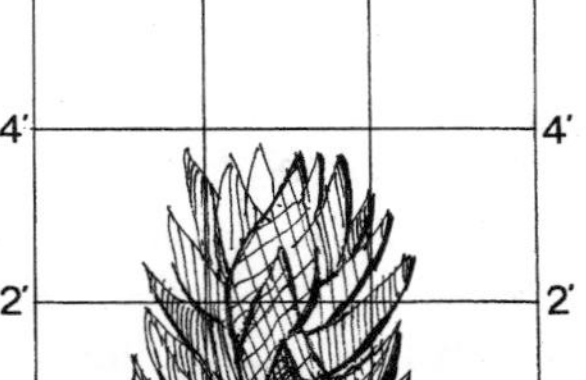

Aloe variegata **Evergreen**
Partridge Breast Aloe

Vertical mass of 5-inch-long, banded, green and white leaves whorling around a central stalk to an occasional height of 5 feet. Reddish-pink flower clusters occur on and off throughout the year. Quite unusual. Moderate growth rate with moderate irrigation.

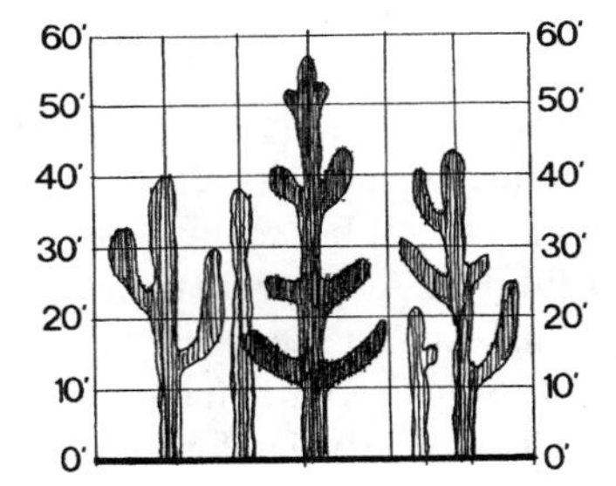

★ *Carnegiea gigantea* **Evergreen**
Saguaro Cactus

The vertical sentinel of the central Sonoran Desert. Probably the most photographed and romanticized Cactus in the world. Grows primarily in the Arizonan part of the Sonoran Desert, although a few are intermingled in Cholla-laden bajadas between Blythe and Desert Center, California. Found at elevations between 1,000 and 3,000 feet; 2,500 feet being optimum. The Sonoran National Monument in Tucson contains the greatest number of Saguaros found anywhere. The Monument is unique in that it is divided into two sections some 15 miles apart. The eastern section which is east of Tucson, contains an older Saguaro forest that, in a lot of respects, is in a state of decline. Cactus found here are 250 years old and older. Nestled in bajadas at the base of the Rincon Mountains, this section of the National Monument is nice, but does not hold a candle to the western half. The western section of the Sonoran National Monument is a sight to behold. The Saguaros in this section are at the peak of their collective lifetimes and acres upon acres of these majestic cacti tower over the terrain of the foothills of the Tucson Mountain Range. Adjacent to this area is the Sonoran Desert Museum, a natural science facility that takes a backseat to no other arboretum or zoo in the country. If you want to observe Saguaros and desert ecology in general, this is the place to visit. The Saguaro Cactus achieves an average height of 40 feet with 60-foot specimens being fairly abundant. When Saguaros are about 60-years old and about 20-feet high, they routinely sprout side branches or arms. These cacti are specified by height and number of arms. Armless Saguaros are called spears and are specified by height. The Saguaro can reach over 3 feet in diameter. It has accordion-like folds, that are armed with 3-inch spines that shrink and swell in response to available water.

All cacti, especially Saguaros, have a skin or cortex. The side of the cortex exposed to the most solar intensity is always thicker. When transplanting Saguaros, they must be aligned in accordance with their cortex. That is, they should be set in the ground with the sun exposure exactly as it was when they were removed. Failure to do this exposes the thin cortex to the sun causing severe burning. Improper planting technique is the primary reason for the failure of large transplants. Experienced plantsmen use a compass to mark north on the trunk prior to digging and reset the cactus with a compass aligning that mark.

Experienced installers are also aware of how a Saguaro, and all barrel-type Cacti for that matter, absorb water. The top of a Saguaro (or Barrel Cactus) is hairy. During intense desert rainstorms, the Cactus can literally absorb water through these hairs directly into its inner pith. While this is a secondary method of drinking in nature, it should be utilized as the primary method of irrigation in replanting. An emitter can be run up and tied to the top of the Cactus and the slowly applied water is readily absorbed by the hairs. Irrigating at grade causes the trunk to rot because the damaged root system simply cannot take up water. The water then sets in the planting hole, becoming progressively warmer and more receptive to disease. With top watering, roots can repair themselves and get a foothold in the Saguaros' new environment.

Saguaros are not native to the Colorado Desert which receives less than half the annual precipitation they are accustomed to and is lower than their optimum range. They will grow, even flourish there, but require supplemental irrigation, especially in the months of July and August when they would be receiving monsoon rain in their natural habitat. It is better to plant younger saguaro spears and let the cactus adapt to their environment. At maturity (± 60 years) Saguaros have spectacular 3-inch-wide white flowers with golden centers which perch on top of the main trunk and arms. Flowers occur at night and persist through the following day. Bloom period is usually mid-May. Red, prune-like fruit follows. This fruit is edible, but usually ripens and splits open, revealing seeds which are relished by birds. Saguaros are strictly protected by the U.S. Department of Agriculture and must be tagged to be legally moved. Specimens over 6 feet in height are extremely heavy and a crane is recommended for ease of handling. Slow growth with minimal water.

Cephalocereus senilis **Evergreen**
Old Man Cactus

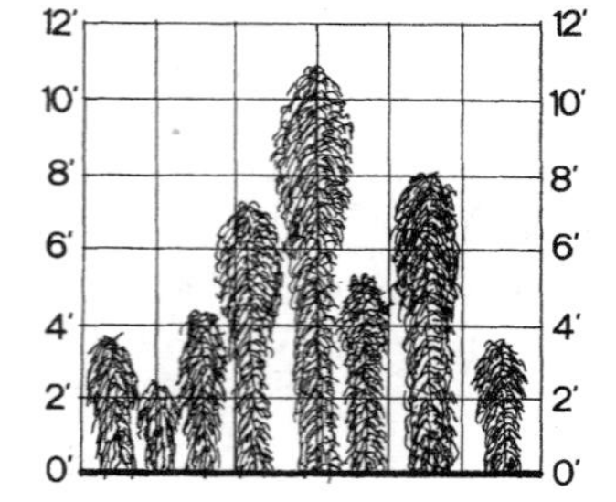

A real horticultural oddity. Prized for its columnar form which is covered with pendulous, almost fur-like, white hairs. Hairs are thick in number and beard-like, giving rise to the common name. This cactus must receive sun and, especially, frost protection to survive in the low desert. In its native Mexico it can achieve a height of 40 feet. In the north, an 8- to 10- foot specimen is a rarity. Excellent potted plants as they grow very slowly. Also a good foreground or accent plant in the cactus garden. Use care in handling — there are 1 1/2-inch yellow spines under all that hair. Mature specimens (10 years and older) have night blooming, rose-colored, pendulous, 2-inch-long flowers arising at the crest of their stems. Extremely slow growth with minimal water.

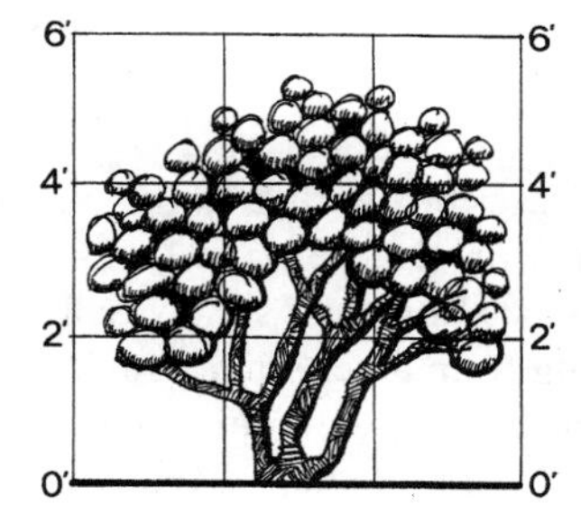

Crassula argentea **Evergreen**
Jade Plant

This exotic succulent must have sun and frost protection to survive in the desert. Very popular worldwide as a houseplant, this Crassula can be grown outdoors in Southern California and, despite its luxuriant appearing foliage, it is very drought tolerant. The plant is most frequently grown for its foliage — flattened, fleshy, bright-green pads tinged in red and about 1 1/2 inches long. These leaves are supported on stout branches arising from an even stouter, thick, and twisted trunk. Mature shape is flat-topped or umbrella-like. Pink, 1/4 inch, star-shaped flowers in clusters bloom in winter to spring, making it a plant for the tourist season. Excellent container subject as it tolerates extreme root crowding. Moderate growth with low to moderate water. Like all succulents, overwatering causes weak growth, root rotting, and toppling of foliage. Avoid overwatering at all costs.

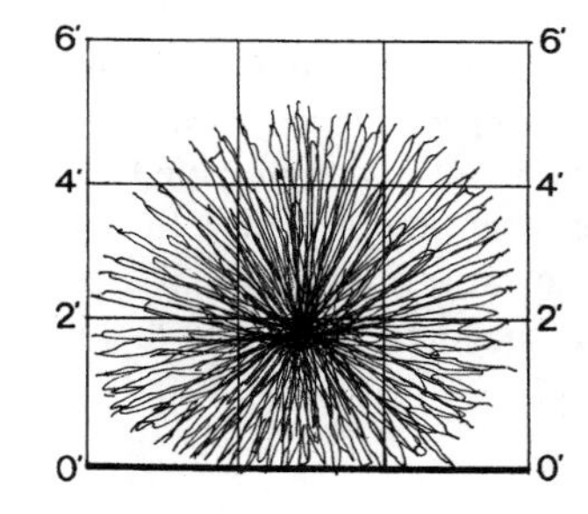

★ ***Dasylirion wheeleri*** **Evergreen**
Desert Spoon

For a number of years, this plant was a well-kept secret. Infrequently used up until the mid-1980s, as most references rated it an inland or chaparral material. Upon introduction to the low and middle desert, it has proven itself a star performer. Full, spikey, gray-green ball. Individual leaves or spines (spoons) are 3 feet long, stiff, sharply pointed, and when pulled from the trunk have a spoon shape. In fact, the leaves were actually used as spoons by the Indians and settlers. They are often used to this day in flower arrangements. The leaf curls inward as response to lower water availability. Plants with a little more irrigation exhibit flatter, fuller, wavy-looking leaves. Like the Agaves, the time of bloom is very unpredictable, except that some desert spoons will bloom between June and October. Unlike the Agaves, the 9-foot flower stalk is not followed by the death of the plant. A fine desert specimen whose only real drawback is that smaller plants are hard to establish. Specify 5-gallon minimum size. Mountain State Nursery is offering *Dasylirion acrotriche*, which is green rather than gray. It is approximately the same size as *Dasylirion wheeleri*. Used together they could provide wonderful color contrast. Slow growth on little irrigation.

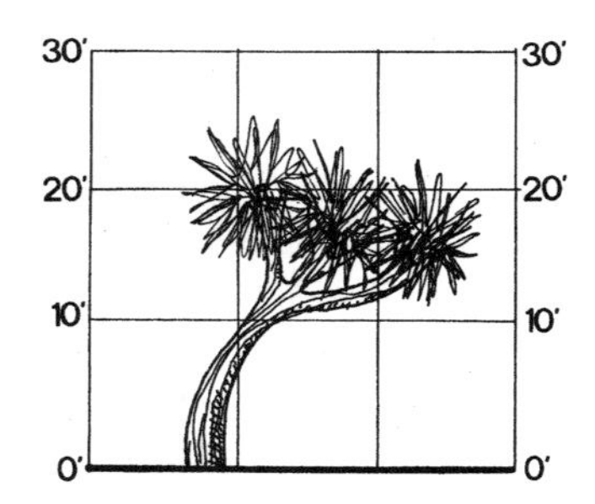

Dracaena draco **Evergreen**
Dragon Tree

Somewhat similar to *Yucca rostrata* described earlier in this section. The main difference is in the leaves, which on the Dracaena are 1 1/2 inch wide at the base, 2 feet long, and taper to a point. Rounded ,spikey balls of leaves rest on top of 3 to 4 beefy stems arising from a very thick trunk. Very slow growing to about 20 feet high. This plant is for the tropical garden and is a conversation piece that needs sun and frost protection. Moderate irrigation produces slow growth.

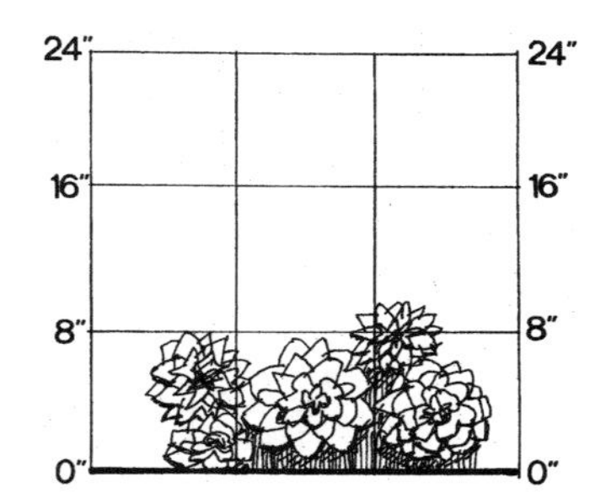

Echeveria imbricata **Evergreen**
Hens and Chickens

Frequently used succulent in home gardens throughout the Southwest. Very pretty plant. Four- to 6- inch diameter rosettes of fleshy, light green leaves tinged with red. Parent plant develops many smaller scale offshoots (pups) that are smaller and dainty — thus the Hen and Chickens common name. The plant will burn in full sun. It needs afternoon shade in summer and frost protection in winter. A good foreground plant in the protected Agave, Aloe, or Yucca garden. Also quite attractive when intermixed with larger species of its own genus. Infrequent flower stalks to 6 inches high arise from the center of the rosette and are usually pink in color. Slow growth with minimal watering.

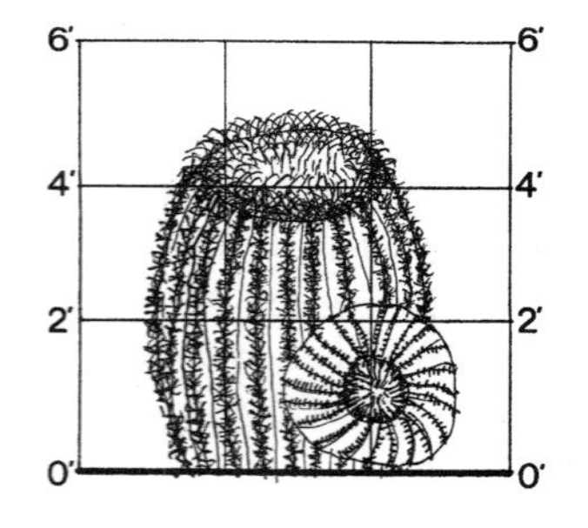

★ ***Echinocactus grusonii*** **Evergreen**
Golden Barrel Cactus

Commonly used specimen of unrivaled beauty. Takes full sun although it appreciates some late afternoon shade in the low desert. Next to the Saguaro, this is likely the most well-known North American cactus. Native to Mexico, it has been planted here to the extent that it can be considered a naturalized plant material. Called the Golden Barrel Cactus because of its 3-inch long yellow spines arch down and over the Saguaro-like ribs. At each main spine location, smaller 1 inch yellow spines fan out in a star shape in all directions across the face of the cactus. The spines act as protection from intruders and also cast shade for sun protection. They cover 50% of the surface area of the cactus. Older specimens (about 5 years old) produce a ring of yellow flowers which spring forth from their hairy yellow crowns in late spring. The flowers occur in daylight and remain on the plant for about 2 weeks if in full sun. Golden Barrels need moderate irrigation when compared to other cactus. In sandy, well-drained soils they require watering every 2 weeks during the hot summer months. Slow growth and high cost are the only serious drawbacks. All Golden Barrel Cactus must be grown from seed as they do not set out pups and cannot realistically be vegetatively propagated.

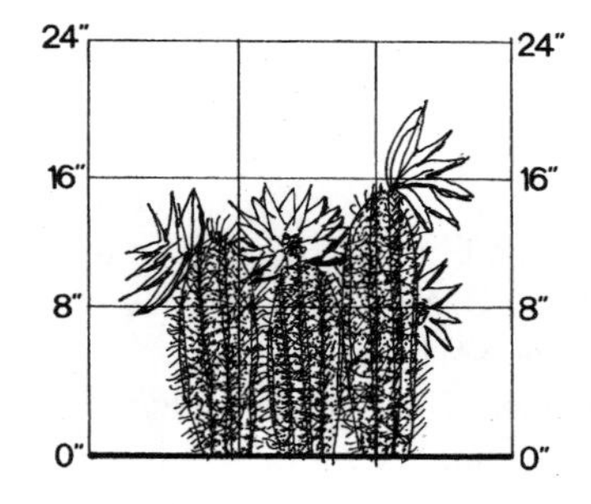

★ *Echinocereus engelmannii* **Evergreen**
Hedgehog Cactus

This little fellow is a spectacular and prolific spring bloomer. Deep violet, 3-inch-wide, cupped flowers with 1-inch yellow centers arise from this ground hugging Cactus and hover about 6 inches off the ground. The Cactus itself spreads about 2 feet and is an earthy green color. As a landscape plant, it is fairly insignificant. The flower show alone, which occurs throughout most of April and into May, justifies cultivation of the plant. Use as a foreground or filler plant in the Cactus or succulent garden. Slow growth on minimal water.

Epiphyllum species **Evergreen/Semi-evergreen**
Christmas Cactus (consult growers' catalogues)

These cacti are best used in raised or hanging pots. Not from the desert, but rather a jungle Cactus that grows in the crotches of trees in a manner similar to Orchids. A houseplant everywhere, this spineless Cactus is easy to grow. It likes sandy, well-drained soil and to be completely dry between waterings. Over 3,000 hybrids (some listed in the Matrix Chart) have been cultivated to utilize the spectacular blossoms to full advantage. Normally a spring bloomer, growers have developed a planting strategy that causes the plant to bloom in winter and it is often available commercially around Christmas — thus the common name. Use in hanging pots or raised planters to serve as an overstory to an understory cactus garden. Fast growth with moderate irrigation.

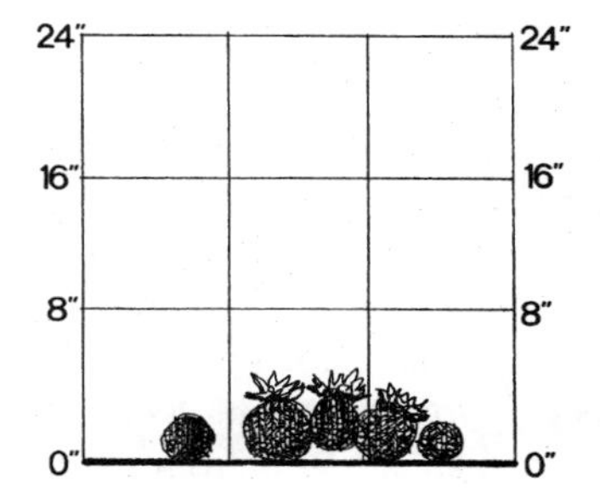

Epithelantha bokei **Evergreen**
Button Cactus

A native to the limestone portions of the Chihuahuan Desert. Not in intense commercial cultivation, this cactus has one desirable and quite unique feature — it is nearly pure white. It also has pure white flowers which is quite a rarity among cacti. Color comes from spines which blanket this tiny baseball-sized Cactus. Its cousin, *Epithelantha micromeris*, is also pure white, a little larger, and more spreading (up to 12 inches) in clumps. Its flowers, however, are light pink. Grows in full sun below 4,000 feet all the way to the desert floor. Would make a startling contrast to the Golden Barrel cactus (*Echinocactus grusonii*). It would probably be a good idea to add some lime to its sandy soil mix when transplanting to emulate its natural growing condition. Slow growth with minimal irrigation.

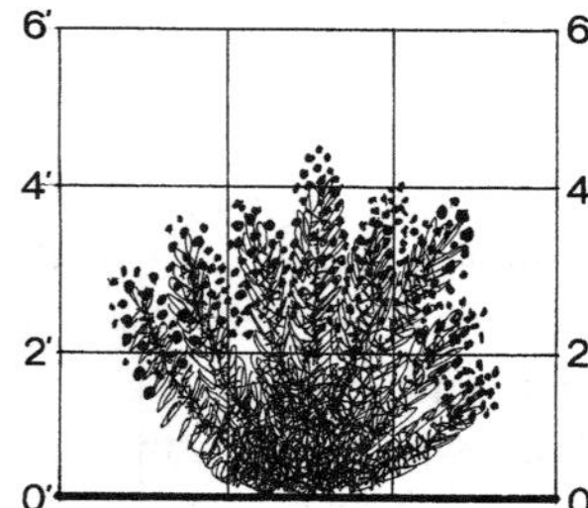

Euphorbia milii **Semi-evergreen**
Crown of Thorns

Greenish stem stalks with occasional long, oval, bright-green leaves. Leaves are found predominately towards the end of the stems. Reminiscent of a miniature Ocotillo (*Fouquieria splendens*), stems are armed with 1/2-inch-long thorns that aid it in climbing. Plant can be trained as a low espalier. Its main attraction, in the eyes of plantsmen, is its nonstop blooming of two-petal, 1/2-inch round flowers in yellow, pink, or red. Needs sun and frost protection. Its ornamental landscape uses are somewhat limited. It does look very nice as a foreground plant to the aforementioned Ocotillo. Fast growth with moderate watering.

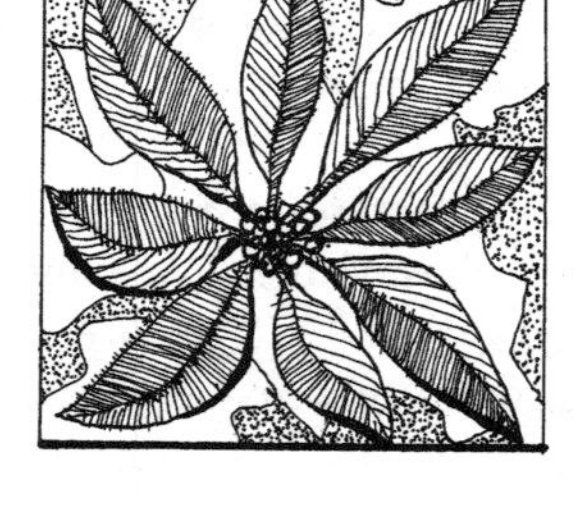

Euphorbia pulcherrima **Semi-evergreen**
Poinsettia

Not truly a succulent, but a Euphorbia (this is a very strange genus) just the same. From Mexico, this has been a long-time Christmas favorite in the U.S. The plants that are used in pots for Christmas gifts and decorations are relatively young. This perennial can attain a height of 10 feet with a 6-foot spread. It can be grown outdoors in well-drained, sandy, and slightly acid (pH 6.5) soil. Grow under protected eaves and out of west sun. Protected from frost, it can be forced into Christmas flowering by stepping up high nitrogen fertilizer applications in October to once a week. The familiar red "petals" are really sepals. The tiny yellow flowers in the center of the bright red bracts are of no consequence. Bright, holly-green leaves are 3 inches long and 2 inches across. Leaves secrete a white sap when cut or crushed. Contrary to popular belief, neither the sap or any other part of the plant is poisonous. Moderate growth with moderate irrigation.

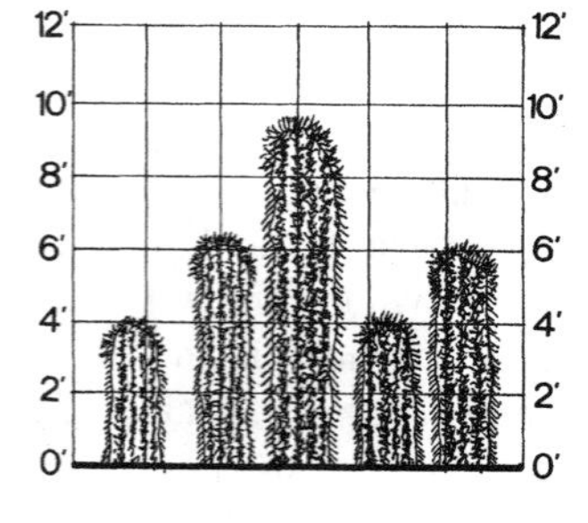

Ferocactus acanthodes **Evergreen**
Compass Barrel Cactus

In shape, this native cactus is similar to a Saguaro (*Carnegiea gigantea*). It has fluted accordion-like skin and it is a single-trunk specimen. Compass Barrel Cactus differs from a Saguaro in that it rarely exceeds 10 feet in height and it produces a line of fishhook-like spines on the centerline of the fluted folds. Several straight spines radiate in a star-shaped pattern out from the main fishhook spines. Spines are not only for predator protection but also to provide shade on the skin of the cactus, shielding it from the sun's rays. Called Compass Barrel Cactus because trunks leans south in response to the north side of the Cactus growing faster because it is shaded. This would be a good fact to remember when setting out the Cactus during planting operations. A ring of yellow, upright, bell-shaped flowers circle the top of the cactus between May and November. Among any given stand of barrels the greater percentage (75%) bloom in late May and June. This small-scale vertical accent looks good as a foreground planting to Saguaros. Slow growth with minimal water. Protected by law.

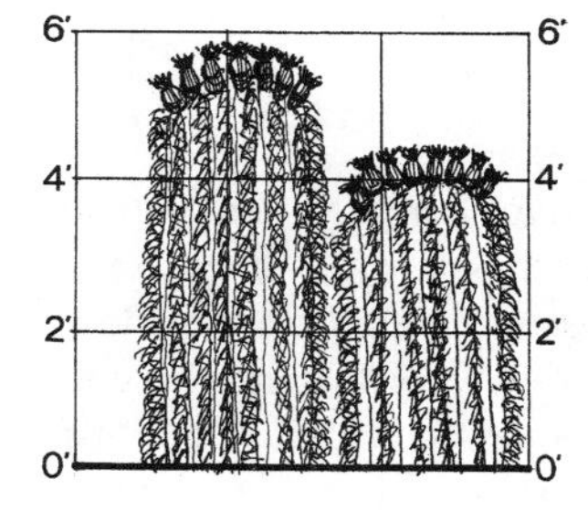

★ ***Ferocactus wislizenii*** **Evergreen**
Fishhook Barrel Cactus

Similar to *Ferocactus acanthodes,* but taller and with more pronounced main spines along the folds. Spines are more yellowish than the tan or reddish spines of *acanthodes*. Flowers are also slightly different, being yellow with reddish edges. Flowers turn to fleshy yellow seed pods (fruit) which stay on the plant for months and look quite attractive. Listed as a star performer because it is extremely attractive — even as a stand-alone specimen. Like *acanthodes*, Fishhook Barrel Cactus is protected by the USDA and only tagged specimens are legal. Slow growth on minimal water to 6 feet high.

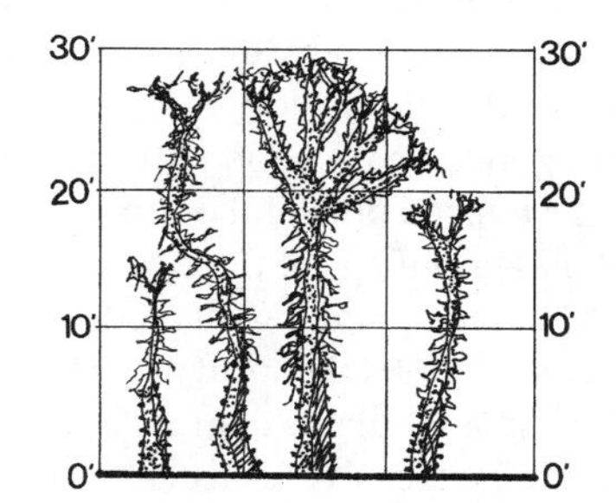

Fouquieria columnaris **Semi-evergreen**
Boojum Tree

An eccentric botanical curiosity from Baja, California. Not frequently grown in the U.S. The stem of the plant is quite wide at its base and tapers consistently, but gradually to a pointed top, looking much like an upside-down carrot. The Boojum Tree's cultural requirements and survival strategies are the same as those of its cousin, the Ocotillo (*Fouquieria splendens*), listed below. The major difference between them is that the Boojum is frost-tender and needs protection when it is away from warm Pacific coastal winter air and north of the border. Fat bases have weird, short, stout thorns similar to the trunk of a Floss Silk Tree (*Chorisia speciosa*). Stems that can extend to 20 feet have horizontal side branchlets which support on-again/off-again leaves which function in the same manner as an Ocotillo. Often, at about 12 feet, the pointed "carrot-top" main stem will "Y" or split into several candelabra-like divisions. Flowers are on 12-inch stalks at the point of the stems. Thrusting upward, they are red in color and about 2 inches long. Not a plant for just any setting because of its bizarre appearance. A stand of five or more Boojums, however, can be remarkably unique. Slow growth on little irrigation.

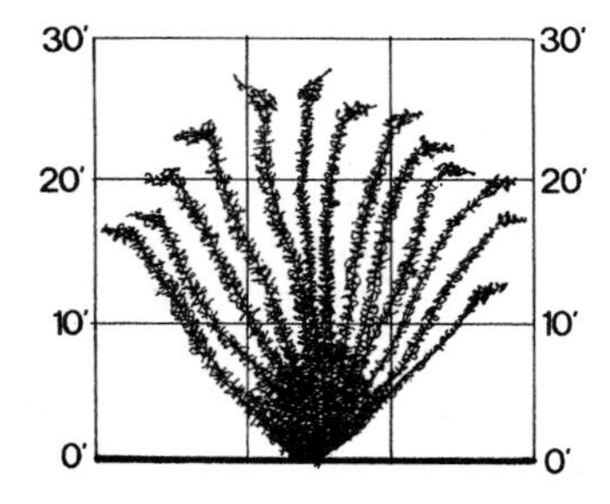

★ *Fouquieria splendens* **Semi-evergreen**
Ocotillo or Desert Barometer

A vase-shaped succulent with many upright stems, called canes, arising from the plant's base. The Desert Barometer is one of the many common names for this unique plant. This plant possesses the ability to develop elongated, rounded, bright-green leaves arranged in whorls along the entire cane in times of rain. When you are in the open desert and the Ocotillos are in full leaf, you know it is the wet season or that a measurable amount of rain has fallen within the past few weeks. The plant can set full leaves in four days and drop them equally as fast as moisture levels recede. Eight-inch-long, brilliant-red flower spikes appear at ends of the canes in spring if rain has fallen and the Ocotillo has set leaves. Flower spikes are loaded with masses of tubular flowers that are a favorite of hummingbirds. Indians brewed a tea from the flower spikes, ate the seeds, and produced waxes and medicines from other parts of the plant. The plant is protected by the USDA and legal specimens must be tagged. Surprisingly, Ocotillo is very easy to transplant bare-rooted and survival rates are very good. Looks good in the foreground to a light-colored background where the twisted play of the canes takes on a kinetic effect. Ocotillos also look better in groupings of three or more plants, as they would be found in the desert. Moderate growth with moderate water. Very slow growth with little or no water. Completely drought-resistant. Using precious quantities of of water to get smaller plants to grow can be easily avoided because large plants are relatively inexpensive, especially when compared to Box Trees. Ocotillo is one of the better landscape buys in the desert.

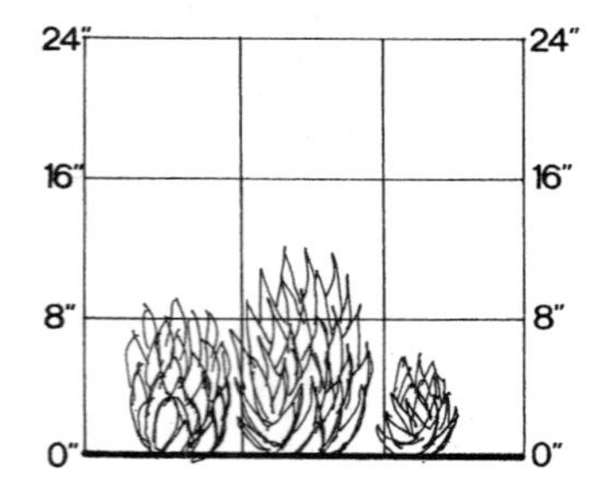

Haworthia attenuata **Evergreen**
White Wart Haworthia

Closely related to the Aloes, the *Haworthia* genus does not receive as much use in desert regions as it should. The *Haworthias* are typified by strong, white horizontal bands across their leaves. Also, as a genus, the leaves themselves are more triangular in cross section, rolling upward from a basal centerline. *Haworthia attenuata* is the largest, being 6 to 8 inches in diameter. The plants spread freely by clumping to form a loose, ground-covering mat. Because of their attractive foliage, smaller size, overall toughness, and generally well-behaved growth habit, the *Haworthias* make excellent pot or container plants. *Attenuata* has the tallest flower spike of the genus. Pink flowers on 2-foot-high stems appear in late spring. Will take all exposures, but prefers some afternoon shade. Slow growth with low water.

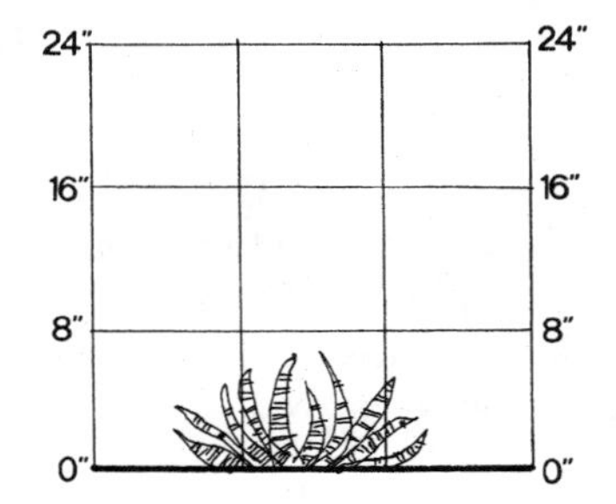

Haworthia fasciata **Evergreen**
Fairy Washboard

Probably the most popular *Haworthia*. Up to 6 inches in diameter, the plant sports a tight rosette of 3-inch-long leaves. The leaves are distinctively banded with smooth white bumps which, from 4 feet away, look like smooth bands. The relative uniform spacing and width of the white bands in contrast to the dark green bands gives a rhythmic, equally spaced, appearance reminiscent of a zebra's coat or a washboard. Leaf tips are tinged pinkish red. Flower spikes arise in late spring, consisting of greenish-white blossoms on a 6-inch stalk. Plant spreads readily by clumping, but it is easy to contain, as clumps can be dug up with minimal effort. Likes afternoon shade. Excellent container subject. Slow growth with minimal irrigation.

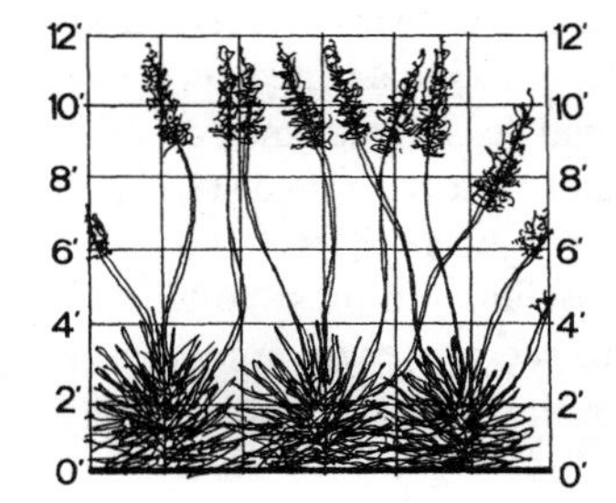

Hesperaloe furifera **Evergreen**
White Yucca

About three times larger in scale than its cousin *Hesperaloe parviflora*. Flower spikes arch upwards to 12 feet supporting greenish white blossoms. Would look good as a backdrop to *parviflora* or especially nice intermixed with Ocotillo (*Fouquieria splendens*) where their verticality would match nicely. Moderate growth with low watering.

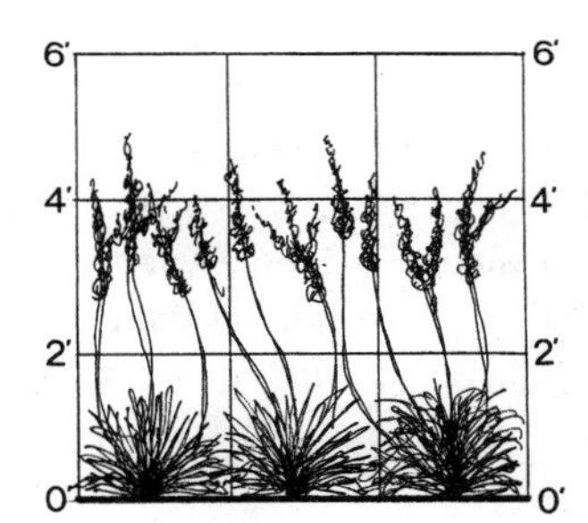

★ ***Hesperaloe parviflora*** **Evergreen**
Red Yucca

A unique perennial that, descriptively, is somewhat like a cross between a grass and a yucca. The gray-green arching leaves are basal and quite loose in appearance. The real feature of the plant is its brilliant red flowers on 4-foot-long arching stalks. Flowers are over an inch long, somewhat bell-shaped, and extend 12 inches from the tip of the stalk towards the center of the plant and appear in late May through July. Very nice flower show gives way to greenish, 1 1/2 inch rounded seed pods which are also pleasing to view. A fine transition to desert edge plant. Mountain States Nursery is starting to offer a yellow-flowering variety which, except for the floral color, is identical to the species. Moderate growth with minimal irrigation. Will tolerate being wetter than it would prefer to be.

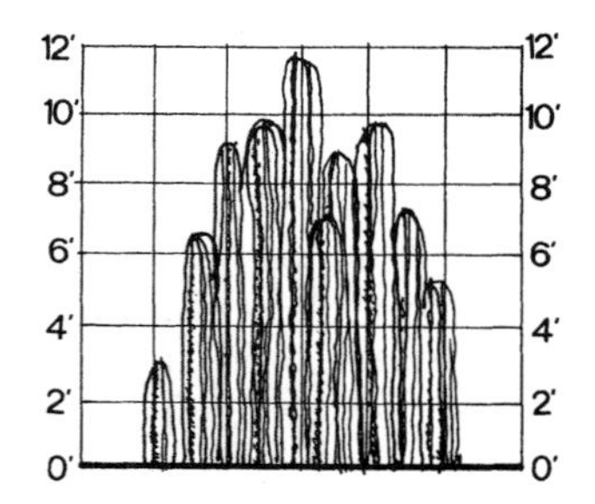

Lemaireocereus marginatas **Evergreen**

Mexican Fence Post

A smaller version (10 feet high) of the famed Organpipe Cactus (*Lemaireoscereus thurberi*), it would work nicely as a foreground planting to its cousing. More readily available from growers. Common name stems from its extremely vertical multi-trunked character. A fine, deeply ribbed specimen. Very slow growth with little to no water.

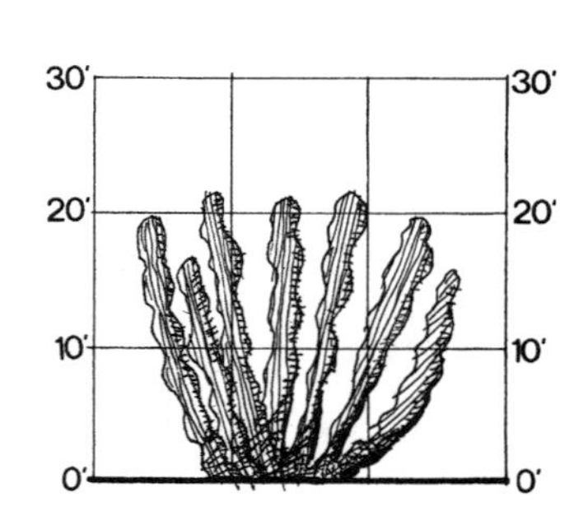

Lemaireocereus thurberi **Evergreen**

Organpipe Cactus

The cactus featured within the Organpipe National Monument in southern Arizona. In a facility that sits on the international border, a joint effort between the U.S. and Mexico has resulted in the setting aside of a large acreage housing these magnificent cacti. A tall cactus with several trunks spreading outward and upwards from a thick base. Individual trunks look like Saguaros (*Carnegiea gigantea*), but they are thinner, less fluted, and contain far smaller spines. Slow growth with minimal water makes younger Organpipe Cactus useful as potted specimens. Can obtain heights of 20 feet and spread as wide. Larger specimens are very difficult to obtain and must be USDA-tagged to be legally planted. It would be nice to see nurserymen take a more active interest in growing one of the giants of the cactus world.

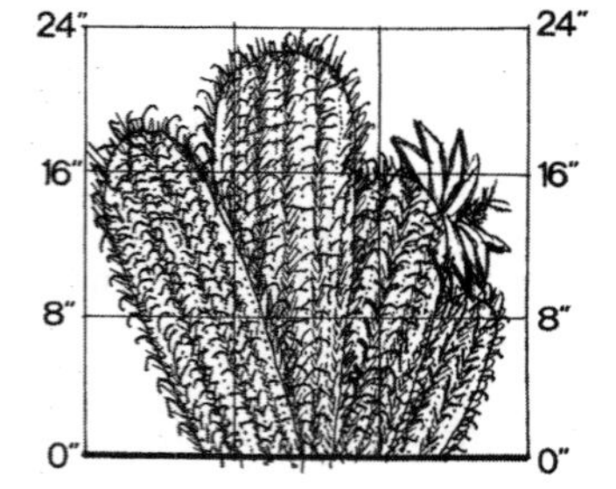

Mammillaria microcarpa **Evergreen**

Fishhook Cactus

A Sonoran Desert native. One of the largest of the Mammillarias reaching heights in excess of 12 inches. Takes full sun and has a striking flower show in midspring. Flowers are multi-pointed and up to 2 inches across, with yellow corollas, deep-pink throats, and fade to light pink at their extremities. Looks good intermixed with Hedgehog Cactus (*Echinocereus engelmannii*). Slow growth with minimal irrigation.

24"
16"
8"
0"

Mammillaria spinosissima **Evergreen**

Red-Headed Irishman

Small cactus to 12 inches high. Completely covered with 1/4 inch, white spines. Tiny, deep lavender flowers in a circular halo configuration occur on the plant in late spring. Quite showy when in bloom, this plant is insignificant when not. Slow growth on infrequent but deep irrigation.

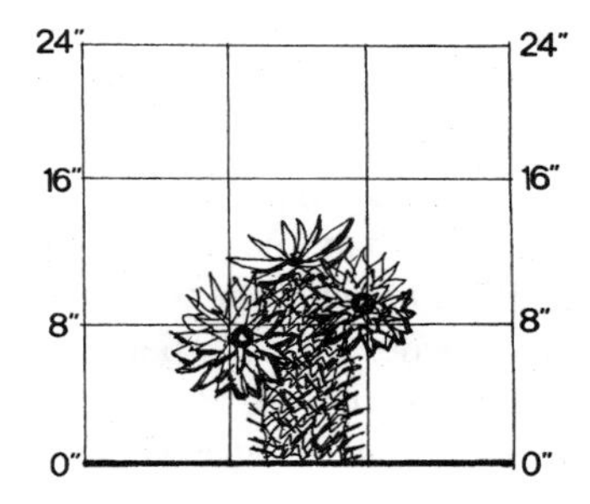

Mammillaria tetrancista **Evergreen**
Fishhook Cactus

Typical of most *Mammilaria*, a small cylinderical cactus rarely exceeding 8 inches in height. Feature of design note are its extremely dark hooked thorns and how they constrast with the delicate rose-purple flowers that encircle the top of each stem. Slow growth with minimum watering.

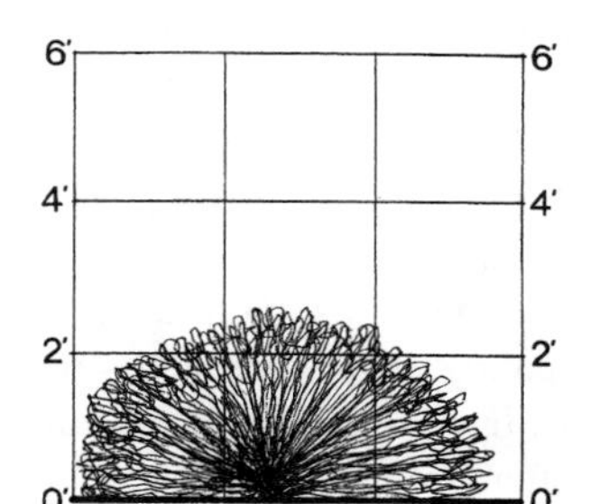

★ ***Muhlenberghia rigens*** **Evergreen**
Deer Grass

A small-scale desert grass that is growing in popularity. Rarely taller than 2 feet, with as wide a spread, it looks like a miniature Pampas Grass (less the plumes). Ideal for bank stabilization. Attractive alongside water features. Moderate growth with little irrigation. With increasing use, this Mohave Desert native has become a star performer.

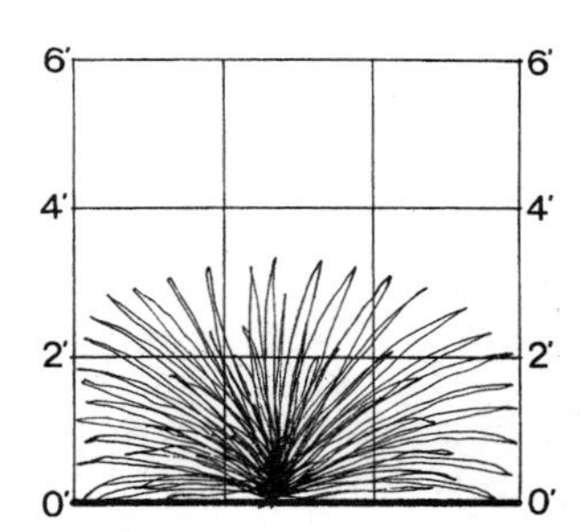

★ ***Nolina parryi*** **Evergreen**
Beargrass

Large, clumping, grass-like plants, 3 feet high and as wide. Dark green in color. Very drought resistant when established. Nice visual effect when used adjacent to water features. This native's only drawback is that it is used in spaces where it becomes overgrown and thus looks out-of-place. When it spreads out, this Nolina can occasionally achieve a 5-foot diameter. Moderate growth with minimum water. Do not overwater.

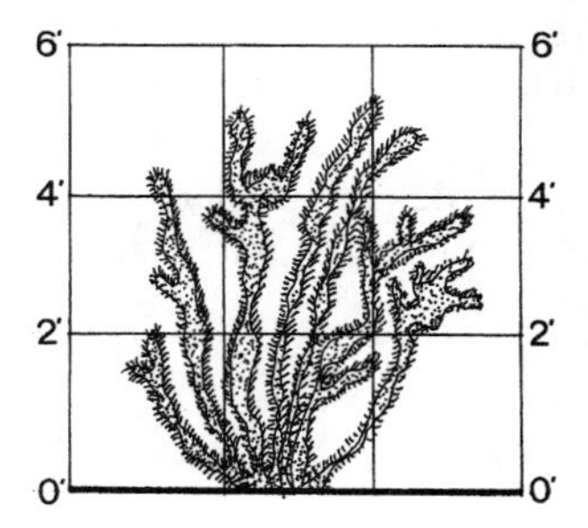

Opuntia acanthocarpa **Evergreen**
Buckhorn Cholla

The Cholla branch of the *Opuntia* genus usually contains plants with rounded stems with 6 to 12 inches between joints. Fat, fuzzy, with profuse spines, this cactus grows to 6 feet tall, but usually stays below 4 feet. It has many branches, giving it the appearance of a buck deer with its horns still in the "velvet" stage. The color of the cactus appears to be buff to tarnish brown when viewed from 20 feet away. Flowers are 3 inches, rounded, cup-shaped, and vary from red to yellow, depending on habitat, with an orangish-red color being the most common. Availability may be a problem, so check with growers before specifying. Slow growth with little irrigation.

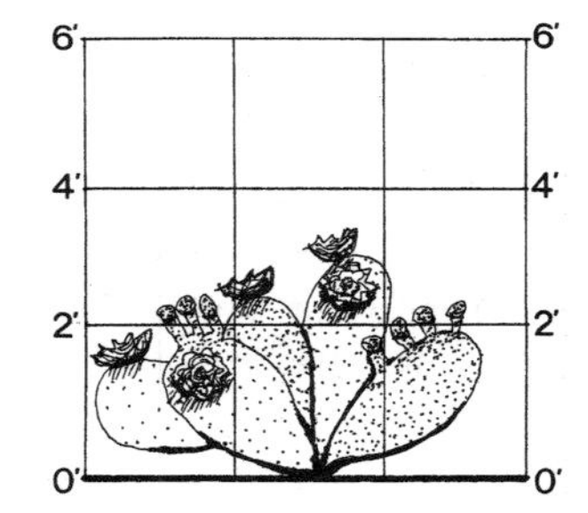

Opuntia basilaris **Evergreen**
Beavertail Cactus

The non-Cholla members of the Opuntia genus are most usually typified by flat, broad pads covered with typical or modified thorns called glochids that are arranged in an almost geometric, grid-like pattern. The beavertail has the wide, fleshy pads typical of the Opuntias under 4 feet in height. Irregular shaped, but loosely following the shape of an undefined rectangle, the plant grows to 4 feet high by 6 feet or so wide. Large stands can exist, as the cactus roots freely from pads that touch or break and fall to the ground. Pads shrink or swell with the availability of water. When spines are removed with a knife or by passing them through an open flame, the pads can be eaten and taste somewhat like green beans. *Opuntia basilaris* is very common at about 3000 feet in deserts. Its magenta, 4- to 6- inch, cupped blossoms are a familiar sight to knowledgeable desert travelers. Indians ate the balled red fruits called tunas, which followed the spiny flowers and ripened by midsummer. Today they are used in a tasty jam, even for candy, or washed and strained for a juice. Good, tough, low-growing cactus. If you desire low growth, insist on tagged specimens, as *Opuntia vulgaris* often becomes mixed in with *basilaris,* and *vulgaris* gets very large. A single vulgaris can get large enough to overpower and ruin a planned small scale cactus garden. *Opuntia basilaris* is a moderate grower with little irrigation.

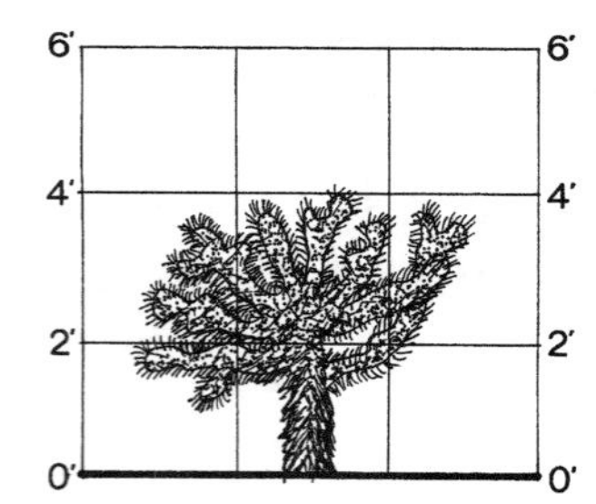

★ ***Opuntia bigelovii*** **Evergreen**
Teddybear Cholla

This is a particularly abundant cactus. Entire stands can be viewed (Teddybear forests) of this species from Interstate 10 between Indio and Blythe, California. There is also an impressive garden at the eastern end of the Joshua Tree National Monument. They occupy rock-strewn bajadas in intense profusion with their golden crowns becoming glistening spots in the sun. Very thick stems to 3 inches round with 1-inch-long spines give this Cholla a fuzzy, teddybear appearance. Cactus can get 6 feet tall, but 3 feet is average. Green-yellow flowers appear in spring, but are insignificant, especially when compared to the foliage. Good back drop to Mexican Golden Barrel Cactus (*Echinocactus grusonii*). Slow growth with little to no irrigation.

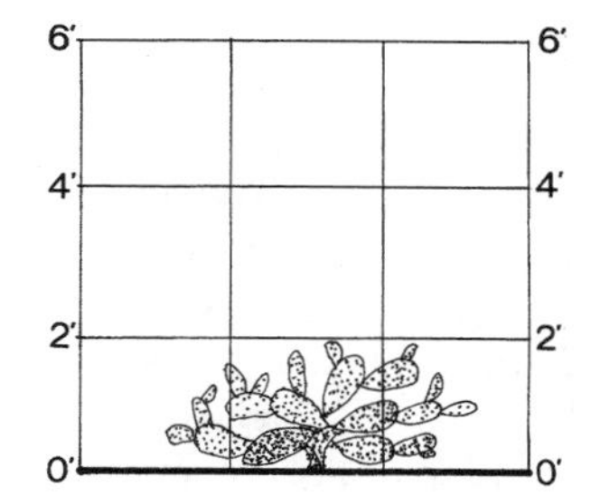

Opuntia microdasys **Evergreen**
Bunny Ears

Small-scale, flat-padded cactus with numerous glochids. Oblong pads look like rabbit ears, making this often potted plant a favorite with children who should look, but not touch as the glochids, which look harmless, have rather nasty little miniature barbs. If you are unfortunate enough to come into contact with them, apply Elmer's Glue, let it dry, and peel it off skin — the glochids usually come with the dried glue. Small, cup-shaped, whitish to yellow flowers in spring. Great plant for silhouette lighting effects. Fast growth with a little less than moderate watering.

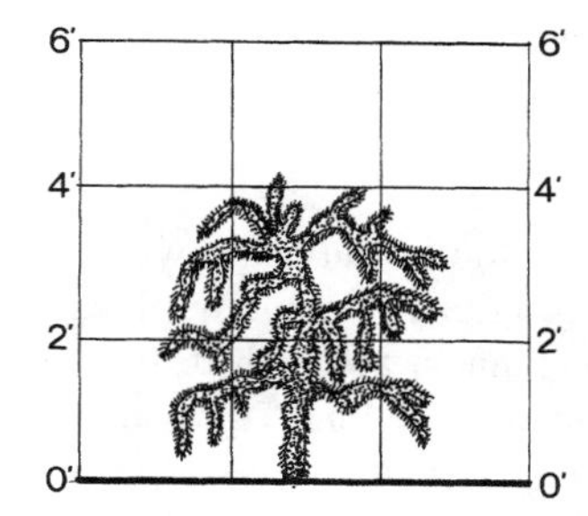

Opuntia ramosissima **Evergreen**
Pencil Cholla

The common name aptly describes the cactus. Very thin, rounded stems covered with 3/4-inch-long spines. Similar in growth habit to the Teddybear Cholla (*Opuntia bigelovii*) except it looks looser and gangly, owing to its thinner branches. Considered by most references to be quite rare, it can be found with regularity in the Indian Canyons area in south Palm Springs. Greenish-white blossom is of little consequence. Slow growth with a small amount of water.

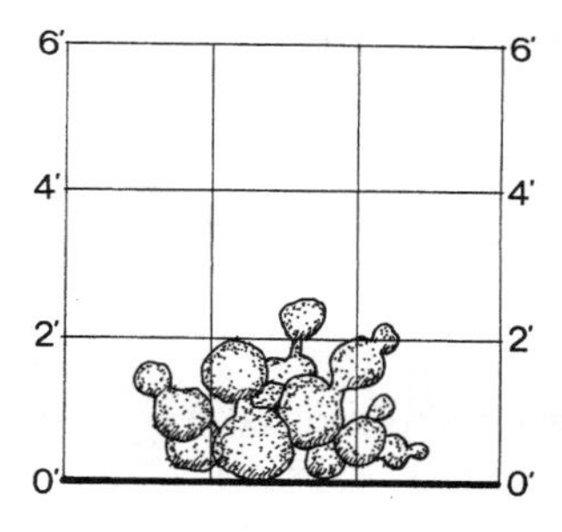

Opuntia violacea 'Santa Rita' **Evergreen**
Blue Blade

Native to the Santa Rita mountain range south of Tucson, Arizona. A beautiful cactus in the beavertail category. Flat pads are, geometrically speaking, almost perfectly round. Color of the pads is bluish-gray to mauve to violet. Cactus is valued for its foliage shape and, in particular, for its color. Yellow flowers are 3 inches round, cup-shaped, and appear in late spring. Like Prickly Pear Cactus (*Opuntia basilaris*), the 1-inch-long oval-shaped fruit is edible. A good medium-sized specimen that is a welcome addition to any cactus garden. Slow growth on a minimum amount of water.

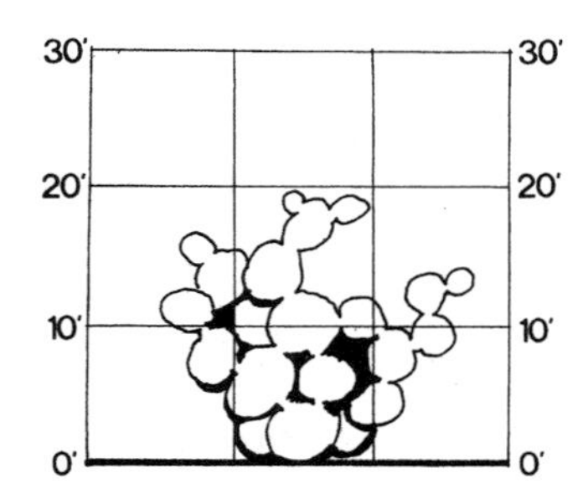

Opuntia vulgaris **Evergreen**
Giant Prickly Pear Cactus

Very large in scale, this cactus can exceed heights of 20 feet, especially in the domesticated ornamental cactus garden where water is frequently more abundant. Roots go deep and wide so this cactus usually gets more water than its neighbors. As a result of more water intake, pads get rounder and more oval-shaped. The Giant Prickly Pear also volunteers itself easily as it roots freely from its somewhat easy-to-break pads. Large, magenta flowers, up to 6 inches across, arrive in spring and are followed by the typical bright red, knobby fruit in summer and fall. Fastest growing of the Opuntias with moderate irrigation.

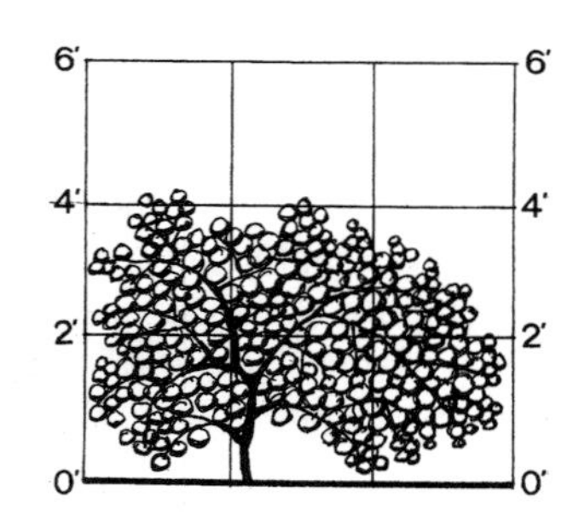

★ ***Portulacaria afra*** **Evergreen**
Elephant's Food

Becoming a very popular plant in the Southest. Can be grown with full sun exposure in the low desert, but needs protection in the middle elevation desert and is better tried only as an interior plant in the high desert. Similar in appearance and cultural requirements to the Jade Plant (*Crassula argentea*), except its leaves are smaller and farther apart on the stems. Open, pendulous character makes this a good potted plant or raised planter section. From South Africa, it has an attractive bloom in its homeland but blooms less frequently here. Succulent foliage is 1/4 inch round, bright yellow-green, and is the main attraction. Looks better with moderate watering and grows surprisingly fast. Older plants can become quite drought resistant.

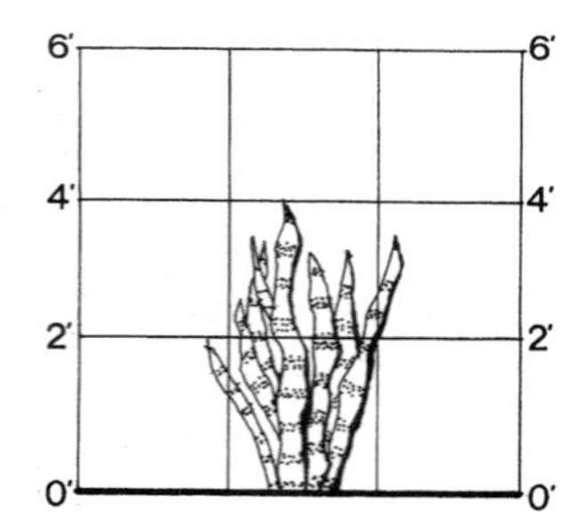

Sansevieria trifasciata **Evergreen**
Mother-in-Law's Tongue

A very tough plant. Valued for its sword-like, twisted leaves that extend vertically upright from a fleshy base. Leaves can approach 4 feet in length. Green leaves are somewhat horizontally striped with grayish bands. If protected from midday and afternoon sun, this plant will withstand what seems like an unlimited amount of neglect. Looks nice bursting through *Asparagus sprengeri* or as a backdrop to any of the *Haworthia* species. Moderate growth on low water.

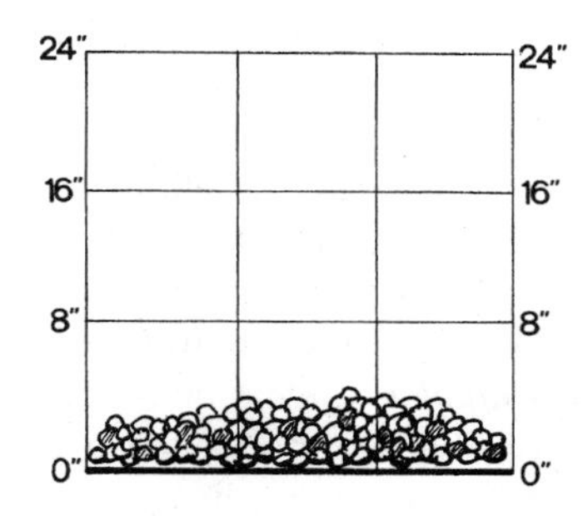

Sedum acre **Evergreen**
Goldmoss Sedum

Needs protection, as do all Sedums in the desert. Genus is valued as foliage plants. Sedums sport fat, rounded, succulent leaves with waxy cuticles. The best desert applications are in atrium gardens or as houseplants. Goldmoss Sedum is a low-growing ground cover to 8 inches high with upright, fleshy, stem-like leaves which root as they go. Spreads to 18 inches. Bright, yellow-green foliage with a reddish tinge. Flowers are not a factor. Slow growth with low to moderate water. The entire genus is worthy of more desert experiments.

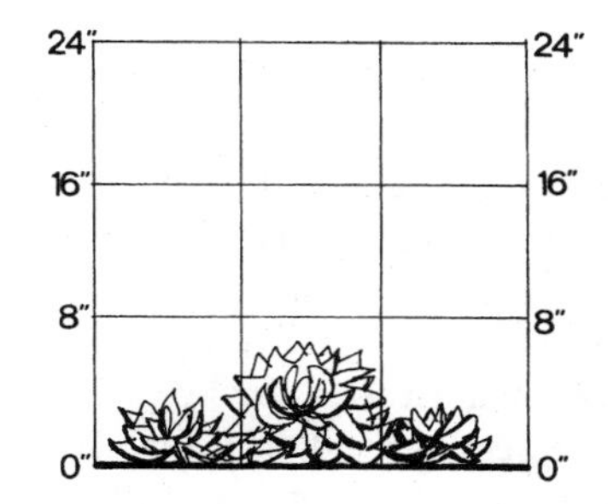

Sempervivum tectorum **Evergreen**
Hen and Chicks

Similar to *Echeveria imbricata* which is also commonly called Hen and Chicks. *Sempervivum tectorum* is larger — 6 to 8 inches across with fewer, but wider and thicker leaves in its rosettes. It spreads by clumping, but clumps less tightly and in less profusion than Echeveria. *S. tectorum* also sets out 2-foot-tall stalks with red clusters of flowers set at the top. A nice plant that needs protection and is more ideally suited to the entry or atrium garden. Moderate growth with moderate water.

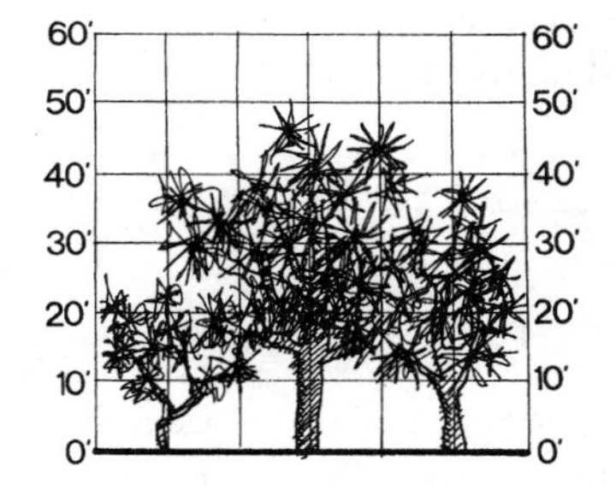

Yucca brevifolia **Evergreen**
Joshua Tree

The signal tree of the Mohave Desert in Southern California. A giant that is preserved within the Joshua Tree National Monument which was founded in 1936. The Yucca is called "Joshua Tree" because Mormon settlers from Utah heading west viewed the plants' upright spreading branches as the uplifted arms of the biblical leader Joshua guiding them towards their promised land. The Joshua Tree flourishes at 4,500 feet and is not really at home in the low-elevation desert. If planted there, it should receive protection from the west sun. Plants outside the native range rarely flower, owing to the absence of the Joshua Tree Moth which is apparently the only insect that can pollinate this Yucca. When planted from containers, it takes an extremely long time to get up off the ground and start its initial trunk formation. Older plants that have the typical branched look are USDA protected and very expensive. Mature plants can achieve a 30 foot height with over a 20 foot spread and possess several (10 or more) uplifted branches. A good Yucca that can be strikingly beautiful in the right setting, Joshua Tree can look just as strikingly awkward in the wrong setting. Slow growth with little to moderate irrigation.

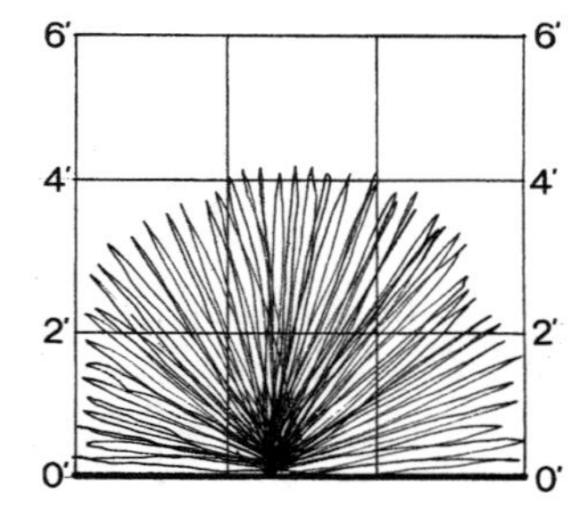

★ *Yucca elata* **Evergreen**
Soaptree Yucca

Similar in many aspects to *Yucca Whipplei,* whose description is to follow. Spikey, gray, 3- to 4-foot rounded ball in youth, *elata* will develop a stalk that grows to heights in excess of 12 feet. The stalks sometimes branch into a "Y" with two or more spikey heads. The thin leaves are formidable and it makes a great barrier plant. Unlike *Y. whipplei*, *Y. elata* does not die after sending out its 8- to 10-foot-tall floral spike. A very popular plant in the desert communities, it is frequently seen in roadway median planters. Moderate growth with minimal irrigation.

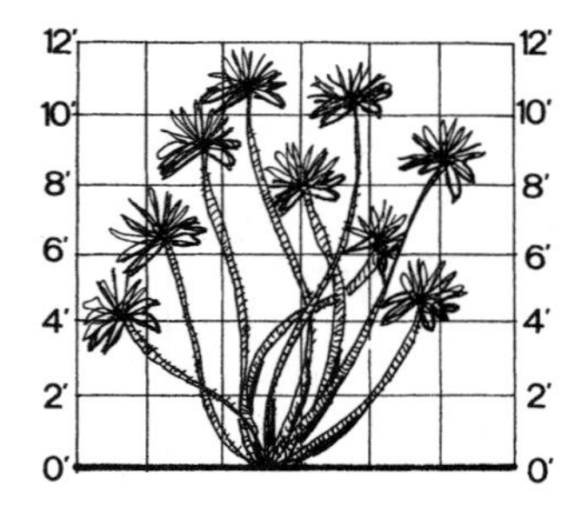

★ *Yucca gloriosa* **Evergreen**
Spanish Dagger

In many respects, this is the most refined and graceful of the Yuccas. Upright, 3-feet long by 2 1/2 inches wide, the leaves are dagger-like in appearance. Plants look best when leaves are peeled from the trunks until a palm-like head becomes apparent. Multi-trunk specimens are especially attractive. Not fussy, but will burn if placed against west-facing glass where it receives intense reflected heat. Up to 8 feet tall and occasionally larger, it looks good in front of windows where it can be viewed to full advantage. Blooms in late summer on stalks that are shorter than most yuccas. White, bell-shaped flowers are attractive. Is quite exotic by its habit and nature. It can fit at home in the tropical garden or fit into a desert scene with equal ease. It can be safely used in pedestrian areas as this is one of the few Yuccas with soft leaf points. Moderate growth on low to moderate water.

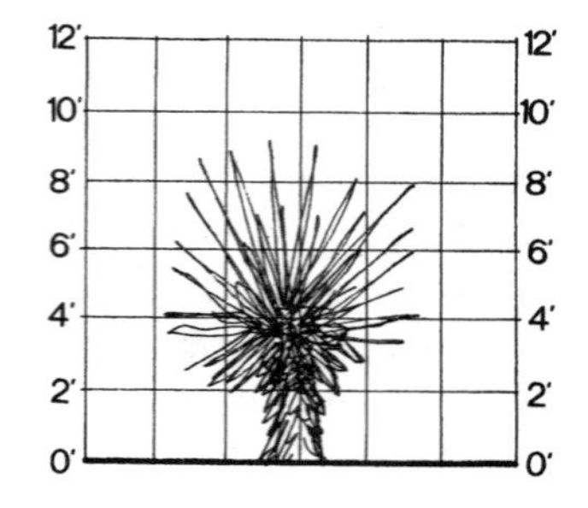

Yucca mohavensis **Evergreen**
Mohave Yucca

As the common name implies, this is a Yucca of the Mohave Desert and grows in the shadows of the famed Joshua Tree (*Yucca brevifolia*). Leaves are yellow-green and very long, sometimes extending to 4 feet. Leaf points, many of which are at eye level, are deadly. This slow-growing plant eventually forms a trunk surrounding by collapsed, downward-pointing dead leaves. Relatively short, 2-foot-high flower stalk has pendulous white flowers tinged purple which appear in late spring. A plant for a large area. Slow growth on minimum water.

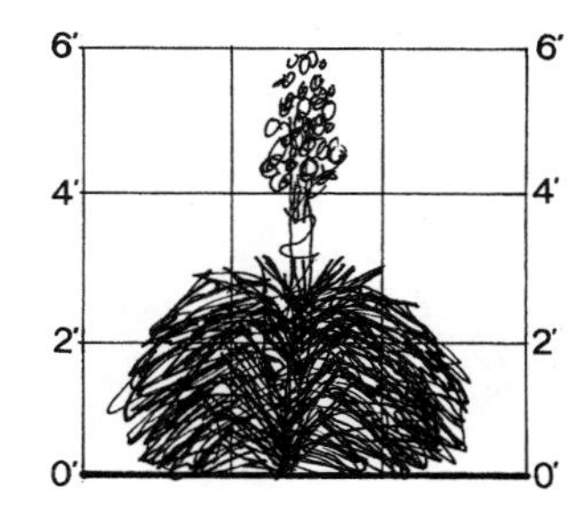

★ *Yucca pendula* **Evergreen**

Pendulous Yucca

Atypical to all the other Yuccas, this plant has dark-green leaves that are soft enough to bend downward 3/4 of their distance away from the trunk. Highly exotic, this plant can find a home in the tropical garden. Does not really fit in the true desert garden. Looks exceptional set among a light-colored ground cover such as Asparagus Fern (*Asparagus sprengeri*). Grows to 3 feet in diameter and 2 feet high. Its 3-foot-high flower stalk is covered with pure white, bell-shaped flowers in late spring. A great plant. Moderate growth rate with moderate irrigation.

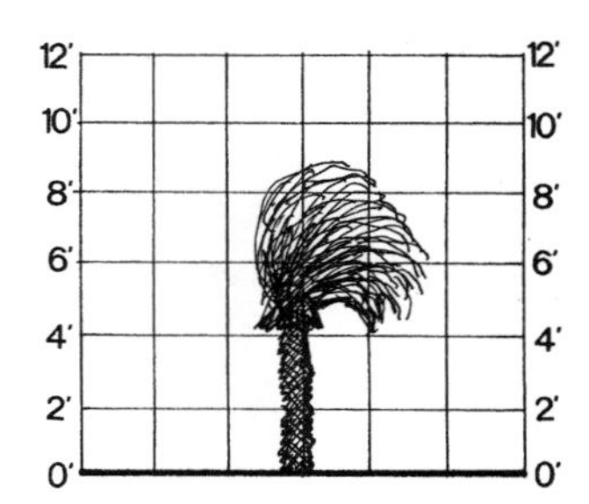

Yucca rostrata **Evergreen**

(No common name)

A horticultural oddity that is not for everyone. Expensive specimens are used on extremely high-end residential projects. It needs sun and, more important, frost protection. Originally from Texas, the plant is valued for its palm-like arching trunk to 8 feet tall. Perched at the top of the trunk is the foliage head. Some think the plant looks like a *Dracaena draco,* but with thinner leaves. The 2-foot-long pendulous pointed leaves are gray-green. A 2-foot-long, thin, flower stalk bearing white flowers appears in spring. Very slow growth on little water.

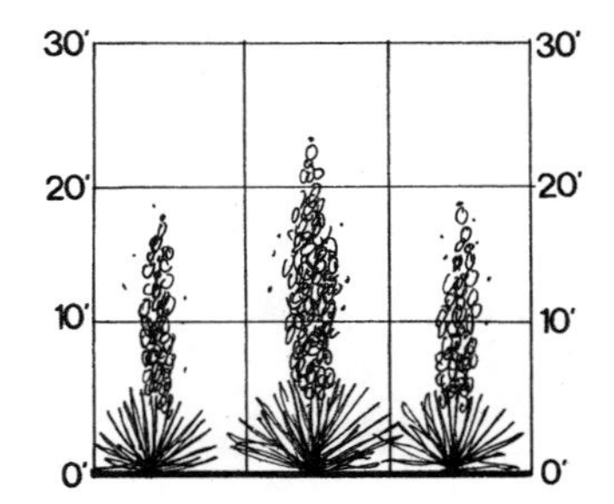

Yucca whipplei **Evergreen**

Our Lord's Candle

An often-photographed native Yucca. Grayish, spiked, 2-foot-long leaves look a lot like *Dasylirion wheeleri*, except they are stiffer and wider. Plant grows readily from seed and is often included in native seed mixes for hillside erosion control. The plant grows to maturity and sometimes, in the spring, after its 15th year of life, sets forth a 10- to 12-foot-tall by 2-foot-wide flower stalk completely covered with dainty, white, downward facing, bell-shaped flowers. It is one of the most spectacularly beautiful flower shows in all of nature. Flowers give way to fat, green, horizontal seed stalks containing rounded, pod-like seed capsules which eventually dry and split open. With the Yucca's life-cycle complete, it unceremoniously dies to the ground. The seeds germinate the following spring and the cycle of life for this magnificent plant begins again. Slow growth with minimal to no irrigation.

Bulbs, Corms, Tubers, and Rhizomes

Bulb display

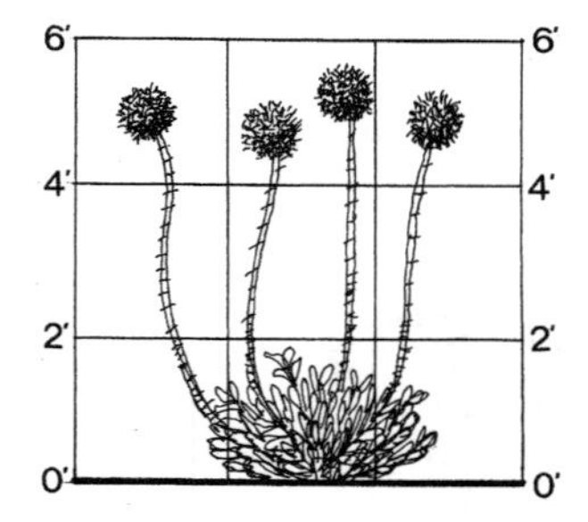

Allium giganteum
Giant Allium

Bulb that blooms in mid-summer with 2-foot high, silvery-gray foliage, providing a nice contrast to adjacent green plants. It is the 5-inch, softball-size flowers that steal the show, however. Perfectly round on their gray-green stalks, they hover 5 feet in the air to stop at eye level and shout for attention. The flowers start green, turn purple, and then fade to gray-green over a 4-week period. Flowers cut just before they turn completely purple will last up to 3 weeks in a vase. Cut foliage to ground after flower show. Fast growth with ample water.

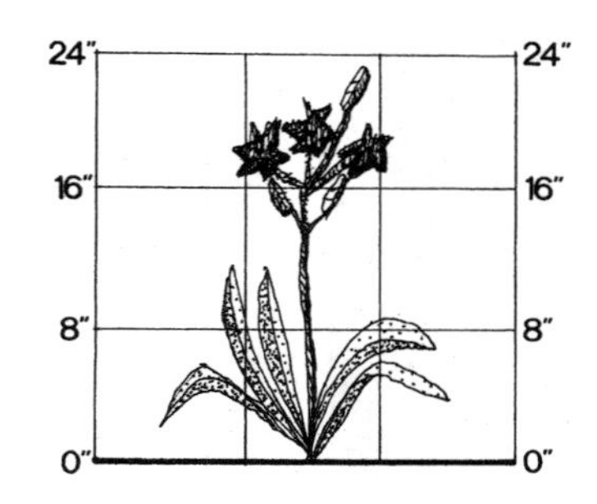

Brodiaea pulchella
Blue Dicks

These dainty, grass-like, flowering plants are corms native to the Pacific coast. They would be a good selection for naturalizing here. Low (8 inches high) grassy clump of leaves produce a thin, 2-foot-high flower stalk. Blossoms consist of sprays of about a dozen deep throated, deep blue, 2-inch-long flowers. Floral show occurs in late April through May. Plant dries out and dies completely to the ground with the onslaught of hot summer weather. Good selection to intermingle with native seed mixes for variety. Apply low to moderate watering to trigger spring growth then allow the plant to go completely dry. Leave corms in soil year round.

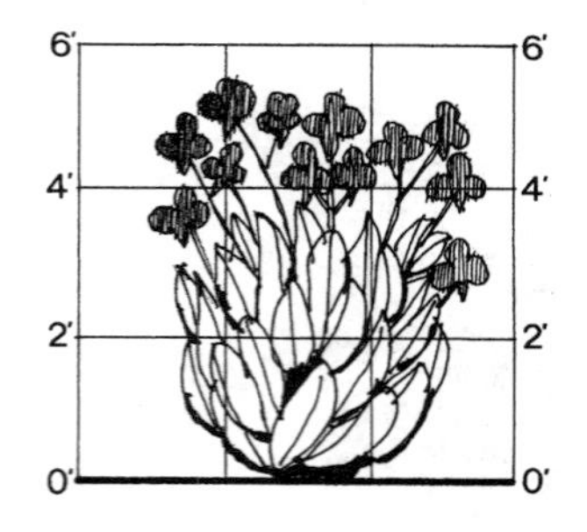

★ ***Canna species***
Canna Lily (consult growers' catalogues)

A tropical tuber. A very large-scale plant with broad banana-like (half the width) curved, bright-green leaves. Needs wet soil and full sun to bloom effectively. Looks good near water features. Many colors are available, but the reds are especially vibrant. Several varieties are used in the Coachella Valley that are fall flowering and in bloom by October which signals the arrival of the tourist season. Fast growth with ample watering. Best maintenance practice is to remove tuberous roots and store them inside through coldest winter months. In the absence of this, foliage should be cut to the ground and removed.

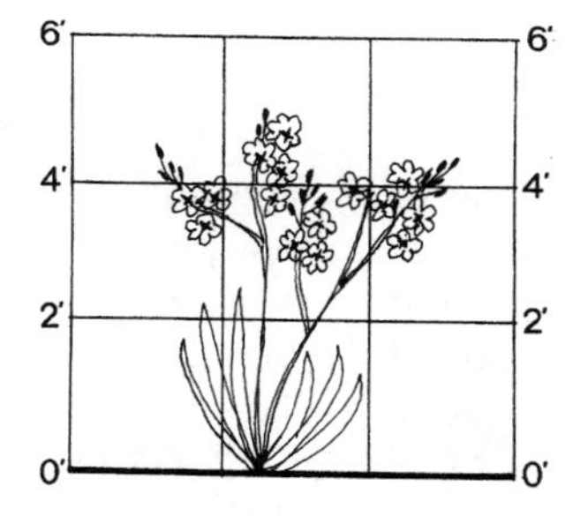

Crocosmia crocosmiiflora
Montbretia

A South African corm that spreads freely and can be quite drought-tolerant. Late spring to early summer bloomer. Blossoms are like those of daylilies (*Hemerocallis fulva*) 1 1/2 inches across, with 6 "petals," and normally orangish-red in color. These flowers are supported on 3- to 4- foot stems which spring up between 1-inch wide by 3-feet tall, bright green, sword-shaped leaves. Leave corms in the ground and simply mow foliage or cut to the ground with a string trimmer when the plant is dormant or out of season. Fast growth in spring on moderate water.

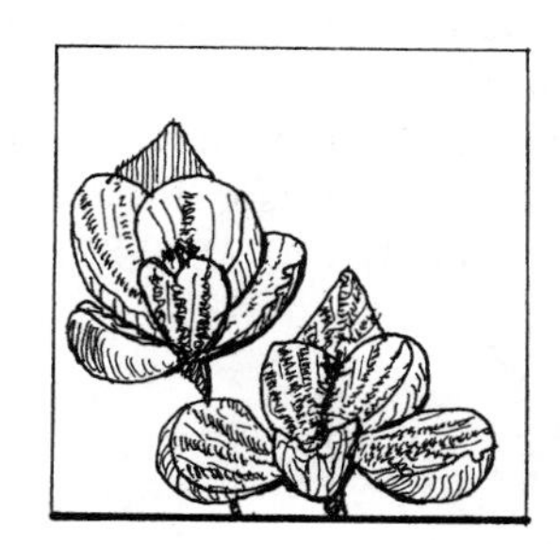

Crocus vernus
Dutch Crocus (consult growers' catalogues)

Varieties within this genus are very popular and widely sold. The species, however, has the largest blossoms. These corms spread quite easily and should be dug up and spread out every three years or so to improve the plant's health and quality of bloom. Low, ground-hugging plants with dark-green, grass-like foliage. Flowers with large petals are 3 inches across, the most popular colors being white, yellow, and purple. You will have to plant 100 or so corms to make an impact. Set corms initially 3 inches apart and 3 inches deep in sandy soil. One of the first plants to rise up and bloom signaling the coming of spring. A nice plant to use under loose, low-growing, ground covers like *Vinca minor*. Trim foliage and flower stalks to grade after bloom period. Fast growth with ample water. Some cultivars are available that bloom in the late fall months.

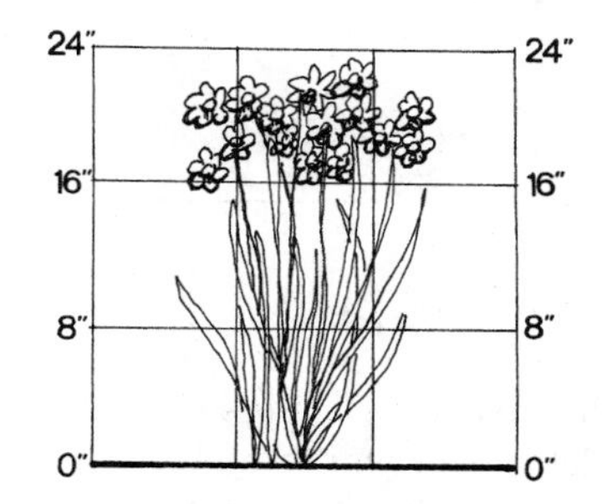

★ ***Freesia armstrongii***
Freesia (consult growers' catalogues)

Corm from South Africa with dull-green, grass-like, basal leaves that are 18 inches high. Freesias are prized for their pleasing scent as well as their floral show. Flower stalks rise slightly above leaf height and bear tubular flowers of either white, pink, or red (many other colors available). Flower stalk is usually bent at the tip that holds flowers, and the flowers are located only on the one side of the stalk that points up towards the sun. Freesias are somewhat invasive. The corms spread rapidly and the flowers set seed which dissipates and readily germinates into new plants. Tough plant, simply allow it to dry out after blooming and cut to the ground until the next growing season. Fast growth with moderate irrigation.

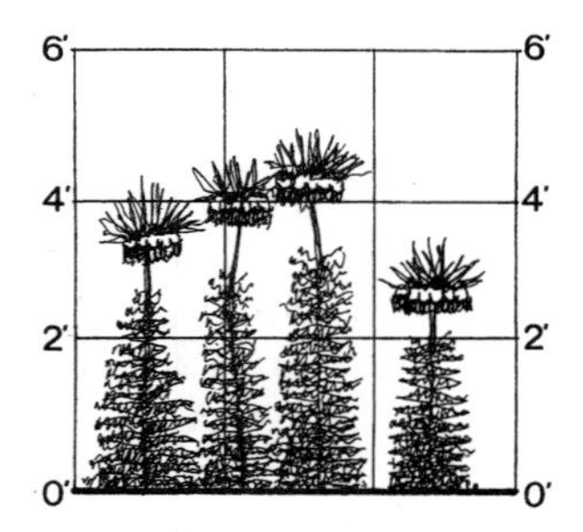

Fritillaria imperialis
Crown Imperial

An exotic bulb that produces a plant with a foliage and flower show that makes it one of the most bizarre, yet beautiful, ornamental plants I have ever seen. An excellent subject for tall narrow containers. Any device that raises the floral show to eye level is a plus. Unfortunately, the flowers smell bad and should be kept out of the prevailing wind. Lily-like leaves in 8- to 10-inch, whorled rosettes, eventually produce a 3-foot-high, 1/2-inch thick flower stalk. Atop the stalk nests a smaller-scale mass of foliage in the same arrangement as the plant's base. Underneath this hovering foliage mass are clusters of red, orange, or yellow Fuchsia-like, pendulous 2-inch long flowers. Truly an eye catcher. Bulbs can remain in the ground after this midspring floral extravaganza. Cut foliage to ground to produce more vigorous plants the following year. Plant Crown Imperial intermittently and in masses if you want a dependable floral show. The plant has a tendency to lie dormant for a year after blooming. It is a well deserved rest. Fast growth with ample watering. You can obtain *Fritillaria imperialis* from: Jackson & Perkins, Bulb Catalogue, 60 Rose Lane, Medford, Oregon 97501-0701, 800/872-7673.

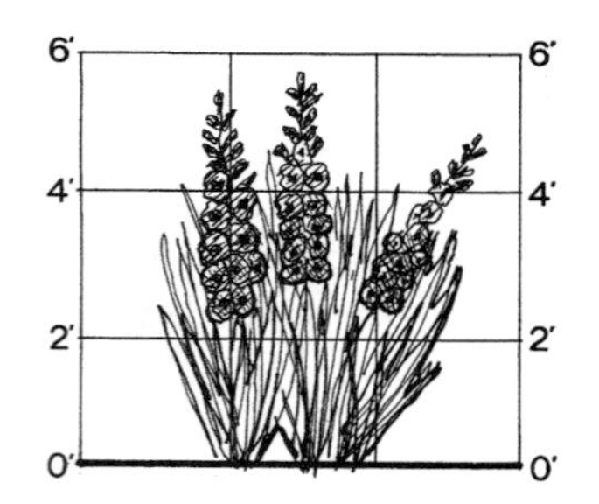

Gladiolus hortulanus
Garden Gladiolus (Consult growers catalogues)

Hortulanus is the most readily available Gladiolus and the most frequently planted. Available in virtually all colors of the rainbow. Bright-green foliage is sword-shaped and basal. Flower stalks are fleshy, 1/4 inch thick, and up to 6 feet high. Flowers are borne on the outward (sun) face of the stalk only. Plant corms in November through February for early to midspring bloom. Dig corms out and dispose of foliage until the start of the next growing season and then repeat this planting process. Fast growth with ample watering.

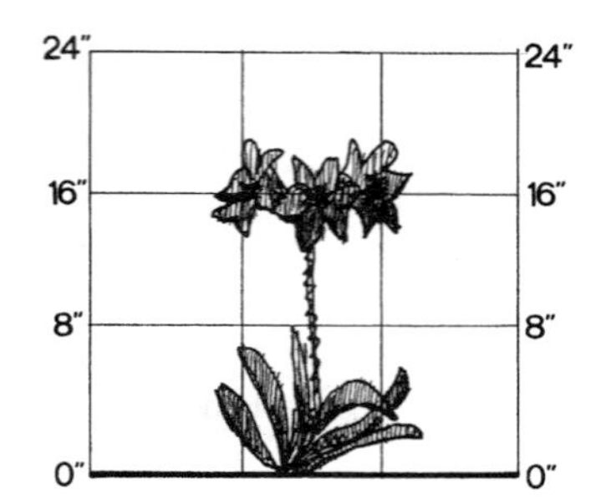

Hippeastrum species
Amaryllis

The long, rounded, dull-green foliage of this bulb plant is so overshadowed by the spectacular blossom that it is relatively insignificant. Usually used as a pot subject, the 8-inch leaf mass sets out a 3/4-inch-diameter, stiff, fleshy stalk. This stalk rises to between 12 and 18 inches and then puts forth a half dozen 8-inch diameter white, pink, or red flowers, sometimes between March and May. Slow growth with moderate water. Cut back to soil line when flowers fade.

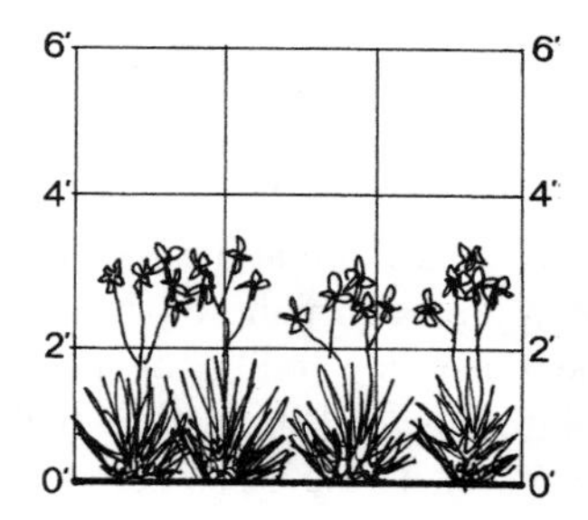

Iris douglasiana
Santa Barbara Iris

As its common name implies, this bulb occurs as a native along the California coast. Good selection for naturalization inland as it spreads freely and is probably the toughest member of a genus that contains over 200 species. The 18 bright-green, knife-like leaf blades are evergreen. However, they will dry in the desert sun without some solar protection and would look better cut to the ground during the summer months. Varieties have cream, yellow, and lavender flowers. These are always the most typical genus colors. Individual plants produce two or three flowers in April. Fast growth with moderate irrigation.

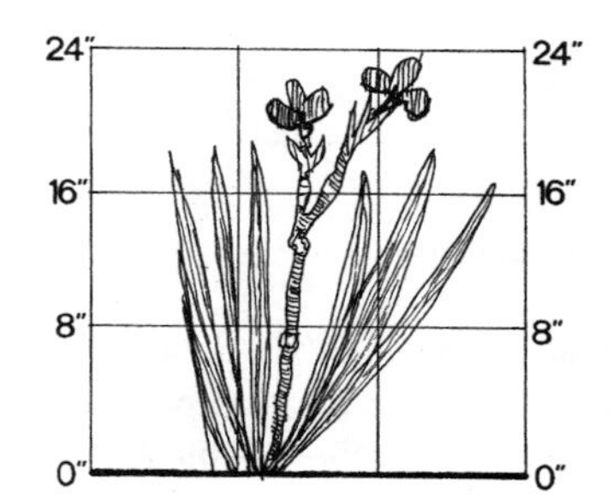

Iris missouriensis
Western Blue Flag

This bulb, native to the western mountain states of the U.S. grows to two feet tall. The flower in spring is very large — up to 3 inches across. Usually bluish purple in color, but whites and yellows are available. Not fussy about cultural conditions. Fast growth with moderate watering. Cut foliage to ground after flower show.

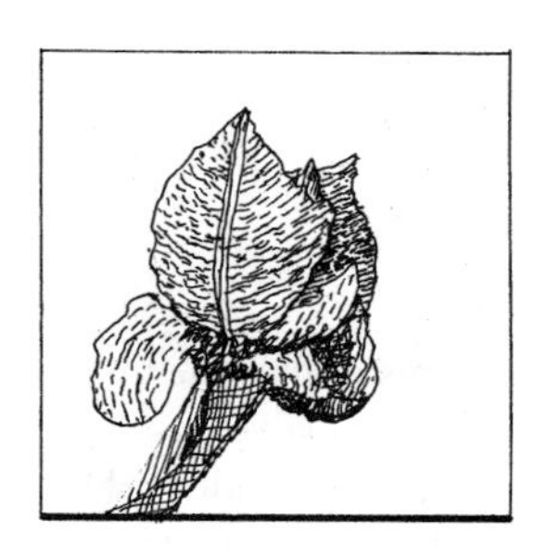

★ ***Iris species***
Tall Bearded Iris (consult growers' catalogues.)

This is, by far, the most widely grown and adored Iris by the general gardening public. Some growers have dedicated their entire operation to producing varieties of this one single plant material. A wide array of colors, although pinks are quite rare and reds do not exist. A spectacular spring bloomer. The three- to four-foot high flower stalks bear 3- to 4-inch deep bearded flowers in late April to June. Cut foliage to ground after unforgettable flower show. Fast growth with ample water. These spectacular bulbs can be obtained just about anywhere, but a reliable grower is: K. Van Bourgondien and Sons, Inc., 245 Farmingdale Road, Babylon, NY, 11702; Tel: 800/552-9996.

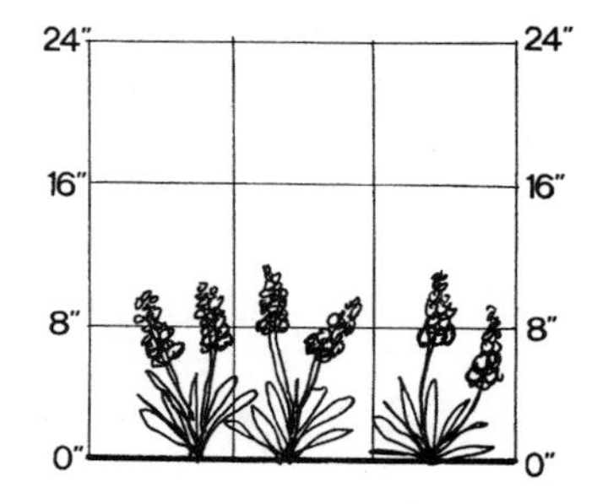

Muscari armeniacum
Grape Hyacinth

This species usually has deep blue, 4-inch-long flower cones. Some white and pink hybrids are offered. Interesting vertical bulb. Fleshy, dark green, strap-like foliage is not a real show stopper but the flowers, that appear in March, are. Little maintenance is required; just cut foliage to ground after flowers die out. Divide bulbs every 3 to 5 years. Moderate growth rate on moderate water.

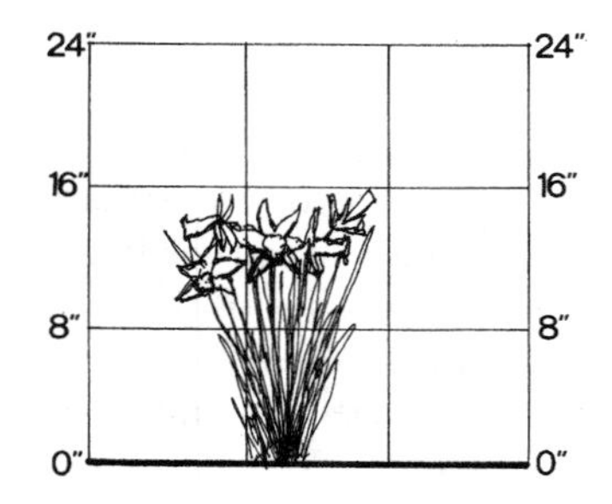

★ *Narcissus cyclamineus 'February Gold'*
Daffodil (consult growers' catalogues)

Along with the ever-popular Tulip, Daffodils are among the best loved bulbs, not only in America, but throughout the world. The familiar flat petals whorled behind a long trumpet with a ruffled end are one of the most noticeable flowers known and also a sure sign of the impending coming of spring. This particular variety is a midsize daffodil in foliage and floral size. 'February Gold' is the hardiest plant with the finest color. These bulbs do not need to be dug up and divided every year but appreciates the process once every 3 years. Cut foliage to ground after flowers fade in late April. Plant bulbs in November after desert soils cool. Fast growth on moderate water. A good supplier for daffodils as well as other bulbs is: Jackson & Perkins, Bulb Catalogue, 60 Rose Lane, Medford, Oregon 97501-0701; Tel: 800/872-7673.

Narcissus jonquilla
Jonquil Daffodil (consult growers' catalogues)

Very attractive mid-size daffodil with back bracket of six petals and a short trumpet. Often the trumpet is a different color than backing petals. Cultural requirements are the same as for *Narcissus cyclamineus* noted above. Fast growth with moderate water.

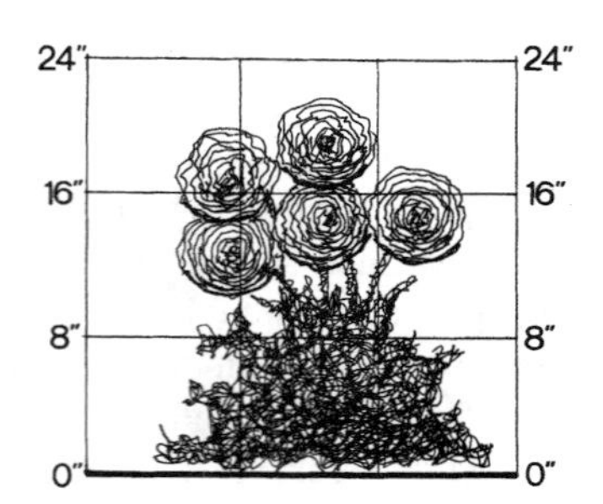

★ ***Ranunculus asiaticus***
Persian Ranunculus

A flower that in shape and pastel-color range resembles the annual, Iceland Poppy (*Papaver rhoeas*). This tuberous flower, however, is so thickly petaled from edge to center that the inner anthers are not noticeable. Flowers in all colors of the rainbow are supported on thin 18 inch stems. Foliage is bright green like Chrysthanthemums, and not a big factor in plant selection. Flowers are between 3 to 5 inches wide and occur in profusion in March and April. Lift tubers and store in cool dry place until the October desert planting season. Moderate growth with moderate irrigation.

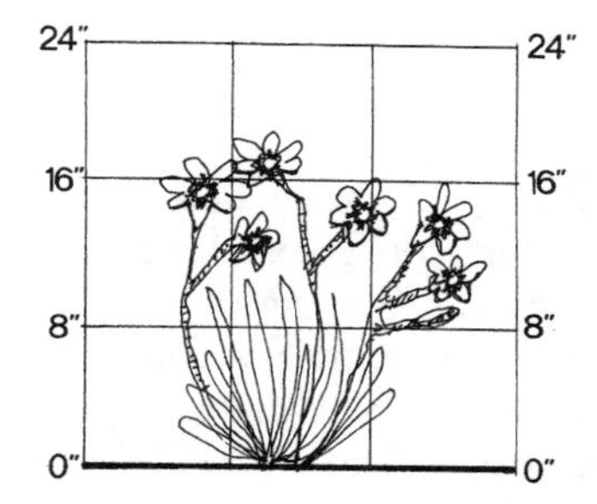

★ ***Sparaxis tricolor***
Harlequin Lily

Delicate, lily-like corms that have tight enough foliage at 8 inches high, and flowers profusely enough to act as a full ground cover if planted close together (12-inch max. centers). Plant corms in spring (April) or store over winter (November) from pots and transplant new plants in spring. Once corms harden-off through their first growing season, they can be left dormant in the ground over winter in all but the coldest areas. Lift and divide corms once every three years. Low desert star performer only. Valued for its flowers with 6 petals, 2 inches wide by 1 inch deep. The flowers are open throated in red, white, purple, yellow, pink, and orange. The tricolor flowers are usually splotched with black at the base of the throat. Mow or trim spiky dull green foliage to ground after flower show has ended. Moderate growth on moderate water. The plant is also highly prized for the length of its late spring to early summer (6 to 8 weeks) bloom period.

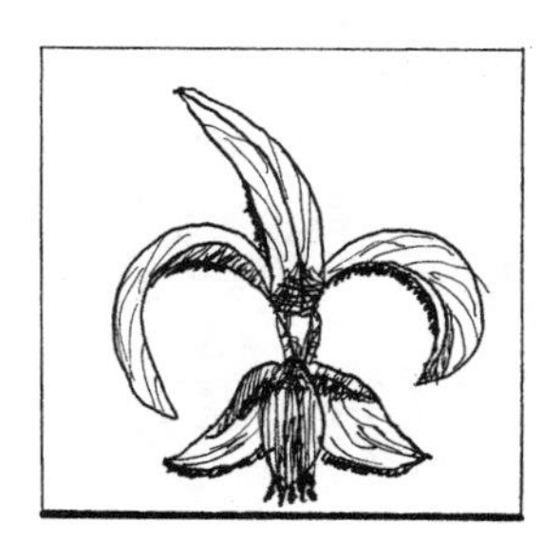

Sprekelia formosissima
Aztec Lily

A bulb from sunny Mexico that produces an exotic crimson, orchid-like flower that virtually shouts olé! Moderately tender plant that may be better displayed (and protected) in pots. In cold winter desert, bulbs should be set out in spring (April). The plant grows daffodil-like foliage to 8 inches and then puts out the exotic flower within 6 weeks of planting. Flowers persist for about a month. Lift bulbs and store in a cool dry place after floral display has ceased. Fast growth on moderate irrigation.

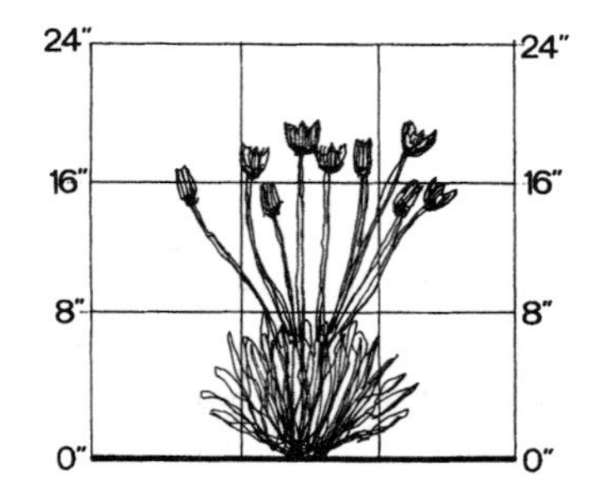

★ ***Tulipa species 'Cottage'***
Cottage Tulip (consult growers' catalogues)

A tall tulip in much the same mold as the famed Darwin tulips (*Tulipa* species 'Darwin') except the flower is narrower, more graceful, with each individual petal being pointed at the end. Tulips are bulbs that prefer cold winter climates where cooler temperatures trigger their growth mechanisms. In the desert, it is a good idea to store bulbs for six weeks in a refrigerator at 40°F before planting them in late November. Also, in the desert, where spring can come early and temperatures often run unseasonably hot for brief periods, it is a good idea not to keep tulips in completely exposed areas. One technique frequently employed is to plant bulbs under the crowns of deciduous trees. The bare crown allows early spring light through to the ground to allow fast initial growth and then the mid- to late-spring leaf-out protects the tulips as hotter weather approaches. After flowering, tulip bulbs should be lifted, dried foliage removed, and stored in a cool dry place until it is time to start the planting process over again. It is always good to fertilize initial growth heavily as it will encourage and improve flower production. Cottage tulips have bright green, foot-long, wavy, spade-like leaves joined at the base. Rising over two feet above the base, on graceful stems, are the delicate flowers which appear throughout May in reds, whites, pinks, golds, and lavender. The whites and lavenders are particularly beautiful. Fast growth with ample watering and fertilization.

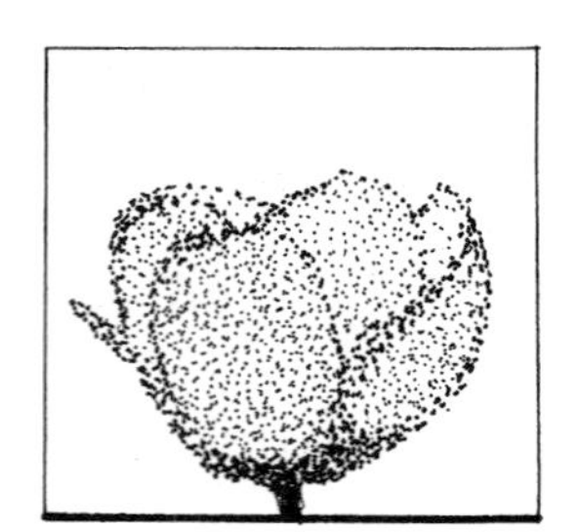

★ ***Tulipa species 'Darwin'***
Darwin tulip (consult growers' catalogues.)

All tulips are star performers, but this tulip is the super star. This is the largest tulip and the most widely hybridized which provides a vast range of color hues. Deep lavenders and purples, bordering on black, are available. Large-cupped flowers to 2 inches wide are supported on 2 1/2 foot stalks. A drift of Darwin tulips on a bright April morning is a majestic sight to witness. Foliage, culture, and care are the same as for 'Cottage' variety noted above. Earlier blooming than the 'Mendel' tulips described below and later blooming than the'Cottage'variety described above. Darwins, therefore, are midspring (April) bloomers and can bridge the floral gap between the other two varieties for a constant spring tulip extravaganza from March to May. Fast growth with ample water and fertilization. A good supplier of the 'Darwin' and other tulips is White Flower Farm, Plantsmen, Litchfield, Connecticut 06759-5050; Tel: 800/888-7756.

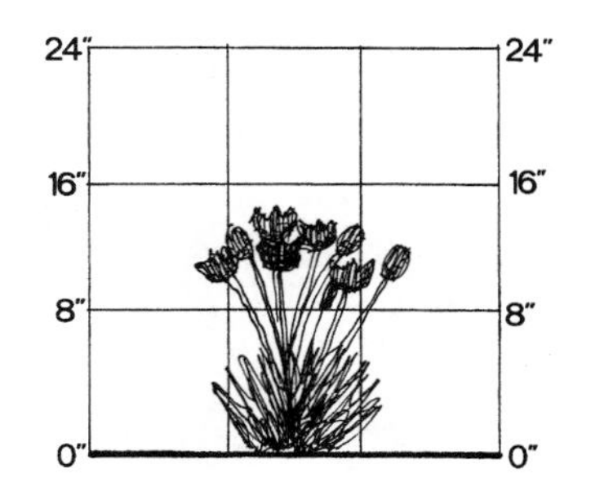

★ ***Tulipa species 'Mendel'***
Mendel Tulip (consult growers' catalogues)

One of the earliest spring blooming tulips. A more traditional, Old World style tulip. Flowers appear in April hoisted up on 18-inch stalks in simple whites, reds, and yellows. Foliage is similar to 'Cottage' varieties but a little shorter. Culture and care are also the same. Fast growth with ample irrigation and applications of fertilizer.

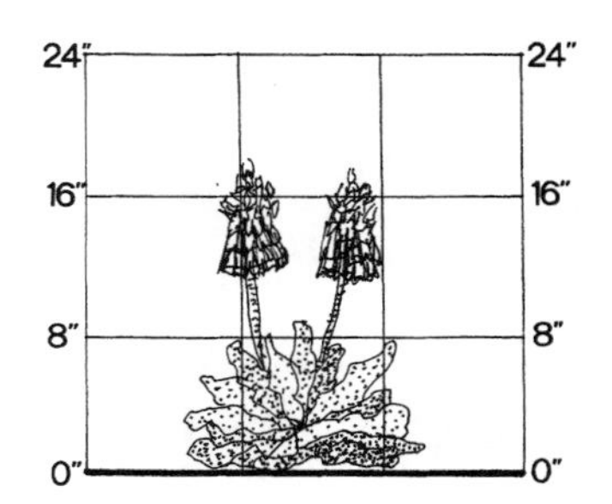

Veltheimia bracteata
(No common name)

A bizarre-looking , spring-blooming bulb on the order of *Fritillaria imperialis* (described earlier). Needs protection from frost and particularly from sun exposure. Foliage, in and of itself, is quite appealing. Leaves are wide, spade-shaped, arching at the midpoint and arranged in an informal rosette. Leaves can be left on the plant year-round, but are summer dormant and would look neater if removed during this period. The flowers are spectacular, somewhat arrow-shaped or spear-tipped. They jut out of the 6-inch foliage mass on other 6-inch stiff brown stalks. It is said the flowers resemble those of the Aloes. Flowers of the species *bracteata* are pink to violet and very subtle in color. (Do not confuse with *Veltheimia capensis* which have red and yellow flowers that are common in nature.) Lift and divide bulbs every three years to encourage healthier and more widespread growth. Moderate growth rate with moderate water.

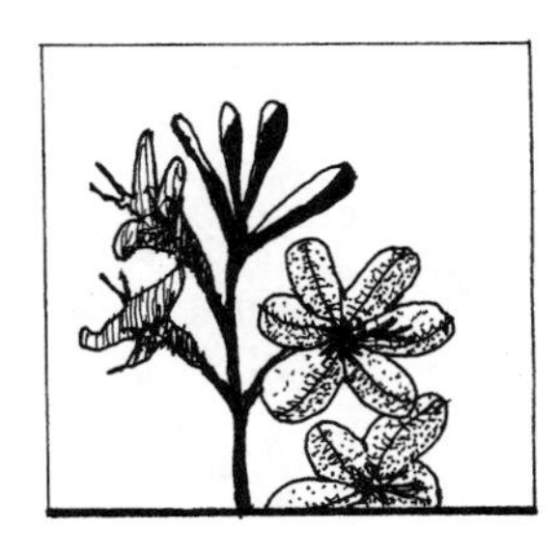

Watsonia beatricus
(No common name)

A tuber with evergreen foliage that is closely related to the popular *Gladiolus hortulanus,* but is better suited to a desert environment. *Watsonia beatricis* is taller than Gladiolus, up to 6 feet at the flower stalks, which rise above the 3- to 4-foot, knife-shaped leaves. Plant has additional benefit of being a mid- to late-summer bloomer (July and August). Floral display consists of tightly clumped, vertically arranged, 3-inch diameter, red-orange blossoms. Cut flower stalks from plant by September, unless there is evidence of continued flower production. In protected areas, leaves can be left on the plant. Where they can burn or freeze, they should be removed. Lift corms and divide every other year for better flower production and to increase planting area of the species. Fast growth on moderate irrigation.

Aquatic Plants

Water lilies

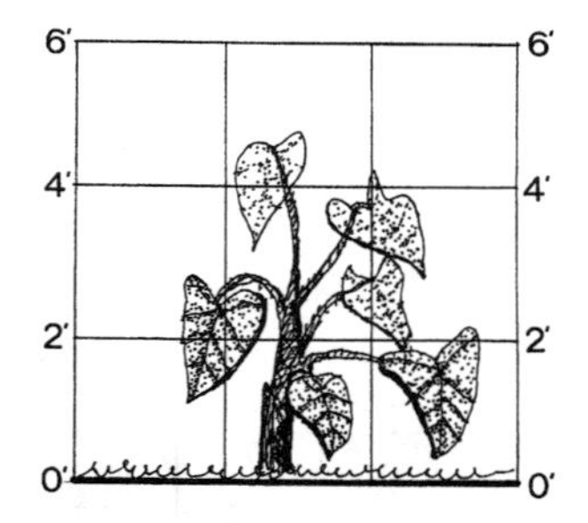

★ ***Colocasia esculenta*** **Semi-evergreen**
Elephant Ear's

A wet soil, water's edge plant. Needs frost protection (30° F) and some afternoon sun protection. In addition, the leaves must be kept out of the wind as they tear and tatter easily. The huge, heart-shaped leaves are the primary attraction of this plant. *Colocasia esculenta* can achieve a height of 6 feet in ideal growing conditions. The harsh desert presents less than ideal growing conditions and a 3-foot high plant can be considered a specimen. Tubers from the elephant ear's root system are a food staple in many South Asian cultures. The plant frequently dies to the ground in winter and, if left in an open area, such a scenario is guaranteed. If frozen or damaged leaves are removed, the plant recovers to a healthy look quickly. Elephant Ear's leaves and weeping habit look especially nice near waterfalls. Plants appreciate a lot of high nitrogen fertilizer when the tubers or seedlings are first set in soil. Flowers are so seldom seen that they are an insignificant factor in plant selection. Fast seasonal growth when in very damp to near completely wet soil.

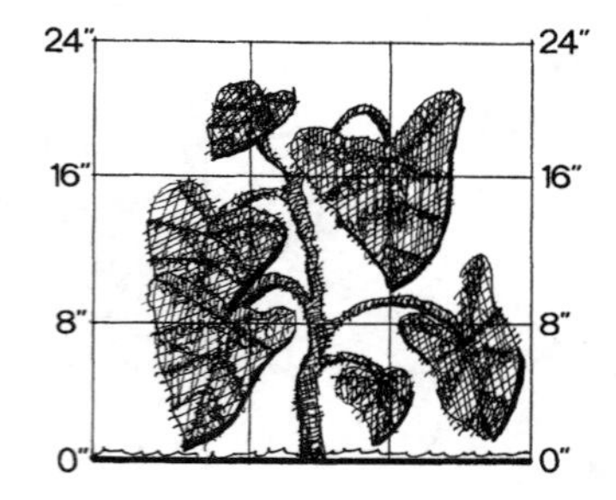

Colocasia indica **Semi-evergreen**
Green Taro

Similar in most respects to *Colocasia esculenta* described above except smaller in height (2 feet) and leaf size. A good selection to intermix with, or to place in front of, *C. esculenta* as a foreground plant. Same cultural requirements. Leaves that receive frost damage should be cut to the ground as they will not recover. Fast growth in wet soil.

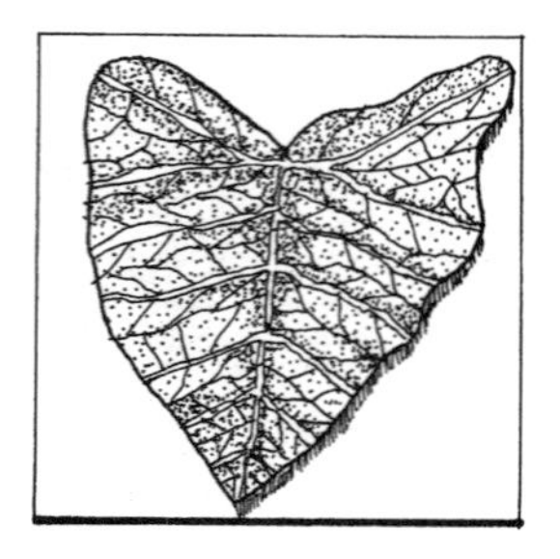

Colocasia violacea **Semi-evergreen**
Violet-Stemmed Taro

The same size and growth habit as *Colocasia indica* noted above. The difference lies in the violet to light maroon color of the foliage. Very exotic and quite unusual. Same culture and care as other Colocasias and looks good intermingled with other members of the genus. Fast growth in wet soil. Remove frozen and damaged leaves.

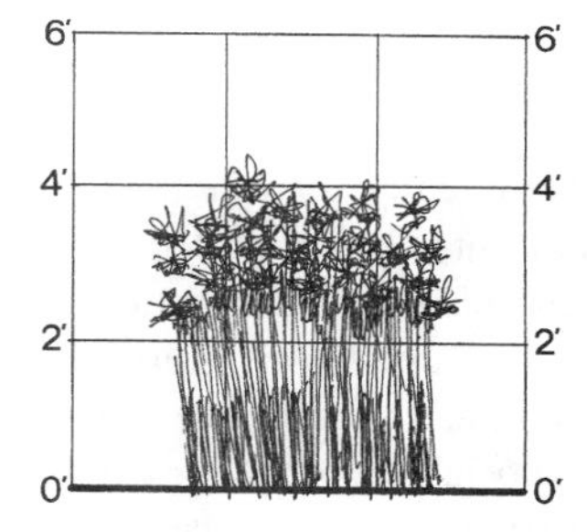

★ ***Cyperus alternifolius*** **Evergreen**
Umbrella Plant

Probably the most frequently used water's-edge, bog-type plant in desert water feature design. It's only real drawback is that it will freeze and completely brown-out at 20° F. It recovers quickly the next growing season, however. The 3- to 4-foot, thin, triangular shaped stems arise basally from central rooting point. Called Umbrella Plant because leaves at apex of stem spread horizontally in five or more evenly spaced directions, giving the appearance of the framework of an umbrella. The Umbrella Plant is a rapid grower and is quite invasive. It will take over a small planting area if not contained either with root barriers or by dividing the constantly expanding rootball and removing older plants on an annual basis. Feathery flower heads occur primarily in spring but will present themselves at anytime. If possible, remove the flower head before it sets seed because the seeds also contribute mightily to the plant's invasive nature. A nice shoreline effect can be created with this plant, which looks very willowy when reflected in moving water. Consider using it mixed with the dwarf variety of the species 'Nanus' which is about half the size and will grow right down and into the water. Very fast growth. A high nitrogen fertilizer helps to green up the foliage in spring.

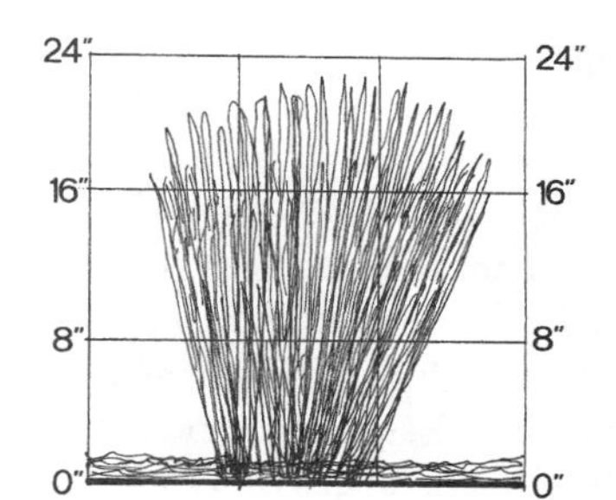

Eleocharis tuberosa **Evergreen**
Chinese Water Chestnut

Delicate, spiky, reed-like plant. Looks very nice as a foreground or basal planting to horsetails (*Equisetum hyemale*) described below. It is not the true edible water chestnut (*Trapa natans*). The small scale, 1 foot high, rush-like leaves have a grassy feel. The plant prefers to grow in about 4 inches of water. Moderate growth. Not considered invasive.

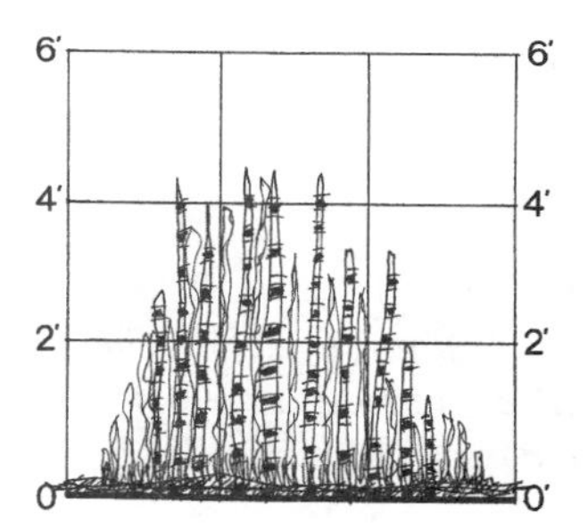

★ ***Equisetum hyemale*** **Evergreen**
Horsetail

Green rush-like foliage with black rings at each node location. This prehistoric relic reproduces by spores borne on a cone-like head that is the crowning glory to the plant's growth cycle. (Technically, considered a fern ally.) Interwoven vertical foliage creates a lacy effect. Acts as a nice backdrop to Chinese water chestnut (*Eleocharis tuberosa*) described above. This plant is extremely invasive and must be contained by root barriers or pavement. Spreads by clumping, which happens at such a rapid rate that it is all but impossible to control by root divisions. Do not plant on the open shoreline. Rather contain the plant in submersible planters or pots. Base of horsetail likes to be underwater but by no more than 4 inches. Fine selection for stream or pond edge treatment. Fast growth.

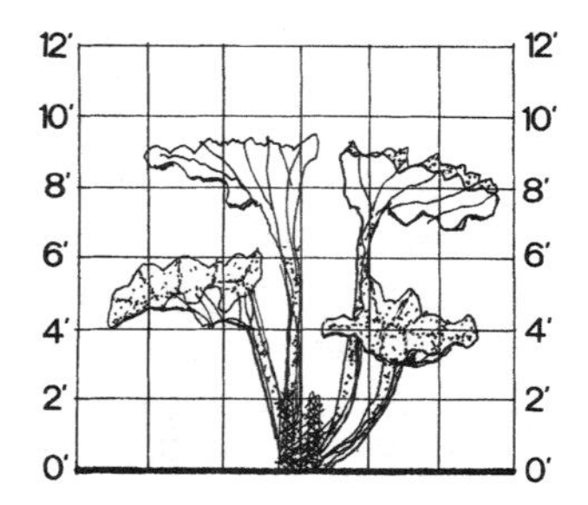

Gunnera chilensis **Evergreen**
(No common name)

This plant puts the "x" in exotic. Although not really rated for the low desert, it can be planted here if provided frost and intense sun protection. The resulting botanical wonder is well worth the effort. This is no downstream plant; it needs plenty of room to spread out. Huge leaves, 4 to 6 feet (yes, feet), across occur on stiff stalks and level off at a height of between 4 and 8 feet. Leaves are upturned, giving them the appearance of having a deep throat, and they turn outward at the edges. Flattened, they have the apearance of huge oak (*Quercus*) leaves. Nice to look up at or down upon in raised areas or sunken atriums. Look very nice as an overstory to a planting of Taros (*Colocasia*). Wash or dust-off leaves occasionally and keep them out of the wind. Flowers that look like tiny corncobs form close to the base of the plant. In cold winter areas the leaves die off and should be removed. The following spring the whole eccentric event happens again. Fast growth when kept in constantly moist, but not wet, soil. Consider growing it in shaded stair wells in conjunction with an underplanting of *Hedera canariensis* which also takes very moist soil. Nice foreground plant to Abyssinian Banana (*Ensete ventricosum*) or Edible Banana (*Musa paradisiaea*). Better leaf production will occur if plant receives a high-nitrogen fertilizer three times a summer.

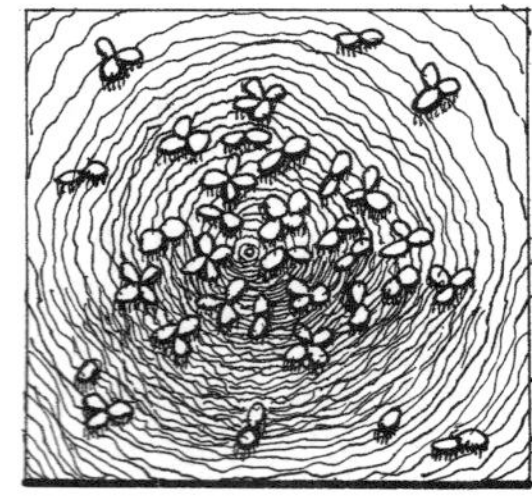
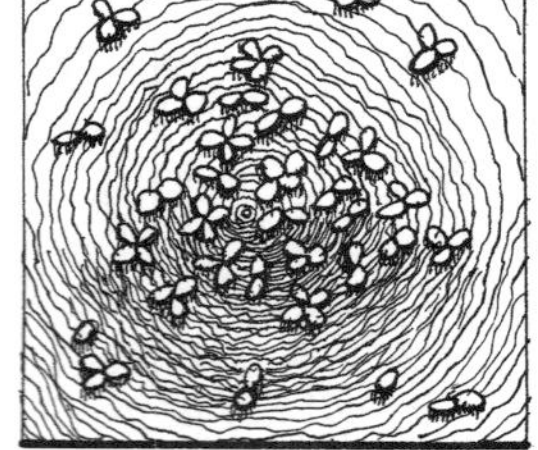

Lemma minor **Evergreen**
Duckweed

Tiny floating plants less than 1/16 of an inch in circumference. Treated as an annual, they occur in such numbers as to be noticeable. They accentuate the movement of water because they float along with it going wherever it goes. This adds a kinetic quality for the pond. Useful as a visual break between other larger water plants. Appreciated by fish and ducks as a food source.

Myriophyllum aquaticum **Evergreen**
Parrot Feather

A floater which trails over rocks and the edges of waterfalls. Foilage consists of tightly whorled, finely cut rosettes somewhat like *Echeveria imbricata*, only a much thinner and yellowish green. Very attractive break from most of the large-scale, broad-leaved water plants. Fish will nibble on the foliage.

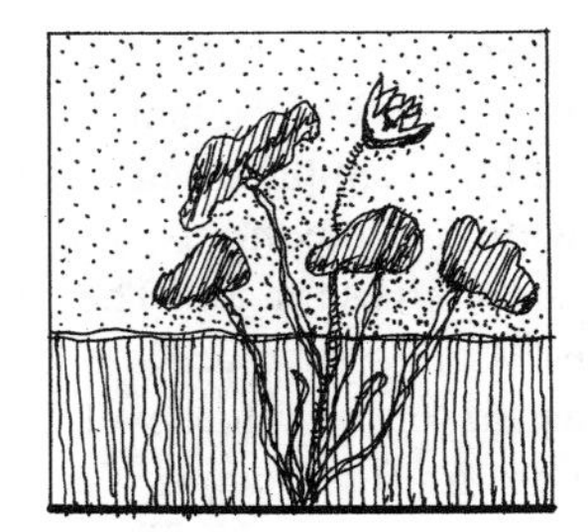

Nelumbo lutea **Evergreen**
American Water Lotus (consult growers' catalogues)

Hardiest of the Water Lotuses and definitely more hardy than the Water Lilies (*Nymphaea* species). Water Lotuses differ from Water Lilies in that their round leaf pads are held in suspension, on thin stalks 8 inches above the water's surface. Water Lily leaves float on the water's surface. Flowers of Water Lotus varieties occur either above or below the leaves. Most plants grown for ornamental landscape purposes are the former type. Water Lotus will not tolerate freezing water temperatures, which is not a problem in the desert. The American species has smaller flowers than its Asiatic counterpart and colors are limited to cream, white, or yellow. Their advantage is their relative toughness and low maintenance requirements. These plants like some shade, particularly during hot summer afternoons. Consult grower catalogues for special cultural requirements. Fast growth.

Nelumbo nucifera **Evergreen**
Asiatic Water Lotus

Larger and more dramatic in every way than the American Water Lotus (*Nelumbo lutea*) described above. The drawback to these plants is that they are less hardy. Round leaves, up to 2 feet in diameter, are held up by stout stalks, 4 feet and even higher above the water. Huge flowers, as much as one foot in diameter, are held singularly, on even stiffer stalks, that project higher than the leaves. Dramatic scale and a wider variety of colors makes this the more frequent Water Lotus of choice. Fast growth.

★ ***Nymphaea species*** **Evergreen**
Water Lily

Like the Water Lotus (*Nelumbo*), there are two main classifications for Water Lilies. These are Hardy and Tropical and they have distinct differences. Water Lilies are probably the most recognized and widely grown water plants in the world. The exotic flowers are startlingly beautiful and always exotic. As outlandish as it may seem, Water Lilies do have a place in desert design, or at least as much of a place in desert design as lakes and ponds, as they are currently used, do. Water features that are not designed to emulate a desert riparian environment and are located on a golf course, or occur well within the oasis zone, are fine candidates for the introduction of Water Lilies. Consider what Water Lilies add to any given pond environment. Their huge, one-foot round pads (leaves) float on the water's surface, providing shade which cools water temperatures and provides a habitat for other organisms. Water Lilies, as well as other aquatic plants, introduce oxygen back into the water as a by-product of photosynthesis. Also, aquatic plants retard the pro-

cess of eutrophication which, simply described, is the way an aquatic environment breathes or releases oxygen and other gases. And then there are the flowers — the icing on the cake. Most types hover 8 to 12 inches above the surface of the water, commanding attention. It is a simple thing to introduce Water Lilies into a lake design. On lakes with gunite bottoms, simply warp or upturn the bottom at the lake edge to create shelves for soil. The top of the planting soil should be 8 inches below the water's surface. The lake construction costs and water expenses must be paid for once the developer commits to building a lake. With a little more design forethought, Water Lilies can be introduced at very little additional expense, especially when their cost is weighed against the visual impact they provide.

As noted earlier, there are two main types of Water Lilies — hardy and tropical. Hardy Water Lilies, as the names implies, are very tough. They grow by rhizomes which harden and become thicker as they mature. Hardy Water Lilies, which bloom from April through summer, can overwinter in desert ponds because the water does not freeze. Tropical Water Lilies should be looked at as annuals although many will overwinter in the desert if a hard freeze does not occur. They grow from fleshy, tender, tubers which can be killed easily in cold weather. Tropicals bloom from June until the first freeze. Both types can be encouraged to bloom, even flourish, during the winter months if the water is heated. The best design choice is to intermix both types. This guarantees constant green on the water's surface and increases the length of color rotation. A unique feature of the tropical variety is that several are night bloomers. This is an added benefit when used in high night use areas like public places, nightclubs, or restaurants. Night-blooming Water Lilies offer dramatic subjects for downlighting or even moonlighting from adjacent trees. Tropical Water Lilies come in all shades of the rainbow. The purples, blues, and reds are the toughest and thus more prolific and longer lasting bloomers. Hardy Water Lilies are limited to whites, pinks, and creamy yellows. Flowers of the hardy Lilies are smaller at 6 to 8 inches in diameter. The flowers of Tropical can get up to a foot or larger. All Water Lilies grow fast if conditions are right. Water Lilies are so beloved and so widely hybridized that virtually hundreds of varieties are available. The plant list contains just a few and the plantsman is encouraged to obtain as much reference information as possible. One of the top growers in the world is Van Ness Water Gardens, 2460 North Euclid Avenue, Upland, CA 91786-1199; Tel: 714-982-2425. The Van Ness catalogue is worth obtaining, as is the book authored by its owner, William C. Uber. *Water Gardening Basics* is listed in the bibliography.

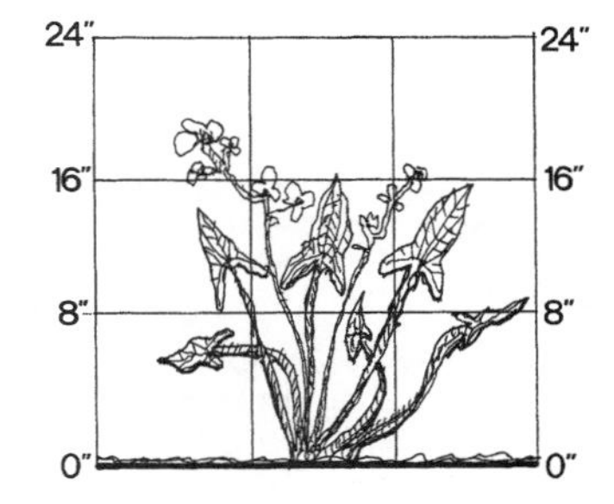

Sagittaria latifolia **Evergreen**
Common Arrowhead

Common Arrowhead needs sun and frost protection in the desert. This plant can grow at the water's edge or out into the pond to a depth of 6 inches, making it a good land-to-water transition plant. It is a rampant grower, spreading by runners. Contain it with pavement or with root barriers or keep it in check with an annual maintenance program of removing new root growth. The plant is most valued for the upward pointing, 3-inch across by 6-inch long, arrow-shaped leaves supported on graceful, 4-foot high stalks. A white flower arises on separate stalks in spring. It has three petals and is 1/2 inch across. Fast growth.

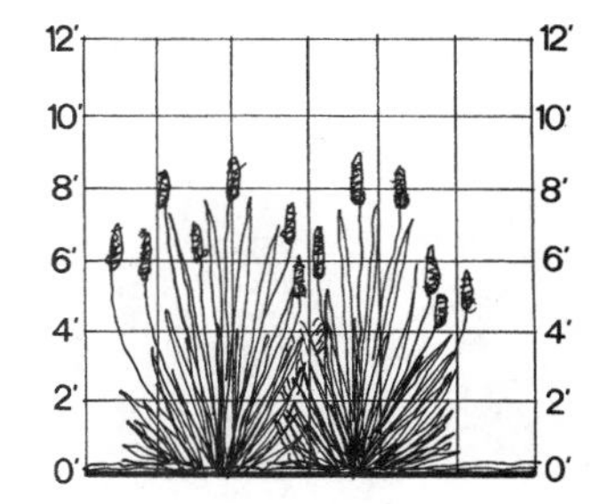

★ ***Typha latifolia*** **Evergreen**
Cattail

The cattail, while being one of the most beautiful water-effect plants in nature, is also one of the most invasive. It cannot be contained by an annual maintenance program. It must be put in containers with solid bottoms to guarantee control. Even at this, the plant seeds rampantly and a wary eye will have to be kept out for new seedlings, which must be immediately pulled. *Typha latifolia* is the most common species. It has the widest (2 inches) and tallest (6 feet) leaves and the largest seed heads. The familiar dark brown cat's tail is in fact several seed structures. The plant is monoecious. The male reproductive parts are at the tip of the tail. The pollen drifts downward onto the female reproductive parts which mature and turn brown. In smaller water-garden settings, you are doing yourself a favor if you cut the tails for dried floral arrangements before they set seed. The species *angustifolia* (Graceful Cattail) is more graceful (thus the common name), somewhat smaller, with thinner leaves to 4 feet high. *Typha minima* is a pygmy-type that grows 12 inches high with tiny tails. Use all three species together for a layering effect. Extremely fast growth. The plant takes all sun exposures, except deep shade, and is quite hardy.

Annuals

Petunias

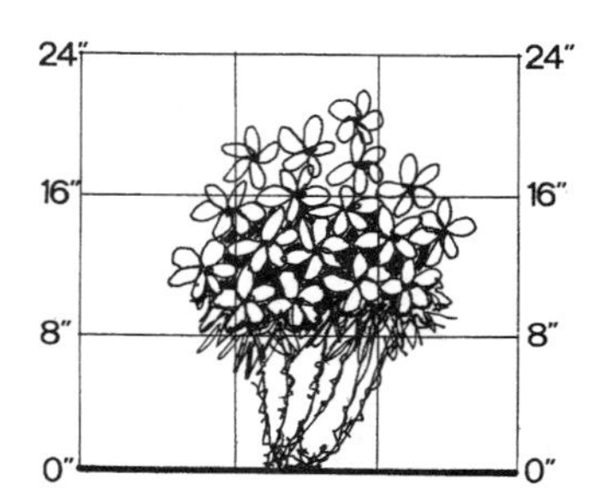

★ ***Abronia villosa***
Sand Verbena

The ultimate low desert naturalized desert annual. It has been used in seed mixes so often that it has spread from 1 end of the Callifornia desert to the other and well into the surrounding foothills. Although other colors are available, it is the familiar purple variety that is depicted by artists in paintings in just about every art gallery in the west. Used extensively with other wildflowers and native grasses in seed mixes for soil stabilization. This star performer hits its peak in late April through early May.

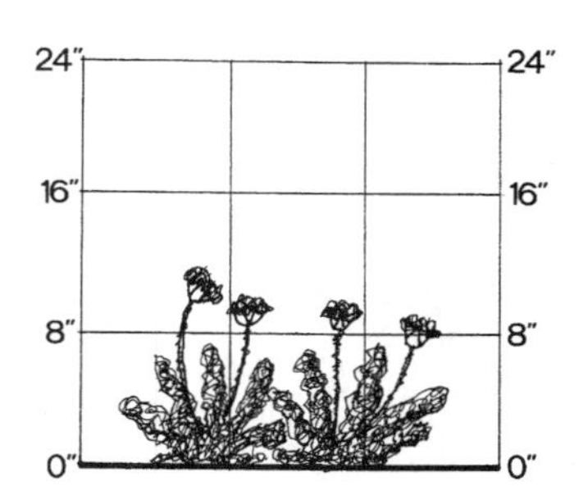

Achillea tomentosa
Woolly Yarrow

Classified in many areas as a perennial, but in the deserts it is treated as an annual. Yellow, flat-topped flowers, in late spring through summer. Foliage forms a flat mat. The species *A.millefolium* is smaller and offers more colors (yellow, red, pink, orange). Its biggest sin seems to be that it is not as well known as *A. tomentosa* but it is well worth looking into.

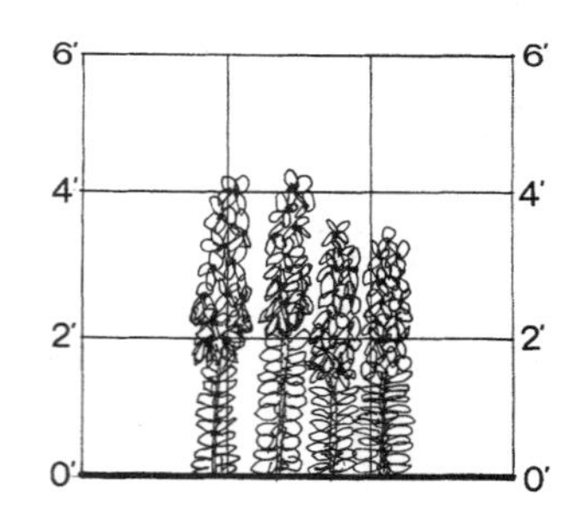

Antirrhinum majus
Snapdragon

Many colors, especially reds, pinks, and white. A midwinter flowering annual in the desert. Flowers snap when pinched giving rise to the common name and delight to children. Plants are tall (2 to 3 feet) and can become floppy when laden with flowers. Consider using as a backdrop to lower and stiffer foreground plants. Plants bloom for over 3 months.

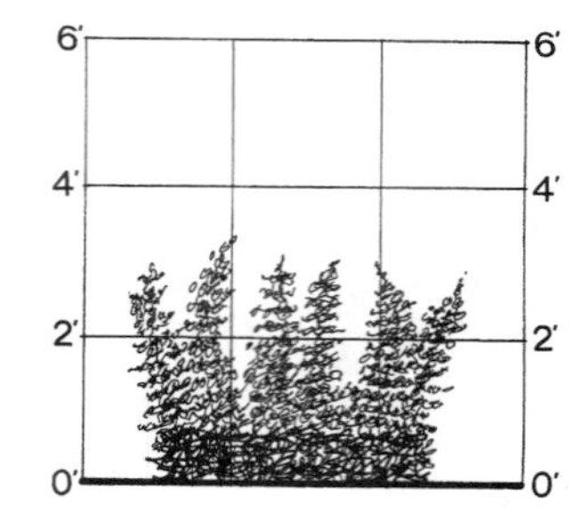

★ ***Astilbe hybrid***
False Spiraea

Perennial elsewhere, but treated as a summer annual in the desert. A recent introduction that is beginning to become more popular. Standard and dwarf varieties. Brilliant reds, several pinks, and a good white. Whenever it is seen, it is a show stopper, especially the red which is one of a precious few deep red annuals you will see in July.

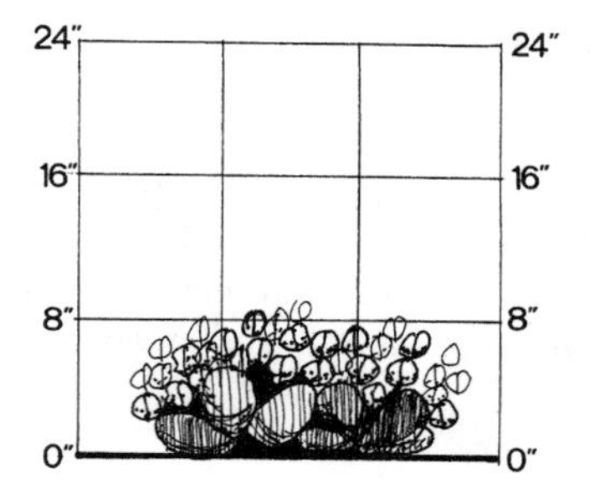

Begonia semperflorens
Bedding or Wax Begonia

Small flowers red, pink, and white in profusion through spring, summer, and into fall. Variety of foliage colors range from green to bronze to some variegated forms. Dwarf varieties, below 6 inches high, are also available. As the common name implies, a good small-scale bedding plant.

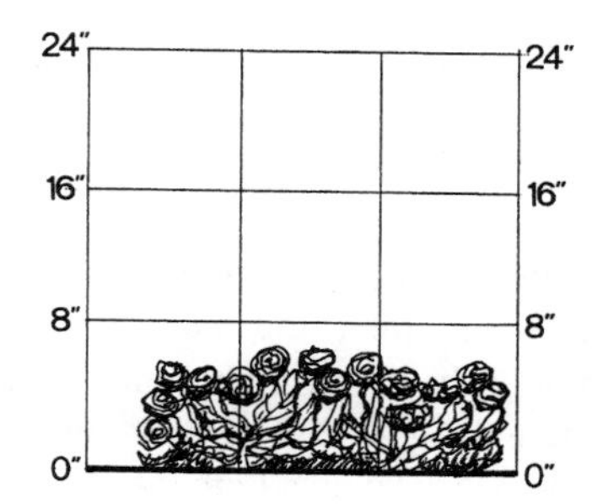

★ ***Begonia tuberhybrida***
Tuberous Begonia

Probably the best known and most widely used Begonia in the west. Fall blooming in all colors except blue. Wide variety of shapes, sizes, and flower types. Grow in filtered light, as it will cook in full sun — even in winter. The bushy upright multiflora variety blooms profusely in several colors with red being the best blossom producer.

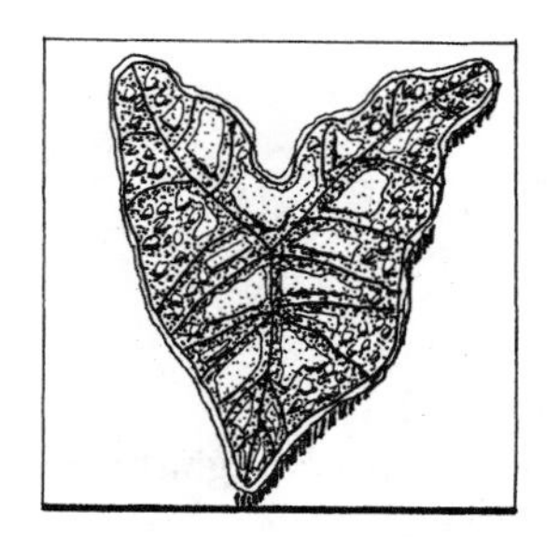

★ ***Caladium bicolor***
Fancy-Leafed Caladium (consult growers' catalogues)

These plants are grown for their showy leaves, which resemble miniature little elephant ears. Although Caladium is technically a bulb, specimens are almost always bought potted and in leaf. It cannot be considered a reliable perennial in the desert. The flowers are insignificant. Species are available with a vast array of leaf patterns and color combinations. Whites, pinks, and reds appear in sections or splotches between green venation or in the reverse arrangement. This is an excellent summer pot subject. Needs shade from noon on. Moderate growth rate with ample watering and frequent applications of high nitrogen fertilizer. An excellent variety of Caladiums are available from: Wayside Gardens, One Garden Lane, Hodges, SC, 29695-0001; Tel: 800/845-1124.

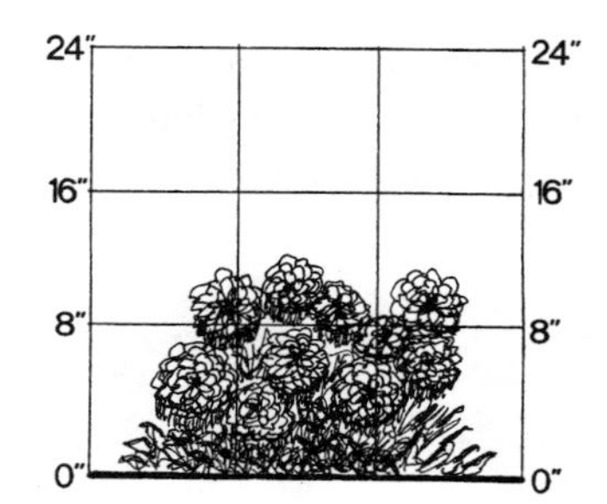

★ ***Calendula officinalis***
Calendula

Also called Pot Marigold. Very similar to the Marigolds except Calendula is winter blooming. Familiar golden-yellow to pale cream flowers. Dwarf variety is 6 to 8 inches high. Does well in full sun and does not like shade. Pick off dead or dying blossoms for better and longer flower show.

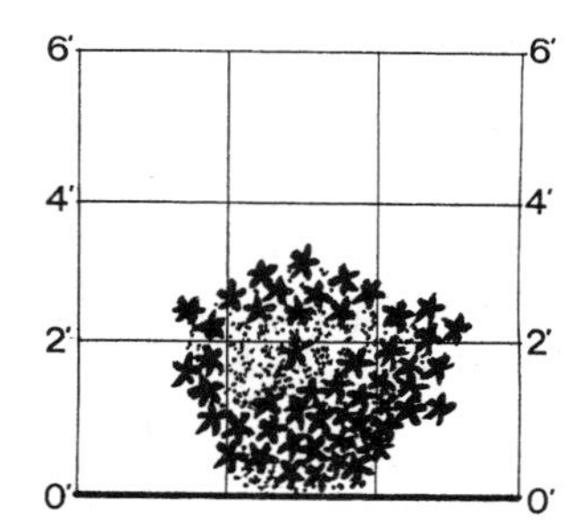

Campanula medium
Canterbury Bells

Deep-blue, bell-shaped flowers of a hue infrequent in the plant kingdom. Other colors available, but they pale in comparison to the blue. Late spring through summer flowers. Keep on the east side or in introduced filtered shade. Prefers slightly acid soil. Divide plants biannually to keep them from overrunning original planting area.

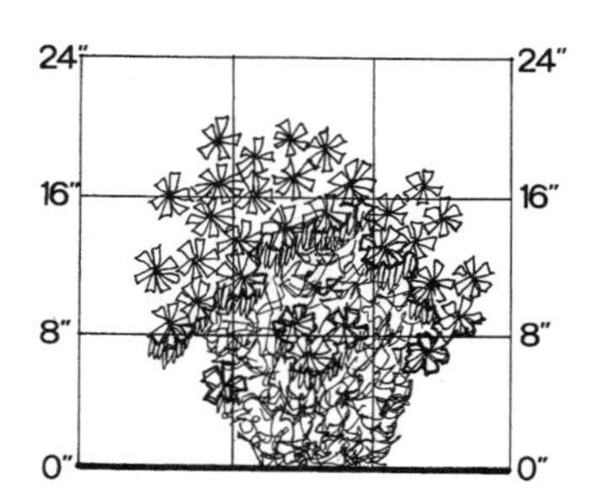

★ ***Catharanthus roseus***
Madagascar Periwinkle

This is the ultimate summer annual in the desert. Accepts full sun, but does appreciate some afternoon shade. White and violet flowers on 18-inch high stems bloom profusely throughout June, July, August, and into September. Hangs on through October, but starts to get leggy. Pull by November. Commonly called Vinca, but not a relative of the true genus *Vinca*. An annual that never disappoints.

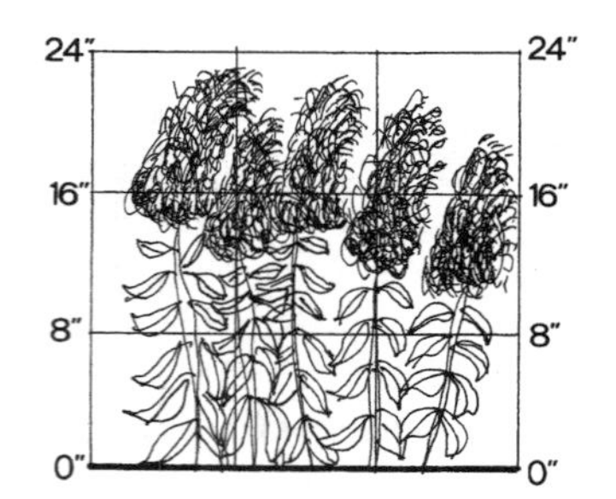

Celosia plumosa
Cockscomb

Similar to Astilbe, except smaller and less color variety — reds, golds, oranges. Takes heat especially well and is somewhat drought-resistant. Do not grow in pots as plants become dwarfed and bloom poorly when root bound. Spring blooming.

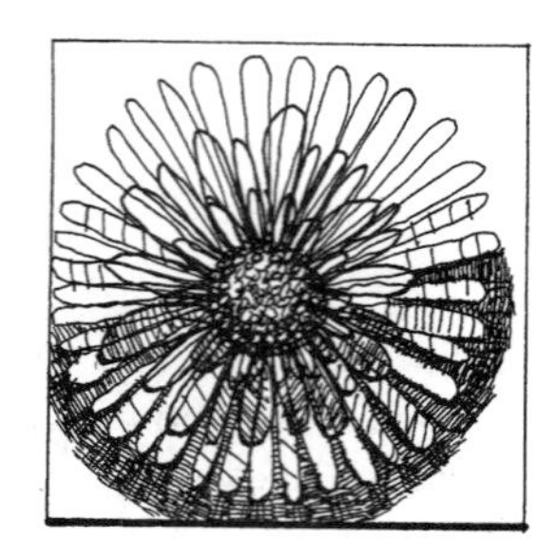

★ ***Chrysanthemum frutescens***
Marguerite

Treated as an annual here, it is rated a perennial elsewhere. White and yellow flowered varieties are the hardiest and most prolific bloomers. Dependable, tough plant for late spring and early summer color.

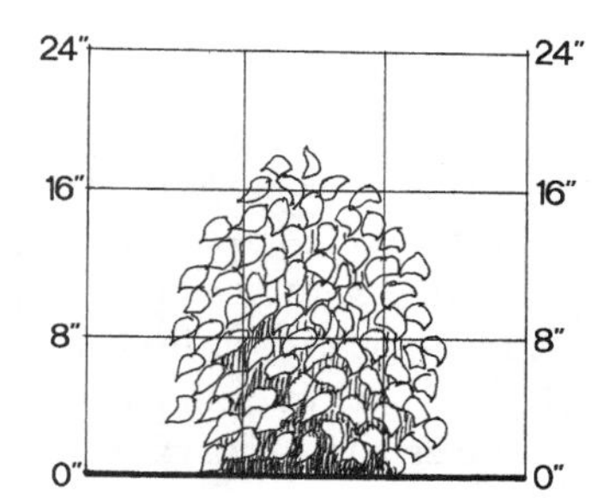

Coleus hybridus
Coleus

Grown more for colorful foliage than for rather uneventful flower show. Leaves display a color show of red, pink, pink on red, pink on green, and several shades in between. Coleus adds interest to border plantings. Needs frost protection and cannot accept full sun. A plant that must be used with care and needs to be pampered, but it is worth the effort.

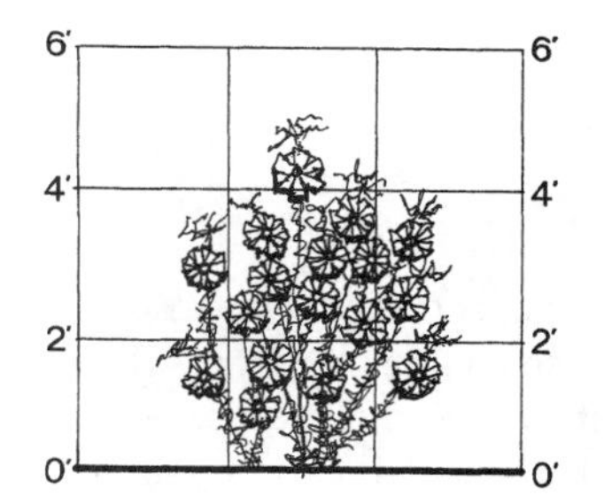

Cosmos bipinnatus
Cosmos

Not as frequently used here as in other parts of the country. Cosmos have daisy-like flowers supported by sparse, fern-like foliage. They look best in mixed color plantings in natural-type gardens. This native American is somewhat drought-tolerant and will take full sun. They can get over 4 feet tall, making them a good selection as a background plant where foreground plants with heavier foliage can screen their sparse leaves. Cosmos is a summer annual that deserves more use in the desert.

Cyclamen persicum
Cycalmen

The ultimate mid-winter bulb in the desert for color. Bold flower form comes in a close second. Heart-shaped leaves. Six- to 8-inch long floral stems support broadly petaled uplifing flowers in reds, pinks, whites, and recently, lavenders. Must have late afternoon shade — even in winter. A terrific potted plant, it looks equally good as a foreground bedding plant in courtyard foundation plantings. Tough, dependable, and increasing in popularity.

Dianthus barbatus
Sweet William

In reality, an outdoors Carnation grown as an annual in the Southwest. It would prefer to be a cool weather annual, so give it some sun protection and consider housing it in a protected courtyard. Excellent cut flowers bloom in late summer (August and September) in many colors, with pink being the sentimental favorite.

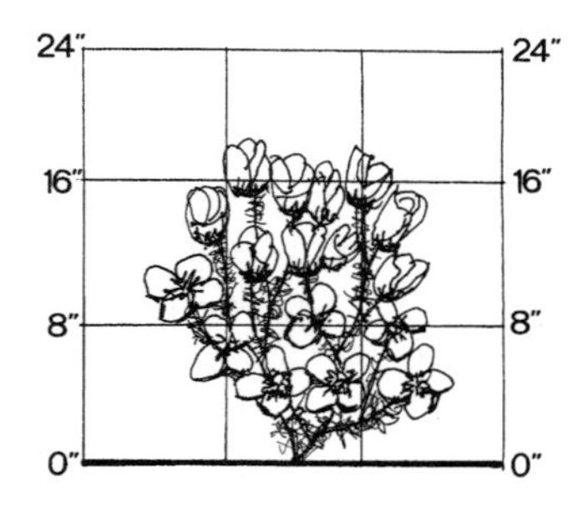

★ ***Eschscholzia californica***
California Poppy

The California state flower and most routinely viewed spring wildflower. Almost always grown from seed. Orange is the color most commonly seen but yellows are readily available and there are roses and whites. Foliage is somewhat ragged so use the plant where it will be viewed from afar where the flowers can dominate the scene. The star performer in any California wildflower seed mix, it is naturalizing further into Arizona, Nevada, and New Mexico.

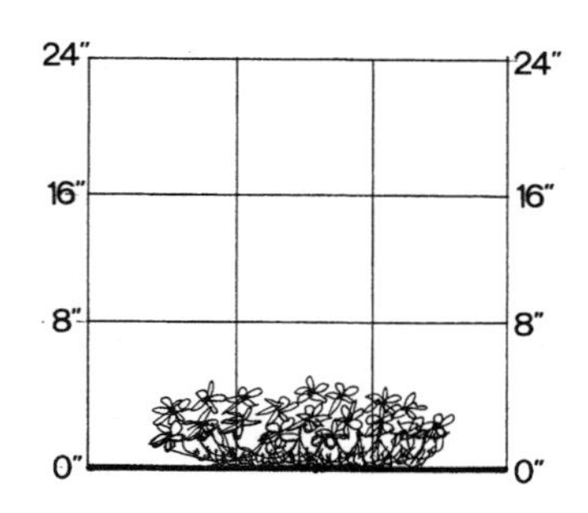

★ ***Gazania splendens***
Clumping Gazania

Like its cousin *Gazania uniflora*, this plant is from South Africa. *Uniflora* is considered a permanent ground cover, spreading by runners. *Splendens* behaves as an annual, perpetuating itself by spreading seeds. Its growth habit is like the common name implies — ball-shaped or clumping. Flowers are yellows, reds, oranges, purples, and some with stripes. Takes full sun and is drought tolerant. Late spring to early summer bloomers in nature. Can be encouraged to bloom in fall and spring with correctly timed seeding and artificial irrigation. The plant is becoming widely used in wildflower seed mixes.

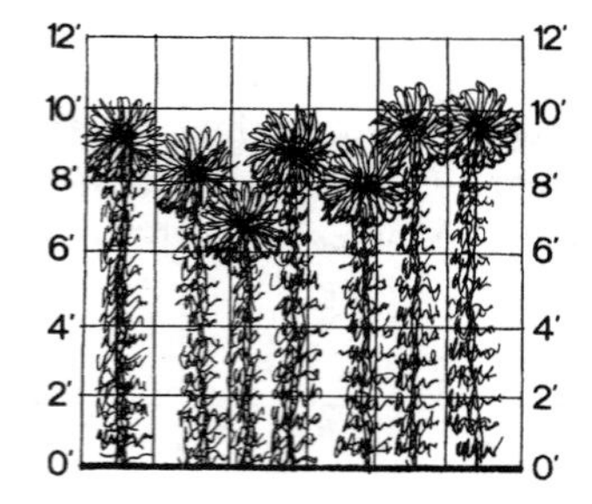

★ ***Helianthus annuus 'Mammoth Russian'***
Sunflower

The species is a fine plant but has smaller flowers. For the massive, 8- to 10-inch across flowers, you need to specify a variety. Huge scale, even gaudy, the plant has a purpose. Stout stems to 10 feet high are strong enough to act as poles. Many gardeners run string from stem to stem and grow sweet peas (*Lathyrus odorathus*) and other climbers on the makeshift trellis. Sunflowers are a favorite of children. They are easy to grow, human in scale, and teach elemental botanical lessons. The seeds, when eaten, are the final lesson in the nature of ecosystems and the structure of the food pyramid. The Sunflower's huge head turns with the sun (heliotropism), teaching an important lesson in solar radiation and its function in plant food manufacturing. Besides all this, the Sunflower is just plain fun to grow and provides a sense of accomplishment. Fast growth with generous watering. Plant in May; it flowers in August. Seeds are edible by September.

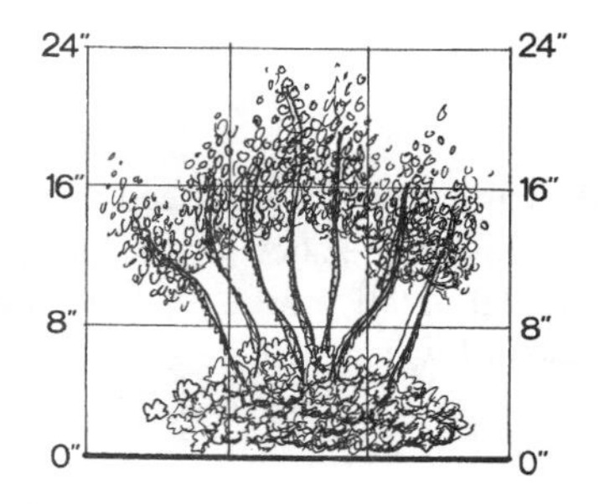

Heuchera sanguinea
Coral Bells

A perennial in protected high-desert areas, but most frequently treated as an annual in the intermediate and low desert. Needs sun protection. East exposure or filtered light are best. Insignificant foliage rarely raises 6 inches above the ground. Plant is valued for 16-inch floral spikes with brilliant red spray-like upright conical blossoms. A breath-taking specimen in the right setting. Would make a great foreground border to Red Yucca (*Hesperaloe parviflora*). Fast growth with minimal irrigation.

★ *Impatiens wallerana*
Impatiens

My all-time favorite desert annual. Reds are the most brilliant you will see anywhere. Reds, pinks, lavenders, and whites — no blues are available to my knowledge, and oranges are uncommon. Can be planted to successfully bloom in fall or spring. Excellent, well-behaved potted plant. Needs some sun protection. Does not like prolonged full sun. A double-petaled, rose-like hybrid and dwarf varieties are available, but nothing can beat the species. Has to have well-drained soil. Move to frost-free areas in early winter to extend blooming period.

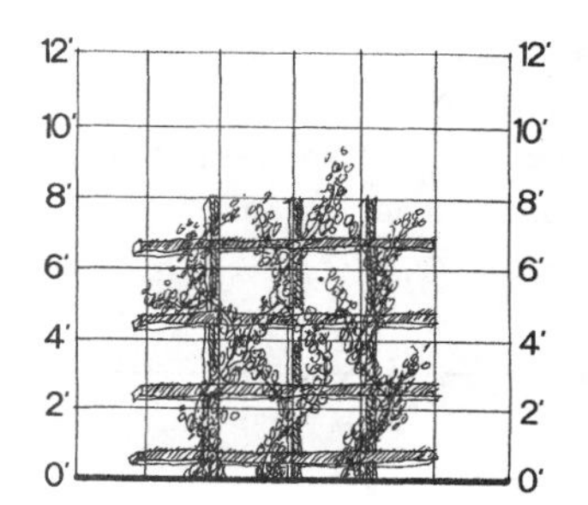

Lathyrus odoratus
Sweet Pea

This very popular annual in other parts of the U.S. is not commonly used in the southwestern deserts, but is a plant that should be used more often. Every color of the rainbow except yellow. Bush and vining varieties as well as spring and summer bloomers. Always started from seeds, which should be soaked in water 24 hours prior to planting. Sweet Peas are known for their very pleasant scent. Vining types can be set in the direction of wind to enhance fragrance. Demands ample water, frequent fertilization, and fast drainage.

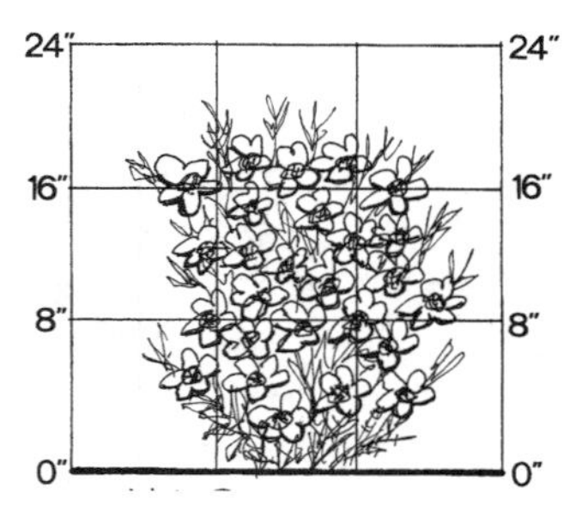

***Linum grandiflorum* 'Rubrum'**
Scarlet Flax

An annual used frequently in spring blooming wildflower seed mixes. Can be used in the domestic landscape with some degree of success. Upright 12-inch high stems allow the plant to be used as a tall border. Give full sun and well-drained soil with minimum amounts of water.

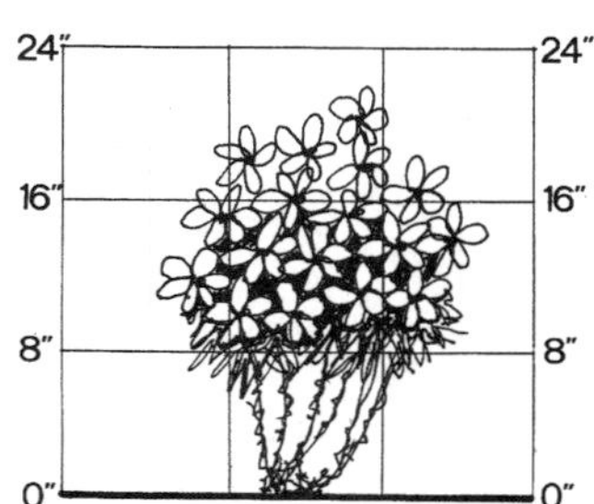

Linum perenne
Perennial Blue Flax

Like its cousin, Scarlet Flax, noted above, this plant is used frequently in desert seed mixes. Deep blue color is a rarity in spring wildflowers. Takes full sun. A useful plant that is not necessarily for the domestic or up-close garden.

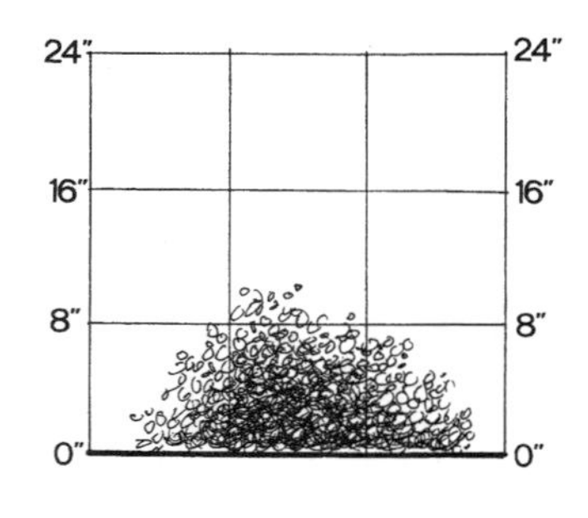

★ *Lobularia maritima*
Sweet Alyssum

Like *Impatiens wallerana*, Sweet Alyssum provides desert gardeners with a spring or fall annual. Use among slower-growing perennial shrubs and ground covers as a nurse plant. (A nurse plant is a plant that takes up space, provides color, and knits soil until the permanent plants crowd it out.) White and purple varieties produce masses of tiny flowers 4 inches off the ground. White is by far the most common. Disliked by some because it seeds and naturalizes freely. I don't really see this as a problem as *Lobularia* gives way easily to stronger species if and when they are introduced.

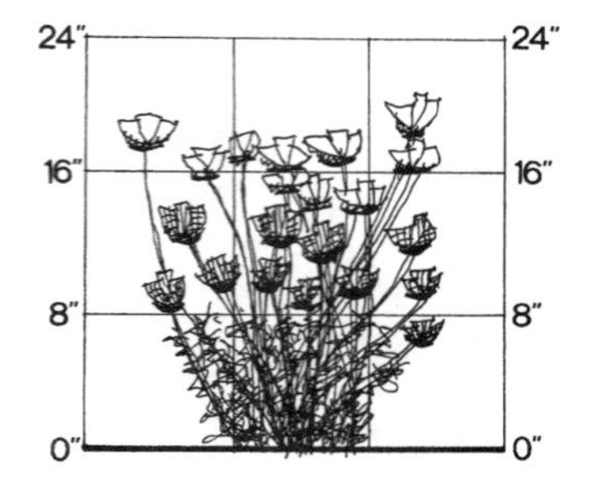

★ *Papaver nudicaule*
Iceland Poppy

Available in all colors except blue. Late spring to midsummer blooming period. Large, saucer-like, 3-inch diameter flowers are impressive in the breeze. Like petunias, pick off the blossoms to increase blooming proficiency and length of blooming period. Started easily from seed, taking less than 2 weeks to germinate. Colors are in a pastel to deep pastel range.

★ ***Pelargonium hortorum***
Common Geranium

One of the most common pot plants in America. Can be seen in the best and worst parts of any city with equal frequency. Red is the most common color. Fall, winter, and occasionally into early spring blooming period. Always dependable, although white and pink varieties are not as hardy. Easy to grow and propagate from cuttings. Pick spent flowers for increased floral production. Does not like to be kept in standing water and will develop stem rot if continually exposed to this condition.

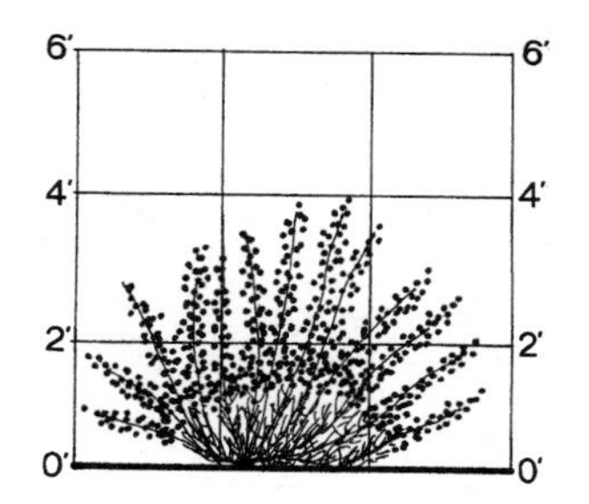

Perovskia atriplicifolia
Russian Sage

A plant noted for its 16-inch-long deep-purple flower spikes that run nearly the length of its 3- to 5-foot-long stems to within 4 inches of the ground. Striking late summer bloomer; will accept full sun and limited water. Beginning to get more use.

★ ***Petunia hybrida***
Common Petunia

Petunias are truly the superstars of the desert fall and winter annuals. They start to die out and get leggy in April and all but disappear by May, giving way to the Vinca (*Catharanthus roseus*) in the typical desert horticultural scheme of things. Petunias have been extensively bred and hybridized to produce every imaginable color — even blue and a near black. They need ample water, plenty of light, large quantities of fertilizer, and above all, constant picking of spent blossoms. With attention, they are worth every bit of the effort. Petunias are classified as grandifloras, which indicates large flowers; and multifloras, which indicates more (multiple) flowers but of smaller size. Both grandifloras and multifloras produce the single-blossom types with connected petals and a pronounced throat and double-blossom types with double rows of petals giving the flower a carnation-like appearance. The single-flowered varieties seem a bit more hardy to desert conditions.

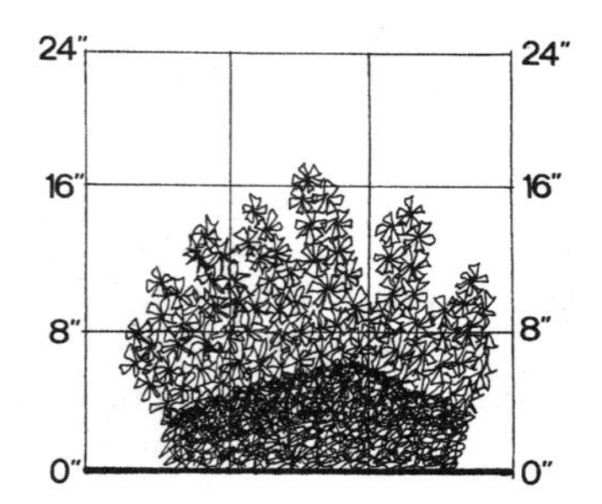

★ ***Phlox drummondii***
Annual Phlox

This plant from Texas comes in all colors. Pick off, or more appropriately, strip spent blossoms to increase future blooming and to keep the plant from forming seeds which disperse rapidly. Late spring to late summer bloomer. Not given a lot of use here, but extremely popular elsewhere.

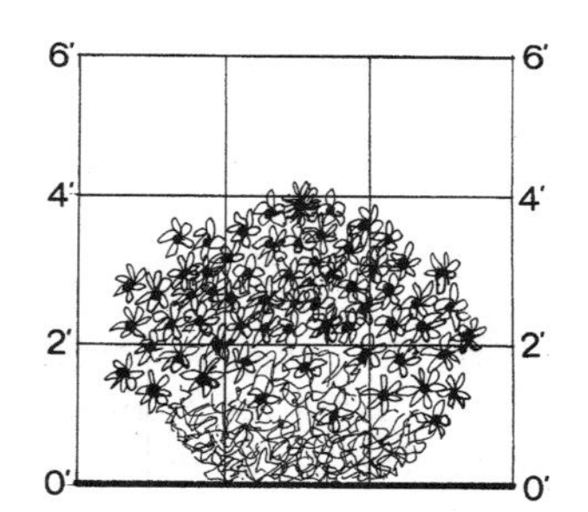

★ ***Rudbeckia hirta***
Black-Eyed Susan

Sentimental favorite. Not commonly seen or used in the domestic flower garden, but does well here as a summer annual. Whorled, yellow flowers with the familiar dark-brown (black) disk (eye). Tall and leggy; best used as a background accent where foreground vegetation can screen the lower foliage.

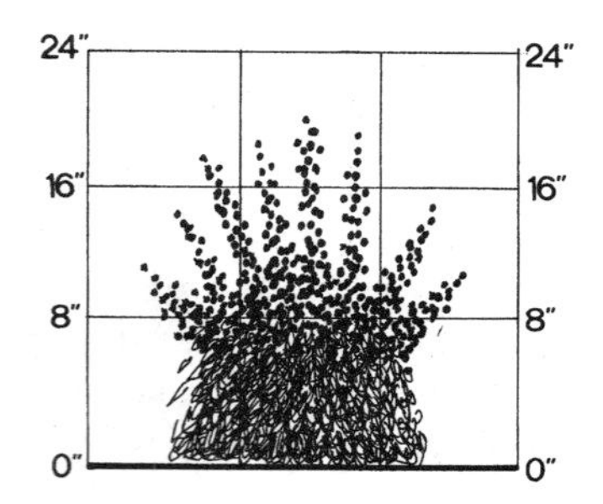

★ ***Salvia officinalis***
Garden Sage

Perennial in most zones. Like several other species of Salvia, this is a splendid desert dweller. Purple variety is the best known and widely sold, but red and white can be found on rare occasions. Beautiful foreground plant. A real eye catcher.

★ ***Tagetes erecta***
American Marigold

This tough American original is an excellent potted plant. Biggest drawback is pungent smell which is disliked by some and loved by others. When planted downwind, it is a star performer in every way. Gold and yellow to nearly orange and rust flowers. Gold is, by far, the most common. Needs well-drained soil. Spring and fall blossoms. Takes full sun when established, but appreciates afternoon shade. Not a large-scale bedding plant. Best used as a stand-alone specimen.

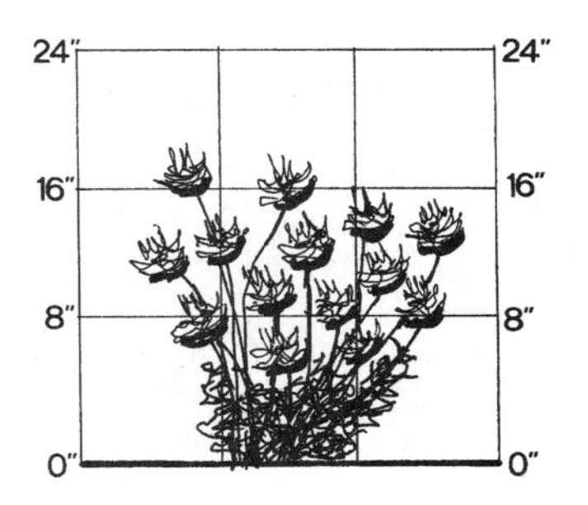

Trollius ledebouri
Globeflower

Gold-orange flowers dance in the breeze supported on stiff stalks. A continual late spring through summer bloomer that follows the California Poppy (*Eschscholzia californica*) and signals the end of summer. Frequently incorporated into wildflower seed mixes.

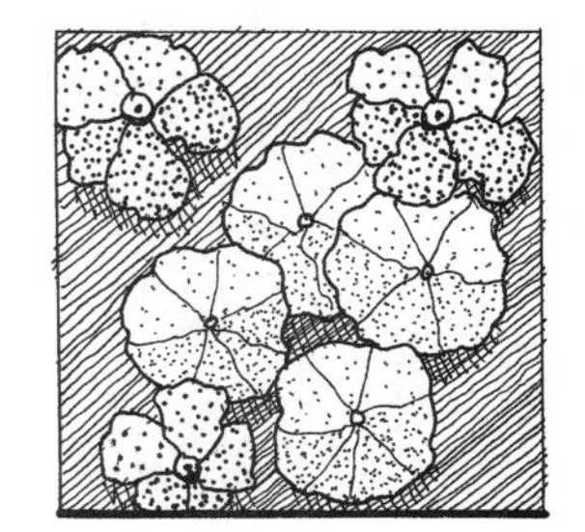

★ ***Tropaeolum majus***
Common Nasturtium

Perennial elsewhere; treated as an annual in the Coachella Valley. Leaves are showy, lobed, almost round, with light centers. Flowers resemble the leaves in size and shape. Orange, yellow, and red are the most common colors, with orange being by far, the most widely planted. Winter bloomer, can be grown from seed sown in the fall. All parts of the plant are edible and used often in southern California salads.

Viola wittrockiana
Pansy

Extremely popular winter annual. The familiar three-splotched black faces of the flower are backed by a multitude of vibrant color selections. Although they are frequently used, I do not rate Pansies as star performers due to both heat and cold tenderness. It can be difficult to time the planting to get the maximum benefit from the plant, and die backs do occur. Like Petunias, the floral show can be increased and prolonged by picking spent blossoms.

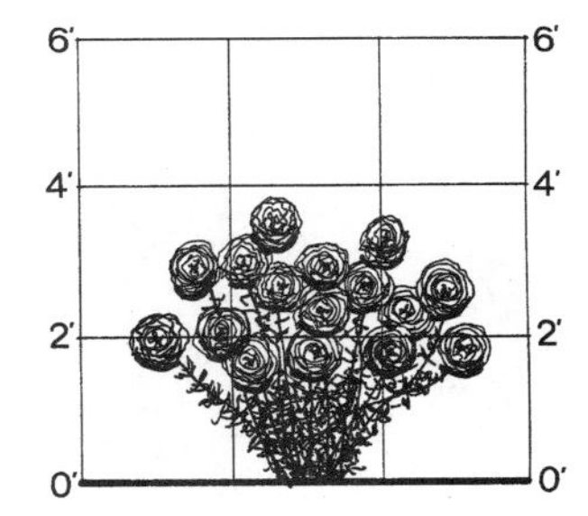

★ ***Zinnia elegans***
Zinnia

Next to Madagascar Periwinkle (*Catharanthus roseus*) this is the midsummer to early fall annual that is seen most frequently throughout the Valley. Yellow, red, copper, and rust marigold-like flowers, 5 to 7 inches across, and supported on 18-inch vertical stalks. Needs well-drained soil and ample water. Fertilize late in the summer to extend blooming period. Do not water by spraying.

Desert Hydroseed

Common Buckwheat

Desert Hydroseed Mixes

Mix #1 (6 inches to 24 inches high) Low Grasses and Wildflowers

This mix is designed to rapidly knit the ground plane of any open desert area. Colorful flowers are selected to provide the longest period of seasonal rotation. Self-seeding species are selected for better long-range soil coverage and perpetuation of species. Consult a seed supplier for amount of seed per 1000 square feet and an individual species percentage to the overall mix. My recommendations are:

Abronia villosa: Desert Sand Verbena
Eriogonum umbellatum: Sulfur Buckwheat
Eschscholzia californica: California Poppy
Euphorbia albomarginata: Rattlesnake Weed
Gaillardia pulchella: Indian Blanket
Gazania splendens: Clumping Gazania
Melampodium leucanthum: Blackfoot Daisy
Oenothera berlandieri: Mexican Primrose
Oryzopsis hymenoides: Indian Ricegrass

Mix #2 (2 feet to 4 feet high)

This mix is designed for desert slopes and the establishment of a more permanent plant community, in terms of hardiness, than Mix #1. Mix #2 is shorter in height, much more colorful, and exhibits a longer color rotation period than either Mix #3 or Mix #4. This mix would knit the desert floor fairly well and encourage invasion of local natives into bare spots. If a complete immediate cover is needed, mix some of Mix #1 in with this mix for faster slope coverage and erosion control. Again, consult a seed company for amount of seed needed per 1000 square feet and other cultural information. Mix #2 consists of:

Ambrosia deltoidea: Bur Sage
Calliandra eriophylla: Fairy Duster
Calochortus kennedyi: Desert Mariposa Lily
Encelia farinosa: Brittlebush
Eircameria laricfolia: Turpentine Bush
Eriogonum fasciculatum: California Buckwheat
Eschscholtzia mexicana: Mexican Gold Poppy
Hibiscus coulteri: Desert Rosemallow
Machaeranthera tortifolia: Mojave Aster
Rafinesquia neomexicana: Desert Chicory
Sphaeralcea ambigua: Desert Globemallow
Thamnosa montana: Turpentine Broom

Mix #3 (4 feet to 8 feet high) Large Shrubs

This mix is intended to be used as a large shrub in-fill to a stable desert floor area that needs some vertical effect or background impact. If spraying seed over open ground with no inherent vegetation, it would be a good idea to select some species from Mix #1 and/or Mix #2 to get some lower, faster-growing plant material to knit the desert soil. Soliciting the advice of a botanist/horticulturist would be a good idea because plants in this mix are quite permanent once established. The large shrubs are:

Beloperone californica: Chuparosa
Fallugia paradoxa: Apache Plume
Isomeris arborea: Bladder Pod
Opuntia basilaris: Beavertail Cactus
Opuntia bigelovii: Teddybear Cactus
Rommneya coulteri: Matilija Poppy
Salvia funerea: Death Valley Sage
Simmondsia chinensis: Jojoba
Yucca whipplei: Our Lord's Candle

Mix #4 (10 feet and higher) Largest Shrubs and Desert Trees

This mix is intended to provide ultimate native desert vertical height. It would be a good mix to use at the base of foothills or on the upper bajada. This mix will not knit slopes by itself. For erosion control you should incorporate species from Mixes #1, #2, and #3. Because of the large-scale nature of the species within this mix it is critical to have a working knowledge of the plant materials listed, as well as enlisting the advice of a botanist/horticulturist. The "grande" desert mix consists of the following species:

Acacia greggii: Catclaw Acacia
Cercidium floridum: Blue Palo Verde
Dalea spinosa: Smoke Tree
Fouquieria splendens: Ocotillo
Larrea tridentata: Creosote Bush
Olneya tesota: Desert Ironwood
Prosopis pubescens: Screwbean Mesquite
Sarobatus vermiculatus: Greasewood

One final note on desert native hydroseed mixes:

Not all species listed are the best plants for the application. Several species not listed may be better. Research and expert advice should be your guide. All species listed will need supplemental irrigation from time to time, especially immediately after hydroseeding to guarantee germination. A temporary irrigation system can be used, but to be honest, it is not a good solution. An occasional irrigation system is more appropriate. This is a below-ground system that is either operated manually or programmed through a controller to be used during selected times of the year. A watering program that starts in late January to early February, for instance, emulates the winter rains that the selected plants are in tune to. This supplemental irrigation will push plants, particularly the wildflowers, into their growth cycles. Most plants selected have the ability to be drought deciduous, meaning watering can be greatly reduced to nonexistent during the hot summer months.

Not all plants in a seed mix germinate and not all plants that germinate will survive. In addition, not all seeds desired will be available. When selecting species for a hydroseed mix, contact seed suppliers as far in advance as possible. This point cannot be stressed enough. Many suppliers are state certified to actually gather seed from plants in the wild. The time of year this can be done, the amount of seed that can be harvested, and the types of seed in stock are all highly variable factors. You will have to be flexible and patient.

Native hydroseeding is a method of planting that is not an exact science. Its more a process of ongoing trial and error. The advantages lies in establishing an environment in much the same way nature would and that is more in tune to ecological processes and niche selection dynamics than any other method of planting. The bottom line is that, although more water is used to get more vegetative cover and faster growth rates than nature would provide, less water is ultimately used with the native hydroseed planting technique than with any other man-induced planting strategy.

Chapter 6

Irrigation Design

Irrigation pipe

Introduction

Of all plant material introduced to arid environments, 90% will not survive without supplemental watering. Even members of the rugged cactus family will need some initial irrigation in order to become established and eventually become drought tolerant. While the irrigation industry has been steadily improving equipment technology and contractors continue to make advancements in installation methodologies, landscape designers are moving away from an active role in irrigation design. Because irrigation design is very dull and technical by nature, it is an area that many creative landscape architects pass off to an irrigation designer without so much as a discussion on design approach or a follow up plan check to see if the resulting design works, much less whether it is water efficient. With all the thought and hard work that goes into a successfully designed project, it seems ludicrous to leave the issue of plant survival up to an outside party with no input or concern on the part of the landscape architect.

Design Concerns

A basic working knowledge of irrigation principles and irrigation design components is essential to any desert landscape architect. Without rudimentary skills in these areas how does one determine:

1. If the irrigation system meets the owner's budget and ongoing maintenance program?
2. If the system meets the needs of the eventual end users and if it protects their health, safety, and welfare?
3. If the system is water efficient and energy conscious?
4. If the system guarantees adequate watering and thus the ultimate survival of all design plant materials?

Whether the landscape architect performs irrigation design in-house or subcontracts the work out to a professional irrigation designer, all parties involved should know:

1. Irrigation requirements of all design plant materials.
2. Source and cost of available water supply; water pressure and available flow volume in gallons per minute.
3. Basic critical site information such as soil characteristics, solar orientation, wind direction, and weather history.
4. Codes and restrictions of ruling governmental agencies. Plan submittal and review processes of these agencies.
5. Expected efficiency of the designed system in terms of water delivery to plant materials, program times, and length of water delivery, ease of ongoing maintenance, and expected life of the system components.

The irrigation designer of today must possess some basic botanical knowledge, understand the fundamental principles of hydraulics, and be on top of rapidly changing technology and evolving product lines. In a competitive marketplace, he makes decisions that balance initial costs with ongoing maintenance budgets, and, above all, he must be cognizant of water conservation. All this acquired knowledge, ongoing research, product selection criteria, and concern for water efficiency must be translated into a design that can be drawn on or transferred to paper and accurately interpreted by an installer. It's a tall order that requires drafting skill and plan clarity. It takes time and commitment to acquire these traits and the irrigation design will represent a large portion of the landscape architect's fee, just as the irrigation installation represents a large portion of the exterior construction budget.

An owner cannot cut corners on the project irrigation system and expect larger scale plant material and attractive hardscape elements to bail the job out. Eventually problems will arise with a cheap irrigation installation that will cost more in the long run to correct than if a quality system were installed at the outset. It is better to meet tight budgets with smaller-scale plants that will grow into the job if they receive adequate irrigation rather than to lose bigger plant material and be forced to abandon a cheap irrigation system for the sole purpose of achieving initial impact. Two years down the road this does not serve any purpose to anyone.

Hydraulics

Any discussion of irrigation design starts with an explanation of the basic principles of hydraulics. Water at rest is said to be hydrostatic. Water in motion is called hydrodynamic. The weight of 1 cubic foot of water is 62.4 pounds. Visually segmenting the cubic foot of water into 12 1-foot-high by 1-inch-square rectangular columns of water helps to illustrate the concept of pounds per square inch. These 1-foot-tall by 1-inch-square columns each weigh 0.433 pounds at their bases. The 1-inch-square column of water is called "X" feet of head, depending upon its height. Thus 1 foot of head, 1-square-inch in cross section, is equal to 0.433 pounds. The term "feet of head" is often used in the design and specifying of pumping equipment to call out pump sizes and performance characteristics.

One pound of water weighs 16 ounces. As we have already noted, a 1-foot-tall by 1-inch-square column of water weighs 0.433 pounds at its base. To weigh 1 pound, this 1-inch-square column of water would have to be 2.31 feet high.

The water resting at the bases of these 1-square inch columns of water has a specific weight determined by the amount of water and its height. Pounds per square inch is the term applied to this phenomenon. In hydraulic and irrigation design, the term "pounds per square inch" (psi) is referred to simply as pressure. The concept of water pressure simply explained, is the force (weight) exerted at the base of the 1-inch-square column of water.

Imagine this column of water contained within a larger water line leading to a tower 150 feet above the ground. One can easily calculate psi of pressure by multiplying 0.433 (weight per foot of head) times 150 (height of contained water) to arrive at 64.95 psi at the base of the column of water. Another way to do this is to divide the height of 1 pound of water into the inch square column which stands at a height of 150 feet. Therefore, 150 divided by 2.31 equals 64.95 psi.

For the purposes of practical irrigation design, the two most important numbers a designer will need to know are 0.433 (1 foot of head) and 0.86 (the side of an equilateral triangle). The 2.31 factor will only come into play in pump design. Until one becomes very adept at irrigation design and all the principles of hydraulics; pump specifications, as well as the liability for performance of the pump, are best left to the experts.

What we will concern ourselves with, for the purpose of this chapter, in the area of hydraulics, will be the amount of water in gallons per minute (gpm) and its pressure in psi. All irrigation design assumes that these two factors are available on site and the design of the irrigation system is determined by available water pressure and gpm at the point of connection. Some research will be required to determine what these factors are and whether adequate pressure is available to design an operable system. A device known as a pressure gauge can be attached to hose bibs and when the water is turned on the gauge will register the available pressure. To gather a pressure reading from a site with no improvements you will have to consult the local water agency to obtain pressure information. The agency will usually give you two readings. The first will be termed "high" or "static" and refers to the normal pressure within the agency's system when not in use or, more frequently, when in average use. Remember that static water pressure represents water that is contained and not moving. Dynamic pressure reflects the pressure of flowing water. The second pressure will be called "peak low" and refers to the pressure (dynamic) in the system when it is in peak use. This normally occurs during early morning hours when users are getting up and preparing to leave for school, work, and other functions and in the early evenings when dinners are being prepared and more people are likely to be in their homes. Irrigation system design should always respond to the peak low pressure as this is the worst case condition. If the system functions well in the worst case it will function well in all cases.

Besides water pressure, which is basically a form of measurement of the weight of water when at rest, the next most important area of hydraulic design that concerns that irrigation designer, is the amount or quantity of water available. This is expressed in gpm and the speed or rate at which water flows is expressed in the term, velocity.

Velocity is an extremely important factor, which will be covered in far greater depth in the area of this chapter which explains pipe sizing. Flow and gpm deal with how much water is actually available to be used for irrigation purposes. System flow and pressure determine meter sizes and the size of all the irrigation equipment downstream of the water meter.

The following is a rule-of-thumb guide to water pressure:

0 to 40 pounds	Too low for normal operation of a conventional system. Suggest incorporation of a system pressure booster pump at the point of connection.
15 to 40 pounds	Ideal pressure for a low-flow drip irrigation emitter system.
41 to 60 pounds	Difficult but workable pressure. The designer must be very careful with hydraulic calculations. Designer must choose low gallonage (thus low precipitation rate) heads that operate at a lower pressure and be generous with valve and pipe sizes for efficient operation of a conventional system. Can be used for drip systems but valves operating drip heads must be a pressure reducing type, and a pressure regulator is recommended downstream of the valve.
61 to 85 pounds	Ideal pressure. Ideal for conventional systems with flow control valves. Will guarantee operation of a wide variety of heads. Valves which operate emitters must be pressure reducing and a pressure regulator downstream of the valve is an absolute necessity.
86 ± pounds	High pressure. If it is a consistent pressure, and especially if it is a peak low pressure, a pressure-regulating valve will be required at the point of connection. It is always a good idea to have pressure-reducing control valves on conventional and drip systems and pressure regulators downstream of the values on drip systems in case the system pressure regulator valve fails at the point of connection.

One of the better irrigation design reference books, *The A, B, C's of Lawn Sprinkler Systems* by A.C. (Chet) Sarsfield (see Bibliography) likens water flow within the piping of an irrigation system to the flow of vehicular traffic leaving a large metropolitan area. In the heart of the city, the volume of cars is largest. Compare this to a water meter where the volume of water (gallonage) is highest. The routes leaving the city have several lanes (larger pipe) in order to handle the flow of traffic. This would represent the irrigation system's mainline. As traffic moves away from the city, cars leave the highway system and exit to the suburbs, which decreases the overall number of automobiles on the road. It would not be economical to continue to use several highway lanes to accommodate fewer and fewer cars as the road system gets further and further away from the city. What happens is that progressively fewer highway lanes (smaller pipe) are employed to handle the diminishing traffic volume.

In irrigation systems, the type and number of individual heads determine the demand for water flow or volume. Think of the irrigation heads as a population center that must be serviced by a highway. The more population centers and the closer they are to one another, the larger the highway system (pipe) needed to adequately serve them. This will be covered in sections dealing with irrigation, head type, selection, and spacing, as well as valve sizing, pipe sizing, and system zoning. Suffice it to say that traffic and water must flow smoothly and efficiently to insure the successful functioning of their respective systems.

Another analogy to use when thinking of water flow within an irrigation system (pipe) is to picture a river system in reverse (as mentioned in Chapter 3, Grading and Drainage). The further back the drainage area in the watershed, the smaller its water flow and its overall size (pipe). As the water within the water shed gets closer and closer to its mouth (water meter), the larger the system becomes.

Irrigation Design

The process of irrigation design includes these steps:

1. Review of site conditions and water availability
2. Analysis of the landscape plan and plant material
3. Define the owner's program
4. Determine watering demand and water delivery

5. Select method of backflow prevention
6. System type and head layout
7. Zoning/circuiting
8. Piping the system
9. Providing related equipment
10. Controller station routing
11. Working Drawings: Drafting, detailing, and specifying
12. Installations: field observation

1. Review of Site Conditions and Water Availability

Any design commission should start with a thorough review of existing site conditions. Such things as elevation above sea level, existing contours and drainage patterns, existing vegetation, and prevailing wind direction should all be noted. If you are not working in conjunction with an architect or civil engineer, it may be hard to obtain a plot plan or footprint of the site. Aerial photographs, tax accessor's maps, or real estate parcel maps could all provide some help. One situation I often encounter is a lack of information for small-scale ("spec") residential work. Owners are frequently first time buyers and relatively unsophisticated in the construction process. It is wise to assume the builder had to locate the building from a plan, no matter how simple, and the procurement of this plan is a point of departure. In the absence of any existing plans, field measurements will become a necessity.

Whether doing your own field measuring or checking the accuracy of an existing site plan, the following information is essential:

- North arrow.
- Scale.
- Wind-direction arrows.
- Type of soil, texture, and note any indications of wind or water erosion.
- Changes in elevation; especially note any slopes which exceed a 3:1 ratio.
- Any existing structures or utilities. Look for overhead wires and any underground pipes or wires.
- Existing vegetation to remain.
- Evidence of the history of previous on site uses and the nature of adjacent site usage.
- Water meter size and location, if available.
- Water pressure reading with a pressure gauge. On sites with no meters or hose bibs, take the reading from the closest adjacent site if possible.

2. Analysis of Landscape Plan and Plant Material

If you are a landscape architect who does his/her own irrigation design or at least controls the process in house, this is not a major step, because several of the planting decisions and material groupings were chosen, hopefully, with ease and efficiency of irrigation in mind. If you are an irrigation designer or a landscape architect working on someone else's plan, you may have inherited more problems than you would have preferred. As this frequently happens, in the real world, and it is often far better to make something work than to criticize why it won't, you will have to study the water requirements of various plant groupings and try to visualize what type of irrigation system or systems will work. The highest percent of the time this system selection will boil down to irrigation head selection, which will be discussed later. In situations where the water requirements of some plant materials are vastly different, you may have to recommend an alternate planting technique such as isolating certain plants with root barriers or in elevated planters. The thing to remember is that irrigation design is not an exact science and that planting design is even less so. Just as some plant material may suffer from incorrect sun or soil exposure, it may become subject to too much or too little watering as a result of compromise in the irrigation design. Incredibly, many desert designs are overwatered. This usually happens either due to a lack of knowledge or by catering to the massive water requirements of one plant to the detriment of its neighbors.

In my opinion, when faced with a design that contains a grouping of plant materials with widely divergent irrigation needs it is better to provide too little water than too much. The plants that are in need of more water will show that fact by stressing. A competent maintenance person can individually irrigate specimens that require more water if the irrigation designer has provided the means for doing so via quick couplers or hose bibs. The basis for this opinion is that you can always apply more water but you can never remove water that has already been applied.

3. Define the Owner's Program

Most, but not all, owners are cost conscious. Some owners are uninformed about the nature of landscape maintenance and are willing to spend a great deal of initial capital on a sophisticated irrigation system but will not pay the salaries of the individuals necessary to manage the system. An irrigation system is an assemblage of moving parts and, as such, there will be eventual breakdowns. If an owner appears unwilling to spend the money to hire competent maintenance personnel or train new or existing personnel, take this as an omen of things to come and design the simplest system possible. Nowhere is this more true than in the area of computerized digital controllers. All the programming capability in the world does not make a bit of difference if the eventual end user does not understand how to operate the controller. There are several controllers that operate like computers but have a mechanical face that is less intimidating, making it much more likely to be programmed. Also, there is nothing wrong with several of the old pin-type controllers. There is nothing wrong with state-of-the-art technology and, indeed, many projects are much better off with it, but remember that in the real world of lower-paid maintenance personnel, advanced equipment often is unused or, worse yet, misused.

There is a tendency for initial controller programs to be set up and then forgotten about. The initial program is inadequate to accommodate the changing climatic and cultural aspects the planting design will encounter. Irrigation designers and/or installers are providing their clients with an important service when they furnish written irrigation schedules that can be programmed into the controller and account for the plant establishment period, ongoing growth rate, seasonal changes, and the eventual maturity of the planting design.

Other examples of the system being above or beyond the capabilities of the maintenance personnel would be in the area of moisture sensors (tensiometers) or the use of a polyethylene (soft pipe) drip system. In these cases the issue becomes a matter of numbers — personnel vs. the hours required to troubleshoot the system.

It is of utmost importance, therefore, when designing an irrigation system, to be practical and perhaps a bit conservative about the abilities of the ultimate end user to comprehend, troubleshoot, maintain, and manage it.

4. Determine Watering Demand and Water Delivery

Talk about a crap shoot. It's time to roll the dice. The good news is that an average irrigation system can more than adequately deliver the water needed to assure the survival of the planting design. The bad news is that very few people (including myself) know exactly or even approximately how much water that is.

Manufacturers, suppliers, and even designers will all try to get you to believe that products and formulas will provide all the answers. They won't; and although it is a cliche, in this case, experience is the best teacher. Here are two facts to ponder. First, even in the desert, most plants are overwatered. Second, with the exception of fruits and vegetables which need the water for optimum product development, most plants can survive at 80% of their optimum water requirement with no noticeable growth deficiencies. On smaller to medium size projects where time and manhours permit, one suggestion to prevent overwatering is to program the controller(s) so that the program can be used in times of vacations, etc. Then put the program on override and irrigate manually through the controller. What I am saying is, it is a mistake to water by rote on a set calendar day if it can be avoided. Most plants prefer infrequent but very deep waterings over the shallow ones that frequently occur due to poor controller programming. This also encourages a deeper and wider root system which will benefit plants greatly in times of severe drought and/or water rationing. By learning to recognize the wilting symptoms of plants, which means they are calling for water, maintenance personnel and homeowners can provide irrigation when it is needed and thus more beneficial to the plant's overall health.

In irrigation formula jargon, you will often hear the term evapotranspiration rate (ET) or potential evapotranspiration rate (PET). Simply put, water is lost to the atmosphere through plant transpiration (T) and surface evaporation (E). This is all part of the hydrological (water) cycle and what we need to do is enter and exit this cycle at the right times. We enter the cycle when conditions are dry and plants need supplemental watering. We exit the cycle when conditions are wet enough for plants to survive on their own and additional watering would be wasteful.

ET is an actual gauged reading, while PET is an educated guess. In a real witches' brew, evapotranspiration rate is based on current temperature, relative humidity, dew point factor, net rainfall, soil temperature, solar radiation, and prevailing wind speed. One can usually acquire the daily evapotranspiration rate from the local weather station. In spite of all the factors considered in compiling the ET, one should note that this is not rocket science nor is it an exact science. The most accurate PET rates are reported as they happen, which leaves very little or no room for preparation. This lack of lead time to react to conditions can be extremely detrimental on large projects. If maintenance personnel wait until plants are undergoing heat stress, several will reach a permanent wilting point before there is enough time available to water them. Thinking ahead and understanding the capabilities of the irrigation system is essential.

The potential evapotranspiration rate is an accumulation of historical weather data and known local factors such as soil type and wind direction. Basic assumptions can be made. Where the PET really comes into play is in the initial irrigation design process when the system must be sized to meet projected worst case scenarios. The irrigation designer must first know how much water the planting design will need. This is usually based on acre feet per year. This acre feet per year estimate is then broken down into an inches per day or week irrigation requirement. This conversion is done so that the demand can be related to the precipitation rate of various irrigation heads which we will discuss later. Suffice it to say that heads must be chosen to be able to deliver the water demand at least on a weekly basis.

The third and final component we will discuss in determining water demand will be the use of in-ground moisture sensors (tensiometers) and above-ground rain gauges. Tensiometers are devices that read or otherwise sense the moisture level in the soil. On systems operated by an electric controller, electronic tensiometers are used. In this application, small, flat metal stakes are inserted into the soil. These stakes are wired to an electronic control (reading) device which in turn interfaces with the irrigation system's main controller. When the moisture level in the soil is inadequate an electrical impulse is sent back to the controller, which in turn activates the valve. When acceptable moisture levels are obtained, the valve is then shut down. The use of tensiometers would, in theory, be the best way to irrigate. The technology associated with tensiometers is relatively new, however, and problems with initial installation and ongoing maintenance can be encountered. The biggest problems with tensiometers, however, is that they are single-point indicators and must be placed in areas that are representative of average conditions within any given hydrozone type.

Rain gauges are cup-like gadgets that are usually affixed to the sides of structures or yard walls. They catch rain and when they become full enough either mechanically (by water weight) or electronically shut down operation of a programmed controller by activating the controller's rain switch. Rain gauges are not extensively used in the desert but they are inexpensive and do occasionally help to save water.

Now that we have discussed water demand and ways to measure it, let's discuss water delivery to the system. Nine times out of ten water will be available through the municipal or water district's potable water system.

In the absence of a domestic metered water supply, most water for irrigation purposes is supplied from deep underground wells and from ground level reservoirs or canals. Reclaimed water is also becoming more widespread. In all instances, this water will need to be pumped (pressurized) in order to function within the irrigation system. If this is the case, it is recommended that the irrigation designer consult a pump consultant or supply house. We will not concern ourselves with pumping design except to add one basic tidbit of information. Pumps function far better pushing water than pulling it. That is, that the elevation of the pump should be as close to or below the elevation of the water line (level) of the water being pumped as possible. If the pump is higher than the water line it will have to virtually suck (pull) water uphill. In this case the suction is, in reality, creating a vacuum. No vacuum can exist beyond the level of atmospheric pressure. All water vacuums rely on atmospheric pressure to push the water from the bottom while the pump creating the vacuum pulls from the top. The limit of atmospheric pressure is 33.94 feet in elevation. No pump, no matter how powerful, can draw water higher (push yes — draw no), as the water would fall downwards when there was no more atmospheric pressure to push it uphill (water always seeks the lowest level). For this reason, place the pump location as close to the water source as possible, even if the pump capacity and performance is being specified by someone else.

This explanation also gives rhyme or reason to ground level reservoirs. It is easier and less costly to store large quantities of water under low flow in holding reservoirs and than pump the water into pressurized irrigation systems then to try to draw water up from a well and directly into an irrigation system. For this reason, lakes are used to irrigate golf courses. They add dramatic beauty, increase the difficulty of play, and contribute water to the course. The reasons for most lakes are not understood by the public-at-large and often they do not deserve the criticism they receive.

Reclaimed water is secondary or tertiary level water recycled from sewage and storm water systems. Several water districts in the Southwest are taking a more active role in providing reclaimed water for irrigation uses. Golf courses are particularly good places to apply reclaimed water, which has slightly higher nitrate levels than potable water. Turf is a voracious consumer of nitrogen and acts as a natural filter before the water enters the underground water table and becomes part of the aquifer. Golf courses themselves, because of the emphasis placed on good subsurface drainage, are very good recyclers of irrigation water. As the need and desire for water conservation continues to gain momentum, reclaimed water will become a more and more viable source of irrigation water.

5. Select Method of Backflow Prevention

In many desert locales, the water district will select the method and type of backflow prevention. On private commissions or on projects with private wells which penetrate into a potable system, it will be up to the irrigation designer to make the selection decision. First, we will look at what backflow prevention means, and then we will look at how it is provided.

On systems originating at a potable water supply, providing backflow prevention is the most important thing the irrigation designer will do. Backflow prevention protects the health, safety, and welfare of all upstream users of the water supply. It also helps to protect the irrigation designer from a lawsuit.

A backflow preventer is a device that allows water contained within a pipe to flow in only one direction. When a back siphonage or suction (vacuum) occurs in the potable water system upstream of the vacuum breaker, potentially contaminated downstream water would, if unobstructed, flow into the potable upstream system, creating what is termed a backflow. There are documented cases where exactly this has happened and people have become sick and even died. A back siphonage happens most frequently when a fire occurs and large quantities of water are rapidly drawn from the municipal water (potable) system. It is also conceivable that a water main or supply dam could break, causing fast depletion of water lines. This, in turn, sucks water backwards into the municipal mainline unless there is something to block off the process.

There are four commonly used types of backflow preventers which are used at the water meter or water source upstream of the project irrigation supply. These are: (1) atmospheric, (2) pressure-type, (3) double-check valve, and (4) reduced-pressure type.

The **atmospheric-vacuum breaker (AVB)**, often referred to in the trade as an antisiphon valve, operates on the simplest principle and is, by far, the cheapest product. The valve is limited in some applications, however, and must be placed a minimum of 6 inches above the highest operating downstream irrigation head. The AVB operates solely by applying the principle of gravity. Under pressure from an open irrigation system control valve, water flows in one direction into the irrigation system. The atmospheric pressure breaker is designed with a floating plunger or poppet that lifts under the pressure of the incoming water, and once elevated, it just floats on top on the moving water. When a back-siphonage occurs, water is sucked backwards out of the system and travels upstream. Due to the way the valve is constructed (it is always a form of angle valve) and due to the fact that the back-siphoned water is moving under far less pressure than the incoming water, the air pressure in the atmosphere enters through ports above the poppet and forces it downward thus shutting off the system line from the potable upstream line and preventing a backflow. The reason the breaker has to be 6 inches higher than the highest downstream head is so that it is the highest point in the system under atmospheric pressure and, as such, receives the maximum benefit from the atmospheric pressure. I do not recommend using this device if you cannot guarantee it will be 6 inches above the highest downstream operable head or on new developments where you cannot predict the nature (and height) of future construction. Because of its method of operation, the AVB must always be installed in an upright (vertical) position. In addition, it must always be installed downstream of a control valve and not between a control valve and the potable pressurized water supply. Atmospheric vacuum brakers are often formed (manufactured) in conjunction with system control valves. These combined valves are of little consequence in commercial applications but are frequently used on smaller sized and lower-budget residential projects.

Pressure-type vacuum breakers (PVB) are a hybrid of the atmospheric-breaker principle described above. The breaker is usually of sturdier, more permanent construction than its cousin. The primary difference is that the disk float assembly (poppet) is spring-loaded or otherwise mechanically assisted to close faster and more firmly.

With the difference in its manufacture, the pressure type vacuum breaker can be installed between the potable pressurized water source and downstream system control valves. As such, there is a need for only one breaker per water source. Because of the increased liability encountered with this backflow preventer's placement, they are required, by code, to be set 12 inches higher than the highest downstream operable head. This allows a full foot of atmospheric pressure (33.94 psi) to assist the spring-loaded poppet in shutting the breaker down. Pressure type backflow preventers are used frequently on midsized residential and smaller sized commercial products.

Double check valve assembly (DCV) backflow preventers are quite good and far more reliable than atmospheric and pressure type breakers but a notch below the reduced pressure backflow preventer in performance. A double check valve has, as its name implies, two check valves that act independently of each other. One is simply backup to the other. A check valve only allows water to flow in one direction. Located at opposite ends of the internally located check valves are two shutoff valves. These shutoffs are not a part of the backflow shutdown process, they are more for servicing and testing other parts of the device. Double check valves can be placed near or below grade, as atmospheric pressure does not factor into their operational principle. Double check valve backflow preventers are acceptable for all sizes and types of projects except schools, hospitals, and health care facilities. These critically important facilities require a reduced pressure backflow preventer as described below.

Reduced pressure type backflow preventers (RVBP) are much more reliable, from a libility standpoint, than the three devices described above. Also, because of the principle under which this device operates, it can be placed at grade, which makes it visually less offensive. Remember, however, that most maintenance personnel would prefer good access to this or any backflow preventer. The internal assembly of this device contains two check valves that operate on a spring loaded poppet principle. Located between these two valves is another valve called a pressure relief valve. The upstream check valve is designed to reduce the incoming water's supply side pressure. This causes the water pressure internal to the backflow mechanism's pressure relief valve housing to be lower than the external supply side pressure. When water on the downstream side of the backflow preventer is sucked backwards through the downstream check valve, it increases pressure within the pressure relief valve's chamber which becomes greater than the upstream valve's pressure and shuts down the upstream check valve. Backflow water now entering the relief valve then drains out through a port to the atmosphere. The mechanical devices within the housing of these breakers are so well-machined and designed that they perform this seemingly impossible task perfectly. All manufacturers are required by law to do perform an extensive battery of tests on each breaker put in the marketplace. The RPBP provides the greatest degree of protection against a backflow condition. I prefer reduced-pressure devices on my private projects. The added safety factor is worth the additional expense and it also reduces professional liability.

When choosing the type of backflow prevention needed for a project, the irrigation designer should balance the site's physical size, type and number of users, and the probability of a catastrophic event, against budget restraints. Each level of backflow prevention covered, while reducing liability, also progressively reduces line pressure. Pressure lost through an atmospheric breaker may be 3 psi while loss through a reduced-pressure breaker could exceed 12 psi. On projects with lower pressures at the point of connection, a less desirable breaker type may have to be chosen simply to make the system work. These devices must be installed in accordance with applicable codes and the manufacturer's explicit instructions. Equipment testing for backflow preventers is done at the factory on a per unit basis and is extensive, so the chances for failure are low. This should not eliminate periodic inspections on the part of the project owner(s) for the cliche "better safe than sorry" was never more appropriate than with backflow prevention. In fact, many health codes and districts require annual testing and certification of all PVB, DCV, and RPBP devices to be done by project owners.

The last thing we will discuss, in the area of backflow prevention, is the subject of hose bibs directly connected to the house or potable water supply. Regular or inverted "Y" hose bibs or quick couplers connected to the irrigation main are already shut off from the potable supply by the system backflow preventer so this point is moot for them. Remember, never drink from these irrigation system-supplied hose bibs because the water they contain could be contaminated. Building-mounted hose bibs are not connected to the irrigation system's mainline and therefore are not on-line with any form of upstream backflow prevention. These building-mounted hose bibs are frequently used for applying fertilizers or pesticides through a garden hose. In addition, water stagnates in the hose. Whatever the case, this water is toxic to humans and animals at this point. A backflow situation in the city water main would suck the hose's bad water back into the building's plumbing system. Hose connection vacuum breakers can prevent this scenario from occurring. These vacuum breakers are female threaded to attach to the hose bib and male threaded to accept the hose. These tiny breakers are comprised of a poppet-type check valve and work quite well. If they are dented or smashed by pliers or from wear and tear they should be immediately replaced as their small cylinders cannot accept the sliding action of the poppet when they are not perfectly round.

6. System Type and Head Layout

We will examine three types of irrigation systems: (1) quick coupler/hose bib systems, (2) drip irrigation systems, and (3) conventional head systems.

Quick Coupler/Hose Bib Systems

A quick coupler is a device which serves the same function as a hose bib. Quick couplers are normally closed valves with spring-loaded seats. The internally threaded valve is long and narrow and stands vertically 6 to 10 inches high. A quick coupler is accessed with a threaded corkscrew-like key that is inserted into the quick coupler's body which opens the valve seat, thus accessing flowing water. A hose bib is a valve that is opened by hand and threaded at its outlet to accept a hose. Quick couplers or hose bib systems, from a design standpoint, do essentially the same thing — provide water at a given point. Committing exclusively to this type of system locks the user into manual operation which is more time consuming than automated systems. Since there is no need for an electric controller, this type of system also eliminates the use of electronic tensiometers to judge water needs and activate the system's watering. Cheaper at the outset because of decreased installation costs, a quick coupler/hose bib system can make maintenance labor expenses skyrocket. Some of the advantages of these systems, coupled with other automated-type systems, would be a good compromise.

The advantages of quick couplers over building-mounted hose bibs is that they require less access space and they can be buried in the ground. Inverted "Y" hose bibs are becoming more popular as they can be housed in a grade-level valve box and do not require a special access key. They do, however, have the disadvantage of being accessible to anyone. Quick couplers can only be accessed by someone with a quick coupler key — presumably project maintenance personnel. This is an advantage in combating vandalism and reduces the risk of unknowing individuals drinking contaminated water.

On smaller sites where the majority of the planting areas are adjacent to the building, the irrigation designer should coordinate design efforts with the plumbing consultant to get as many exterior hose bibs with applicable backflow preventers as possible mounted to the building's exterior in accessible areas. These hose bibs are much easier to use and, with the added advantage of being firmly mounted to the building's exterior wall, they are more permanent fixtures. Quick couplers and hose bibs connected to the irrigation system mainline are often abused by the pulling and jerking of hoses attached to them. This often puts stress at the point of connection to the mainline and creates leaks and even breakage.

As alluded to earlier, the best way to use quick couplers and hose bibs is in conjunction with other types of systems. All system types rely on a mainline for water supply. Once the expense of the mainline is a foregone conclusion, it is an easy matter to add quick couplers and hose bibs to it at strategic locations throughout the system. The cost of these devices is minimal when compared to the benefits they provide. First, they act as backup in the event that a valve malfunctions (freezes) or a number of irrigation heads needs replacement, or a mainline breaks upstream of the coupler or bib. Maintenance personnel can temporarily hand water affected plant material until appropriate repairs are made. Installation of quick couplers or hose bibs speeds the construction process as a mainline can be initially installed and hand watering of new plant materials can follow the path of construction while the remainder of the irrigation installation to surrounding areas occurs simultaneously. These devices also aid installation by providing accessible water for trench settling, water-truck refill, equipment and site cleaning, etc.

Drip Irrigation

The term "drip" refers to irrigation heads with extremely small orifices that emit such small amounts of water over such an extended period of time that their discharge rate is calculated in gallons per hour while conventional-type irrigation heads are rated in gallons per minute.

The theory is to apply water to plant material slowly, thus allowing the plant time to take up all the water before it leaches below the root zone or is lost to runoff. Water drips directly at the emitter's outlet, so there is the added benefit of no overspray falling onto walks, windows, or roadways. The only area wetted is around the plant's immediate root zone, which discourages the number and growth rate of competitor plants and weeds. The essence of the theory is that more of the water gets to the vegetation for which it is intended. Since the water is applied so slowly, the gpm through any given control valve can service a far greater number of plants than if the same valve were used on a conventional system. This results in less equipment, smaller pipe sizes, fewer stations required per controller, fertilizer injection, less weed control, and better water conservation. It seems too good to be true and, in some applications, it is.

The drawbacks to an emitter system are:

1. **Clogging of emitters** — Orifices are so tiny that root hairs, soil particles, and buildups of calcium from the water supply can choke off the emitter. The solution is good system design, troubleshooting for malfunctions, regular cleaning of heads, and/or eventual head replacement. None of these solutions is as effective as proper water filtration just downstream of the control valve.
2. **Controller type and operating times** — Emitters sometimes take so long to meet the gallonage of the plantings' water demand that there are not enough hours in a day to get through a less sophisticated controller program, so a more expensive, dual program type, controller is required.
3. **Valve life** — Valves are open over such long periods of time that diaphragms, seats, and springs become stressed and worn. This requires repair and/or replacement.
4. **Cheap installations** — Many emitters are designed to be inserted directly into polyethylene tubing which is cheaper to buy and easier to work with than polyvinylchloride (PVC) hose or pipe. This type of application is fine for agriculture and nurseries where emitters first began to receive widespread use in just this manner. It is not, however, appropriate for long-term or high-end ornamental landscaping. The tubing, under the best conditions, has a 5-year life expectancy and that is being generous. In Arizona, where poly tubing is used more extensively than in Southern California, the soils

have a higher clay content. This holds surface moisture around the emitters and the tubing which, in turn, cools them and limits thermal expansion. In California and many other areas of the Southwest, soils are predominately sandy and fast draining. This makes surface soils hot and dry which accelerates the rate of deterioration of polyethylene. Life expectancy for poly tubing used in these areas is often less than 2 years, and 3 years is pushing the issue. Wherever it is used, the tubing can be cut or crushed fairly easily and it is hard to locate the problem. In addition, thinner spaghetti tubing is oftentimes run long distances from the emitter. This tubing is even easier to damage than the larger size polyethylene. Spaghetti tubing which is used to transport water from a central emitter to an individual plant 2 to 4 feet away will oftentimes widen at the base of its connection with the emitter and eventually leak or pull away from it. This separates plants from their immediate water source and they frequently die from lack of water.

5. **Salt buildup** — Occurs at the edges of what is called an emitter's wetted pattern. This buildup of salts can be evidenced by a white ring at the outer edge of the wetted pattern. The reason salt buildup is more prevalent with emitters than conventional systems is that soil irrigated by emitters stays wet a longer period of time and does not drain quickly (leach); this allows salts to virtually float their way to the soil surface. Two methods have been developed to lessen the harmful effects of salt buildup. The first is emitter placement. On individual emitters, the closer the emitter is to the center of the plant, the further out the salts will travel in a concentric pattern. On double or triple emitter placement, the more the center of each emitter's wetted pattern overlaps the other, the further out towards the edges of the joint wetted patterns the salts will float. Second, the easiest way to get rid of salts, especially in sandy soils, is to leach them out of the root zone by overspraying them by use of a hose or other form of temporary watering. This gives reason to the strategic placement of quick couplers and hose bibs along a drip system's main supply line. In emitter system design, they can be employed to help leach salts into the soil substrata and they can also occasionally wash dust off plant leaves, since the placement and nature of emitters does not accommodate foliage washing as other systems do.

In the desert, where water conservation is of ultimate concern, the advantages of drip systems far outweigh the disadvantages. The easiest way to combat most of the drawbacks of emitters is to hardline the system — that is, to use rigid PVC pipe throughout and install all the necessary adapters needed to have rigid risers to all emitters. While this is a more expensive system initially, money will be saved over the long term in reduced maintenance costs and water bills.

Liquid fertilizer injection through the emitter system to individual plant material has proven to be very efficient and has been extremely successful in agricultural applications. The fertilizer spreads evenly through the root zone at a rate whereby the plant can absorb it without burning. Man hours are greatly reduced because fertilizer hookup occurs at any given control valve or at the system point of connection (downstream of required RPBP), as opposed to fertilizer application to every individual plant. Also, workers are free to do other tasks until the fertilizer bottle runs dry.

A subsurface or geoflow type of emitter system is beginning to receive serious consideration. In this application, flexible PVC tubing is laid 8 inches underground, usually in rows 12 inches apart. Plug-in type, in-line emitters are placed at 12-inch centers for turf areas forming a consistent grid. In shrub and ground cover areas, the emitters may occur at the 18 inch centers or be on the same spacing as the plant materials if they are wider apart. Maintenance and life expectancy of the system does not raise as much objection as the more expensive flexible PVC is used as opposed to poly tubing. Also, the orifices are underground where temperatures at the point of connection to the flexible PVC are much cooler. A herbicide in the emitter opening prevents roots from clogging the orifice. Evaporation and vandalism are deterred. Maintenance, in the event of a line leak, is more difficult. When using this system in sandy soils, I would recommend that all affected soil areas receive polymers applied per the manufacturer's recommendations to the same depth as the system. This would encourage moisture to move horizontally through the root zone. Assuming that allowances can be made to provide temporary watering for the establishment of possible grass seed or necessary winter rye grass, although relatively untested, the concept behind this system is sound. Consider what subsurface irrigation could mean to sporting facilities and golf courses. Irrigation would not interrupt play and could occur at any time of the day. thus requiring less sophisticated controllers. On ball fields, the absence of grade mounted heads limits the probability of injury and thus limits liability. Fungus diseases aided by standing water are also likely to decrease. This system is worth investigating, and although not for everyone, may satisfy a need.

Drip irrigation technology is advancing rapidly, especially in the area of emitter design. Microspray heads are now available in radii of up to 4 feet and beyond. While somewhat maintenance intensive, these mini- or microsprayers do deliver water in gallons per hour rather than gallons per minute, which accommodates steep slopes, clay soils, and above all, water conservation. The conscientious irrigation designer must strive to learn all he can about drip irrigation because, in desert irrigation design, the future is now.

Conventional Irrigation

Conventional systems comprise those irrigation heads that were in popular use before emitters came to the fore and exclude quick coupler or hose bib systems which, in reality, are specialized valves. The irrigation heads we will discuss are:

- **Sprayheads:** pop-up
fixed riser
- **Rotating sprinklers:** pop-up
fixed riser
ball or cam driven
gear-driven
impact driven
- **Bubblers:** pop-up
fixed riser
flood
spider or short radius
pressure compensating

Sprayheads are the most commonly used and easily recognized of all the conventional head types. The spray is created by pressurized water flowing through tiny machined orifices which are commonly called nozzles. Distribution of spray is not aided by any mechanical device: thus the maximum spray distance that radiates out from the head is usually 8, 12, and 15 feet. There is even a 4 foot wide by 30-foot-long rectangular pattern available for small strip areas. In addition, there are numerous speciality arc and pattern nozzles available for unusual circumstances.

The pattern of spray refers to how water is distributed or falls to the ground. Owing to the type of nozzle and the way it is machined, patterns range from quarter circle (90 degrees), to half circle (180 degrees), to full circle (360 degrees), with just about every other angle in between being accommodated by specialized head design.

Sprayheads can be mounted on a fixed riser above the ground and frequently are in shrub and ground cover beds, especially when viewed from a distance where the head and riser are not easily noticeable and thus not visually objectionable. In turf areas and in planting beds adjacent to walks, drives, and other pavement surfaces, the pop-up spray is not as visually obtrusive and is more viable from a maintenance and safety standpoint. Pop-up spray heads in turf are usually 3 inches high and occasionally 6 inches high. Pop-up sprays in planting beds are 6, 12, or 18 inches high, and 24 and 36 inch heights are available for special circumstances. The nozzle of the head is housed in a brass or plastic body which contains a retractable stainless steel spring. Water pressure forces the nozzle body up through the head to the designated height. When water pressure is removed (water shut off), the spring pulls the nozzle body down, retracting it back into the body of the head. A water-tight and usually sand-tight wiper seal protects the opening at the surface of the head body from unwanted elements getting caught in the nozzle body path and creating wear and tear which eventually causes leaking or pop-down failure.

The areas of coverage for most sprayhead radii are at 8, 12, and 15 feet.

Of the conventional head types, sprayheads have, by far, the most reliable and efficient pattern of water distribution and are a better head on slopes and hillsides, although the rotating heads are often employed instead, due to cost restraints. Sprayheads can also be depended upon to deliver the most consistent precipitation rate (explored later in this chapter). Like all forms of machinery, the more moving parts there are, the more chance for failure to occur. Pop-up heads will stick either up or down and a good troubleshooting maintenance program to correct this condition is a necessity.

Rotating Sprinklers are, as their name implies, operated by some manner of rotating device that distributes water across the individual head's pattern of spray. Because they are designed to distribute water in a narrow high pressure stream, these sprinklers can throw water farther than sprayheads and are employed for irrigating large areas. Of the head types used on ballfields or golf courses, for example, 90% will be rotating sprinklers. Radii for these sprinklers will range from 30 feet to well over 100 feet. In day-to-day ornamental landscape irrigation design, on average size projects, any head that throws over 60 to 75 feet is a rarity and considered a big head.

The high-velocity, slowly rotating stream of water that disseminates from the head is distributed by three main types of mechanical systems.

Ball- or cam-driven heads operate on a principle which channels water inside the body of the head in such a way that the water hits a cam or ball-like mechanism that in turn hits against an anvil and turns the head one notch. These heads do not have a return mechanism like an impact head. Rather, a plate slides in front of the nozzle which continues to rotate in one direction until such time as it is in position to resume its pattern of spray. These heads are adjustable in radius and are relatively maintenance free. It takes a high volume of water under high pressure to operate these heads effectively and they are not particularly efficient in pattern of spray under the best of circumstances. For the latter reasons I recommend they be used with discretion, if at all.

The gear-driven rotating head is the most efficient in terms of pattern of spray. They are also the most reliable in delivering their designed precipitation rate to be discussed later. The head's nozzle is rotated in a smooth consistent radius by a system of water-driven gears. The biggest drawback to these heads is their performance in sandy soils. Sand can cause severe damage to the gear system and also to the pop-up nozzle body. Wiper seals for this type of head are extremely tight and the retracting spring will give your fingernails a real test when you try to pull the nozzle out from the body. Several manufacturers have developed specialized wrenches to aid in this endeavor. Gear driven heads are popular in institutional design because their positive retraction and relatively small surface area (at the top) discourages vandalism. Of gear-driven heads, 90% are of the pop-up variety. In fixed-riser, above ground applications, irrigation designers usually opt for the less expensive and easier to maintain impact rotors.

Impact rotors are often referred to as "machine-gun heads," owing to their appearance, method of operation, and sound. These heads are employed for irrigating the largest landscape areas. Fixed-riser, above groun impact rotors are efficient and maintainable for large beds of shrubbery and ground covers. Sometimes these heads are attached to quick coupler keys and manually inserted into an equally spaced quick coupler temporary or occasional use type irrigation system. Such would be the case for flood-irrigated ball fields which need temporary irrigation only in spring and fall to reestablish Bermuda grass or overseed with Rye grass. Native hydroseed mixtures are frequently established or pushed into their seasonal growth cycles by irrigating in this manner.

Impact rotors have an impact or driver arm that is sometimes called a vane. This flat metallic arm extends in front of the nozzle. High velocity water exiting the nozzle hits the arm which first acts to widen the stream of spray and, second, moves the head a notch. A high tension spring moves the arm back into position in front of the nozzle and the process repeats itself and the head moves another notch. When the head reaches the end of its intended arc, the spring returns it to its starting position and it goes through the pattern again. Sometimes impact rotors have two nozzles. One which is shorter, shoots out the back of the head and trips a modified vane or rocker arm. This is called the drive nozzle because it drives the head. The other nozzle, called the range nozzle, disperses water over the head's intended pattern of spray (range). This type of impact rotor is frequently employed in pop-up applications as it is smaller in overall size and thus easier to house in an underground body. As you may have guessed, the head's retract spring is very strong and special wrenches or pry bars aid greatly in working with them. Except when working with very large areas (+50), a gear-driven pop-up head is usually a better choice. Also, avoid using these heads within the play area of ball fields. Impact rotors have a wide surface-mounted top which can increase the chances of an injury when someone falls on them or by causing players to trip over them.

Rotating heads serve a purpose in that they irrigate the largest areas. On larger projects with large land areas (e.g., golf courses), rotating heads represent the most cost-effective installation on a per head basis. These heads are not, however, as efficient in pattern of spray coverage as the smaller radius spray heads. Although there are a lot of gallons of water within their stream, owing to the size of the area they must cover, they apply water relatively slowly and take a long time to get complete coverage. Because of the slow application rate, many manufacturers rate the head a low precipitation head, but I disagree. The head's stream of water falling over any given area has a lot of precipitation (gallons); it's just that there is a lot of area to cover. For practical, everyday purposes remember that there is a difference between application time and precipitation rate. This factor comes into play on slopes and hillsides where, if an irrigation designer believes that several rotating heads will have a low precipitation rate, their installation could cause severe erosion problems. As a rule of thumb, keep rotating heads on as level a grade as possible and if they must be used on sloping land, opt for the gear driven heads which have the lowest and most reliable precipitation rates among the rotating heads.

Bubblers are irrigation heads designed to apply water to limited soil surface areas. In a lot of ways, they are similar to emitters described earlier in this chapter. In fact, bubblers are the forerunners of emitters, the primary difference being precipitation rate. Bubblers apply water in GPM while emitters apply water in GPH. This represents a big difference.

Flood bubblers simply flood water out of an orifice at the top of the head. Most flood bubblers have a head twist adjustment or adjustment screw at the top of the head to regulate water flow from maximum gpm (usually 2 or 3) to completely off.

Spider bubblers have anywhere from 2 to 8 tiny drilled orifices which squirt water 2 feet or so in an arched-like (spider leg) pattern onto the ground. They are used to get a better pattern of surface application than a flood bubbler, while operating in an area too tight for a spray head.

Pressure compensating bubblers are a hybrid between a flood bubbler and an emitter. They are designed to be used with hard line systems and screw directly onto conventional risers in the same manner as bubblers. In addition, the orifice of a pressure compensating bubbler is designed with a special diaphragm similar to an emitter. This specialized diaphragm adjusts pressure ranging between 20 and 80 pounds psi to a pressure that is consistent throughout every bubbler on the same zone or circuit. Flow rates are always the same. Rates are in gpm but are very low and very dependable. Usual rates are 1/4, 1/2, 1, or 2 gpm. Heads are designed to operate at the same flow rate, even when mixed with other differently rated pressure compensating bubblers. This allows 1/4-, 1/2-, 1-gpm, and 2-gpm heads all to be used on the same circuit. Many installers argue that the same results can be achieved by adjusting flood bubblers, but they cannot. First, the flood bubbler does not have the pressure compensating diaphragm necessary for consistent low flow, and second, the adjustments may be mistakenly changed by anyone, to the detriment of all the other heads in the zone.

In sandy soils, water from bubblers soaks into the soil extremely fast. The pattern of coverage is where water hits and usually no more. The irrigation designer cannot expect flood bubblers to really flood a sandy soil area — it just doesn't happen. Water penetrates the soil subsurface so fast that it leaches below the root zone before it can be utilized by plant materials and is, in effect, wasted. There are several methods to combat this process. The most frequently used is to program dual or multiple program controllers to activate bubbler zones for short periods of time during several waterings. This supplies irrigation demand to the plant materials over a time frame that enables them to absorb the water efficiently. This method can have the drawback of encouraging shallow rooting. The method I prefer is to add the previously mentioned soil polymers to the soil mixture at the time of planting. Polymers act like miniature sponges that are capable of expanding to ten times their dry volume when absorbing water. These polymers hold water in suspension in the root zone longer until the plant material can utilize it. Soil polymers are especially effective in raised planters and pots where the type and amount of soil mixture can be controlled.

Bubblers are used in very narrow planters (e.g., parking lot strips) or in areas that are virtually impossible to water with any other type of head (e.g., 4-inch strips between concrete stepping pads). Bubblers are also used in areas adjacent to glass where the back spray or windblown spray from other head types would hit on and smear the glass or cause annoying calcium buildups. Overspray onto walks in high pedestrian traffic areas can present a safety hazard. Flood or pressure-compensating bubblers are often used as backup irrigation to trees in turf areas and occasionally shrub areas. These backup bubblers provide supplemental gallonage to meet the tree's larger water demand and also encourage deep rooting which prevents the tree's robbing the turf of surface moisture and nutrients. The backup bubbler system also acts as a true backup in times of drought where, if turf irrigation were eliminated, there would still be a system in place to irrigate and insure the survival of specimen trees.

With the exception of spider bubblers, there is no need to raise the bubbler head more than 1 inch above the soil surface. I usually specify 4 inches maximum on my details for flood and pressure-compensating bubblers so maintenance personnel can find the head and 6 inches minimum for spider bubblers to accommodate the pattern of spray. One axiom of irrigation design you can always count on is that the higher a fixed riser the higher the rate of damage or vandalism and thus the higher the cost of maintenance. If there is a need to elevate a bubbler higher than 6 inches, I recommend going to a pop-up bubbler head.

Head Ratings

Head layout is the primary factor in determining the level of success or failure in any irrigation system. Assuming that water capacity is available, the owner's program is not too restrictive, and the soil is of average quality; the next design step, after surveying the site, is to lay out the system. The three principal issues in head selection are the size of the area to be irrigated, the type of plant material specified, and the absorption rate of the soil within that area.

Irrigation equipment supply is an extremely competitive business and there is an abundance of irrigation equipment catalogues available for the asking. Within these catalogues are all the head types discussed earlier. Different heads with different characteristics are given separate model or call numbers and are designed to be used with other heads within what is commonly called a family of heads.

Any given family of heads is manufactured to have matched precipitation rates. On most of the charts provided, the first bit of information will be a head's pattern of spray (1/4, 1/3, 1/2, 2/3, 3/4, or full circle). Next is given the pounds per square inch of water pressure that will be required for the head to operate properly. Next will be the head's expected radius of throw in feet and, frequently, the radius of throw will increase as pressure increases. Following will be the head's expected water usage in gallons per minute (GPM rating is an extremely important category as it determines the number of heads on a zone and pipe size). Last is the head's precipitation rate, sometimes called application rate. Precipitation rate estimates how many inches of water a head will apply over the course of an hour. The rate is important to know in determining the head's ability to meet the water requirements of various plant material and how a head will relate to the absorption rate of various soil types. Note that I differentiate between a manufacturer's stated precipitation rate and actual ground application rate. The reasons for this are discussed in other portions of this chapter.

On smaller (radius of 15 feet and less) spray heads, some manufacturers will also list the trajectory or angle of the spray. This is important to note in windy areas, as heads with a low angle or flat spray will prove more efficient since there is likely to be less wind blown misplaced water.

This myriad of information will seem impossibly confusing to the irrigation design newcomer but is relatively easy to digest after a few practice designs. Do not mix one family of heads with another family within any given zone unless absolutely necessary. Even though their characteristics may seem quite similar on paper, there are subtle design differences which can affect the overall performance of the system in the field. Heads from just one family, on one zone, will also make things a lot easier on the installer and the maintenance man.

Of all the factors to consider in head selection, once a head's radius of throw is determined to be suitable for the area, the pattern of head layout will be the most critical. Several design texts discuss different levels of head overlapping as a percentage of how much one circle of coverage from one head overlaps the circle of coverage from another head. In the desert, coverage overlap should be a minimum of 50%. In other words, there should be head to head coverage. This means that the spray from one head at its outer periphery, should land at the base of the next available head and that head should do the same.

Consider how most heads spray. Water arcs from the nozzle to a point on the perimeter of the circle where it can go no further. Along this stream, or arc, water falls to the ground at various rates. This is often referred to as a sprinkler's distribution curve and, typically, more water falls at the outer area of the curve. This means that less water falls in the area adjacent to the head. By throwing head to head, water from the wet part of one head's distribution curve falls into the dry area of the other head's distribution curve. This overlapping to accommodate the variation in distribution curves guarantees uniformity of coverage which, in turn, guarantees a consistent water application rate over the entire area to be irrigated. Each manufacturer's distribution curve is slightly different, even for head types rated at the same radius and GPM For this reason, mixing of different "equivalent" heads will almost always guarantee poor coverage uniformity on the ground plane. Wet spots and/or dry spots will occur within the coverage areas of any given valve circuit. This again reinforces the design axiom of staying within the same family of heads on any given zone.

Head Layout

When laying out heads, the desert irrigation designer chooses heads of a pattern and radius to meet the head to head coverage requirement. Heads are laid out in an equally spaced grid pattern or an even more efficient equilateral triangular spacing pattern. To figure the distance between equally spaced triangular rows of heads multiply the width between heads (the head's radius) by .86. Triangular spacing takes fewer heads to cover an area and accommodates windy conditions better than a grid pattern. Often a free form or combination of patterns will have to be employed to meet the demands of irregular area configurations. Frequently an area can be covered quite nicely, except at one side where a strip about half the width or less of all the previous rows of heads occurs. This will necessitate backup heads which are choked down and throw in one direction into the dry distribution curve area of the heads in the preceding row. Because the head is choked down, its own distribution pattern drops more water than normal into its own distribution curve's dry area. Remember that irrigation design is not an exact science and this is especially true in the area of head layout. Another rule of thumb in desert irrigation design is that it is always better to have too much coverage than not enough which, in turn, means it is far better, from a coverage standpoint, to have too many heads as opposed to too few. When designing on a hillside or slope and a backup row of heads is required, always place the backup row at the bottom of the slope. The logic is that more water lands further uphill and flows downhill over a larger surface area as opposed to being thrown downhill and flowing nowhere (creating a wet spot) or off the area to be irrigated.

7. Zoning and Circuiting

Knowing the capabilities of the different head types and selecting the appropriate head for the diverse areas encountered in an average planting design is the irrigation designer's biggest challenge. Next he must start to bring it all together in an effort to connect the project irrigation system into a unified whole, to impart logic and order to an assemblage of smaller and dissimilar pieces.

This is sometimes called valving, because each zone type receives a separate valve. The amount of water required to irrigate these planting zones also represents specialized zones called hydrozones. The concept of hydrozones is gaining popularity. The thrust of the concept is that zones (valves) are separated in accordance with the unique water requirement of different groupings of plant materials. For example, more water is required in areas that contain more lush plant materials. These are areas which are somewhat shaded, or turf areas which are most often located in proximity to oasis areas. With the addition of water, these planting zones become cooler while the subsurface hydrozones become wetter. As the lushness and water requirements of plant materials fade, the design likewise fades back to the desert and the hydrozones become less and less water demanding.

Creating hydrozones by circuiting heads onto separate valves is determined by the following factors:

- Available water pressure and flow in gallons per minute. This will determine the maximum number of individual heads that can be put on any given zone.
- Type of heads — do not mix families of heads.
- Sun exposure.
- Wind exposure.
- Soil type and adsorption rate.
- Degree (gradient) of slope.
- Species of plant materials being irrigated.

The major factor to consider in zoning a system is the available water flow in gallons per minute. This will always determine the maximum size a zone can be in terms of gpm and thus determine the maximum number of heads that can be dedicated to any given zone operated by any given valve. Available flow depends on water pressure and the type of equipment used. Assuming that adequate gallonage and pressure is available at the point of connection, the amount of available gallonage for zoning will depend on the size of equipment upstream of the heads in the zone. Only so much water can push (flow) through service lines, water meters, backflow prevention devices, the inside walls of pipe, and the valve itself. As water flows through this equipment, water pressure is decreased due to friction loss which, in turn, will slow water delivery, which equates to less gpm.

For the purposes of explaining zoning, assume for the moment that adequate water pressure will be available at the base of the individual irrigation heads to meet their operating requirements.

Another component that is directly related to water flow is the concept of velocity. Velocity is the term used to describe the speed at which water flows. Do not confuse velocity with pressure, as pressure equals force. Velocity is easier to understand when thinking of water confined in a pipe. To maintain the same amount of flow (gpm) through successively smaller pipe, the speed of the water must increase. Think of a river coming to a narrow canyon. The speed of the water must pick up in order for the volume of water to traverse the canyon without backing up upstream flow. All practical interpretations of irrigation design revolve around the principles of water capacity, water pressure, and rate of flow (water velocity). Water flowing too rapidly can be a destructive element in an irrigation system just as fast moving water can be an erosive element in nature. The rule of thumb to remember concerning water velocity within the irrigation system is that under no circumstances should water flow at a rate exceeding 5 feet per second (fps) through any given piece of equipment. There is a plethora of charts, diagrams, and graphs which illustrate the effects of water flow through various equipment sizes and the velocity created. Select equipment that keeps velocity below 5 fps and you will be safe.

Valve sizes that adhere to the under 5 fps velocity rule are as follows:

GPM	Valve Size (in.)
0 – 0	3/4
11 – 20	1
21 – 35	1 and 1/4
36 – 55	1 and 1/2
46 – 60	2

Pipe size, as it relates to velocity, will be discussed a little later but there is one thing that should be said about valve size as it relates to pipe size. Valves that are smaller than the water delivery line (system mainline) restrict flow while valves that are larger do not impede flow. Where velocity is a concern and needs to be slowed, make valves the same size or larger than the delivery line on the upstream side of the valve. On the downstream side of the valve where water is being delivered through pipes called laterals to operate the heads, the valve should be of the same size or no more than one size smaller than the connecting lateral. To make the valve size significantly larger than the outgoing lateral will cause water flow to exceed 5 fps within the lateral.

There is, as stated before, a lot of reference information available to aid the irrigation designer in calculating velocity. These are available from all the major manufacturers in their product catalogues and technical literature. The charts are, of course, based on technical formulas which are tried and true and beyond the scope of my limited understanding. My advice is to save time and effort and to simply just consult this readily available information.

How does the irrigation designer know how many gallons per minute are available to be used at any given valve? If the water is supplied by a water meter and velocity is not to exceed 5 fps, here is a breakdown of flow immediately downstream of the meter:

Meter size (inches)	GPM
5/8	20
3/4	30
1	50
1 and 1/2	100
2	160
3	300
4	500

Most meter gpm ratings should be figured at 75% of maximum capacity to compensate for unforeseen circumstances. In most ornamental landscape irrigation systems, it will be rare that a meter size exceeds 2 inches. On larger projects where system demand at any given time exceeds 120 gpm (75% of 160 gpm) other meters, sized appropriately, should be added to meet the demand.

Assuming the average valve will be open (supplying water to the heads) for 30 minutes a day for 4 times a week (2 hours total); let's look at the number of valves a given water meter operating on a 1/2 day (nighttime), 3/4 day (nighttime and morning), or full day (24 hours a day) schedule can operate. With the programming capabilities of today's automatic controllers this is not an unreasonable assumption.

Number of valves @ 2 hours per valve

Meter Size (in.)	System GPM	# of Valves at Maximum GPM	1/2 Day Schedule	3/4 Day Schedule	Full Day Schedule
3/4	30 @ 75%=23	1 @ 23	42	63	84
1	50 @ 75%=38	1 @ 38	42	63	84
1 1/2	100 @ 75%=75	2 @ 38	84	126	168
2	160 @ 75%=120	3 @ 40	126	189	252
		2 @ 60	84	126	168

What this diagram illustrates is that bigger meters mean bigger flows which accommodate more zones and a higher gpm per zone. When the irrigation designer begins to group individual heads into individual hydrozones, he totals the gpm rating through all the heads and knows where he must cut off an area or where he has maxed out a given valve.

The old school of thought used to be to balance valves. That was, to try to match gallons per minute through each individual valve. Assume a hydrozone on a 1-0 inch water meter with the heads totaling 50 gpm. You could install one 1 1/2-inch valve at 35 gpm and a 1-inch valve at 15 gpm or you could install two 11/4-inch valves at 25 gpm. The two 1 1/4-inch valves at 25 gpm is the best selection for treating the same hydrozone. If two different hydrozones total 35 gpm and 15 gpm respectively, it would not be advisable to split them into two 25 gpm zones just to balance valves, as the watering requirements for the two different zones are now on one or the other (or both) valves. Something will be overwatered and something will go dry. Also, consider a hydrozone of similar planting on a steep slope. Although the valve may be able to accommodate the gpm of all the heads, it is still advisable to separate the uphill row of heads from the downhill row of heads because water will accumulate on these different parts of the slope differently. *Always supply water per hydrozone requirement.* If one valve is at 10 gpm operating one hydrozone type and an adjacent, different, hydrozone type has a valve running at 50 gpm, so be it. The purpose of irrigation design is to keep plants alive, not to balance valve legends.

A discussion about control valve operation would be in order at this juncture. There are normally open and normally closed valves. In addition, there are electric valves and hydraulic valves. We are primarily concerned with normally closed solenoid valves that are activated to open by an electric impulse from an automatic controller and closed the same way. Normally closed manual control valves deserve mention but they are of limited use, usually only for the small property and they require constant personal attention. Hydraulic valves are opened by an injection of water or hydraulic fluid from narrow, water holding tubes. I do not recommend the use of hydraulic valves as the tubing is subject to failure.

Valves are of brass or plastic construction. The only cases in which I would recommend plastic is for residential use, temporary use, or on low budget projects. Their expected life span is shorter. Brass valves, by and large, are the best, and since valves are the heart of the system, they are well worth the extra expense. Some brass valves have a built in pressure regulator which is a nice feature as backup to a system pressure regulator and as an upstream aid to an emitter system's pressure regulator. In summary, electric brass valves with built in pressure regulators are the best for use on a serious irrigation system.

Once the gpm of each hydrozone is calculated and an appropriate valve size is assigned per hydrozone, the irrigation designer knows immediately what size (number of stations) the controller must be and has a good idea of how to route mainline pipe and laterals. The number and type of zones will give the irrigation designer an insight into what type of related equipment would be beneficial to overall system efficiency and ongoing maintenance. With good head coverage and proper hydrozone valving, the irrigation designer has dedicated the right amount of water for the right plant material. Now water must be delivered, through pipe, to distribution points in the overall irrigation system.

8. Piping the System

Pipe is a conduit that contains water. Water within a pipe will flow in a given direction in response to pressure. Water moving away from a source of pressure does so at a certain speed or velocity. Pipe is to the landscape irrigation system what arteries and veins are to the human body. Pipe is the transportation system for life giving fluids.

For the purposes of this chapter, we will concern ourselves with copper and plastic PVC pipe. PVC is far and away the pipe of choice in modern irrigation systems, and most references to pipe throughout this portion of the chapter pertain to it.

Copper pipe or, more appropriately, copper tubing is used primarily for tapping into or hookup of the potable water supply to the irrigation system. In order to screen the backflow preventer from view, for instance, type "K" copper tubing will have to be used at the point of connection at the domestic (potable) water supply (usually a meter) and routed to the breaker's final location. Copper is less likely to crack than PVC and, owing to the fact that it must be soldered at its fittings, copper is much less likely to develop leaks. Copper, because it weathers nicely by developing a chalky green patina, is occasionally also used for sprinkler risers and in exposed pipe situations.

On 95% of irrigation systems all pipe downstream of the backflow preventer will be PVC. There are two rating systems used to describe PVC— schedule and class. Schedule was a term originally used to classify wrought iron or steel pipe and refers to the thickness of the pipe's wall. In PVC pipe, schedule 40 and schedule 80 are used primarily for pipe fittings and connections. Schedule 40 is thinner than schedule 80 and much more commonly used. Schedule 80 is specified in some high pressure (above 80 to 90 psi) situations. In all but unusual circumstances, a minimum schedule 40 mainline is required for irrigation systems by most desert municipalities. The mainline is the irrigation system's water supply line that connects the water source to the system valves. All pipes downstream of the valves are referred to as laterals PVC, by virtue of the fact that it is plastic, expands and contracts readily. For this reason, specifications frequently call for pipe to be "snaked" from side to side in underground trenches.

Lateral pipe is usually specified by class. Class is derived from a rating system that also categorizes pipe according to wall thickness. The rating system is called S.D.R. (standard dimensional ratio) and is based upon a proportional increase in the outside diameter (O.D.) of the pipe. The inside diameter (I.D.) stays constant; thus the wall thickness increases as class designation increases. The three most commonly used classes in irrigation design from thinnest to thickest are 160, 200, and 315. The wall thickness of class 315 is thicker than schedule 40 and this pipe is sometimes used in lieu of the minimum schedule 40 mainline in high pressure situations. Most lateral pipe is class 200 and, on smaller jobs, class 160 is acceptable. Class designations correspond directly to the amount of pressure a pipe can withstand. Class 200, for example, withstands 200 psi in all pipe sizes.

Valves that service any given set of hydrozone lateral pipes should always split the hydrozone pipe and head layout by being in or connecting to the middle of the zone. This allows for equal water distribution and also equalizes pressure loss by cutting water travel distances in half. Since gpm demand is split, lateral pipes can be smaller, which is more cost effective.

Pressure Loss

The subject of pipe wall thickness makes a good point of departure for a discussion of line pressure loss. When pipe, especially PVC, is manufactured it is formed by mechanical processes. The inside wall of a pipe, while it may feel smooth to the touch, has a certain amount of surface roughness. As water passes through the pipe, it brushes against its inside wall and friction is created which, in turn, causes turbulence. This turbulence causes water to slow, and slower moving water, in effect, loses pressure. Thinner classes of pipe have less friction loss characteristics because their inside walls are smoother. Therefore, 1 inch schedule 40 (because its wall is thicker) will lose more pressure than comparably sized class 160 applied exactly the same way. The smaller the size of the pipe and the higher the class, the higher the pressure loss.

Most pressure loss charts depict pounds of pressure lost through a certain class and size of pipe carrying a specified gpm. If the irrigation designer can choose a pipe large enough to carry the hydrozone gpm demand, at a velocity below 5 psi, and deliver adequate pressure to the heads (check manufacturer's recommended pressure at the base of heads), then he has an operable system, providing pressure loss for other equipment is accounted for.

Here is how system pressure loss is usually determined for an entire irrigation system, starting the calculation at the point of connection (downstream of the water meter):

System Pressure Loss

Available pressure at P.O.C.	P
Less backflow preventer	2X
Less mainline pipe	2X
Plus or minus elevation (.433/foot)	6X
Less valves	2X
Less laterals	2X
Subtotal of system pressure loss	P
Less pressure at the base of irrigation head rating	2X
Remaining pressure	P

P = if a plus, the system is a go.
P = if a minus, the system needs a rework.

As another rule of thumb, note that in 90% of irrigation design, the highest pressure loss will be in the mainline pipe, second highest will be through the backflow prevention device, and third highest is through any given hydrozone valve. If you calculate the loss through these three areas and are 10 pounds higher than the head's pressure requirement, the odds are good that the system will work just fine. An absolute given will always be that as equipment size increases, pressure loss decreases. This rule must be used with discretion as it can lead to over design and unnecessary expense.

In our discussion concerning valves, we looked at the importance of maintaining an acceptable rate of velocity. This is just as important in pipe design. The reason velocity should be kept below 5 fps in pipe is a phenomenon called water hammer. Water surges in pipe when valves are opened or closed. Air pushed in front of this surge literally smashes against anything in its path, sometimes with tremendous force. When PVC pipe is glued together, it looses roughly half its strength. Remember this fact when specifying pipe class, especially mainline that is under static (constant) pressure. Class rating should always exceed twice the pressure reading. Piping is the most critical factor in determining the life of and ease of maintenance in a system. Pipe that receives water under acceptable pressure will last a great deal longer than pipe that receives water under too high a pressure, because the effects of water hammer are greatly negated with the former. Under unacceptable pressure conditions not only will pipe fail but heads will virtually blow off their risers. A system pressure regulator will reduce pressure and is a relatively inexpensive item when initial costs are balanced against ongoing maintenance costs. The pipe size chart shown below will guarantee that water velocity is kept below 5 fps.

Laterial Pipe Sizing Chart

GPM	Pipe size (inches)
0–5	1/2
6–10	3/4
11–20	1
21–30	1 and 1/4
31–45	1 and 1/2
46–60	2

The final rule of thumb about piping and, by far, the most helpful one is: looping mainline pipe cuts pressure loss in half. This is because water flows in two directions from its source, cutting flow and pressure loss inside the pipe in half. This will bail you out of a low pressure situation time and time again. Often, it is well worth the expense of an extra 300 or 500 feet of mainline to save a critical 10 to 20 pounds of pressure. Add this rule to your bag of tricks, and in borderline pressure situations, use it.

Occasionally, in low pressure situations, nothing in the irrigation designer's arsenal will result in adequate system pressure. It is here that a pressure booster pump will need to be specified. As long as gallonage is available, a booster pump is a viable way to make the system operable. The specifying of booster pumps is best left to qualified pump designers and/or suppliers.

9. Providing Related Equipment

All the equipment mentioned to this juncture with the exception of a controller would make for an operable irrigation system, but not an optimum irrigation system. The irrigation designer must weigh the value of the following and decide if they warrant inclusion into the base system:

Gate or shut-off valves: These are in-line valves to the system mainline that shut off or isolate sections of the irrigation system. They are of value in that they allow contractors and maintenance personnel to isolate smaller areas of the overall system or an individual hydrozone for work or repair without having to shut the entire system down. Initially, this allows the installer to work away from (downstream of) the point of connection (usually the backflow preventer) in stages. He can get one area of the landscape installation up and running and then move on to the next. With a downstream shut-off valve near the end of a section of mainline, the irrigation contractor can simply connect each area, turn on the valve, and proceed to the next phase of work. Each additional phase can be brought on line by temporarily shutting the gate valve, making the connection, and then reopening it. Believe me, on large systems, these isolation valves can be worth their weight in gold.

Excess flow valves: Sometimes mistakenly referred to as check valves, these units are coming to the forefront in desert irrigation design. This piece of equipment can correctly be referred to as a hydraulic circuit breaker or specialized type of antidrain valve. This is an in line valve that functions like a coupler with female threads on both ends. When mounted within the riser assembly of a sprinkler head, it has a flow sensitive poppet (preset at 5 or 10 gpm) that closes when too much flow is present. This device saves some water when the hydrozone valve shuts down and all the water within the lateral pipe drains towards the low head in the system. The main purpose of this valve, however, is its excess flow shut off feature. When an irrigation head is vandalized, damaged, or blows, most of the water in the system (when the valve is on) will exit at that point. This can be evidenced by a gusher, which not only wastes massive quantities of water and elicits the criticism of all witnesses but also deprives the remaining plant material on the given zone of proper irrigation. Hydraulic circuit breakers are recommended for systems where heads are not maintained on a regular basis and for heads that line driveways and sidewalks, for courtesy and safety.

Irrigation system master valve: This is a normally open valve that is placed in the system mainline just downstream of the backflow preventer and always upstream of all other system valves. If there is a mainline break or a normally closed hydrozone valve sticks open, the master valve, through an electric impulse from the controller, which senses the problem, will shut the entire system down. On projects with a large mainline carrying massive GPM (2 in. and up), this is a very good feature to provide.

10. Controller Station Routing

Today's automatic controllers contain some of the best features technology has to offer. Like remote control valves, there are electric and hydraulic controllers, but we will concern ourselves with electric only here. Think of an electric controller as being comparable to the typical television VCR. There is a clock, a calendar, and an on/off device. On a controller, the on/off device accesses a remote control valve instead of a television.

In addition to the basics listed above, most controllers offer a manual operation mode through the controller. An override switch allows the controller to bypass stations as directed or in conjunction with a rain gauge. Dual or multiple programming capabilities mean that varying programs (watering schedules) can be utilized for, say a summer and a winter watering program or a seasonal turf establishment program, as directed by the operator. Most new computer type controllers interface with other electronic equipment that allows for the use of moisture sensors (tensiometers) and flow sensors.

Many controllers also have a master valve circuit for operation of a system master valve. Also, on projects where the water source requires pumping for flow or to boost pressure, controllers are available with a pump control circuit that calls for water to be pumped into the system just prior to demand by the hydrozone valves. The pump is shut down when the irrigation system is not in operation, thus saving electricity and wear and tear on the pump itself.

Controllers are powered by a standard 115-volt alternating current (AC) electrical source. A transformer housed within the cabinet of the controller provides low voltage outlets at 24 V for the operation of the low-voltage (24 V) electric hydrozone valves. Low voltage operation allows for the use of direct burial wire as this amount of electrical current does not represent a health risk. Direct burial wire makes installation easier and more cost effective. Just as PVC is snaked side to side in its trenches to accommodate thermal expansion and contraction the same should be done for control wire. Many details specify that wire be coiled in a 20-foot loop at every change in direction and also be coiled in a 10-foot loop in valve boxes. The wire coiled in valve boxes allows for maintenance and repairs as the valve bonnet can be easily lifted from the box for servicing and old wire can be cut away as wear and tear dictate.

Once individual hydrozone valves are counted and a controller or controllers with the appropriate number of stations and desired program features are selected, the irrigation designer must decide how to route the system. The first given is to position the controller in a location that is as central to all the hydrozone valve locations as possible. This splits wire runs in half a well as walking time and distance for maintenance personnel. I like to separate all different hydrozone types into separate blocks on a controller. That is, all turf zones occupying successive stations, then all shrub zones, then all bubbler zones, and finally all emitter zones. On very large projects it is advisable to use separate controllers for separate blocks. This method enables a programmer to concentrate on one hydrozone type at a time and also allows a troubleshooter to walk the system in an organized, logical manner. The people maintaining the irrigation system should be able to start at the controller, walk through one block type, and arrive back at the controller in a continuous route. Each block type should circulate in the same direction and start and finish at the controller. Even when utilizing the new hand held remote control devices which can command any station within the controller from anywhere in the project, it is still a good idea to program the controller(s) in blocks as it is a logical process and the remote controls are usually in the hands of a supervisor, who is frequently elsewhere when troubleshooting takes place or a malfunction occurs.

The actual physical location of the controller should be an exterior equipment yard or other easily accessible place. I always opt to locate the controller on the outside, even on projects with dedicated equipment rooms. The reason for this is that the landscape maintenance man is usually not the preferred holder of the maintenance room key. Controllers located in planting areas can be hard to find, difficult to access, and worst of all, shorted out by water from the hydrozone spray heads that has pooled around the cabinet. Occasionally, on larger projects, controllers will have to be pedestal mounted, but even these should be protected from being sprayed with water.

Controllers should be hard-wired into electrical junction boxes. This prevents vandals or others from pulling out plugs which would render the controller ineffective. It cannot be stressed enough, for the best results do not allow for plug-in use as the controller is useless unplugged. Most controllers have a back-up battery pack which is designed to keep a controller up and running in the event of a power failure. These back up batteries run down quickly when they are being drawn upon to operate a controller and, in the real world, they are usually forgotten about and sit dead in a controller cabinet. To be effective, batteries need to be tested on a monthly basis. Note: Batteries won't open valves; they only hold memory.

11. Working Drawings: Drafting, Detailing, and Specifying

Careful and accurate drafting is of utmost importance when assembling irrigation working drawings. Head spacing, valve placement, mainline routing, hydrozone piping, and the location of backflow prevention devices and automatic controllers require exacting line work and specific notation. As the majority of the eventual equipment will be underground, the irrigation designer's intentions must be diagrammatically portrayed in a fashion that can be comprehended by the system installer.

The working drawing drafting process closely follows the design process. Most of the front-end research such as water pressure and unusual site conditions are picked up in notes, as you cannot draw something like water pressure. Equipment legends are especially helpful in irrigation design. Most legends will have equipment catalogue call numbers and other pertinent information that relates to the thoughts or reasons for the system layout being the way it is shown. Legends are especially useful in head design as minimum operational pressure, radius of throw, and gallons per minute (or hour) can be noted one time rather than for each individual head. I like to use valve legends, even for extremely large projects. Valve legends assign a valve number, size, and gpm to each valve in the system. If you find it difficult to show 100 or so valves on a legend, just imagine how difficult it is for a contractor to find these same valves strewn all over the plan sheet or set of sheets.

A pipe size schedule is another thing I prefer, as opposed to actually sizing every length of pipe. This is a matter of designer preference, as is the way equipment connections are called out and pipe sleeving is noted. The important thing to note is that most of the items discussed so far are more easily described than they are to draw.

Actual drawing almost always starts with head layout. Most of the major equipment manufacturers provide designers with equipment templates free of charge. The templates are used to draft any number of graphic symbols, most of which are head depictions. Once heads are shown and hydrozones, utilizing various heads, are selected, it is time to route the mainline. Mainlines are usually shown as a solid or a dashed line, and the lateral lines should always be the opposite of the mainline for clarity. I believe that a graphic convention showing sleeves should be on the plan. It is not enough to assume an irrigation contractor will provide sleeves or even pick up a note concerning their placement. Sleeves are open pipes through which water-bearing pipe is inserted. Sleeves are used under all paved surfaces and through all walls. The main purpose of sleeves is to allow broken pipe to be pulled out through them for repair. I prefer to have sleeves at least two times larger than the inside pipe. This allows for bending and also provides a route for remote control wire, low-voltage light cable, and any additional lateral pipe needed to accommodate field changes. Under expensive pavement it is better to have too many sleeves as opposed to too few.

Once the mainline has been routed, valves should be located as close to the middle of every hydrozone as possible. In high-end residential design and on sport fields, this may be difficult because valve boxes should be located out of turf areas for the sake of aesthetics and safety. Even when valves are located away from the center of a hydrozone, try to have the first water delivery lateral from the valve split the hydrozone. After valves are located, lateral pipes connecting all the specific hydrozone heads are drawn in. Laterals that cross a mainline or any other lateral should hop over the line by a graphic half circle or simply be a broken line.

Method of backflow connection and the breaker location are shown, as is the location of the automatic controller(s). Finally, important related equipment such as quick couplers, gate valves, and master control valves are shown. On phased projects, I like to cap off the mainline and locate it in a valve box with an upstream gate valve just inside the next phase line. This allows for easy continuation of the main if project hydraulics allow or at least provides a temporary water source for new construction until move permanent measures can be brought on line. Pipe and zone the entire system before locating quick couplers or inverted hose bibs since it is easier to see where they are needed. It is also a very good idea to show any hose bibs on adjacent structures as it would be wasteful to locate a quick coupler next to a building mounted hose bib. Gate valve location should definitely be done in the final drafting stages. At this point it is easier to see the actual mainline route and all the valve locations. This gives insight into where hydrozone valves can be efficiently isolated by gate valves. When isolating valves on a mainline that is looped, remember to provide gate valves on both sides of the valve(s) to be isolated because water in a looped mainline is flowing in two directions. Where possible, the irrigation designer should also make every effort to locate valves in groups as this minimizes the number of valve boxes and gate valves as well as lowering maintenance personnel search time.

On large projects of three sheets or more, it is a good idea to provide an "irrigation mainline plan." This plan is done at a larger scale than the other sheets, and its purpose is to show the entire site at a glance. All major equipment plus the mainline route are shown on one sheet. Space allowing, this sheet is also a great place to show the overall site valve legend. This greatly aids the installation and maintenance contractors. Heads and lateral pipe are a detail item better shown on separate sheets at a smaller (larger actual drawing) scale. The mainline plan is broad in scope. Having the major equipment on one sheet aids inventorying and acts as a quick system check for any glaring mistakes. Estimators and suppliers have told me that even the simplest irrigation mainline plan, if complete, will cut their bidding time in half.

Once the entire system is graphically depicted on the drawings, installation details showing equipment relationships and method of installation are provided. Heights of risers, types of unions, and placement of related components (e.g., emitter system control head) are especially important since they not only affect system operation, but also show code compliance. Most of the larger equipment manufacturers supply very good details free of charge. These manufacturers' details can be edited and then sticky-backed directly onto working drawings or separate detail sheets. This saves time and expense and provides industry uniformity.

Finally, the specifications are written. Landscape architects and irrigation designers, pay particular attention to what is in your specifications. First, allow no conflicts between the spec and what is on the plans. Secondly, and most important, always give yourself an out. In this day of shot gun lawsuits, you will be sued in conjunction with owners, installers, and anyone else that can be squeezed onto the complaint. If someone trips on a sprinkler riser or jogs over an open valve box, you stand an excellent chance of being sued. In my 17 years of private practice I have been named in four lawsuits. All four were related to irrigation design and all four were summarily dismissed based primarily on the clarity and completeness of my irrigation specifications. A good spec can nip lawsuits in the bud. While many people do get hurt outside (and inside as well), many others simply pretend to get hurt. Do not allow yourself to be the target of such greedy, unscrupulous behavior. Aside from injuries derived from equipment placement, a lack of water pressure or flow will make your life uncomfortable. Language such as "...meet all applicable codes...", "...verify...", "...notify landscape architect if a discrepancy occurs...", or "...provide equipment as needed to guarantee proper operation..." will help to alleviate legal disputes. While dry and boring, experience will prove specifications to be your best friend. Attorneys and judges may have a difficult time understanding drawings but they read better than anyone. What they read should vindicate you.

12. Installation: Field Observation

Just as graphic clarity is needed to depict system design because components are located underground, field observation must be ongoing and intense because this equipment is buried. While plants can be downsized to save construction costs and quality ongoing maintenance will save the project, down-grading an irrigation system will create maintenance nightmares and eventually ruin the project.

Equipment has a life span, and the cheaper the equipment the shorter its life will be. The first rule of irrigation field observation is to assure that the type of equipment specified is the type of equipment installed. The second rule is to make sure all the equipment specified is indeed installed. Then check the quality of the installation. You will have to make the call if the specified 12-inch-deep trenches are consistently 8 inches deep. Sleeves are often missed, and check valves seem to be forgotten about. Pipe class and size can mysteriously change and sometimes even heads "grow legs" and move to a wider spacing. Trench backfill can be trash and sometimes trench settling occurs with initial watering and not as a result of proper floating. Believe me, corners can be, and routinely are, cut in the area of irrigation system installation and you must watch for it. Because many project owners call for field observation on the part of the landscape architect, after installation of the irrigation system, as a cost saving measure, it behooves you to recommend only proven and reputable irrigation contractors and divorce yourself from the project (in writing) if they are not used.

The irrigation observation schedule in Chapter 8 will prove usefu, but remember that if someone really wants to cut corners, the installation of an irrigation system is the easiest place for them to do it. While many landscape architects dislike the dull mechanics of an irrigation system, they should at least know what equipment is specified and how it is to be installed. Any changes or discrepancies at this juncture could make for real problems in the future.

Not only should the field observer check the equipment, he should watch the system operate. This shows head coverage, compliance with planned controller programming, and any significant leakage. Constant adjustments and even some layout changes occur in the field on a daily basis. The irrigation field man needs to be flexible, knowledgeable, and dedicated. No related design area is more important to the success of the project — *plants die in the desert without water* — it's that simple. A well designed and installed irrigation system will guarantee plant survival, and that is the bottom line, the assurance of the landscape in landscape architecture.

Water Conservation

Before closing on the subject of irrigation design, a word needs to be said about water conservation as it relates to landscape irrigation. First, irrigation designers and project owners have been given a bad rap from an uninformed public. True, some 75% of all residential water usage can go towards landscape watering. Consider that at least a third of this percentage is wasted water in the form of overwatering and faulty equipment maintenance — both the homeowner's responsibility. On commercial projects designed, installed, and maintained by professionals, the efficiency of the irrigation system is much better. Also, as noted earlier, lakes and golf courses are not nearly the water-guzzling culprits they appear to be. Golf courses, in fact, can filter and purify reclaimed water before it leaches back into the underground aquifer. Irrigation designers and the systems they create do, indeed, need to be monitored and controlled, but the public must also play its part in other areas.

Simple measures like only doing dishes or laundry when there is a full load, not flushing evening toilets until morning, using toilet dams and faucet low-flow devices, and above all, prudent landscape watering will greatly aid the noble cause of water conservation.

Reclaimed water needs to be utilized and the concept of utilizing gray water on an individual homeowner basis needs to be explored. The average homeowner does not have the wherewithal to set up a reclaimed water system. But a gray water system that filters and recycles sink, tub, dishwasher, and laundry water for landscape irrigation is an objective that is obtainable by everyone.

Since it takes three glasses of water to wash one glass, paper cups should be considered. Foot, knee, and pedal-operated sinks would save many gallons of water during cooking, shaving, and hand washing. Air blowers instead of hose washing should be utilized to clean pavement. If the need for a swimming pool is marginal, consider alternatives such as an outdoor shower. Outdoor fountains should be justified.

Water conservation is the responsibility of every citizen and a community effort is needed; those who use the most water should pay the most, and those that waste it should be fined. The water supply we have in the Southwest deserts should be looked upon as a blessing, not a birthright.

Backflow Prevention

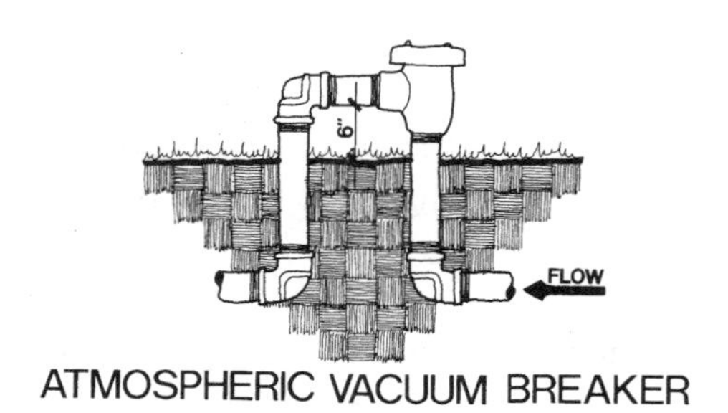

ATMOSPHERIC VACUUM BREAKER

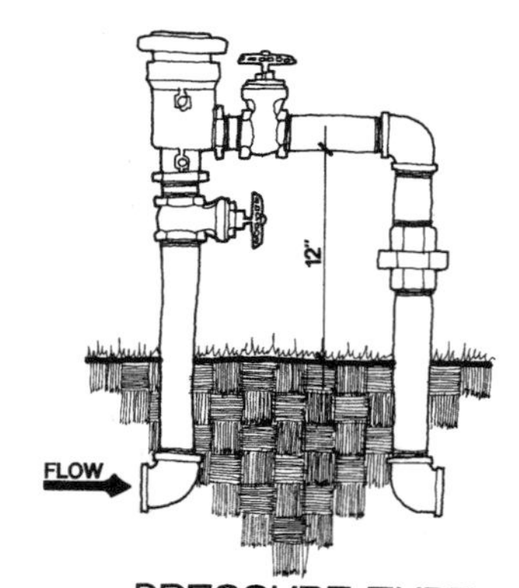

PRESSURE TYPE VACUUM BREAKER ASSEMBLY

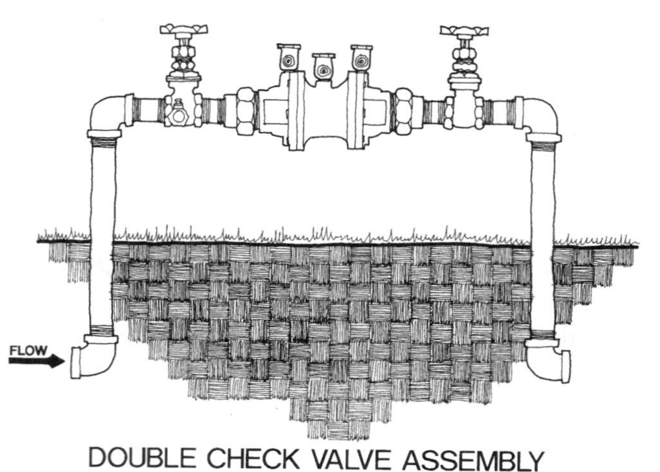

DOUBLE CHECK VALVE ASSEMBLY

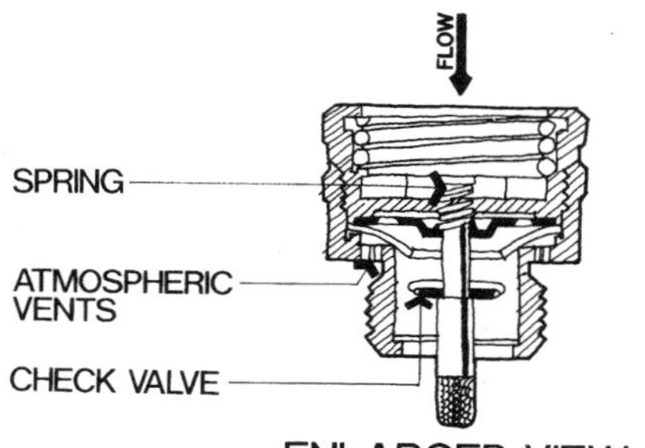

ENLARGED VIEW OF HOSE BREAKER

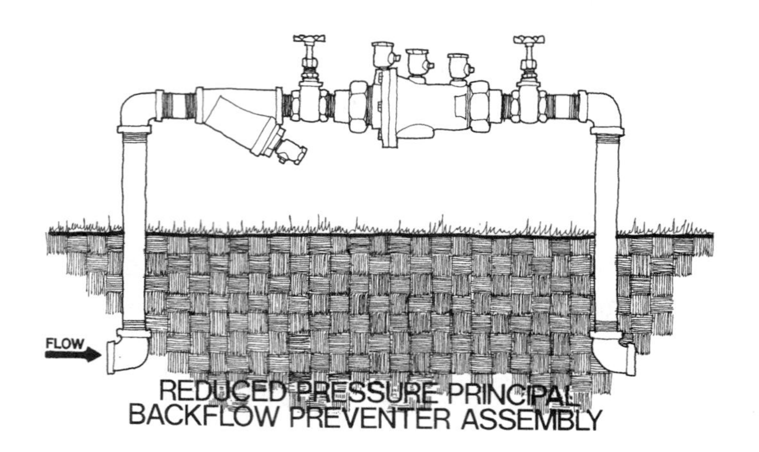

REDUCED PRESSURE PRINCIPAL BACKFLOW PREVENTER ASSEMBLY

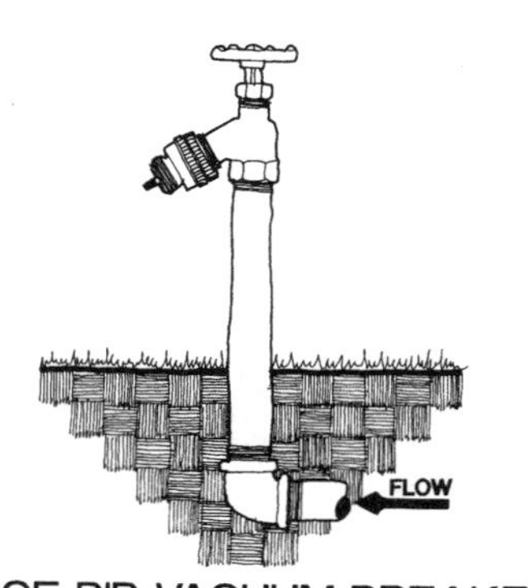

HOSE BIB VACUUM BREAKER

Conventional System Equipment

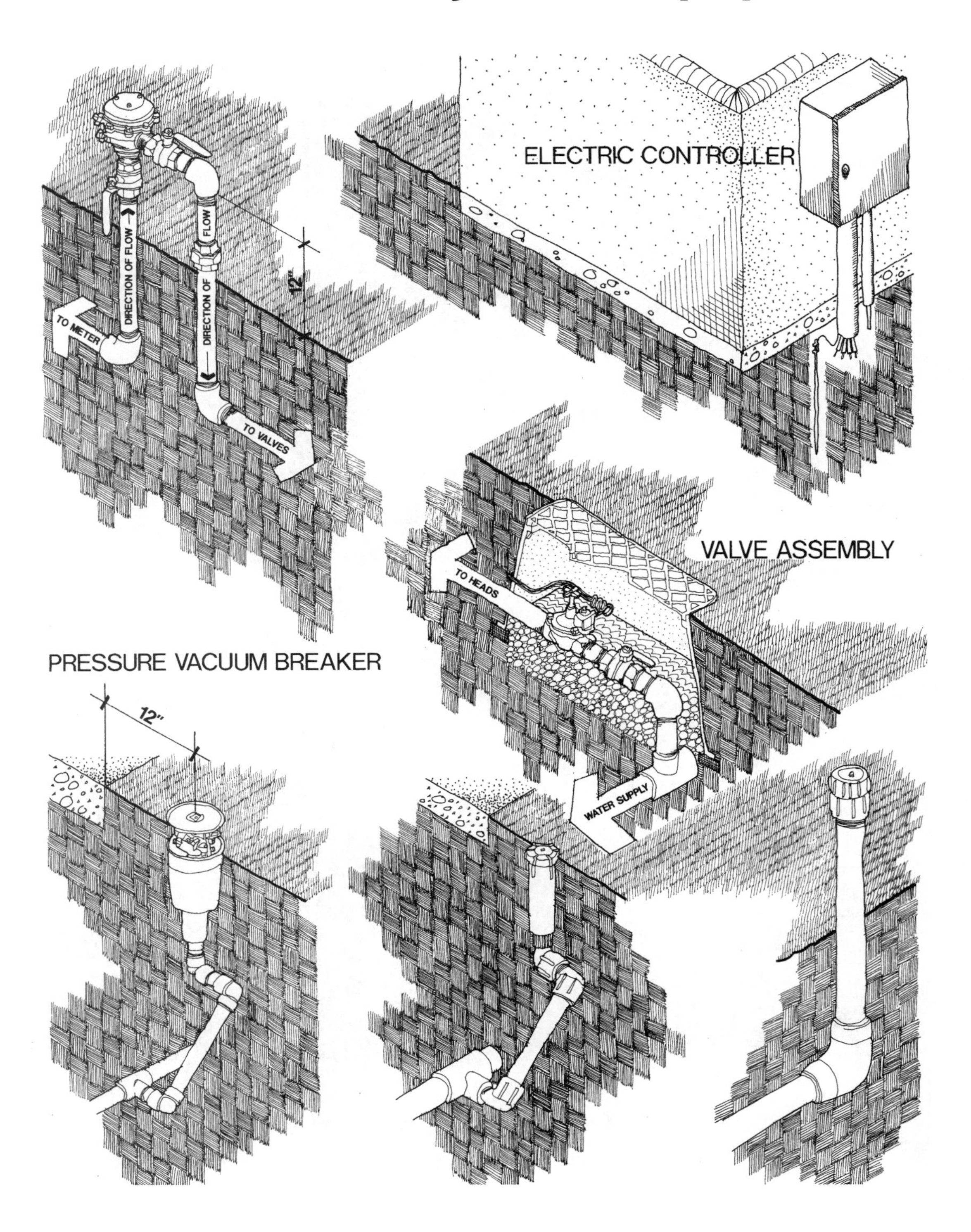

Emitter System Equipment

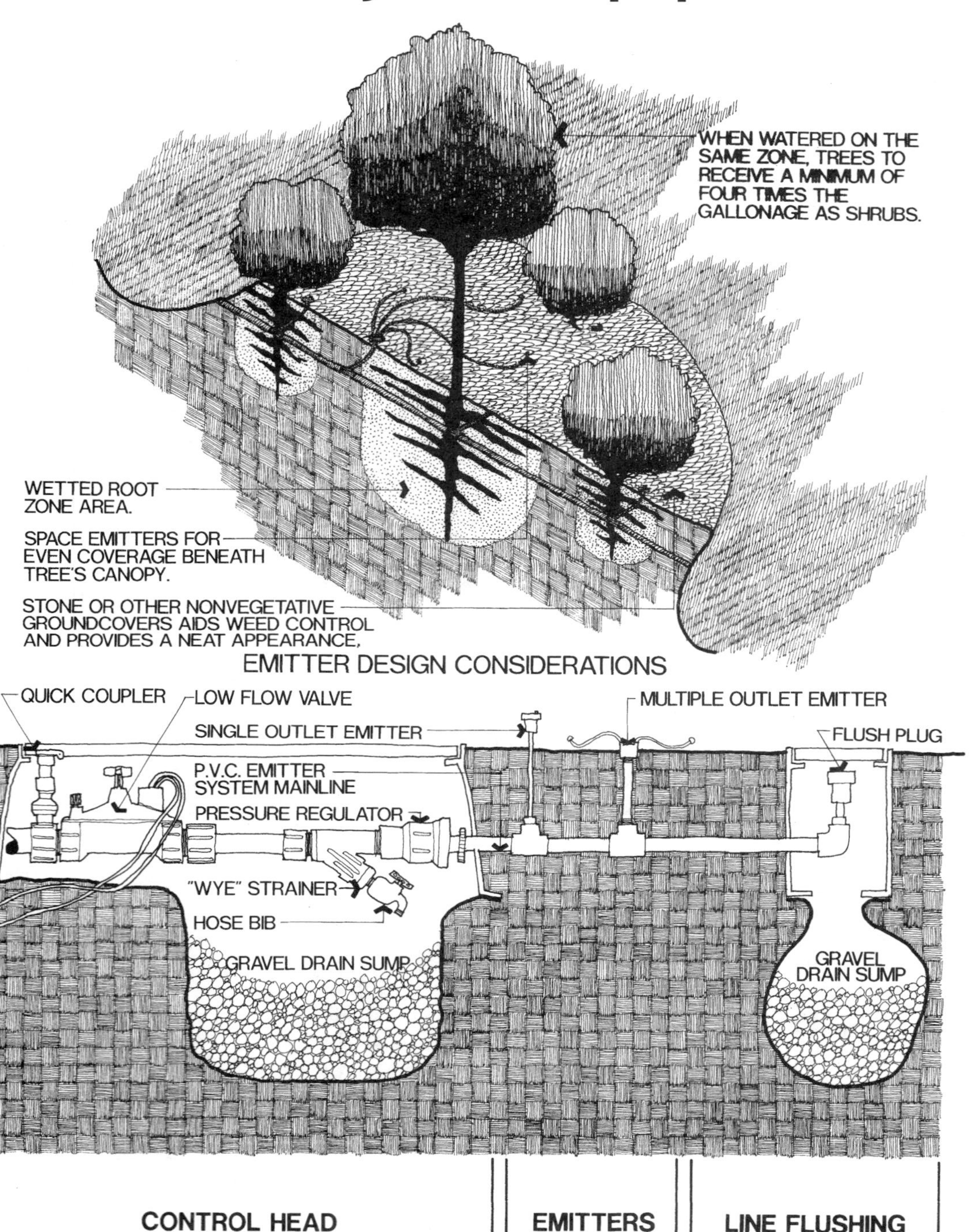
WHEN WATERED ON THE SAME ZONE, TREES TO RECEIVE A MINIMUM OF FOUR TIMES THE GALLONAGE AS SHRUBS.
WETTED ROOT ZONE AREA.
SPACE EMITTERS FOR EVEN COVERAGE BENEATH TREE'S CANOPY.
STONE OR OTHER NONVEGETATIVE GROUNDCOVERS AIDS WEED CONTROL AND PROVIDES A NEAT APPEARANCE.
EMITTER DESIGN CONSIDERATIONS
QUICK COUPLER
LOW FLOW VALVE
MULTIPLE OUTLET EMITTER
SINGLE OUTLET EMITTER
FLUSH PLUG
P.V.C. EMITTER SYSTEM MAINLINE
PRESSURE REGULATOR
"WYE" STRAINER
HOSE BIB
GRAVEL DRAIN SUMP
GRAVEL DRAIN SUMP
CONTROL HEAD
EMITTERS
LINE FLUSHING
SYSTEM ASSEMBLY

Emitter System Irrigation Detail

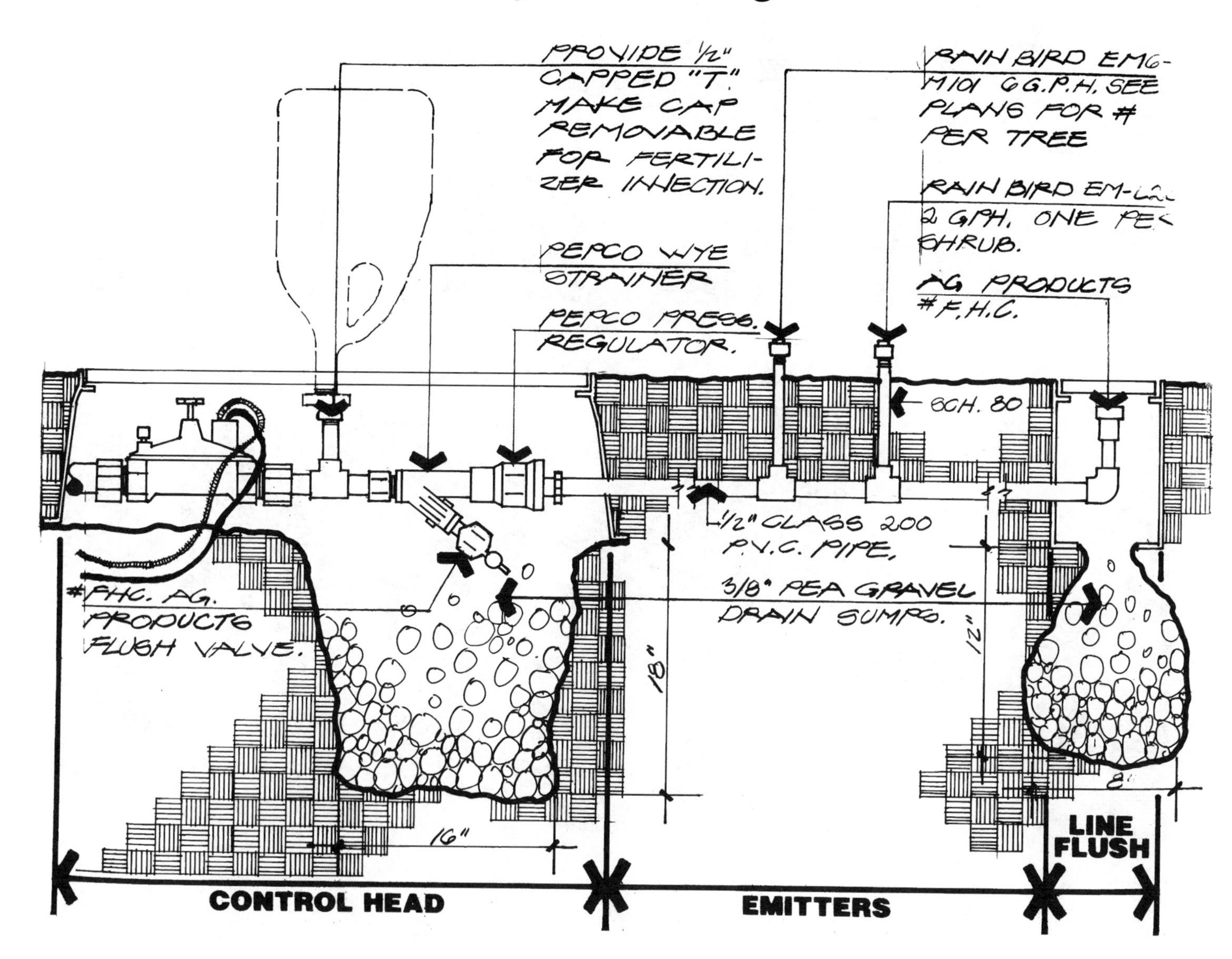

Deep-Watering Assembly Irrigation Detail

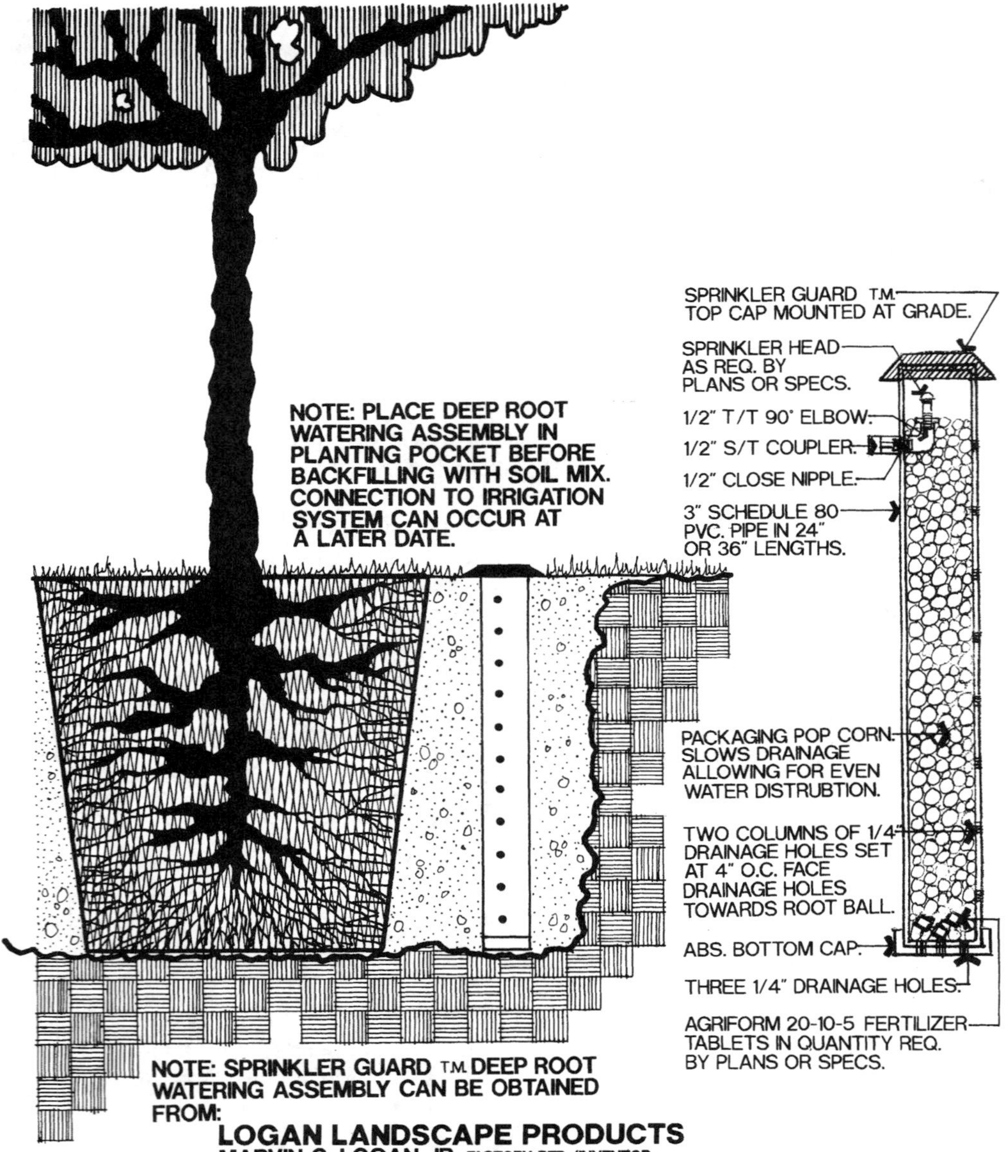
NOTE: PLACE DEEP ROOT WATERING ASSEMBLY IN PLANTING POCKET BEFORE BACKFILLING WITH SOIL MIX. CONNECTION TO IRRIGATION SYSTEM CAN OCCUR AT A LATER DATE.
SPRINKLER GUARD T.M. TOP CAP MOUNTED AT GRADE.
SPRINKLER HEAD AS REQ. BY PLANS OR SPECS.
1/2" T/T 90° ELBOW
1/2" S/T COUPLER
1/2" CLOSE NIPPLE
3" SCHEDULE 80 PVC. PIPE IN 24" OR 36" LENGTHS.
PACKAGING POP CORN SLOWS DRAINAGE ALLOWING FOR EVEN WATER DISTRUBTION.
TWO COLUMNS OF 1/4" DRAINAGE HOLES SET AT 4" O.C. FACE DRAINAGE HOLES TOWARDS ROOT BALL.
ABS. BOTTOM CAP
THREE 1/4" DRAINAGE HOLES
AGRIFORM 20-10-5 FERTILIZER TABLETS IN QUANTITY REQ. BY PLANS OR SPECS.
NOTE: SPRINKLER GUARD T.M. DEEP ROOT WATERING ASSEMBLY CAN BE OBTAINED FROM:
LOGAN LANDSCAPE PRODUCTS
MARVIN C. LOGAN JR. FACTORY REP./INVENTOR
30015 LOS NINOS CATHEDRAL CITY, CA. 92234
LOCAL: (619) 770-2832 TOLL FREE: (800) 232-4948
SPRINKLER GUARD T.M.
NO SCALE:
DETAIL #
DEEP ROOT WATERING ASSEMBLY
NOTE: THIS "STICKY BACK" MASTER PROVIDED AS A COURTESY FROM SUPPLIER.

Mainline Plan

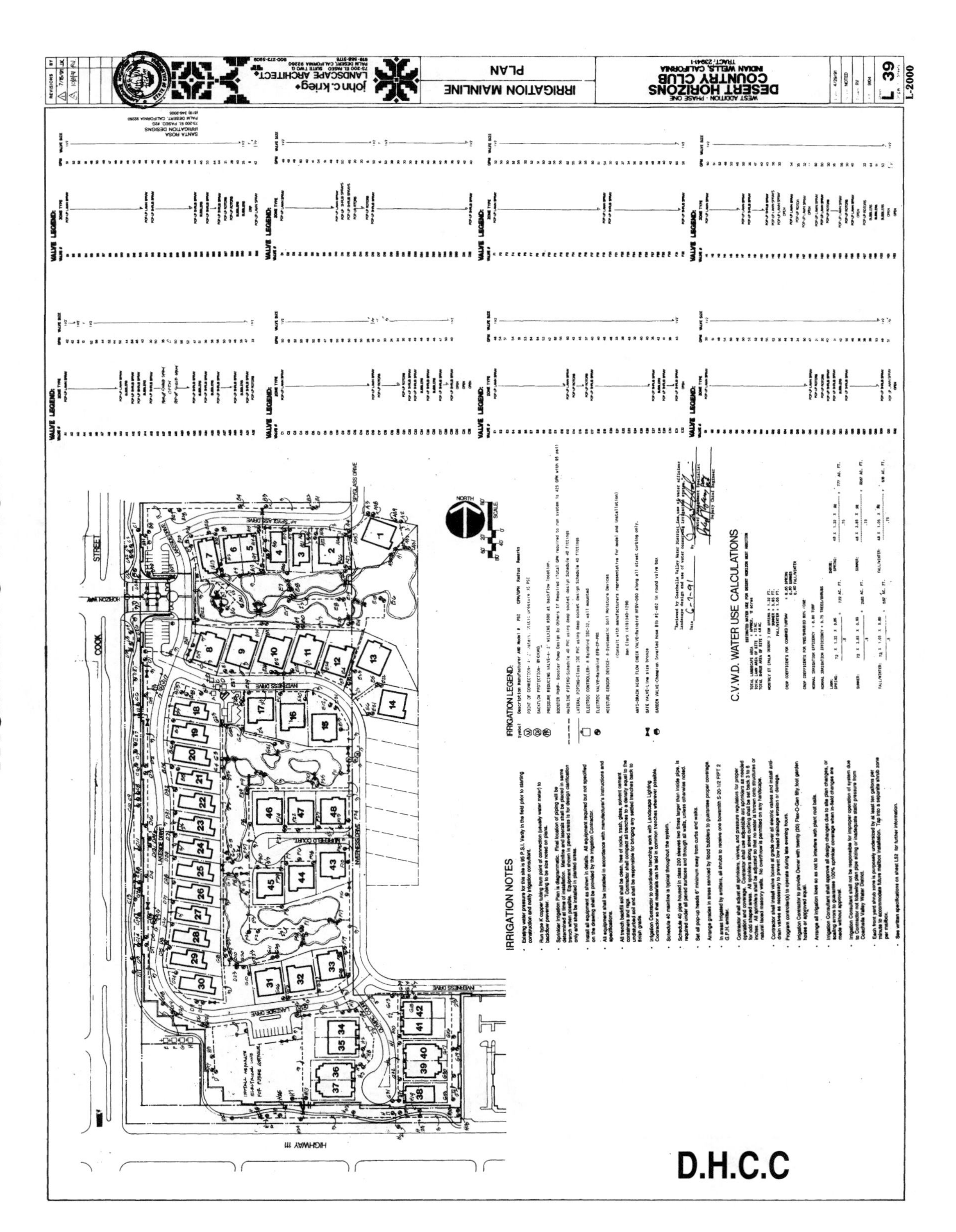

System Layout with Valve Legend

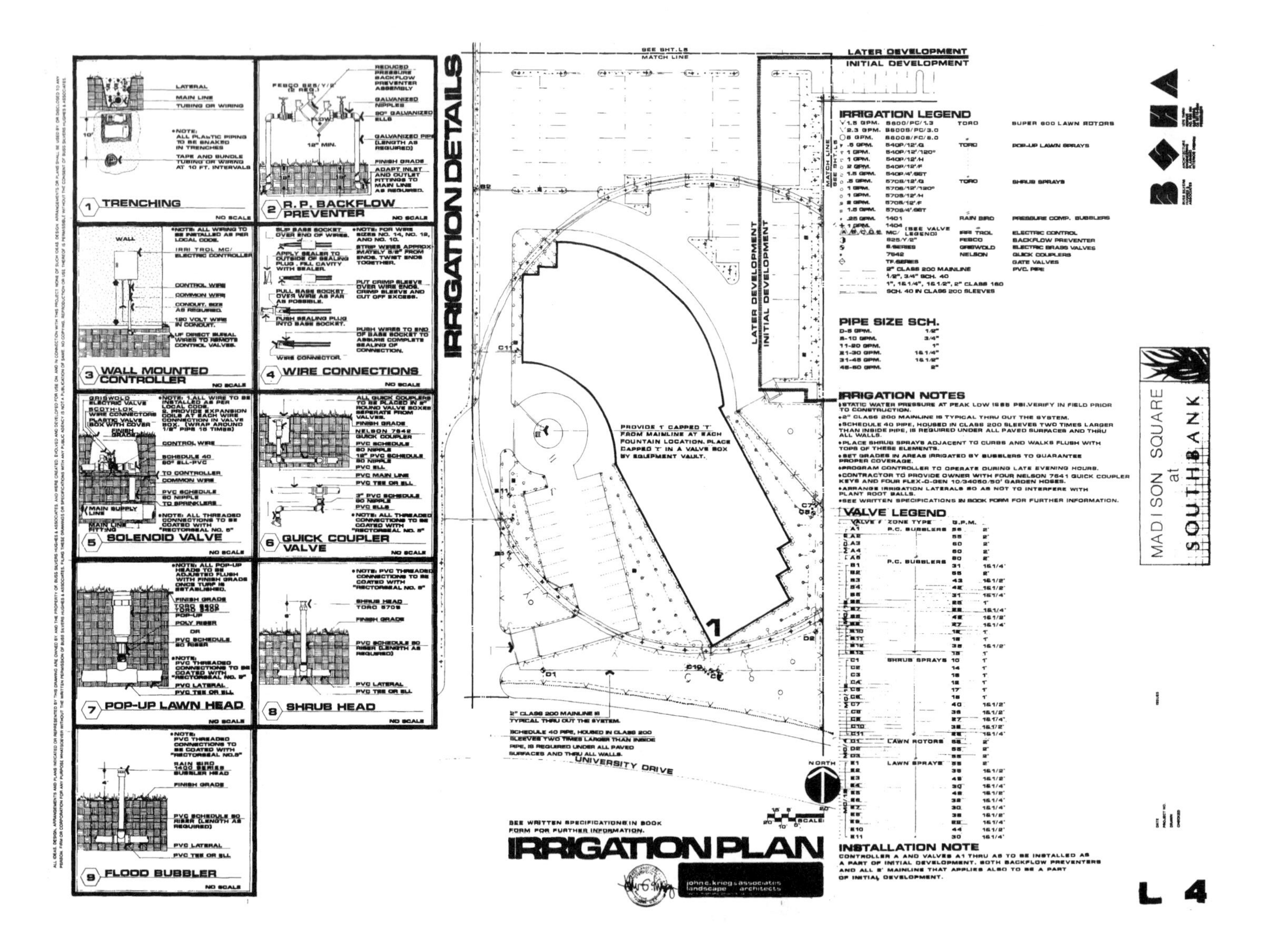

Irrigation Equipment

Backflow prevention

Automatic controllers

Pop-up sprinkler head

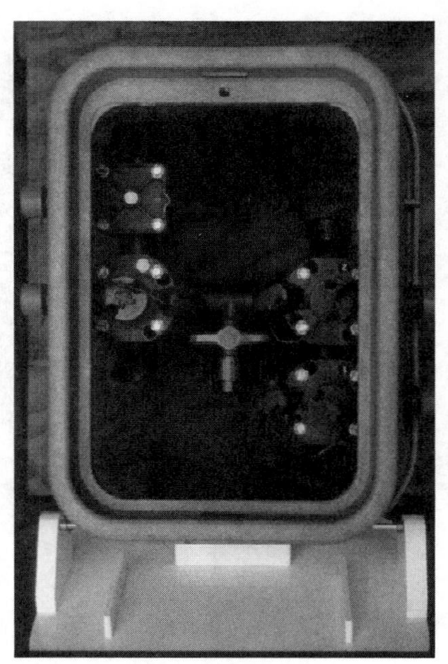

Valve assembly

Drip Irrigation Equipment

Conventional Irrigation Equipment

Computer Chip

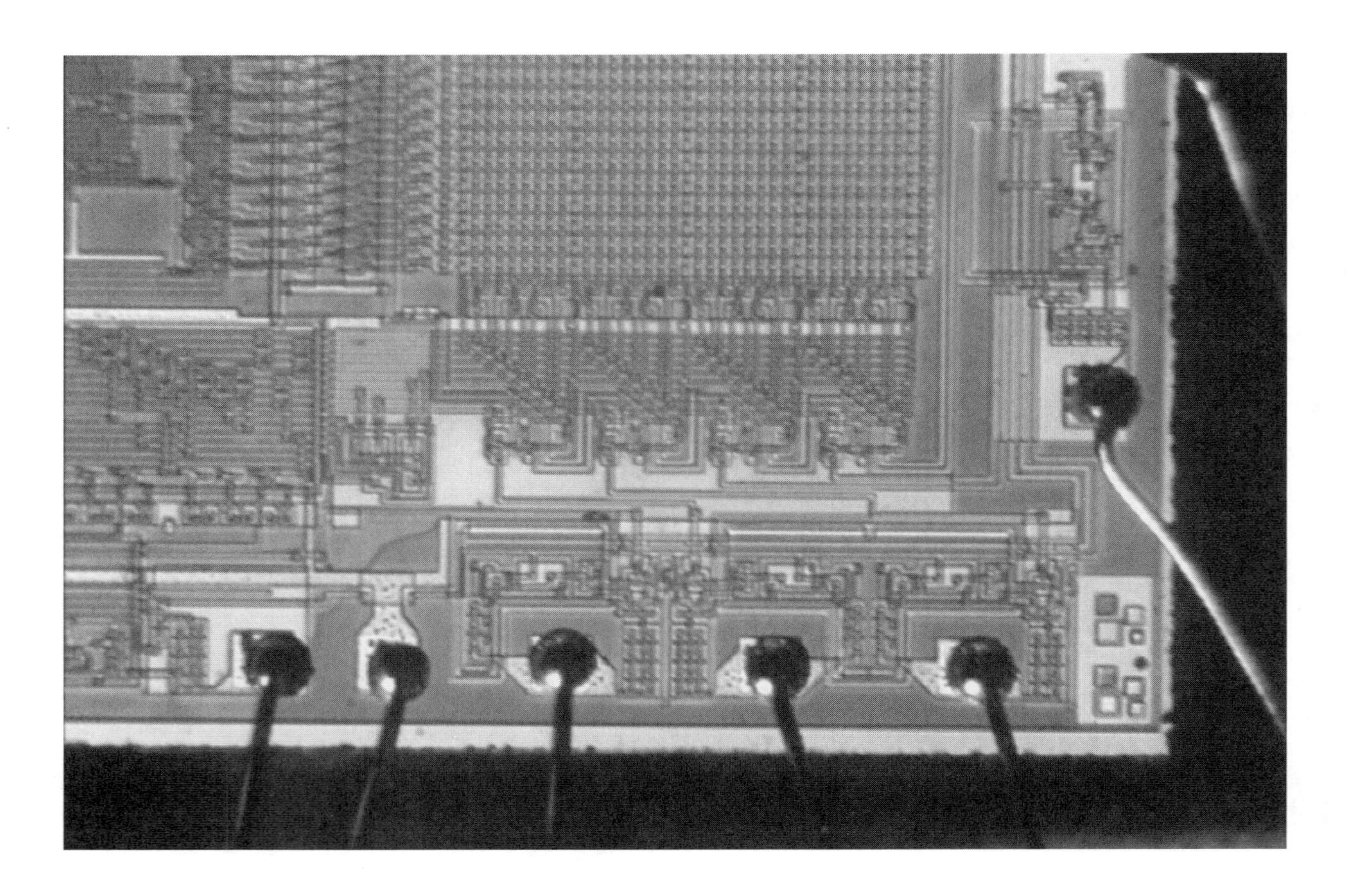

Central Arizona Project

Glossary

Angle valve: A valve that discharges water at 90° from the opening where it was received.

Application rate: The true amount of water that actually falls on a given ground surface area.

Atmospheric pressure: Air pressure, of which the maximum vertical limit is 33.94 feet. No pump can draw (suck) water higher than this.

Atmospheric vacuum breaker (AVB): This device has a poppet which floats on top of incoming pressurized water. In the event of a backflow, atmospheric pressure will force the poppet down as the water changes direction. This, in turn, will block the backflow.

Automatic controller: Electrical device that is, in actuality, an automatic timer. At set times the controller sends electronic impulses to the valves, activating the valve to open and operate. These times are collectively referred to as the controller's program. In industry jargon, controllers are often called clocks.

Backflow prevention: Providing a mechanical device downstream of the potable water supply that prevents nonpotable water from being drawn (sucked) backwards into the potable supply.

Backup heads: Irrigation heads that occur in odd size or irregularly shaped areas that are choked down and are intended to irrigate just these edge areas.

Ball- or cam-driven rotor: Large rotating head. Water driven into the head's body forces a ball to hit against an anvil, which turns the head one notch with each hit.

Breaker: Slang for backflow preventer.

Check valve: A valve designed and manufactured so as to allow water to flow in only one direction.

Circuiting: Dedicating certain valves to operate certain hydrozones (circuits). Sometimes called sectioning or zoning.

Class: Pertains to pipe wall thickness. The thicker the wall, the higher the number of the class rating. Class 160 is thinner than class 200 which, in turn, is thinner than class 315.

Copper tubing: Must be used and soldered to all direct connections into the potable water supply.

Cubic foot: As it applies to this chapter, a cube of water 12 inches square (12 in wide by 12 in. deep by 12 in. high). A cubic foot of water weighs 62.37 pounds and contains 7.4805 gallons.

Diaphragm: A thin piece of plastic or hardened rubber that serves as a partition. Diaphrams control rate of water flow through valves and pressure compensating heads.

Drip irrigation: Colloquial term used to describe an irrigation system that uses emitters for delivering water to plant materials. The emitters are low flow and literally drip water slowly, giving rise to the name.

Double check valve backflow preventer (DCV): Breaker that contains two check valves. One valve simply acts as a backup to the other.

Emitter: An extremely low flow irrigation device that delivers water in GPH.

Emitter system: A method of irrigation which utilizes individual emitters to water individual plant materials.

Equilateral triangle: A triangle formed by three equal sides. Triangular head spacing covers the most area with the least number of heads.

Evapotranspiration rate (E.T.): Water lost to the atmosphere through plant transpiration and ground plane surface evaporation.

Excess flow valve: As it applies to this chapter, a valve mounted to the vertical riser of an irrigation head. Also called an antidrain valve or hydraulic circuit breaker. The valve shuts down in the event of head failure, thus preventing wasted water.

Feet of head: .433 psi per foot.

Feet per second (fps): Term used to express the rate of speed at which water travels in a pipe. In irrigation design, equipment and pipe should be sized so that water will travel no faster than 5 fps.

Fertilizer injection: Liquid fertilizer attached to some point in the irrigation system downstream of the backflow preventer. When the system is running, the liquid fertilizer mixes with the water and is dispersed through the heads.

Fixed riser: A rigid riser supporting an irrigation head above the ground.

Flood bubbler: Irrigation head that releases water in gpm directly at the head location.

Flood irrigation: Canal or well water that is channeled through trenches and is allowed to simply flood over confined areas.

Gate (shut-off) valve: A valve that opens or closes via a gate that slides up or down in a track within the valve body. Water passes through the valve in a straight (180_) line.

Gallon: Four quarts of water. One gallon weights 8.3 pounds.

Gallons per minute (GPM): Term used to express the measurable amount of water (gallons) that flows through pipe, valves, or heads over the course of 1 minute. Also, referred to as rate of flow.

Gear driven rotor: Large rotating head. Water passing through the head's body drives a series of gears which turn the head's nozzle.

Globe valve: Valve through which water passes in an "S"-shaped flow pattern. Valve is opened or closed via a threaded plunger that rises from or lowers into a valve seat.

Gray water: All water drained from a home or facility that is not sewage from toilets.

Head to head coverage: Designing head placement so that the outer periphery of one head's pattern of spray touches the base of an opposite or adjacent head. Best type of coverage to provide in desert environments.

Hose bib: A globe valve that is male threaded to accept the female end of a hose.

Hose connection vacuum breaker: A simple check valve that is placed on hose bibs and connects directly to the potable water supply. These breakers prevent water inside the hose from getting sucked into the potable system in the event of a backflow.

Hydraulics: Study of the nature and properties of liquids in motion.

Hydrodynamic: Relating to water in motion.

Hydrological cycle: All water on earth is part of a closed system which simply recycles itself. This is known as the hydrological cycle.

Hydrostatic: Water at rest.

Hydrozones: Areas in the irrigation design that are valved or circuited separate from other areas. Each hydrozone occurs due to microclimatic location, similarity in the water requirements of plant materials within the zone, or similarity in the degree of slope for heads within the zone.

Impact-driven rotor: Large rotating head. These heads have a spring-loaded arm which is tripped when water splashes against it. Every time the arm trips it turns the head a notch in its rotation.

Inside diameter (I.D.): Refers to the size of pipe measured in cross section from inside wall to inside wall.

Inverted "Y" hose bib: Functions as a quick coupler but is easier to use. The bib connects to the system mainline, is accessed through a valve box, and is easy to connect the hose to as the male threads face up.

Irrigation contractor: An individual who by education, experience and state licensing is deemed knowledgeable, capable, and legally able to install irrigation systems.

Irrigation designer: An individual who by training and/or experience is knowledgeable and adept in the design of irrigation systems capable of maintaining plant material in a healthy condition.

Irrigation mainline plan: A plan provided on projects with three or more sheets. This plan is usually at a large scale so that the boundaries of the entire project can be shown on one sheet. Shows the mainline routing, location of all valves and equipment, and controller location(s). When accompanied by an overall site valve legend this sheet allows contractors and maintenance personnel to review the entire project (minus heads) at a glance.

Lateral pipe: Any irrigation line that is not under continuous pressure. Pipe composing this line is called laterial pipe.

Mainline pipe: The system mainline which is under constant pressure and provides water to all the valves and thus to all the lateral pipe.

Master controller: On large projects this is a more powerful, centrally located controller that sends commands to several satellite controllers. Employed frequently in golf course design and most often programmed and operated by the golf course superintendent.

Master valve: Acts as system backup. If a mainline is ruptured or a hydrozone valve sticks open, this valve is designed to shut the entire system down. Always located downstream of the breaker and upstream of the valves.

Normally closed valve: Requires an electric impulse from the controller to open. Almost all electric valves are of this type.

Normally open valve: Requires an electric impulse from the controller to shut down.

Orifice: An opening. In irrigation terminology, the term is used to describe the type of openings in irrigation heads that control the amount of water flow and type of spray or water delivery pattern.

Outside diameter (O.D.): Refers to size of pipe measured in cross section from outside wall to outside wall.

Pattern of spray: The geometric pattern of water that spray heads are designed and machined to deliver onto the ground plane. Usually a percentage of a circle, but squares and rectangles are available.

Point of connection (P.O.C.): Term used in irrigation design that refers to the point where water is brought into the irrigation system. This can be a water meter, well, canal, or lake.

Polyethylene tubing: Flexible plastic tubing used frequently to deliver water to emitters that are inserted directly into the tubing of in line drip systems.

Polyvinylchloride (PVC): Rigid plastic pipe used in conventional type irrigation systems and for hard line drip systems. There is now flexible PVC available which is much more durable than polyethylene and is becoming more commonly used with in line drip systems.

Poppet: A vertically sliding valve that physically opens by lifting (floating) from its seat.

Pop-up heads: Sprinklers whose bodies house a sliding, spring retractable nozzle. Water pressure causes the nozzle to slide vertically out of the sprinkler body when the head is operating. When water is shut off, the spring pulls the nozzle back into the head's body. This head can therefore be mounted at grade which is safer and more visually pleasing.

Pounds per square inch (psi): Pressure or force exerted by 1 square inch of water on a 1" x 1" surface. A 1-foot (12 inches)-tall times 1 square inch column of water exerts .433 psi at its base.

Polymers: Acrylics that are tiny crystals when dry but swell to ten times their dry size when wetted.

Potential evapotranspiration rate (P.E.T.): Calculation of what the actual E.T. will be on a given date-based upon recorded past E.T.s and predicted weather conditions.

Potable water: Any water fit for human consumption.

Precipitation rate: The volume of water manufacturers claim their irrigation heads will deliver to a 1 square foot area over a 1 hour period. Since these rates are determined in controlled wind-free laboratory situations, they are not to be confused with or taken to be the same as an application rate. See application rate.

Pressure: Force exerted on a given surface area.

Pressure booster pump: Pump placed at the irrigation system's point of connection which increases water presure in the downstream line.

Pressure-compensating bubbler: Bubblers with specialized diaphragms located at their orifices that equalize the pressure for all the similar bubblers in the line and thus equalize flow.

Pressure-compensating emitters: Emitters with specialized diaphragms located at their orifices that equalize the pressure for all similar emitters in the line and thus equalize flow.

Pressure gauge: A device that can be attached to a hose bib or other male threaded valve. When the valve is opened, the gauge will measure the water pressure.

Pressure loss: Hydrodynamic water will lose pressure due to friction loss as it passes through irrigation lines and equipment or when it travels uphill.

Pressure regulator: A valve that reduces pressure and will keep it at a set level.

Pressure type vacuum breaker (PVB): Similar to an atmospheric vacuum breaker. Has a floating poppet, but the poppet itself is spring loaded. This spring assists the poppet in closing the internal check valve faster and more firmly.

Program: As it applies to this chapter, the watering schedule assigned to an automatic controller.

Quick coupler: A valve that is machined to be accessed with a special key. This coupler key forces a spring-loaded valve seat to open. Essentially used for the same functions as a hose bib.

Quick coupler key: A brass device which screws into a quick coupler throat and forces open a valve seat, thus accessing flowing water.

Radius of throw: The radius that a manufacturer rates (claims) a spray or rotating head will throw water under a given pressure. Does not account for wind conditions.

Rain gauge: A cup-like device that catches rain water and either mechanically (by its full weight) or electronically shuts down an irrigation controller until such time as it empties (due to evaporation during drier weather), and the controller's normal program is resumed.

Reclaimed water: Recycled sewage water that can be used for irrigation of plant materials. All reclaimed water used in the Coachella Valley must meet a tertiary or higher level of treatment before it can be used for landscape irrigation. Golf courses are excellent users and filters for reclaimed water.

Reduced pressure backflow preventer (RPBP): The safest backflow preventer. Has two check valves with a pressure relief valve in between. Operates on the principle of pressure differential between the check valves at the instant a back flow occurs. The downstream valve remains open while the upstream valve closes. This causes the irrigation system water to exit the breaker through the relief valve. This type of breaker must be used for hospitals, schools, and many other types of public installations in the state of California, as well as when fertilizer injection equipment is employed.

Satellite controllers: Field controllers with less power and programming capability than the master controller which interfaces with them. Frequently employed in golf course design.

Schedule: A rating used to describe pipe wall thickness. Most PVC fittings are either schedule 40 or schedule 80. Thickness increases as the schedule number increases; thus schedule 80 is thicker and stronger than schedule 40.

Sleeving: Providing open pipe under pavement surfaces and through walls to accommodate future pipe and wiring run interior to the sleeve. This provides for future service and repairs as pipe and wires can be pulled from and reinserted through the sleeve.

Snaking: Zigzagging pipe and wire from side to side in open trenches to allow for thermal contraction and expansion as well as service and repairs.

Spider bubblers: Bubblers whose orifices are machined so that the outgoing stream(s) of water arches like the leg of a spider.

Standard dimensional ratio (S.D.R.): A rating used to describe pipe wall thickness. S.D.R. is called class. See Class.

Surge: Flowing water within the walls of a pipe has a certain velocity. When the water flow is shut down and the water pressure momentarily increases due to atmospheric pressure (33.94) entering the line, a surge condition exists.

Tensiometer: Moisture sensing device that reads the moisture content in soil. Electronic tensiometers interface with automatic controllers and, in effect, tell the controller to open and close various hydrozone valves at the appropriate times to keep soil moisture at the right level.

Trenches: Narrow soil excavations that run in straight or gently curving lines. Trenches are where irrigation pipe and control wire are installed.

Turbulence: Flowing water that is disturbed, agitated, or otherwise not moving smoothly is said to be in a state of turbulence.

Valve: Mechanical device that controls the flow of liquids.

Valving: See circuiting.

Velocity: The speed of water traveling through pipe that is expressed in feet per second (fps). Under no circumstances should velocity exceed 5 fps in irrigation design.

Water hammer: Within a closed irrigation system, the smashing (hammering) of water against the side walls of pipe and equipment as a result of surge or water velocity.

Water meter: Device that measures the flow of water. Usually a metered valve that provides potable water from an agency or municipality to individual sites on an individual (1 meter per site) basis.

Chapter 7

Lighting Design

Island at night

Introduction

Think about this: depending on the time of year, roughly 1/3 to 1/2 of the 24 hours in a day are nighttime hours. This affords the landscape architect or lighting designer an excellent opportunity to perform lightscaping that rivals the drama and impact of daytime landscaping. Indeed, a lot of design time and construction money is spent on outdoor lighting. What is disturbing is that there is a lot of incoherent and outright bad lighting design. It is very disappointing that, in an area of such visual importance, very little information is available. There are no hard-and-fast rules or design axioms in lighting design such as there are in other types of design. Probably the most alluring thing about lighting design is that the designer has the power to control what is seen. In daytime design, the designer attempts to direct vision and create impact but cannot guarantee the viewer's line of sight or level of overall comprehension. With the correct type and application of night lighting, it is guaranteed that the viewer will usually see what is intended or see practically nothing at all. Outdoor lighting design, as it relates to this chapter, serves three primary purposes: (1) safety; (2) security; and (3) aesthetics.

Safety may or may not be as obvious a need as security and, for the purposes of applying a definition, let's say it's for the benefit of friendly site users. This is to say that the lighting is applied to areas that may prove harmful to family, friends, and normal site users if left unlighted. Steps, stairs, grade changes, and unexpected walls or curbs would all be more negotiable if night lighted in some fashion.

Security lighting provides the site user protection from intruders — real and imagined. The level of security lighting depends on several factors, ranging from the type of neighborhood a site is in to the actual fear level of the users. Carports, porch lights, and alley flood lights are all examples of security lighting. Street lights, parking lot lights, and enclosed corridor lighting are examples of public area security lighting. The two main features of security lighting that are of key importance are that the light source (luminaire) is vandal proof and that bulbs are maintained regularly. It does little good to have a security light fixture with a dead bulb.

Aesthetics in lighting, as in all forms of design, involves personal taste and an awareness of one's surroundings. The focus of this chapter will be on aesthetic types of lighting — the objects to be lighted and the effects that can be created by utilizing various lighting techniques. Aesthetic lighting can be used in conjunction with other types of lighting to form a unified site lighting scheme.

When attempting to analyze all the light that can be utilized in or that impacts upon an overall site-lighting scheme, consider all sources that contribute to outdoor light. A partial list would include:

1. Off-site sources such as street lights or light from other structures or facilities (e.g., ball stadium).
2. Overwash or cast interior light out of the windows of site structures.
3. Surface-mounted exterior light from the site structures. This would include safety and security lighting and could also include informational (sign, street numbers) lighting.
4. Pool, spa, and water-feature lighting.
5. Built-in light fixtures such as step or wall lights.
6. Free-standing aesthetic light fixtures.
7. Light cast from controlled fire.
8. Moonlight from a full moon at certain times of the month.

As you can see, some light sources can be absolutely controlled while other sources will have to be accepted as given and lived with. Before embarking into a full-fledged dissertation of lighting design and techniques, let us first look at the nature of electricity and some common electrical components.

Electrical Terminology

For the purposes of this discussion, a working knowledge of hydraulics in an irrigation system would be helpful, because flowing electrical current, oddly enough, is similar to flowing water.

Water in a pipe is under pressure. Electrical current in a conductor (wire) also is under a form of pressure called volts. The amount of water which passes through a pipe is measured in gallons, while the amount of electricity passing through an electrical conductor or component is expressed as amperes. The term "watts" is used to quantify how much electricity is actually being used. A kilowatt equals 1000 watts, while a kilowatt hour equates to 100 watts used over a 1-hour period. A kilowatt hour is the measurable (metered) unit that is used in the sale of electricity from utility companies to private vendors.

Electricity flows within a closed circuit, which is to say there is a source, a conductor, a user, and a return to the source. Flowing electricity is frequently referred to as current. There are two types of current — direct and alternating. Direct current (DC) means that positive and negative electricity flow in one pathway or direction. Car batteries operate on direct current. Positive electrical energy leaves the battery and drives a mechanism. Upon leaving the mechanism, the electrical energy is returned to the battery as negative electricity. Energy is contained within a closed loop flowing out of and back into the source in only one direction. By and large, most of the electricity encountered in outdoor lighting design will be derived from an alternating current (AC). Here the current within a conductor is constantly changing directions. Every two directional changes is defined as a cycle, and the number of cycles per second determines the current's frequency. Most wiring described in this chapter is 60 cycle (or hertz) wire. A directional change in electrical current 1/60 second hardly leaves enough time for an electrical appliance to turm on or shutoff. The appliance simply reads the current as being constant and stays on until the current is removed, at which time the appliance shuts off.

Alternating current (AC) is always carried by two wires — the hot wire, usually sheathed in black, and the neutral wire, usually sheathed in white. Both wires must originate at a service panel. The hot wire originates at the service panel circuit and is routed to the users (fixtures and appliances). The neutral wire, in reality, originates at the users and returns to the service panel, being connected to what is called a bus bar. With the hot wire going out from the service panel circuit and the neutral wire, in effect, returning to the service panel, a complete loop or circuit is established. The users merely draw upon and use electricity as it is passing through this loop. All modern electrical systems must be grounded. Most cables containing the hot and neutral wires will also contain a green or bare ground wire. What the ground does is intercept any interruption to the energized loop, sending the flowing electricity to the ground. In our appliance dependent society, if an appliance shorts or malfunctions, the current will travel from the point of the short to a grounded surface or connection and eventually to the ground itself. A grounded electrical system will not prevent a shock if someone directly contacts a conductor. The system simply reroutes interrupted electricity to a safe place.

In the case of human contact, the electricity simply reads the human as a conductor and flows through the human to a ground. This may cause electrocution which would, in turn, create a considerable liability problem. In order to assure that this situation does not occur, the use of a ground fault circuit interrupter (GFCI) is employed. These devices can sense current leakage out of the normal flow path and automatically shut the affected circuit down within milliseconds. GFCIs or GFIs are required on all outdoor lighting and water-feature circuits.

Just as water flowing within a closed pipe encounters resistance in the form of turbulence against the pipe walls, electricity flowing in a conductor encounters resistance. This resistance is measured in ohms. Ohms are an important factor in wire sizing because a larger wire exhibits fewer ohms, just as a larger water pipe creates less turbulence.

How is electrical demand determined? Let us return to the concept of watts. The formula: volts × amperes = watts is important to all electrical work. Conversely, the formula: volts ÷ watts = amps (w/v = a) can be applied when trying to determine the electrical current capacity of any given appliance.

When a utility company brings power (service) to a typical residence, it brings the electricity in the form of two 120-volt wires and one neutral or ground potential wire. This is referred to as three wire service. In older homes, built more than 25 years ago, service was frequently supplied by two-wire service. With one wire hot at 120 volts and the other wire neutral, two things occurred. First, the home could not readily utilize 240-volt appliances, and second, the overall amperage rating for the house was low which, in turn, limited the amount of wattage that could be utilized at any given time, thus greatly limiting the number of appliances that could be run at one time. Consider the following equations:

Two-Wire Service	Three-Wire Service
120 volts @ 60 amps = 7,200 watts	240 volts @ 60 amps = 14,400 watts
120 volts @ 100 amps = 12,000 watts	240 volts @ 100 amps = 24,000 watts
120 volts @ 150 amps = 18,000 watts	240 volts @ 150 amps = 36,000 watts
120 volts @ 200 amps = 24,000 watts	240 volts @ 200 amps = 48,000 watts

It is easy to see that a three-wire service at any given amperage rating provides twice the power of a two-wire service. The 240 volts number for three-wire service is arrived at because there are two hot 120-volt wires. In older homes a 60-amp electrical panel was not uncommon. Today this would not drive very many of the typical 1500 watt appliances that are readily available. Most modern homes start with 100-amp three-wire service with two 120-volt lines for a minimum of 24,000 available watts. Today's homes are usually three times more powerful than their counterparts of 25 years ago. Demand is calculated in many ways, but a minimum of two 240-volt (30-amp) circuits are usually provided for large appliances such as a kitchen range or washer/dryer hookup. Four 120-volt circuits (15 amps) are distributed over the rest of the home. Houses of 150 amp to 200 amp capacity are not uncommon. A frequently used rule of thumb is to add up the number of watts required for all large and small appliances and then add an additional 3 watts per each square foot of floor area. A total wattage is arrived at, and this wattage is divided by the 240 volts (w/v = a) available from two-wire service. The house service rating should exceed the amperage arrived at in the equation. The amperage rating and overall wattage of any or all available circuits at the house electrical panel or on a subpanel will be of primary concern to the outdoor lighting designer when it comes time to determine the power supply to drive his system design.

All outdoor lighting of a conventional nature is rated 120 volts, with typical lamp wattages of 100 to 150 watts. Occasionally a 250- to 400-watt lamp will be used in underwater lighting, or even for aboveground security lights, but nine times out of ten, a 250-watt lamp will be the largest in the system.

In a rough comparison of conventional irrigation to drip irrigation, one could also compare conventional light fixtures to low voltage outdoor light fixtures. These low-voltage fixtures operate on 24-volt or 12-volt electrical current, with 12 volt being, by far, the most common. Power from a 120-volt circuit is routed into a transformer. A transformer decreases voltage (transforming it) to a lower amount. While this does decrease power demand, the primary advantages of low voltage systems are that smaller size and cheaper direct burial wire can be used, saving installation time and expense. A low-voltage system is also user friendly downstream of the transformer becaues 12 volts does not represent a life threatening electrical shock. A low-voltage system may be the only viable way to add on to an existing circuit as six to ten lights can be gained with only 250 to 500 watts expended at the transformer.

Let's look at how electricity is supplied to an electrical panel, broken down into various circuits, and ultimately routed through (wire) to eventual users, conductors, or lighting fixtures.

Electricity is brought to a home or site by a utility company. This utility, following the dictates of the National Electrical Code (NEC), houses the electrical supply in an electrical panel. There is a main circuit breaker upstream of this panel, which can inactivate the panel by cutting off the power supply. Individual circuits within the panel each have a separately dedicated circuit breaker which cuts off power to that circuit only. (In older installations, glass-faced fuses were used as circuit breakers.) All electrical work downstream of the panel must also conform to the N.E.C. and any local governmental codes or restrictions, as well.

When examining an existing site for power supply there are two things which will give you an immediate insight into the age of an electrical installation. A service panel comprised primarily of fuses indicates an older installation, as does an electrical meter with four dials. Modern meters have five dials. Most meters will also have a face plate which indicates 120-volt (two-wire) or 240-volt (three-wire) service.

Electrical meters actually house a tiny electronic motor that drives the dials when power is being used. Whenever a dial is read and the arrow falls between two numbers, the lower number is always taken, even if the arrow is actually closer to the higher number. The readout on the meter gets subtracted by the previous readout and the resulting number indicates present kilowatt hours Aside from counting fuses and/or circuit breakers or looking at meter dials, the easiest way to determine a system's age is to add up the amperage capacity of all circuits. If the amps total less than 100, the odds are good the system is over 25 years old. Any total amperage that is obviously below what could be expected by applying the volts ÷ watts = amps formula to current usage can raise suspicion that the system is an older one.

Unlike steel wire discussed in Chapter 4, which gets physically larger as its numerical designation increases, electrical wire always decreases in size as the numerical designation increases. As discussed earlier, an ohm is a unit of measurement used in determining electrical resistance, and the larger a wire is (the smaller the number) the less ohms it will draw. Wire size and how the wire is insulated (covered) are very important safety factors since electrical resistance equates to energy loss which is given off as heat. Too many ohms in too small a wire will literally melt the insulation, resulting in a possible short circuit, a definite safety hazard, or in the worst case, a fire.

Electrical Wire and Cable

Wire, in reality, refers to just the metal conductor. This conductor, when combined with the outer sheath or insulation that houses the wire(s), is correctly called a cable. Wires are comprised of copper, copper-clad aluminum, or aluminum. Copper is a better conductor of electricity than aluminum, meaning that aluminum or aluminum-clad wire will always have to be a minimum of two size ratings larger than copper wire to carry an equal amount of electrical current at the same ohm capacity. For the purposes of this chapter, from here on, all references to wire shall be to copper wire. Following is a listing of wire sizes and their common uses.

Wire Size	Usage
2/0 1/0 2 4 6 8	Service entrance by utility companies. 240 -volt appliance circuits. Note that all wire in this size category is actually comprised of several smaller stranded wires.
10 12 14	120-Volt service. Doubled to supply 240-volt service. #12 and #10 used for direct burial hookup to low-voltage lighting systems. #14 is minimum size for interior lighting.
16 18	Very low-voltage hookups to doorbells, thermostats, time clocks, and internal wiring of very small appliances (e.g, radios).

Cables are identified by the number of internal wires they contain and the size of the wires. A #12-2 designation means two (2) #12 wires (hot plus neutral) with ground (G). There are four types of cable we will concern ourselves with, two of which we will frequently encounter in lighting design.

They are:

1. **Type NM:** Nonmetallic sheathed cable. Contains all three wires with the ground usually bare or colored green. Used in dry interior locations only. Usually used with solid wire sizes 10 through 18.
2. **Type UF:** Underground feeder cable. Contains all three wires within a solid plastic sheath. Cable lies flat for interior stapling. Must be routed in conduit on all exterior locations. Although not recommended, UF cable can be directly buried for underground uses. Underground conduit is a better way to go. Cable used for all conventional outdoor lighting fixtures. Most frequently houses solid wire sizes 10, 12, and 14.
3. **Type SE:** Service-entrance cable. Contains two 120-volt wires and one neutral wire. Within the service panel, this neutral ground potential wire becomes a true ground. Cable is rounded, hard plastic with an inner fiber layer. Sizes for SE wire range between 2/0 to 8. All wire within SE cable is stranded.
4. **Type AC or BX:** Armored cable. This is a flexible steel conduit used in the same manner as nonmetallic sheathed (NM) cable. AC or BX cable is used where accidents or damage to the internal wire could occur. The steel armor stands a far better chance of withstanding any anticipated abuse. Internal wire sizes are typically 10, 12, and 14 but can be larger in some cases. Whenever the cable is cut to expose internal wire, a fiber bushing is inserted that protects the wire from being cut by the edge of the cable.

Type NM and UF cable are frequently used in outdoor lighting design. You will encounter type BX on occasion and should not have anything to do with SE cable unless under the tutelage of a professional electrician. The only other wire that is frequently used in outdoor lighting design is stranded low voltage wire either in semihard PVC insulation or in flexible rubber insulation. While solid #10 or #12 wire is sometimes used, the stranded type is more flexible in its insulation and does not exhibit as much voltage drop.

Volts, like water pressure, drop as they pass through a line at a certain rate over a specified length. Voltage drop in a low-voltage circuit should never exceed 2 volts and is readily noticeable by dimming and yellowing of the lights at the end of the run. Voltage drop in conventional 120-volt lines should not exceed 5 volts. The NEC and several equipment manufacturers provide voltage drop charts in conjunction with wire types and sizes over a given distance. Most voltage drop problems in conventional systems can be solved by upsizing the electric supply wire. Voltage drop in low-voltage systems is chartable but a little less cut and dried. A general rule of thumb is that any run over 150 feet will prove to cause excessive voltage drop. Never allow a low-voltage system's aggregate wattage to exceed the design wattage of the system transformer. In irrigation design, where pressure loss is a problem, valves are placed in a manner to equally divide the length of pipe in the downstream hydrozone, thereby cutting potential pressure loss in half. Comparing this valve to the power source in a lighting circuit and knowing volts equate to pressure, we can apply the same principle to lighting design. If possible, split the wire run in two directions of equal or near equal length from the service panel or low voltage transformer. This will significantly lessen voltage drop. Most lighting designers cover their bases concerning voltage drop by incorporating in their project specifications that the lighting contractor verify line voltage drop to be within an adequate range and to notify the designer of any potential problems that could occur in this area.

Electronic Devices

On conventional lighting systems leading from any given circuit on a service panel electrical conductors (wire) housed in appropriate conduit connect to these electronic devices: switches, receptacles, junction boxes, and light fixtures.

Switches are devices that connect or disconnect the flow of electricity. There are two-way, three-way, and four-way switches. The designation comes from the number of screw terminals used to connect wiring at the switch body, not the number of locations (switches) from which a fixture can be operated. To clarify, a two-way switch is operated from one location; a three-way switch from two locations; and a four-way switch from three or more locations depending on intermediate wiring. Outdoor switches are located in waterproof boxes, either wall mounted or conduit riser mounted, at least 18 inches above grade. A dimmer switche has the capability to control the level of light within fixtures on its circuit from normal (100%) to dim (10%). Dimmers work best on incandescent lamps and offer a great deal of design flexibility in this type of circuit. In the category of a switch, but somewhat of a hybrid, are photocells. Photocells react to certain levels of daylight. When daylight levels are too low, the photocell trips a circuit on and will, conversely, trip a circuit off when ensuing daylight brightens. Photocells are a tremendous convenience over time clocks and recommended at least for all safety and security lighting. In areas that are unsightly or impractical to light all evening, but where security is desired, motion sensors have come to the fore. These devices detect motion and kick on a circuit for a preset time period and then shut down the circuit.

Receptacles are outlets for direct plug in of electric cords to operate various electronic devices. Receptacles are usually single or double outlet and occasionally triple outlet. Wall mounted receptacles are frequently joined together or ganged in line when more than three outlets are needed.

Junction boxes generally serve the same function as receptacles, except there is no external outlet on the face of the box. Electronic devices to receive service are hardwired to conductors and grounded inside the box. This is the best way to hook up electronic controllers and most conventional lighting fixtures. This is the only way to hook up underwater lighting fixtures. In fact, many outdoor lighting fixtures are set directly on top of junction boxes and connected by any number of conduit type fittings. Exterior junction boxes must be waterproof, and direct burial junction boxes must be even more so. NEC specifications, as always, must be met.

Light fixtures comprise a myriad of lighting devices. A partial list would include:

- Large area and parking lot downlights
- High street lights

- Medium-height mall lights
- Human-scale (±6 foot high) lights
- Ceiling or soffit lights
- Wall-mounted lights
- Bollards
- Uplights
- Well lights
- Underwater lights
- Low-voltage path lights
- Low-voltage step or strip lights

It is obvious that the lighting designer has a wide variety of lighting types to choose from. How light is defined and what types of lamps deliver certain types and qualities of illumination will be examined next.

Illumination and Lamps

All artificial and nighttime lighting is measured in foot candles. A foot candle is the amount of light from a lumen of lighting that falls on a square foot of surface area. A lumen is defined as the amount of light emitted from one standard candle measured at the candle. Listed below are examples of foot candle illumination:

- 1 foot candle = moonlight
- 2 to 4 foot candles = dim light
- 6 to 8 foot candles = medium light
- 3 to 5 foot candles = amount of light emitted from standard outdoor fixtures
- 5 foot candles = maximum garden light, provide by any one fixture
- 8+ foot candles = bright light
- 20 foot candles = maximum garden brightness provided by four or more fixtures
- 30 foot candles = reading light
- 50 to 70 foot candles = residential light
- 75 to 150 foot candles = office light

Lamp Type	Advantages	Disadvantages
Fluorescent	Consistent bright cool white glow; better lumen per watt ratio than incandescent; long-lived; good light for signage and wall illumination; frequently used for business and office lighting.	Primary usage is as an uplight; does not adapt to in-ground well light fixtures; very difficult light to apply dimmers to; poor color rendering.
High-pressure sodium	Longest-lived of all the light bulbs; yellowish light does not draw insects.	Yellowish light is not attractive; lamp is used primarily in commercial and safety/security applications;. poor quality color rendering.
Incandescent	The most inexpensive and common lamp available; light emitted is soft warm yellow-glowing variety; common household bulb; nice light for moonlighting effect; most lights now have a tungsten filament; older carbon filaments were much less efficient; good lamp for dimmers and low voltage applications.	Short lived; relative softness of light mutes graphic detail in items like signage; lowest lumen per watt ratio of all the lamps.
Quartz incandescent	Much more efficient than the tungsten filament conventional incandescent; brighter and whiter light than its cousin; better for illuminating detail items like house numbers and signage; good low voltage lamp; excellent color rendering.	Not as easily dimmable as other incandescents; relatively expensive.
Mercury vapor	Very energy efficient; very good light for street lighting and commercial areas.	Color rendering is not the best; gives off a bluish-green tint; longer-lived than incandescent but shorter than all others.
Metal halide	Very bright light that is greenish white in color.	Not as readily available as the other lamp types.

Do not confuse the foot candle rating of a light with your anticipated level of illumination. Remember, 1 foot candle covers 1 square foot. The fixture or fixtures have to be rated to cover the square footage of the area you want to light. The major difference between daytime and nighttime light is that daytime light is much brighter and will cast longer shadows in one direction at a given sun angle. Nighttime light illuminates a much smaller and more defined area, fades quickly once outside the boundaries of that area, and casts far shorter shadows in many directions. Color rendering in nighttime lighting changes in value, intensity, and hue. A color does not change to gray or white but remains what it is. The difference is that the level of reflected light changes how the color is perceived by the human eye.

The shape of the pattern of coverage for lights, especially downlight varieties, is much like that of irrigation spray heads on the ground or surface plane. The difference between the two patterns is that, while an irrigation head usually throws more water at the middle and outer periphery of its radius, a light bulb will always throw the most foot candles immediately adjacent to its fixture and the level of illumination will progressively fade as the light radiates out form its central source. The good news is that the lighting designer will not have to have head to head coverage to have a consistent level of illumination. An overthrow of 30 to 50% will usually represent fairly even coverage.

Lighting manufacturers, like irrigation equipment manufacturers, issue a plethora of equipment catalogues and supporting technical data. There are frequently available graphic gridded drawings called photometric charts which show a lamp's pattern of coverage and level of light intensity over a given surface area (the grid). Note that the light intensity always fades as its pattern of throw radiates further from the fixture. The lighting designer of a parking lot, for example, must determine what is the minimum level of acceptable light and then space his fixtures accordingly.

All the lamps, with the exception of the incandescent types, require a ballast which will physically increase the size of the fixture. Outdoor lighting fixtures can be fitted with any type of lamp listed in the chart above. Remember that just as you would not normally mix head types on any given irrigation hydrozone, you would not normally change lamp types on any given individual lighting circuit.

When selecting lamps, the lighting designer must weigh the owner's program and budget against such factors as levels of illumination, color rendering, and visual appeal. Sometimes a lamp that would not be the designers first choice, will become the obvious best choice because it meets the bulk of the design criteria. Once lamps for circuits are chosen, it is hard, from an electronic and cost standpoint, to switch out to another lamp type. A survey of installations will be helpful in determining how a lamp type performs in the field. Manufacturers and suppliers are more than willing to supply useful information. On larger or more important projects the lighting designer can often request an on-site evening demonstration of various lamp types. The earlier in the design process this nighttime mockup takes place, the more beneficial it will be to the overall lighting design process. Trial and error in lamp types is the best, if sometimes a brutal teacher.

Lighting Design

As with all forms of design, the lighting design process starts with a determination of what is needed and atttempts to arrive at a solution which will appropriately fulfill those needs. Budget allowing, any additions to the lighting design, beyond the base needs, is purely for aesthetic viewing and enhanced site usage. By varying the levels of brightness and type of fixtures within the lighting design, a hierarchy of importance can be established as well as variety and order. Here is a short list of the types of lighting effects that the lighting designer can draw from:

- Uplighting
- Downlighting
- Backlighting
- Moonlighting
- Accent or spot lighting
- Surface (grazing) lighting
- Circulation lighting
- Funnel lighting
- Underwater lighting

Uplighting: Very popular in high-end residential areas. Well lights with fixtures mounted at grade and lamps housed below grade are gaining in popularity as the fixture itself is not readily seen, especially during daylight hours. Of the aboveground uplights, fluorescent fixtures and the bullet type incandescent fixtures are the most popular. Uplighting is good for wall and sign illumination. Multitrunk trees or interesting tree canopies are presented well through the use of uplighting. In order for uplighting or any lighting, for that matter, to be most effective, it is better if the fixture is hidden from view as much as possible.

Downlighting: Creates good ground plane illumination. Downlighting depends on a stucture or pole to support the actual fixture. Downlighting also depends on a low subject. The closer the subject is to the fixture the more eye level glare will be created. Nothing in lighting design looks more artificial or is more visually annoying than glare. Downlighting is a good source for safety and security lighting especially in high use areas. Soffit- or lattice-mounted lights are efficient and relatively inexpensive.

Backlighting: Can be used to draw subtle attention to a background element. This form of lighting is also often employed to create silhouettes. The dark picturesque outline of a shrub or sculpture seen against a softly lit backdrop can be very appealing. Backlight is often used to illuminate signage and address numbers. Backlighting through stained glass, glass blocks, or translucent corian panels can provide breathtaking effects. The most important thing to remember when backlighting is that too much light will always be worse than not enough. The harsher the light source the more diminished in importance foreground elements become.

Moonlighting: A somewhat ambiguous term. The concept is to provide a light source that emulates the effect of a full moon. By definition this requires dim light. Because the effect is very natural, it is of utmost importance that the lamp cannot be seen. Moonlighting is most frequently employed when there are tall trees on site. Crossing the beams of lights mounted in a tree will create interesting shadow patterns on the ground plane; this is particularly true when there is a breeze present.

Accent or spotlighting: Really variations on the same thing — to light an interesting subject and forego surrounding elements.

Accent lighting usually applies to small-scale items. Spotlighting is used to draw attention to larger objects. The strength of this lighting concept lies in narrow beam focus and a dark, or less bright, surrounding area. The object lit, therefore, takes on primary importance within its immediate surroundings. In the design process, this form of lighting comes into play as site details become more important, and in areas where there is the time and setting to notice such things.

Surface or grazing light: Refers to a beam of light which falls across a plane element, usually a wall. Stone and brick textures are brought to life as the shadow patterns created form a rich texture. Glare will defeat this lighting concept every time. For this reason, softer lights of the incandescent types are recommended. A dimmer may add greatly to the success of grazing light because a 10% change in brightness may make a world of difference.

Circulation lighting: Not only provides safety but adds rhythm to a design. Driveway and path lights portray the essence of the circulation system. Level of illumination should reflect the level of importance of the path and respond to traveling speed of the user. When using circulation lighting it is of utmost importance to clearly define the beginning and the end of the route. Intermediate lighting should be so spaced as to allow the user to be reasonably confident that he is on the right path.

Funnel lighting: Sometimes referred to a vista or perspective lighting. This type of lighting leads the eye to a distant point. Changing the level of brightness as the lights travel away from the viewer can be quite dramatic. Strong light becoming progressively dimmer makes the distant object appear further away and subtle. Dim light becoming progressively brighter brings the object visually closer and can create a sense of awe. The thing to remember most, when applying this concept, is that the lighting fixtures should be of enough frequency and intensity to definitely funnel the viewer's eye to the object. With this type of lighting, it is acceptable to see the fixtures, since the light source is not as important as the object that the eye is encouraged to focus upon.

Underwater lighting: Can create soft consistent panels of ground plane light. In lakes with waterfalls, a few underwater uplights at the base of the falls can really highlight the cascading play of water in a manner that it is not usually seen. I always use dimmers with underwater lights, as lamps are not as easy to change out and different user moods at different times can be enhanced with the right level of illumination. The most common mistake found with underwater lighting is that fixtures are pointed in the direction of the viewer or towards the area from which the majority of viewing will occur. This causes light to shine directly at the viewer's eyes. For some reason, lighting designers forget that fixtures can be seen underwater. Pointing fixtures directly away from a residence, for example, will eliminate the typical hot spot at the fixture location and lead the eye out away from the house, allowing the property to appear larger.

Design Techniques

Different lighting techniques used in conjunction with varying levels of brilliance create a visual nighttime dance that has rhythm, line, and above all else, harmony. With lighting design, more than all other types of design, the quality of application is much more important than the quantity of application. A few lights properly directed will have more visual impact than several bright lights inappropriately and arbitrarily pointed into space.

A good base lighting design should have the inherent ability to accommodate festival and holiday lighting. The two should complement one another rather than compete for the viewer's attention. Lighting design for private use should always enhance, rather than distract, and should always be tasteful and possess a simple elegance.

When safety and security are an issue, the lighting should, indeed, provide these necessary functions and not just be an individual site token that drops the user into an immediate off-site pool of darkness. Efforts to coordinate security lighting between adjacent properties is to the benefit of all parties concerned and creates a real sense of neighborhood.

Safety lighting does not have to be dull and boring. For example, the strip step lights used to define risers are quite attractive. The deeper the lights are set under the tread the more soft and glowing the light becomes. Downlighting in entries and carports initially designed for safety serves double duty if it illuminates an interesting paving pattern.

Hopefully, more creativity will be used in outdoor fixture design. The Southwest affords the use of more natural materials. Clay bodies, pounded tin, and even glass block can be utilized in a wide array of local vernacular-type forms and patterns. With exposed fixtures, how the light is presented is almost as important as the illumination provided. Lighting design has been preoccupied with seeing and not with what is seen. A nice lighting scheme at night can be diluted by the presence of annoying unattractive fixtures seen during the day.

Sight is the most heavily relied upon sense people have. Lighting design works with this sense to evoke and create emotions. Light is one of the most powerful tools in the landscape architect's arsenal.

Working Drawings

Depicting lighting design is usually done in a looser fashion than in other design areas. This acknowledges the fact that there will be a need for more input and interpretation on the part of the installer.

Fixture location and the number of fixtures on any given circuit are shown easily enough. The routing of wire is usually another matter entirely.

Since it is extremely important that lights be directed onto their intended subjects, it is beneficial to show fixture locations on the planting plan. Most lighting designers will have a screened reproducible run of the planting plan before notes and other information are applied. This screened reproducible run prints lighter than the lighting line work. The lighting designer can show where the beam of light is to be directed by using arrows and other graphic conventions. All lights on one circuit are connected with a heavy curving line. As in irrigation design, where lines cross, one must hop over the other or break.

How and where circuits receive power is shown. This includes the type of switching and any related equipment such as dimmers or photocells. In low-voltage lighting, transformer locations must be shown.

The heart of lighting working drawings is the legends and/or schedules. On the legend the graphic symbols are assigned a definite meaning and the schedule provides information impossible to show graphically. A typical schedule will call out fixture type, lamp type and wattage, manufacturers's exact catalogue number, and any useful descriptions or remarks.

Similar to irrigation design, lighting details should show equipment assembly and how one piece of equipment relates to another. In no other area of landscape architectural design is good detailing and information about details so lacking as in the area of lighting design. Lighting equipment manufacturers are starting to take a cue from irrigation manufacturers and are beginning to provide standard details.

In any given set of working drawings, for any given project, the fact remains that the lighting details will be the weakest and fewest in number. What is needed is more importance placed on lighting details and some creativity applied towards incorporating catalogue cut sheets directly onto the lighting plans.

Until lighting details dramatically improve, lighting designers should rely heavily on the strength of the lighting specification. The language of this specification should always protect the health, safety, and welfare of the general public. It should also protect the professional career of the lighting designer. A landscape architect is unlikely to encounter another design area in which disaster could occur as quickly or with such finality, as in lighting design. Two notes to be included that are crucial are:

1. All work shall be in accordance with the latest version of the National Electrical Code (NEC) and applicable state and local codes, industry standards of workmanship, and manufacturer's instructions and specifications. All electrical equipment shall be Underwriters Laboratories (UL) approved and shall comply with all National Electrical Manufacturers Association (NEMA) standards.

2. The electrical contractor shall promptly notify the landscape architect and general contractor of any work outlined on the plans or specifications that is not in accordance with applicable laws, codes, and regulations. Without such notice and appropriate modifications by the landscape architect, the electrical contractor shall assume full responsibility for any work executed which is contrary to such laws, codes, and regulations.

As with any other type of specification, always give yourself an out. This is not to shirk responsibility, but rather to avoid inappropriate blame for circumstances beyond your control.

Refer to Chapter 8 for lighting field observation recommendations and a construction review schedule. Municipalities conduct several of their own electrical inspections, owing to the importance of the work. This should relieve you somewhat but not completely. In order to avoid catastrophe, always be conscientious in providing graphic clarity and an air tight specification. Also insist on qualified and reputable contractors. If you have doubts about a lighting contractor, it is better to sever yourself (in writing) from the field observation portion of the project rather than to stick it out and see your worst fears realized.

Lighting Techniques

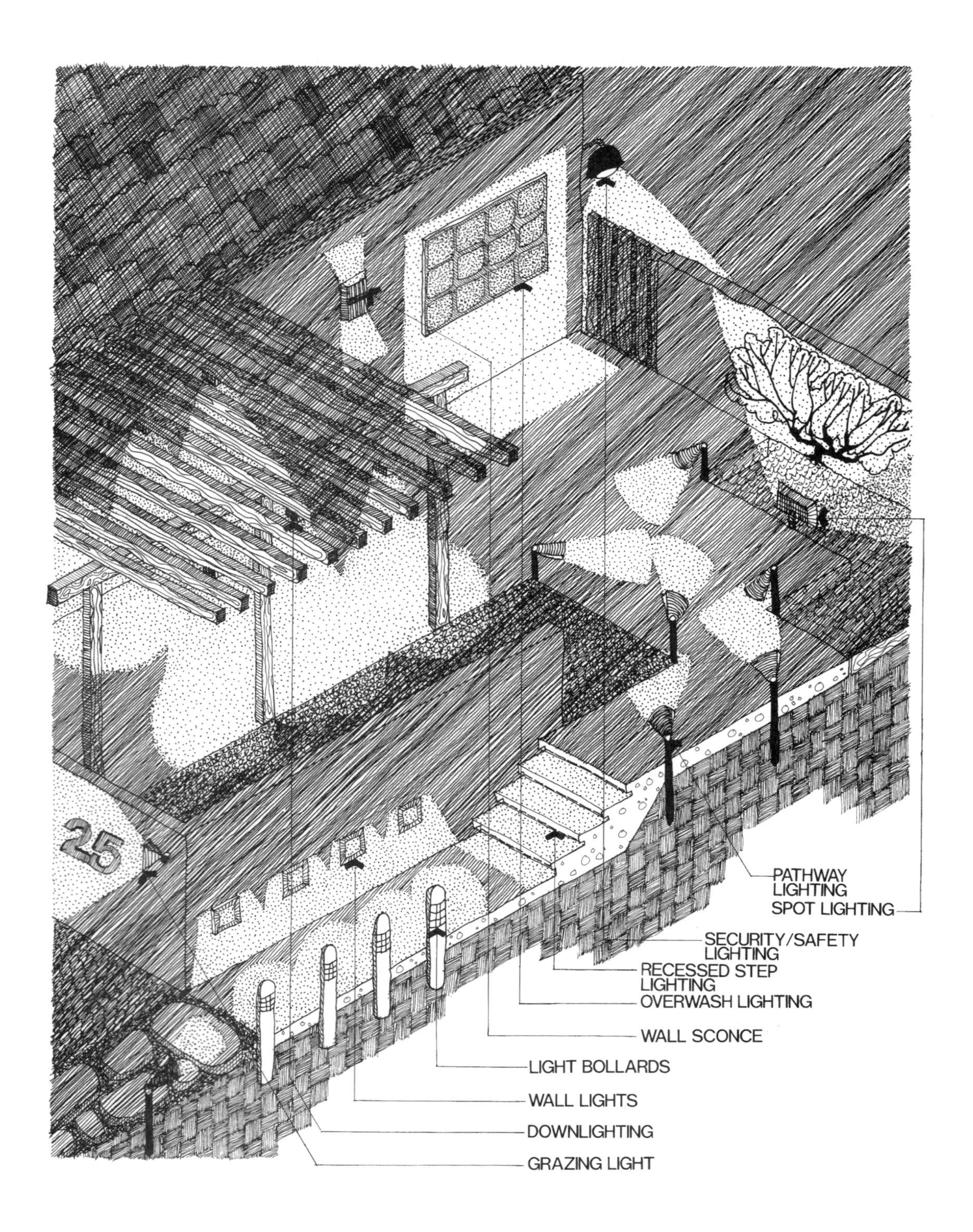

Lighting Techniques

CIRCULATION/PATH LIGHTING
WITH MINI-BOLLARDS
MOONLIGHTING
WITH BULLET TYPE DOWNLIGHTS
FLOODLIGHTING
WITH FLOURESCENT FIXTURE
SPOTLIGHTING
WITH LOW VOLTAGE HOODED ACCENT LIGHTING FIXTURE
UPLIGHTING
WITH WELL LIGHTS

Electrical Components

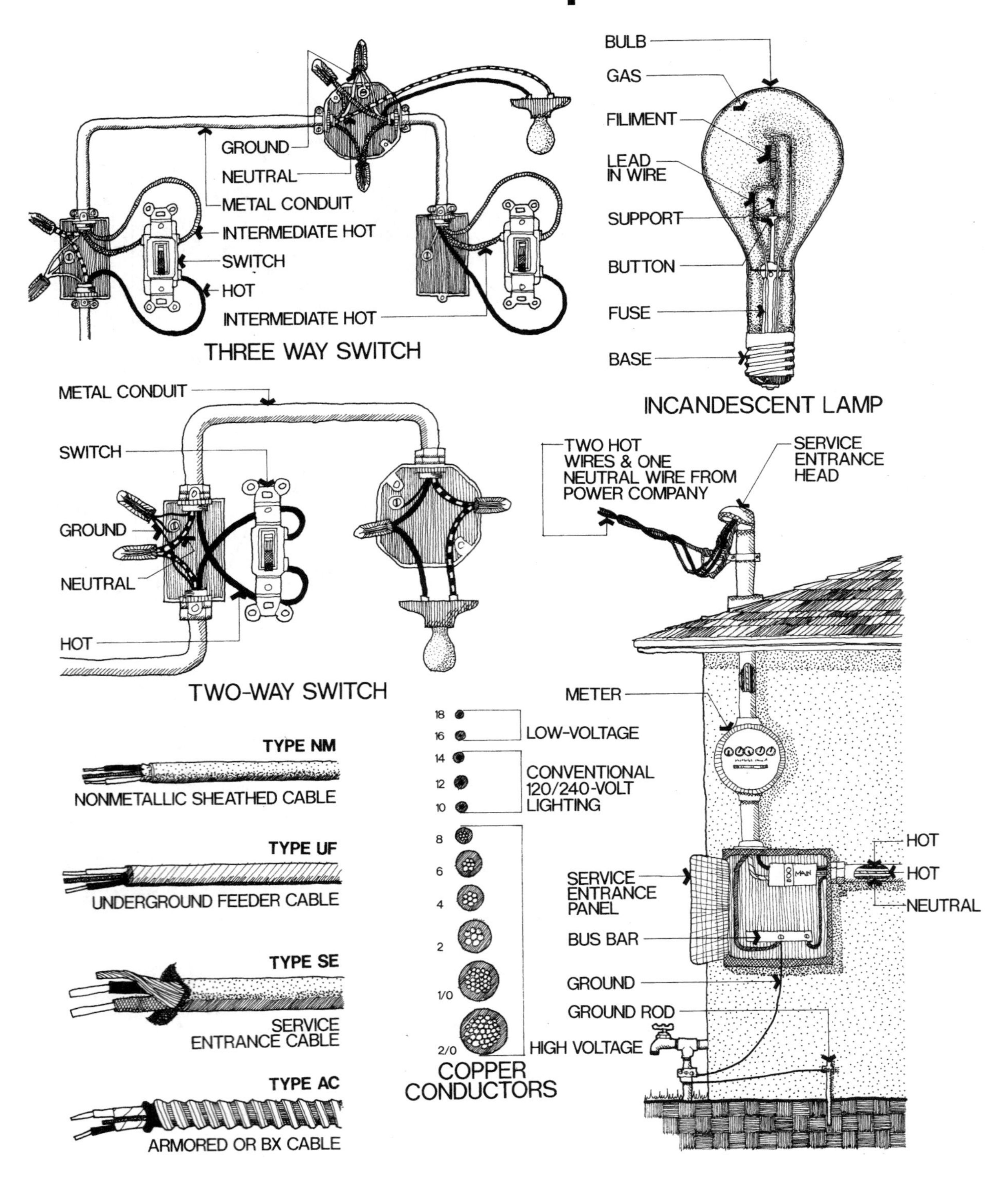

GROUND
NEUTRAL
METAL CONDUIT
INTERMEDIATE HOT
SWITCH
HOT
INTERMEDIATE HOT
THREE WAY SWITCH
BULB
GAS
FILIMENT
LEAD IN WIRE
SUPPORT
BUTTON
FUSE
BASE
INCANDESCENT LAMP
METAL CONDUIT
SWITCH
GROUND
NEUTRAL
HOT
TWO-WAY SWITCH
TWO HOT WIRES & ONE NEUTRAL WIRE FROM POWER COMPANY
SERVICE ENTRANCE HEAD
METER
TYPE NM
NONMETALLIC SHEATHED CABLE
TYPE UF
UNDERGROUND FEEDER CABLE
TYPE SE
SERVICE ENTRANCE CABLE
TYPE AC
ARMORED OR BX CABLE
18
16
LOW-VOLTAGE
14
12
10
CONVENTIONAL 120/240-VOLT LIGHTING
8
6
4
2
1/0
2/0
HIGH VOLTAGE
COPPER CONDUCTORS
SERVICE ENTRANCE PANEL
BUS BAR
GROUND
GROUND ROD
HOT
HOT
NEUTRAL

Lighting Details and Specifications

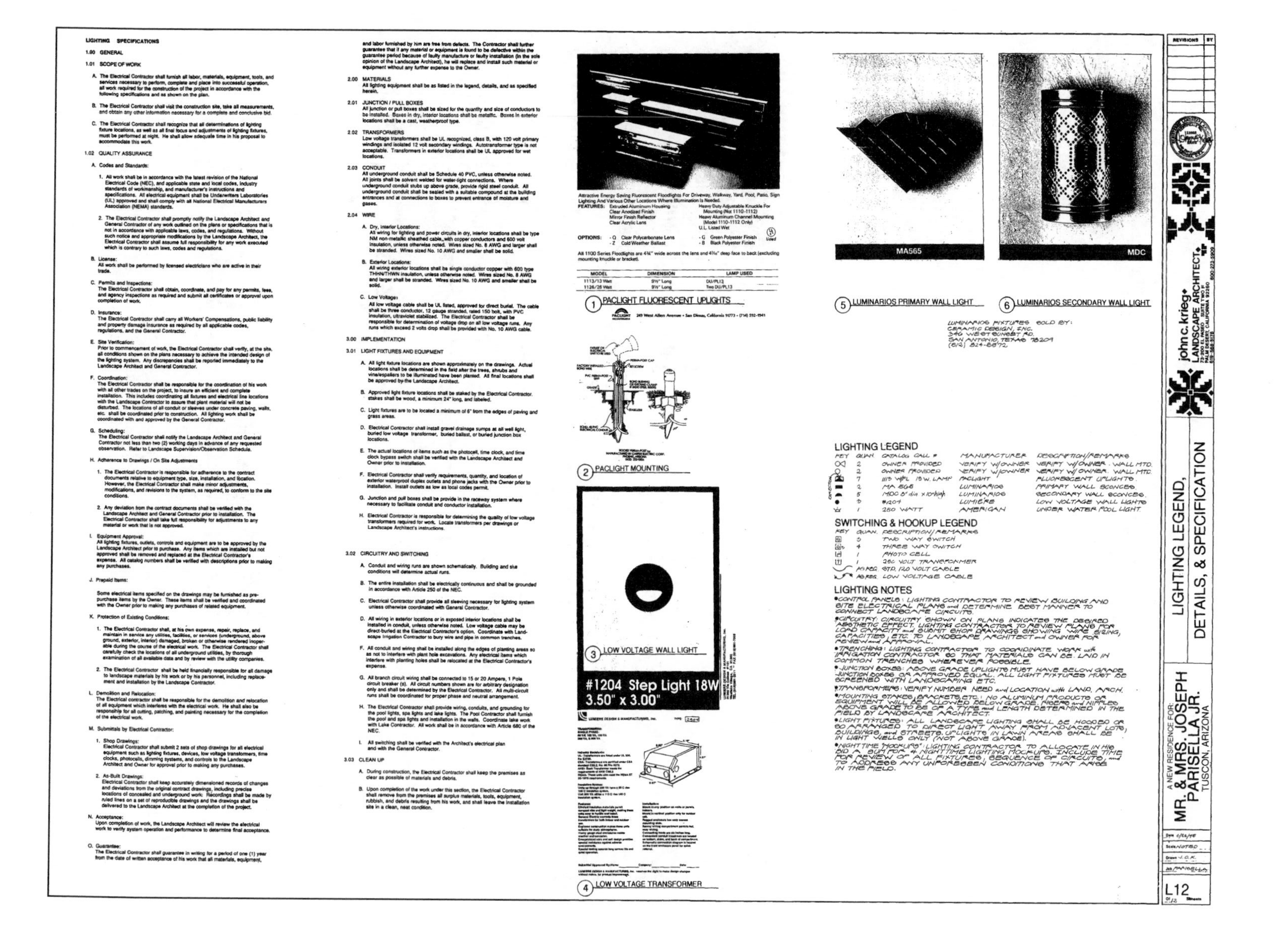

LIGHTING SPECIFICATIONS

1.00 GENERAL

1.01 SCOPE OF WORK

A. The Electrical Contractor shall furnish all labor, materials, equipment, tools, and services necessary to perform, complete and place into successful operation, all work required for the construction of the project in accordance with the following specifications and as shown on the plan.

B. The Electrical Contractor shall visit the construction site, take all measurements, and obtain any other information necessary for a complete and conclusive bid.

C. The Electrical Contractor shall recognize that all determinations of lighting fixture locations, as well as all final focus and adjustments of lighting fixtures, must be performed at night. He shall allow adequate time in his proposal to accommodate this work.

1.02 QUALITY ASSURANCE

A. Codes and Standards:

1. All work shall be in accordance with the latest revision of the National Electrical Code (NEC), and applicable state and local codes, industry standards of workmanship, and manufacturer's instructions and specifications. All electrical equipment shall be Underwriters Laboratories (UL) approved and shall comply with all National Electrical Manufacturers Association (NEMA) standards.

2. The Electrical Contractor shall promptly notify the Landscape Architect and General Contractor of any work outlined on the plans or specifications that is not in accordance with applicable laws, codes, and regulations. Without such notice and appropriate modifications by the Landscape Architect, the Electrical Contractor shall assume full responsibility for any work executed which is contrary to such laws, codes and regulations.

B. License:
All work shall be performed by licensed electricians who are active in their trade.

C. Permits and Inspections:
The Electrical Contractor shall obtain, coordinate, and pay for any permits, fees, and agency inspections as required and submit all certificates or approval upon completion of work.

D. Insurance:
The Electrical Contractor shall carry all Workers' Compensations, public liability and property damage insurance as required by all applicable codes, regulations, and the General Contractor.

E. Site Verification:
Prior to commencement of work, the Electrical Contractor shall verify, at the site, all conditions shown on the plans necessary to achieve the intended design of the lighting system. Any discrepancies shall be reported immediately to the Landscape Architect and General Contractor.

F. Coordination:
The Electrical Contractor shall be responsible for the coordination of his work with all other trades on the project, to insure an efficient and complete installation. This includes coordinating all fixtures and electrical line locations with the Landscape Contractor to assure that plant material will not be disturbed. The locations of all conduit or sleeves under concrete paving, walls, etc. shall be coordinated prior to construction. All lighting work shall be coordinated with and approved by the General Contractor.

G. Scheduling:
The Electrical Contractor shall notify the Landscape Architect and General Contractor not less than two (2) working days in advance of any requested observation. Refer to Landscape Supervision/Observation Schedule.

H. Adherence to Drawings / On Site Adjustments

1. The Electrical Contractor is responsible for adherence to the contract documents relative to equipment type, size, installation, and location. However, the Electrical Contractor shall make minor adjustments, modifications, and revisions to the system, as required, to conform to the site conditions.

2. Any deviation from the contract documents shall be verified with the Landscape Architect and General Contractor prior to installation. The Electrical Contractor shall take full responsibility for adjustments to any material or work that is not approved.

I. Equipment Approval:
All lighting fixtures, outlets, controls and equipment are to be approved by the Landscape Architect prior to purchase. Any items which are installed but not approved shall be removed and replaced at the Electrical Contractor's expense. All catalog numbers shall be verified with descriptions prior to making any purchases.

J. Prepaid Items:

Some electrical items specified on the drawings may be furnished as pre-purchase items by the Owner. These items shall be verified and coordinated with the Owner prior to making any purchases of related equipment.

K. Protection of Existing Conditions:

1. The Electrical Contractor shall, at his own expense, repair, replace, and maintain in service any utilities, facilities, or services (underground, above ground, exterior, interior) damaged, broken or otherwise rendered inoperable during the course of the electrical work. The Electrical Contractor shall carefully check the locations of all underground utilities, by thorough examination of all available data and by review with the utility companies.

2. The Electrical Contractor shall be held financially responsible for all damage to landscape materials by his work or by his personnel, including replacement and installation by the Landscape Contractor.

L. Demolition and Relocation:
The Electrical contractor shall be responsible for the demolition and relocation of all equipment which interferes with the electrical work. He shall also be responsible for all cutting, patching, and painting necessary for the completion of the electrical work.

M. Submittals by Electrical Contractor:

1. Shop Drawings:
Electrical Contractor shall submit 2 sets of shop drawings for all electrical equipment such as lighting fixtures, devices, low voltage transformers, time clocks, photocells, dimming systems, and controls to the Landscape Architect and Owner for approval prior to making any purchases.

2. As-Built Drawings:
Electrical Contractor shall keep accurately dimensioned records of changes and deviations from the original contract drawings, including precise locations of concealed and underground work. Recordings shall be made by ruled lines on a set of reproducible drawings and the drawings shall be delivered to the Landscape Architect at the completion of the project.

N. Acceptance:
Upon completion of work, the Landscape Architect will review the electrical work to verify system operation and performance to determine final acceptance.

O. Guarantee:
The Electrical Contractor shall guarantee in writing for a period of one (1) year from the date of written acceptance of his work that all materials, equipment, and labor furnished by him are free from defects. The Contractor shall further guarantee that if any material or equipment is found to be defective within the guarantee period because of faulty manufacture or faulty installation (in the sole opinion of the Landscape Architect), he will replace and install such material or equipment without any further expense to the Owner.

2.00 MATERIALS
All lighting equipment shall be as listed in the legend, details, and as specified herein.

2.01 JUNCTION / PULL BOXES
All junction or pull boxes shall be sized for the quantity and size of conductors to be installed. Boxes in dry, interior locations shall be metallic. Boxes in exterior locations shall be a cast, weatherproof type.

2.02 TRANSFORMERS
Low voltage transformers shall be UL recognized, class B, with 120 volt primary windings and isolated 12 volt secondary windings. Autotransformer type is not acceptable. Transformers in exterior locations shall be UL approved for wet locations.

2.03 CONDUIT
All underground conduit shall be Schedule 40 PVC, unless otherwise noted. All joints shall be solvent welded for water-tight connections. Where underground conduit stubs up above grade, provide rigid steel conduit. All underground conduit shall be sealed with a suitable compound at the building entrances and at connections to boxes to prevent entrance of moisture and gases.

2.04 WIRE

A. Dry, Interior Locations:
All wiring for lighting and power circuits in dry, interior locations shall be type NM non-metallic sheathed cable, with copper conductors and 600 volt insulation, unless otherwise noted. Wires sized No. 8 AWG and larger shall be stranded. Wires sized No. 10 AWG and smaller shall be solid.

B. Exterior Locations:
All wiring exterior locations shall be single conductor copper with 600 type THHN/THWN insulation, unless otherwise noted. Wires sized No. 8 AWG and larger shall be stranded. Wires sized No. 10 AWG and smaller shall be solid.

C. Low Voltage:
All low voltage cable shall be UL listed, approved for direct burial. The cable shall be three conductor, 12 gauge stranded, rated 150 bolt, with PVC insulation, ultraviolet stabilized. The Electrical Contractor shall be responsible for determination of voltage drop on all low voltage runs. Any runs which exceed 2 volts drop shall be provided with No. 10 AWG cable.

3.00 IMPLEMENTATION

3.01 LIGHT FIXTURES AND EQUIPMENT

A. All light fixture locations are shown approximately on the drawings. Actual locations shall be determined in the field after the trees, shrubs and vine/espaliers to be illuminated have been planted. All final locations shall be approved by the Landscape Architect.

B. Approved light fixture locations shall be staked by the Electrical Contractor. stakes shall be wood, a minimum 24" long, and labeled.

C. Light fixtures are to be located a minimum of 6" from the edges of paving and grass areas.

D. Electrical Contractor shall install gravel drainage sumps at all well light, buried low voltage transformer, buried ballast, or buried junction box locations.

E. The actual locations of items such as the photocell, time clock, and time clock bypass switch shall be verified with the Landscape Architect and Owner prior to installation.

F. Electrical Contractor shall verify requirements, quantity, and location of exterior waterproof duplex outlets and phone jacks with the Owner prior to installation. Install outlets as low as local codes permit.

G. Junction and pull boxes shall be provide in the raceway system where necessary to facilitate conduit and conductor installation.

H. Electrical Contractor is responsible for determining the quality of low voltage transformers required for work. Locate transformers per drawings or Landscape Architect's instructions.

3.02 CIRCUITRY AND SWITCHING

A. Conduit and wiring runs are shown schematically. Building and site conditions will determine actual runs.

B. The entire installation shall be electrically continuous and shall be grounded in accordance with Article 250 of the NEC.

C. Electrical Contractor shall provide all sleeving necessary for lighting system unless otherwise coordinated with General Contractor.

D. All wiring in exterior locations or in exposed interior locations shall be installed in conduit, unless otherwise noted. Low voltage cable may be direct-buried at the Electrical Contractor's option. Coordinate with Landscape Irrigation Contractor to bury wire and pipe in common trenches.

F. All conduit and wiring shall be installed along the edges of planting areas so as not to interfere with plant hole excavations. Any electrical items which interfere with planting holes shall be relocated at the Electrical Contractor's expense.

G. All branch circuit wiring shall be connected to 15 or 20 Ampere, 1 Pole circuit breaker (s). All circuit numbers shown are for arbitrary designation only and shall be determined by the Electrical Contractor. All multi-circuit runs shall be coordinated for proper phase and neutral arrangement.

H. The Electrical Contractor shall provide wiring, conduits, and grounding for the pool lights, spa lights and lake lights. The Pool Contractor shall furnish the pool and spa lights and installation in the walls. Coordinate lake work with Lake Contractor. All work shall be in accordance with Article 680 of the NEC.

I. All switching shall be verified with the Architect's electrical plan and with the General Contractor.

3.03 CLEAN UP

A. During construction, the Electrical Contractor shall keep the premises as clear as possible of materials and debris.

B. Upon completion of the work under this section, the Electrical Contractor shall remove from the premises all surplus materials, tools, equipment, rubbish, and debris resulting from his work, and shall leave the installation site in a clean, neat condition.

Lighting Plan

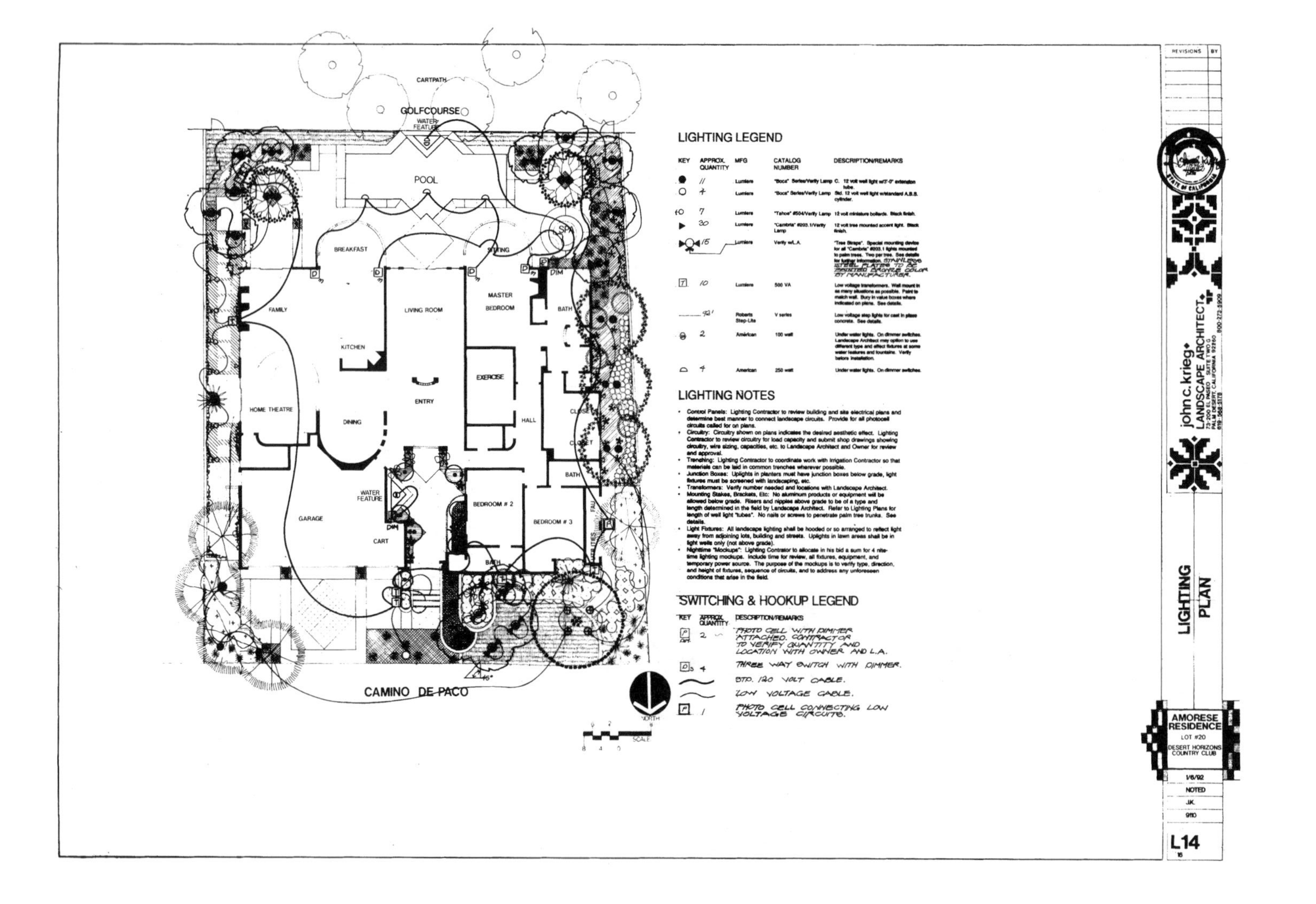

Moonlighting and Uplighting

Installed Lighting Techniques

Uplit tree

Down lighting

Mini bollard

Backlit glass block

Glossary

Alternating current: Electric current that constantly changes directions as it flows through a wire. This happens instantaneously, and every two reversals in direction is termed a cycle.

Ampere: Measurement of the flow of electrical current.

Ballast: Device that controls the flow of electrical current into gaseous lamps. Housed within the light fixture, ballasts are required on fluorescent, metal halide, sodium, and mercury vapor lamps.

Cable: Two or more electrical wires housed within a common insulated sheathing are collectively called a cable.

Circuit: The path electrical current takes as it leaves a source and travels through various switches, receptacles, lights and/or appliances before returning back to the source.

Conductor: Electrical wire which carries electrical current. In a broader sense, anything capable of transporting electrical current.

Cycle: Term interchangeable with hertz. See alternating current.

Direct current: Electric current that is capable of flowing in only one direction.

Electrical contractor: An individual who by education, experience, and state licensing is deemed knowledgeable, capable, and is legally permitted to perform electrical hookups and connections as well as route wiring and install fixtures.

Fixture: As it applies to this chapter, the entire unit that houses a light bulb or lamp.

Fluorescent lamp: Lamp which creates light from a mixture of heated gases which act upon a white coating on the inside glass of the bulb. Most energy efficient lamp.

Foot candle: Measurement of the level of illumination created by a light. The term derives from the amount of light generated by a lighted candle held 1-foot away from a 1-square foot surface.

Glare: Looking directly into very bright light.

Grounded: Giving electrical current a path to the ground. This is safety requirement as a system short or wire break would pass to the ground instead of to a downstream user. Ground wires are always green or bare.

Hertz: Term interchangeable with cycle. See alternating current.

Hot spot: A light fixture placed so close to the subject to be lighted that glare occurs on the subject in a confined and unattractive area.

Illumination: A source of light. A measurable amount of light.

Incandescent: A lamp which creates light when electrical current heats a filament which glows. Most common type of lamp. Emits a soft yellow glow.

Junction box: A closed box where electrical wire connections are housed.

Kilowatt: 1000 watts of electricity.

Kilowatt hour: 1000 wats of electricity being used over a 1 hour period. Most electric companies bill based on this unit of measurement.

Lamp: Light bulb comprised of glass housing, metal connector, interior gases, and any filaments. The contents of a lamp, when excited by electricity, produce light.

Low voltage: Typically, lights of 12 or 24 volts. Low-voltage systems require a transformer to reduce standard 120-volt current to the lower current requirement.

Lumen: Similar to a foot candle, a lumen is a measure of light taken at the light source, and is equal to 1 candle of light at that point.

Mercury vapor lamp: Lamps that produce high intensity bluish-green light from radiated mercury vapor excited by electicity.

Metal halide lamp: Lamp containing metal compounds which radiate high intensity grenish-white light. Very bright light.

National Electric Code (NEC): Protects health, safety, and welfare of the general public by establishing rules and standards governing electrical appliances, fixtures, methods of installation and workmanship. The code most adopted by municipalities. Revised every 3 years.

National Electrical Manufacturers Association (NEMA): Sets product and safety standards for appliances and fixtures.

Ohm: Measurement of electrical current resistance within a wire or appliance. Ohms determine wire sizes.

Receptacle: Also called an outlet. Device that accepts a plug and supplies electricity to the downstream appliance or fixture.

Service panel: Box where electricity supplied from the utility company is connected to circuits dedicated to be used to supply the building or project needs. Often called the house panel. Main circuit breakers and fuses are also located here.

Sodium lamp: A lamp in which light is created by housing sodium vapor under high pressure. Electricity excites the sodium which emits a noticeable yellow glow. Cost-effective lamp used frequently for security lighting.

Switch: A device that either interrupts electrical current or allows it to flow.

Three-wire service: Two 120-volt wires and one neutral or ground wire.

Transformer: Reduces (transforms) 120 volt current to 12 or 24 volts for use in low voltage lighting systems.

Two-wire service: One 120-volt wire and one neutral or ground wire.

Underwriters Laboratories (UL): Does the majority of testing of electrical appliances and fixtures and sets minimum acceptable performance standards. Most electrical products must be UL approved to be insurable.

Volt: Unit of electrical pressure.

Watt: Unit used to measure electrical power. Expressed in the formula volts × amperes = watts used.

Chapter 8

Installation and Maintenance

Tree pruning using handcutters

Introduction

In order for any landscape design to be considered a success, the quality of the installation and the maintenance that follows must be of a high level and inextricably linked. A good installation can get the plant material established, the irrigation system up and running, and provide all other features and systems in good working order. It is the maintenance contractor, however, who will inherit the job and be responsible for its ongoing prosperity or ultimate failure.

The Maintenance Program

Good maintenance is the lifeblood of a landscape design. When the drawings start to yellow and age, after the installer has left the job site for good, subsequent to the grandest of Grand Openings — the job remains. The project falls into the lap of the maintenance contractor or the owner's maintenance staff. This is when the trouble usually starts and the finger-pointing begins. The maintenance contractor blames the landscape contractor, the landscape contractor blames the landscape architect, the landscape architect blames the owner, and the owner blames everyone. Obviously this is not going to further the careers or emotional stability of any of the parties concerned. Let us look at some of the reasons for project failure:

- Initial program was too ambitious. Scope of project was beyond the capabilities of the budget to deliver the desired end product.
- Initial program was vague and undefined. Owner was either unwilling or unable to comment on merits of the schematic and/or preliminary design.
- Design deviates from established program. The landscape architect becomes so carried away with his design that components are added that were not a part of the initial program.
- Installation is downsized or intentionally cheapened either with the owner's knowledge or as a part of the installer's cost-cutting measures.
- Project maintenance is poorly performed. Overall "look" of the project suffers or parts or sections of planting design are intentionally removed.

Initial programming revolves around project leadership and product knowledge. Not every owner is a dynamic leader, but if they are knowledgeable about what they want and what they need, a program can be established. Sometimes an owner is an absolute tyrant, while his level of project knowledge leaves something to be desired. This is the very worst set of circumstances that, if they **can** be handled, are best handled with tact and frequent written documentation. Frequently the owner looks to the landscape architect for leadership. This is fine if the landscape architect accepts the challenge, and the owner is somewhat wiling to let go of the reins. Project knowledge can be gained with dedicated research and the ability to ask the right questions. Project leadership is another issue. It would behoove all parties concerned to remember that in order for one to lead, the others must be willing to follow. Early on in the process, it is important for the landscape architect to identify the project leadership or to step forward and become the leader. An inability to do this results in chaos, and chaos breeds ineffective programs.

Even with defined programs, designs frequently digress, due to preconceptions about, or disagreement with, the project's direction. Owners frequently complain that designers, in general, do not listen, do not know or care about costs, and often ignore even a written program. Unfortunately, this is true much of the time. It is important for designers to remember that even though they may be involved in several projects a year, most owners have only one project, and often it represents the crowning achievement of their careers. Even if the designer feels he is adding an improvement to the final product, owners who get something they do not want or who do not understand what they do get are likely to view the project as a disaster.

State laws bind landscape architects to the laws of fiduciary. Simply put, this means the landscape architect usually acts as an agent to the owner (whom he contracts with) and as such, puts the owner's wishes ahead of all others including his own. The only way to end a fiduciary relationship logically and legally is to terminate the contract.

Often the landscape contractor is required to change and downsize the project in order to meet cost restraints. If this is done with the owner's knowledge and is agreeable to both parties, then the resulting installation would have to be acceptable. If this is done without the owner's knowledge then a dispute is likely to occur. The final outcome of this dispute may have to be decided in a court of law. Sometimes, in the real world, it is easy to see that an owner is squeezing a contractor or that a contractor is cutting corners. While this is unfortunate, it is beyond the landscape architect's control. A fiduciary relationship lies with the party who holds the contract. It is up to the landscape architect to represent the owner, not necessarily to agree with his tactics. This representation requires a determination as to the quality of the installation and as to whether all items called for were, indeed, installed. Getting caught up in personal battles, personality conflicts, and issues of fairness has nothing to do with the facts. Either the installation meets the drawing, detail, and specification requirements or it does not. This is all that needs to be commented upon.

Finally, the maintenance contractor inherits the job. A poor maintenance contractor can make a good installation look bad very quickly. A good maintenance contractor can make a poor installation look good, but never great. Suffice it to say that a good installation is mandatory in order to establish a solid base to work from. Whether that base improves, stays the same, or declines will be dependent on the quality of the project maintenance. Installers often get better treatment and payment than maintenance people. This derives from two common misconceptions. First, it is felt that a higher level of expertise is required to install the project. This is simply not true. In fact, a truly knowledgeable maintenance man is probably one of the most intelligent individuals in the industry. Second, owners are product delivery conscious. They recognize a roof, wall, or pavement. These elements, when installed correctly, can last 10 years or longer before any real maintenance or upkeep may be required. Owners pay for these items and, for the time being, forget about them. Plants are living, growing organisms in a constant state of change. Irrigation systems demand consistent troubleshooting to work properly. These products are delivered, but cannot be forgotten about at any time. Most owners breathe a sigh of relief when a punch list is completed. They feel that their major expenses are over, and indeed, inside the building walls, this is true for the short term. Maintenance of the exterior is required immediately, however, and often an owner is not aware of, or prepared to, incur this expense. What happens frequently is that the maintenance budget is very low, and service conforms to the old adage, "You get what you pay for." Some of these unfortunate occurrences can be avoided if landscape architects can do a better job of informing owners early in the design process that maintenance costs will be ongoing and can be substantial. As a rule of thumb, the first year's maintenance costs can be 10% of the overall exterior installation cost, and at least

5% in each successive year. This can be startling news to someone who thinks his expenses end at project occupancy. An owner has the right to know the facts and make an informed decision whether to tone down the installation to cover a percentage of maintenance expenses or to find a way to budget for these expenses. He can do neither if he has no idea what these expenses will be.

Installation Costs

Installation costs are directly impacted by the following:

1. Quantity of items
2. Size of items
3. Complexity of installation
4. Installer unfamiliar with items or method of installation
5. Unavailability of materials
6. Work load of installer
7. Current economic conditions

1. Quantity of items could mean anything from the number of a certain plant type in a specific container size to the overall square footage of slate decking. The point is, each item has what is referred to as a *unit cost*. While discounts may be given for bulk orders, two units will always cost more than one, and three more than two, and so on. The more of anything, the higher the costs.

2. Size of items due to bulk, weight, or longevity of life (trees) will increase as they get larger. The only exception to this would be mature agricultural trees that are difficult to harvest or are considered to be in a state of decline. Take, for example, this schedule of container plant prices at 1996 approximate figures:

Container	Price	Container	Price
1 gallon	$ 7.00	36" box	$ 550.00
5 gallon	18.00	42" box	975.00
15 gallon	100.00	48" box	1,200.00
24" box	275.00	60" box	1,800.00

These are installed prices and, as you can see, each jump in container size has a corresponding quantum leap in actual cost. Downsizing a project refers to choosing to go to a lower container size. If the plant material is healthy, the installation good, the intent and integrity of the irrigation system left intact, and the maintenance reliable, then downsizing to meet budget constraints is not necessarily a bad thing. It depends on how long an owner is willing to wait to achieve mature growth. Downsizing can refer to hardscape items as well. The term applies more to reducing area square footages, heights of walls, or depths and widths of water features.

Do not confuse downsizing with downgrading, which is another matter entirely and can really hurt a job. Changes of materials or going to cheaper stock items (e.g., inferior pipe class or from brass to plastic irrigation valves) may bring the project within budget, but will also increase maintenance costs and shorten the life of the job.

3. Complexity of installation refers to the difficulty encountered in building site features or in accessing areas of the site. Any work beyond the scope of what is normally performed can be considered complex.

4. Installer unfamiliar with items or method of installation is closely related to project complexity, but is not exactly the same thing. The major difference is that a product or building system that is new is not necessarily complex. In fact, most new technology strives for a level of simplicity. The similarity lies in the way a complex system and a new system are viewed by a bidder. Unfamiliarity with the product creates what is called a "fear factor," and this will usually raise costs. This should not preclude the use of new materials but rather necessitates a good explanation of the product or design approach and the ample distribution of any technical or support information.

5. Unavailability of materials, especially plant materials, can be a project killer. Sometimes the unavailability is due to a shortage but, more frequently, it occurs as a unacceptable delay in material delivery. With plant material, a grower's contract to assure availability can be called for, but if the owner is unwilling to front the contractor the money for a down payment to the grower then the chances of this occurring are slim. The same can be said for materials. Suppliers will not ship materials without some down payment or good faith money. Problems with unavailability also occur due to indecision. Interior designers, in particular, will often not commit to a decision on a material (e.g., pavement) until the structure is up out of the ground or worse yet, finished. This does not allow enough time for ordering quality specialty material when the remaining time to finish construction is 3 months or less. Unavailability caused by a lack of knowledge concerning local grower and supplier conditions is the fault of the landscape architect. Unavailability due to lack of project coordination, unwillingness to release minimal funds, or indecision is the fault of human fragilities and inflated egos in which no one benefits and the project unduly suffers.

6. Work load of the installer will affect his bid. It is a well-known fact that hungry contractors will bid a project tighter. A busy contractor is much more likely to submit a high bid, not really needing the job and considering it to be gravy if he gets it. This is not unethical but rather a reflection of market conditions. Contractors are frequently subjected to a bidding process that amounts to little more than a crapshoot and are expected to honor their bid and perform even when they have obviously underbid and are suffering economic distress because of it. Who is to say a high bid is unfair? Business revolves around the concept of "let the buyer beware." If a high bidder performs, all that has happpened is that he got paid more than what someone else wanted — nothing more. The buyer received the desired end product and that is the bottom line.

7. Examining current economic conditions is similar to analyzing a specific contractor's work load. It differs in that an average or mean condition is likely to exist. That is, the majority of the bids are usually quite close or fall within a close range of one another. In a tight economy, expect lower and more competitive bidding. While this is logical enough and not of much significance on small-sized projects, it can have a major impact on larger developments. Knowing the construction market is a leading (as in first to be affected) economic indicator, a wise developer can often save major sums just by having a sense of good timing.

When cost is a concern (and when is it not?) remember these ten axioms:

1. Costs increase if the site has import and/or export soil. Import soil, in particular, is expensive as the cost is for transportation plus material, not just transportation.
2. Costs increase as the underground drainage system becomes more elaborate.
3. Costs increase if earth needs to be retained by retaining walls.
4. Costs increase with each successive increase in plant size. Box trees, in particular, become dramatically more expensive with each increase in size.
5. Costs increase with additional irrigation equipment. Cost of hardline emitter systems is more expensive than a conventional system as there are more heads in the drip system and costs are based on a per unit (head) basis.
6. Costs increase with additional square footage of any specific type of hardscape or walls. The same applies for additional square footgage of sod.
7. Costs increase with more cubic footage of water features.
8. Costs increase with detail quantity (in the set of drawings), complexity, and unfamiliarity. Any detail the contractor has not previously installed can create a fear factor.
9. Costs increase with sculpture and any other form of fine art.
10. Costs increase with poor project leadership and with any lack of coordination between various building trades.

As experience is gained on certain types of projects, a broad-scale rule of thumb can be applied to new projects by reviewing completed ones and dividing final costs by landscape or hardscape square footage.

Here is a rough breakdown of cost in 1997:

Installation Costs/Unit Prices

Price/Sq.Ft.	Item
$ 0.10	Hydroseeded turf
0.25	Native seed mix
0.70	Decomposed granite
0.55	Sod
1.00	Salt River stone
1.00	Seeded turf with irrigation
1.75	Sod with irrigation
1.50	Decomposed granite with irrigation and small plant materials
2.00	Minimum cost large areas (+500 sq.ft.) of concrete
2.50	Decent, small scale, landscape/irrigation installation with small plant material
3.50	Good landscape/irrigation installation with moderately sized plant material
6.00	Great landscape/irrigation installation with large plant materials
10.00	Great landscape/irrigation installation with moderate plant materials, hardscape, and simple water features

It is recommended that the $1.00, $2.50, $3.50, $6.00, and $10.00 installation figures only be applied to areas larger than 5000 square feet. A point of diminishing returns is reached when trying to apply a rule of thumb figure to a small area. Also, on landscape areas over one acre (43,560 sq. ft.) these numbers begin to decrease.

Installation Techniques

In Chapter 2, in the discussion about project specifications, it was stated that most project specifications are performance specifications. This is important to note, as the language and intent of a specification begin to rise in stature the closer a project is to completion. A performance specification does not tell a contractor how to do his job, but rather what is expected as the final result of his workmanship. This is the essence of a landscape architect's field observation input — to assure the final outcome of the project reflects the design intent.

A landscape architect is involved in installation techniques when he assures that:

1. Site is properly prepared and ready for respective subcontracting trades to begin their segment of the overall installation.
2. Materials are accounted for, delivered to the site, properly handled, and correctly installed.
3. Workmanship conforms to an acceptable level of quality.
4. Punch list items are picked up. Installation portion of project is closed out. Smooth transition of project responsibility occurs from installer(s) to maintenance contractor(s).

Site preparation depends on one key factor — coordination and cooperation between the general contractor and project subcontractors and between all subcontractors. The best way to see if this is going to occur is to call for a preconstruction conference involving all affected parties once their identities are known. The purpose of the preconstruction conference is to discuss project approach, time schedules, and construction sequence. A review of the plans, details, and specifications is warranted and beneficial with all parties present. Any questions and concerns can be addressed at this time and potential problem areas can be identified. This seems like a very simple procedure and, indeed, it should be. It is amazing, however, that this preconstruction conference is often ignored.

The result is that the project proceeds haphazardly until the date of final completion approaches. Then the majority of subcontractors are brought onto the site in unison. No subcontractor has satisfactory site preparation. They scurry about bumping into each other, arguing about who is supposed to do what first and that one cannot get started until the other finishes. No one gets hurt worse than the landscape contractor. If he takes the lead and installs plant material, it seems that stucco men and painters make it their sole objective in life to step on every plug of ground cover and see to it that no tree well is spared having excess paint and cleaning water dumped into it. Paint kills trees — it's that simple. Believe me, I have seen it time and time again; if the painters are not finished, you are asking for trouble if you commence with planting operations. Salt from salt-finished concrete washed into planting beds will also wreck havoc with plants.

The biggest problem in project coordination is in the area of grade preparation (alluded to earlier in Chapter 3). Even when properly documented by design consultants and comprehended by the general contractor, it usually falls on the shoulders of the landscape contractor. Here again, the landscape contractor takes a beating. It is impossible to install the job correctly with no established base or rough grade to work from. This means is that he will either be forced to do the grading himself or ignore the landscape architect's plans. This is one of the biggest issues to iron out and document, in writing, to the project owner at a preconstruction conference.

Site preparation can also include such things as determining construction access onto the site, arranging for a materials stockpiling yard, or procuring a temporary water meter. Other items which appear minor, such as sleeves for irrigation lines and electrical conduit, fall under the category of site preparation. While an easy enough thing to do before pavement is installed, it is a major undertaking afterwards.

Materials delivery is dependent on accurate scheduling. The closer material is delivered to the actual time of installation the less the chances of damage, vandalism, and theft. A fenced and locked materials yard is a real asset, especially on larger projects. Such a yard does not, however, protect plants from wind-blown dust and drying out in their boxes. Plant materials, in particular, have a much better survival rate when installed and watered in at their final location as soon as possible after delivery to the site.

Poor material handling can cause problems after installation. Irrigation pipe exposed to intense sun, trees that have dried out in boxes, broken root balls, and hairline cracks in paving materials can all spell eventual failure.

As noted continually throughout this book, it is a luxury to work with reputable contractors. Knowing a contractor wants the same thing the landscape architect wants — to provide an exceptional project — makes it a lot easier to perform these field observation schedules.

Grading and Drainage Field Observation Schedule:

1. Preconstruction conference with general and grading contractors.
2. Review of rough grades, mounding, and adherence to grading intent.
3. Drain lines, catch basin, and dry-well review prior to backfilling.
4. Slot, trench, floor, and area drain layout.
5. Mounding and retention basin review and approval.
6. Inspection of all work and punch list.
7. Punch list completed, final cleanup, and final approval.

Hardscape Field Observation Schedule:

1. Preconstruction conference with general contractor and related trades.
2. Layout of all water features.
3. On-site boulder approval and selection.
4. Boulder placement observation.
5. Wall layout, overall height, and change in height locations.
6. All concrete form work and expansion-joint layout prior to pouring.
7. On-site stone approval.
8. Stone paver, band, steps, stepping pad, and coping layout.
9. On-site mounding review prior to grading as it affects hardscape.
10. Wall plaster application/finish review and approval.
11. Deck sealant application review and approval.
12. Inspection of all work and punch list.
13. Punch list completed, final cleanup, and final approval.

Landscape Field Observation Schedule:

1. Preconstruction conference with general and landscape contractors.
2. Rough grades and mounding.
3. Header location lined out on-site.
4. Boulder placement observation.

5. Staked tree locations.
6. Plant approval — on-site, in containers.
7. Tree placement and facing, under direction of landscape architect
8. Soil amendment installation.
9. Plant location approval — all shrubs, vines, espaliers, and ground covers, in containers set in their locations.
10. Pre-emergent weed control application.
11. Pot location and installation review.
12. Inspection of all work and punch list. Project cleanup.
13. On-site punch list completion review for substantial completion and final cleanup.
14. 30-day walk-through of contract maintenance.
15. 60-day walk-through of contract maintenance.
16. 90-day walk-through of contract maintenance for final acceptance.

Irrigation Field Observation Schedule:

1. Preconstruction conference with general and irrigation contractors.
2. Backflow prevention hook-up review.
3. Sleeving installation review.
4. Mainline installation — open trench review.
5. Irrigation equipment, layout, and open trench lateral review.
6. Pot drainage, irrigation stub location review.
7. System operation and head coverage review.
8. Inspection of work and punch list.
9. Punch list completed, final cleanup, and final acceptance. Additional specified equipment turned over to owner. System as-built drawings supplied to owner by irrigation contractor.

Lighting Field Observation Schedule:

1. Preconstruction conference with general and lighting contractors.
2. Staked light location review.
3. Fixture review and adjustment.
4. Nighttime mock-up(s).
5. Inspection of work and punch list.
6. Punch list completed, final cleanup, and final acceptance. System as-built drawings supplied to owner from lighting contractor.

Maintenance Costs and Techniques

This area, as explained earlier, can often turn out to be a real shock for the project owner. The owner is frequently caught unaware, because most landscape specifications call for a 60- or 90-day maintenance period after the installation is substantially complete, and the landscape contractor is usually the last trade on and off the job site. At this point in time, the owner frequently is faced with a maintenance proposal after he feels his expenses are over. As stated earlier, some forewarning that this event looms in the future, on the part of the landscape architect, will help an owner to brace himself for a case of sticker-shock.

Following is a partial list of items covered in most landscape maintenance proposals:

1. Lawn mowing and maintenance
2. Shrub and tree trimming and pruning
3. Weeding of planting beds
4. Trash and leaf litter removal
5. Pest and weed control
6. Disease control
7. Fertilization program
8. Rotation of annual color program
9. Irrigation system upkeep and seasonal controller programming
10. Lamp replacement in lighting fixtures

Most bids will be for some form of basic service. Replacement of damaged material and equipment (trees, irrigation heads, light fixtures) are usually billed as an extra, at unit cost plus labor. As with all contracts, it is important to note what is and what is not included. Furthermore, a complete weekly, quarterly, and annual schedule helps to clarify the maintenance contractor's need for site access and how the presence of his crews can be coordinated with other site users. Let's look at the noted maintenance items in more detail.

1. Lawn mowing and maintenance is not nearly as simple as it seems. Quality Bermuda grass needs to be cut and edged at least once every two weeks during the summer months to look its best. Annual Rye Grass should be mowed at least once every 10 days once it is established. For winter overseeding, Bermuda needs to be scalped and should be power raked. (Scalping refers to cutting the turf back completely to grade. Power raking is a process whereby stolons and thatch are cut [sometimes called verti-cutting] and removed.) Rye grass should be scalped about mid-March to allow for the seasonal onslaught of Bermuda. At least every 2 years, turf should be aerated. Aeration is performed by a machine that spikes soil cores out of the turf usually at about 12 inches on center and 4 inches deep. A competent turf maintenance program requires a variety of specialized equipment. Even mowers for the two types of turf should be different. Bermuda responds better to reel mowers, while Rye has to be cut with a rotary mower. This describes just a standard turf maintenance program for commercial and residential developments and does not come close to the level of care given to golf courses.

2. Shrub and tree trimming and pruning are a major source of conflict and remorse. Except for a real formal type design, the original intent of most landscape architects is not to have cubed shrubs and lollypop trees. This happens due to lack of training concerning maintenance personnel. It is somewhat unrealistic to expect an individual making minimum wage, or frequently less, to be very knowledgeable or to seek some form of training. These individuals have to be better supervised or paid more, and a combination of the two would be best. The reason plant materials are sheared into geometric forms is that such a form is easy to recognize and repeat. Landscape architects can help to alleviate this botanic abuse in three ways: first, by being willing to devote more of their on-site time to training, especially when the project responsibility changes from the original installer to the first maintenance contractor; second, by offering project maintenance manuals akin to installation specifications as a part of their scope of services; and last, by adhering to the old adage that if a tree or shrub has to be pruned more than twice a growing season, then it is the wrong plant selection for the space it occupies.

When pruning most trees, it is necessary to cut only those branches that are out of character with its natural head and canopy and those branches which endanger the health of the tree. Crossing branches which rub together, branches that grow into the head of the tree, and branches that are in danger of wind or pedestrian breakage should all be removed to safeguard the health of the tree. Smaller branches can be cut with smaller hand-held anvil or hook-and-blade type shears. Always have the anvil or hook (the dull side) below the branch, because cutting from above tends to limit the tearing of bark. Also, cut a branch so that a noticeable nub protrudes from the stem or trunk. This leaves a smaller surface area for new bark growth to cover. Always cut smaller branches just above a node. This initiates quicker hardening off. Consult the diagrams on pruning at the end of this chapter. Bigger branches are cut with pruning loppers that are larger and held with both hands. Major branches are cut by saws. When using a saw, make three cuts. Undercut 6 inches up the branch, from the trunk, and halfway into the branch. Cut from the top to the position of the first undercut. Allow the branch to fall to the ground. Cut the remaining stub at an appropriate length.

There are some forms of specialty pruning, such as pollarding, to maintain a bosque of trees (e.g. Sycamores) at a controlled height. Also, fruit trees are heavily pruned, and citrus trees are literally sheared to enhance crop harvesting. Be judicious in pruning flowering trees, because heavily pruned trees flower poorly. Pleaching is a practice whereby the leaders of small trees are interlaced to create a natural arbor.

Trimming of most shrubs closely follows the techniques of tree pruning. The primary difference is that there will almost always be a need to remove more dead wood from the interior of a shrub's crown. There are espaliers which require heavier pruning and accompanying weaving and tying to supports. Unfortunately, most espaliers flower in less profusion than their counterparts that are left in their natural form. In the small garden, an espalier may be the only plant that the space can accommodate and compromises will have to be made. Formal hedges are frequently sheared in geometric shapes. Squared hedges should always have a slight batter — that is, the bottom should always be wider than the top to allow sunlight to reach all of the branches. Shrubs trimmed in a vase shape tend to acquire dead wood at their bases owing to the lack of light.

Just as some trees receive specialty pruning some shrubs are used (or misused) in the art of topiary. Topiary utilizes plant materials to mimic animal life or other desired forms. (Personally, I hate it with a passion, but many owners just love it, and topiary will be a fact of life on some projects.)

3. Weeding of planting beds refers to hand-pulling of nuisance plants. Chemical weed control comes more under the heading of pest and weed control (see item 5 below) and requires a higher level of expertise. Hand weeding is labor intensive and, seemingly, never ending. This form of weeding usually takes place in ground cover and annual beds. Instruction basically involves identifying what not to pull and having all other low lying plants removed.

4. Trash and leaf litter removal can be a much larger task than originally anticipated. Projects with a large quantity of deciduous trees can require an enormous raking effort. There are also flowering trees and shrubs to consider. Jacaranda trees and Bougainvillea, for example, can create a lot of litter when spent blossoms fall to the ground. The owner or project manager will have to determine the level of trash removal. Dumpster and street-side garbage can service is usually contracted out to a separate waste disposal company. But what about wind-blown trash, common and pool area trash cans, walk, parking lot, and street sweeping, etc? This is something that needs to be clearly defined as more than a few disputes have and will occur over this issue.

5. Pest and weed control frequently involves chemical treatment and a higher level of expertise than that possessed by the average lawn man. Pests are animals and insects. Natural methods of deterring these pests are always more environmentally sensitive than chemical applications. Deer, coyotes, and dogs can all be deterred by organic scent repellents. When employing this approach, be sure to isolate and identify the real culprit. Bone meal will repel deer, for example, but attracts dogs. Snails will literally drown themselves in a thin bowl of beer. Some insect species are considered beneficial. Ladybugs thrive on aphids and lacewing wasps are fond of the larvae of whiteflies. Neither of these predatory insects is harmful to plant material. Fencing, ranging from chicken wire to chain link, can turn away birds, rabbits, mice, and deer. Sometimes traps can prove effective for mice and gophers.

As a last resort, chemicals will have to be applied, especially for weeds. Rat, mouse, and gopher poisons are available that are relatively harmless to the environment. Chemical insecticides (insect sprays) and herbicides (weed killers) are another matter entirely. The two most commonly applied insect sprays are Diazinon and Malathion. Diazinon should only be used for insects that occur close to the ground, as it is toxic to birds. Malathion is termed a broad-spectrum insecticide and is the most commonly used, above grade, chemical for agricultural and ornamental plants. Malathion should only be used after pollination has occurred (the simplest way to tell is if the plant has set fruit), because it will kill bees.

The two types of most frequently applied weed killers are preemergents and postemergents. Preemergents retard germination and attack very small seedlings. These chemicals are applied right after soil preparation and can be used with larger plants, since they affect only smaller specimens. Dacthal and Surflan are the most widely used preemergents. Postemergents are employed after weeds and other undesirable plant material have started mature leaf growth. These chemicals are spot sprayed on the leaves for contact killing or diluted and applied to the root zone. Any herbicide which is absorbed by the plant is termed a systemic, because it disrupts the plant's metabolism or (system). A product called Roundup™ by Monsanto Chemical Corporation is a popular contact herbicide, while Glyphosate is a prevalent systemic.

Great care needs to be exercised with the application of all insecticides and herbicides. Manufacturer's instructions need to be followed to the letter. Environmentally speaking, it is always better to have too weak a solution than too strong. This is especially true of herbicides, where more applications are easily performed while it is virtually impossible to remove an overdose. Retaining a licensed firm that has personnel trained in the proper application of pesticides is a worthwhile expense if there is any doubt as to the nature of the chemical or the competency of the current personnel.

Insects and weeds are an eternal problem. They can be controlled but not easily eradicated. The project owner will need to determine at which level of excellence the project needs to be kept and what can be tolerated. It is a balancing act between budget and aesthetics, and it is ongoing. This is the essence of what industry professionals commonly refer to as an integrated pest management (IPM) program.

6. Disease control involves retarding and combating invasions of bacteria and fungus. In the desert, bacteria type diseases occur more frequently than fungus diseases because, as a general rule, most bacteria tolerate higher air temperatures than do fungi. Fungus does occur, especially soil-borne diseases such as Texas Root Rot and Verticillium Wilt. In predominately sandy and well-drained soils, most fungus diseases are the direct result of prolonged overwatering and can easily be avoided. The most common type of bacterial disease is fire blight, which occasionally infests Pyracanthas, Roses, and various fruit trees. The easiest and most reliable way to control fire blight (and other bacterial diseases as well) is to simply remove the infected branches by pruning. Disinfect shears and saws after every cut by dipping in alcohol or other commercially available solutions. Prevention can be achieved if copper-based sprays are applied in early spring when this disease is most likely to occur.

Bacterial and fungal diseases are chemically treated with sprays or powders. Powders are usually more effective, if slightly more difficult to work with. Captan or common sulfur are the oldest and most widely used powders for a variety of diseases. A final word on plant diseases is that several are very difficult to diagnose. A qualified horticulturist or aboriculturist is a valuable asset. County Agricultural Extension Agents are usually quite helpful or can recommend competent specialists. These specialists are well worth their fees if consulted early when a problem first becomes apparent and has not gotten a real foothold. No professional on earth is going to be of much help in the event of a full blown infestation. In this event, things have to run their course. In short, just as in human disease, early detection and prevention are of utmost importance in fighting plant diseases.

7. A fertilization program is influenced by two main factors — the type of plant materials and their age. As a general rule, the more shallow rooted the plant material, the more it will appreciate fertilization. This would include turf and most low-lying ground covers. Any plant in a position to expend a great amount of energy over a short time span can be aided by fertilization. Initial spring flowering and leaf budding are energy-consuming events in trees and shrubs. Even evergreen plants that go somewhat dormant in winter can be spurned into faster, lusher spring growth. The primary law of annual color rotation is to fertilize early and often.

Then there is the other side of the coin. With established plants living in good soil and exhibiting a satisfactory growth rate it may be advisable not to fertilize. Fertilizer increases the growth rate, and thus increases the water consumption of plants. Besides requiring more irrigation water, this will necessitate more pruning, increase leaf and litter removal, and deplete inherent soil nutrients faster.

The owner's objectives for the ongoing look and feel of the project, coupled with budget constraints, will help to determine the nature of the project fertilization program. Often a "fertilize as needed" approach is the best solution. Here key areas and beds of annual color within the public eye receive the most fertilizer. Side yards, screen hedges, and mature trees are left alone until it becomes apparent that they would look better with occasional fertilization. As plants mature they become recipients of programmed fertilization.

The goal is to provide healthy, well formed plant materials over the longest life span possible. A good fertilization program creates an aesthetic asset, while a bad one can prove to be a waste of money.

8. Rotation of annual color is a major maintenance cost item. On most well designed projects, annual color is located in the highest visual impact areas. Requiring the greatest amount of water, fertilizer, and attention, annuals are located in important but limited areas. Seasonal rotation usually relates to spring and fall annuals, but there are an increasing number of summer, and even some winter annuals.

Annuals are generally expensive to procure and time-consuming to plant. Planting annuals frequently requires a sense of good timing, so that the greatest profusion of color can coincide with an important target date such as a project grand opening or seasonal event.

Most annuals bloom more heavily and longer when spent blossoms are picked from the plant. This assures that no important energy is wasted on dying tissue. Unfortunately, this practice will also increase labor time. Balance this fact against the costs of replanting, and it may be better to stretch a blooming period another 3 weeks to a month by picking dead blossoms.

As with any design or maintenance program, color rotation will be determined by actual need, aesthetic impact, and expense.

9. Irrigation system upkeep is an absolute necessity. Without water, the project or sections of it are lost. When dealing within the constraints of a tight budget this is one aspect of the maintenance program that simply cannot be ignored. Better the seasonal turf stay brown a little longer or off-season summer annuals go unplanted, or the trees get pruned every other year than to compromise the irrigation system.

An irrigation system is an assemblage of moving parts, and it is a sad fact of mechanical life that moving parts eventually wear out. Heads will blow, valves will freeze, pipes will burst, and controllers will malfunction. All will require constant monitoring and immediate repair. The time requirement alone, to walk the system to troubleshoot broken and jammed heads, can be substantial. Locating a line leak or finding a low-voltage wire short can be extremely frustrating, as well as time consuming. A cheap or shoddy installation of the irrigation system will rear its ugly head repeatedly. Poor maintenance of a good system assures a slow death. Good maintenance of a poor system will chew up a major portion of the overall maintenance budget.

The most difficult and demanding irrigation task is seasonal controller programming. A programmer needs to know the system layout, seasonal water demand, and irrigation requirements of the plant materials affected. He also needs to know the effective features and limitations of the controller(s) operating the system. Merely checking the controller's station routing takes ample time.

Keeping the irrigation system up and running is usually the most time-absorbing maintenance task. This, coupled with the replacement costs of various articles of equipment, will make the upkeep of the irrigation system the most limiting factor in the maintenance program.

10. Lamp replacement in lighting fixtures does not appear to be a very large maintenance item, yet it is one element of the maintenance program that is often lacking. First, maintenance personnel are often off-site when the problem is most likely to be noticed — during the evening hours. Second, many types of replacement bulbs are prohibitively expensive. The per unit cost of some low-voltage bulbs can be staggering. Lights located in difficult areas can be hard to service. Well lights, even in open turf areas, have a tendency to freeze at their lids, making access a major chore, often resulting in damage to the fixture. The glass lenses of many fixtures, over time, will yellow due to water or mineral deposits, thus making the internal lamp appear dim.

Perhaps in no other area of initial site design should the question of ongoing maintenance of the units be addressed more than with lighting. Fewer lights functioning properly are more effective than many lights with 10 to 20% of the lamps burned out.

Miscellaneous Maintenance Considerations

The landscape maintenance program can address some or all of the items discussed above and still fall short of being a comprehensive site maintenance program. Pools, spas, and water features, while usually a part of a separate contract, should be mentioned here. Pool maintenance during the summer months is a weekly task. The clean out of drainage system area drains, catch basins, and dry wells is usually required at least once a year. Painting of common area screen walls and the sealing of decks and wood trellises will need to be assigned to someone. Parking lot sweeping, as well as painting and sealing, are important maintenance issues, as is the resurfacing of tennis and other sport courts. Sometimes sidewalks receive chemical treatment to clean and roughen their surface texture as a safety precaution. Entry gates will require occasional servicing. The erection and dismantling of holiday lighting can be surprisingly time intensive, as well as difficult.

In closing, it is well to remember that projects do not maintain themselves — people do. In the landscape industry, these people are frequently not fluent in English nor well educated. This does not mean they are stupid or second-class citizens. It certainly does not mean they are lazy, as they are among the hardest working individuals in the workforce. Some people are going to have a hard time conducting construction business in the Southwest if they cannot give the Hispanic man an even break.

There is a real lack of quality reference material in the area of maintenance. Not only would more books be nice, but videos would be especially helpful — in English and Spanish. Experience is undoubtedly the best teacher but, in this competitive segment of the industry, very few experienced people are willing to teach. Maintenance needs to be recognized as a more important part of the industry, and landscape architects need to give it more prominent consideration earlier on in the design process.

Maintenance Scheduling

Good project maintenance is not just a function of cost control coupled with product and project familiarity, but it also requires an excellent feel for environmental conditions and having a sense of good timing.

Performing the right task, at the appropriate time, is almost as important as how the task is performed. Following is an incomplete but, hopefully helpful, breakdown of a calendar year of maintenance recommendations, tasks, and requirements.

January

- Dismantling of seasonal and Christmas decorations.
- Best time to prune deciduous trees and shrubs as branch structure and overall crown appearance can be easily studied without foliage

February

- Deep-drill fertilization of older trees, especially those used for spring flower show
- Late month is a good time to provide supplemental water to native wildflower areas in order to trigger blossoming

March

- Early month is the best time to plant spring annual color
- Late-month scalping of seasonal Rye grass to allow for transition to Bermuda grass
- Aeration of lawn after scalping

April

- Midmonth: first application of high-nitrogen lawn fertilizer; Follow with biweekly applications up until the end of August

May

- Late month pulling of spring annuals
- Plant summer annuals

June

- Aeration of Bermuda grass
- Plant summer annual color

July

- Lift bulbs, corms, and tubers, as required
- Lowest tourist area population level:. good time to stripe and seal parking lots and paint or refinish other items

August

- Cut back irrigation to some specialty plant material such as Bougainvillea and Floss Silk tree in order to encourage a more vivid fall color show

September

- Late month: scalp Bermuda grass and overseed with Rye grass; apply steer manure or other types of top dressing for fertilization and to discourage birds from eating seed

October

- Preparations for most tourist areas season begin in earnest. Most project owners will want their best look by Thanksgiving weekend
- Mid to late month best time for planting fall annuals, especially Petunias

November

- Plant winter annual color

December

- Put up Christmas and other seasonal decorations

Summary

Remember that installation and maintenance are only as good as the individuals performing these tasks. Methodologies and techniques are constantly evolving and undergoing the process of trial and error. Landscape architects will benefit greatly by being receptive to suggestions and new ideas. Maintenance personnel who live with the project on a day-to-day basis will come to know its strengths and weaknesses. An occasional follow-up visit to job sites in the ensuing years, after the initial installation, will reveal many things and provide some real world education. Admittedly, often projects ultimately turn out to be big disappointments. While this can be, and often is, the fault of poor maintenance, it is also just as often the fault of poor initial design. As always, experience is the best teacher and sometimes a punishing one.

Maintenance Considerations

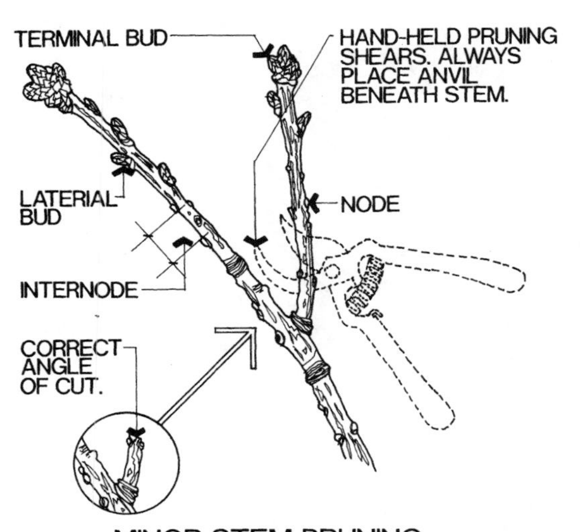

MINOR STEM PRUNING

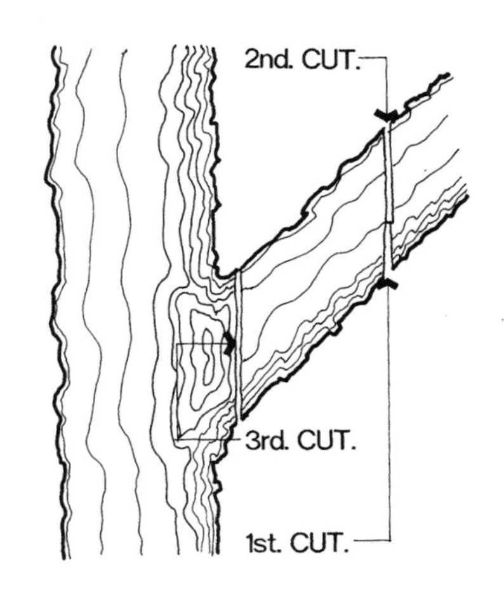

MAJOR BRANCH PRUNING

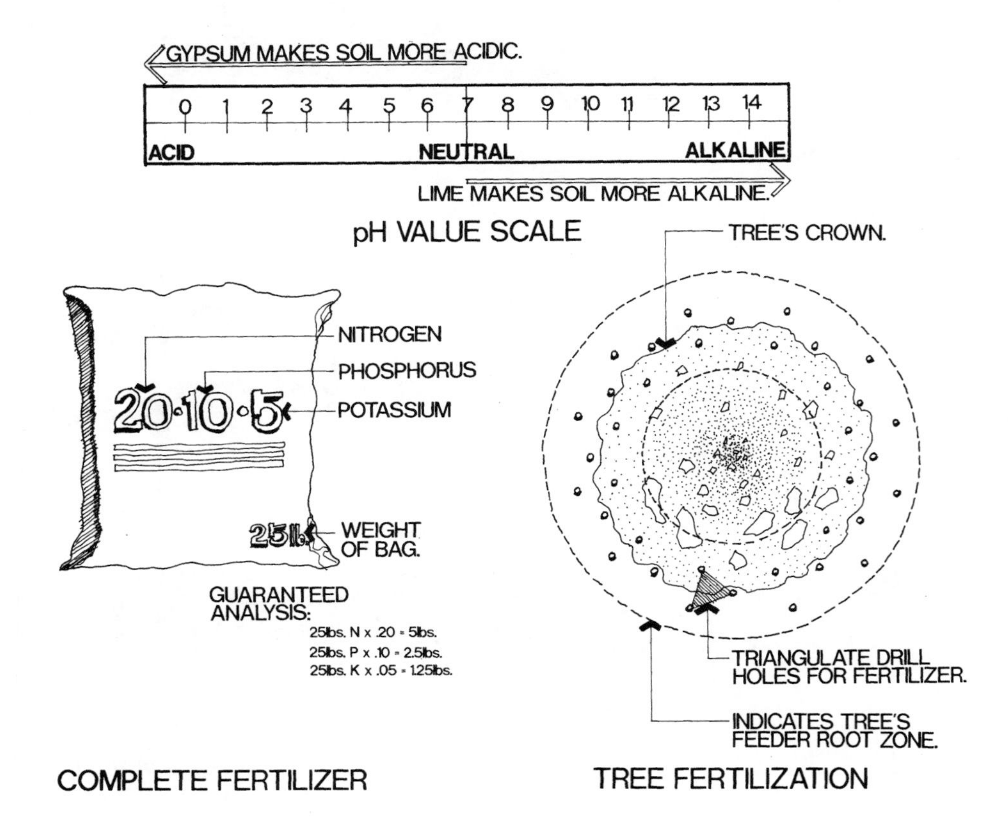

COMPLETE FERTILIZER

TREE FERTILIZATION

Tree Maintenance

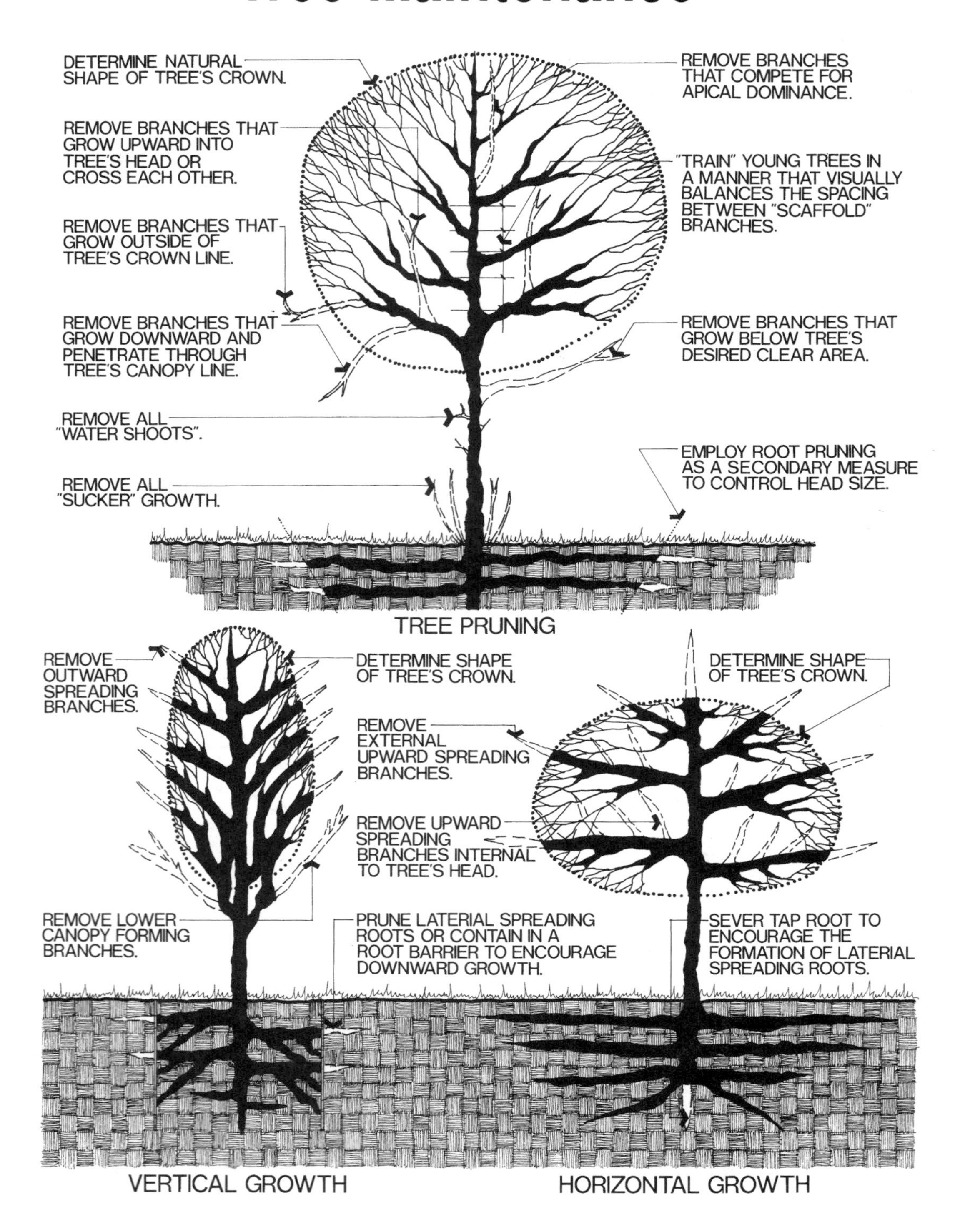
DETERMINE NATURAL SHAPE OF TREE'S CROWN.
REMOVE BRANCHES THAT GROW UPWARD INTO TREE'S HEAD OR CROSS EACH OTHER.
REMOVE BRANCHES THAT GROW OUTSIDE OF TREE'S CROWN LINE.
REMOVE BRANCHES THAT GROW DOWNWARD AND PENETRATE THROUGH TREE'S CANOPY LINE.
REMOVE ALL "WATER SHOOTS".
REMOVE ALL "SUCKER" GROWTH.
REMOVE BRANCHES THAT COMPETE FOR APICAL DOMINANCE.
"TRAIN" YOUNG TREES IN A MANNER THAT VISUALLY BALANCES THE SPACING BETWEEN "SCAFFOLD" BRANCHES.
REMOVE BRANCHES THAT GROW BELOW TREE'S DESIRED CLEAR AREA.
EMPLOY ROOT PRUNING AS A SECONDARY MEASURE TO CONTROL HEAD SIZE.
TREE PRUNING
REMOVE OUTWARD SPREADING BRANCHES.
DETERMINE SHAPE OF TREE'S CROWN.
REMOVE EXTERNAL UPWARD SPREADING BRANCHES.
REMOVE UPWARD SPREADING BRANCHES INTERNAL TO TREE'S HEAD.
DETERMINE SHAPE OF TREE'S CROWN.
REMOVE LOWER CANOPY FORMING BRANCHES.
PRUNE LATERIAL SPREADING ROOTS OR CONTAIN IN A ROOT BARRIER TO ENCOURAGE DOWNWARD GROWTH.
SEVER TAP ROOT TO ENCOURAGE THE FORMATION OF LATERIAL SPREADING ROOTS.
VERTICAL GROWTH
HORIZONTAL GROWTH

Shrub Maintenance

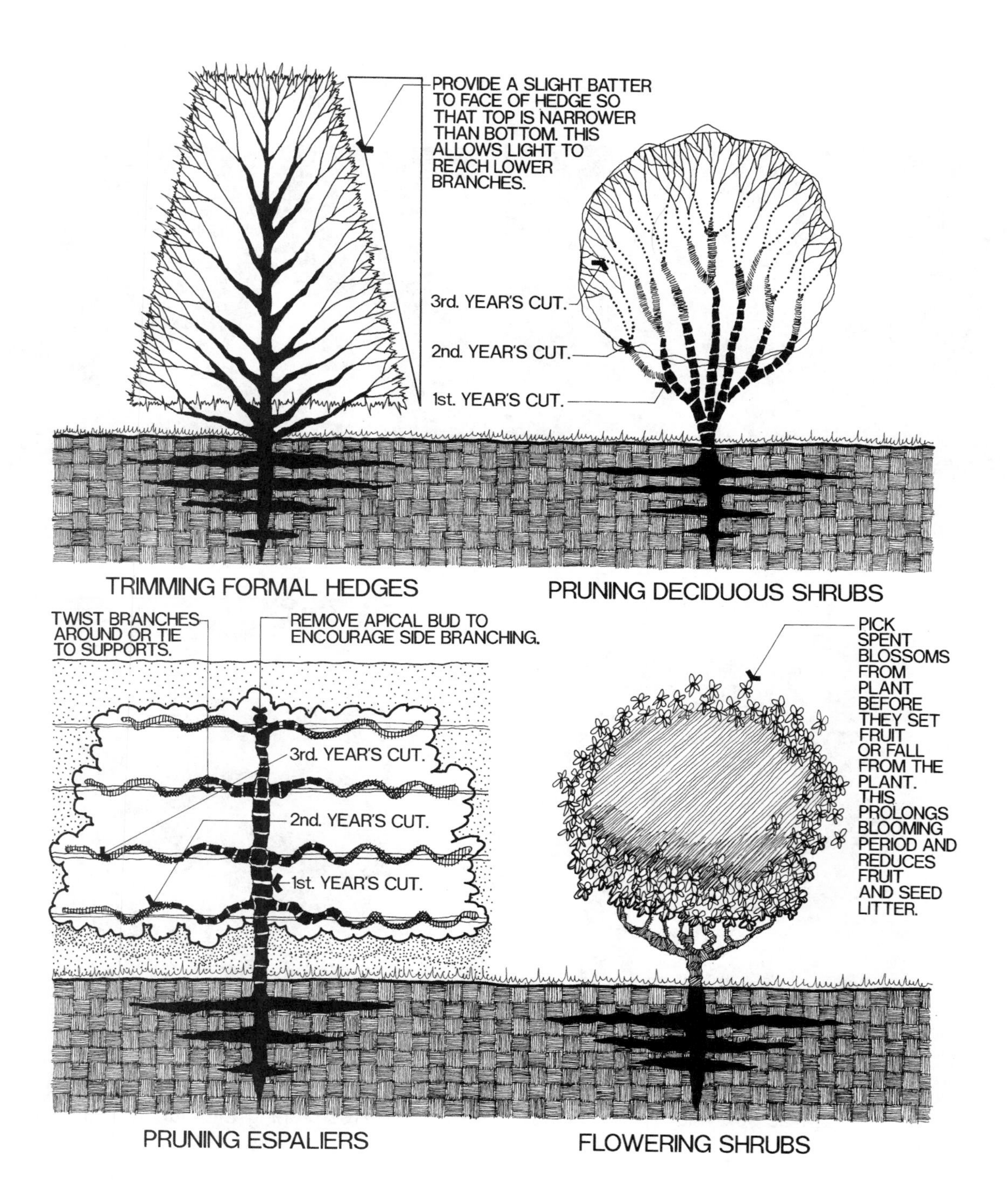
PROVIDE A SLIGHT BATTER TO FACE OF HEDGE SO THAT TOP IS NARROWER THAN BOTTOM. THIS ALLOWS LIGHT TO REACH LOWER BRANCHES.
3rd. YEAR'S CUT.
2nd. YEAR'S CUT.
1st. YEAR'S CUT.
TRIMMING FORMAL HEDGES
PRUNING DECIDUOUS SHRUBS
TWIST BRANCHES AROUND OR TIE TO SUPPORTS.
REMOVE APICAL BUD TO ENCOURAGE SIDE BRANCHING.
3rd. YEAR'S CUT.
2nd. YEAR'S CUT.
1st. YEAR'S CUT.
PICK SPENT BLOSSOMS FROM PLANT BEFORE THEY SET FRUIT OR FALL FROM THE PLANT. THIS PROLONGS BLOOMING PERIOD AND REDUCES FRUIT AND SEED LITTER.
PRUNING ESPALIERS
FLOWERING SHRUBS

Maintenance Tasks

Box Palm prior to backfilling

Box Palm backfilling with prepared soil mix

Tree spraying

Tree pruning with hand loppers

Palm Planting

Large palm planting

Glossary

Aerating: Drilling holes into turf areas to introduce air to the root zone. Sometimes called plugging.

Arboriculture: Growing and caring for trees that are primarily used for agriculture or ornamental horticultural purposes.

Arborculturist: An individual who by education and training is knowledgeable in the practice of arborculture.

Annual color rotation: Refers to the minimum biannual changing of annual species to maintain constant or near constant color within a planting bed or pot. Annuals that are environmentally adapted to specific climatic conditions are utilized during the season in which they provide peak blooming performance.

Bacteria: Microorganisms that cause disease and decay. Usually wind borne in desert environments.

Bidding process: Methodology whereby a contractor provides a written bid (estimate) for a defined scope of construction along with documentation (performance bonds) that he will stand by his estimate. At this point the bid usually cannot be changed if it is accepted by the owner.

Bosque: Massing or grouping of trees of the same species in a, more or less, formal or geometric pattern.

Chemical insect control: Using licensed and approved chemicals to eradicate unwanted or destructive insects.

Chemical pest control: Using licensed and approved chemicals to eradicate or drive away animal pests.

Chemical weed control: Using licensed and approved chemicals to eradicate noxious weeds.

County Agricultural Extension Agent: Individual employed by the County Agricultural Extension Service who is knowledgeable in local agricultural and ornamental horticultural conditions and practices. This agent is on hand to answer questions from the public.

Cubic footage: Volume of an area in cubic feet, determined by calculating or measuring. Usually comes into play in grading design and swimming pool equipment sizing and construction. The square footage (length times width) of an item times its height will yield the cubic footage.

Disinfect: To remove a source of infection. Also, to sterilize pruning instruments with chemicals when pruning infected material.

Downsizing: To reduce gallon or box sizes of plant materials. To reduce square footage of hardscape and/or planting areas. To reduce cubic footage (volume) of earthwork and water features.

Environmental pest control: Utilizing natural methods to eradicate or drive away insect or animal pests. This method is most frequently used to control insect pests. Insects that are predators of the pest but not harmful to the surrounding environment are released in infested areas. For example, ladybugs are used to control aphids.

Export soil: Earth that must be removed from a site during grading operations to accommodate a new finish grade.

Fear factor: Colloquial term that means new products or installation methodologies will usually prompt a higher bid on the part of a contractor who is not familiar with them.

Fertilization program: A planned program that determines what plant material will receive fertilization during what season. The type and amount of fertilizer is also determined. This aids in maintenance scheduling and determining manpower requirements.

Fiduciary relationship: As it applies to contracts, a legal and binding agreement between an owner and an agent (contractor, designer). Acting as an agent, one must hold the owner's interests highest. Simply put, an agent is required to be responsible to the person who holds his contract.

Field observation: Reviewing the project installation during the course of construction and issuing reports as to whether the work meets the requirements of the plans and specifications.

Field observation schedule: Specific points during the course of construction where work must be reviewed. These points are noted in a schedule so that all parties concerned can make arrangements to be available on site.

Final inspection: That point in time when the project is considered complete and guarantees and/or warranties on the part of the contractor are put into effect.

Fungus: Group of plant material that contain no carbohydrates and are incapable of producing it. Thus fungi must receive nourishment by becoming parasitic on other plants or animals. For the purposes of this chapter, fungus means plant disease.

Fungicide: Chemical that controls or eradicates fungi.

General contractor: An individual who by education, experience, and state licensing is deemed knowledgeable, capable, and legally able to oversee all aspects of building and site installations. General contractors must also be bonded and insured to guarantee a minimum level of compliance with state law.

Hand-held pruning shears: Used for removing smaller branches, stems, and twigs. These shears have a flat anvil and sharp blade. The anvil should always rest underneath the cutting area.

Herbicides: Chemicals used to eradicate unwanted herbaceous plant material. Commonly called weed killers.

Horticulture: The science and art of propagating and growing plant material.

Horticulturist: An individual who by experience and/or education is knowledgeable in the practice of horticulture.

Import soil: Earth that must be brought on to a site during grading operations to accommodate a new finish grade.

Insecticide: A chemical used to eradicate unwanted or destructive insects.

Installation: A project where construction work is performed and the site is somehow physically improved.

Integrated Pest Management (IPM): A program that prioritizes the need for chemical and environmental pest control and schedules times for the most efficient applications of these elements. IPM attempts to consider the big picture and not just narrow in on one pest.

Landscape contractor: An individual who by education, experience, and state licensing is deemed knowledgeable, capable, and legally able to perform landscape installations.

Lawn edging: Creating a clean, crisp, noteceable line where turf meets hardscape or planting beds.

Lawn mowing: Physicially cutting turf by use of machines with sharpened blades. Bermuda grass requires a reel-type mower, while Rye grass requires a rotary-type mower.

Maintenance: To keep various elements of a project in top condition and good working order; also, to keep plant materials healthy.

Maintenance budget: Funds allocated to perform project maintenance functions.

Maintenance contractor: An individual who by experience and/or education is knowledgeable in and capable of performing maintenance functions.

Maintenance period: Usually a 60- or 90-day period that begins after the substantial completion inspection of the construction contract where the installing contractor maintains the project while punch list (pick up) items are addressed.

Maintenance program: A comprehensive schedule as to what maintnance functions need to be performed and when to do them.

Maintenance staff: An owner's in-house (employees) maintenance crew.

Nighttime mock-up: Review of lighting fixtures and lighting installations during nighttime hours.

Noxious weeds: Unwanted plants that are extremely difficult to eradicate. Soil specifications frequently state that import soil must be free from noxious weeds. Soil borne seeds, stems, and roots of these weeds are capable of germinating and spreading rapidly, when exposed to irrigation water, at a new site.

Nuisance plants: Any species that is not a part of the planting program and is unwanted.

Nurseryman: An individual who by experience and/or education is knowledgeable in and capable of running a nursery operation. This includes, but is not limited to, propagation, growing, transplanting, fertilizing, pruning, and plant identification.

Overseeding: Application of Rye grass seed over scalped Bermuda grass to produce a green winter lawn. Overseeding can be successfully performed after September 21.

Pesticides: Chemicals used to eradicate unwanted animals.

Pests: Animal life that is unwanted, especially insects.

Pleaching: Twining or interlacing the leaders of small trees to form an overhead arbor or canopy.

Pollarding: Method of pruning deciduous trees where branches are cut at the same node every season. This greatly reduces the canopy and creates gnarly, grotesque nubs at the node when the tree is out of leaf. Useful for controlling tree size in pedestrian plaza areas.

Post emergent: Herbicides that attack immature weeds or contact sprays that are applied to the leaves of older weeds.

Power raking (verti-cutting): Removing thatch from turf after it has been scalped by use of a special cutting machine. Sometimes called de-thatching.

Preconstruction conference: Initial site meeting between the general contractor, landscape architect, related subcontractors, and owner's representative. The purpose of the meeting is to answer questions and determine the most efficient course of construction.

Preemergent: Herbicide that attacks weed seedlings, killing them before they develop true leaves.

Propagation: To reproduce plant material through natural or vegetative processes. In the case of vegetative propagation, plants are capable of regenerating cells due to growth of meristematic cells and cambium. This makes possible all manner of stem, leaf, and even root cuttings. Many species also produce reproductive tissue such as bulbs and rhizomes that are capable of producing replicas of the parent plant. Many hybrids must be propagated vegetatively, as their seeds are often sterile or, genetically, they do not breed true. See Chapter 5 Glossary for information and terms concerning propagation from seeds.

Pruning: Removing growth from plants to improve their health, appearance, flower, or fruit production. Also, a method of controlling the size and shape of plant material.

Pruning loppers: Large pruning shears of the anvil and blade type to be used with two hands and designed to remove larger branches than the hand-held variety.

Punch list: List of items to be addressed, completed, or modified that is complied during the substantial completion inspection.

Reel mowers: Lawn mowers with many blades that roll (reel) in a vertically circular direction.

Rotary mowers: Lawn mowers with two blades that rotate in a horizontally circular motion.

Scalping: Cutting turf to grade.

Square footage: The length times the width of a plane surface will yield the square footage.

String trimmer: Often called weed eaters. Machines that employ short, fast-rotating nylon cord (string) to cut turf and weeds, particularly in limited areas or areas a mower cannot reach. String trimmers can easily girdle the trunks of young trees, so protective measures need to be taken to prevent this.

Substantial completion inspection: Usually performed when a project is 85% finished. A punch list of items is compiled and the landscape contractor is started on his 60- or 90-day maintenance period if the majority of the installation is found satisfactory.

Systemic: A herbicide that is mixed with water. Weeds take up the treated water and the herbicide attacks their internal systems.

Topiary: Pruning and shearing certain types of plant materials into geometric or animal shapes.

Top soil: Technically, the top layer of the ground that is usually darker and more fertile due to an accumulation of organic matter. In industry terminology, the term usually refers to any soil that is heavily amended to enhance plant growth.

Trimming: Light pruning.

Unit cost: The price of a product on an individual (per unit) basis.

Weeds: Unwanted plants.

Weeding: Physically removing weeds by pulling them from the soil.

Weed killers: See herbicides.

Workmanship: As it applies to this chapter, the level of quality a contractor applies to his trade.

Conclusion

(A message to other landscape architects)

Just as professional speakers have panic attacks as they approach the podium, or theatre actors get weak in the knees before going on stage, the designer often has his moment of doubt. All the factors to be considered, all the options to be explored, the client's unending criticism and unrealistic time schedule often prompts the question, "where do I start?"

Much as the speaker and actor must utter the first word, you must start at the beginning. Put all your research, training, and uncertainty aside for one moment and draw the first line on paper — the rest will follow.

Frederick Law Olmsted, the father of landscape architecture, died in a sanitorium. L'Enfant, who master-planned our nation's capitol, died in its streets, complaining that he was never understood. As landscape architects, we often let our work become our consuming passion, to the detriment of our staffs, our friends, and even our families.

A word of caution about design to designers. We tend to take our work and ourselves too seriously. Clients view what we do as something that should please them, and indeed they are the ones paying the bill. They are not concerned about the turmoil they create inside of us. Criticism and changes will plague a designer all his life. Just as a writer feels his best work is often found at the bottom of an editor's trash basket, a designer will feel the slings and arrows of various insensitive and cost-conscious clients throughout his career.

In programming and design, even in determining the contractual scope of services, a landscape architect needs to define what is appropriate. Appropriateness is a concept whose time has come. Determining what is actually needed and how to provide it is the essence of good service. Learn to spend more time communicating ideas, and drawing rough, explanatory plans and sketches (the type you don't mind throwing out).

Our drawings are not works of art, although they should be graphically pleasing. Don't lament too much the hacking apart of your finest drawings, but do try to preserve the substance of your design intent. Above all, as trite as it sounds, be a good listener. This will keep the hacking down to an acceptable level.

When you leave this earth you will leave some semblance of a body of work behind you. In the final analysis, what is in the ground and can be seen by those that remain behind is all that will matter. Try to enjoy what you do. Visit your favorite projects often, not only to learn from them, but to cherish them. Any line of work has its problems. With the wrong attitude, any business can be a tough business. Come on, lighten up, and now — get to work!

Bibliography

Chapter 1

Colorful Cacti of the American Deserts, Edgar and Brian Lamb, Mcmillan Publishing, Co., New York, 1974.

Flowers of the Southwest Deserts, Natt N. Dodge, Southwest Parks and Monuments Association, Tucson, AZ, 1985.

Desert Palm Oasis, James W. Cornett, Champion Press, Santa Barbara, CA,1989.

Deserts: The Audubon Society Nature Guides, James A. MacMahon, Chanticleer Press, New York, 1985.

The Desert: Time Life Books, A. Starker Leopold, Time Inc., New York, 1962.

Drylands, Philip Hyde, Random House, New York, 1987.

The Desert Realm: Lands Of Majesty And Mystery, Prepared by the Special Publications Division, National Geographic Society, Washington, D.C., 1982.

Times Island: The California Desert, T.H. Watkins, Peregrine Smith Books, 1989.

Trees And Shrubs Of The Southwestern Deserts, Lyman Benson and Robert A. Darrows, University of Arizona Press, Tucson, AZ, 1981.

Chapter 2

Anatomy of a Park, Albert J. Rutledge, McGraw-Hill Book Company, New York, 1971.

Basic Elements of Landscape Architectural Design, Norman K. Booth, Elsevier Science, New York,1983.

Cost Effective Site Planning, National Association of Home Builders, 1976.

Desert Southwest Gardens, Paula Pauich and Nora Burba Trulsson, Photography by Terry Moore, Bantam Books, New York, 1990.

Design with Nature, Ian L. McHarg, Falcon Press, Philadelphia, PA, 1969.

Earthscape: A Manual Of Environmental Planning, John Ormsbee Simonds, McGraw-Hill, New York, 1978.

Gardens are for People, 2nd edition, Thomas D. Church, Grace Hall, Michael Laurie, McGraw-Hill, New York, 1983.

Garden Design: History, Principles, Elements, Practice, William Lake Douglas, Susan R. Frey, Norman K. Johnson, Susan Littlefield and Michael Van Valkenburgh, Simon and Schuster, New York, 1984.

Golf Course Design and Construction, National Golf Foundation, 1150 South U.S. Highway One, Jupiter, FL, 1990.

Landscape Architecture (The Shaping of Man's Environment), John Ormsbee Simonds, McGraw-Hill, New York, 1961.

Landscaping Your Home, William R. Nelson, Jr., Cooperative Extension Service, University of Illinois at Urbana, Champaign, IL, 1963.

Modern Landscape Architecture, Felice Frankel and Jorg Johnson, Cross River Press, 1991.

Site Planning, 2nd edition, Kevin Lynch, M.I.T. Press, 1971.

The Gardens of Roberto Burle Marx, Sima Eliovson, Harry N. Abrams/Sagapress, New York, 1991.

The Golf Course, Geoffrey S. Cornish and Ronald E. Whitter, Rutledge Press, New York, 1981 (revised 1988).

The Landscape We See, Garrett Eckbo, McGraw-Hill, New York, 1969.

The Landscape Architect's Reference Manual, Bethard and Cathcart, Basic Information Services, 1976.

Chapter 3

A Guide to Site and Environmental Planning, Harvey M. Rubenstein, John Wiley & Sons, New York, 1969.

Construction Design for Landscape Architects, Able E. Munson, P.E., L.A., McGraw-Hill, New York, 1974.

Grade Easy, Richard K. Untermann, Landscape Architecture Foundation, 1973.

Handbook of Landscape Architectural Construction, D. Carpenter, Editor, Landscape Architecture Foundation, 1976.

Landscape Architecture Construction, Harlow C. Landphair and Fred Klatt, Jr., Elsevier Science, New York, 1979.

Simplified Site Engineering for Architects and Builders, Harry Parker and John W. MacGuire, John Wiley & Sons, New York, 1954.

Site, Space, and Structure, Kim W. Todd, Van Nostrand Reinhold Company, New York, 1985.

Soil Science: Principles and Practices, R. L. Hausenbuiller, William C. Brown, Dubuque, IA, 1972.

Time-Saver Standards for Site Planning, Joseph De Chiara and Lee E. Koppelman, McGraw-Hill, New York, 1984.

Chapter 4

Architectural Graphic Standards, 6th Edition, Charles G. Ramsey and Harold R. Sleeper, John Wiley & Son, New York, 1970.

Barrier Free Site Design, American Society of Landscape Architects Foundation, U.S. Dept.of Housing and Urban Development, Washington, D.C., 1975.

Central City Malls, Harvey M. Rubenstein, John Wiley & Sons, New York, 1978.

Cities, 2nd Edition, Lawrence Halprin, M.I.T. Press, Cambridge, MA, 1972.

Construction Materials (Types, Uses And Applications, Caleb Hornbostel, D.P.L.G., R.A., John Wiley and Sons, New York, 1978.

Construction Materials & Processes, Don A. Watson, McGraw-Hill, New York, 1972.

Dictionary Of Architecture And Construction, Cyril M. Harris, McGraw-Hill Book, New York, 1975.

Fountains and Pools, C. Douglas Aurand, PDA Publishers, Mesa, AZ, 1986.

Graphic Standards for Landscape Architects, Richard L. Austin, Thomas R. Dunbar, J. Kip Hulvershorn, Kim W. Todd, Van Nostrand Reinhold Company, New York, 1986.

Landscape Architectural Site Construction Details, Gary O. Robinette, Editor, Environmental Design Press, 1976

Materials in yhe Architecture of Arizona, 1870–1920, Bernard Michael Boyle, Architecture Foundation of the College of Architecture, Arizona State University, Tempe, AZ, 1976.

Site Design And Construction Detailing, Theodore D. Walker, PDA Publishers, West Lafayette, IN, 1978.

Reader's Digest: Complete Do-It-Yourself Manual, Reader's Digest Association, Pleasantville, New York, 1973.

The Craft of the Potter, Michael Casson, Barron's Educational Series, Woodbury, New York, 1977.

The Garden Book, John Brookes, Crown Publishers, New York, 1984.

Chapter 5

Beautiful Gardens, Eric A. Johnson and Scott Millard, Ironwood Press, Tucson, AZ, 1991.

Botany, Wilson and Loomis, Rinehart and Winston, New York, 1971.

Botany For Gardeners: An Introduction And Guide, Brian Capon, Timber Press, Portland, OR, 1990.

Botany Made Simple, Victor A. Grenlach, Ph.D., Doubleday and Company, Inc., Garden City, NY, 1968.

Burpee American Gardening Series: Annuals, Suzanne Frutig Bales, Prentice Hall Press, New York, 1991.

Cactus and Succulents, Editors of Sunset Books and Sunset Magazine, Lane Publishing, Menlo Park, CA, 1978.

California Gardening (The Los Angeles Times), Robert Smaus, Harry N. Abrams, New York, 1983.

Flowering Plants in the Landscape, Mildred E. Mathias, Editor, University of California Press, Berkeley, CA, 1982.

Gardening in Dry Climates, Scott Millard, Ortho Books, Chevron Chemical Company, San Ramon, CA, 1989.

Gardening in the Southwest, Editors of Taylor's Encyclopedia of Gardening, Houghton Mifflin, Boston, MA, 1992.

Lush and Efficient: A Guide to Coachella Valley Landscaping, Eric A. Johnson and David Harbison, Desert Printing, Bermuda Dunes, CA, 1988.

Natural Landscaping: Designing with Native Plant Communities, John Diekelmann and Robert Schuster, McGraw-Hill, New York, 1982.

Planting Design: A Manual of Theory and Practice, William R. Nelson, Stipes Publishing, Champaign, IL, 1985.

Plants for Dry Climates, Mary Rose Duffield and Warren D. Jones, Price, Stern, Sloan, Los Angeles, CA, 1981.

Roadside Plants of Southern California, Thomas J. Belzer, Mountain Press, Missoula, MN, 1984.

Selected California Native Plants in Color, Saratoga Horticultural Foundation, Woolford Associates, San Francisco, CA, 1980.

Simon & Schuster's Guide to Trees, Stanley Schuler, Editor, Simon & Schuster, New York, 1977 .

Trees and Shrubs for Dry California Landscapes, Bob Perry, Land Design Publishing, Claremont, CA, 1989.

Trees for Architecture and the Landscape, Robert L. Zion, Van Nostrand Reinhold, New York, 1968.

Trees for Every Purpose, Joseph Hudak, McGraw-Hill, New York, 198

Trees in Urban Design, Henry F. Arnold, Van Nostrand Reinhold, New York, 1980.

The Audubon Society Book of Trees, Les Line, Ann Sutton, and Myron Sutton, Harry N. Abrams, New York, 1981.

The Plants, Frits W. Went and the Editors of Time-Life Books, Time, New York, 1963.

Water Gardening Basics, William C. Uber, Dragonflyer Press, Upland, CA, 1988.

Water Saving Gardening, Editors of Taylor's Encyclopedia of Gardening, Houghton Mifflin, Boston, MA, 1990.

Waterwise Gardening, Editors of Sunset Books and Sunset Magazine, Lane Publishing, Menlo Park, CA, 1989.

Western Garden Book, Editorial Director: Kathleen Norris Brenzel, and the editors of Sunset Books and Sunset Magazine, Lane Publishing, Menlo Park, CA, 1995.

Chapter 6

Buckner: Irrigation Systems Design Manual, Buckner, Fresno, CA., 1988.

Irrigation, 4th edition, Irrigation Association Authors, Irrigation Association, Arlington, VA, 1983.

Lawn Sprinklers: A Do-It-Yourself Guide, Richard L. Austin, Tab Books, Blue Ridge Summit, PA, 1990.

Rain Bird: Landscape Drip Irrigation Design Manual, Keith Shepersky, Rain Bird Sales, Turf Division, 1984.

Rain Bird: Landscape Irrigation Design Manual, Keith Shepersky, Rain Bird Sales, Turf Division, 1984.

Rain Bird: Trickle Irrigation Design, Jack Keller, and David Karmeli, Rain Bird Sprinkler Manufacturing Corporation, 1975.

The A, B, C's of Lawn Sprinkler Systems, A.C. "Chet" Sarsfield, Irrigation Technical Services Publications Division, 1977.

Landscaping to Save Water in the Desert, Eric A. Johnson and David G. Harbison, E&H Products, Rancho Mirage, CA, 1985.

The American Society of Irrigation Consultants: Minimum Standards for Landscape Irrigation, 3rd edition, Standards Review Committee, American Society of Irrigation Consultants, 1992.

Turf Irrigation Manual, James A. Watkins, Telsco Industries, Dallas, TX, 1990.

40 Ways to Save Water in Your Yard and Garden, L. Ken Smith, Landscape Architect, published by the author. Can be purchased by sending $1.00 to 253 Beech Road, Newbury Park, CA. 91320

Chapter 7

American Electrician's Handbook, 12th edition, Terrell Croft and Wilford I. Summers, McGraw Hill, New York, 1992.

House Wiring Simplified, Floyd M. Mix, Goodheart-Wilcox Company, 1991.

How to Design and Install Outdoor Lighting, Ortho Books, Chevron Chemical Company, 1984.

Mcgraw Hill's National Electrical Code Handbook, 20th edition, Joseph F. McPartland and Brian McPartland, McGraw Hill, New York, 1990.

Sunset: Basic Home Wiring Illustrated, Linda J. Selden, Editor, Lane Publishing Co., Menlo Park, CA, 1987.

Chapter 8

Complete Guide to Basic Gardening, Michael MacCaskey (project editor), HP Books, Los Angeles, CA, 1986.

Gardening Techniques, Alan Tickmarsh, Simon and Schuster, New York, 1981.

Landscaping, 2nd edition, Jack E. Ingels, Delmar Publishers, Albany, NY, 1983.

Lawns and Groundcovers, Michael MacCaskey, HP Books, Los Angeles, CA, 1982.

Plant Propagation, Philip McMillan Bowse, Simon and Schuster, New York, 1979.

Plants in the Landscape, Philip L. Carpenter, Theodore D. Walker, and Frederick O. Lanphear, W.H. Freeman and Company, San Francisco, CA, 1975.

Pruning, Christopher Brickell, Simon and Schuster, New York, 1979.

Pruning Planting & Care, Eric A. Johnson, Ironwood Press, Tucson, AZ, 1997.

The Gardener's Year, John Ferguson and Burkhard Mücke Barrons, New York, 1991.

The Low-Water Flower Gardener, Eric A. Johnson and Scott Millard, Ironwood Press, Tucson, AZ, 1993.

The Time-Life Encyclopedia of Gardening: Lawns and Ground Covers, James Underwood Crockett, Time-Life Books, New York, 1971.

The Time-Life Encyclopedia of Gardening: Trees, James Underwood Crockett, Time-Life Books, New York, 1972.

Appendices

Appendix A

List of Abbreviations

CL	centerline
PD	perpendicular
RND	round
ABV	above
AFF	above finished floor
AGG	aggregate
ALN	align
ALT	alternate
APPROX	approximate
ARCH	architect
AD	area drain
BLK	block
BLKG	blocking
BS	both sides
BW	both ways
BOT	bottom
BLDG	building
CIPC	cast-in-place concrete
CST	cast stone
CB	catch basin
CK	calk(ing) caulk(ing)
CHAM	chamfer
CLR	clear(ance)
COL	column
CONC	concrete
CONST	construction
CONT	continuous or continue
CONTR	contract(or)
CJT	control joint
DIA	diameter
DR	door
DBL	double
DN	down
DWG	drawing
EA	each
EW	each way
EQ	equal
EQPT	equipment
EX	existing
EJ	expansion joint
EXP	exposed
EXT	exterior
FIN	finish(ed)
FFE	finished floor elevation
FTG	footing
GR	grade, grading
HDR	header
HORIZ	horizontal
HB	hose bib
ID	inside diameter
JT	joint
LA	landscape architect
MAX	maximum
MIN	minimum
NIC	not in contact
NTS	not to scale
NO/#	number
OC	on center(s)
OPP	opposite
OD	outside diameter
PAR	parallel
PV	pave(d), (ing)
PVMT	pavement
PLTG	planting
PCC	precast concrete
PL	property line
RDWD	redwood
REM	remove
REQ	required
RM	room
SECT	section
SHT	sheet
SIM	similar
SP	space
SQ	square
SST	stainless steel
STD	standard
STL	steel
TBS	to be selected
THK	thick(ness)
TYP	typical
VER	verify
VERT	vertical
WP	waterproofing
WIN	window
W/	with
WO	without

Appendix B

Technical Information

Avoirdupois Weight

1 ton	=	2,000 pounds
1 pound	=	6 ounces
1 ounce	=	16 drams
1 dram	=	27.34 grains
1 grain	=	0.0648 gram
1 cubic foot water	=	62.4 pounds

U.S. Liquid Measure

1 gallon	=	4 quarts (128 fluid ounces)
1 quart	=	2 pints (32 fluid ounces)
1 pint	=	4 gills (16 fluid ounces)
1 gill	=	4 fluid ounces (1 cup)

U.S. Dry Measure

1 bushel	=	4 pecks
1 peck	=	8 quarts
1 quart	=	2 pints
1 pint	=	33.6 cubic inches

U.S. Cubic Measure

1 cubic yard	=	27 cubic feet
1 cubic foot	=	1,728 cubic inches

U.S. Square Measure

1 square mile	=	640 acres		
1 acre	=	43,560 square feet	=	160 square rods
1 square rod	=	30˘ square yards	=	272˘ square feet
1 square yard	=	9 square feet		
1 square foot	=	144 square inches		

U.S. Linear Measure

1 land league	=	3 miles
1 statute mile	=	5,280 feet
1 furlong	=	40 rods
1 rod	=	5 yards
1 yard	=	3 feet
1 foot	=	12 inches
1 inch	=	2.54 centimeters

U.S. Land Measure

1 township	=	36 square miles (36 sections)
1 square mile	=	640 acres (1 section)
1 acre	=	43,560 square feet (10 square chains)
1 square chain	=	16 square poles
1 square pole	=	625 square links

Angular Measure

60 seconds	=	1 minute
60 minutes	=	1 degree
360 degrees	=	1 circle
90 degrees	=	1 quadrant
60 degrees	=	1 sextant

Weights of Commonly Used Construction Materials:

Material		Material	
4≤ brickwork	35	Clay (dug)	63
4≤ concrete block	35	Clay (wet)	100
4≤ lightweight concrete block	22	Earth (dry)	75–95
6≤ concrete block	50	Earth (wet)	80–120
6≤ lightweight concrete block	30	Gravel or sand (dry)	90–110
8≤ concrete block	58	Gravel or sand (wet)	100–120
8≤ lightweight concrete block	36	Concrete (wet)	130–150
12≤concrete block	90	Cast iron	450
12≤lightweight concrete block	58	Cedar	22
		Redwood	28
		Water	62.4

Diagrammatic System of Land Surveying

Within each region of the U.S., an east-west base line and north-south principal meridian have been established, and to these all subsequent land subdivision and title descriptions are related. Townships are numbered north and south of the base line, and ranges east and west of the principal meridian.

The principal units of land within counties are townships, 6 miles on a side, comprised of 36 sections, each approximately 1 mile square.

Sections are further subdivided as shown. Lots or parcels are described by bearings and distances or "metes and bounds" from stated reference points within a given area of the survey grid.

Appendix C

Agencies and Organizations

NOTE: The agencies and organizations listed herein frequently provide free technical data, furnish a membership roster, and publish newsletters and/or magazines. In addition, several provide endowments and other methods of financial support to individuals showing a need in their respective areas of interest. Many are also great bodies to be affiliated with for information exchange and professional support. All addresses and phone numbers given were current as of September 1996.

United States Government Agencies

Department of Agriculture
Independence Avenue between 12th and 14th Streets SW
Washington, DC 20250
201-720-2791

Environmental Protection Agency
401 M St. SW
Washington, DC 20460
202-260-2090

Department of Housing and Urban Development
451 7th St. SW
Washington, DC 20410
202-208-1422

Department of the Interior
1849 C St. NW
Washington, DC 20240
202-208-3100

Library of Congress
101 Independence Avenue SE
Washington, DC 20540
202-707-5000

National Park Service
National Headquarters Office
18th and C Sts. NW
P.O. Box 37127
Washington, DC 20013-7127
202-208-4747

National Science Foundation
1800 G. St. NW
Washington, DC 20550
202-357-5000

Engineering, Technological, & Natural Sciences Organizations

American Architectural Foundation (AAF)
1735 New York Avenue, NW
Washington, DC 20006
202-626-7500

American Institute of Architects (AIA)
1735 New York Avenue, NW
Washington, DC 20006
202-626-7300

American Society of Engineers and Architects
511 Garfield Avenue
South Pasadena, CA 91030
213-682-1161

American Society of Interior Designers (ASID)
8687 Melrose Avenue, Suite 52
Los Angeles, CA 90069
310-659-8998

American Society of Golf Course Architects (ASGCA)
221 N. La Salle St.
Chicago, IL 60601
312-372-7090

American Society of Landscape Architects (ASLA)
4401 Connecticut Avenue, NW
Washington, DC 20008
202-686-2752

Institute for Urban Design
4253 Karensue Avenue
San Diego, CA 92122
619-455-1251

Landscape Architecture Foundation (LAF)
4401 Connecticut Avenue, NW, 5th Floor
Washington, DC 20008
202-886-2752

American Phytopathological Society (Botany) (APS)
3340 Pilot Knob Road
St. Paul, MN 55121
612-454-7250

American Society of Horticultural Science (ASHS)
113 S. West St., Suite 400
Alexandria, VA 22314-2824
703-836-4606

American Society of Plant Physiologists (ASPP)
15501 Monona Drive
Rockville, MD 20855
310-251-0560

American Society of Plant Taxonomists (ASPT)
University of Georgia
Department of Botany
Athens, GA 30602
404-542-1802

Arizona Cactus and Succulent Research (ACSR)
8 Mulberry Lane
Bisbee, AZ 85603
602-432-7040

Association of Environmental Professionals
c/o George Stefan Associates
1333 36th St.
Sacramento, CA 95186-5401
916-737-2371

Botanical Society of America (BSA)
c/o Christopher Hanfler
University of Kansas
Department of Botany
Haworth Hall
Lawrence, KS 66045-2106
913-864-4301

American Bulb Society (IBS)
UCI Arboretum
University of California
Irvine, CA 92717
714-725-2909

International Organization of Citrus Virologists (IOCV)
c/o Dr. L. W. Timmer
University of Florida
Research and Education Center
700 Experiment Station Road
Lake Alfred, FL 33850
813-956-4631

International Palm Society (IPS)
P.O. Box 1897
Lawrence, KS
66044-8897

International Society of Citriculture
Department of Botany and Plant Science
University of California
Riverside, CA 92251
714-787-4412

International Turfgrass Society
Virginia Tech
International Turfgrass Corp. and Soil Environmental Science
Blacksburg, VA 24061-0404
703-231-9736

National Wildflower Research Center (NWRC)
2600 F.M., 973 North
Austin, TX 78725-4201
512-929-3600

American Concrete Institute (ACI)
P.O. Box 19150
Detroit, MI 48219
313-532-2600

Association of Asphalt Paving Technologists (AAPT)
1404 Concordia Avenue
St. Paul, MN 55014
612-642-1350

Construction Specifications Institute (CSI)
601 Madison Street
Alexandria, VA 22314-1791
703-684-0300

Epiphyllum Society of America
P.O. Box 1395
Monrovia, CA 91017
818-447-9688

The Masonry Society (TMS)
2619 Spruce St., Suite B
Boulder, CO 80302-3808
303-939-9700

American Society of Cost Engineers (AACE)
c/o Kenneth K. Humphreys
P.O. Box 1557
Morgantown, WV 26507-1557
304-296-8444

Institute of Electrical and Electronics Engineers (IEEE)
345 E. 47th St.
New York, NY 10017
212-705-7900

American Society of Agricultural Engineers (ASAE)
2450 Niles Road
St. Joseph, MI 49085-9659
616-429-0300

American Society of Civil Engineers (ASCE)
345 E. 47th St.
New York, NY 10017
212-705-7496

American Society of Plumbing Engineers (ASPE)
3617 Thousand Oaks Blvd., #210
Westlake, CA 91362
805-495-7120

National Society of Professional Engineers (NSPE)
1420 King St.
Alexandria, VA 22314
703-684-2800

National Geographic Society (NGS)
17th and M Streets, N.W.
Washington, DC 20036
202-857-7000

Geological Society of America (GSA)
3300 Penrose Place
P.O. Box 9140
Boulder, CO 80301-9140
303-447-2020

American Design Drafting Association (ADDA)
P.O. Box 799
Rockville, MD 20848-0799
310-460-6875

Illuminating Engineering Society of North America (IESNA)
345 E. 47th St.
New York, NY 10017
212-705-7913

American Society of Mechanical Engineers (ASME)
345 E. 4th St.
New York, NY 10017
212-705-7722

American Museum of Natural History (AMNH)
Central Park W. at 79th St.
New York, NY 10024
212-769-5100

Southwest Parks and Monuments Association (SPMA)
221 N. Court Ave.
Tucson, AZ 85701
602-622-1999

American Society for Photogrammetry and Remote Sensing (ASPRS)
5410 Grosvenor Ln., Suite 210
Bethesda, MD 20814-2160
301-493-0290

Seismological Society of America (SSA)
El Cerrito Professional Bldg., Suite 201
El Cerrito, CA 94530
415-525-5474

Soil Science Society of America (Sssa)
677 S. Segal Rd.
Madison, WI 53711
608-273-8080

Solar Energy Industries Association (SEIA)
777 N. Capitol St. NE, Suite 805
Washington, DC 22202
202-408-0660

American Congress On Surveying and Mapping (ACSM)
5410 Grosvenor Ln.
Bethesda, MD 20814-2122
301-493-0200

American Society of Testing Materials (ASTM)
1916 Race St.
Philadelphia, PA 19103-1187
215-977-9679

American Institute of Hydrology (AIH)
3416 University Avenue SE
Minneapolis, MN 55414-3328
612-379-1030

American Society of Irrigation Consultants (ASIC)
425 Oak St.
Brentwood, CA 94513
510-516-1300

American Water Resources Association (AWRA)
5410 Grosvenor Ln., Suite 220
Bethesda, MD 20814-2192
301-493-8600

Association of Groundwater Scientists and Engineers (AGWSE)
6375 Riverside Dr.
Dublin, OH 43017
614-761-1711

Colorado River Assocation (CPA)
417 S. Hill St., Rm. 1024
Los Angeles, CA 90013
213-626-4621

National Xeriscape Council, Inc. (Nxci)
P.O. Box 163172
Austin, TX 78716-3172
512-392-6225

American Wind Energy Association (AWEA)
777 N. Capitol St., Suite 805
Washington, DC 20002
202-408-8988

Trade, Business & Commercial Organizations

Asphalt Institute (AI)
Research Park Dr.
P.O. Box 10452
Lexington, KY 40512-4052
606-288-4960

Ceramic Tile Distributors Association (CTDA)
15 Salt Creek Lane, Suite 422
Hinsdale, IL 60521
708-655-3270

National Asphalt Pavement Association (NAPA)
NAPA Bldg.
5100 Forbes Blvd.
Lanham, MD 20706-4413
301-731-4748

National Association of Brick Distributors (NABD)
212 S. Henry St.
Alexandria, VA 22314
703-549-2555

National Patio Enclosure Association (NPEA)
1015 E. Chapman Ave., B
Fullerton, CA 92631
714-525-3405

National Computer Graphics Association (NCGA)
2722 Merrilee Dr., Suite 200
Fairfax, VA 22031
703-698-9600

National Concrete Masonry Association (NCMA)
P.O. Box 781
Herndon, VA 22070-0781
703-435-4900

National Precast Concrete Association (NPCA)
825 E. 64th St.
Indianapolis, IN 46220
317-253-0486

National Ready Mixed Concrete Association (NRMCA)
900 Spring St.
Silver Springs, MD 20910
301-587-1400

Portland Cement Association (PCA)
5420 Old Orchard Rd.
Skokie, IL 60077
708-966-6200

Prestressed Concrete Institute (PCI)
175 W. Jackson Blvd.
Chicago, IL 60604
312-786-0300

American Society of Concrete Construction (ASCC)
1902 Techny Ct.
Northbrook, IL 60062
312-291-0270

Associated General Contractors of America (AGC)
1957 E. St. NW
Washington, DC 20006
202-393-2040

Construction Financial Management Association (CFMA)
Princeton Gateway Corporate Campus
707 State Rd., Suite 223
Princeton, NJ 08540-1413
609-683-5000

Gunite/Shotcrete Association (GCA)
12306 Van Nuys Blvd.
Lakeview Terrace, CA 91342
818-896-9199

National association of home builders of the U.S. (NAHB)
15th and M Streets NW
Washington, DC 20005
202-822-0200

National Electrical Contractors Association (NECA)
7315 Wisconsin Ave.
Bethesda, MD 20814
301-657-3110

Painting and Decorating Contractors of America (PDCA)
3913 Old Lee Hwy., Suite 33B
Fairfax, VA 22030
703-359-0826

Professional Construction Estimators Association of America (PCEA)
P.O. Box 11626
Charlotte, NC 28220-1626
704-522-6376

International Association of Electrical Inspectors (IAEI)
901 Waterfall Way
Richardson, TX 75080
708-696-1455

National Electrical Manufacturer's Association (NEMA)
2101 L St. NW
Washington, DC 20037
202-457-8400

American Electronics Association (AEA)
5201 Great America Pkwy, Suite 250
Santa Clara, CA 95054
408-987-4200

International Hardwood Products Association (IHPA)
P.O. Box 1308
Alexandria, VA 22313
703-836-6696

National Forest Products Association (NFPA)
1250 Connecticut Ave. NW, Suite 200
Washington, DC 20036
202-463-2700

Southern Forest Products Association (SFPA)
P.O. Box 52468
New Orleans, LA 70152
504-433-4464

Timber Operators Council (TOC)
6825 SW Sandburg St.
Tigrad, OR 97223
503-620-1710

Western Building Materials Association (WBMA)
P.O. Box 1699
Olympia, WA 98507
206-943-3054

Western Wood Products Association (WWPA)
Yeon Bldg.
522 SW 5th Ave.
Portland, OR 97204-2122
503-224-3930

American Plywood Association (APA)
P.O. Box 11700
Tacoma, WA 98411
206-565-6600

American Wood Preservers Association (AWPA)
4128 I 12 California Ave., SW No. 171
Seattle, WA 98116
206-937-5338

Art Glass Suppliers Association (AGSA)
1100-H Brandywine Blvd.
P.O. Box 2188
Zanesville, OH 43072-2188
614-452-4541

National Glass Association (NGA)
8200 Greensboro Dr., Suite 302
McLean, VA 22102
703-442-4890

Stained Glass Association of American (SGAA)
6 SW 2nd St., No. 7
Lees Summit, MO 64063-2348
800-888-7422

National Golf Foundation (NGF)
1150 South U.S. Highway One
Jupiter, FL 33477
800-733-6006

Interior Design Society (IDS)
P.O. Box 2396
High Point, NC 27261
800-888-9590

Interior Plantscape Division (ALCA/IPD)
405 N. Washington St., Suite 104
Falls Church, VA 22046
703-241-4007

International Association of Lighting Designers (IALD)
18 E. 16th St., Suite 208
New York, NY 10003
212-206-1281

International Society of Interior Designers (ISID)
433 S. Spring St., 10th Fl.
Los Angeles, CA 90013
213-680-4240

Associated Landscape Contractors of America (ALCA)
405 N. Washington St., Suite 104
Falls Church, VA 22046
703-241-4004

Garden Council (GC)
500 N. Michigan Ave., Suite 1400
Chicago, IL 60611
312-661-1700

National Landscape Association (NLA)
1250 I St. NW, Suite 500
Washington, DC 20005
202-789-2900

National Lawn and Garden Distributors Association (NLGDA)
1900 Arch St.
Philadelphia, PA 19103
215-564-3484

Professional Lawn Care Association of America (PLCAA)
1000 Johnson Ferry Rd., Suite C-135
Marietta, GA 30068
404-977-5222

Aluminum Association (AA)
900 19th St. NW, Suite 300
Washington, DC 20006
202-862-5100

American Copper Council (ACC)
2 South End Ave., No. 4C
New York, NY 10280
212-945-4990

American Iron and Steel Institute (AISI)
1101 17th St. NW
Washington, DC 20036-4700
202-463-6573

American Tin Trade Association (ATTA)
P.O. Box 1347
New York, NY 10150
908-364-2280

Copper and Brass Fabricators Council (CBFC)
1050 17th St. NW, Suite 440
Washington, DC 20036
202-833-8575

National Paint and Coatings Association (NPCA)
1500 Rhode Island Ave. NW
Washington, DC 20005
202-462-6272

Society of the Plastics Industry (SPI)
1275 K St. NW, Suite 400
Washington, DC 20005
202-371-5200

American Supply Association (ASA) (Plumbing)
222 Merchandise Mart, Suite 1360
Chicago, IL 60654
312-464-0090

National Pool and Spa Institute (NSPI)
2111 Eisenhower Ave.
Alexandria, VA 22314
703-838-0083

Allied Stone Industries (ASI)
c/o Jack Van Etter
P.O. Box 288145
Chicago, IL 60628
312-928-4800

Building Stone Institute (BSI)
P.O. Box 5047
White Plains, NY 10602-5047
914-232-5725

Marble Institute of America (MIA)
33505 State St.
Farmington, MI 48335
313-476-5558

National Aggregates Association (NAA)
900 Spring St.
Silver Spring, MD 20910
301-587-1400

National Building Granite Quarries (NBGQA)
P.O. Box 482
Barre, VT 05641
802-476-3115

National Quartz Producers Council (NQPC)
P.O. Box 1719
Wheat Ridge, CO 80034
303-430-1307

National Stone Association (NSA)
1415 Elliott Pl. NW
Washington, DC 20007
800-342-1415

Stucco Manufacturers Association
507 Evergreen Road
Pacific Grove, CA 93950-3804
408-649-3466

Environmental & Agricultural Organizations

Agricultural Council of America (ACA)
1250 J St. NW, Suite 601
Washington, DC 20005
202-682-9200

American Society of Agronomy (ASA)
677 S. Segal Rd.
Madison, WI 53711
608-273-8080

Chihuahuan Desert Research Institute (CDRI)
Box 1334
Alpine, TX 79831
915-837-8370

Desert Fishes Council (DFC)
P.O. Box 337
Bishop, CA 93515
619-872-8751

Desert Protective Council (DPC)
P.O. Box 4294
Palm Springs, CA 92263
760-397-4264

Desert Tortoise Preserve Committee (DTPC)
P.O. Box 2910
San Bernardino, CA 92406
213-548-0962

National Audubon Society (NAS)
950 3rd Ave.
New York, NY 10022
212-832-3200

National Wildlife Federation (NWF)
1400 16th NW
Washington, DC 20036-2266
202-797-6800

Native Seeds/Search (NS/S)
2509 N. Campbell Ave. No. 325
Tucson, AZ 85719
602-327-9123

The Nature Conservancy
213 Stearns Wharf
Santa Barbara, CA 93101
805-962-9111

Soil and Water Conservation Society (SWCS)
7515 NE Ankeny Rd.
Ankeny, IA 50021
515-289-2331

Treepeople (TP)
12601 Mulholland Dr.
Beverly Hills, CA 90210
818-753-4600

The Wilderness Society
900 17th St. NW
Washington, DC 20006-2596
202-833-2300

Sierra Club (SC)
730 Polk St.
San Francisco, CA 94109
415-776-2211

National Tree Society
P.O. Box 10800
Bakersfield, CA 93389
805-589-6912

American Society of Consulting Arborists (ASCA)
3895 Upham St., No. 12
Wheatridge, CO 80033
303-420-9554

American Sod Producers Association (ASPA)
1855-A Hicks Rd.
Rolling Meadows, IL 60008
708-705-9898

Professional Grounds Management Society (PGMS)
10402 Ridgland Rd., Suite 4
Cockeysville, MD 21030
301-667-1833

American Association of Nurseymen (AAN)
1250 J St. NW, Suite 500
Washington, DC 20005
202-789-2900

Garden Centers of America (GCA)
1250 J St. NW, Suite 500
Washington, DC 20005
202-789-2900

Horticultural Research Institute (HRI)
1250 J St. NW, Suite 500
Washington, DC 20005
202-789-2900

Landscape Nursery Council (LANCO)
1315 Talbott Tower
Dayton, OH 45402
513-222-1071

Professional Plant Growers Association (PPGA)
P.O. Box 27517
Lansing, MI 48909
517-694-7700

Wholesale Nursery Growers of America (WHGA)
1250 J St. NW, Suite 580
Washington, DC 20005
202-789-2900

International Society of Aborculture (ISA)
303 W. University Avenue
P.O. Box 908
Urbana, IL 61801
217-328-2032

National Arborist Association (NAA)
The Meeting Place Mall
Rt. 101, P.O. Box 1094
Amherst, NH 03031
603-673-3311

Committee for National Arbor Day
P.O. Box 333
West Orange, NY 07052
201-731-0840

National Arbor Day Foundation (NADF)
100 Arbor Drive
Nebraska City, NE 68410
402-474-5655

Appendix D

Large-Scale Project Checklist

Project Name: ______________________________

Project Location: ______________________________

Date: ______________

Programming

1. Facility type? ______________________________
2. Makeup of users? ______________________________
3. Site square footage needed? ______________________________
4. Building square footage needed? ______________________________
5. Parking requirements? ______________________________
6. Growth and expansion projections and time frame? ______________

Demographics

Current regional population? ______________________________

Current local population? ______________________________

Site Inventory

1. Location:

Surrounding municipalities? ______________________________

Proximity to rail, trucking, and air traffic? ______________

Path of growth? ______________________________

Connecting vehicular transit system(s)? ______________

Nature of adjacent sites? ______________________________

2. Environment:

Prevailing wind? ______________________________

Earthquake fault line proximity? ______________________________

Flood plain? ______________________________

Noise? ______________________________

Air quality? ______________________________

Odors? ______________________________
Water quality? ______________________________
Wildlife? ______________________________
Trees? ______________________________
Protected species? ______________________________

3. Physical Characteristics:
Topography? ______________________________
Soil type? ______________________________
Degree of slope? ______________________________
Groundwater? ______________________________
Soil type? ______________________________
Washes? ______________________________
Vegetative cover? ______________________________

4. Utilities:
Domestic water? _____ Yes _____ No
TV cable?
Electricity? _____ Yes _____ No
Sanitary sewer? _____ Yes _____ No
Natural gas? _____ Yes _____ No
Storm sewer? _____ Yes _____ No
Telephone? _____ Yes _____ No

5. Services:
Police? _____ Yes _____ No
Schools? _____ Yes _____ No
Fire? _____ Yes _____ No
Shopping? _____ Yes _____ No
Medical? _____ Yes _____ No
Parks and recreation? _____ Yes _____ No
Solid waste disposal? _____ Yes _____ No

Review Agency Analysis

1. Federal input? (E.I.S.) _____ Yes _____ No
2. State input? (E.I.R.) _____ Yes _____ No
3. County input? (Specific plan) _____ Yes _____ No
4. City or town input? _____ Yes _____ No
5. Country club input? _____ Yes _____ No
6. Highway Dept. input? _____ Yes _____ No
7. Water agency input? _____ Yes _____ No
8. Agricultural committee input? _____ Yes _____ No

9. Private development codes, covenants, restrictions? _____ Yes _____ No
10. Design standards from any/all of the above? _____ Yes _____ No
11. Allowed drawing scales? ____
12. Allowed plan sheet sizes? ____
13. Colored renderings required? ____

Coordination with Other Design Disciplines

1. Architect ____
2. Civil engineer ____
3. Structural engineer ____
4. Interior designer ____
5. Irrigation designer ____
6. Water feature consultant ____
7. Soils testing laboratory ____
8. Arboriculturist ____
9. Other ____
10. Other ____
11. Other ____
12. Other ____

Conceptual Design

1. Identify all site use from information garnered during the programming phase.
2. Generate balloon or bubble diagrams showing ideal use area, optimum locations, and relationship to one another.
3. Dovetail use areas to site realities.
4. Review work with client.

Schematic Design

1. Generate loose site plan.
2. Develop recommended hardscape materials selections.
3. Develop a general recommended palette of plant materials.
4. Review work with client.

Preliminary Design

1. Generate site plan and any area enlargements at a defined scale.
2. Refine hardscape materials selections.
3. Refine plant palette.
4. Develop a grading and drainage concept.
5. Develop an irrigation concept.

6. Develop a lighting concept.
7. Generate a preliminary cost estimate.
8. Colored presentation graphics.
9. Review work with client.
10. Inform client of various design review fees.
11. Submit work for all appropriate design review agencies, boards, and individuals.

Working Drawings

1. Verify availability of hardscape materials.
2. Verify availability of plant materials.
3. Produce, oversee, or coordinate Grading and Drainage Plans.
4. Produce, oversee, or coordinate Staking Plans.
5. Produce, oversee, or coordinate Planting Plans.
6. Produce, oversee, or coordinate Irrigation Plans.
7. Produce, oversee, or coordinate Lighting Plans.
8. Detail package for all of the above.
9. Specifications for all of the above.
10. Revise and update preliminary cost estimate. Include all plan review fees, permit, and utility hookup fees.
11. Review work with client.
12. Inform client of various design review fees.
13. Submit work to all appropriate design review agencies, boards, and individuals.

Bidding

1. Select and approve all bidders.
2. Issue bid documents with bidding instructions.
3. Issue any addenda during bid period.
4. Receive bids and open on a specified date.
5. Negotiate with low or preferred bidder, if necessary.

Initial Construction

1. Organize preconstruction conferences.
2. Check all grades and soil suitability before they are turned over to landscape contractor.
3. Check adequacy of soil preparation.
4. Check water hookup and verify water pressure.
5. Check irrigation trenches and equipment.
6. Check quality of plant materials.
7. Issue field reports for owner and all applicable contractors.

Substantial Completion

1. Watch irrigation system operate.
2. Check health and status of all plant materials.
3. Check status of weeds.
4. Check tree staking and guying.
5. Check stand of grass in any lawn areas.
6. Determine if project is 85% complete for payment.
7. Issue field report to owner and all applicable contractors.

Final Completion

1. Reject poor plant materials.
2. Watch irrigation system operate.
3. Check status of weeds.
4. Check stand of grass in any lawn areas.
5. Determine if project is 100% complete for payment.
6. Issue notice of final completion to owner and all applicable contractors.
7. Letter or manual to owner outlining on-going maintenance requirements.

Appendix E

Homeowner's Residential Landscape Design Process

I. **Evaluate your property and surrounding areas for design clues.**

   A. Take a new and fresh look at your property (get rid of all pre-conceived ideas).
   Walk your property and take note of items such as:

      a. sun exposure and angle
      b. types of vegetation growing (on and off your property)
      c. views
      d. slopes
      e. special features
      f. "feel" of the neighborhood (green, 1/2 and 1/2, desert, etc.)
      g. any unpleasant items such as odors or noise

   B. Take note of other residences which you like and determine why.

II. Draft a base plan; Collect needed information to compile a plan on which the design may be worked out on.

   A. Plan should include the following (these should be actually shown on the plan):

      1. north
      2. scale
      3. wind direction
      4. property lines
      5. location of any existing structures
      6. existing vegetation
      7. walks and drives
      8. streets and street lights
      9. streams, washes, or drainage swells
      10. other man-made features
      11. topography (degree of slope and surface characteristic of the ground plane.)

B. Gather this information from
   1. site layout from building designer or architect
   2. plot plan from the builder of your home
   3. hire a surveyor
   4. measure the property yourself
   5. tax map from the County Assessor's office

III. Site Analysis. Take note of any natural and man-made forces which are being exerted on your property which will effect what you will develop (this can be done on a blueprint, xerox, or overlay of your base plan.)
   A. Sun orientation
      1. winter
      2. summer
   B. Wind direction (predominate)
      1. winter
      2. summer
   C. Views
      1. desirable
      2. undesirable
      3. on site
      4. off site
   D. Zoning restrictions
      1. set-back lines for fences, swimming pools, overhead structures, etc.
      2. height restrictions for overhead structures and fences
      3. types of plant materials that may be restricted
   E. Utilities.
      1. water
      2. electricity
      3. gas
      4. telephone wires and TV and cable lines
      5. sanitary sewer or septic tank
      6. storm sewer

F. Soil
   1. Type
      a. Sandy
      b. Loam
      c. Clay
   2. Quality
      a. pH level
      b. Fertility level
      c. Salinity level

G. Topography
   1. Slopes
      a. Steep or gentle slopes
      b. Evidence of erosion
   2. Drainage areas
   3. Surface characteristics
      a. Rocky
      b. Sandy
      c. Existing turf
      d. Tree cover

IV. Goals for your outdoor space: evaluate your needs and interests.

A. List these needs and interests. For example:
   1. Vegetable garden
   2. Swimming pool
   3. Outdoor shower
   4. Spa
   5. Enlarged patio area
   6. Bar-B-Q area
   7. Private area
   8. Play area
   9. Service area

B. Rate these items in order of importance on a scale of 1 to 5, with 5 being the highest.

V. Balloon (functional) diagram; divide the property up into different activity areas or uses. Place these areas on the plan according to approximate size requirements and desired location.
   A. Consider the importance between a use area's location and its interaction between existing and/or proposed activities
   B. Consider ways that use areas could be combined to maximize limited space.

VI. Preliminary design.
   A. Goals of good design to be considered while preparing the preliminary plan
      1. Privacy
      2. Physical comfort
      3. Low maintenance
      4. Entertaining
      5. Practicality
      6. Safety
      7. Adaptability
      8. Beauty
   B. Guidelines for elements of design
      1. Form
      2. Scale
      3. Space
      4. Rhythm, line, and harmony
      5. Balance
      6. Emphasis
      7. Texture
      8. Light
      9. Color

VII. Finalize design:
   A. Refine use areas and start to work out details
      1. Show circulation
      2. Establish area buffers where needed

3. Consider hardscape materials:
    a. Walks, patios, and drives
    b. Overheads
    c. Fences
    d. Walls
    e. Water features
4. Consider plant materials
    a. Study the relationship between the plant material in relation to their:
        size
        form
        texture
        color
        soil requirements
        irrigation requirements
    b. Study the function or use of the plants you will need:
        shade giving trees
        screen plants
        accent plants
        colorful shrubs
        ground covers
        colorful and/or fragrant annuals?
        erosion control
        etc.
    c. Determine specific plants

B. Draw all of these items, such as the plant materials, fences, patios, etc., all to scale on the base plan

Appendix F

Residential Client Questionnaire

I. Family information
   A. Number in family ____________________
   B. Ages
   C. Male ______ Female ______
   D. Hobbie ____________ ____________________
   E. Pets ____________________

II. How long do you expect to reside in the house? ____________________

III. How many hours/week do you intend to spend on maintenance? ____________________

IV. What is your installation budget? ____________________

V. Do you entertain? _____ Yes _____ No
   Large groups or small? ____________________

VI. Who will be doing the installation? _____ Contractor? _____ Yourself? _____ Both?

VII. Plant preferences
   A. What do you like? ____________________
   B. What do you dislike? ____________________
   C. Are you allergic to any plants? ____________________

VIII. Design input
   A. Public Area
      1. Adequate parking ____________________
         a. Number of cars? ____________________
         b. Guest parking? ____________________

2. Privacy from street
    a. Noise. Level of tolerance? ______________________
    b. Vehicle headlights? ______________________
    c. Privacy from public view? ______________________
    d. Mailbox access? ______________________

B. Entry area
    1. Image desired? ______________________
    2. Courtyard? ______________________
    3. Lighting? ______________________
    4. Benches? ______________________
    5. Fountain? ______________________
    6. Address numbers? ______________________

C. Outdoor living area
    1. Patio/deck? ______________________
    2. Overhead/climate control? ______________________
    3. Pool? ______________________
    4. Spa? ______________________
    5. Outdoor shower? ______________________
    6. Fountains/water features? ______________________
    7. Outdoor cooking (perm./port.)? ______________________
        a. Electricity? ______________________
        b. Gas? ______________________
        c. Water for sink? ______________________
        d. Refrigerator/ice maker? ______________________
    8. Outdoor furniture? ______________________
        a.. Chairs and tables? ______________________
        b. Benches? ______________________
        c. Umbrellas? ______________________
    9. Lighting? ______________________
    10. Screening? ______________________

D. Private area (usually off bedrooms)
    1. Terrace? ______________________
    2. Spa? ______________________
    3. Fountain? ______________________
    4. Benches? ______________________

E. Play areas
    1. Sports (volleyball, basketball, tennis) ______________
    2. Children's play area ______________
        a. play equipment/structures? ______________
        b. bicycle paths? ______________
F. Service areas
    1. Clothesline? ______________
    2. Storage areas? ______________
    3. Equipment storage? ______________
    4. Dog house/run? ______________
    5. Trash enclosure? ______________
    6. R.V. or boat storage? ______________
    7. Service garden? ______________
G. Garden area
    1. Citrus? ______________
    2. Vegetables? ______________
    3. Herbs? ______________
    4. Cut flowers? ______________
H. Special features
    1. Sculptures? ______________
    2. Fountains? ______________
    3. Exotic plants? ______________
    4. Preserve existing views? ______________
    5. Block existing poor views? ______________
    6. Special animal environment? ______________
    7. Potted plants? ______________
I. Design tastes
    1. Green environment (oasis)? ______________
    2. Semigreen environment (transition)? ______________
    3. Natural/native environment (desert)? ______________
    4. Favorite color(s)? ______________
    5. Favorite material(s)? ______________

Appendix G

Plant Information Sheet

Botanical Name:	Common Name:

☐ Trees & Palms	☐ Shrubs	☐ Espaliers
☐ Vines	☐ Groundcovers	☐ Turf Grasses
☐ Cacti, Succulents, etc.	☐ Bulbs, Corms, Tubers, Rhizomes	☐ Aquatic Plants
☐ Annuals		☐ Wildflowers
☐ Annual	☐ Biannual	☐ Perennial
☐ Native	☐ Naturalized	☐ Exotic
☐ Deciduous	☐ Evergreen	☐ Semi-Evergreen
☐ Oasis	☐ Transition	☐ Desert
☐ Presently Available	☐ Limited Availability	☐ Hard to Find

Form	Branching Habit
Ultimate Height	Ultimate Width
Root System Type	Bud Type
Leaf Type	Flower Type
Fruit Type	Propagation Method
Temperature Range	Soil Preference & p.H.
Growth Per Year	Life Span
Thorns: _______ Yes _______ No	Poisonous: _______ Yes _______ No

CHARACTERISTICS

SEX	☐ Dioecious	☐ Monoecious	☐ Other
STEM	☐ Single	☐ Multiple (3 to 5)	☐ Profuse
FOLIAGE - TACTILE	☐ Fine	☐ Medium	☐ Coarse
FOLIAGE - VISUAL	☐ Light	☐ Medium	☐ Dense
GROWTH	☐ Slow	☐ Moderate	☐ Fast
HARDINESS	☐ Tender	☐ Intermediate	☐ Hardy
EXPOSURE	☐ Shade	☐ Filtered Sun	☐ Sun
PESTILENCE	☐ Susceptible	☐ Moderate	☐ Resistant
WATER	☐ Low	☐ Moderate	☐ High
FERTILIZER	☐ Low	☐ Moderate	☐ High
MAINTENANCE	☐ Low	☐ Moderate	☐ High

Appendix H

MASTER PLANT MATERIALS MATRIX

PLANT CATEGORY

BOTANICAL NAME	COMMON NAME	ENVIRON. GROUPING				SIZE		MACRO ZONE			MICRO ZONE					DESIGN USE			WATER REQ.			LEAF HABIT			FLOWER SHOW				F. C.	★
DESCRIBED		NATIVE	NATURALIZED	EXOTIC	TROPICAL	HEIGHT	WIDTH	LOW DESERT	INTERMEDIATE DESERT	HIGH DESERT	A — SUNNY	B — PART SUNNY	C — LITTLE SUNNY	D — INTRO. SHADE	E — DEEP SHADE	OASIS	TRANSITION	DESERT	LOW WATER	MODERATE WATER	HIGH WATER	EVERGREEN	SEMI EVERGREEN	DECIDUOUS	SPRING FLOWERS	SUMMER FLOWERS	FALL FLOWERS	WINTER FLOWERS	FALL COLOR	STAR PERFORMER

Appendix I

Annual Maintenance Expense Checklist

	TASK	PERFORMED PER					ACTUAL COST PER YR.	IN-HOUSE	PRIVATE VENDOR
		WK.	BI-WK.	MO.	YR.	OTHER			
☐	Lawn mowing	4	4				$	☐	☐
☐	Scalping and overseeding turf					4 Bi-Yearly	$	☐	☐
☐	Tree and shrub trimming and pruning			4	4		$	☐	☐
☐	Weeding of planting beds		4	4			$	☐	☐
☐	Trash and leaf litter removal		4			4 Sometimes Daily	$	☐	☐
☐	Dumpster trash pickup	4	4				$	☐	☐
☐	Pest and weed control		4	4			$	☐	☐
☐	Disease control			4	4		$	☐	☐
☐	Fertilization program		4	4			$	☐	☐
☐	Rotation of annual color			4	4	4 Bi-Yearly or Quarterly	$	☐	☐
☐	Irrigation system manitenance	4					$	☐	☐
☐	Irrigation system controller program					4 Quarterly	$	☐	☐
☐	Lamp replacement in lighting fixtures		4	4			$	☐	☐
☐	Pool/spa/water feature cleaning	4	4				$	☐	☐
☐	Pool/spa/water feature replastering				4	4	$	☐	☐
☐	Street and parking lot sweeping			4			$	☐	☐
☐	Street and parking resealing					4	$	☐	☐
☐	Parking lot restriping					4	$	☐	☐

TASK	PERFORMED PER					ACTUAL COST PER YR.	IN-HOUSE	PRIVATE VENDOR
	WK.	BI-WK.	MO.	YR.	OTHER			
☐ Sidewalk cleaning					4	$	☐	☐
☐ Pool deck resurfacing					4	$	☐	☐
☐ Stonework resealing					4	$	☐	☐
☐ Re-stuccoing					4	$	☐	☐
☐ Repainting of walls					4	$	☐	☐
☐ Repainting of ironwork						$	☐	☐
☐ Clean out drainage structures					4	$	☐	☐
☐ Christmas decorations				4		$	☐	☐
☐ Gate repair				4		$	☐	☐
☐ Other						$	☐	☐
☐ Other						$	☐	☐
☐ Other						$	☐	☐

ESTIMATED ANNUAL MAINTENANCE EXPENSES:

$

Comments:

Appendix J

Places to Visit

Anza-Borrego Desert State Park
P.O. Box 299
Borrego Springs, CA 92004
760-767-4684

Arizona Cactus Botanical Garden
c/o Arizona Cactus and Succulent Research Inc.
8 Mulberry Lane
Bisbee, AZ 85603
602-432-7040

Big Morongo Canyon Preserve
P.O. Box 780
Morongo Valley, CA 92256

Boyce Thompson Southwestern Arboretum
P.O. Box AB
Superior, AZ 85273
602-689-2811

Coachella Valley Museum And Cultural Center
82-616 Miles Avenue
Indio, CA 92201
760-342-6651

Coachella Valley Preserve
P.O. Box 188
Thousand Palms, CA 92276
760-343-1234

Coachella Valley Water District Demonstration Garden
District Headquarters
Avenue 52 and Highway 111
P.O. Box 1058
Coachella, CA 92236
760-398-2651

Death Valley National Monument
Furnace Creek Headquarters
Death Valley, CA 92328
619-786-2331

Desert Botanical Garden
120 North Galvin Parkway
Phoenix, AZ 85008
602-941-1225

Desert Water Agency Demonstration Garden
1200 Gene Autry Trail, South
Palm Springs, CA 92264
760-323-4971

Ethel M. Botanic garden
2 Cactus Garden Drive
Henderson, NV 89014
702-458-8864

Heard Museum
22 E. Monte Vista Road
Phoenix, AZ 85012
602-252-8848

Hi-Desert Nature Museum
57-117 Twentynine Palms Highway
Yucca Valley, CA 92284
760-228-5452

Jaeger Preserve
Interstate 10, Eagle Mountain Exit
Owned and operated by: Biology Department
La Sierra University
Riverside, CA 92515
714-785-2105

Joshua Tree National Monument
74485 National Monument Drive
Twentynine Palms, CA 92277
760-367-7511

Malki Museum
11795 Fields Road
Banning, CA 92220
714-849-7289

Moorten Botanical Garden
1702 South Palm Canyon Drive
Palm Springs, CA 92264
760-327-6555

Old Pueblo Museum At Foothills Center
7401 North La Cholla Boulevard
Tucson, AZ 85741
602-742-7191

Organ Pipe Cactus National Monument
Route 1, P.O. Box 100
Ajo, AZ 85321
602-387-6849

Rancho Santa Ana Botanic Gardens
1500 North College Avenue
Claremont, CA 91711
714-625-8767

Saguaro National Monument East
Rincon Mountain District
3693 South Old Spanish Trail
Tucson, AZ 85730
602-296-8576

Saguaro National Monument West
Tucson Mountain District
2700 West Kinney Road
Tucson, AZ 85743
602-888-6366

Salton Sea National Wildlife Refuge
906 West Sinclair
Calipatria, CA 92233
619-348-5278

Santa Barbara Botanic Garden
1212 Mission Canyon Road
Santa Barbara, CA 93105
805-563-4726

The Arizona-Sonora Desert Museum
2021 North Kinney Road
Tucson, AZ 85743
602-883-2702

The Living Desert
47900 Portola Avenue
Palm Desert, CA 92260
760-346-5694

The Palm Springs Desert Museum
101 Museum Drive
Palm Springs, CA 92262
760-325-0189

The Palm Springs Historical Society
221 South Palm Canyon Drive
Palm Springs, CA 92262
760-323-8297

Tucson Botanical Gardens
2150 North Alvernon Way
Tucson, AZ 85712
602-326-9255

Other places of interest:

Index

M

N

O

P

Q

R

S

T